A SOURCEBOOK OF AFRICAN
CUSTOMARY LAW FOR SOUTHERN AFRICA

A Sourcebook of African Customary Law for Southern Africa

T W Bennett

assisted by

N S Peart

Juta & Co, Ltd

CAPE TOWN   WETTON   JOHANNESBURG

First Edition 1991

© Juta & Co, Ltd
PO Box 14373, Kenwyn 7790

The publishers and the author wish to thank the Attorneys Fidelity Fund for generous financial assistance towards the publication of this book, and the South African Legal Rights Foundation, PO Box 391, Isando 1600, South Africa, telephone 011–9742966. The Foundation is a non-profit, non-political organization which was founded with the object of promoting an understanding of the law and legal rights to the general public.

The views expressed in this publication are those of the author and are not necessarily shared by the Foundation, or the Fidelity Fund.

Cover design by

Susan Abraham

ISBN 0 7021 2546 6

SET, PRINTED AND BOUND IN THE REPUBLIC OF SOUTH AFRICA
BY THE RUSTICA PRESS (PTY) LTD, WYNBERG, CAPE
D33

Preface

In comparison with other branches of the South African legal system customary law is small game. It would be generous to attribute the want of attention to an unconscious neglect; it is more probably the result of a deliberate policy to exclude Africans from full participation in the South African legal system. And, because customary law has been marginalized, it has been ignored in the legislative processes that, in the past two decades, have preceded reform of the common law of divorce, intestate succession and matrimonial property.

In a purely formal sense customary law has also become isolated. Legal positivism has succeeded in decontextualizing the subject by abstracting it from its social and moral/ethical background. The courts are empowered by the so-called repugnancy proviso to delete or amend any rule of customary law that is contrary to the principles of public policy or natural justice. The fact that they have not invoked this proviso for the past forty years has been commended as an enlightened sympathy for cultural relativism. It could equally be interpreted as a symptom of neglect.

Wider horizons in both a literal (geographic) and a metaphorical (academic) sense would have encouraged fresh interpretations and could have suggested goals for development. The revolution in western systems of family law that were prompted by changes in the status of women and children, marriage and the family structure, might have provided models for the reform of customary law. And local customary law would be better understood if more attention were paid to research in developing countries. The poor and ill-educated the world over face common social and economic problems: we could have learned much from the extensive body of literature on issues as disparate as the position of customary law in Papua New Guinea, family law reform in East Africa, modes of processing disputes in Brazil and Mexico, and the relationship between official and unofficial law in Indonesia.

As a result of this neglect, South African customary law is now at variance with contemporary social conditions. There is always some discrepancy between legal theory and social reality, but in the case of customary law this discrepancy has been exaggerated until it has become a serious disjunction. For this, the one-sided political process is largely responsible. Nearly all law-making aimed at Africans has been concerned to control their movement, education, work, residence etc; because Africans have been excluded from government, their domestic legal needs are seldom (if ever) voiced. And, for the South African legal profession, African family law is financially unrewarding work.

Apathy and lack of interest found a convenient justification in the policy of cultural self-determination: it is not for Whites to interfere; Blacks are responsible for their own domestic affairs. Ironically, even liberal political views have discouraged consideration of customary law: the subject suffers the taint of apartheid politics and in consequence it must be condemned along with all other products of the system. It should also be appreciated that the current version of customary law suits a large and conservative African constituency: any reform would inevitably bring an improvement in the status of women, something few men would support.

Proposals to restructure the South African legal order, a process that implies expunging the evils of apartheid and securing a better deal for the dispossessed section of the population, now afford an opportunity to reconsider customary law and its position in the legal system. Yet, even in these favourable circumstances, customary law—an unhappy reminder of an out-of-date and politically undesirable legal regime—is in danger of being overlooked. To overlook it would, however, be indefensible. This law (admittedly not always in the form in which it is officially depicted) is still integral to the lives of numerous people, and its enforcement gives effect to a pre-eminent right of self-determination.

At present customary law seems to have an assured future in the South African legal system. It rests on a secure judicial infrastructure dating from the middle of the last century, and the ANC (the political party most likely to argue for its abolition) has given no indication of wanting to change this. Albie Sachs, for instance, when arguing for a bill of rights, calls for a 'special tolerance' for traditional law and custom:

> 'This is a question where extensive discussion with the people is required, so that all that is rich and meaningful to the people can be retained and progressively developed, while that which is divisive, exploitative and out of keeping with the times—especially that which has been distorted by colonialism and apartheid—can be eliminated.' (*The Future of Roman Dutch Law in a Non-racial Democratic South Africa* (1989) 19)

Customary law will be an item on any agenda for reform, but future law-makers will be confronted with the product of years of neglect and, what is more insidious, a subject of doubtful authenticity, a so-called 'invented tradition'.

Customary law is supposed to develop spontaneously in a given jural community. The adjective 'customary' implies that the rules were not fashioned by a professional class of lawyers. Over the past decade, however, it has become apparent that this is a misconception. The alienation of customary law from its community origins began with the colonial policy of indirect rule, when indigenous laws were co-opted to the received European law. As the price of recognition customary law had to conform to the dominant legal culture. The claim that this transformed law represented a genuine precolonial tradition or a continuing evolution of social norms was not true, but the banner of tradition encouraged subject peoples to believe that they retained some sort of legal autonomy. The inverted commas now regularly flanking the term 'customary law' signify the scepticism felt about its authenticity. Three quite different meanings of this term must be distinguished: the official body of law employed in the courts and by the administration (this diverges most markedly from actual social practice); the law used by academics for teaching purposes; and the law actually lived by the people. Our knowledge of customary law in the last sense is, for want of up-to-date empirical studies, necessarily a matter of conjecture.

The preservation of customary law as a distinct legal system found its justification in the cultural uniqueness of the African people. The African heritage is its culture, the symbols of group identity that mark the people as distinct and different. As such, culture is a political and social resource for an emergent African national consciousness.

In southern Africa, however, culture can equally be read as the basis of apartheid. Culture was the keystone of divide-and-rule politics, resulting in the fragmentation of the country. It was also the foundation of a policy of legal segregation that subjected all Africans to an outmoded and often oppressive law, whatever their individual preferences might have been. The actual social/cultural groups that dictated these policies were, of course, neither immanent nor static: there can be no exact dividing line between a notionally traditional, African group and a modern, western group, although by implication this distinction underlies the criteria for applying customary law. None the less, artificially created ethnic divisions persist in South Africa and continue to exacerbate political inequalities. It is hardly surprising that the concept of culture is highly suspect.

Here, as a purely technical aside, it might be noted that one undesirable consequence of the political segregation of South Africa has been an alarming multiplication of new laws, which is proving difficult to control. The independent homelands naturally have absolute legislative autonomy, and two at least have exercised their powers in private-law matters (the Transkei Marriage Act 21 of 1978 and the Bophuthatswana Succession Act 23 of 1982). Each of the self-governing territories, so far as their citizens are concerned, also has legislative competence in family-law matters. A notable exercise of this power was the promulgation of a separate code of Zulu law in KwaZulu, instituting several changes in the customary law formerly applicable under the Natal Code. It is now becoming evident that legal pluralism, if it is to be seriously enforced, is a complex and a costly business that the South African legal profession is in no position to undertake.

A decisive year in the history of customary law was 1927, the date of the enactment of the Native Administration Act (No 38). This statute separated the white and the African judicial structures; it made customary law a preserve of the lower courts (chiefs' and commissioners' courts) subject to the administrative control of the Department of Native Affairs. The Act was intended to introduce stability and order into a chaotic legal system inherited from the nineteenth century; and in fact the regime established by the Native Administration Act remained unchanged for the next fifty-eight years. When the government was finally spurred to action, the results were disappointing.

In 1985, the newly established South African Law Commission initiated an inquiry into customary and civil marriages contracted by Africans (*Marriages and Customary Unions of Black Persons*, Working Paper 10, Project 51). Legislation was forestalled by subsequent political turmoil and the State of Emergency. What finally emerged four years later was a very modest enactment, concerned only with civil/Christian marriage (Marriage and Matrimonial Property Law Amendment Act 3 of 1988).

More important was the abolition, in 1986, of the unpopular commissioners' courts and their courts of appeal (Act 34 of 1986). This was primarily a political move, aimed at cleansing the judicial system of the stigma of apartheid. The courts were unified into a single hierarchy, and in 1988, for the first time, all the courts of the land were authorized to take judicial notice of customary law (Law of Evidence Amendment Act 45 of 1988). These might be thought to be real advances, but there is little reason for optimism.

If customary law is an 'invented tradition', a body of rules appropriated from its social matrix and now lacking genuine social acceptance, it seems pointless for the courts to persist in the pretence that it is a product of African culture. These rules may no longer serve the interests of the community they are alleged to come from, and law reform seems to lack the initiative or capability to discover what these interests really are. In any event, further judicial development of customary law has been cut short. Because of litigation costs, customary law is now confined to lower courts whose judgments are not reported. Thus a major source of new law has been lost. Finally, can customary law, in its present form at least, meet the challenge posed by the norms of human rights? This is a particularly cogent question in view of the probable introduction of a bill of rights in South Africa.

The talk about human rights that currently permeates discussions about South African law has its origins in the international and constitutional human rights movement. The universality claimed for this movement should not obscure its actual cultural provenance. Although the accession of many developing countries to United Nations' declarations and international conventions gives a superficial impression of universalism, human rights are the product of bourgeois western values. In many parts of Africa this has given cause for suspicion about a renewed attempt to impose western cultural hegemony.

Opposition to human rights has rested on two main arguments. The first contends that Africa has an indigenous doctrine of rights that was not perceived by European colonists, who were too patronizing to believe that the continent could produce such a moral code. In respect of political and judicial processes, this argument has some truth (although the protection of due process was parochial in that it extended only to those within local jurisdictions, not to outsiders), but it overlooks important substantive issues such as sexual discrimination. The second, more plausible argument is that human rights are irrelevant to the situation in Africa because there is no social need to be met. This might have been valid for precolonial Africa, but conditions have so changed this century that it is no longer true. Feminist studies, for instance, have revealed that women used to be assured of material protection and support within the network of the extended family; after the introduction of capitalism, however, the system of labour migration caused the breakdown of this family structure to the detriment of women (amongst others). They have now been rendered vulnerable, and at the same time forced to undertake roles (for which they have no formal legal powers) that were previously prescribed for men.

Although patriarchy was probably a feature of all sub-Saharan African societies, it took on an extreme manifestation in South Africa. Women have always been able to mitigate the strictures of male domination in ways that depended on the character of the women concerned, their domestic circumstances and the attitude of the communities in which they lived. The inherent flexibility of customary law would have tolerated this. But any such local variations were ignored by the South African courts in favour of a uniform rule that deprived all women of legal capacity. No doubt this was believed to be in conformity with African attitudes, but it is certainly no longer an accurate reflection of women's social roles. Here the appellation 'invented tradition' is an apt description of the judicial code of customary law, and the application of a more authentic version may go part of the way to correcting some of the worst excesses of this regime. Even so, if customary law is to find a place in a progressive legal system that is in keeping with international norms, more than this will be required. According to the 1948 United Nations Declaration of Human Rights, spouses enjoy equality of status during marriage; and the 1979 Convention on the Elimination of Discrimination against Women goes even further: it obliges States Parties to modify all prejudices and cultural patterns of conduct that encourage 'the idea of the inferiority . . . of either of the sexes' (art 5).

The status of children is an issue less emotive than women's emancipation but equally pressing. International conventions require elimination of the status of illegitimacy and freedom from exploitation. Children from economically depressed families are expected to contribute to the family livelihood at the earliest possible age; this widespread social practice, combined with the customary rule that all earnings of household inmates accrue to the head of the family, could well conspire to produce a situation of economic exploitation. Significant too is the effect that human rights norms may have on support obligations and the structure of the family: the natural parents are contemplated as duty bearers vis-à-vis the child; this runs counter to the African principle that children belong to a patrilineal extended family.

A more subtle challenge emerges in the form of the property rights guaranteed in certain human rights instruments. Customary law, in particular customary land tenure, cannot be read to contain 'rights of ownership' in the common-law sense of absolute ownership. The customary ideas about property holding were predicated on an extended family system that was cemented by an ethic of generosity towards kin. All major assets were considered to be family property; the fortunes of the individual and those of the family were one. Material security rested on personal rights and duties of support. It is argued in this book that social changes in Africa are such that people must now find security principally in the form of individual rights to property. Where an individual cannot expect the support of kinfolk as a matter of course, an assured right to property becomes a necessity. And any move to ameliorate the position of women and children inevitably involves removal of the privileges of patriarchy, the first of which is control of property.

The strictly racial division of the courts' jurisdictional powers and the rigid application of customary law in the past has done little to recommend the system established by the Black Administration Act in 1927. Africans, especially women, have found that they were bound by a personal law, the dictates of which they were unable to escape regardless of their own predilections. Customary law must be reconceived, new questions must be formulated about its role in South African law, and new goals must be posed for its development. So far as the goals are concerned, in this book extensive use is made of materials from local common law and legal systems abroad; and the proposed bill of human rights, even if it is not made justiciable, will inevitably inform decision-making as a source of ideas on public policy.

*   *   *

The format of this book needs a special word of explanation. As the title 'sourcebook' suggests, it is a compilation of the sources, both legal and anthropological, from which customary law is constructed. South Africa has always been noted for its scholarly tradition in anthropology and many of the great names of the British school, such as Radcliffe-Brown, Gluckman, Schapera and Wilson, have had a lasting influence on customary law. Full tribute is paid here to their ethnographic studies and their provocative theories about law and society.

By emphasizing primary sources, the book is intended to reflect the diversity of customary law in place, time and source. Contrary to what the official version might lead one to believe, there is in reality no monolithic code of customary law, not even a code representing the law of the Zulu or Tswana or any other 'tribe'. The customary nature of the law implies its origin and application in parochial communities. These may be no larger than a neighbourhood centred on a local headman's court, or, where there is a stable tradition of central government (as in Lesotho), the community may embrace a larger political unit. Western legal formalism obliterates these particularities, reducing all law to the same set of conceptual formulae: contract, property, delict, crime etc. An acknowledgement of the diversity of customary law, however, does not imply that each system differs so markedly from its neighbours that a general work on southern Africa is impossible. Tendencies towards uniformity can be found in the influence of common social, economic and political structures, especially those that have resulted from the penetration of capitalism and the forces of industrialization.

Some of the sources are now quite clearly dated. But, apart from the fact that the writer of a book that is to cover a region as heterogeneous as South Africa cannot afford to be too discriminating, many of these early works are valuable demonstrations of the transformations necessary to incorporate custom into a legal code. The decisions of the former Native Appeal Courts are a case in point. They provide good examples of the interface between local custom and the demands of western legalism. Thus a constant although unspoken propensity to generalize from the particular case (compounded by the courts' insistence on the doctrine of stare decisis) is always evident in the courts' judgments. Similarly, a logical coherence has been imposed on the mixed repertoire of norms derived from various parts of the country. From this followed the gradual compilation of a single national code of law, and in this respect the Natal Code, despite protestations to the contrary, was influential way beyond the borders of the province.

*   *   *

Our grateful thanks are due to Kate Coleman, Diane Davis, Tessa Dogon and Ian Jennings, for their help in proof-reading, research and checking references, and to Lesley Shapiro for her faultless typing. Thanks are also due to the Association of Law Societies, the University of Cape Town and the South African Legal Rights Foundation for the generous financial assistance which made publication of this book possible. Finally, the Alexander von Humboldt Foundation warrants special mention for making possible a sabbatical year during which many of the ideas in this work came to fruition.

Contents

Case Index

Bibliography

ABEL R L 'Customary laws of wrongs in Kenya: an essay in research method' (1969) 17 *Am J Comp L* 573
—— 'A comparative theory of dispute institutions in society' (1973) 8 *Law & Soc R* 217
—— 'Conservative conflict and the reproduction of capitalism: the role of informal justice' (1981) 9 *Int J Sociology L* 245
—— (ed) *The Politics of Informal Justice* 2v 1982 New York Academic Press
ABITBOL E 'La famille conjugale et le droit nouveau du mariage en Côte d'Ivoire' (1966) 10 *JAL* 141
ADAM H (ed) *South Africa: Sociological Perspectives* 1971 OUP
ADAM L 'Modern ethnological jurisprudence in theory and in practice' (1934) 16 *J Comp Leg* 216
AFRICA PUBLICATIONS TRUST *The Children of Apartheid: a study of the effects of migratory labour on family life in the Ciskei* 1974 London
AFSHAR H (ed) *Women, State and Ideology* 1987 Macmillan Press London
AKANKI O 'Proof of customary law in Nigerian courts' (1970) 4 *Nigerian LJ* 20
ALBERTI L (trans W Fehr) *Account of the Tribal Life and Customs of the Xhosa in 1807* 1968 AA Balkema Cape Town
ALLAN K 'Nation; tribalism and national language: Nigeria's case' (1978–9) 18 *Cahiers d'Études Africaines* 397
ALLEN Sir C K *Legal Duties, and other Essays in Jurisprudence* 1931 Clarendon Press Oxford
—— *Law in the Making* 7ed 1964 Clarendon Press Oxford
ALLOTT A N 'Methods of legal research into customary law' (1953) 5 *J Afr Admin* 172
—— 'The judicial ascertainment of customary law in British Africa' (1957) 20 *MLR* 244
—— 'Marriage and internal conflict of laws in Ghana' (1958) 2 *JAL* 164
—— (ed) *Conference [on the] Future of Customary Law in Africa 1959–1960* 1960 Butterworths London
—— *Essays in African Law, with special reference to the law of Ghana* 1960 Butterworths London
—— 'Towards a definition of absolute ownership' (1961) 5 *JAL* 99
—— 'Towards the unification of laws in Africa' (1965) 14 *ICLQ* 366
—— 'The law of inheritance, family structure and modern economic order in Africa' (1970) 71 *Zeitschrift für Vergleichende Rechtswissenschaft* 105
—— (ed) *Judicial and Legal Systems in Africa* 1ed 1960; 2ed 1970 Butterworths London
—— *New Essays in African Law* 1970 Butterworths London
—— 'The people as law-makers: custom, practice and public opinion as sources of law in Africa and England' (1977) 21 *JAL* 1
—— *The Limits of Law* 1980 Butterworths London
ALLOTT A N & G WOODMAN (eds) *People's Law and State Law* (The Bellagio Papers) 1985 Foris Publications Dordrecht
ANDERSON J N D (ed) *Family Law in Asia and Africa* 1968 George Allen & Unwin Ltd London
ARDENER E (ed) *Social Anthropology and Language* 1971 Tavistock London
ARGYLE J & E PRESTON-WHYTE *Social System and Tradition in Southern Africa* 1978 OUP Cape Town
ARIÈS P (trans R Baldick) *Centuries of Childhood; a social history of family life* 1964 Random House New York
ARMSTRONG A K & R T NHLAPO *Law and the Other Sex; the legal position of women in Swaziland* 1985 Univ of Swaziland Kwaluseni
ARMSTRONG A K *Women and Law in Southern Africa* 1987 Zimbabwe Publishing House Harare
ARMSTRONG G M 'From the fetishism of commodities to the regulated market: the rise and decline of property' (1987) 82 *Northwestern LR* 79
ASANTE S K B *Property Law and Social Goals in Ghana 1844–1966* 1975 Ghana UP
ASHTON H *The Basuto* 1952 OUP
AUBERT V (ed) *Sociology of Law, selected readings* 1969 Penguin Harmondsworth
AUSTIN J *Lectures on Jurisprudence or the Philosophy of Positive Law* (5ed by R Campbell) v1 1885 John Murray London
—— *The Province of Jurisprudence Determined and the Uses of the Study of Jurisprudence* 1954 Weidenfeld & Nicolson London
BACHOFEN J J *Das Mutterrecht* 1897 Benno Schwabe Verlagsbuchhandlung Basel
BALBUS I D 'Commodity form and legal form: an essay in the "relative autonomy" of the law' (1976–77) 11 *Law & Soc R* 571
BAPELA M S W *The People's Courts in a Customary Law Perspective* Unpublished paper 1988 UNISA

BATES F (ed) *The Child and the Law* 2v 1976 Oceana Publications Inc Dobbs Ferry

BAXI U 'People's law, development, justice' (1979) 12 *Verfassung u Recht* 97

BAXTER I F G & M A EBERTS *The Child and the Courts* 1978 Carswell Co Toronto and Sweet & Maxwell London

BEATTIE J *Other Cultures; aims, methods and achievements in social anthropology* 1966 Routledge & Kegan Paul London

BEATTIE J H M 'Informal judicial activity in Bunyoro' (1957) 9 *J Afr Admin* 188

BEINART B 'Liability of a deceased estate for maintenance' 1958 *AJ* 92

BEINART W *The Political Economy of Pondoland 1860–1930* 1982 Ravan Press Johannesburg

BEKKER J C 'Is emancipation of Bantu women in Natal still necessary?' (1975) 38 *THRHR* 394

—— 'Regspraak soos beoefen in die Noord-oostelike Bantoe-appèlhof' (1975) 8 *De Jure* 148

—— 'Judisiële kennisname van Bantoereg en -gewoonte' (1976) 39 *THRHR* 359

—— 'Grounds of divorce in African customary marriages in Natal' (1976) 9 *CILSA* 346

BEKKER J C & J J J COERTZE 'The role of official witnesses in African customary marriages in Natal' 1976 *De Rebus* 601

BEKKER J C *Seymour's Customary Law in Southern Africa* 5ed 1989 Juta Cape Town

BENNETT T W 'The African court system in Rhodesia: an appraisal' (1975) 15 *Rhod LJ* 133

BENNETT T W & W M SCHOLTZ 'Witchcraft: a problem of fault and causation' (1979) 12 *CILSA* 288

BENNETT T W 'The application of common law and customary law in commissioners' courts' (1979) 96 *SALJ* 399

BENNETT T W & T VERMEULEN 'Codification of customary law' (1980) 24 *JAL* 206

BENNETT T W 'Conflict of laws in South Africa: cases involving customary law' (1980) 43 *THRHR* 27

—— 'The interpersonal conflict of laws: a technique for adapting to social change in Africa' (1980) 18 *J Mod Afr Studies* 127

—— 'Maintenance of minor children: a problem of adapting customary law to meet social change' 1980 *AJ* 115

—— 'Conflict of laws—the application of customary law and the common law in Zimbabwe' (1981) 30 *ICLQ* 59

BENNETT T W & N S PEART 'The dualism of marriage laws in Africa' 1983 *AJ* 145

BENNETT T W 'Terminology and land tenure in customary law: an exercise in linguistic theory' 1985 *AJ* 173

—— *The Application of Customary Law in Southern Africa, the conflict of personal laws* 1985 Juta Cape Town

BENTSI-ENCHILL K 'Do African systems of land tenure require a special terminology?' (1965) 9 *JAL* 114

—— 'Intestate succession revisited I' (1972) 9 *Univ Ghana LJ* 123

—— 'Structural variations in property law' (1973) 6 *IECL* ch 2

BERGLUND A-I *Zulu Thought-patterns and Symbolism* 1976 C Hurst & Co London

BERNARD J *Women and the Public Interest* 1971 Aldine Atherton Chicago

BLANC-JOUVAN X 'Remarques sur la codification du droit privé à Madagascar' (1967) 43 *Rev Jur du Congo* 159

BLANKENBURG E et al (eds) 'Alternative Rechtsformen und Alternativen zum Recht' 1980 *Jahrbuch für Rechtssoziologie und Rechtstheorie* Band VI Westdeutscher Verlag Wiesbaden

BLOCH M (ed) *Marxist Analyses and Social Anthropology* 1975 Malaby Press London

—— *Marxism and Anthropology: the history of a relationship* 1983 Clarendon Press Oxford

BOBERG P Q R *The Law of Persons and the Family* 1977 Juta Cape Town

BOCK P (ed) *Peasants in the Modern World* 1969 Univ of New Mexico Press

BODDINGTON E 'The participation of women in the South African labour force' 1979 *Africa Perspective* 7

BOHANNAN P *Justice and Judgment among the Tiv* 1957 OUP London

—— *Social Anthropology* 1963 Holt, Rinehart & Winston New York

—— (ed) *Law and Warfare: studies in the anthropology of conflict* 1967 Natural History Press New York

BOONZAIER E & J SHARP *South African Keywords: the uses and abuses of political concepts* 1988 David Philip Cape Town

BOSERUP E *Women's Role in Economic Development* 1970 George Allen & Unwin London

BOURDILLON M F C *The Shona Peoples; an ethnography of the contemporary Shona with special reference to their religion* 1976 Mambo Press Gwelo

BOZZOLI B 'Marxism, feminism and South African studies' (1983) 9 *JSAS* 139

BRANDEL M 'Urban lobolo attitudes: a preliminary report' (1958) 17 *Afr Studies* 34

BRITTEN H 'Twala—the need for registration of customary unions' (1930) 4 *Bantu Studies* 269

BROOKE N J 'The changing character of customary courts' (1954) 6 *J Afr Admin* 67

BROOKES E H *The History of Native Policy in South Africa from 1830 to the Present Day* 1924 Nasionale Pers Cape Town
—— *The Colour Problems of South Africa* 1934 Lovedale Press Lovedale and Kegan Paul, Trench, Trubner & Co London
BROPHY J 'Parental rights and children's welfare: some problems of feminists' strategy in the 1920s' (1982) 10 *Int J Sociology L* 149
BROWN J T *Among the Bantu Nomads* 1924 Seeley, Service & Co Lippincott
BRUNET E 'Questioning the quality of alternate dispute resolution' (1987) 62 *Tulane LR* 1
BRYANT A T *The Zulu People* 1949 Shuter & Shooter Pietermaritzburg
BRYDE B-O *The Politics and Sociology of African Legal Development* 1976 Alfred Metzner Verlag Frankfurt
BUDLENDER G M 'Incorporation and exclusion: recent developments in labour law and influx control' (1985) 1 *SAJHR* 3
BUKH J *The Village Woman in Ghana* 1979 Scandinavian Institute of African Studies Uppsala
BUNDY C *The Rise and Decline of the South African Peasantry* 1979 Heinemann London
BURMAN S B 'Cape policies towards African law in Cape tribal territories 1872–1883' unpublished PhD thesis 1973 Univ of Cape Town
—— 'Symbolic dimensions of the enforcement of law' (1976) 3 *Brit J L & Soc* 204
—— 'Use and abuse of the "modern" versus "traditional" law dichotomy in South Africa' (1979) 12 *Verfassung u Recht* 129
BURMAN S B & B E HARRELL-BOND (eds) *The Imposition of Law* 1979 Academic Press London and New York
BURMAN S B 'Roman-Dutch family law for Africans: the Black Divorce Court in action' 1983 *AJ* 171
BURMAN S B & R FUCHS *Custody in Divorce in Apartheid South Africa* 1984 Paper presented at the 20th Anniversary Meeting of the Law and Society Association
BURMAN S B & J BARRY 'Divorce and deprivation in South Africa' 1984 Second Carnegie Inquiry into Poverty and Development in Southern Africa Paper No 87 Cape Town
BURMAN S B 'The interaction of legislation relating to urban Africans and the laws regulating family relationships' 1984 *AJ* 89
—— 'Legislation for social change in a "multicultural" society' (1985) 14 *Quaderni Fiorentini* 175
BURMAN S B & P REYNOLDS (eds) *Growing up in a Divided Society; the contexts of childhood in South Africa* 1986 Ravan Press Johannesburg
BURMAN S B 'Marriage break-up in South Africa: holding want at bay?' (1987) 1 *Int J Law & Family* 206
BURMAN S B & S BERGER 'When family support fails: the problems of maintenance payments in apartheid South Africa' (1988) 4 *SAJHR* 194 and 334
BURMAN S B & W SCHARF *Informal Justice and People's Courts in a Changing South Africa* Unpublished paper 1989 Univ of Cape Town
—— 'Creating people's justice: Street committees and people's courts in a South African city' (1990) 24 *Law & Soc R* 693
BURN E H (ed) *Cheshire's Modern Law of Real Property* 11ed 1972 Butterworths London
BURNS A et al (eds) *The Family in the Modern World; Australian Perspective* 1983 George Allen & Unwin Sydney
CAIN M & K KULCSAR 'Thinking disputes: an essay on the origins of the dispute industry' (1981) 16 *L & Soc R* 375
—— *Disputes and the Law* 1983 Akadémiai Kiadó Budapest
CAMPBELL A 'baNgwaketse marriage and dissolution of marriage' (1970) 3 *CILSA* 212 and 325
CAPE OF GOOD HOPE COMMISSION ON NATIVE LAWS AND CUSTOMS Report on Proceedings, with appendices of the Government Commission on Native Laws and Customs 1883 Government Printers Cape Town
CAPPELLETTI M (ed) *Access to Justice* 4v 1978–79 Sijthoff & Noordhoff Alphen aan den Rijn
CENTRE FOR CONTEMPORARY CULTURAL STUDIES *On Ideology* 1978 Hutchinson London
CHANOCK M 'Neo-traditionalism and the customary law in Malawi' (1978) 16 *Afr L Studies* 80
—— *Law, Custom and Social Order, the colonial experience in Malawi and Zambia* 1985 CUP
CHASKALSON A 'The right of black persons to seek employment and be employed in the Republic of South Africa' 1984 *AJ* 33
CHEATER A P 'Fighting over property: the articulation of dominant and subordinate legal systems governing the inheritance of immovable property among Blacks in Zimbabwe' (1987) 57 *Africa* 173
CHIGWEDERE A *Lobola—the Pros and Cons* 1982 Books for Africa Harare
CHILD H F *The History and Extent of Recognition of Tribal Law in Rhodesia* 2ed 1976 Government Printer Harare

CHINYENZE M 'A critique of Chigwedere's book "Lobolo—the pros and cons" in relation to the emancipation of women in Zimbabwe' (1983–84) 1–2 *Zimb LR* 229

CHRISTIE R H 'Editorial' in (1967) 7 *Rhod LJ* 1

CHURCH J 'Guardianship as an incident of the customary law of parent and child—with reference to Transkei' (1979) 12 *CILSA* 326

CLARK H 'The new marriage' (1976) 12 *Willamette LJ* 441

CLERC A 'The marriage laws of the Ronga tribe' (1938) 12 *Bantu Studies* 75

CLIFFORD J & G E MARCUS (eds) *Writing Culture: the poetics and politics of ethnography* 1986 Univ of California Press

CLIGNET R *Many Wives, Many Powers* 1970 Northwestern Univ Press Evanston

COCK J *Maids and Madams; a study in the politics of exploitation* 1980 Ravan Press Johannesburg

COERTZE P J *Inleiding tot die Algemene Volkekunde* 3ed 1977 Voortrekkerpers Johannesburg

COERTZE R D *Die Familie-, Erf- en Opvolgingsreg van die Bafokeng van Rustenburg* 1971 SABRA Pretoria

COKER G B A *Family Property among the Yorubas* 1958 Sweet & Maxwell London

COLDHAM S F R 'The law of succession in Zambia: recent proposals for reform' (1983) 27 *JAL* 162

COLLIER J *Law and Social Change in Zinacantan* 1973 Stanford Univ Press Stanford

COLSON E 'Possible repercussions of the right to make wills upon the Plateau Tonga of Northern Rhodesia' (1950) 2 *J Afr Admin* 24

——— *Tradition and Contract: the problem of order* 1975 Heinemann London

COMAROFF J L & S ROBERTS 'Marriage and extra-marital sexuality, the dialectics of legal change among the Kgatla' (1977) 21 *JAL* 97

COMAROFF J L (ed) *The Meaning of Marriage Payments* 1980 Academic Press London and New York

COMAROFF J L & S ROBERTS *Rules and Processes* 1981 Chicago UP

COOK P A W *Social Organizations and Ceremonial Institutions of the Bomvana* 1931 Juta Cape Town

COONTZ S & P HENDERSON *Women's Work, Men's Property: the origins of gender and class* 1986 Verso London

CORBETT M M, H R HAHLO & G HOFMEYR *The Law of Succession in South Africa* 1980 Juta Cape Town

CORDER H 'The rights and conditions of entry into and residence in urban areas by Africans' 1984 *AJ* 45

CORDER H (ed) *Democracy and the Judiciary* 1989 IDASA Cape Town

COTRAN E 'The unification of laws in East Africa' (1963) 1 *J Mod Afr Studies* 209

——— 'African conference on local courts and customary law' (1965) 4 *J Local Admin Overseas* 128

COTRAN E & N N RUBIN (eds) *Readings in African Law* 2v 1970 Africana Publishing Corp New York

CRETNEY S 'The maintenance quagmire' (1970) 33 *MLR* 662

DANET B 'Language in the legal process' (1979) 14 *Law & Soc R* 445

DANIELS W C E *The Common Law in West Africa* 1964 Butterworths London

——— 'Recent reforms in Ghana's family law' (1987) 31 *JAL* 93

DANZIG R 'Toward the creation of a complementary, decentralized system of criminal justice' (1973) 26 *Stanford LR* 1

DANZIG R & M J LOWY 'Everyday disputes and mediation in the United States: a reply to Professor Felstiner' (1975) 9 *Law & Soc R* 675

DAVID R 'A civil code for Ethiopia: considerations on the codification of the civil law in African countries' (1962–3) 37 *Tulane LR* 187

——— 'La refonte du code civil dans les états africaines' 1962 *Annales Africaines* 160

DAVIS G et al 'Divorce: who supports the family?' (1983) 13 *Family L* 217

DEAN W H B 'A citizen of Transkei' (1978) 11 *CILSA* 66

DE JAGER E J (ed) *Man: anthropological essays presented to O F Raum* 1971 C Struik (Pty) Ltd Cape Town

DE SOUSA SANTOS B 'The law of the oppressed: the construction and reproduction of legality in Pasargada' (1977–8) 12 *Law & Soc R* 4

——— 'Law and community: the changing nature of state power in late capitalism' (1980) 8 *Int J Sociology L* 379

——— 'From customary law to popular justice' (1984) 28 *JAL* 90

DHLODHLO A E B 'Traditional burial, "ukuncindisa" and mourning ceremonies of the Zulus' (1984) 13 *Speculum Juris* 96

DIAMOND A S 'Book review: The Law of Primitive Man—a study in comparative legal dynamics by E Adamson Hoebel and The Judicial Process among the Barotse of Northern Rhodesia by Max Gluckman' (1956) 5 *ICLQ* 624

—— *Primitive Law, Past and Present* 1971 Methuen & Co London
DIAMOND S 'The rule of law versus the order of custom' (1971) 38 *Social Research* 42
DICKENS B M 'The modern function and limits of parental rights' (1981) 97 *LQR* 462
DLAMINI C R M 'Recognition of a customary marriage' 1982 *De Rebus* 593
—— *A Juridical Analysis and Critical Evaluation of Ilobolo in a Changing Zulu Society* unpublished LLD thesis 1983 Univ of Zululand
—— *The New Legal Status of Zulu Women* 1983 Univ of Zululand KwaDlangezwa
—— 'The transformation of a customary marriage in Zulu law' (1983) 16 *CILSA* 383
—— 'The modern legal significance of *ilobolo* in Zulu society' 1984 *De Jure* 148
—— 'Maintenance of minor children: the role of the courts in updating customary law to meet socio-economic changes' (1984) 101 *SALJ* 346
—— 'Should ilobolo be abolished? A reply to Hlophe' (1985) 18 *CILSA* 361
DONZELOT J (trans by R Hurley) *The Policing of Families* 1980 Hutchinson London
DRIBERG J H 'Primitive law in eastern Africa' (1928) 1 *Africa* 65
—— 'The African conception of law' (1934) 16 *J Comp Leg* 230
DUBOW S 'Holding "a just balance between white and black": the Native Affairs Department in South Africa c.1920–33' (1986) 12 *JSAS* 217
DUGARD J 'South Africa's "independent" homelands: an exercise in denationalization' (1980) 10 *Denver J Int L & Policy* 11
DUNCAN P *Sotho Laws and Customs* 1960 OUP Cape Town
DURAND J J F *Swartman, Stad en Toekoms* 1970 Tafelberg Uitgewers Kaapstad
EEKELAAR J M & E CLIVE *Custody after Divorce* 1977 Centre for Socio-Legal Studies Oxford
EEKELAAR J M *Family Law and Social Policy* 1978 Weidenfeld & Nicolson London
—— 'Some principles of financial and property adjustment on divorce' 1979 *LQR* 253
EEKELAAR J M & S N KATZ (eds) *Marriage and Cohabitation in Contemporary Societies* 1980 Butterworth & Co Toronto
—— *The Resolution of Family Conflict, comparative legal perspectives* 1984 Butterworth & Co Toronto
EEKELAAR J M & M MACLEAN *Maintenance after Divorce* 1985 Clarendon Press Oxford; OUP New York
EEKELAAR J M 'The emergence of children's rights' (1986) 6 *Oxford J Legal Studies* 161
EGAN S (ed) *S M Otieno, Kenya's Unique Burial Saga* 1987 The Nation Nairobi
EHRLICH E *Fundamental Principles of the Sociology of Law* (trans by W L Moll) 1936 Harvard Univ Press Cambridge
EISENSTADT S N 'African age groups: a comparative study' (1954) 24 *Africa* 100
ELIAS T O *The Nature of African Customary Law* 1956 Manchester UP
ELLIOTT E D 'The evolutionary tradition in jurisprudence' (1985) 85 *Columbia LR* 38
ELOFF J F & R D COERTZE *Etnografiese Studies in Suidelike Afrika* 1972 Van Schaik Pretoria
EMANÉ J 'Les droits patrimoniaux de la femme mariée ivorienne' 1967 *Annales Africaines* 86
ENGELS F *The Origin of the Family, Private Property and the State* (trans by E Untermann) 1902 Charles M Kerr Chicago
EPSTEIN A L 'Some aspects of the conflict of law and urban courts in Northern Rhodesia' (1951) 12 *Human Problems* 31
—— *The Administration of Justice and the Urban African* 1953 Colonial Office HMSO London
—— *Juridical Techniques and the Judicial Process* 1954 Manchester UP
—— *Politics in an Urban African Community* 1958 Manchester UP
—— *The Craft of Social Anthropology* 1967 Tavistock London
—— 'The reasonable man revisited: some problems in the anthropology of law' (1972) 7 *Law & Soc R* 643
—— *Urbanization and Kinship, the domestic domain in the Copperbelt of Zambia 1950–1956* 1981 Academic Press London
ERASMUS H J, C G VAN DER MERWE & A H VAN WYK *Lee & Honoré: Family, Things and Succession* 2ed 1983 Butterworths Durban
ETIENNE M & E LEACOCK (eds) *Women and Colonization, anthropological perspectives* 1980 Praeger New York
EVANS-PRITCHARD E E *The Nuer: a description of the modes of livelihood and political institutions of a Nilotic people* 1940 Clarendon Press Oxford
—— 'Bridewealth among the Nuer' (1947) 6 *Afr Studies* 181
—— *Kinship and Marriage among the Nuer* 1951 Clarendon Press Oxford
FALLERS L A *Law without Precedent* 1969 Chicago UP
FAUL E 'Origins, development and crisis of the idea of progress' (1985) 31 *Law & State* 7
FELSTINER W L F 'Influences of social organization on dispute processing' (1974) 9 *Law & Soc R* 63
FINE B et al (eds) *Capitalism and the Rule of Law* 1979 Hutchinson London

FINER REPORT *Report of the Committee on One-Parent Families* 2v 1974 Cmnd 5629 HMSO London
FITZPATRICK P *Law and State in Papua New Guinea* 1980 Academic Press London
FORSYTH C F '*Jus inter gentes*: section 11(2) of the Black Administration Act 1927' (1979) 96 *SALJ* 418
—— *Private International Law* 2ed 1990 Juta Cape Town
FORTES M & E E EVANS-PRITCHARD (eds) *African Political Systems* 1940 OUP
FORTES M *The Dynamics of Clanship among the Tallensi* 1945 OUP London
—— *Kinship and the Social Order* 1970 Routledge & Kegan Paul London
FORTES M & S PATTERSON (eds) *Studies in African Social Anthropology* 1975 Academic Press London
FOX R *Kinship and Marriage, an anthropological perspective* 1967 Penguin Harmondsworth
FRANCIS M J D 'Two problems with Bantu civil marriages' 1967 *AJ* 149
FREEMAN M D A & C M LYON *Cohabitation without Marriage: an essay in law and social policy* 1983 Gower Guildford
FREEMAN M D A *The Rights and Wrongs of Children* 1983 Frances Pinter London
—— (ed) *The State, the Law, and the Family: critical perspectives* 1984 Tavistock and Sweet & Maxwell London and New York
—— 'Towards a critical theory of family law' 1985 *Current Legal Problems* 153
FRIEDMAN L M 'On legal development' (1969) 24 *Rutgers LR* 11
FRIEDMAN L M & R V PERCIVAL 'A tale of two courts: litigation in Alameda and San Benito counties' (1976) 10 *Law & Soc R* 267
FRIEDMAN L M *Law and Society: an introduction* 1977 Prentice Hall Englewood Cliffs NJ
FULLER L L 'Consideration and form' (1941) 41 *Columbia LR* 799
GALANTER M 'Why the "haves" come out ahead: speculations on the limits of legal change' (1974) 9 *Law & Soc R* 95
—— 'Justice in many rooms: courts, private ordering and indigenous law' (1981) 19 *J Legal Pluralism* 1
GALEN D P 'Internal conflicts between customary law and general law in Zimbabwe: family law as a case study' (1983–4) 1/2 *Zimb LR* 3
GEERTZ C (ed) *Old Societies and New States: the quest for modernity in Asia and Africa* 1963 Free Press New York
GEERTZ C *Local Knowledge: further essays in interpretative anthropology* 1983 Basic Books New York
GERBER B A & S P NEWMAN *Soweto's Children: the development of attitudes* 1980 Academic Press London
GHAI Y 'Law, development and African scholarship' (1987) 50 *MLR* 750
GIBBS J L 'Marital instability among the Kpelle' (1963) 65 *Am Anthropologist* 552
GLENDON M A *State, Law and Family: family law in transition in the United States and Western Europe* 1977 North Holland Oxford
—— *The New Family and the New Property* 1981 Butterworths Toronto
GLUCKMAN M 'Bridewealth and the stability of marriage' (1953) 53 *Man* 141
—— *Analysis of a Social Situation in Modern Zululand* 1958 (Rhodes-Livingstone Institute Papers No28) Manchester UP
—— *Essays in the Ritual of Social Relations* 1962 Manchester UP
—— *Politics, Law and Ritual in Tribal Society* 1965 Blackwell Oxford
—— *The Judicial Process among the Barotse of Northern Rhodesia* 2ed 1967 Manchester UP
GLUCKMAN M (ed) *Ideas and Procedures in African Customary Law* 1969 OUP
—— *The Allocation of Responsibility* 1972 Manchester UP
GLUCKMAN M *The Ideas in Barotse Jurisprudence* 1972 (reprint) Manchester UP
—— 'Limitations of the case-method in the study of tribal law' (1972–3) 7 *Law & Soc R* 611
GOLDSTEIN J et al *Beyond the Best Interests of the Child* 1973 The Free Press New York
—— *Before the Best Interests of the Child* 1979 The Free Press New York
GOODE W J *World Revolution and Family Patterns* 1963 Free Press New York
—— *The Family* 1964 Prentice Hall Englewood Cliffs NJ
GOODHART A L 'The importance of a definition of law' (1951) 3 *J Afr Admin* 106
GOODRICH P 'The antinomies of legal theory: an introductory survey' (1983) 3 *Legal Studies* 1
—— *Reading the Law* 1986 Blackwell Oxford
GOODY J *The Developmental Cycle in Domestic Groups* 1958 CUP
—— *Death, Property and the Ancestors. A study of the mortuary customs of the Lodagaa of West Africa* 1962 Tavistock London
GOODY J (ed) *Succession to High Office* 1966 CUP
—— *Kinship, selected readings* 1971 Penguin Harmondsworth
GOODY J & S J TAMBIAH *Bridewealth and Dowry* 1973 CUP
GOODY J (ed) *The Character of Kinship* 1973 CUP

GOODY J et al *Family and Inheritance; rural society in Western Europe 1200–1800* 1976 CUP
GOODY J *Production and Reproduction* 1976 CUP
—— *The Development of the Family and Marriage in Europe* 1983 CUP
—— *The Interface between the Written and the Oral* 1987 CUP.
GORDON R J & M J MEGGITT *Law and Order in the New Guinea Highlands: encounters with Enga* 1985 Univ Press of New England Hanover and London
GORDON R 'The white man's burden: *ersatz* customary law and internal pacification in South Africa' (1989) 2 *J Historical Sociology* 41
GOULDNER A W *The Coming Crisis of Western Sociology* 1970 Heinemann London
GRAY K J *Reallocation of Property on Divorce* 1977 Professional Books Abingdon
GRAY R F & GULLIVER P H (eds) *The Family Estate in Africa* 1964 Routledge & Kegan Paul London
GREAT BRITAIN Report on the Royal Commission of Enquiry into the Administration of Justice in Kenya, Uganda and Tanganyika in Criminal Matters (Bushe Commission) 1934 HMSO London
GRIFFITHS A 'The problem of informal justice: family dispute processing among the Bakwena—a case study' (1986) 14 *Int J Sociology L* 359
GUEST A G (ed) *Oxford Essays in Jurisprudence* 1961 OUP
GULLIVER P H *Social Control in an African Society: a study of the Arusha* 1963 Routledge & Kegan Paul London
—— (ed) *Tradition and Transition in East Africa* 1969 Routledge & Kegan Paul London
GULLIVER P H 'Negotiations as a mode of dispute settlement: towards a general model' (1973) 7 *Law & Soc R* 667
—— *Disputes and Negotiations: a cross-cultural perspective* 1979 Academic Press New York
GUTKIND P C W & P WATERMAN (eds) *African Social Studies: a radical reader* 1977 Heinemann London
GUTTO S B O (ed) *Children and the Law in Kenya* 1979 Institute for Development Studies Nairobi Univ
HAFKIN N J & E G BAY *Women in Africa, studies in social and economic change* 1976 Stanford Univ Press
HAHLO H R & E KAHN (ed) *South Africa: the development of its laws and constitution* 1960 Juta Cape Town
HAHLO H R 'Here lies the common law: rest in peace' (1967) 30 *MLR* 241
HAHLO H R & E KAHN *The South African Legal System and its Background* 1968 Juta Cape Town
HAHLO H R & J D SINCLAIR *The Reform of the South African Law of Divorce* 1980 Juta Cape Town
HAHLO H R *The South African Law of Husband and Wife* 5ed 1985 Juta Cape Town
HAILEY LORD *An African Survey: a study of problems arising in Africa south of the Sahara* 2ed 1945 OUP
HALL M 'The myth of the Zulu homestead: archaeology and ethnography' (1984) 54 *Africa* 76
—— *The Changing Past: farmers, kings and traders in southern Africa 200–1860* 1987 David Philip Cape Town
HAMMOND-TOOKE W D *The Bhaca Society: a people of the Transkeian uplands, South Africa* 1962 OUP Cape Town
—— (ed) *The Bantu-speaking Peoples of Southern Africa* 2ed 1974 Routledge & Kegan Paul London
—— *Boundaries and Belief, the structure of a Sotho worldview* 1981 Wits Univ Press
—— 'Descent groups, chiefdoms and South African historiography' (1985) 11 *JSAS* 305
—— 'Who worships whom: agnates and ancestors among Nguni' (1985) 44 *Afr Studies* 47
HAMNETT I *Chieftainship and Legitimacy; an anthropological study of executive law in Lesotho* 1975 Routledge & Kegan Paul London
—— (ed) *Social Anthropology and Law* 1977 Academic Press London
HANNIGAN A St J J 'Native custom, its similarity to English conventional custom and its mode of proof' (1958) 2 *JAL* 101
HARE A P, G WIENDIECK & M H VON BROEMBSEN (eds) *South Africa: sociological analyses* 1979 OUP Cape Town
HARRELL-BOND B A 'The influence of legislative change on behaviour: a case study on the status of illegitimate children in Sierra Leone' (1975) 8 *Verfassung u Recht* 447
HARRIES C L *The Laws and Customs of the Bapedi and Cognate Tribes of the Transvaal* 1929 Hortors Ltd Johannesburg
HART H L A *The Concept of Law* 1961 Clarendon Press Oxford
HARTLAND E S *Primitive Law* 1924 Methuen & Co Ltd London
HASTINGS A *Christian Marriage in Africa* 1973 Hollen Street Press Ltd London
HAY M J & M WRIGHT (eds) *African Women and the Law: historical perspectives* 1982 Boston Univ Press Boston

HAYDEN R M 'A note on caste panchayats and government courts in India' (1984) 22 *J Legal Pluralism* 43

HAYSOM N *Mabangalala: the rise of right-wing vigilantes in South Africa* 1986 Occasional Paper 10 Centre for Applied Legal Studies Univ of Witwatersrand

HELLMANN E *Rooiyard; a sociological survey of an urban native slum yard* 1948 Rhodes-Livingstone (Institute) Papers No 13

HERSKOVITS M J *Economic Anthropology; the economic life of primitive peoples* 1965 W W Norton & Co New York

HIMSWORTH C M G 'The Botswana Customary Law Act, 1969' (1972) 16 *JAL* 4

HINDESS B & P Q HIRST *Pre-capitalist Modes of Production* 1975 Routledge & Kegan Paul London

HINDSON D C 'Orderly urbanization and influx control' (1985) 25 *Cahiers d'Études Africaines* 401

HIRSCHON R (ed) *Women and Property/Women as Property* 1984 Croom Helm London

HIRST P & P WOOLLEY *Social Relations and Human Attributes* 1982 Tavistock London

HLOPHE J M 'The Kwazulu Act on the Code of Zulu Law, 6 of 1981—a guide to intending spouses and some comments on the custom of lobolo' (1984) 17 *CILSA* 163

HOEBEL E A 'Fundamental legal concepts as applied in the study of primitive law' (1941–2) 51 *Yale LJ* 951

—— 'Three studies in African law' (1961) 13 *Stanford LR* 418

—— *The Law of Primitive Man: a study in comparative legal dynamics* 1976 Atheneum New York

HOFMAN J 'The development of the canon law of marriage' 1983 *AJ* 23

HOHFELD W N (COOK W W ed) *Fundamental Legal Conceptions* 1919 Yale UP New Haven

HOLLEMAN J F 'Die twee-eenheidsbeginsel in die sosiale en politieke samelewing van die Zulu' (1940) 14 *Bantu Studies* 31

—— 'An anthropological approach to Bantu law with special reference to Shona law' (1950) 10 *Human Problems* 51

—— *Shona Customary Law, with reference to kinship, marriage, the family and the estate* 1952 OUP Cape Town

—— *African Interlude* 1958 Nasionale Boekhandel Johannesburg

—— 'Die Bantoehuwelik op die kruispad' (1960) 11 *J Racial Affairs* 82

—— (ed) *Experiment in Swaziland* 1964 OUP Cape Town

—— *Chief, Council and Commissioner: some problems of government in Rhodesia* 1969 Royal Van Gorcum Ltd Assen

—— 'Customary law and legal reform' (1972–3) 7 *Law & Soc R* 585

—— 'Trouble-cases and trouble-less cases in the study of customary law and legal reform' (1973) 7 *Law & Soc R* 585

—— *Issues in African Law* 1974 Mouton The Hague

—— 'Disparities and uncertainties in African law and jurisdictions: a Rhodesian case study' (1979) 17 *Afr L Studies* 1

HOLMES O W 'Law in science and science in law' (1899) 12 *Harvard LR* 444

—— *Collected Legal Papers* 1920 Constable & Co Ltd London

HOOKER M B *Legal Pluralism: an introduction to colonial and neo-colonial laws* 1975 Clarendon Press Oxford

HORRELL M *The Rights of African Women, some suggested reforms* 1968 SA Institute of Race Relations Johannesburg

—— *The African Homelands of South Africa* 1973 SA Institute of Race Relations Johannesburg

HOWARD R E *Human Rights in Commonwealth Africa* 1984 Rowman & Littlefield Totowa New Jersey

—— 'Legitimacy and class rule in Commonwealth Africa: constitutionalism and the rule of law' (1985) 7 *Third World Quarterly* 323

HUBER H *Marriage and the Family in Rural Bukwaya (Tanzania)* 1973 Fribourg UP

HUGHES A J B *Land Tenure, Land Rights and Land Communities on Swazi National Land in Swaziland: a discussion of some inter-relationships between the traditional tenurial system and problems of agrarian development* 1972 Institute for Social Research Univ of Natal Durban

HUND J 'Legal and sociological approaches to indigenous law in southern Africa' (1982) 8 *Social Dynamics* 29

HUND J & M KOTU-RAMMOPU 'Justice in a South African township: the sociology of makgotla' (1983) 16 *CILSA* 179

HUND J & H W VAN DER MERWE *Legal Ideology and Politics in South Africa: a social science approach* 1986 Lanham Univ Press

HUNTER M 'Results of culture contact on the Pondo and Xosa family' (1932) 29 *SA J of Science* 681

—— *Reaction to Conquest* 2ed 1961 OUP London

HUTCHINSON T W et al (eds) *Africa and Law: developing legal systems in African Commonwealth nations* 1968 Wisconsin UP Madison
IFE UNIVERSITY *Integration of Customary Law and Modern Legal Systems in Africa* (Conference held at Ibadan 1964) Ife UP & Africana Publishing Ile-Ife & New York
ISON T G 'Small claims' (1972) 35 *MLR* 18
IZZARD W 'Migrants and mothers: case studies from Botswana' (1985) 11 *JSAS* 258
JACKSON B S *Semiotics and Legal Theory* 1985 Routledge & Kegan Paul London
JAMES D 'Family and household in a Lebowa village' (1985) 44 *Afr Studies* 159
—— 'Land shortage and inheritance in a Lebowa village' (1988) 14 *Social Dynamics* 36
JANISCH M 'Some administrative aspects of Native marriage problems' (1941) 15 *Bantu Studies* 1
JEFFREYS M D 'Lobolo is child-price' (1951) 10 *Afr Studies* 145
JEPPE W J O *Bophuthatswana: land tenure and development* 1980 Maskew Miller Cape Town
JUNOD H A *The Life of a South African Tribe* 2v 1912 Attinger Neuchâtel
—— 'Bantu marriage and Christian society' (1941) 15 *Bantu Studies* 25
KAHN J S & J R LLOBERA *The Anthropology of Pre-Capitalist Societies* 1981 Macmillan London
KAMENKA E, R BROWN & E R TAY (eds) *Law and Society, the crisis in legal ideals* 1978 Edward Arnold London
KAPFERER B (ed) *Transaction and Meaning; directions in the anthropology of exchange and symbolic behaviour* 1976 Institute for the Study of Human Issues Philadelphia
KAPLAN D & R A MANNERS *Culture Theory* 1972 Prentice Hall Englewood Cliffs NJ
KASUNMU A B & R W JAMES *Alienation of Family Property in Southern Nigeria* 1966 Caxton Press (West Africa) Ltd Ibadan
KEESING R M *Cultural Anthropology: a contemporary perspective* 2ed 1981 Holt, Rinehart & Winston New York
KELSEN H *The Pure Theory of Law* 1967 California UP Berkley LA
KENNEY H *Architect of Apartheid: H F Verwoerd—an appraisal* 1980 Jonathan Ball Johannesburg
KERR A J 'Liability in delict for wrongfully causing the death of a Native man married according to Native law' (1956) 73 *SALJ* 402
—— 'The application of Native law in the Supreme Court' (1957) 74 *SALJ* 313
—— 'The reception and codification of systems of law in southern Africa' (1958) 2 *JAL* 82
—— 'Roman-Dutch law marriages and the *lobola* contract' 1960 *AJ* 334
—— 'Implied *lobola* contracts ancillary to Roman-Dutch law marriages' 1963 *AJ* 49
—— 'Does a minor need two natural guardians in two systems of law to assist him at the same time?' (1965) 82 *SALJ* 487
—— 'Guardianship of children of Bantu customary unions: the inter-personal conflict of laws problem' (1973) 90 *SALJ* 4
—— *The Customary Law of Immovable Property and of Succession* 2ed 1976 Rhodes Univ Grahamstown
—— 'Customary law in the Small Claims Court' (1984) 101 *SALJ* 726
—— 'The Cape Government Commission on Native Laws and Customs (1883)' 1986 *Transkei LJ* 11
KHUMALO J A M *Civil Practice and Procedure of all Courts for Blacks in Southern Africa* 3ed 1984 Juta Cape Town
—— Supplement *Practice and Procedure of Customary Courts of the Republic of Botswana* 1977
KIDD D *Kafir Socialism and the Dawn of Individualism* 1908 Adam & Charles Black London
KIDDER R L 'The end of the road? Problems in the analysis of disputes' (1981) 15 *Law & Soc R* 717
—— *Connecting Law and Society: an introduction to research and theory* 1983 Prentice-Hall Englewood Cliffs NJ
KING M 'Playing with symbols—custody and the Law Commission' (1987) 17 *Family L* 186
KLOPPERS H P & T F COERTZE *Bantu Divorce Courts* 2ed 1976 Juta Cape Town
KLUDZE A K P 'Problems of intestate succession in Ghana' (1972) 9 *Univ Ghana LJ* 89
—— 'Accountability of the head of family in Ghana: a statutory solution in search of a problem' (1987) 31 *JAL* 107
KOCH K-F *War and Peace in Jalemo: the management of conflict in Highland New Guinea* 1974 Harvard UP Cambridge
KOCH K-F et al 'Political and psychological correlates of conflict management: a cross-cultural study' (1976) 10 *Law & Soc R* 443
KOHLER M *Marriage Customs in Southern Natal* 1933 Department of Native Affairs, Ethnological Publications vol 4, Government Printer Pretoria
KÖNZ P 'Legal development in developing countries' (1969) 63 *Proceedings of the Am Soc of Int Law* 91
KOYANA D S *Customary Law in a Changing Society* 1980 Juta Cape Town
KRAUSE H D 'Creation of Relations of Kinship' (1976) 4 *IECL* ch 6 Mohr Tübingen
—— 'Reflections on child support' (1983–4) 17 *Family LQ* 109

KRIGE E J 'Changing conditions in marital relations and parental duties among urbanized Natives'
(1936) 9 *Africa* 5
KRIGE E J *The Social System of the Zulus* 1936 Longmans Green London
KRIGE E J & J D KRIGE *The Realm of a Rain-Queen; a study of the pattern of Lovedu society* 1943
OUP London
KRIGE E J 'Woman-marriage, with special reference to the Lovedu—its significance for the definition
of marriage' (1974) 44 *Africa* 11
KRIGE E J & J L COMAROFF *Essays on African Marriage in Southern Africa* 1981 Juta Cape Town
KRIGE J D 'The significance of cattle exchanges in Lovedu social structure' (1939) 12 *Africa* 393
—— 'Some aspects of Lovedu judicial arrangements' (1939) 13 *Bantu Studies* 113
KUHN A & A WOLPE *Feminism and Materialism; women and modes of production* 1978 Routledge &
Kegan Paul London
KUPER A 'The Kgalagari and the jural consequences of marriage' (1970) 5 *Man* 466
—— 'The man in the study and the man in the field' (1980) 21 *European J Sociology* 14
—— 'Symbolic dimensions of the Southern Bantu homestead' (1980) 50 *Africa* 8
—— *Wives for Cattle; bridewealth and marriage in Southern Africa* 1982 Routledge & Kegan Paul
London
—— *Anthropology and Anthropologists; the modern British school* rev ed 1983 Routledge & Kegan Paul
London
KUPER A & J KUPER *The Social Science Encyclopaedia* 1985 Routledge & Kegan Paul London
KUPER A *South Africa and the Anthropologist* 1987 Routledge & Kegan Paul London
KUPER H *An African Aristocracy—rank among the Swazi* 1947 OUP London
—— *The Swazi; a South African kingdom* 1963 Holt, Rinehart & Winston New York
KUPER H & L KUPER (eds) *African Law: adaptation and development* 1965 Univ of California
Berkeley LA
KURCZEWSKI J & A PODGORECKI 'The disparity between law and social reality' (1975) 1 *Kroniek
van Afrika* 3
LABUSCHAGNE J M T 'Strafregsprekersbevoegdheid van Bantoekapteins en -hoofmanne in Suid- en
Suidwes-Afrika' (1974) 7 *De Jure* 38
—— 'Die Bantoehowe, vandag en môre' (1976) 1 *TRW* 59
LABUSCHAGNE J M T & D J SWANEPOEL 'Regspleging van die stedelike swartman in Suid-Afrika'
(1979) 12 *De Jure* 17
LABUSCHAGNE J M T 'Verjaring in die inheemse reg' (1987) 50 *THRHR* 87
—— 'Die inheemse *ukuthwala*-gebruik, wederregtelikheidsbewussyn en strafregtelike aanspreeklikheid
weens ontvoering' (1988) 13 *TRW* 33
LADLEY A S 'Changing the courts in Zimbabwe: the Customary Law and Primary Courts Act' (1982)
26 *JAL* 95
—— 'Courts and authority: a study of a Shona village court in rural Zimbabwe' unpublished PhD Thesis
1985 Univ of London
LANGBEIN J H 'The twentieth-century revolution in family wealth transmission' (1988) 86 *Michigan
LR* 722
LAPCHICK R E & S URDANG *Oppression and Resistance, the struggle of women in southern Africa*
1982 Greenwood Press Westport Connecticut
LAUBSCHER B J F *Sex, Custom and Psychopathology: a study of South African pagan Natives* 1937
George Routledge & Sons Ltd London
LEACH E R *Pul Eliya* 1961 CUP
LEACOCK E B *Myths of Male Dominance* 1981 Monthly Review Press New York
LEMPERT R 'More tales of two courts: exploring changes in the "dispute settlement function" of trial
courts' (1978) 13 *Law & Soc R* 91
LETSOALO E M *Land Reform in South Africa: a black perspective* 1987 Skotaville Johannesburg
LÉVI-STRAUSS C *Structural Anthropology* 1958 (trans C Jacobsen & B G Schoepf) 1963 Basic Books
New York
LEWIN J 'Some legal aspects of marriage by natives in South Africa' (1941) 15 *Bantu Studies* 13
—— 'The conflict of tribal laws' (1944) 61 *SALJ* 269
—— *Studies in African Native Law* 1947 African Bookman Cape Town
LEYS C *Underdevelopment in Kenya* 1977 Heinemann London
LLOYD P C 'Family property among the Yoruba' (1959) 3 *JAL* 105
—— *Yoruba Land Law* 1962 OUP London
LUCKHAM R (ed) *Law and Social Enquiry: case studies of research* 1981 Scandinavian Institute of
African Studies Uppsala
LUGG N C 'The practice of lobolo in Natal' (1945) 4 *Afr Studies* 23

LLEWELLYN K N 'Some realism about realism—responding to Dean Pound' (1931) 44 *Harvard LR* 1222

LLEWELLYN K N & E A HOEBEL *The Cheyenne Way* 1941 Univ of Oklahoma

LYE W F & C MURRAY *Transformations on the Highveld: the Tswana and Southern Sotho* 1980 David Philip Cape Town

MACCORMACK C P & M STRATHERN *Nature, Culture and Gender* 1980 CUP

MACCORMACK G 'Problems in the description of African systems of landholding' (1983) 21 *J Legal Pluralism* 1

MACLEAN COLONEL J *Compendium of Kafir Laws and Customs* 1906 J Slater Grahamstown

MAFEJE A 'The ideology of tribalism' (1971) 9 *J Mod Afr Studies* 253

MAGUBANE B 'The "Xhosa" in town, revisited. Urban social anthropology: a failure of method and theory' (1973) 75 *Am Anthropologist* 1701

MAIDMENT S 'A study in child custody' (1976) 6 *Family L* 195 and 236

—— *Child Custody and Divorce* 1984 Croom Helm London

MAINE SIR HENRY S *Ancient Law* 1861 John Murray London; 1917 Everyman ed J M Dent

—— *Lectures on the Early History of Institutions* 1905 John Murray London

MAIR L *Marriage* 1971 Penguin Harmondsworth

MAKAMURE K 'A comparative study of comrades' courts under socialist legal systems and Zimbabwe's village courts' (1985) 3 *Zimb LR* 34

MALINOWSKI B *Crime and Custom in Savage Society* 1926 Kegan Paul Trench & Trubner London

MANGANYI C & A DU TOIT (eds) *Political Violence and the Struggle in South Africa* 1990 Southern Cape Town; MacMillan London

MANONA C W 'Impact of urbanization on rural areas: the case of white-owned farms in the Eastern Cape' (1988) 47 *Afr Studies* 1

MAQUTU W C M 'Lesotho's African marriage is not a "customary union"' (1983) 16 *CILSA* 374

MARKS S & A ATMORE (eds) *Economy and Society in Pre-Industrial South Africa* 1980 Longman London

MARKS S & R RATHBONE (eds) *Industrialisation and Social Change in South Africa; African class formation, culture and consciousness 1870–1930* 1982 Longman New York

MARWICK B A *The Swazi; an ethnographic account of the natives of the Swaziland Protectorate* 1940 CUP

MASSELL G J 'Law as an instrument of revolutionary change in a traditional milieu' (1968) 2 *Law & Soc R* 179

MATTHEWS Z K 'Marriage customs among the Barolong' (1940) 13 *Africa* 1

MATHEWSON E 'Impact of urbanization on "Lobola"' (1959) 10 *J Racial Affairs* 72

MAY J *Zimbabwean Women in Customary and Colonial Law* 1983 Mambo Press Gweru

MAYER P (ed) *Socialization: the approach from social anthropology* 1970 Tavistock Publications London

MAYER P *Townsmen or Tribesmen* 1971 OUP Cape Town

MAYER P (ed) *Black Villagers in an Industrial Society* 1980 OUP Cape Town

MAYLAM P *A History of the African People of South Africa: from the early Iron Age to the 1970s* 1986 Croom Helm London; David Philip Cape Town

M'BEYE K 'L'expérience sénégalaise de la réforme du droit' (1970) 22 *Rev Int Droit Comparé* 38

MBILINYI M J 'The "new woman" and traditional norms in Tanzania' (1972) 10 *J Mod Afr Studies* 57

—— 'Runaway wives in colonial Tanganyika: forced labour and forced marriage in Rungwe District 1919–1961' (1988) 16 *Int J Sociology L* 1

MCNALLY N J 'Law in a changing society: a view from north of the Limpopo' (1988) 105 *SALJ* 434

MCQUOID-MASON D J *An Outline of Legal Aid in South Africa* 1982 Butterworths Durban

MCINTOSH W '150 Years of litigation and dispute settlement: a court tale' (1981) 15 *Law & Soc R* 823

MEAD M *Sex and Temperament in Three Primitive Societies* 3ed 1963 Morrow New York

MEILLASSOUX C 'From reproduction to production' (1972) 1 *Economy & Society* 102

—— *Anthropologie Économique des Gouro de Côte d'Ivoire* 3ed 1974 Mouton Paris

MERRY S E 'Going to court: strategies of dispute management in an American urban neighborhood' (1979) 13 *Law & Soc R* 891

MERRYMAN J 'Comparative law and social change: on the origin, style, decline and revival of the law and development movement' (1977) 25 *Am J Comp L* 457

MEULDERS-KLEIN M T & J EEKELAAR *Family, State and Individual Economic Security* 1988 2v Story-Scientia Brussels

MILL J S *On Liberty* 1962 Fontana London

—— *Utilitarianism* 2nd imp 1962 Collins London

MILLER J G *The Machinery of Succession* 1977 Professional Books Abingdon

MILLETT K *Sexual Politics* 1971 Hart-Davis London

MITCHELL J *Woman's Estate* 1971 C Nicholls & Co Manchester
MNOOKIN R 'Child-custody adjudication: judicial functions in the face of indeterminacy' (1975) 39 *Law & Contemporary Problems* 226
MNOOKIN R & L KORNHAUSER 'Bargaining in the shadow of the law: the case of divorce' (1979) 32 *Current Legal Problems* 65; also in (1979) 88 *Yale LJ* 950
MOHOHLO D 'Bophuthatswana Succession Act—a résumé with particular reference to customary marriages' 1987 *De Rebus* 31
MOLLER V & G J WELCH *Polygamy and Well-being among Zulu Migrants* 1987 Univ of Natal Durban
MONAMA R *Is This Justice?; a study of the Johannesburg Commissioners' ('pass') Courts* 1983 Centre for Applied Legal Studies Wits University Johannesburg
MÖNNIG H O *The Pedi* 1967 Van Schaik Pretoria
MOORE S F *Law as Process; an anthropological approach* 1978 Routledge & Kegan Paul London
—— 'Archaic law and modern times on the Zambezi' (1979) 7 *Int J Sociology L* 3
—— *Social Facts and Fabrications; 'customary' law on Kilimanjaro, 1880–1980* 1986 CUP
MORGAN L H *Ancient Society* 1877 Henry Holt & Co New York; 1967 Meridian Books
MORRIS C 'Law, reason and sociology' (1958) 107 *Univ Pennsylvania LR* 147
MORRIS H F 'Attitudes towards succession law in Nigeria during the colonial period' (1970) 14 *JAL* 5
—— 'Ghana: The Matrimonial Causes Act, 1971' (1972) 16 *JAL* 71
MORRIS H F & J S READ *Indirect Rule and the Search for Justice; essays in East African Legal History* 1972 Clarendon Press Oxford
MORSE B W & G R WOODMAN (eds) *Indigenous Law and the State* 1987 Foris Publications Dordrecht
MOTSHEKGA M S *Alternative Legal Institutions in Southern Africa* Unpublished paper 1989 UNISA
MQEKE R B 'Protection of a customary union wife' 1980 *De Rebus* 597
MÜNKNER H-H 'Law and development, a new discipline of scientific research and teaching' (1983) 4 *Jahrbuch Afrikanisches Recht* 99
MURCH M *Justice and Welfare in Divorce* 1980 Sweet & Maxwell London
MURDOCH G P *Social Structure* 1949 Macmillan New York
MURRAY C 'Marital strategy in Lesotho: the redistribution of migrant earnings' (1976) 35 *Afr Studies* 99
—— 'High bridewealth, migrant labour and the position of women in Lesotho' (1977) 21 *JAL* 79
—— 'The effects of migrant labour: a review of the evidence from Lesotho' (1980) 6 *SA Labour Bulletin* 21
—— 'Migrant labour and changing family structure in the rural periphery of southern Africa' (1980) 6 *JSAS* 139
—— *Families Divided; the impact of migrant labour in Lesotho* 1981 CUP; Ravan Johannesburg
MYBURGH A C 'Perspectives of South African Bantu law' (1965) 6(2) *Codicillus* 10
MYBURGH A C (ed) *Indigenous Criminal Law in Bophuthatswana* 1980 UNISA Pretoria
—— *Anthropology for Southern Africa* 1981 Van Schaik Pretoria
—— *Papers on Indigenous Law in Southern Africa* 1985 Van Schaik Pretoria
MYBURGH A C & M W PRINSLOO *Indigenous Public Law in KwaNdebele* 1985 Van Schaik Pretoria
NADEL S F *The Foundations of Social Anthropology* 1951 Cohen & West London
—— 'Reason and unreason in African law' (1956) 26 *Africa* 160
NADER L (ed) *Law in Culture and Society* 1969 Aldine Publishing Co Chicago
NADER L & L R SINGER 'Law in the future: what are the choices: dispute resolution' (1976) 51 *Calif State Bar J* 281
NADER L & H F TODD (eds) *The Disputing Process—Law in Ten Societies* 1978 Columbia Univ Press New York
NADER L (ed) *No Access to Law: alternatives to the American Judicial System* 1980 Academic Press New York
NATAL Commission appointed to inquire into the past and present state of the kafirs in the District of Natal *Report and Proceedings* 1852–3 Pietermaritzburg
NDULO M 'Widows under Zambian customary law and the response of the courts' (1985) 18 *CILSA* 90
NEWMAN K S *Law and Economic Organization: a comparative study of preindustrial societies* 1983 CUP
NHLAPO R T *Women and the Law* 1983 Reports of Proceedings of Two Seminars Univ of Swaziland KwaLuseni
—— 'International protection of human rights and the family: African variations on a common theme' (1989) 3 *Int J Law & Family* 1
NICHOLAS B *An Introduction to Roman Law* 1962 Clarendon Press Oxford

NIEHAUS I A 'Domestic dynamics and wage labour: a case study among urban residents in QwaQwa' (1988) 47 *Afr Studies* 121

NKRUMAH K 'Law in Africa' (1962) 6 *JAL* 103

NORRIE A 'Pashukanis and the "commodity form theory": a reply to Warrington' (1982) 10 *Int J Sociology L* 419

NSEREKO D D 'The nature and function of marriage gifts in customary African marriages' (1975) 23 *Am J Comp L* 682

OAKLEY A *Sex, Gender and Society* 1972 Maurice Temple Smith Ltd London

—— *Housewife* 1974 Penguin Harmondsworth

OBBO C *African Women, their struggle for economic independence* 1980 Zed Press London

OBI S N C *The Ibo Law of Property* 1963 Butterworths London

—— *Modern Family Law in Southern Nigeria* 1966 Sweet & Maxwell London

OCRAN T 'Law, African economic development, and social engineering: a social nexus' (1971–2) 3/4 *Zambia LJ* 16

O'DONOVAN K 'Should all maintenance of spouses be abolished?' (1982) 45 *MLR* 424

—— *Sexual Divisions in Law* 1985 Weidenfeld & Nicolson London

OKORO N *The Customary Laws of Succession in Eastern Nigeria and the statutory and judicial rules governing their application* 1966 Sweet & Maxwell London

OLIVIER N 'Property rights in urban areas' (1988) 3 *SA Public L* 23

OLIVIER N J J et al *Die Privaatreg van die Suid-Afrikaanse Bantoetaalsprekendes* 3ed 1989 Butterworths Durban

OLLENNU N A 'Comments with special reference to customary law' (1969) 5 *East African LJ* 97

OLSEN F E 'The family and the market: a study of ideology and legal reform' (1983) 96 *Harvard LR* 1497

OPOKU K 'African law: existence and unity' (1976) 9 *Verfassung u Recht* 65

OXAAL I et al (eds) *Beyond the Sociology of Development: economy and society in Latin America and Africa* 1975 Routledge & Kegan Paul London

PALMER R & N PARSONS (eds) *The Roots of Rural Poverty in Central and Southern Africa* 1977 Heinemann London

PALMER V V *The Roman-Dutch and Sesotho Law of Delict* 1970 Sijthoff Leiden

PARKER S 'The Marriage Act 1753: a case study in family law-making' (1987) 1 *Int J Law & Family* 133

PARKINSON L 'Conciliation: Pros and cons' (1983) 13 *Family L* 22 and 183

PARSONS T *Essays in Sociological Theory* 1954 The Free Press Glencoe Illinois

—— 'The kinship system of the contemporary United States' (1943) 45 *Am Anthropologist* 22

PASHUKANIS E B *Law and Marxism, a general theory* (trans B Einhorn) 1978 Ink Links Ltd London

PATON G W *A Textbook of Jurisprudence* (edited by Paton G W & D P Derham) 4ed 1972 Clarendon Press Oxford

PAULME D (ed) *Women of Tropical Africa* (trans H M Wright) 1963 Routledge & Kegan Paul London

PAUW B A *The Second Generation; a study of the family among urbanized Bantu in East London* 1973 OUP Cape Town

PEARSON H W (ed) *The Livelihood of Man: Karl Polanyi* 1977 Academic Press New York

PEART N S 'Section 11(1) of the Black Administration Act No 38 of 1927: the application of the repugnancy clause' 1982 *AJ* 110

—— 'Civil or Christian marriage and customary unions: the legal position of the "discarded" spouse and children' (1983) 16 *CILSA* 39

—— 'The lobola agreement and the civil or Christian marriage' (1984) 47 *THRHR* 158

PÉDAMON M 'Les grandes tendances du droit de la famille à Madagascar' (1965) 2 *Annales de l'Univ Madagascar* 59

PELZER A N (ed) *Verwoerd Speaks* 1966 APB Publishers Johannesburg

PENDLETON W C *Katutura: a place where we do not stay* 1974 San Diego State Univ Press

PENNOCK J R & J W CHAPMAN (eds) *Property* 1980 Nomos XXII NY Univ Press New York

PERLMAN J E *The Myth of Marginality; urban poverty and politics in Rio de Janeiro* 1976 California UP Berkley

PETERS P 'Gender, developmental cycles and historical process: a critique of recent research on women in Botswana' (1983) 10 *JSAS* 100

PHILLIPS A & H F MORRIS *Marriage Laws in Africa* 1971 OUP London

PHILLIPS A (ed) *Survey of African Marriage and Family Life* 1953 OUP London

PHILLIPS R E *The Bantu in the City; a study of cultural adjustment in the Witwatersrand* 1938 Lovedale Press Lovedale

PLATZKY L & C WALKER *The Surplus People; forced removals in South Africa* 1985 Ravan Press Johannesburg

POSPISIL L *Anthropology of Law* 1971 Harper & Rowe New York
—— 'Modern and traditional administration of justice in New Guinea' (1981) 19 *J Legal Pluralism* 93
POULTER S M 'An essay on African customary law research techniques: some experiences from Lesotho' (1975) 2 *JSAS* 181
—— *Family Law and Litigation in Basotho Society* 1976 Clarendon Press Oxford
—— *Legal Dualism in Lesotho: a study of the choice of law question in family matters* 1979 Morija Sesuto Book Depot Morija
PRESTON-WHYTE E & H SIBISI 'Ethnographic oddity or ecological sense? Nyuswa-Zulu descent groups and land allocation' (1975) 34 *Afr Studies* 283
PRINSLOO M W 'Die nuut geïntegreerde hofstelsel en die toepassing van inheemse reg' (1987) 20 *De Jure* 67
QUINN N 'Anthropological studies on women's status' (1977) 6 *Annual R of Anthrop* 181
RADCLIFFE-BROWN A R & D FORDE (eds) *African Systems of Kinship and Marriage* 1950 OUP London
RADCLIFFE-BROWN A R *Structure and Function in Primitive Society* 1952 Cohen & West Ltd London
RAMSAY T D *Tsonga Law in the Transvaal* 1941 Department of Native Affairs Pretoria
RAUM O F & E J DE JAGER *Transition and Change in a Rural Community* 1972 Fort Hare UP Alice
READ J S 'Marriage and divorce: a new look for the law in Kenya?' (1969) 5 *East African LJ* 107
—— 'A milestone in the integration of personal laws: the new law of marriage and divorce in Tanzania' (1972) 16 *JAL* 19
READER D H *The Black Man's Portion; history, demography and living conditions in the native locations of East London, Cape Province* 1961 OUP Cape Town
—— *Zulu Tribe in Transition—the Makhanya of Southern Natal* 1966 Manchester UP
REICH C A 'The new property' (1964) 73 *Yale LJ* 733
RENNER K *The Institutions of Private Law and their Social Functions* (trans A Schwarzschild) (1949 ed by O Kahn-Freund) Routledge & Kegan Paul London
REUTER A *Native Marriages in South Africa, according to law and custom* 1963 Aschendorffsche Verlagsbuchhandlung Münster
REYNOLDS P F *Men without Children* 1984 Second Carnegie Inquiry into Poverty and Development in Southern Africa Paper No 5
RHEINSTEIN M (ed) *Max Weber on Law in Economy and Society* (trans E Shils & M Rheinstein) 1954 Harvard UP Cambridge
RHEINSTEIN M & R KÖNIG *Persons and Family* (1972) 4 *IECL* ch 1 Mohr Tübingen; Mouton The Hague
RHEINSTEIN M & M A GLENDON *Persons and Family* (1980) 4 *IECL* ch 4 Mohr Tübingen; Sijthoff & Noordhoff Alphen
RHODESIA Commission of Inquiry into the Administrative and Judicial Functions in the Native Affairs and District Courts Department (Robinson Commission) 1961
RICH P B 'Administrative ideology, urban social control and the origins of apartheid theory 1930–1939' (1980) 7 *J Afr Studies* 70
RIP C M *Black Pre-marital Illegitimacy in Pretoria* 1977 SAHSRC Pretoria
ROBERT A 'A comprehensive study of legislation and customary law courts in the French, Belgian and Portuguese territories in Africa' (1959) 11 *J Afr Admin* 124
ROBERTS S 'A revolution in the law of succession in Malawi' (1966) 10 *JAL* 21
—— 'The Malawi law of succession: another attempt at reform' (1968) 12 *JAL* 81
—— 'The recording of customary law: some problems of method' (1971) 3 *Botswana Notes & Records* 12
—— 'The settlement of family disputes in the Kgatla customary courts: some new approaches' (1971) 15 *JAL* 60
—— *Botswana I: Tswana Family Law* (Restatement of African Law: 5) 1972 Sweet & Maxwell London
—— 'The survival of the traditional Tswana courts in the national legal system of Botswana' (1972) 16 *JAL* 103
—— 'Law and the study of social control in small-scale societies' (1976) 39 *MLR* 663
—— (ed) *Law and the Family in Africa* 1977 Mouton The Hague
—— *Order and Dispute: an introduction to legal anthropology* 1979 Penguin Harmondsworth
—— 'Tradition and change at Mochudi: competing jurisdictions in Botswana' (1979) 17 *Afr L Studies* 37
—— 'Imposition, choice and change: some conflicting perceptions of the relationship between state law and indigenous institutions in contemporary Africa' (1981) 2 *Jahrbuch Afrikanisches Recht* 99
—— 'Mediation in family disputes' (1983) 46 *MLR* 537
—— 'Introduction: some notes on "African Customary Law"' (1984) 28 *JAL* 1
ROBINSON R E 'The administration of African customary law' (1949) 1 *J Afr Admin* 158

ROGERS H *Native Administration in the Union of South Africa* 2ed 1949 Government Printer Pretoria
ROSALDO M Z & L LAMPHERE *Woman, Culture and Society* 1974 Stanford UP
ROSE N 'Beyond the public/private division: law, power and the family' (1987) 14 *J Law & Soc* 61
ROSENN K S 'The jeito: Brazil's institutional bypass of the formal legal system and its developmental implications' (1971) 19 *Am J Comp L* 514
ROWBOTHAM S *Women, Resistance and Revolution* 1972 Chaucer Press Suffolk
RUBIN N 'The Swazi law of succession: a restatement' (1965) 9 *JAL* 90
RUGEGE S 'The struggle over the restructuring of the Basotho or chiefs' courts in Lesotho: 1903–50' (1987) 3 *Lesotho LJ* 159
RWEZAURA B A 'The integration of personal laws: Tanzania's experience' (1983–4) 1/2 *Zimb LR* 85
RWEZAURA B A & U WANITZEK 'Family law reform in Tanzania: a socio-legal report' (1988) 2 *Int J Law & Family* 20
RYCROFT A et al (eds) *Race and the Law in South Africa* 1987 Juta Cape Town
SACHS A 'Changing the terms of the debate: a visit to a popular tribunal in Mozambique' (1984) 28 *JAL* 99
—— 'The two dimensions of Socialist legality: recent experience in Mozambique' (1985) 13 *Int J Sociology L* 133
SAFFIOTI H I B *Women in Class Society* (trans M Vale) 1978 Monthly Review Press New York
SALACUSE J W *An Introduction to Law in French-speaking Africa* VI 1969 Michie Charlottesville
SANDAY P R *Female Power and Male Dominance; on the origins of sexual inequality* 1981 CUP
SANDERS A J G M (ed) *Southern Africa in Need of Law Reform* 1981 Butterworths Durban
—— 'Ten years of the Botswana Matrimonial Causes Act—further proposals for divorce reform' (1982) 26 *JAL* 163
—— 'How customary is African customary law?' (1987) 20 *CILSA* 405
SANTOS . . . see DE SOUSA SANTOS
SARBAH J M *Fanti Customary Laws: a brief introduction to the principles of the native laws and customs of the Fanti and Akan districts of the Gold Coast* 3ed 1968 Frank Cass & Co Ltd London
SAWER G *Law in Society* 1965 Clarendon Press Oxford
SCANDINAVIAN INSTITUTE OF AFRICAN STUDIES *Law and Development, the future of law and development research* 1974 Research Advisory Committee on Law and Development of the International Legal Centre Uppsala
SCHÄFER I 'Family courts—reconsideration invited' 1983 *AJ* 191
SCHAPERA I 'Premarital pregnancy and Native opinion (1933) 6 *Africa* 59
—— 'The social structure of the Tswana ward' (1935) 9 *Bantu Studies* 203
—— *Tribal Legislation among the Tswana of the Bechuanaland Protectorate, a study in the mechanism of cultural change* 1943 Percy Lund, Humphries & Co London
—— 'The work of tribal courts in the Bechuanaland Protectorate' (1943) 2 *Afr Studies* 27
—— *Migrant Labour and Tribal Life: a study of conditions in the Bechuanaland Protectorate* 1947 OUP
—— *The Ethnic Composition of Tswana Tribes* 1952 London School of Economics, Monographs on Soc Anth No 11 London
—— *A Handbook of Tswana Law and Custom* 2ed 1955 OUP London
—— *Government and Politics in Tribal Societies* 1956 C A Watts & Co London
—— (ed) *The Bantu-speaking Tribes of South Africa* 1956 Maskew Miller Cape Town
—— *Married Life in an African Tribe* 1971 Penguin Harmondsworth
SCHAPERA I & S ROBERTS 'Rampedi revisited: another look at a Kgatla ward' (1975) 45 *Africa* 258
SCHÄRF W 'Community policing in South Africa' 1989 *AJ* 209
SCHILLER A A 'The draft legislation and customary law' (1969) 5 *East African LJ* 88
SCHLEGEL A (ed) *Sexual Stratification, a cross-cultural view* 1977 Columbia UP New York
SCHOOMBEE H & D DAVIS 'Abolishing influx control—fundamental or cosmetic change?' (1986) 2 *SAJHR* 208
SCHOULER J *A Treatise on the Law of Marriage, Divorce, Separation and Domestic Relations* 6ed (trans A W Blakemore) 3v 1921 Matthew Bender & Co Inc Albany NY
SCOTT-McNAB D 'Mediation in the family context' (1988) 105 *SALJ* 709
SEAGLE W *The History of Law* 1946 Tudor Publishing New York
SEDDON D (ed) *Relations of Production: Marxist approaches to economic anthropology* 1978 Frank Cass London
SEEKINGS J 'People's courts and popular politics' (1989) 5 *SA Review* 119
SEGALEN M *Historical Anthropology of the Family* (trans J C Whitehouse & S Matthews) 1986 CUP
SEIDMAN R B 'Witch murder and *mens rea*: a problem of society under radical social change' (1965) 28 *MLR* 46
—— 'Law and stagnation in Africa' (1973) 5 *Zambia LJ* 39

—— *The State, Law and Development* 1978 Croom Helm London
—— 'Rules of recognition in the primary courts of Zimbabwe: on lawyers' reasonings and customary law' (1983) 32 *ICLQ* 871
SEYMOUR WOOD G 'Some reflections on the Bantu courts: present and future' 1966 *Speculum Juris* 17
SHARP J 'Unit of study, context and culture: towards an historical anthropology' (1985) 44 *Afr Studies* 65
SHARP J & A D SPIEGEL 'Vulnerability to impoverishment in South African rural areas: the erosion of kinship and neighbourhood as social resources' (1985) 55 *Africa* 133
SHEDDICK V G J *The Southern Sotho* 1953 International African Institute London
—— *Land Tenure in Basutoland* 1954 HMSO London
SHOWERS K 'A note on women, conflict and migrant labour' (1980) 6 *SA Labour Bulletin* 54
SHROPSHIRE D W T *The Bantu Woman under the Natal Code of Native Law; an investigation* 1941 Lovedale Press Lovedale
—— *Primitive Marriage and European Law: a South African investigation* 1976 Frank Cass London
SILBERMAN L & A SCHEPARD 'Court-ordered mediation in family disputes: the New York proposal' (1986) 14 *NY Univ R of L Social Change* 741
SIMKINS C E W 'The economic implications of African resettlement' in SAIRR (ed) *Resettlement: papers given at the 51st Annual Council Meeting* 1981 South African Institute of Race Relations Johannesburg
—— *Four Essays on the Past, Present and Possible Future Distribution of the Black Population of South Africa* 1983 SALDRU Univ of Cape Town
SIMMEL G *Conflict and The Web of Group-affiliations* (trans by K H Wolff and R Bendix respectively) 1955 Free Press Glencoe
SIMONS H J 'Customary unions in a changing society' 1958 *AJ* 320
—— 'Marriage and succession among Africans' 1960 *AJ* 312
—— 'The status of customary unions' 1961 *AJ* 17
—— *African Women; their legal status in South Africa* 1968 C Hurst London
SINCLAIR J D 'Financial provision on divorce—need, compensation or entitlement?' (1981) 98 *SALJ* 469
SMART C 'Regulating families or legitimating patriarchy? Family law in Britain' (1982) 10 *Int J Sociology L* 129
—— *The Ties that Bind: law, marriage and the reproduction of patriarchal relations* 1984 Routledge & Kegan Paul London
SMITH D N 'Man and law in urban Africa: a role for customary courts in the urbanisation process' (1972) 20 *Am J Comp L* 223
SMITH J et al (eds) *Households and the World-economy* 1984 Sage Publications Beverly Hills
SNYDER F G 'Law and development in the light of dependency theory' (1980) 14 *Law & Soc R* 723
—— 'Anthropology, dispute processes and law: a critical introduction' (1981) 8 *Brit J L & Soc* 141
—— *Capitalism and Legal Change, an African Transformation* 1981 Academic Press London
—— 'Colonialism and legal form—the creation of "customary law" in Senegal' (1981) 19 *J Legal Pluralism* 49
SOGA J H *The Ama-Xosa: life and customs* (1931) Lovedale Press Lovedale
SORNARAJAH M 'Parental custody: the recent trends' (1973) 90 *SALJ* 131
SOUTH AFRICA Native Affairs Commission 1903–5 *Report* v 5 1905 Cape Times Ltd Printers Cape Town
SOUTH AFRICA Native Affairs Commission 1930–1932 *Report* 1932 Government Printer Pretoria
SOUTH AFRICA Commission of Inquiry into Legislation affecting the Utilization of Manpower (excluding the legislation administered by the Departments of Labour and Mines) (Riekert Commission) *Report* 1979 Government Printer Pretoria
SOUTH AFRICA Commission of Inquiry into the Structure and Functioning of the Courts (Hoexter Commission) *Report* 1983 Government Printer Pretoria
SOUTH AFRICAN LAW COMMISSION *Report on the Law of Divorce and Matters Incidental Thereto* 1978 Government Printer Pretoria
—— *Investigation into the Legal Position of Illegitimate Children* 1984 Project 38 Government Printer Pretoria
—— *Marriages and Customary Unions of Black Persons* 1985 Working Paper 10 Project 51 Government Printer Pretoria
—— *Investigation into the Advancement of the Age of Majority* 1985 Government Printer Pretoria
—— *Review of the Law of Succession: the introduction of a legitimate portion or the granting of a right to maintenance to the surviving spouse* 1987 Project 22 Government Printer Pretoria
SOUTHALL A W (ed) *Social Change in Modern Africa* 1961 OUP London

SPALDING F D et al '"One nation, one judiciary": the lower courts of Zambia' (1970) 2 *Zambia LJ* 1
SPIEGEL A D 'The fluidity of household composition in Matatiele, Transkei: a methodological problem' (1986) 45 *Afr Studies* 17
SPIRO E *Law of Parent and Child* 4ed 1985 Juta Cape Town
STAFFORD W G & E FRANKLIN *Principles of Native Law and the Natal Code* 1950 Shuter & Shooter Pietermaritzburg
STARR J O *Dispute and Settlement in Rural Turkey: an ethnography of law* 1978 E J Brill Leiden
STAYT H A *The Bavenda* 1931 OUP London
STEPHENS W N *The Family in Cross-Cultural Perspective* 1963 Holt Rinehart & Winston New York
STEWART J E 'The widow's lot—a remedy? The application of spoliation orders in customary succession' (1983–4) 1&2 *Zimb LR* 72
STEYN A F & C M RIP 'The changing urban Bantu family' (1968) 30 *J Marriage & Family* 499
STEYN A F (ed) *Marriage and Family Life in South Africa: research priorities* 1987 HSRC Pretoria
STOLJAR S J *Children, Parents and Guardians* (1971) 4 *IECL* ch 7 Mohr Tübingen; Mouton The Hague; Oceana Dobbs Ferry
STONE F F 'A primer on codification' (1955) 29 *Tulane LR* 303
STOPFORTH P *Two Aspects of Social Change: Highfield African Township* 1973 Univ of Rhodesia Harare
SUGARMAN D (ed) *Legality, Ideology and the State* 1983 Academic Press London
SUMNER C (ed) *Crime, Justice and Underdevelopment* 1982 Heinemann London
SUTTNER R S 'Towards judicial and legal integration in South Africa' (1968) 85 *SALJ* 435
—— 'Legal pluralism in South Africa: a reappraisal of policy' (1970) 19 *ICLQ* 134
—— 'African Customary Law—its social and ideological function in South Africa' 1983 Unpublished paper African Studies Univ of the Witwatersrand
—— 'The social and ideological function of African Customary Law in South Africa' (1985) 11 *Social Dynamics* 49
SWANEPOEL D J 'Appelle vanaf kapteinshowe na Bantoesakekommissarishowe in siviele sake' (1977) 10 *De Jure* 350 and (1978) 11 *De Jure* 113
—— 'Die Erkenning en Toepassing van die *Bogadi*-gebruik by sekere Tswanastamme in die Suid-Afrikaanse Reg' 1977 Unpublished LLM Thesis PUCHO
SWANTZ M-L *Women in Development: a creative role denied? the case of Tanzania* 1985 C Hurst & Co London
TERRAY E *Marxism and 'Primitive' Societies* 1969 (trans M Klopper) 1972 Modern Reader New York
THOMAS J A C *Textbook of Roman Law* 1976 North-Holland Publishing Co Amsterdam
THOMPSON L (ed) *African Societies in Southern Africa* 1969 Heinemann London
TIERSMA P M 'Rites of passage: legal ritual in Roman Law and anthropological analogues' (1988) 9 *J Legal History* 3
TORDAY E 'The principles of Bantu marriage' (1929) 2 *Africa* 255
TRANSVAAL (Province) Local Government Commission (Stallard Commission) *Report* 1922 Government Printer Pretoria
TRUBEK D M 'Max Weber on law and the rise of capitalism' 1972 *Wisconsin LR* 720
—— 'Toward a social theory of law: an essay on the study of law and development' (1972) 82 *Yale LJ* 1
TURNER V W *Schism and Continuity in an African Society* 1957 Manchester UP
TWINING W *The Place of Customary Law in the National Legal Systems of East Africa* 1963 Law School Chicago UP
—— 'The restatement of African customary law: a comment' (1963) 1 *J Mod Afr Studies* 221
—— 'Two works of Karl Llewellyn—II' (1968) 31 *MLR* 165
—— 'Law and anthropology: a case study in inter-disciplinary collaboration' (1972–3) 7 *Law & Soc R* 561
TYLOR E B *Primitive Culture, researches into the development of mythology, philosophy, religion, language, art and custom* 2v 4ed 1920 John Murray London
UNGER R M *Law in Modern Society: toward a criticism of social theory* 1976 Free Press New York
—— 'The critical legal studies movement' (1983) 96 *Harvard LR* 563
UNIVERSITY OF NATAL *Legal Aid in South Africa* 1974 Univ of Natal Durban
UTZ S G 'Maine's *Ancient Law* and legal theory' (1984) 16 *Connecticut LR* 821
VAIL L (ed) *The Creation of Tribalism in Southern Africa* 1989 James Currey London
VAN DER MERWE N J & C J ROWLAND *Die Suid-Afrikaanse Erfreg* 2ed 1974 J P van der Walt Pretoria
VAN DER VYVER J D 'Artikel 31 van die Wysigingswet op Bantoewetgewing, 1963' (1964) 27 *THRHR* 94
VAN DER WESTHUIZEN J et al (eds) *Paul van Warmelo: huldigingsbundel* 1984 Univ of SA Pretoria

VAN DOORNE J H 'Situational analysis: its potential and limitations for anthropological research on social change in Africa' (1981) 21 *Cahiers d'Études Africaines* 479

VAN DOREN J W 'Death African style: the case of S M Otieno' (1988) 36 *Am J Comp L* 329

VAN GENNEP A *The Rites of Passage* (trans M B Vizedom & G L Caffee) 1960 Routledge & Kegan Paul London

VAN HOUTTE J & C DE VOCHT 'The obligation to provide maintenance between divorced husband and wife in Belgium' (1981–2) 16 *Law & Soc R* 321

VAN LOGGERENBERG C 'The Transkeian Marriage Act of 1978—a new blend of family law' 1981 *Obiter* 1

VAN NIEKERK B v D 'Some thoughts on custom as a formative source of South African law' (1968) 85 *SALJ* 279

VAN NIEKERK G J 'People's courts and people's justice in South Africa' (1988) 21 *De Jure* 292

VAN ROUVEROY VAN NIEUWAAL E A B 'Unité du droit ou diversité du droit' (1979) 12 *Verfassung u Recht* 143

VANSINA J *Oral Tradition, a study in historical methodology* (trans H M Wright) 1965 Routledge & Kegan Paul London

VAN TROMP J *Xhosa Law of Persons: a treatise on the legal principles of family relations among the Ama Xhosa* 1947 Juta Cape Town

VAN VELSEN J *The Politics of Kinship* 1964 Manchester UP

VAN WARMELO N J & W M D PHOPHI *Venda Law* Parts 1–3 1948; Part 4 1949; Part 5 1967 Government Printer Pretoria

VAN WARMELO P 'Die abintestaat erfopvolging' (1959) 21 *THRHR* 91

VENTER F 'The government of Blacks in urban areas in South Africa' 1984 *AJ* 17

VERRYN T D (ed) *Church and Marriage in Modern Africa* 1975 Ecumenical Research Unit Greenkloof RSA

VILAKAZI A *Zulu Transformations; a study of the dynamics of social change* 1962 Univ of Natal Pietermaritzburg

VON BENDA-BECKMANN F 'Case note' (1968) 12 *JAL* 173

—— 'Forum shopping and shopping forums: dispute processing in a Minangkabau village in West Sumatra' (1981) 19 *J Legal Pluralism* 117

WALLERSTEIN I *The Modern World System; capitalist agriculture and the origins of the European world economy in the sixteenth century* 1974 Academic Press New York

WARRINGTON R 'Pashukanis and the commodity form theory' (1981) 9 *Int J Sociology L* 1

WEBSTER D *Family and Household in KwaDapha, KwaZulu* 1987 Paper presented at Conference of SA Anthropologists Univ of Cape Town

WEINER M (ed) *Modernization: the dynamics of growth* 1966 Basic Books New York

WEINRICH A K H *Chiefs and Councils in Rhodesia* 1971 Heinemann London

—— *African Marriage in Zimbabwe and the Impact of Christianity* 1980 Mambo Press Gweru

WEITZMAN L J *The Divorce Revolution: the unexpected social and economic consequences for women and children in America* 1985 Free Press New York

WELCH C E & R I MELTZER (eds) *Human Rights and Development in Africa* 1984 State Univ of NY Press Albany

WELSH D *The Roots of Segregation: Native policy in colonial Natal 1845–1910* 2ed 1973 OUP Cape Town

WENGLER W 'The general principles of private international law' (1961 III) 104 *Recueil des Cours* 279

WEST M 'From pass courts to deportation: changing patterns of influx control in Cape Town' (1982) 81 *African Affairs* 463

WESTERMANN D *The African Today and Tomorrow* 1939 OUP London

WESTON A B 'Law in Swahili—problems in developing the national language' (1965) 1 *East African LJ* 60

WHITFIELD G M B *South African Native Law* 2ed 1948 Juta Cape Town

WHORF B L (ed J B Carroll) *Language, Thought and Reality* 1956 MIT Press Cambridge Mass; John Wiley New York

WILSON M et al *Keiskammahoek Rural Survey* v3 *Social Structure* 1952 Shuter & Shooter Pietermaritzburg

WILSON M & A MAFEJE *Langa. A study of social groups in an African township* 1963 OUP Cape Town

WILSON M *The Changing Status of African Women* 1974 National Council of Women of SA

WOLPE H 'Capitalism and cheap labour power in South Africa: from segregation to apartheid' (1972) 1 *Economy & Society* 425

—— (ed) *The Articulation of Modes of Production: essays from economy and society* 1980 Routledge & Kegan Paul London

WOODMAN G R 'Ghana reforms the law of intestate succession' (1985) 29 *JAL* 118

YAWITCH J 'Tightening the noose: African women and influx control in South Africa 1950–1980' 1984 Second Carnegie Inquiry into Poverty and Development in Southern Africa Paper No 82 Cape Town

YNGVESSON B & P HENNESSEY 'Small claims, complex disputes: a review of the small claims literature' (1975) 9 *Law & Soc R* 219

ZAMBIAN GOVERNMENT LAW DEVELOPMENT COMMISSION *Report on the Law of Succession* 1982 Government Printer Lusaka

ZEMANS F H (ed) *Perspectives on Legal Aid* 1979 Frances Pinter London

Principal Works Cited, with Mode of Citation

Afr L Studies	*African Law Studies*
Afr Studies	*African Studies*
AJ	*Acta Juridica*
Allott *New Essays*	Allott, A N *New Essays in African Law* (1970)
Am Anthropologist	*American Anthropologist*
Am J Comp L	*American Journal of Comparative Law*
Annales d l'Univ Madagascar	*Annales de l'Université de Madagascar*
Annual R of Anthrop	*Annual Review of Anthropology*
Ashton	Ashton, H *The Basuto* (1952)
Bekker	Bekker, J C *Seymour's Customary Law in Southern Africa* (1989)
Bennett	Bennett, T W *The Application of Customary Law in Southern Africa, the conflict of personal laws* (1985)
Boberg	Boberg, P Q R *The Law of Persons and the Family* (1977)
Bohannan *Justice and Judgment*	Bohannan, P *Justice and Judgment among the Tiv* (1957)
Bourdillon	Bourdillon, M F C *The Shona Peoples* (1976)
Brit J L & Soc	*British Journal of Law and Society*
Calif State Bar J	*California State Bar Journal*
CILSA	*Comparative and International Law Journal of Southern Africa*
Coertze	Coertze, R D *Die Familie-, Erf- en Opvolgingsreg van die Bafokeng van Rustenburg* (1971)
Columbia LR	*Columbia Law Review*
Connecticut LR	*Connecticut Law Review*
Corbett	Corbett, M M, H R Hahlo & G Hofmeyer *The Law of Succession in South Africa* (1980)
Denver J Int L & Policy	*Denver Journal of International Law and Policy*
Dlamini	Dlamini, C R M *A Juridical Analysis and Critical Evaluation of Ilobolo in a Changing Zulu Society* (1983)
Duncan	Duncan, P *Sotho Laws and Customs* (1960)
East African LJ	*East African Law Journal*
European J Sociology	*European Journal of Sociology*
Family L	*Family Law*
Family LQ	*Family Law Quarterly*
Forsyth	Forsyth, C F *Private International Law* (1990)
Gulliver	Gulliver, P H *Social Control in an African Society* (1963)
Hahlo	Hahlo, H R *The South African Law of Husband and Wife* (1985)
Hahlo & Kahn	Hahlo, H R & E Kahn *The South African Legal System and its Background* (1968)
Hahlo & Kahn *South Africa*	Hahlo, H R & E Kahn *South Africa: the Development of its Laws and Constitution* (1960)
Hailey *African Survey*	Hailey, Lord *An African Survey: a study of problems arising in Africa South of the Sahara* (1945)
Hammond-Tooke	Hammond-Tooke, W D *The Bhaca Society* (1962)
Hammond-Tooke *Bantu-speaking Peoples*	Hammond-Tooke, W D *The Bantu-speaking Peoples of Southern Africa* (1974)
Harries	Harries, C L *The Laws and Customs of the Bapedi and Cognate Tribes of the Transvaal* (1929)
Harvard LR	*Harvard Law Review*
Holleman	Holleman, J F *Shona Customary Law* (1952)
Human Problems	*Human Problems in British Central Africa*
Hunter	Hunter, M *Reaction to Conquest* (1961)

ICLQ	*International and Comparative Law Quarterly*
IECL	*International Encyclopaedia of Comparative Law*
ILM	*International Legal Materials*
Int J Law & Family	*International Journal of Law and the Family*
Int J Sociology L	*International Journal of the Sociology of Law*
J Afr Admin	*Journal of African Administration*
J Afr Studies	*Journal of African Studies*
Jahrbuch Afrikanisches Recht	*Jahrbuch für Afrikanisches Recht*
JAL	*Journal of African Law*
J Comp Leg	*Journal of Comparative Legislation and International Law*
J Historical Sociology	*Journal of Historical Sociology*
J Law & Soc	*Journal of Law and Society*
J Legal History	*Journal of Legal History*
J Legal Pluralism	*Journal of Legal Pluralism and Unofficial Law*
J Local Admin Overseas	*Journal of Local Administration Overseas*
J Marriage & Family	*Journal of Marriage and the Family*
J Mod Afr Studies	*Journal of Modern African Studies*
J Racial Affairs	*Journal of Racial Affairs*
JSAS	*Journal of Southern African Studies*
Junod	Junod, H A *The Life of a South African Tribe* (1912)
Kerr	Kerr, A J *The Customary Law of Immovable Property and of Succession* (1976)
Khumalo	Khumalo, J A M *Civil Practice and Procedure of all Courts for Blacks in Southern Africa* (1984)
Krige	Krige, E J *The Social System of the Zulus* (1936)
Krige & Krige	Krige, E J & J D Krige *The Realm of a Rain-Queen* (1943)
Kuper	Kuper, H *The Swazi; a South African Kingdom* (1963)
Law & Soc R	*Law and Society Review*
Lesotho LJ	*Lesotho Law Journal*
LQR	*Law Quarterly Review*
MacLean	MacLean, Colonel J *Compendium of Kafir Laws and Customs* (1906)
Marwick	Marwick, B A *The Swazi* (1940)
Mayer	Mayer, P *Townsmen or Tribesmen* (1971)
Michigan LR	*Michigan Law Review*
MLR	*Modern Law Review*
Mönnig	Mönnig, H O *The Pedi* (1967)
Nigerian LJ	*Nigerian Law Journal*
NY Univ R of L & Social Change	*New York University Review of Law and Social Change*
Olivier	Olivier, N J J, N J J & W H Olivier *Die Privaatreg van die Suid-Afrikaanse Bantoetaalsprekendes* (1989)
Oxford J Legal Studies	*Oxford Journal of Legal Studies*
Pauw	Pauw, B A *The Second Generation* (1973)
Phillips	Phillips, A *Survey of African Marriage and Family Life* (1953)
Poulter	Poulter, S M *Family Law and Litigation in Basotho Society* (1976)
Quaderni Fiorentini	*Quaderni Fiorentini per la Storia del Pensiero Giuridico Moderno*
Radcliffe-Brown & Forde	Radcliffe-Brown, A R & D Forde *African Systems of Kinship and Marriage* (1950)
Ramsay	Ramsay, T D *Tsonga Law in the Transvaal* (1941)
Reader	Reader, D H *Zulu Tribe in Transition—the Makhanya of Southern Natal* (1966)
Rev Int Droit Comparé	*Revue International du Droit Comparé*
Rev Jur du Congo	*Revue Juridique du Congo*
Rhod LJ	*Rhodesian Law Journal*
Roberts	Roberts, S *Botswana I: Tswana Family Law (Restatement of African Law 5)* (1972)
Rutgers LR	*Rutgers Law Review*
SAJHR	*South African Journal on Human Rights*

SAJ of Science	*South African Journal of Science*
SA Labour Bulletin	*South African Labour Bulletin*
SALJ	*South African Law Journal*
SA Public L	*South African Public Law*
SA Review	*South African Review*
Schapera	Schapera, I *A Handbook of Tswana Law and Custom* (1955)
Schapera *Married Life*	Schapera, I *Married Life in an African Tribe* (1971)
Simons	Simons, H J *African Women: their legal status in South Africa* (1968)
Soga	Soga, J H *The Ama-Xosa* (1931)
Spiro	Spiro, E *Law of Parent and Child* (1985)
Stafford & Franklin	Stafford, W G & E Franklin *Principles of Native Law and the Natal Code* (1950)
Stanford LR	*Stanford Law Review*
Stayt	Stayt, H A *The Bavenda* (1931)
THRHR	*Tydskrif vir Hedendaagse Romeins-Hollandse Reg*
Transkei LJ	*Transkei Law Journal*
TRW	*Tydskrif vir Regswetenskap*
Tulane LR	*Tulane Law Review*
Univ Ghana LJ	*University of Ghana Law Journal*
Univ Pennsylvania LR	*University of Pennsylvania Law Review*
Van Tromp	Van Tromp, J *Xhosa Law of Persons* (1947)
Van Warmelo & Phophi	Van Warmelo, N J & W M D Phophi *Venda Law* (1948–67)
Verfassung u Recht	*Verfassung und Recht in Übersee*
Whitfield	Whitfield, G M B *South African Native Law* (1948)
Wisconsin LR	*Wisconsin Law Review*
Yale LR	*Yale Law Review*
Zambia LJ	*Zambia Law Journal*
Zimb LR	*Zimbabwe Law Review*

CHAPTER 1

Customary Law in Theory

I CUSTOMARY LAW AND POSITIVISM

Customary law is the law of small-scale communities. The people living in these communities take it for granted because it is part of their everyday experience, but outsiders are by definition excluded. They must be told about customary law or they must read about it; in either case their information is once removed from the source. This means that few, if any, texts on customary law can claim to be direct, personal accounts of community practice. They are the work of many informants, each of whom brings to bear on the subject his or her own preconceptions and prejudices. The ultimate, and the most distinctive imprint is that of the final author.

A text that aims to be strictly legal would overlook the contingencies that shaped the product. Legal practitioners need a systematic code of rules, one that is clear and consistent. Once this has been written, there is little more to be said, even though such an account might diverge sharply from the social realities it claims to describe. More discerning lawyers, especially those with a more tolerant attitude to the social sciences, have criticized the obvious shortcomings of this approach, and in general today more is expected of a work on customary law. Answers must be provided to a range of questions that formerly were not considered to be within the province of lawyers. Why did a particular rule develop in the way that it did? How does customary law relate to the social, political and economic changes occurring in a particular society? How should customary law be interpreted to allow expression of individual rights and freedoms?

A great number of the existing records of customary law were written during the time of colonial rule and the first impressions of the colonial authors were not auspicious. Many institutions fundamental to African life—bridewealth and polygyny being the most notorious—were condemned out of hand. Not only content but also form was censured. The amorphousness and lack of system so characteristic of customary law made it difficult for lawyers to identify norms which they could confidently call 'law'. None of this of course reflected well on African people. In *Re Southern Rhodesia*[1] the Privy Council patronizingly remarked:

> 'Some tribes are so low in the scale of social organization that their usages and conceptions of rights and duties are not to be reconciled with the institutions or the legal ideas of civilized society.'

However low the esteem in which indigenous law was held, it could not be indefinitely ignored. The colonial governments were in no position to impose their own laws on an uncomprehending population; they had neither the finance nor the manpower necessary to force obedience and they were wary of provoking rebellion.[2] Some compromise had to be made, and so it was decided to recognize certain of the less offensive areas of customary law. This pragmatic approach, later celebrated as an enlightened policy of indirect rule,[3] led to the creation of the complex code of rules which is now known as 'customary' (or 'indigenous') law.

At the time that this code was being compiled, during the late nineteenth and early twentieth centuries, western legal thought was heavily influenced by positivism, a philosophy which has had a long-lasting and generally a malign effect on customary law. Positivism contributed nothing to the understanding of customary law; but it provided a series of assumptions about the relationship of law and society which have been responsible for the distinctively 'legalistic' attitude that has characterized much subsequent work on the subject.

[1] SEIDMAN *THE STATE, LAW AND DEVELOPMENT* 31–4

The colonial decision to impose English law on Africa was rooted in part in the perception of Colonial Office lawyers of the function of law in society. That perception stemmed largely from the then dominant jurisprudential theory, analytical positivism. Theories that purport to explain the world inevitably become the rationale for policy.... Analytical positivism arose to guide investigations within the legal framework of nineteenth-century England. It became, however, the philosophical guide for structuring the legal order of tropical Africa.

Max Weber argued that the principal capitalist legal requirement was predictability.[1] Entrepreneurs must so far as possible reduce their risk. Lawyers can advise their business clients only if they can calculate how the state will act towards their clients' activities. Predictability, lawyers believed, required that the legal order minimize official discretion, and that "independent" courts decide, as it were, like computers, whether state power should be applied in specific cases. Predictability was impossible if the judge might decide the case according to his subjective ethical notions. Weber said that predictability in law demanded "logical formal rationality", that is, decisions in particular cases that relied exclusively for their justification upon materials drawn from the legal order itself, derived by a specialized deductive mode of legal thought. Positivism therefore purported to limit the courts' function to law-finding, not law-making. This system implies a model of the

---

[1] [1919] AC 211 at 233–4.
[2] Allott *New Essays* 12–13.
[3] See below, [30].

legal order that has been denoted as "legalism". That model defines the law as a "logically consistent set of rules constructed in a specialized fashion", which are the exclusive rules for settling disputes. There must be a "clear differentiation of law from other sources of normative ordering. Law must become both autonomous and supreme".[2] A system of law enforced through courts appears autonomous par excellence.

The school of jurisprudence called analytical positivism met these requirements. John Austin, its nineteenth-century author, announced a single, thundering proposition. All law, he said, was the command of the sovereign.[3] His system limited the function of the lawyer to determining not what the law ought to be, but what it is. It confined the study of law to examining the universe of legal rules, to harmonizing and elucidating them. As an empirically grounded hypothesis, Austin's major affirmation was nonsense. As an intellectual construct, it matched all the demands made upon the lawyer. It explained to him why he directed his attention not to how the rules worked in society, but to the rules as guides to judicial decisions. The legal order became not a normative system ordering social life, but the rules of the litigation game. Positivism directed the lawyer's attention towards what Austin called the Province of Jurisprudence, and away from the Province of Legislation. Analytical positivism pretended that the corpus of the law was a gapless web. If a gap appeared, one could deduce from legal materials and logic alone, what the law covering the supposed gap had to be. Analytical positivism therefore directed attention to the internal elegance and logical consistency of the rules, not to the relative desirability of the behaviour the rules prescribed. If its internal elegance and consistency, rather than its consequences for society, defines good law, then good law in one time and place must be equally good in other times and places.

The Colonial Office imposed English law on Africa without considering what sort of society the new law would mould. . . . British lawyers imposed the law they knew, and therefore, the law they believed to be "good". In fact, the reception statutes facilitated imperial exploitation of Africa. . . .

An attractive investment climate is a necessary condition to capitalist investment. The government can, as a minimum, supply law and order, and a judicial system to protect property and enforce contracts. The colonial powers everywhere imposed a centralized bureaucracy and courts upon their dependent territories. The mere existence of courts and law became a hallmark of "development".

English law apparently came to Africa, however, not out of deep laid plots by imperialists intent on Africa's exploitation, but out of the pervasive insularity of analytical positivism. Nevertheless, English law in Africa as in England nicely served the interests of British entrepreneurs, now at the expense of African peasants. Where necessary to advance English interests, the colonial power readily changed it; but the fact that English law in its larger outlines remained largely unchanged down to independence demonstrates its effectiveness in serving English rather than African concerns.

Analytical positivism, although powerfully challenged, remained the dominant jurisprudence for practising lawyers in independent Africa. It remained concerned with legal elegance, not legal content. When drafting a new law, African lawyers and their expatriate advisers all but invariably copied the laws of the former metropole.

Notes

1. D M Trubek 1972 *Wis LR* 730.
2. Trubek op cit 736.
3. J Austin *Province of Jurisprudence Determined* v1 101ff.

At a time that was critical for its formulation and development, customary law was being applied by people who had a peculiarly narrow view of law. A central axiom of positivism was that lawyers should concern themselves exclusively with the study of law. In consequence a precise definition of law was essential to demarcate the appropriate area of study. And here Austin's simple pronouncement was decisive: law was a rule laid down by a sovereign or political superior. If the acephalous societies of Africa did not fit the political model implied, then it followed that they had no law.[4] This so-called 'Austinian handicap' stigmatized customary law as a lesser normative order, and gave lawyers an excuse to abandon it to missionaries and anthropologists.

There were other, more obviously political reasons for this lack of interest. The business of the colonial administration was not so much with the welfare of the African people as with the maintenance of a submissive population. The law-makers were preoccupied with the public-law enactments designed to secure this obedience and not with customary law which, as a body of private law intended to facilitate domestic interaction, was of little concern to the policy makers.[5]

Later, twentieth-century positivists made special provision for systems of customary law in their definitions of law.[6] Hart has been the most influential in this regard.[7] By discarding the usual unitary definition of law, and by focusing on the differences that mark simple and developed societies,[8] he could accept the possibility of there being 'law' in small-scale, acephalous societies. To explain the dissimilarities between their law and that of complex societies, he posited a dual system of rules. Primary rules constitute the normative order (ie standards of behaviour) in simple societies; secondary rules, which emerge only later, specify the manner in which the primary rules can be ascertained, varied and applied. Hart acknowledged that simple societies could function without secondary rules but, he said, the status of the rules would be uncertain, there would be difficulty in changing them, and they would be inefficiently administered.[9]

The sharp distinction that western jurisprudence requires between law and religion, ethics, custom and morals is arguably a reflex of professionalism.[10] Because occupations in simple societies are relatively unspecialized, there is no group of people dedicated solely to the practice and study of law; and without a legal profession law is differentiated from other normative orders only partially, if at all.[11]

The normative order of simple societies is readily identifiable with the 'custom' of common law, although in strictly legal terms custom is a matter of fact. It is behaviour, what people actually do. Law is a body of norms, what people *ought* to do. By an enigmatic process that has never been fully understood the 'is' of custom may become the 'ought' of law.[12] In the practice of the courts this involves the calling of witnesses and a determination that the custom in

---

[4] See, eg, Evans-Pritchard *The Nuer* 6.
[5] Hund & Van der Merwe *Legal Ideology and Politics in South Africa* 27–9.
[6] Mainly in order to accommodate Public International law: Kelsen *The Pure Theory of Law* 225, 228 and 320–8.
[7] *The Concept of Law* 89–98.
[8] See below, 21ff.
[9] See Seidman (1983) 32 *ICLQ* 871 for an application of Hart's theory.
[10] Friedman *Law and Society* 21.
[11] In its turn, occupational specialization is symptomatic of increased social complexity. This of course was Durkheim's thesis: *The Division of Labour in Society* (1893).
[12] Allott (1977) 21 *JAL* 5.

question was certain, reasonable, uniform, and well established.[13] Custom therefore is conceived as a primitive or basic norm that a litigant may ask to have co-opted to the legal code for the purposes of a particular case.[14]

From the colonial government's point of view the question whether or not customary law deserved the appellation 'law' was insignificant compared with the question whether the social practices of the people should be recognized. Accordingly, once the content of the rules had been approved, their form (as law or non-law) became irrelevant. And today, although at a theoretical level the debate about the legal nature of customary law continues, it has lost its heat. A typical modern argument would concede that law is a product peculiar to a certain type of socio-political structure, the state; thus it would be wrong to say that African societies have the same or an equivalent institution because they are (or were) not state societies.[15] Yet even this type of argument is felt to be academic and speculative. It lacks the topicality of other, more socially relevant issues,[16] such as the co-existence of different normative orders (customary and state law), how they interact, and whether customary institutions (notably patriarchy) are tolerable in modern states.

In jurisprudence too the question of the legal nature of customary law has become stale, and so for all intents and purposes the problem of definition has been disregarded. Most writers, such as Hamnett below, are more interested in describing the characteristics of customary law than defining it.

[2] HAMNETT *CHIEFTAINSHIP AND LEGITIMACY* 9–16

Even the term "customary systems" raises an initial problem, at least in so far as the word "system" implies a rigorous, logically ordered and complete array of juristic propositions and normative rules. In the ideal legal "system", at least, all norms are mutually consistent in themselves and in their implications; there are no gaps in it—no juristic vacuum; and each item can be derived from some other item (a concept or a rule) of higher order. Customary law falls short of all these requirements. The concepts it employs are not rigorously defined; logical ordering exists more by chance than on principles of structure; the scope for deduction is very limited; it is far from being logically complete; and its rules are not always mutually consistent.[1]. . . Perhaps more consonantly with modern usage it could be called an open set. But to say that customary law is a set of normative rules is trivial, indeed almost truistic. It fails to suggest the specific features that distinguish *customary* law from any other unsystematic set of norms. The special qualities of customary law cannot be purely negative; no satisfactory conception of customary law can be arrived at simply by taking a systematic legal order and eliminating from it in turn its consistency, its conceptual precision, its completeness and its logic and supposing that the residue constitutes customary law.

The word "customary" itself suggests a more positive approach. Although the term "customary" has misleading overtones for English-speaking lawyers, it has the virtue of bringing out a central characteristic of certain forms of legal order. It deflects attention away from those who teach or interpret the law, and directs it instead towards those who

---

[13] See below, 141.

[14] The procedure involves application of Hart's secondary rules. Bohannan *Law and Warfare* 45ff terms this a process of 'reinstitutionalization'.

[15] See Bohannan 212 and Alliot in Ife University *Integration of Customary Law* 74ff; cf Woodman in Allott & Woodman *People's Law and State Law* 157–8.

[16] Cf Hamnett *Social Anthropology and Law* 3–4.

live it and use it. Customary law emerges from what people do, or—more accurately—from what people believe they ought to do, rather than from what a class of legal specialists consider they should do or believe. This is not to deny that, in any society, some people are credited with a more acute sensitivity to such obligations than others, or even that the incumbents of certain statuses (defined often by age or seniority) have a *prima facie* claim to possess this greater sensitivity. Differences in human qualities are universally recognised, and in hierarchically ordered societies the senior grades will be assumed to be more, rather than less, generously endowed with wisdom, understanding and insight than other people. Yet the ultimate test is not, "what does this judge say?" but rather "what do the *participants* in the law regard as the rights and duties that apply to them?" The real task of the customary jurist is to answer this last question, not to apply deductive or analytic reasoning to a set of professionally formulated legal concepts.

Again, the word "customary" itself points to this conclusion, suggesting as it does a law that emerges, not from jurisprudential interpretation, but from the "customs" in terms of which the actors themselves determine their actions. However, there are serious dangers in relying too much on the concept of custom—whether in its technical or in its everyday sense—for an understanding of customary law. The first danger arises from the fact that, at least in the English doctrine, "custom", if it is to have the force of law, must have a series of attributes not all of which have any formal application to the kind of law now under discussion. . . . Customary law is pre-eminently embodied in a set of concrete principles, the detailed application of which to particular cases is flexible and subject to change. The principle is unchanging, no doubt, but it is not always an easy matter to determine when any given norm or rule is an authentic principle or is nothing more than the practical application of a general norm to a particular case. If, therefore, custom is to be described as stable or immutable or unchanging, this permanency must be attributed only to the most general norms and not to the subordinate or contingent norms that emerge when a given principle is applied in a concrete case. These subordinate norms can, should and do change, in response to varying social situations. Moreover, when a general rule is applied in a concrete case, the law is not, as it is in systems that recognise the binding precedent, thereby made more specific or narrow. When the case is concluded, the law returns, as it were, from its brief excursion into detail and reverts to its normal condition of generality.

A further stipulation found in modern systems of law is that custom must be observed as of right. This requirement is different in kind from the other rules, and is in principle fully applicable to customary law, indeed it is crucial to any analysis. Besides the misunderstandings to which the technical lawyer is liable, . . . there is a further danger of an opposite kind, namely that custom may be interpreted to mean no more than *practice*. If law is to be looked for not in those who expound it as professionals but in those who live it and use it, it could be supposed that it can be found simply by looking at what people do—law becomes simply a function of practice. No misunderstanding could be more complete. To make practice the formal source of law in the customary field is to be untrue to the facts, where people recognise in normative law a moral authority, a legitimacy, that they do not accord to practice or usage as a whole. No approach to customary law that fails to take this indigenous recognition into account can ever be satisfactory. The certainty of this distinction is not affected by the difficulty of drawing a precise line of demarcation. People may not be sure whether certain intermediate norms are authoritative or not, but they may still be clear that X is in a real sense "law" while Y is definitely "not law". This is all that is necessary in order to make the point. Moreover, norms can never be equated with practice since so much of practice is contrary to the norms. Customary law does not say that a man should not steal his neighbour's chickens more than occasionally, or graze his cattle on another man's field more than anybody else does. It says that these things may not be done at all. For these reasons, the test of observance as a right, if interpreted as an affirmation of the authoritative and regulatory character of normative rules, is a critical feature of customary as of any other law.

Another way of putting this would perhaps be to say that practice is not, and cannot be, the *formal* source of customary law. It remains, of course its *material* source, in that customary law is materially abstracted or derived from practice, rather than by a series of logical operations upon a legal formula or proposition. It is not just that the *original* rule of common law was derived from practice, but was then made the object of jurisprudential operations in the course of its later development. In customary law, not only the original but also the derived norms are related to those who *participate*—to the actors in the social situation—and not only to a professional body of specialised teachers and judges.

The phrase "actors in the social situation" points to the last formal characteristic of customary law to be discussed: its social origin and character. This might seem an obvious feature of all law, and hardly worth insisting upon. However, if the ultimate test of customary law is not "what does the judge say?" but "what do the participants regard as the rule?" the question arises of the eccentric participant or actor who regards as a *rule* some private and personal predilection of his own. If customary law derives from practices that are endowed with authority by the practitioners, how is it possible to deal (analytically) with idiosyncratic practitioners? It is to close this gap that it becomes necessary to stress the social character of customary law. The argument here is not that a total "society"—whatever that may be—defines one homogeneous law by derivation from universally sanctioned practice; though in fact this meets the case in certain instances, it would be much too rigorous an assumption for most non-literate societies. To say that law is social and not individual is not to imply that between the individual and the total society to which he belongs there are no intermediate social groups whose corporate and semi-independent character validates their own local law. Clans, sub-clans, lineages and even individual families can constitute social groups in this sense, in such a way that the norms to which they attribute authority are socially and not merely individually legitimised. The exact nature of the groups that possess this, so to speak, "public" character will vary from society to society. Moreover, the domain within which this public character exists will vary according to the kind of rule or subject-matter involved. Thus, as in Sotho law, questions of inheritance may be determinable by the immediate agnatic kinsmen of the deceased, while questions of succession to office may be determined by some more widely defined group, and questions of land-tenure may be referred to some other authority again. So variations may be expected not only from society to society, but also, within any one society, from one type of case or subject-matter to another. The essential fact is that the law is always socially defined. In no known society is it open to each individual to find his own law. The legitimacy, the imputed authority with which customary law is clothed, is not transmitted by a legislative assembly or a specialist judge, but neither is it the product of an individual's idiosyncrasy.

The argument so far has raised a number of substantive and not merely definitional issues and suggests a formula that omits purely contingent and accidental features and yet is not entirely trivial. *Customary law can be regarded as a set of norms which the actors in a social situation abstract from practice and which they invest with binding authority.* The positive content of this definition may be taken as fourfold: the relation of norms to *practice* rather than to "lawyers' reasoning"; the dominant role of the *actors* or participants in the determination of law; the *authoritative* or legitimate, rather than merely factual or utilitarian, character of the emergent rules; and the essentially *social* nature of their validation and status. . . .

Nor does the formulation suggested above ignore the fact that some people may be regarded as more authoritative exponents of the law than others. The incumbents of certain positions, typically the hereditary position of chief, may be especially privileged in this regard. . . . [T]oo much can be made of the "essentially democratic" character of traditional monarchy. To stress the social and in a certain sense "popular" character of customary law, in chiefly societies as in others, is certainly to recall something of what is implied in the American term "folk-ways"; but this does not exclude the indubitable truth, neatly expressed by Professor Goebel, that a folk-way may be the way of the folk in power. . . . A hereditary chieftainship develops its own interests as an ascriptive status-group, which are analytically (and can become empirically) separate from those of the community. Where chieftainship is *itself* a central political value in the society, the ambiguities of its domination grow to create a broad area of "indeterminacy", and it is precisely here that "force" is mediated to "law". . . .

An empirical feature of most customary law is that it is unwritten.[2] This is more than a simple descriptive fact, for it has implications for the *kind* of law that emerges. When law is written, it is possible to isolate it from its social context and to seal it off in books; jurisprudential analysis can then begin. The fact that customary law is unwritten is one reason why it remains both general and concrete. It remains *general* because its detailed applications in different places are not made known to all, only the principle being universally remembered, and *concrete* because detailed logical analysis is impracticable when the analyst has got no accurate and objective reports on which to rely. The doctrine of precedent is hard to set up when there is no written record of earlier decisions.[3] This allows customary norms to be flexible and adaptable, and to function, in Plucknett's words, as "instruments for legal change rather than the fossilised remnants of a dead past".[4] But it is not just a matter of saying that pre-literate societies lack certain cultural techniques and that therefore their law is what it is. It is hardly too much of a paradox to reverse the order of cause and effect and assert that the unwritten character of customary law is the product or effect of its general nature, rather than the reverse. Max Weber has shown[5] how essential writing is for the functioning of a modern rational bureaucratic system. But the relevant point in the present context is that it is not the mere fact of writing but the use to which it is put that is crucial. In Lesotho, it happens to be the fact that written records of the proceedings and judgments of most courts and tribunals are kept, but this is not enough to constitute a "written law", since the records are not, on the whole, then used as a basis for analysis, the establishment of precedent, or the abstract manipulation of concepts. At least until very recently, writing might as well not exist for all the part that it has played in the shaping of the law.

Notes

1. See, eg, J F Holleman *Issues in African Law* 13.

2. A generalization obscuring the fact that there have been at least two indigenous codes of customary law: the Laws of Lerotholi drawn up in 1903 by the Basutoland National Council; and from 1828, the Merina monarchs of Madagascar began to issue written codes: Deschamps in M Gluckman *Ideas and Procedures in African Customary Law* 169ff.

3. See M Gluckman *The Judicial Process among the Barotse* 253ff and also L A Fallers *Law without Precedent* 18–20.

4. T F T Plucknett *Legislation of Edward I* (1949) 7.

5. M Rheinstein *Max Weber: Law in Economy and Society* ch 9.

II CUSTOMARY LAW AND ANTHROPOLOGY

(1) Anthropological jurisprudence

Customary law, usually identified with exotic, 'tribal' societies, inevitably attracted the interest of anthropologists, and much of our information on the subject (information which has been gradually incorporated into the legal code via commissions of inquiry, court decisions, codes, textbooks and restatements) was originally gathered by anthropologists. Their interests of course extend far beyond the narrow domain of law, which they see as only one aspect of social control. It comes as no surprise then that anthropology (and its sister science, sociology) have been a fruitful source of ideas about the relationship of law and society.

The close association between anthropology and customary law led to the development of a specialized discipline, 'anthropological jurisprudence'.[17] Sir Henry Maine is generally considered to be its founder. His major work—*Ancient Law* (1861)—was inspired by the topical issue of his time: evolution. Early anthropologists (notably Morgan and McLennan) transposed the newly discovered biological laws to their studies of society, and it was widely believed that all societies progressed through clear and inescapable stages of development. Maine applied this idea to law.[18] By comparing various archaic legal systems—Roman, Hindu, English and Celtic—he sought to discover a universal pattern of legal development. Implicit in this thesis was the understanding that by comparison of disparate phenomena a general evolutionary direction could be charted, from a lower, primitive, to a higher, more civilized, state. Political structure was regarded as the determinant of legal change. The earliest polity was the family, later the tribe, and finally the state; changes occurring in each of these structures provoked consequential changes in the legal system.

Evolutionist theorizing yielded provocative ideas about social change but most of them were highly conjectural, and the non-empirical method was later regarded as a fatal defect. A more pervasive problem, which has never been completely overcome, was an intrinsically ethnocentric bias. This was responsible for the belief that western European society represented the apogee and goal of all development, a belief that conveniently endorsed the racial prejudices of the imperial powers. Although evolutionism was later discredited by functionalist anthropology, it survived in popular thinking, and long after it had lost any plausibility in academic circles, it continued to influence thinking in the colonial administration.[19]

The typing and the evolution of different legal systems according to their socio-economic and political milieu was also a concern of sociology, and in this regard Weber's book *Economy and Society* (1922–5) was an influential source of ideas. He sought to explain the role of law in the formation of industrial or bourgeois capitalism in western Europe.[20] While Weber acknowledged that most organized societies had law, the European legal systems (and here he would except English law) differed significantly from the others.[21] Their unique quality lay not so much in the content of legal rules as in their *forms* of organization and process. Judicial decisions, for example, were based on the application of notionally universal rules, and were free from political intervention. The qualities peculiar to western law—its autonomy, the purposiveness of its legislation, the generality and universality of its rules—were captured in the epithet 'rationality'.[22]

---

[17] A term coined in 1886 by the German scholar Post; see Adam (1934) 16 *J Comp Leg* 216.
[18] See the work of a modern evolutionist: Diamond *Primitive Law, Past and Present*.
[19] Chanock *Law, Custom and Social Order* 74.
[20] See Trubek 1972 *Wisconsin LR* 721.
[21] See Rheinstein *Max Weber on Law in Economy and Society* xlviii.
[22] Morris (1958) 107 *Univ Pennsylvania LR* 141; Trubek op cit 724.

Weber typed legal systems according to another variable, their basis of legitimation.[23] He identified three ideal forms: charismatic, traditional and legal. Where the legitimacy of a legal system derived from the charisma of the law-giver, it would be his or her extraordinary or exemplary characteristics that would incline members of the social order to obey any commands given. Conversely, the source of rules in primordial custom or the practice of the ancestors (as is the case with customary systems of law) provided a traditional basis of legitimacy. The hallmark of a 'modern' legal system is, in Weberian terms, its legal rationality. In a substantive sense this means that predetermined, generalized rules provide the sole criteria for law-making and law-finding; in a formal sense, it means that the unique features of individual cases are not allowed to obtrude into the legislative or judicial processes.[24]

Weber's typology has done much to inform the modern legislative programmes of the law and development movement.[25] If custom (including customary law) is not 'rational' in the sense that western law is, then it follows that its rules are not the product of purposive law-making. (This helps to explain the persistent belief that customary law never originates in legislation.)[26] As a result custom is believed to operate as a check on behaviour, never as a goal or an incentive, with the implication that customary law cannot be used to achieve a predetermined end. In Weber's theory (as in evolutionism) simple 'tribal' societies lay passively imprisoned and unthinking in the bonds of tradition. And in one respect at least this coincided with positivism: the tranquillity of tribal societies was explained, in the absence of all the trappings of a *legal* order, by an unconscious conformity to habits deeply ingrained.[27]

The break with this view, in particular with evolutionism, can be dated to a new perspective opened by Malinowski in a work on the Trobriand Islands: *Crime and Custom in Savage Society* (1926). His first concern was to destroy the illusion that

> '[the "savage"] obeys [laws] "slavishly", "unwittingly", "spontaneously", through "mental inertia", combined with the fear of public opinion or of supernatural punishment; or again through a pervading "group sentiment if not group instinct"'.[28]

Malinowski showed that order on the islands flowed from the economic circumstances of the people, circumstances which compelled a calculated reciprocity of behaviour.[29]

Perhaps even more important than this finding was Malinowski's research method. It opened new possibilities for legal anthropology and for the social sciences in general. Two characteristics marked this method as 'scientific', and so distinguished it from the speculative tendencies of evolutionism. In the first place, it was empirical, requiring actual observation of native life; in the second

---

[23] In other words, the claim that authorities can make to have their commands obeyed or to justify their exercise of power. See Rheinstein op cit n21 336–7 and Trubek op cit n20 731–9.

[24] Either generically determined facts or legal concepts provide cues for the application of the rules.

[25] It also underlies the dichotomy between law and custom. See further below, 41ff.

[26] Despite evidence to the contrary, such as Schapera's *Tribal Legislation among the Tswana*.

[27] Hartland *Primitive Law* 2, 5 and 8.

[28] Op cit 10.

[29] Op cit 58.

place, each culture was to be evaluated on its own terms, without reference to a notionally superior or more civilized external standard. By implication this meant rejection of the comparative, theoretical approach of evolutionism.[30] This was perhaps inevitable. The suppositions of the evolutionists were being confounded by first-hand evidence of native life in the colonies, and in any event, interest was shifting from conjecture about prehistoric societies to the understanding of existing ones.

During the 1920s in the United States the concerns of jurisprudence were also changing. Roscoe Pound and Oliver Wendell Holmes had succeeded in diverting attention from analytical positivism, with its preoccupation with what law *is*, to the more practical matter of what law *does*. In consequence the focus of investigation became the courts in action, not the law in abstract. The school of American Realism, as it came to be called, sprang from Holmes's famous dictum: 'The prophecies of what the courts will do in fact, and nothing more pretentious, are what I mean by the law.'[31] At this point law and anthropology merge, because the frame of reference for jurisprudence expanded to include the social context in which law was applied. One of Holmes's many aphorisms was: 'It is perfectly proper to regard and study the law simply as a great anthropological document.'[32]

Llewellyn and Hoebel were both disciples of the Realist movement and they applied its tenets to the study of systems of customary law. In a seminal work, *The Cheyenne Way* (1941), they set anthropological jurisprudence on a new course, one which it still follows. In keeping with the precepts of Realism they concentrated on the

'peculiar job [law has] of cleaning up social messes when they have been made. Law exists for the event of breach of law and has a major portion of its essence in the doing of something about such breach.'[33]

This had far-reaching implications for research method.

Llewellyn and Hoebel identified three possible ways of investigating customary law.[34] The first they called 'ideological', implying an examination of the rules which a society deemed to be 'proper for channeling and controlling behaviour'. To construct a code of tribal law the field-worker had only to ask the elders of a community what they considered the rules to be. More recently this has come to be called a 'rule-centred' paradigm[35] which rests on an assumption that 'normal behaviour [is] the product of compliance with established normative precepts'. This approach typifies several famous southern African works, Schapera's *Handbook of Tswana Law and Custom* (1938) being a classic

---

[30] Kuper (1980) 21 *European J Sociology* 14ff.
[31] *Collected Legal Papers* 173.
[32] (1899) 12 *Harvard LR* 444. And see Llewellyn (1931) 44 *Harvard LR* 1222. Twining (1972–3) 7 *Law & Soc R* 561 describes one of the early examples of interdisciplinary collaboration, that of Llewellyn and Hoebel.
[33] Op cit 20. The definition of law was correspondingly less significant. More important was the concept of the court, because law could be defined only with reference to the rules regularly enforced by a court: Hoebel *The Law of Primitive Man* 37.
[34] *The Cheyenne Way* 20–9 and Twining (1968) 31 *MLR* 165.
[35] Comaroff & Roberts *Rules and Processes* 5ff.

example, and currently it is the basis of the so-called 'jural school' of legal anthropology centred in Pretoria.[36] It was also the preferred method of the restatement projects undertaken by the School of Oriental and African Studies of London University.[37]

A rule-centred or ideological approach is inevitably favoured by lawyers because it is conducive to their needs. They want precise, clear statements of rules; any circumstantial information about social context is an irrelevant distraction to be excluded.[38] It is not difficult to trace a conceptual link between this need for certainty and positivism.[39]

[3] ALLOTT *FUTURE OF LAW IN AFRICA* 14–15

One of the major problems in administering customary law today is in determining what is the appropriate customary law to be applied in any particular case. The lack of certainty is due to various causes: (i) it may be inherent in the character of customary law itself; (ii) there may be uncertainties as to the application of customary law; and (iii) there may be uncertainty due to the deficiencies in the process for the ascertainment of customary law.

As to the character of customary law itself, the first point to be noticed is that there may be a lack of fixed rules for dealing with different situations, and judges in African courts may merely apply what they consider to be justice and common sense in the light of the special circumstances of the case. The problem of the definition of customary law is also relevant here; the question, for instance, which norms are legal and which are merely social, moral or religious, arises. . . .

As regards the second point—the uncertainty as to the application of customary law in particular cases—this often arises because of possible conflict between customary law and English law and doubts as to which system should be applied in any particular case. There is also the difficulty arising from the lack of uniformity in the customary law as between one tribe or one area and another.

As regards the judicial ascertainment of the customary law, a distinction ought to be made between the position in the superior or non-African courts of a territory, and in the African or native courts. The basic rule in the non-African courts is that until a custom has become notorious by repeated proof the courts cannot take judicial notice of it. . . .

As regards ascertainment of the customary law by African or native courts, the position is entirely different. In the African courts the customary law is supposed to be in the breasts of the judges, and there is no question of proving the law by evidence. Several speakers made the point that uncertainty as to the customary law existed only in the minds of foreigners and not in the minds of those who were themselves subject to the customary law. It was pointed out that in some areas today the young men may not be learning the customary law and hence the traditional knowledge of customs may be lost by the new generation. Uncertainty might arise in the African courts as to what customary law to apply if there were so-called "gaps" in the customary law. Such gaps might occur if new situations faced the courts for which there was no existing appropriate and applicable rule of customary law. In such a case it might be necessary to create new customary law, and many delegates made the point that this was a contradiction in terms. On the other hand, it was stated that there were no gaps in fact in the law which was

---

[36] See, e g, Myburgh *Papers on Indigenous Law*. This also draws heavily on the tradition of volkekunde scholarship: Hund & Van der Merwe op cit n5 32; Hund (1982) 8 *Social Dynamics* 30–1. See Roberts (1976) 39 *MLR* 663.

[37] Allott and Cotran in Ife University op cit n15 26–7 and 33–6 respectively. And see: Twining (1963) 1 *J Mod Afr Studies* 221.

[38] See Allott (1953) 5 *J Afr Admin* 172; cf Poulter (1975) 2 *JSAS* 181.

[39] See, e g, Hoebel op cit n33 28 and Pospisil *Anthropology of Law* 39–96.

administered in most areas, and the courts would usually devise a rule to fit each case which came before them. In other words, the African courts were evolving rules to deal with present-day circumstances; but legislation might be necessary in order to supplement the law in certain aspects.

The rule-centred paradigm further assumes that fundamental legal concepts, such as law, property, crime and delict, are universal and thus observable in all legal systems. This assumption, of course, is at best debatable, and many would say completely wrong. An even more telling defect of the paradigm is that it 'contents itself, for the most part, with an almost passive acceptance of ideal norms as truly representing the law'.[40] The opinions and statements of the norm collected by the field-worker, give only a partial view of social reality. They do not necessarily reflect the way that people actually behave, since every rule allows leeway for deviance. An ideological approach tends to obscure the difference between the ideal and the reality.

The second method identified by Llewellyn and Hoebel is in essence descriptive. From observation of how people in a community behave, law may be inferred. On its own, observation is generally acknowledged to be insufficient, as there is no guarantee that the field-worker will be in a position to witness all relevant behaviour or that he or she will draw the correct inferences about its significance. But when the data are supplemented with the views of native informants, a more rounded image of a legal system can be constructed.

Llewellyn and Hoebel personally advocated a third method, one culled from American Realism, which they claimed was especially appropriate for the study of law: the case-study method.[41]

[4] ROBERTS (1971) 3 *BOTSWANA NOTES & RECORDS* 12–14

The practical importance of the arguments about methodology was soon brought home to the writer of this note when he found himself in the field. In the course of investigating the nature of interests in arable land held under customary forms of tenure, I asked several elderly men whether payment was ever made where fields were transferred from one person to another. All were emphatic that such payments were "against the law" and never happened. However, I had already discovered, reading through the records of the Chief's Court of their tribe, that payment was permitted by that court provided that the land in question had been cleared for cultivation (the idea being that such payments were referable to the cost of improvements carried out on the land). Later on, as I got to know the area better, I found that it was quite a common practice for payment to be demanded even where interests in uncleared land were transferred (particularly where such land was favourably sited in relation to water supplies and centres of population), even though people knew that this was not permitted by the Chief's Court. So here were three methods of investigation—talking to informants, investigating actual decisions of the court and observing the day-to-day habits and practices of tribesmen—each revealing a different picture of the law. Each picture was true in a sense, as what the old men said was probably the traditional position, whereas the discrepancy between the court records and everyday

---

[40] Hoebel op cit n33 29; see further Abel (1969) 17 *Am J Comp L* 573–82; Roberts (1971) 3 *Botswana Notes & Records* 12–15.

[41] Hoebel op cit n33 37; Llewellyn & Hoebel op cit n34 23. See further: Poulter (1975) 2 *JSAS* 181; Allott loc cit n38 and Abel op cit 573. Schapera (1943) 1 *Afr Studies* 27 esp 40 had independently made the same discovery. He worked with the written case records of chiefs' courts in Botswana.

behaviour could be explained on the basis that the courts had not caught up with generally accepted practice (a common enough phenomenon in any legal system). The lesson to be gained was that the picture of the law formed might well be heavily dependent upon the method of investigation used; a possibility the full implications of which I had not really considered.

Previous investigations of Tswana customary law had been almost entirely carried out through interviews with informants. This method formed the basis of the research upon which Schapera's classic, *A Handbook of Tswana Law and Custom*, was written. . . . However, other researchers, notably anthropologists, have investigated customary law through the examination of actual disputes. Some have used the technique of observing disputes while they are actually in progress, while others have relied upon written records kept by customary courts. Latterly, some lawyers have also been won over to this method.

Recent arguments about the methods of recording customary law have been largely concerned with the respective merits of the two approaches, and rather damaging attacks have been made upon investigations based upon interviews with informants. Such criticism has been made on two levels. First, it is said, such investigations tend to be directed towards obtaining a set of abstract rules, or "disembodied propositions" about the law, and fail to reveal the function which these rules have in the social system and the mechanics of their operation. These criticisms, which are also fashionably directed at rule-centred legal research in common law systems as well, seem well founded as far as much of the work so far produced by the Restatement of African Law Project is concerned. The restatements so far published do largely consist of abstract rules inadequately anchored to the social context in which they are alleged to apply, and they are also very weak as far as procedural aspects of the law are concerned. However, these defects are not inevitably inherent in research conducted through discussion with informants, a fact which seems to be overlooked by some critics of the Restatement of African Law Project.

The other kind of criticism levelled at investigation through interviews is that a defective picture of the law is obtained on account of the individual opinions and preconceptions of the interviewer or the person interviewed. First, there is the problem that the range and kind of information obtained is circumscribed by the questions asked by the investigator. Any questions the recorder asks must be determined by his preconceptions as to what the legal system he is investigating is like; where his training has been in another legal system and he has not had an opportunity to watch the one he is investigating for a long time at close quarters, the questions asked may well be wrong ones, or, at least, peripheral matters may be laboured and central ones utterly neglected. There are also wrong ways of asking questions; a fact well known and guarded against by investigators in some areas of the social sciences, but seldom given much attention by lawyers. Secondly, there is the risk of distortion on the part of the informant: he may tell you what he thinks you would like the answer to be; what he would like the answer to be; or, what the answer might have been in the past. Of all these problems, the one that worried me most was the problem of dating information obtained from informants. My impression was that most informants talked most easily about the past, and lapsed back into this tense despite continual reminders. Of course, this difficulty was greatest where an informant considered that the present law had taken an unfavourable turn. An example of this may be cited from the context of the law of procedure. Older informants always said that a young married couple might not bring a matrimonial dispute before a ward court before referring it to their senior relations, who had also to be present at the ward court proceedings. Similarly, it was regularly said that a young woman who had been impregnated might not bring proceedings herself, but that this had to be done by her father or guardian. No doubt this was true in the past, but the most limited personal experience of court procedure today discloses that this is no longer the case.

It was my experience that both of the dangers stressed in the previous paragraph could be greatly reduced by an examination of actual disputes, as opposed to posing theoretical questions to informants. For this it is necessary to look to the customary courts as a primary source of information. This involves sitting in these courts, watching and listening, or finding out what happens in them by other means. While it is indispensable to spend some time watching and listening, it is certainly impossible in this way to obtain a comprehensive picture of the law within the time likely to be available to most investigators (except, perhaps, anthropologists). In view of this it is necessary to investigate actual disputes by building up accounts of them from discussion with informants or by examining the records of proceedings kept by the courts. It is certainly possible to build up a picture of past disputes by talking to informants, and on the whole men's memories of the details of past litigation seem curiously extensive, but the method is laborious and there is always the fear that crucial features of a piece of litigation have been forgotten with time. A well-prepared contemporary written record, on the other hand, provides a starkly neutral account of what took place in court. Although such a record is open to interpretation by the investigator, it can in no way be influenced in form or content by his preconceptions.

Reliance on the study of cases to the exclusion of any other approach, however, has its own shortcomings. First, the occurrence of a particular type of case may be influenced by variables that have nothing to do with the norms involved. For instance, many people are reluctant to litigate about their domestic problems, a phenomenon that tends to obscure norms which might be socially very important. Secondly, the construction of rules for the purposes of individual cases does not necessarily determine how they will fare in later suits. Each case is in essence an excursion from the general to the particular; unless the doctrine of stare decisis is strictly enforced there can be no guarantee that from one hearing the particular will become the general. In any event the actual manifestation and application of a rule during a trial is determined by a multitude of factors, including the litigants' style of argument, the community's views, and the judge's forensic ability. Thirdly, concentration on court cases tends to deflect attention from extra-judicial institutions, such as conclaves of elders, where norms are also constructed and developed.[42] Llewellyn and Hoebel themselves were not prepared to abandon the study of rules completely, but they did insist that the rules be placed in a proper context—the trial—where the limits of deviance from ideal norms could be more accurately fixed.

Even the simple observation of the trial is now seen as unduly restrictive; a case should rather be studied in its full setting, from the beginnings of a grievance, embedded in its social matrix, to the effect of the judgment on the subsequent relations of the litigants.[43] This is the so-called 'extended' case method. It heralded a move away from trial/judgment accounts of dispute to studies of social conflict that were far less discriminating.[44]

In recent years, the case-study method has come to be associated with what is called a 'processual' paradigm of customary law.[45] The interest in process is part

---

[42] For criticisms of the case-study approach see: Gluckman (1972–3) 7 *Law & Soc R* 611 and *Politics, Law and Ritual* 235–42; and Holleman (1973) 7 *Law & Soc R* 585. Other complementary methods are discussed in Luckham *Law and Social Enquiry*.

[43] Gluckman in Epstein *The Craft of Social Anthropology* xv; Gulliver in Nader *Law in Culture and Society* 17–19.

[44] Roberts *Order and Dispute* is an example.

[45] Which is usually opposed to the rule-centred paradigm. See Comaroff & Roberts op cit n35 5ff and Hund op cit n36 31ff.

of a broad concern with social control, a tribute to the lasting influence of Malinowski.[46] One of the tenets of this approach is the belief that social conflict is neither unusual nor pathological. The focus of research tends to fall on the constraints on behaviour that are derived from 'the intrinsic properties of social relations—obligations, expectations, and reciprocities—and by the exigencies of interaction'.[47] The dichotomy between rules and processes also owes much to the distinction drawn between law and politics.[48] Unlike the legal process, which depends on the impartial application of rules, politics focuses on the exercise of power.[49] Study of process rather than rule, and politics rather than law has resulted in the overall demystification of the legalism characteristic of western legal systems, viz the formal equality of the parties before the court and impartial adjudication according to a fixed code of rules.

At the time that Llewellyn and Hoebel were writing, the theoretical dogma of anthropology was functionalism (usually called structural-functionalism). One of the canons of functionalism was cultural relativity: exotic data were to be accounted for only in terms of the native cultural system. This meant that each item of information, if its meaning were to be explained, had to be viewed in relation to other items, a process of reasoning that suggested the logical connection of all information in a coherent system.[50] This entailed a conception of society as a system rather than as an aggregate of individuals. What made the group something more than the totality of its component parts was the relationship of the parts to each other in specific ways, relationships that were patterned in a manner analogous to the laws of nature. A biological metaphor was usually invoked to show how a society functioned: each part of an organism contributed to overall good health. This meant that explanations of social data were inevitably teleological: all social life depended on the fulfilment of certain requirements functional to a society's survival.

While functionalism was applauded for its value-free, empirical method, there were serious flaws in its premises. It assumed, for instance, that all parts of a system were integrated into a unified whole—the society or culture under investigation[51]—and that the natural state of this unit was one of changeless equilibrium.[52] This detracted from influences extrinsic to the society in question. Yet, in keeping with the metaphor of a healthy organism, it seemed that the introduction of any foreign matter would disrupt the function of the organism, and would therefore be pathological.

Of special importance in the context of Africa was the bearing this had on colonial policy. Africans were presumed to be divided on ethnic or tribal lines; each tribe was studied as if it were, and ought to remain, free from the subversive influences of European culture. It followed that change was socially harmful,

---

[46] See Moore *Law as Process* 220.
[47] Comaroff & Roberts op cit n35 12.
[48] Gulliver *Social Control in an African Society* 297.
[49] Gulliver op cit 298; Moore op cit n46 181ff; Gulliver in Nader op cit n43 11–13.
[50] Cf Kaplan & Manners *Culture Theory* 55ff.
[51] See below, 19–20.
[52] Cf Driberg (1928) 1 *Africa* 65 and (1934) 16 *J Comp Leg* 231.

and that when two cultures were brought into contact with one another, there was bound to be conflict.[53] This understanding operated politically to suggest the desirability of segregation and the safeguarding an antique 'tribal' ideal against the innovations imported from the West.

Of the other objections to functionalism, possibly the most important, was the charge that it was not, in fact, objective. With the emergence of a critical anthropology based on Marxist theory, the value-free stance of functionalism was debunked, revealing that much of the work done during the colonial era was directed by, or at least disposed towards, the interests of the colonial governments.[54]

(2) Key concepts

(a) Culture

Culture has conventionally been regarded as the raw material of anthropology. In much the same way that definitions of law delimited the scope of study for lawyers, so definitions of culture have specified the proper area for study by anthropologists. Most of these definitions can be traced to Tylor's:

> 'Culture or Civilization . . . is that complex whole which includes knowledge, belief, art, morals, law, custom, and any other capabilities . . . acquired by man as a member of society.'[55]

In this broad sense culture is normally taken to mean the totality of human behaviour and artifacts that are socially, as opposed to genetically, transmitted. In a narrower sense, however, culture is used to denote different social units.

[5] KAPLAN & MANNERS *CULTURE THEORY* 2–4

[S]ince the emergence of anthropology as a systematic field of inquiry in the late nineteenth century, the issues that anthropologists have been concerned with can be subsumed under two broad and interrelated questions: (1) How do different cultural systems work? and (2) How have these cultural systems, in their considerable variety, come to be as they are? Note that these questions are addressed to the *differences*—in space as well as over time—among cultures. If all cultures were identical, there would probably be no need for the discipline of anthropology. Human biology viewed broadly would be the discipline through which we would seek explanations of human behaviour. This is not to say, however, that anthropologists have not been concerned with the *similarities* among cultures. They have, but cultural similarities arise as issues to be explored when they are seen against the contrasting background of other human, or in some cases infrahuman, differences.

If, as all anthropologists assume, it is true that the various populations of the world belong to a single species, *Homo sapiens*, and if it is also true—following this—that the psychobiological nature of each of these populations is roughly the same, we should expect to find that all human societies would look pretty much alike or, at least, that they would

---

[53] Van Doorne (1981) 21 *Cahiers d'Études Africaines* 480–1. This article is based on a provocative study by Gluckman *Analysis of a Social Situation in Modern Zululand* that documented the opening of a bridge in Zululand, an event which, despite the notional hostility of the two racial groups involved, was marked by harmony and co-operation. Van Doorne suggests that in actual situations social constructs such as race and culture are less relevant than would theoretically be expected.

[54] Kuper *Anthropology and Anthropologists* 99ff; cf Gluckman in Fortes & Patterson *Studies in African Social Anthropology* 21ff.

[55] *Primitive Culture* v1 1.

exhibit certain broad similarities. And indeed in certain respects they do. To put it somewhat more concretely: if it is the case—and nobody has been able to demonstrate the contrary—that the psychobiological makeup of, let us say, the Trobriand Islanders and the Europeans is not significantly different, then it would be logical to assume that since both "groups" have occupied the planet as *Homo sapiens* for the same length of time, their cultures or lifeways should be much more alike in structure and content than they are. However, having noted the *differences* between the Trobrianders and the Europeans, we generally tend to be more impressed by these than by the apparent similarities evidenced by their cultures. Not only are we impressed, but we are likely to ask why the differences exist. If the psychobiological infrastructure is indeed a constant, it is obvious that we cannot look to it to provide us with an answer to our question. For while psychobiology may account for many of the broad cultural resemblances that we observe, it cannot at the same time explain the differences.

In addition to the cultural similarities that may be attributed to the psychobiological "unity" of man, there are other similarities which cannot be explained by this unity. We refer to those resemblances in cultural form and pattern that arise from convergent processes of growth, change, or development—for example, the similarities, despite certain persisting dissimilarities in culture content, between industrial Japan and industrial Germany. They interest us in this connection because we know that the sociocultural systems of these two countries differed profoundly in the era immediately preceding the launching of their industrial revolutions. Thus, parallel processes of industrialization clearly led to increasing similarities in ideology and social structure. . . . Throughout this entire period of intense change, the psychobiological features of these two populations, so far as one can tell, remained constant.

Anthropology's central problems, then, are the explanation of cultural similarities and differences, of cultural maintenance as well as cultural change over time. As change may be seen only against the background of cultural stability or maintenance, so stability may be understood only against a background of change. If cultures did not differ from each other, and if they did not change, questions about the mechanisms of change or stability would never arise. But we observe that cultures do differ from each other and—at varying rates—do change over time. We cannot fall back on intraspecific variation to account for the cultural differences found so often among populations in the past as well as in the present.

Only in examining those mechanisms, structures, and devices lying outside of man—the means by which he achieves his own transformation—can we learn why some groups differ in their beliefs, values, behaviour, and social forms from others. . . .

Those collective mechanisms, structures, and devices lying outside of man (outside in an analytic rather than in some metaphysical sense) are what anthropologists have called culture.

In popular thinking differences of culture explain the persistence and especially the change of social institutions. Typically, it would be argued that African family structures changed when people migrated to the cities because there they came into contact with European culture, which influenced their behaviour and way of thinking. The process of *acculturation* was thus the key to explaining social change.[56] As an analytical device this has been found to be too vague, and anthropologists now look instead to other criteria, in particular economic or political forces.[57]

Successive governments in South Africa have used culture as a device to legitimize their policies. Racial segregation and the fragmentation of the country

[56] See Myburgh *Anthropology for Southern Africa* 30–4. And further see below, 152–3.
[57] Sharp (1985) 44 *Afr Studies* 65ff.

into separate homelands was justified by the understanding that the population was naturally divided into different (and implicitly hostile) cultures, whose competing interests could be accommodated only by territorial and social separation. By promoting this process as an ostensible *right* of cultural self-determination, the government could vindicate the maintenance of unequal power relations on the ground that they happened to coincide with cultural differences.

[6] THORNTON in BOONZAIER & SHARP *SOUTH AFRICAN KEYWORDS* 17–24

One textbook goes so far as to say, "*Soveel volke wat daar is, soveel kulture bestaan daar*" (There are as many cultures as there are peoples.)[1] Another widely used textbook, *An Introduction to Anthropology*, by D P Stoffberg, says that culture is "the expression of an ethnic group's speech, thought processes, actions and aspirations. An ethnic group and its culture develop organically and simultaneously to become an indivisible, homogeneous group."[2]

A C Myburgh approaches the issue from the other side by defining "a people" as "a human group producing and maintaining a culture"[3], while B Levitas in yet another textbook claims that the members of a group "ie a people, possess a common way of life and share a common culture", and goes on to say: "All South Africans are classified into races . . . [and] . . . consist of many peoples, the Xhosa, Zulu and Tswana, etc., each with a distinct language and culture."[4] We find similar views world-wide. Elvin Hatch, for instance, defines culture as "the way of life of a people" in the 1985 edition of *The Social Science Encyclopedia*.[5]

. . . [T]he assertion of cultural differences distinctive of different "peoples" or *volke* is apparently contradicted daily by the very fact that the ideology of differences is communicated easily across all of the "cultural barriers" that we are told exist. In the marketplace and workplace, listening to music or watching television, at homes and in churches, people in fact experience the same desires, profess the same religions, follow the same leaders, and eat the same cornflakes, notwithstanding their "multicultural" condition!

The problem is the little "*s*" that makes "cultures" from "culture". Most of the textbooks just cited acknowledge that culture is what makes the species Homo sapiens specifically human, but once this is said, all agree that humanity is divided by its many cultures. . . . [M]uch more than the scientific definition of "culture" is at stake here. The very act of defining "culture" is itself a declaration of what it is to be human—that is, a moral statement—and a statement of identity—in other words, a political statement. This is because the attempt to understand and to define culture is also part of culture. Unlike the attempt to say precisely how microbes cause disease or specify the exact composition of a piece of granite, to discuss culture is to be part of culture, to have an effect on it, and ultimately to change the very nature of the "object" itself. Although this concept is difficult to grasp, it is essential if our understanding of culture is to be more than a restatement in different terms of the moral and political ideas of our times.

The idea of culture and its context
The idea of culture as it is used in the modern period acquired the main features of its meaning in the nineteenth century. It shares a complex intellectual history with the ideas of "society", "nation" and "organism", all of which appeared with their contemporary sense around the beginning of the nineteenth century. They have in common the idea of self-contained and self-regulating *wholeness*. Several intellectual sciences developed around these ideas, and today form the content of the academic disciplines of anthropology and/or ethnology, sociology, political economy and/or political science, and biology. The powerful ideas that these sciences have contributed to the world have transformed it completely in the two centuries in which they have been current.

These ideas have interacted with each other too. The idea of "culture" has frequently been fused with that of "society", and they have been used interchangeably to refer to a general social state of affairs or to a more or less clearly recognisable group of people. Ideas about "cultures" and "organisms" have also influenced each other in the development of theories of evolution, both cultural and biological. Sometimes people have argued that cultures are like organisms, or even that cultures are a *kind* of organism or "super-organism". Such notions have supported the idea that nations are endowed with unique cultures—something like the genetic component of an organism—which must be protected in order to preserve "society". Unfortunately, these ideas are confused and contribute nothing to a useful understanding of culture.

Worse still, these ideas have been used to justify repressive and brutal forms of government by arguing that, like an organism, a culture or a nation must defend itself against internal, as well as external, enemies. If the initial premise that cultures are "owned" by nations is accepted, the activities of repressive state bureaucracies may be justified as a form of political hygiene. But in many cases the apparent similarities that exist between ideas of "cultures", "organisms", "nations" and "societies" are the result of the historical development of these ideas in a common intellectual and political context, and not the expression of genuine insight into the human condition. . . .

In the twentieth century, the Modernist idea of culture retained the notion that culture is uniquely associated with a single society or nation. But unlike the Romantic notion, it asserts that culture functions to maintain society (or nations), and that culture is historical and changes over time, often in relation to (or determined by) changes in "society" (or economy). Because culture—in the form of myths, political speeches, religious beliefs, ideologies, histories and traditions—is held to have a social function, the theory requires that each "culture" exists as a *whole* within a "society".

Anthropologists who wrote according to this concept of culture often spoke about groups of people living on islands, or isolated from others by forests or mountains. Even where the people they wrote about were not isolated in any physical way, simply the fact that they were written about in a book, usually titled something like *The Life of a South African Tribe* (H A Junod, 1912), *The Bantu-speaking Tribes of South Africa* (Schapera, 1937), or *The Pedi* (Mönnig, 1967), suggested their uniqueness and boundedness. The boundaries of so-called national states reflect, in many cases, the limits of a nineteenth-century dictionary which defined a "language" (such as Tswana), or the designation of map-makers who, from the vantage point of Cape Town, distinguished between "this side" (*cis-*) and "that side" (*trans-*) of the Kei River. Elsewhere, culture has been written directly into legislation, administered by bureaucracies, and enforced by armed intervention. Indeed, in South Africa, it is often the history of ethnological *publications*, rather than the real history of South African people, that has had most influence in the shaping of political boundaries. . . .

One of the factors that determines the perspective of the observer most forcefully is the distribution of wealth and power among the people the observer observes, and this is precisely what most earlier concepts of culture left out—or rather left for others to consider. Since the study of culture takes place in the discipline of anthropology, and the study of power, economy, and biology is pursued by other disciplines, part of the problem is the history of disciplines themselves.

The fact that the observer must also be part of the social situation that is observed was left out of earlier descriptions of "cultures". This created the effect of "cultures" existing by themselves, the objects of scientific and disinterested observation. In fact, there are many reasons why observers observe and writers write about peoples' culture. But in order to write about the differences between people, observers must be *there*. No matter how different they may seem to themselves or to those they describe, observers must look and listen, sometimes understanding and sometimes misunderstanding. They must buy, sell, negotiate—in short, interact in a human and social way. The fact that books which detail all the *differences* of "cultures" can be written at all negates the idea that cultures are *fundamentally* different.

Many anthropologists now feel that we have come to the end of an age. Some call it post-Modernism, for lack of a better term, to indicate that we have now entered an intellectual age that can dispense with some of the ideas on which the oppressive weight of the modern state rests. It is clear, too, that many concepts that have been fundamental to the sciences which appeared and grew during this age—biology, sociology, anthropology, and others—have changed. The concept of culture, one of the most politically and intellectually powerful ideas of the Romantic and Modern times, is also changing.

Notes

1. P J Coertze *Inleiding tot die Algemene Volkekunde* 61.
2. D P Stoffberg *Introduction to Anthropology* 1.
3. A C Myburgh *Anthropology for Southern Africa* 31.
4. B Levitas *Ethnology: an introduction to the peoples and cultures of southern Africa* 19.
5. A Kuper & J Kuper (eds) *Social Science Encyclopedia* 178.

(b) The simple society

All works on customary law are formulated with particular ideas of society in mind. One of the most influential in this regard is an opposition between simple and complex societies. The former type (usually identified with Tönnies' *Gemeinschaft* relationships) implies a homogeneous group of people with shared values and interests; the latter (identified with *Gesellschaft* relationships) is the antithesis. Systems of customary law are identified with the normative orders of simple societies and predictably western-style legal systems are associated with complex societies.[58] The distinctive features of the two legal types are predicated by this dichotomy;[59] for example, customary law is believed to be consensual in origin, and the law-making process is thought to be more democratic[60] than in complex societies.[61]

Gluckman elaborated the concept of the simple society (which in the extract below he terms 'tribal') in order to explain the operation and evolution of the legal institutions he was going to describe.

[7] GLUCKMAN *THE IDEAS IN BAROTSE JURISPRUDENCE* 4–5

I distinguish a society as "tribal" by several interrelated characteristics: there are only relatively simple tools, so that each worker produces little beyond what he can himself consume of the basic primary goods; since a wealthy man cannot eat more than a certain amount of food, wear luxurious clothes when only materials like skin, barkcloth, and a little cotton are available, or live in a palace when habitations are made of skin, grass, mud, and similar materials, these societies are marked by a basically egalitarian standard of living; trade goods may travel from hand to hand in a series of exchanges over distances, but the total volume of trade is limited.

Two important general results flow from this situation. First, the wealthy and powerful do not form what might be called a separate "class", cut off from the poor by a quite different style of life. Those of varying power and riches mix fairly freely with one another, and intermarriage can occur between their families without provoking a public scandal. They can thus be kin to one another. In fact, the powerful and wealthy use the lands and goods they control to attract followers, and a man's prestige is determined by the number

---

[58] Sawer *Law in Society* 27ff.
[59] And so too is Hart's theory of law: Fallers *Law without Precedent* 14.
[60] Cf Allen *Law in the Making* 92ff.
[61] Smith in Kuper & Kuper *African Law* 26–7 and Bohannan op cit n14 50ff.

of dependants or subjects he has, much more than by mere possession and use of goods. Prestige and power are important in all these societies and enable a man to control the actions of others; but he gains that control through establishing relationships of personal dependence with as many others as he can.

Second, the usual settlements of these societies are camps, hamlets, or villages of a number of closely related families—what Ehrlich called "genetic associations". The core of organization of these settlements may be a number of men related to one another by descent through the agnatic line, or in other tribes through the matrilineal line; or the core may be in yet other tribes a number of females related to one another by descent through the female line. These are the most clearly defined possibilities. But extremely complex situations are also found, in which men and women may choose to live with any kinsfolk, as among the Barotse, so that families within a settlement are related to one another in a most complex pattern.

Despite these variations, in all societies of this type a grouping of some kind of kinsmen and/or kinswomen, with their spouses and usually their children, tend to live together. As a group, sometimes through particular representatives, they own certain rights ... of access to land, in which they have other rights as members of smaller units and as individuals. As we shall see, goods are appropriated by the individual who produces them, despite some collaboration in productive activities, but consumption involves considerable and constant sharing. Since there are no specialized priests, these groups also form congregations, worshipping the spirits of their dead kin or supplicating at common land shrines or other ritual objects. There are no schools, and children are educated as well as reared in the settlement. The settlement also tends to form a political unit for important purposes, whether or not the tribe be organized under a chief. Relations among the members of these groups are thus directed to a multiplicity of purposes, and I have therefore named them *multiplex*. It is this situation that I describe continuously as one "dominated by status".

These ties establish the most important sets of obligations between persons, and hence transactions between persons are determined by their status (in Maine's sense) relative to one another. The relations involved stand in sharp contrast with the relations, arising out of single interests, in which we nowadays become associated with other persons through the many contracts into which we enter throughout our daily lives.

In the next extract the differences between simple and complex societies are further refined, again with particular reference to Africa. The principal organizing feature alluded to—the degree of political centralization—is of special interest to lawyers because of the positivist concern with political sovereignty.[62] The models presented below have been highly influential in explaining, inter alia: the content of rules of law, whether the societies in question actually have 'law', modes of processing disputes,[63] and methods of law-making.

[8] FORTES & EVANS-PRITCHARD *AFRICAN POLITICAL SYSTEMS* 5, 14–16

It will be noted that the political systems described in this book fall into two main categories. One group, which we refer to as Group A, consists of those societies which have centralized authority, administrative machinery, and judicial institutions—in short, a government—and in which cleavages of wealth, privilege, and status correspond to the distribution of power and authority.... The other group, which we refer to as Group B, consists of those societies which lack centralized authority, administrative machinery, and

---

[62] See Austin and Hart above, 3–4.
[63] See below, 54, [20].

constituted judicial institutions—in short which lack government—and in which there are no sharp divisions of rank, status, or wealth. . . . Those who consider that a state should be defined by the presence of governmental institutions will regard the first group as primitive states and the second group as stateless societies. . . .

In our judgement, the most significant characteristic distinguishing the centralized, pyramidal, state-like forms of government of the Ngwato, Bemba, &c., from the segmentary political systems of the Logoli, the Tallensi, and the Nuer is the incidence and function of organized force in the system. In the former group of societies, the principal sanction of a ruler's rights and prerogatives, and of the authority exercised by his subordinate chiefs, is the command of organized force. This may enable an African king to rule oppressively for a time, if he is inclined to do so, but a good ruler uses the armed forces under his control in the public interest, as an accepted instrument of government—that is, for the defence of the society as a whole or of any section of it, for offence against a common enemy, and as a coercive sanction to enforce the law or respect for the constitution. The king and his delegates and advisers use organized force with the consent of their subjects to keep going a political system which the latter take for granted as the foundation of their social order.

In societies of Group B there is no association, class, or segment which has a dominant place in the political structure through the command of greater organized force than is at the disposal of any of its congeners. If force is resorted to in a dispute between segments it will be met with equal force. If one segment defeats another it does not attempt to establish political dominance over it; in the absence of an administrative machinery there is, in fact, no means by which it could do so. In the language of political philosophy, there is no individual or group in which sovereignty can be said to rest. In such a system, stability is maintained by an equilibrium at every line of cleavage and every point of divergent interests in the social structure. This balance is sustained by a distribution of the command of force corresponding to the distribution of like, but competitive, interests amongst the homologous segments of the society. Whereas a constituted judicial machinery is possible and is always found in societies of Group A, since it has the backing of organized force, the jural institutions of the Logoli, the Tallensi and the Nuer rest on the right of self-help.

Differences in response to European rule

The distinctions we have noted between the two categories into which these eight societies fall, especially in the kind of balance characteristic of each, are very marked in their adjustment to the rule of colonial governments. Most of these societies have been conquered or have submitted to European rule from fear of invasion. They would not acquiesce in it if the threat of force were withdrawn; and this fact determines the part now played in their political life by European administrations.

In the societies of Group A, the paramount ruler is prohibited, by the constraint of colonial government, from using the organized force at his command on his responsibility. This has everywhere resulted in diminishing his authority and of increasing the power and independence of his subordinates. He no longer rules right, but as the agent of the colonial government. The pyramidal structure is now maintained by the latter's taking his place as paramount. If he he may become a mere puppet of the colonial government. He lo people because the pattern of reciprocal rights and duties which destroyed. Alternatively, he may be able to safeguard his form openly or covertly leading the opposition which his peor rule. Very often he is in the equivocal position of havi roles as representative of his people against the ce against his people. He becomes the pivot on which

In the societies of Group B, European rule ha government cannot administer through aggregat segments, but has to employ administrative agents.

persons who can be assimilated to the stereotyped notion of an African chief. These agents for the first time have the backing of force behind their authority, now, moreover, extending into spheres for which there is no precedent. Direct resort to force in the form of self-help in defence of the rights of individuals or of groups is no longer permitted; for there is now, for the first time, a paramount authority exacting obedience in virtue of superior force which enables it to establish courts of justice to replace self-help. This tends to lead to the whole system of mutually balancing segments collapsing and a bureaucratic European system taking its place. An organization more like that of a centralized state comes into being.

A polity taken to be characteristic of simple societies is the chiefdom. This is considered to be a body of people united by ties of kinship under the leadership of a senior member of the leading clan. Flowing from their genetic links, the people share a common language, culture and law.[64]

Simple societies are generally believed to be traditionalist and static, a view that can be directly attributed to the theory of evolution. Connected with this is the belief that simple societies are unable to develop of their own accord, and that any changes that do occur are random, unplanned and imposed by extrinsic forces. All these ideas have a certain geographic dimension: simple societies are rural phenomena, whereas the complex society is a product of urbanization. Customary law has inevitably been associated with backward, rural regimes; with them, it is locked into an unchanging past.

(c) Tribe

The tribe as a unit of study has provided the parameters for most works on customary law.[65] In anthropological parlance, Africans south of the Zambezi belong to one large unit designated the 'Southern Bantu'. These people are supposed to have a common historical origin further to the north; they have many linguistic similarities, (see the diagram of the distribution of languages opposite); and most importantly they share a culture, marked by such features as a patrilineal system of succession and the giving of bridewealth.

People south of the Limpopo have been further classified into two broad categories: the Nguni and the Sotho-Tswana. (Neither of these appellations is necessarily used by the people themselves; they are terms of convenience attributed by colonial historians, administrators and anthropologists.)[66] The Nguni occupy the eastern coastal plain of southern Africa, broadly the area from Swaziland southwards to the Great Fish River. A distinctive mode of dispersed residence, a strictly exogamous regime for marriage, and above all a certain linguistic uniformity (despite numerous differences of dialect) are common characteristics. Using the same cultural and linguistic criteria, the Nguni are further divided into a northern group, comprising broadly the Swazi and Zulu

om in Hammond-Tooke *Bantu-speaking Peoples* 262–3. The belief that the chiefdom was the ical unit of pre- (and indeed post-) conquest southern Africa is now being questioned, in light nd archaeological evidence to the contrary. See Hall *The Changing Past* 74ff.
ks on tribal law, such as Whitfield (1948), were regularly produced to meet the he colonial administration. See Hund & Van der Merwe op cit n5 36–7.
o in Hammond-Tooke op cit n64 59ff.

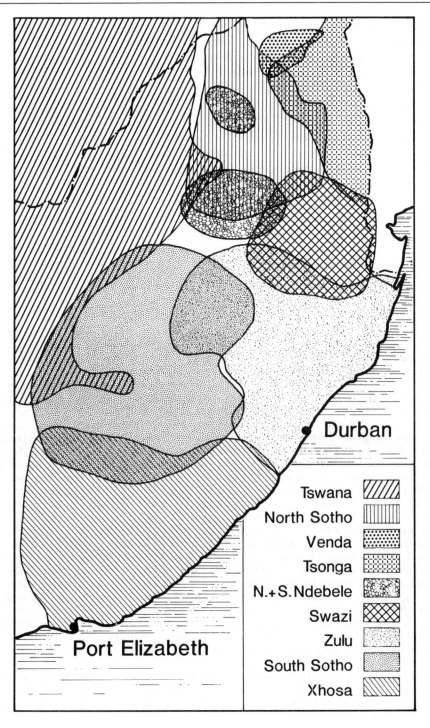

Tswana	
North Sotho	
Venda	
Tsonga	
N.+S.Ndebele	
Swazi	
Zulu	
South Sotho	
Xhosa	

Distribution of Languages

kingdoms, and a southern group, comprising a loose association of chiefdoms: the Xhosa, Pondo, Bhaca, Pondomise, Thembu, Bomvana, Mfengu.

The Sotho-Tswana peoples inhabit the interior plateau. In contrast to the Nguni, they live in more concentrated settlements (or towns) and they have a system of preferred cousin marriage. The Tswana chiefdoms are located mainly on the dry savannah bordering the Kalahari, although the people are scattered throughout the Orange Free State, northern Cape, Botswana and Transvaal. The Sotho are divided into two branches—Northern and Southern—again principally on geographic grounds. The Southern Sotho can claim as a heartland the historic kingdom of Lesotho; the Northern Sotho, constituted mainly by the Pedi and Lovedu, are located in the northern Transvaal.

Somewhat neglected in this classification are three peoples of the Transvaal: the Tsonga, Ndebele and Venda. The following extract describes in some detail how the Tsonga 'tribe' was constructed over a hundred-year period, despite the absence of any significant unifying features, such as culture, language or polity. This type of historical research has placed in question many previous assumptions made about southern African tribal groupings.

[9] HARRIES in VAIL *CREATION OF TRIBALISM IN SOUTHERN AFRICA* 83–107

The Migration of Tsonga-speakers

In the early nineteenth century people who were later to be defined as Tsonga-speakers occupied the whole of Mozambique south of the Sabi river except for the enclaves of territory surrounding and immediately to the south of the town of Inhambane. For the major part of the century the chiefdoms to the north of Delagoa Bay fell under the hegemony of the Gaza Nguni; those to the west of the bay were heavily influenced by the Swazi; while the Zulu dominated the chiefdoms to the south of the bay. All three states incorporated, both politically and culturally, many of the people living on their borders who spoke language forms later to be classified as Tsonga. These people, particularly traders and hunters from the areas around Inhambane and Lourenço Marques, had for many years operated in the high and lowveld areas to the west of the Lebombo mountains. Here their commercial skills, rites, customs and organization bound them together and, together with their foreignness, singled them out as a distinctly separate group. But it was only in the second quarter of the nineteenth century that coastal peoples settled the area that was later to become the northern and eastern Transvaal in a purposeful way.

During the 1820s a number of Nguni refugee groups fleeing from the disturbances in Natal associated with the growth of the Zulu state passed through southern Mozambique. In the late 1830s one of these groups, led by Soshangane, took advantage of a decline in Zulu power following the battle of Blood River and reoccupied the fertile lower Limpopo. According to missionary historians who gathered evidence a half-century after the event, Soshangane's return to the south initiated a "general exodus" of people living between the Nkomati and Limpopo rivers. The refugees travelled along the trade routes flanking two rivers, the Olifants and Limpopo-Levubu, that passed through the thinly populated lowveld and gave access to the healthier, well-watered areas to the west. The second major wave of immigrants entered the Transvaal as a result of the Gaza civil war and ecological upsets of 1858–62. Raids into the coastal and northern Delagoa Bay hinterland by the defeated heir to the Gaza throne and his Swazi allies continued into the 1870s, causing the movement of people into the Transvaal to continue unabated. The flow of war refugees was continually augmented by people fleeing from natural upheavals such as drought, famine and smallpox.

These immigrants settled under virtually every chief living on the escarpment and eastern highveld. Although they often shifted their political allegiances, they were

welcomed by chiefs to whom they paid tribute in labour and in goods. They were attached
to homesteads as individuals or, as small groups under their own headmen, were scattered
throughout the veld, colonizing those areas where human and animal diseases, poor soils
or lack of water had previously restricted settlement. Coming from a different ecological
area, East Coast immigrants introduced new types of food such as fowls, cassava, certain
kinds of groundnuts, various grain and potato strains and, especially, maize. These new
foodstuffs, together with their techniques of preparation and cooking, served as cultural
markers that defined these displaced people, in the eyes of the autochthonous population,
as outsiders. Chiefs competed with each other to attract these East Coast immigrants by
offering them security and access to a means of production. . . .

By the 1860s four small semi-independent clusters of East Coast refugees had begun to
emerge in the Transvaal. The middle and lower Levubu river was largely settled by
members of the Maluleke clan who were perennially under Gaza hegemony. The
heterogeneous population in the Spelonken hills accepted the overlordship of Albasini and
his chiefs. To the south the other major groups, consisting mainly of Baloyi and Nkuna
clan members, lived in the Haenertsberg under various North Sotho-speaking chiefs.
Smaller settlements, many of whose members were described as "Hlangaan", developed to
the south of the Olifants river around Pedi, immigrant Boer and Swazi communities. The
discovery of alluvial goldfields in this area in the 1870s attracted large numbers of coastal
immigrants who settled as labour tenants on company lands surrounding the mining
villages. The final major wave of East Coast refugees, consisting of several thousand Gaza
Nguni, settled in the eastern and northern Transvaal in 1897 following their defeat in the
second Luso-Gaza war. In the twentieth century the movement of Mozambicans into the
Transvaal, drawn by better living conditions, continued unabated despite a legislative
attempt in 1913 to restrict this immigration.

By the early twentieth century East Coast immigrants were scattered throughout the
northern and eastern Transvaal; many barriers divided them from each other and,
although they tended to settle in low-lying areas and river valleys, no natural frontier
separated them from their neighbours. Even where borders can be distinguished,
immigrant communities were surrounded by wide belts of mixed settlement, and islands
of linguistic minorities existed on both sides. In 1896 a northern Transvaal newspaper
remarked of the immigrants from the East Coast that they were "an admixture of
refugees . . . they have no recognized king, but subject themselves to the most wealthy,
who assumes the leadership under the title of induna or headman". It is ironic that the
geographically diffuse and politically amorphous form of settlement practised by these
nineteenth century immigrants was also recognized by N J van Warmelo, the government
ethnologist who was later to play a leading role in their definition and delimitation as a
"population group" with its own "homeland". In 1937 he wrote that:

"the Tsonga-speaking refugees came over the border in small parties and settled down
wherever they could. Very often they became the subjects of Sotho and Venda chiefs
and, though the tendency to reassemble and live together was there, they usually failed
to muster sufficient strength to form tribes of any importance."

Even to use the term "Tsonga-speaking" with reference to nineteenth century is
misleading as it invokes an erroneous linguistic unity. No single language linked the early
East Coast refugees who were settled throughout the northern and eastern Transvaal.
Instead, they spoke a rich variety of language forms that reflected their diverse
geographical origins. The codification and categorization of Tsonga as a language was
only undertaken at the end of the nineteenth century by missionaries who, trained to
categorize and classify national groups and characteristics according to language, reified
this linguistic category into an ethnic group—into a "tribe".

Missionaries and the Definition of the "Tsonga Tribe"

During the nineteenth century a number of popular stereotypes were applied in a rough
way to those people living in, or originating from, the region east of the Lebombos and

north of Zululand. The term "Tonga" entered the English language as a borrowing from the Zulu who used it in the nineteenth century to refer to all the conquered peoples of the coastal areas north of Zululand. It was used in a similarly pejorative way by several chiefdoms in southern Mozambique, at least one of which was later to be classified as Tsonga-speaking.... Despite the imprecision with which the Zulu used the term, the Natal colonists adopted the word as a general term applied to those people living along the coast north of the Zulu border regardless of their actual linguistic or cultural affiliations. Because of the derogatory overtones with which the term was imbued, however, it was never used by the people to whom it was applied. It was only in the twentieth century that linguists expurgated the abusive connotations from the term, initially by introducing an aspirated /h/ and finally by adopting the term "Tsonga".

The Portuguese at Lourenço Marques distinguished between intrusive Vatua or Nguni-speakers and the indigenous Landims, a practice that has led some historians to view the terms "Tsonga" and "Landim" as synonymous. In the Transvaal, East Coast immigrants were given various general labels by the people with whom they came into contact, such as "Knobnoses", given to them by Europeans because of the distinctive nasal cicatrization practised by some of the coastal peoples, and "Gwambas", a term applied by indigenous Africans living in the Zoutpansberg and Spelonken hills. This label, initially derived from the name of a chief near Inhambane whose followers had traded in the northern Transvaal, had evolved into a synonym for "easterner". On the diamond and gold fields, "East Coasters" were also called "Shangaans", a term that, correctly used, should be applied to those people who adopted the material culture of the Gaza Nguni chief Soshangane. Thus, in present-day South Africa, only the descendants of the Gaza Nguni immigrants who entered the eastern Transvaal after the second Luso-Gaza war of 1897, are officially classified "Shangaan" or "Tshangana" and in this way distinguished from the descendants of earlier immigrants, the Tsonga, who were in most cases never under Gaza rule. Yet the word "Shangaan" has become an all-embracing term used to refer to the Tsonga-speaking peoples of southeast Africa and, in a more general way, to all Mozambicans employed on the South African mines. It is obvious that during the nineteenth century these terms were used in a generic and popular way to embrace diverse peoples and chiefdoms with no common name and, as ethnographic terms, they are of very little value.

A far more scholarly attempt to delineate an ethnic group emerged at the end of the nineteenth century out of a heated debate within the Swiss mission over the linguistic relationship between their followers in the Transvaal Spelonken and those living on the East Coast.... One of the first steps taken by the Swiss missionaries to ease their work was to reduce the various dialects spoken by the East Coast refugees amongst whom they lived to a single written language. This resulted in the publication in the early 1880s and early 1890s of a language primer and several religious works in a *lingua franca* which the missionaries named "Gwamba". In compiling this language the missionaries had been strongly influenced by the northern Delagoa Bay dialect spoken by their assistants and by most of the immigrants in the Spelonken....

To avoid being viewed as foreigners from the north, or "Karangas", Henri A Junod, one of the missionaries in the Lourenço Marques area, started to codify another local *lingua franca* which he called "Ronga". In 1894 Junod produced a basic Ronga reader and over the following three years he completed a grammar and collection of folktales and an extensive ethnographic work on what he then referred to as "the Ronga people". It was this division of the "Ronga", both linguistically and socially, from the "Gwamba" in the Spelonken area that sparked off the debate within the Swiss mission over how to categorize the people among whom they worked....

After spending several years in the Transvaal, Junod published in 1907 an Elementary Grammar of the Thonga/Shangaan Language, which marked the abandonment of the geographically and politically imprecise term "Gwamba".... Within a few years distinct

Ronga and Thonga/Shangaan (formerly "Gwamba") written languages had been established on the basis of separate grammars and orthographies. Ronga came to dominate southern Mozambique and Thonga/Shangaan the northern Transvaal and central-southern Mozambique. Meanwhile, American missionaries working in the Inhambane area delineated a third related language which they named "Tswa". Despite the defeat of the movement calling for one written Tsonga dialect, the ideal of a single unifying language is still expressed in missionary circles. . . .

Encouraged by evolutionism and by Sir James Frazer, the classicist-turned-anthropologist, Junod used the same schema to make sense of the complex and confusing African world into which he had plunged. But to make African societies fit the European pattern, he resorted to pseudo-history by hypothesizing that at some time in the distant past, migrants originating from different areas had imposed themselves on an earlier proto-Thonga people and had adopted their language. Working from this shaky and, at best, historically speculative premise, Junod saw language as the common thread holding together the Thonga as a "tribe" or "nation". By 1905 he ascribed the "recognition of the Thonga as a tribe" largely to the work of the Swiss mission. Seven years later in his two-volume *Life of a South African Tribe*, which he published in English in order to reach an influential audience, he divided the Thonga into the "northern clans", who spoke Thonga/Shangaan, and the Mozambican Ronga who occupied the area south of the Nkomati river. Yet Junod had never been to the southern half of what he defined as the Ronga area nor had he visited the extensive Thonga/Shangaan area north of the Nkomati river or that of the "Tswa" to the west and north of Inhambane. But because he automatically associated language with culture he unconsciously imbued all the people who spoke these two artificially defined languages with distinctive social customs and traits. His distinction between the Ronga and Thonga/Shangaan was not always clear and, consequently, many historians and others have conflated them into a single Tsonga ethnic group. . . .

In fact, there was no "pure" Tsonga culture that could be regarded as a uniform or static entity, for Tsonga-speaking immigrants in the Transvaal did not come from a common cultural pool. The material culture expressed by an individual was not static or "traditional", nor was it bound by linguistic affiliations. The cultural markers exhibited by Tsonga-speakers such as diet, tools, clothing, custom and language were, moreover, marked by continual adaptations to changing social and environmental situations. The division of the people of southern Mozambique into various linguistic sub-groups was therefore totally arbitrary and nowhere did they present a common bounded and static linguistic entity.

East Coast traders, hunters and later waves of refugees who entered the Transvaal at different times and from different areas brought with them elements of various material cultures which were, because of their foreign origin, distinguishable from local cultures. But here again, these were factors of exclusion rather than cohesion and the line became blurred as Tsonga-speaking immigrants adapted themselves to their new surroundings. Long distance migrations demanded that fish- or beef-eaters who moved westwards into dry, riverless or tsetse-ridden areas of the Lowveld were obliged to adapt their diet and production strategies to the new environment. In an attempt to assimilate to local norms, some Tsonga-speaking immigrants attended initiation lodges run by host chiefdoms while others adopted local totems. Some continued to practise circumcision which on the East Coast had largely been abandoned by those chiefdoms dominated by Nguni-speakers. Their music was influenced to differing degrees by the Pedi and by people today classified as Venda, Lovedu, Chopi and Ndau, many of whose instruments they have adopted. Many Tsonga-speakers were incorporated, through the ideology of kinship, into host clans in the Transvaal, alongside whose members they constituted a single production unit. This process of individual assimilation was so advanced that it led one anthropologist to speculate that an entire Venda-speaking clan had its roots east of the Lebombos, while another believed that the Tsonga-speaking Baloyi clan had once spoken a Shona-based dialect. An ecologically symbiotic relationship also existed between Tsonga-speaking agriculturalists who colonized malarial and tsetse infested river valleys and plains and the cattle-keepers living above the valley.

As long as male immigrants stressed their independence by clinging to foreign customs, especially those that were related to sexuality, such as puberty rites and marriage patterns, intermarriage with local people was generally precluded. As outsiders who practised "barbarous" customs and spoke the local language badly, they were considered inferiors and classified as such by being labelled "Tonga". For immigrants to benefit fully from the patronage of members of the host clan they had to resort to fictive filiation and suffer the exploitation as junior members that this often implied. When immigrants arrived in a group under their own chief, however, their position was far stronger and they were more likely to maintain their distinctive material culture.

The cultural boundaries first defined and established by missionary anthropologists at the turn of the century have been extrapolated back into the past by historians who see "the Tsonga" as a primeval ethnic group occupying a large part of south-east Africa. . . .

The African Mode of Self-Identification

In reality, however, the Africans conceptualized the structure and order of their world in an entirely different way. The basis of African political and social life was the chiefdom. This grouped together members of the same productive unit and was dominated by the members of one clan. Membership of the clan was expressed through the use of a common patronymic, or *shibongo*, through which an individual identified himself as a member of his clan leader's house. Outsiders who professed fealty to the clan leader or chief defined themselves as being "from the land of" their host clan while the latter's unifying ideology of agnatic descent provided for their gradual incorporation through the adoption of the clan patronymic. Junod referred to the chiefdom, or *tiko*, as "the true national unit" in which political identity was rooted.

Various symbols bound the members of the chiefdom together and distinguished one chiefdom from another. Foremost amongst these was the institution of chieftaincy, for the chief, as the believed direct descendant of the founding ancestors and as the senior member of the kin group, was the embodiment of clan unity and the centre of its corporate identity. He administered a form of justice that was entirely based on the moral community of the clan and the chiefdom, protected the army with his war medicines, interceded with the clan ancestors and generally regulated production strategies. The chief gave to his followers a sense of belonging and unity by using symbols of office that were believed to invest him with special powers and by organizing various rites that were limited to clan members, such as first fruit ceremonies and entry to the age regiments. The cohesion of the clan and the differences between clans were accentuated by marriage patterns which stressed clan endogamy, by the accreditation to each clan of a separate area of origin and migration and by particularities of dialect. . . .

Tsonga-speaking chiefdoms in the Transvaal remained small and independent of one another and manifested no tendency to grow through conquest. But the roots of ethnic consciousness cutting across the divisions of clan and chiefdom may be discerned by the beginning of the twentieth century. Clan endogamy had broken down entirely in areas of the Transvaal like the Spelonken where large numbers of refugees had gathered. Men were meeting and working on the mines and plantations as "Shangaans" and "Tongas" and literacy in Thonga/Shangaan, although limited to a small number of people, provided Christians and traders from different areas with a common means of communication. But the vast majority of the population remained illiterate and the individual's world remained largely a small personal one, limited to the chiefdom with whose members he or she shared symbols and rituals that gave meaning to their lives. Poor communications and a limited area of social and economic exchange further restricted the development of a political consciousness extending beyond the clan and chiefdom. What defined the Tsonga in the final instance were their neighbours. The Tsonga/Knobnoses/Gwamba/Shangaans, as their various neighbours called them, only took on or adopted an ethnic identity later in the twentieth century. This new identity emerged as a result of the politicization of the old classificatory ethnicity—a politicization that was the product of the new economic infrastructure introduced by capitalist development. . . .

The Waning of Chiefly Power

In frontier areas like the Zoutpansberg, where the ratio of blacks to whites in the first decade of the twentieth century was estimated at 100 :1 and where a police force of fifty had to cope with a population of over 300,000, chiefs had of necessity performed the role of paid civil servants. They were obliged to help collect taxes and supply labour for public works and farms and prevent what the government declared to be poaching, the destruction of state forests and the consumption of illicit liquor. Native Commissioners were unanimously opposed to the detribalization process as the chiefs "were of great assistance in maintaining law and order". . . .

This perspective dovetailed with that of ethnologists and evolutionist anthropologists such as Henri Junod who feared that urbanization and the loss of chiefly control would lead to the "demoralization" and "degeneration" (i.e. proletarianization) of the African population. . . . Emerging from the same mould, the young liberal segregationist Edgar Brookes supported the creation of reserves in which Africans could "develop along their own lines and under their own chiefs". At a time when 60 per cent of the African population lived as tenants on white farms or in the cities of South Africa, it was nonetheless commonly believed that Africans lived in "traditional tribes"! This historically static view was perhaps best expressed in a handbook sponsored in 1934 by the South African inter-university committee for African Studies, Isaac Schapera's seminal collection, *The Bantu Speaking Tribes of South Africa*. Although this book claimed and probably achieved the status of "a manual of South African ethnography", the introduction frankly stated that "the greater part [92.5 per cent] of the book is devoted to an account of the Bantu as they were before affected by the intrusion of white civilization". Like Schapera, Junod hoped that his work would influence native administrators to understand the exoticisms of tribal life.

At the ideological level the Native Affairs Department was strongly influenced by this strain of anthropology. Members of the Department established compilations of "traditional laws" by drawing borders that were ethnically conceived around regularities of rite and custom. At the economic level they became increasingly aware of the need to conserve within the reserves the elements of non-capitalist society that bore a large part of the costs of the reproduction of the urban labour force. . . . To check this process, various laws were passed in the 1920s in an attempt to bolster the powers of the chiefs and preserve "the tribes". In many cases, this amounted to creating chiefdoms where none had previously existed.

The 1936 Natives Trust and Land Act "released" large areas of land in the northern Transvaal for African settlement. All "scheduled" and "released" land was henceforth to be purchased on a tribal basis and a Trust fund was established "to acquire land for and on behalf of specific tribes in order to provide necessary extensions to the tribal locations". People forced off white farms by the anti-squatter section of the act would be settled under chiefs in these areas. Chiefs were also given the power to levy special taxes on their followers for the purchase of tribal land. They remained a central element in Native Administration: in 1938 the Native Affairs Commission recognized that:
"hereditary chiefs with their headmen are the instruments through which native administration works. Without their assistance it would be very much more difficult and very much more expensive to maintain the customary law and order and respect for authority which characterizes the Bantu rural population."[1]

But attempts to bolster the power of the chiefs were not merely aimed at strengthening the Native Affairs system; they were also, perhaps primarily, aimed at supporting the chiefs whose political power was increasingly threatened by the rising African petty bourgeoisie. . . .

Land alienation, together with tenant and freehold forms of African land tenure had undermined the chiefs' major source of political power: their ability to control the distribution of land. Opposition from white farmers to the sale of land released by the 1936 act continued to deprive the chiefs of any real power. As the Native Affairs Commission complained in 1938, "the authority of the chiefs and respect for tribal institutions is under continual attack owing to the landless condition of the head of the tribe. This . . . militates against the maintenance of that necessary tribal unity and control which it is the policy of the state to foster." The popularity of the chiefs had also declined: much of the democratic element in chieftaincy as an institution had disappeared when the size of the chiefdom was petrified and chiefs became civil servants appointed by and responsible to the Native Affairs Department rather than to their own followers. . . .

The Consolidation of a Tsonga/Shangaan Ethnic Awareness

As the chiefs lost their power of protection and patronage, the chiefdom and clan declined as a focus of political consciousness. . . .

The petty bourgeoisie emerged as an alternative source of political leadership to that of the chiefs. . . . The ethnic consciousness expressed by the Tsonga-speaking petty bourgeoisie tended to be a defensive reaction to the politicization of ethnicity. . . . The assertiveness expressed by numerically larger and politically more centralized and confident ethnic groups such as the Swazi and Zulu surged forward in the late 1920s and early 1930s. Encouraged by white segregationists, this ethnic assertiveness found expression at all levels of African society and threatened to marginalize disparate and unorganized peoples such as those considered to be "Tsongas". Ethnicity had to be mobilized to maintain the balance of power within the African nationalist movement. The rise of ethnic awareness also indicated a shift in the awareness of the petty bourgeoisie away from politics at the national level, with its more abstract concern for civil rights, towards local issues. These had become of crucial importance because of the extreme social and economic dislocation in the rural areas caused by proletarianization and betterment schemes. Tsonga-speakers also laboured under the very real fear, first expressed at the time of the land commissions, that, as immigrants into the northern Transvaal, they did not have a secure historical tenure to their land. They were subject to attacks such as that made by a Venda headman when addressing the Eastern Transvaal Natives' Land Commission in 1916:

> "You must take no notice of these Shangaans. They are no good. We are Bawendas here. These Shangaans came to the country. . . . You must remove the Shangaans. There will not be enough room [for us both]. Take the Shangaans away."[2]

Tsonga-speakers were not the product of a military tradition and had no paramount chief to represent their interests, factors which made them inferior to the more politically centralized ethnic groups in the eyes of many whites and blacks. Consequently, Tsonga-speakers were divided by the Native Affairs Department into administrative districts dominated by Venda or Northern Sotho chiefs, while within the black urban areas they were marginalized as a minority group. . . .

The Role of the Apartheid System

In 1948 the Afrikaner National Party came to power with a policy aimed at transforming the reserves into African homelands. In numerous speeches, the new government's ministers stressed the central role of the chief and tribe in the implementation of apartheid in the rural areas. . . .

The first step was the passage of the Bantu Authorities Act of 1951 which bolstered the power of the chiefs by modernizing and expanding their tax basis to include all the members of the tribal authority. This gave the chiefs a new element of patronage through their control of the tribal account and through their participation in the decisions of the Regional Authority. . . .

The Bantu Authorities Act of 1951 did not affect the ethnically heterogeneous nature of the population living in the northern Transvaal reserves. A Tsonga homeland was not envisaged and Tsonga-speaking Tribal Authorities were grouped administratively in Regional Authorities, dominated by Venda and North Sotho-speakers in, respectively, the northern and eastern Transvaal. The first move towards an ethnic segregation of the area came from a number of northern Tsonga-speaking chiefs who felt their Regional Authority was dominated by Venda-speaking chiefs. . . . But it was only in 1959 with the promulgation of the Bantu Self-government Act that Pretoria asserted that "The Bantu people of South Africa do not constitute a homogeneous people, but form separate national units on the basis of language and culture." This act formally declared the "Shangane/Tsonga" to constitute a "national unit" and allowed the government to accede to the Tsonga chiefs' wishes for a separate homeland. Four Regional Authorities dominated by Tsonga-speakers were then cut out of the old multi-ethnic regional authorities in the northern and eastern Transvaal and in November 1962 they combined to form the Matshangana Territorial Authority. Seven years later a Tsonga-Shangane commissioner-general was installed and a legislative assembly was opened at the newly-constructed capital at Giyani.

The segregation of the rural areas into ethnically-defined units was paralleled by similar movements in the urban areas. In Johannesburg, culturally mixed communities like Sophiatown were torn down and replaced by townships, like Soweto, that were built on an ethnic grid. . . . Thus apartheid blocked the process of social integration and cultural hybridization that had emerged as the economy required a geographically mobile African workforce. Under apartheid, the movement to the towns, both spiritual and material, was increasingly directed along ethnic conduits.

The government's new divide-and-rule policy . . . generated bitter ethnic conflicts over local resources, for in the early 1960s the northern Transvaal reserves remained crushingly overpopulated and overgrazed. . . .

In 1973, the year that the Territorial Authority became the "self-governing" Bantustan of Gazankulu, the delineation of one of its southern borders led to threats of war being made in the Giyani legislature against the Northern Sotho of the Lebowa Bantustan. Further ethnic hostility arose over the allocation of the eastern Transvaal Shiluvane mission hospital to Gazankulu in mid-1981. . . .

Notes

1. Quoted by Morris in H Wolpe (ed) *The Articulation of Modes of Production* 230.
2. Evidence before Natives' Lands Commission UG 22–1916 p 70.

Revisionist historians have produced an entirely new version of preconquest and colonial history in southern Africa. They have shown, for example, that much of the writing on Zulu and Sotho origins was based on the work of A T Bryant, the missionary and author who collected Zulu oral traditions in the fifty years after 1883.[67] Now it is thought that his work is flawed both in detail and in its larger conception.[68] And, in retrospect, the idea of a neatly bounded tribal unit seems unconvincing. Given the rapid and often violent change that marked southern

---

[67] *The Zulu People* (1949).
[68] Maylam *A History of the African People of South Africa* 23; Marks in Thompson *African Societies in Southern Africa* 126ff.

Africa in the last two centuries, cultural and political boundaries must have been imprecise and permeable.[69]

As a scientific concept, tribe has been completely discredited because it is both vague and misleading. On the one hand, the criteria used to define it are so various (language, political affiliation, culture, ethnicity, genetic association, etc) that it has no value left for analytical purposes;[70] on the other hand, the government has intervened so often to amalgamate, divide or constitute tribes (and to appoint tribal authorities) that the current 'tribes' may bear little or no resemblance to the groups originally found here.[71]

Finally, bound up with the concept of tribe, is the idea of 'tribalism'. This connoted, in a negative sense, the primitive and barbaric, in a positive sense, the simple and uncorrupted. Both meanings have been influential in government policy, the first during the early days of colonization, the second from the 1920s onwards.

> 'The glorification of tribalism and all the old customs, precisely because they are old, a kind of twentieth century adaptation of the "noble savage" theory, has had direct effects upon the Union Native Policy, for here what I have called the "Anthropological School" came into immediate contact with life. It stands behind many of the provisions of the Native Administration Act of 1927, by which the chief has been made an important part of the administrative machinery. One of the chief complaints made against the Act has been that it tends to assimilate all Natives to the position of Tribal Natives in the Reserve. Others may exist, they may even form the majority, but they are an embarrassing phenomenon. They do not live as the social anthropologist thinks they ought to live. They do not think on the lines which the Department considers suitable for natives.'[72]

State policies in South Africa have rested on a triad of concepts: culture, tribe and chiefdom. Racial differences originally provided the occasion for territorial segregation under the Black Land Act.[73] Subsequently, the land set aside under this Act (the 'reserves') and the later Development Trust and Land Act[74] formed the core of the apartheid 'bantustans', which were to become the 'homelands' of the future. Segregation also required separate political institutions for Africans: thus the African franchise was scrapped[75] and a bantustan political structure was created, in which chiefs were given most of the power.[76] The corollary of these enactments was the Promotion of Black Self-Government Act,[77] which established eight African national units and provided for the development of their self-government and ultimate independence. For the purposes of the Act, the entire African population was divided into eight (later nine) tribal units, each

---

[69] Skalnik in Boonzaier & Sharp *South African Keywords* 74–5.

[70] Hammond-Tooke op cit n64 xv; Mafeje (1971) 9 *J Mod Afr Studies* 253; Gulliver *Tradition and Transition in East Africa* 7–35; and Vail *The Creation of Tribalism in Southern Africa*.

[71] Section 5 of the Black Administration Act 38 of 1927 and ss 2 and 3 of the Black Authorities Act 68 of 1951. See generally Skalnik in Boonzaier & Sharp op cit n69 68ff.

[72] Brookes *The Colour Problems of South Africa* 137.

[73] 27 of 1913. This was welcomed by the white population as the only solution to the 'native problem': *House of Assembly* Debates 1913 col 2515. See Pelzer *Verwoerd Speaks* XXX–XXXI.

[74] 18 of 1936.

[75] Act 12 of 1936.

[76] When apartheid was formally introduced, the Black Authorities Act 68 of 1951 was passed. This established a three-tier hierarchy of government, based on chiefs and their councillors.

[77] 46 of 1959.

one being allotted a portion of the reserves as its 'national homeland':
North-Sotho (Lebowa), South-Sotho (Qwaqwa), Swazi (Kangwane), Tsonga
(Gazankulu), Tswana (Bophuthatswana), Venda (Venda), Ndebele (KwaNde-
bele), Xhosa (Transkei and Ciskei) and Zulu (KwaZulu).[78]

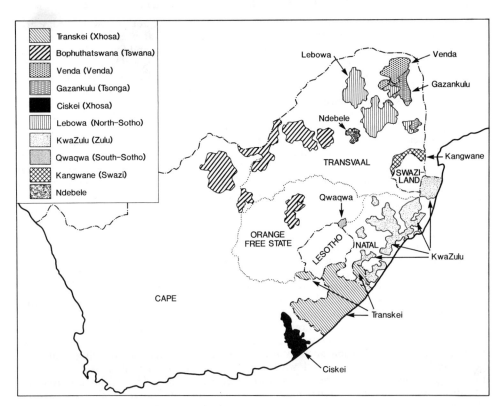

This multifaceted programme was justified, particularly for the sceptical
international audience, by the right of cultural self-determination.

'South Africa is in fact and in the first place a multi-national country, rather than a
multi-racial country. Apart from the South African nation of European stock, the country
comprises the homelands of a number of other nations. These have their own separate
identities, each with its own undeniable right to separate nationhood in a land which, too,
has been its own. I am, of course, referring to the various Bantu nations, differing from one
another in language, culture, tradition, and in everything else that determines national
identities, rights and aspirations. . . . We must bring about a situation where peaceful
co-existence of the various nations in our country will be possible. We believe that this can
be achieved only by the independent development of each of these peoples towards the full
realisation of its separate nationhood and the recognition of the right of each nation to
govern itself in accordance with its own national tradition and aspiration.'[79]

---

[78] Cf Kenney *Architect of Apartheid* 157; West in Boonzaier & Sharp op cit n69 106.
[79] Helgaard Muller *Address to the General Assembly of the UN* 1964.

The division of the South African population into different ethnic groups, long regarded as obvious and somehow natural,[80] is now being challenged on many fronts.

[10] LYE & MURRAY *TRANSFORMATIONS ON THE HIGHVELD* 20–2

Does the phrase Sotho-Tswana society have any meaning? The Sotho-Tswana today are distributed across several international boundaries. They are at present subject to the administration of six governments: those of Lesotho, Botswana and South Africa; of the newly "independent" Transkei and BophuthaTswana; and of QwaQwa, the Southern Sotho "homeland". They are peasant cultivators, commercial livestock farmers, urban commuters. They are Christians and traditionalists, they are down-to-earth country people and sophisticated townspeople. Many of them spend their working lives as migrants who oscillate between their rural homes and employment in the "white" urban areas of South Africa, in the mining, manufacturing, construction and service industries. Many of them are unemployed, and their families have the greatest difficulties in making ends meet. Differences of this kind are found within the population of Southern Africa as a whole. Therefore there is no bounded set of social relationships today that we can usefully identify as Sotho-Tswana society. Many years ago Isaac Schapera, the anthropologist who is best known for his exhaustive historical and anthropological studies of the Tswana, insisted that chief and district administrator, missionary and medicineman, trader and teacher, migrant miner and peasant, all had to be studied as participants in a single social system, that of Southern Africa as a whole. We share this view. It poses the problem of what perspective is appropriate for seeking to understand the experience of the Sotho-Tswana, defined as a minority population within Southern Africa.

Let us briefly outline two possible approaches. Neither is adequate in itself. One approach would be to reconstruct, from oral tradition and written sources, a social system which no longer exists but which may be considered approximately representative of the Sotho-Tswana tradition. The unit of analysis would be a tribe or a chiefdom, an independent polity having its own territorial base, a hierarchy of hereditary offices, and a relatively self-sustaining economy based on livestock and crop cultivation, with some trade and craft specialisation such as iron-working. We would discover high rates of polygyny—men marrying several wives—among the ruling families; preferences for marrying women defined as cousins in kinship terms; rituals of kinship for propitiating the ancestors and marking births, marriages and deaths; communal rituals for initiating the youth, for invoking the rain and for ensuring protection from malevolent powers; and elaborate social arrangements for ensuring the transmission of property, office and tradition from generation to generation.

An alternative approach would be to develop a perspective within which to understand the lives of Africans who live in the rural areas of Southern Africa. We would describe and analyse conditions which are not peculiar to the Sotho-Tswana peoples but which are typical of the labour reserves from which migrant workers are drawn to meet the needs of South African industry. These labour reserves are the black "homelands" within South Africa itself, including the Transkei and BophuthaTswana; the independent kingdoms of Lesotho and Swaziland, and the Republic of Botswana. Southern Moçambique and Malawi may also be included as historically important suppliers of labour to the mining industry. Collectively these areas comprise what may be called the rural periphery of Southern Africa, by contrast with the industrial core where migrants are employed—the mines of the Witwatersrand, the Orange Free State and Natal—and the heartlands of secondary industry: the major conurbations of the Pretoria-Johannesburg-Vereeniging complex, Durban, Port Elizabeth and Cape Town. The terms rural periphery and industrial core are analytically convenient because they enable us to transcend the

---

[80] Gordon (1989) 2 *J Historical Sociology* 43ff.

boundaries of nation-states when seeking to understand the regional economy of Southern Africa. The flow of migrants across these international boundaries on a large scale makes it impossible to understand the economy of any one of these countries in isolation.

Because of South African influx control and pass laws, migrant workers' families remain behind in the rural areas, where many live in overcrowded squalor and where they seek to scrape a partial livelihood from exhausted and over-grazed soils. Our analysis would focus on the relationships between migrants and their dependent families, and on the consequences for the elderly, the young, the sick and the unemployed of general dependence on the earnings of absentees. We would find a gross imbalance between the sexes in the rural populations—women far outnumber men, especially amongst young and middle-aged adults. Family life is ravaged by the separation of spouses and the absence of fathers. There is a crisis of security in old age. The energies of the vast majority of people are devoted to sheer survival under difficult conditions. We would also find evidence of increasing differentiation between rural households—most people are poor, but some are very much poorer than others.

The challenge in presenting an account of the Sotho-Tswana today is to integrate these two approaches. They would appear to have little in common. No traditional chiefdoms survive as independent political entities, with the partial exception of Lesotho. It is impossible to conceptualise a Sotho-Tswana economic system today, for the Sotho-Tswana participate, variously but inevitably, in the regional economic system of Southern Africa as a whole. But custom seldom merely dies. Some aspects of it are undermined with the passage of time. Other aspects of it are invigorated. Social relationships do not merely wither away—they are transformed. The Sotho-Tswana still engage in disputes within the framework of customary law, and rationalise their behaviour with reference to the morality of their grandfathers. They have also acquired new values—with education, with Christianity and the habits of an urban consumer life-style. New forms of religious behaviour have partly replaced the old forms, but the new idiom is often inspired by the old idiom. Many of the younger generation in Lesotho still go to initiation schools. Other Sotho-Tswana despise these schools as relics from the past.

The object of our study is therefore the transformations that have taken place in political, economic, kinship and ritual relations. Much of Sotho-Tswana custom persists. In this sense people remain, in Setiloane's phrase, "stubbornly Sotho-Tswana". But it is misleading to represent the persistence of custom as cultural bedrock impervious to superficial change. The changes in people's lives are themselves fundamental. Rituals for the ancestors persist, even amongst members of Christian congregations. Many Sotho-Tswana, both rural and urban, continue to perform their customary obligations in this respect, and fear the mystical consequences, in the form of illness or misfortune inflicted by the ancestors, of failure to do so. The dead, in other words, are still regarded as moral arbiters of relations among the living. Yet the pattern of relations among the living—between elders and juniors, between men and women—has undergone significant change. This suggests that the relationship between ritual practice and everyday life is a very complex one. Likewise, the institution of bridewealth persists among many of the Sotho-Tswana peoples. As will be seen, however, it is not the same institution in the late twentieth century as it was in the middle of the nineteenth century. Accordingly the problem which recurs in the later chapters is how to analyse the relationship of Sotho-Tswana custom to the changing lives of the Sotho-Tswana themselves. We are particularly concerned with those who retain their roots in rural communities.

(3) Language and writing

A problem encountered in all cross-cultural studies is the use of terms appropriate to describe the data. Language is not simply an obstacle to comprehension; when conceived as a symbolic system representing thought, it can be appreciated as the principal point of access to a foreign culture: 'social behaviour . . . is in large measure linguistic behaviour'.[81] Language allows admission to a thought system and a people's vision of the world.[82]

When the field-worker's objective is to record a foreign system of law, the difficulties of language are compounded by the technicality of legal terms. Western lawyers/anthropologists have always been tempted to transcribe foreign data into a technical vocabulary, on the assumption that the terms and concepts they use, are universal and culture-free.[83] Bohannan was a resolute opponent of this undiscriminating approach. He was strongly influenced by an American school of ethno-linguistics, which contended that a language predisposed its users to perceive and think in the categories and relationships that were encoded into its vocabulary and grammar.[84] Accordingly, Bohannan advocated discarding European legal terminology in favour of 'folk' systems of language and thought. By spelling out native concepts and categories in detail and by using the appropriate vernacular terms, he personally was able to expose distinctively Tiv conceptions of various institutions, notably law and court.[85]

Gluckman then entered what was to become a widely publicized debate.[86]

[11] MOORE in NADER *LAW IN CULTURE AND SOCIETY* 340–2

A great deal of discussion between Gluckman and Bohannan takes place in the form of an argument about what is a suitable language in which to describe another people's legal system. Bohannan argues that the vocabulary of English jurisprudence is a vocabulary developed for talking about English law and is unsuitable for the description of the folk systems of other peoples. His case is that to describe another people's system, one must spell out at length the implications of native terms and categories in order to approximate as closely as possible the indigenous system being examined, and then one must use these native terms rather than substitute English equivalents. Then, and only then, can one begin to think about making comparisons. This part of his argument starts as an argument against an ethnocentric Anglo-American legal vocabulary. Then he faces the difficulties inherent in trying to use indigenous vocabularies when making comparisons. In his paper Bohannan proposes that this problem may be dealt with in the future by means of a "new logical and independent language", and he suggests that Fortran or some other computer language may be the most suitable medium into which to translate folk concepts for comparative purposes. His argument is fundamentally that English legal terms are so inextricably bound up with the content of English law that they cannot be used effectively to describe another system. The number of redefinitions and qualifiers that must be used to make a term of English law fit an alien legal category is such that, in his view, it is less distorting and less confusing to use certain key indigenous terms and try to describe their referents. This last, since he is writing in English, he does in English words, but with an effort to avoid technical legal terms as far as he can.

Gluckman agrees that the first task of the ethnographer is to describe what Bohannan has called the folk system. He also agrees that vernacular African terms sometimes have no English equivalents, and that in such cases indigenous terms must continue to be used

---

[81] Nadel *The Foundations of Social Anthropology* 40.

[82] The semiotic triangle graphically depicts the relationship between *words/terms* (physically manifested in sound or writing), *concepts* (intellectually conceived in the abstract) and the *referents* (the concrete existence of the latter two in reality); cf Jackson *Semiotics and Legal Theory* 14–17.

[83] Such as ownership. See below, 384–5.

[84] Whorf *Language, Thought and Reality* 213–14. See generally Ardener *Social Anthropology and Language*.

[85] *Justice and Judgment among the Tiv* 101 and 210–14.

[86] *The Ideas in Barotse Jurisprudence* xxiv and 254ff; Moore op cit n46 ch 4.

after they have been explained in English. However, where it is practical to use English terms without having to add too many qualifiers—where, in short, there is a satisfactory English equivalent or approximation—he not only sees no objection to using English (or whatever is the language of the investigator), but also thinks it far preferable to do so. He argues that only if the same term is used to cover the notions of diverse legal systems is it possible to discuss where the notions in each system differ, as well as the common elements across the systems. What Gluckman does, further, is to argue that after the notions of an African legal system have been described, they can be compared profitably with those of English law at various stages of its development. Similarly, he also draws on the terms and ideas of Roman law and other legal systems where they seem appropriate.

Presented in this way, there seems a limited area of disagreement between the two. After giving and explaining native terms, Gluckman is prepared to shift to terms of English law more readily than Bohannan, and he has a strong interest in particular comparisons of African with English legal notions that Bohannan does not share. Bohannan explains in English and then continues to use more indigenous terms and makes a studied effort to avoid terms of English law when he can. Both are acutely aware of the difficulties of translation and definition in the task of describing an alien legal system, and both realize that those difficulties are multiplied when the level of analysis and comparison is reached.

The dispute about terminology is incidental to a more profound difference of method. Bohannan's interest was in the way that cultures classify reality into categories;[87] every culture has certain critical words/concepts in its language which the ethnographer must communicate in order to give some understanding of the culture being studied.[88] Once these concepts have been discerned and understood, they may be compared with like concepts in other cultures. Gluckman's concern was different. He saw words/concepts as tools within legal systems that could be utilized for different purposes, not merely as reflexes of thought systems. He looked to social and economic structures for the broader, underlying explanations of legal concepts.[89] To demonstrate this relationship, he used a comparative method, referring to different legal systems embedded in like socio-economic structures.

Allott proposed a compromise of sorts:[90] the use of a simple, non-technical vocabulary which, while still consisting of English words, was stripped of legalism. While this might serve the needs of research workers well, it has not been adopted in legal circles.[91] And, in courts applying common law, minimal use is made of vernacular languages.[92]

The problem of language goes far beyond difficulties of translation. A person recording a system of customary law has to tap an oral tradition. Any testimony given by an informant is no more than a 'mirage of the reality it describes';[93] and the reliability of these sources is hardly up to the standards usually demanded in

---

[87] *Social Anthropology* 46.
[88] Op cit 11–12.
[89] Gluckman op cit n86 xiv.
[90] In respect of land tenure: in Anderson *Family Law in Asia and Africa* 121ff.
[91] Goodrich (1983) 3 *Legal Studies* 1 has explanations.
[92] Bennett 1985 *AJ* 173. On the problem of developing Swahili as a national legal language see: Weston (1965) 1 *East African LJ* 60ff. And on the selection of a national language in Nigeria see: Allan (1978–9) 18 *Cahiers d'Études Africaines* 397. See generally on language and dispute processing: Danet (1979–80) 14 *Law & Soc R* 445.
[93] Vansina *Oral Tradition* 76.

western legal systems. In the first place, an oral tradition, which implies an
anonymous authorship, permits no method of checking what had originally
happened: the event is locked forever in an inaccessible past. In the second place,
there is the problem of memory. In preliterate cultures there is a wide range of
auditory mnemonic devices to monitor the accuracy of transmission. These
devices are largely ones of style or genre, and include rhythm, metre, rhyme, etc.
But such clear stylistic formalities, as characterize epic poetry or saga, do not
exist in the case of customary law. With so few checks on the transmission, a
number of divergent versions of the same thing may easily be produced, each of
greater or lesser reliability. In non-western courts, such imprecision would not
be a particular problem, because, although law always involves a measure of
continuity and thus demands a relatively stable tradition, certainty is less
important where conciliation is the primary aim of litigation.[94]

The initial informant in an oral tradition gives, either deliberately or
otherwise, a partial account of what happened because he[95] sees only some aspect
of it and he places his own interpretation on it. This testimony is coloured by his
own personality, stamped by his private interests, and set within a framework of
reference provided by the society in which he happens to live. The first
testimony then undergoes alterations and distortions by all other informants in
the chain of transmission, down to and including the very last one, all of them
being influenced by factors similar to those working on the first.[96] The
assumption has always been that writing was a transparent medium, allowing the
reader direct access to the experiences of the informant. Yet there is no
'metalanguage', no system capable of transcending language for the use of
objective description. Language is inherently metaphorical, ambiguous and
partial. Once this is realized it becomes evident that ethnographies have more in
common with literary creations than with scientific reports.[97]

In the court room precise norms have to be extracted from the mixed
repertoire of rules that constituted the oral tradition; and according to the
doctrine of precedent the rules chosen for the particular case have to be preserved
for later cases. In this manner the oral tradition is translated into a written one,
a process that involves a further distancing from the original source.[98]

The encoding of law into writing is arguably the most momentous event in
legal history, stimulating, in Weberian terms, the transformation of a
'traditional' order into a 'legal' one.[99] Recent developments in jurisprudence and
anthropology, in this instance influenced by literature and linguistics, have come
to focus ever more narrowly on the significance of this event. Writing facilitates

---

[94] See below, 54–5 and 75–6.

[95] The gender of the informant is usually male, which obviously influences the information given. See below, 305.

[96] Vansina op cit n93 76.

[97] Clifford & Marcus *Writing Culture* 2 and 22.

[98] Twining *The Place of Customary Law in the National Legal Systems of East Africa* 32.

[99] Writing is often a reaction to a popular demand for greater availability of the law (viz the Twelve Tables of Roman law) and thus a restraint on the arbitrary exercise of power; but writing creates the need for specialist interpreters, and historically it is true that as soon as law has been written down a professional class emerges to interpret it to the people: Goodrich *Reading the Law* 21.

more objective reflection on a society's intellectual culture; it stimulates the classification of ideas and a gradual systematization of rules. Hence writing goes hand in hand with the development of a more ordered and rational legal system.[100]

III THE RISE OF CRITICAL LEGAL SCHOLARSHIP

(1) Customary law in the Decade of Development

By the close of the 1950s the African colonies were contemplating their independence. As part of the decolonization programme, the Western powers pledged them aid for their economic development, a goal that was universalized when it was taken up by the United Nations: in 1961 the General Assembly proclaimed the First Development Decade. The new states were aspiring to standards set in the industrialized nations, which implied that development was an endeavour to transcend local traditionalism in favour of western modernity.[101]

Customary law was generally considered as an obstacle to these aims because it was inherently conservative.[102] African systems of land tenure were a prime example: rural lands were still under the control of chiefly authorities; the methods of farming were technologically backward; and agriculture was oriented to subsistence. Modernization required innovation and individual initiative but in Africa these requirements were hampered by the demands of kinfolk. The attachment to the past and the population explosion were believed to be jointly responsible for trapping people into a cycle of poverty, which in turn stifled the enterprise necessary to generate capital needed for export growth. Customary law—a symbol of the tribal past—had to be modified or abolished.[103]

Probably overriding even the desire for development was the need for national unity. The new states were fragile polities threatened by the tensions of linguistic, ethnic and religious diversity. Customary law represented a tribal pluralism inimical to national unity. It therefore had to be sacrificed in favour of a single, uniform legal system.[104]

On the other hand, customary law also stood for an African consciousness that had nurtured and reinforced the sentiments of African nationalism.[105] Politicians could not afford to ignore its power as a cultural symbol.

These views were debated in the context of the then current theories about development. The advanced industrial economies of the West were regarded as exportable commodities, and so too was the law that facilitated them. This suggested that law was a type of technology, a value-free instrument that could

---

[100] J Goody *Interface between the Written and the Oral* ch 11.

[101] See Schiller (1969) 5 *E African LJ* 88 regarding the ambiguous position of customary law. Galanter in Weiner *Modernization* 153 lists the requirements of a 'modern' legal system. Münkner (1983) 4 *Jahrbuch Afrikanisches Recht* 99 describes 'development law'.

[102] Van Rouveroy van Nieuwaal (1979) 12 *Verfassung u Recht* 143; Seidman in Hutchinson *Africa and Law* 9.

[103] David 1962 *Annales Africaines* 161 and (1962–3) 37 *Tulane LR* 188–9.

[104] Allott *The Limits of Law* 176–7 and 182ff.

[105] Nkrumah (1962) 6 *JAL* 103ff; M'Beye (1970) 22 *Rev Int Droit Comparé* 38.

be used to change society.[106] Another, complementary strand of thought, based on legal positivism, held that 'good' law was logical and coherent law regardless of its responsiveness to particular socio-economic conditions. By implication a technically advanced legal system, such as a European one, could successfully be applied anywhere else in the world.[107]

(2) Disillusionment and Marxist theory

Even by the end of the Decade of Development it was apparent that the grand experiment to transform the developing world was not working. The assurance of the theorists faltered, and in what became a general crisis of academic confidence, open dissatisfaction with orthodox scholarship began to emerge. In anthropology, functionalist empiricism was found inadequate to contend with the rapid changes taking place in Africa.[108] Economists were at a loss to explain the increasing poverty of what was now branded the 'Third World'. Similarly, when the western-inspired legislative programmes of the new states failed to find acceptance with the majority of the population, the myopic vision of positivism was found wanting.

The failure of the legal transplants stimulated a new trend in research, still mainly functionalist in orientation, to discover the reasons.[109] Much of this work demonstrated a need to overcome the barriers that had compartmentalized the academic disciplines. These divisions were quite arbitrary, stemming from an unquestioned tradition of western universities. Little had been achieved in the past by the narrow view each discipline had of its area of study, and interdisciplinary co-operation was now much in vogue.[110] Such research could hardly be expected to yield conclusive results, but it did at least establish that the effect of imposing alien law is unpredictable[111] and that neglect of local attitudes will skew statutory objectives.[112]

One of the main targets for criticism was the empirical approach that had been so characteristic of anthropology in the colonial period. The challenge came first in the 1960s with the work of Lévi-Strauss, the progenitor of structuralism. Lévi-Strauss disputed the main premise of empiricism: that information may be validly gained only by sense perception or observation. In terms of a structuralist perspective the explanatory value of raw data must be rejected; meaning can be deduced only from the occurrence of the data within an overall and necessarily

---

[106] Friedman op cit n10 46 and (1969) 24 *Rutgers LR* 29; Scandinavian Institute of African Studies *Law and Development* 16; Ocran (1971–2) 3/4 *Zambia LJ* 23.

[107] Allott op cit n104 109; Seidman (1975) 5 *Zambia LJ* 39. And see generally: Trubek (1972) 82 *Yale LJ* 1.

[108] Kaplan & Manners op cit n50 ch 5. Magubane (1973) 75 *Am Anthropologist* 1701 gives a critique of South African scholarship.

[109] Although the future for such scholarship is bleak: Ghai (1987) 50 *MLR* 750.

[110] Cf Merryman (1977) 25 *Am J Comp L* 457.

[111] See, e g, Harrell-Bond (1975) 8 *Verfassung u Recht* 447 and Kidder in Burman & Harrell-Bond *The Imposition of Law* 292. More generally see: Allott op cit n104 ch 4. For the explanation of compliance with imposed law see: Lloyd-Bostock and Aubert in Burman & Harrell-Bond op cit 10ff and 27ff respectively; Massell (1968) 2 *Law & Soc R* 179 and Friedman (1969) 24 *Rutgers LR* 48.

[112] Könz (1969) 63 *Proceedings of American Soc of Int Law* 94; Baxi (1979) 12 *Verfassung u Recht* 97; Kurczewski & Podgorecki (1975) 1 *Kroniek van Afrika* 3.

transparent structure. This theory borrowed heavily from linguistics. The physical manifestation of language—words—is meaningful only within the framework of the whole language, especially its grammar. Hence, when the particular
term is seen in the context of the larger structure, meaning can emerge.[113] This
meant that the focus of attention had to move from the conscious/perceptible to
the unconscious/abstract. It followed that a field-worker's observations of
society were of little value until related to a broader explanatory structure.

It was Marxism, however, that offered the most comprehensive answers to the
questions that arose out of the crisis of the social sciences.[114] By adopting a
definite point of view, one aligned with the African peasantry and the nascent
urban proletariat, Marxism actively contested the impartiality of functionalism;
but of course it would also have denied the possibility of ever achieving
functionalism's vaunted claim of objectivity through empirical observation.
(Here Marxism revealed common ground with structuralism. Information is not
gained solely by sense perception; logical deduction is an equally valid way of
understanding the world.)

The distinctive theory of social change contained in Marxism also offered an
attractive explanation of the changes sweeping Africa.[115] According to the
Marxist model (unlike its functionalist counterpart), society was inherently
unstable. In the primordial form, economic production was communal; when
workers were alienated from what they produced and subjected to the
production process, class divisions appeared. The conflict latent in class/state
society and the contradictions that inevitably surfaced between the forces and
relations of production were continually resolving themselves in a dialectical
process.

Until the 1960s Marxism had had little serious appeal for anthropology outside
the Soviet Union. Whereas Marx's work was concentrated on capitalist society,
anthropologists were normally interested in simpler societies, lacking the
panoply of state and apparently also lacking a class structure. Marx, however,
had posited five main historical eras—Asiatic, ancient, feudal, capitalist and
socialist—each taking its character from a particular mode of production. This
concept became the keystone of neo-Marxist anthropology in the 1960s and
70s.[116] As the mode of production changed, so did the non-productive
superstructure of society, including its law, religion and politics. The kinship
system—the cement of simple societies—was a problematic factor. Theoretically it should have been a superstructural element but it was difficult to
demonstrate how the economic base determined kinship; rather it seemed that
kinship determined the economy.

---

[113] Lévi-Strauss *Structural Anthropology* 33.
[114] Copans in Gutkind & Waterman *African Social Studies* 24–7.
[115] This theory was inspired by the nineteenth-century anthropologist, Morgan: Bloch *Marxism and Anthropology* 8ff; Terray *Marxism and 'Primitive' Societies* 5ff.
[116] It designates the forces (natural resources, labour power and technology peculiar to a society) and the relations of production (social relationships regulating the distribution of property and power).

The appearance of a creative, non-dogmatic Marxism, owing much to the work of Althusser, overcame certain of these conceptual barriers.[117] Althusser and his associates offered a new reading of Marx, synthesizing many intellectual trends in France, notably structuralism. Most importantly he refined the conception of the mode of production (which had never been clearly defined by Marx) and rejected the outright economic determinism associated with earlier Marxist work.[118] This fresh conceptual apparatus opened up new avenues of exploration for anthropology.[119] The mode of production was no longer tied to capitalism: as a heuristic device it could be used for the investigation of African societies,[120] and new modes (village/lineage, tributary and communal) were devised to illuminate particular situations.[121] The persistence of indigenous economies and social structures within a capitalist-dominated colonial state[122] could be explained by positing the articulation of two or more modes of production with one another.[123] Thus, although the problems of kinship and class remained unresolved, the French anthropologists of the 1960s and 70s made possible a new understanding of African societies.[124]

(3) Dependency theory

Among the first beneficiaries of the revival in theoretical Marxism was the group of writers that has come to be known as the dependency theorists.[125] They sought to explain the poverty of the developing countries not as a result of stubborn traditionalism (the general view of liberal economists), but as a continuance of colonial exploitation. The demands of international capitalism caused a drain on the resources of the developing countries, forcing them into a position of dependency on First World nations.[126] The model used to signify this relationship was the 'centre-periphery':[127] the world economic system, centred in Europe and North America, incorporated the territories of the former colonies—the periphery—and continued to exploit them. Previously, states in the periphery had been politically bound to Europe, but even after decolonization they remained economically dependent, a notion captured in the terms 'neo-colonialism' or 'underdevelopment'.[128]

Social relations *within* the periphery are often explained by use of the same centre-periphery model: the metropolis, dominated by export interests and the cultural influence of the West, functions as centre to the backward and conservative areas of the rural periphery. The developing state suffers all the

[117] See Kahn & Llobera *Anthropology of Pre-Capitalist Societies* 274–7; Bloch op cit n115 152–7.

[118] At the most, Althusser allowed that the economic structure would determine 'in the last resort'.

[119] See Copans & Seddon in *Relations of Production* 1ff, and to a lesser extent, law: Newman *Law and Economic Organization*.

[120] And here Meillassoux *Anthropologie économique des Gouro* (1964) was a forerunner.

[121] Hindess & Hirst *Precapitalist Modes of Production*.

[122] Wolpe 'Introduction' in *The Articulation of Modes of Production*.

[123] See Terray op cit n115 93ff.

[124] Copans & Seddon op cit n119 36ff and Bloch op cit n115 162–4.

[125] See Snyder (1980) 14 *Law & Soc R* 724.

[126] Leys *Underdevelopment in Kenya* 8ff and 26–7.

[127] Wallerstein *The Modern World-System* ch 6.

[128] Leys op cit n126 ch 1; Palmer & Parsons *Roots of Rural Poverty* 4 and 13.

problems caused by extreme inequalities. The productive, export-oriented enclave of the metropolis is modern and technologically advanced; productivity is high and most amenities are concentrated here. Western values connected with work, family life and civic duty predominate. The lives of the population in the remainder of the country, however, are prescribed by a subsistence economy. This imbalance results in a persistent rural-urban migration, the main attraction being the higher income available in the cities.[129] The inequalities typifying developing countries are signified in the term 'internal colonialism', which connotes the economic and political subordination of the indigenous population by a people originating in or affiliated to the capitalist West.[130]

The effect of this theory has been to redirect scholarly objectives and to reformulate research methods. The gathering of empirical data is now only one aspect of the field-worker's task; as important is relating this data to the structure underlying the observable world. This suggests an expansion of the boundaries of the unit of study, in both time and space.

> 'The lives peasants lead in Zinacantan or rural India, the lives of urban squatters in the favelas of Rio de Janeiro, can be understood only in terms of their place in a scheme of things we cannot see simply by participating as ethnographers in these communities. If we find landless untouchables working in virtual bondage for an Indian landlord, we need not simply find out about their social organization and kinship and religion; we need to find out how and why their fathers and grandfathers lost their land, how the landlord's wealth was created and how it is sustained. We need to follow the circles of interconnection out in space, and back in time, until they join us to the history of a British past as well as an Indian one, to the political economy of wealth and class as well as caste. Life in an Indian village or on a landlord's estate is inseparably linked to events in Bombay and Delhi, and ultimately to events in New York and London and Tokyo.'[131]

At least two comprehensive accounts of customary law were shaped by such a global perspective: Fitzpatrick *Law and State in Papua New Guinea* (1980) and Snyder *Capitalism and Legal Change* (1981).[132] In both of them customary law was studied in the context of a social formation in which the dominant capitalist modes interacted with one or more autochthonous modes of production. Customary law, a facet of the indigenous modes of production, was embedded in the precapitalist way of life. Yet, at the same time, it had been extracted and transformed by colonial (and post-colonial) courts to serve policies dictated by the interests of world capitalism. The authors had to explain both the persistence of precapitalist institutions and the changes they underwent. They reasoned that these institutions functioned as a social security system providing a base of support for workers in the capitalist enclave, both in order to subsidize low wages and to provide refuge in times of unemployment, sickness or old age;[133] aside from which, the promotion of traditional social and political structures inhibited the consolidation of a working class.[134]

---

[129] See below, 151ff.
[130] Wolpe op cit n122 and see Wolpe in Oxaal et al *Beyond the Sociology of Development* ch 11.
[131] Keesing *Cultural Anthropolgy* 458.
[132] And see Fitzpatrick and Snyder in Allott & Woodman op cit n15 249ff and 262ff respectively.
[133] Meillassoux (1972) 1 *Economy & Society* 102.
[134] Fitzpatrick *Law and State in Papua New Guinea* 247–8. And see below, 114–15 and 151–2.

(4) An 'invented tradition'

The Marxist theorists who devoted their attention to law in western European states were interested mainly in its ideological function, a concern that followed from the position of law as a superstructural element. As first conceived, ideology was thought somewhat simplisticly to be a distortion of reality, an illusion perpetuated by the ruling class. This understanding changed radically after the work of Gramsci. He showed that class domination resulted as much from the consensus of the dominated as from their physical repression;[135] and institutions such as law, education and the media sustained existing social relations by winning general acceptance—the notion of ideological hegemony.[136] As further developed, the notion of ideology came to mean less of an illusion and more of a representation of reality. Thus the world of the oppressed, a world in which they lived and which they took for granted, was constructed for them. It determined their choices because it had predisposed them to think in certain ways.

Customary law was one such ideological construct. State courts were supposed to be applying 'the law of the people', a law inherited from the founding fathers of the African tribes. A critical examination of this assumption revealed that much customary law was in fact the creation of the colonial courts.[137] Although this law had no authentic ancestry, it functioned to legitimate state control of the people.[138] The notion of tradition offered a sense of continuity with the past to a people whose lives had been disrupted by colonial conquest. This was a past that could be moulded and interpreted in ways consonant with state policies. For both colonial, and for many modern African governments,[139] tradition is vital for the preservation of a compliant population and existing social structures.

[12] ROBERTS (1984) 28 *JOURNAL OF AFRICAN LAW* 1–5

The very label "African Customary Law" has a flavour of the 1950s and 60s about it, recalling that new and exciting area of study which Allott marked out single handed and then enthusiastically encouraged others to join him in developing. The assumption was then that we were dealing with a living, specifically African repertoire of norms and procedures which could be put to work in helping to shape some African "future". Since then the nature and provenance of this repertoire and the merits of that ambition have been the subject of a lively re-examination. . . .

The profitable continuation of that discussion requires that we are clear about the range of meanings which "African customary law" may carry. My own, subjective, marking-out of the field would be along the following lines. Much writing about African customary law takes for granted that a base-line can be located in terms of the normative commitments which different groups of Africans entertained, and of the governmental arrangements to

---

[135] Hall et al in Centre for Contemporary Cultural Studies *On Ideology* 45ff.

[136] Althusser made a further major contribution to the understanding of ideology; see McLennan in Centre for Contemporary Cultural Studies op cit 77ff. And, for an application of his views to customary law, see: Suttner (1985) 11 *Social Dynamics* 49–64.

[137] Snyder in Sumner *Crime, Justice and Underdevelopment* 90ff and (1981) 19 *J Legal Pluralism* 49.

[138] See, eg, Burman (1979) 12 *Verfassung u Recht* 129 and Gordon & Meggitt *Law and Order in the New Guinea Highlands* 206–9.

[139] See Chanock (1978) 16 *African L Studies* 80ff.

which those Africans were subject, prior to European contact and penetration. So one conceivable focus of attention must be upon ascertaining the truth about the pre-colonial African "past". Second, we may think in terms of the survival, transformation or displacement of those commitments and governmental forms during the colonial period. What were the normative commitments of Africans and what were the government realities, under colonial rule? Third, there was that "customary law", arguably a very different phenomenon, which was "applied" in the system of courts established in the colonial period, and which had a life in legislation, governmental reports, and in the heads of expatriate administrators and Africans caught up in "indirect rule". The relationships between these second and third meanings is certainly complex and problematic; I come back to that. Fourth, there was that "customary law" which was retrieved and written down, sometimes by Africans themselves (e.g. Sarbah in Ghana, Matthews in Botswana), but more often by European observers, typically anthropologists and lawyers. Then there is that "customary law" which "survives" today, which forms part of the lifeworld of contemporary Africans. Last, and arguably different yet again, is the law which is presently administered in "local", "traditional" or "customary" courts, or in tribunals of "popular justice". While there may be links between these phenomena, there are at the least important differences between them and it is crucial to be clear which we have in mind when we speak of "customary law".

In trying to elucidate these different meanings, I begin with the African "past". The truth is that we know sadly little about the governmental arrangements prevailing in different regions of Africa prior to the colonial period, and less still about the cognitive and normative "maps" which Africans entertained. Most of this is now, of course, irrecoverable. But what little survives, how far can we now generalise along the grand lines confidently attempted by Maine, Marx, Tönnies, Durkheim and Weber? All of these scholars seems to have held recognisably similar conceptions of "traditional" societies. These were essentially kin-based groups, in which "order" was a matter of compliance with a shared repertoire of norms, and in which the "individual" actor was rather more submerged in the community than was his European counterpart in the second half of the nineteenth century. But the differences are important. For Maine, Marx and Weber, this was a history of government; for Durkheim and perhaps Tönnies too, it was more a history of different forms of solidarity, and a story of "order" rather than "domination". There are differences too as to how far they were talking of external constraint, as against internal commitment; about conscious compliance with rule, as against the habitual and the automatic. For all five, the "past" was also a construct, a largely unexamined foil against which the more interesting "present" could be brought into sharp focus. The past was not being looked to for its own sake. These exercises, while in part constituting attempts to isolate the definitive qualities of traditional as against modern societies, also revealed the varied forms of "solidarity" and "domination" which any society might exhibit.

Overall, the result is that our inheritance of preconceptions about "custom" and "tradition" from these classical theorists is something of a jumble. We link custom with the past, and yet it is still with us. We see traditional solidarity in terms of unthinking, habitual routine *and* of attentive compliance with rule. "Tribal" societies may be stable acephalous groups or groups ruled by despotic patriarchs. Customary law represents at once an affair of norms and affair of government. Behind all this, there is the transition from the said and the remembered to the written record, from an oral to a literate culture.

What of all this seems correct today? First, the undisputed shift from an oral to a literate culture—a transition which is still in progress. Clearly, this was important—but how important? In what ways does literacy make people think differently about their world; in what ways does the availability of writing and print make a difference to government? These questions are widely debated, but there is not yet general agreement as to how they should be answered. What is amply clear, however, is that lower level courts in Africa, and elsewhere in the third world, today provide a unique meeting point of cultures, and the modes of discourse found in them deserve detailed study.

Many African "societies" of the pre-colonial period certainly were small, kin-based groups in which most relationships tended to be multiplex. But no generic label such as "archaic", "tribal" or "traditional" could hope to bear the load imposed by the very diverse forms of social and political organisation now known to have been present in pre-colonial Africa. The presence of tiny, fiercely egalitarian nomadic bands, as well as large centralised kingdoms, indicates that Maine was incorrect to see the history of "society" as the history of "government". Similarly, even in the narrow sphere of the normative we now know that there was wide variation; that the clarity and detail in which commitments were articulated and the manner in which they were treated varied considerably.

Again, these classical theorists all lived in the pre-Malinowskian world. Even if we regard Malinowski as guilty of exaggeration, a vision of mechanical solidarity, of unrelenting normative constraint, can never be reimposed on non-western societies. The implications of reciprocal obligation, of interdependence, were just as important as they are today, even if in some cases specialisation was far less pronounced. However different cognitive and normative maps may have been drawn, people in pre-colonial Africa actively navigated their ways around their worlds, just as people do today.

One other aspect of the overall picture has now come to be revised. On the whole, the classic vision of a customary order was of a rather static condition, a long-standing equilibrium, in which the rate of change was slow, probably scarcely perceptible to those involved. Africa in the nineteenth century does not fit such a picture. In many areas, the period prior to European penetration was characterised by upheaval, migration and war .... So, however we see the establishment of European rule, it was not superimposed upon existing conditions of tranquil continuity.

When we come to consider the fate of African communities under colonial rule, radically different views of what happened are now available. In general, older accounts offer a picture of order and continuity, later ones of abrupt transformation. The earlier view showed colonial rule being imposed upon a stable egalitarian consensus. Life in most encapsulated communities was said to have altered little: at first, because the colonial power lacked the resources to bring about rapid, ameliorating change; later, because survival and continuity of "traditional" life was deliberately fostered under the policies of "indirect rule".

Present accounts ... tend to contradict this picture sharply. The revision tells a story of discontinuities, abrupt transition and coercive domination, which left members of encapsulated communities exposed to the arbitrary rule of neo-traditional authorities and drawn to their disadvantage into new forms of economic relations. Colonial local government is presented as having scanty links with the past: authorities had to be "found" and placed in charge of formerly acephalous groups; or, at best, holders of existing office were made to perform roles quite different to their accustomed ones. The "customary law" which was recognised in colonial legislation, and developed and "applied" in the newly established "native" courts was a tendentious montage with slender links to the past, supportive of the project of colonial rule, and entrenching the position of elders over juniors, men over women. It has even been given by some the vivid label of an "invented tradition".

Overall, this revision is a valuable one, a necessary antidote to earlier accounts which had postulated a deceptively harmonious and egalitarian pre-colonial context, and which had over-emphasised the extent to which long-standing indigenous institutions had been there in the first place and then survived. There is no doubt, either, of the coercive nature of "indirect rule", or about the disruption of the lives of Africans through their association, often involuntary, with European economic operations.

Nevertheless, the new picture is still arguably an incomplete one, and care must now be taken to avoid distortions of an opposite kind to those present in earlier sentimental accounts. There are real difficulties in seeing "customary law" solely in terms of domination. Similarly there are problems in seeing it as being of entirely recent manufacture. Lastly, there must be doubts as to how far "colonial customary law" was successfully transmitted to, and assimilated in, the lifeworlds of most Africans.

First, while the extent and nature of colonial domination needed to be revealed in view of the degree of consensus implied in earlier writings about customary law, "domination" cannot be allowed to appear as the total account. Even if we freely concede the coercive nature of local government in the colonial period, and the ideological quality of what passed for "customary law", an exclusively one-way, top-down view of the colonial encounter must mislead. There is no need to repeat here the now well-articulated and generally accepted worries about placing too literal a reliance upon a conception of "sovereign" power. "Power" resides at different levels, takes on diverse forms, and runs in all directions. So, while "customary law" in the sense of the repertoire of rules applied in the colonial courts *did* provide an instrument of rule, it also offered avenues of escape and resistance for the ruled. Similarly, "customary law" in the different sense of the meanings and commitments which furnished the lifeworlds of Africans, while subject to covert penetration and co-option, also provided the means of qualified autonomy.

The insistence of scholars like Chanock, Snyder and Ranger that "customary law" is of recent manufacture, a creature of the colonial period rather than the pre-colonial past, is helpful in a number of ways. It is essential that we be prepared to recognise the relationship between contemporary and past forms as at the very least problematic. Also the association between "custom" and a supposedly egalitarian context must be questioned. Further, the specific idea of "invention" restores and ensures prominence for a conception of agency, the essential notion that custom is linked to the goings on of living men and women, that it is both at the root of action and the product of it. But there are difficulties in pressing this view of customary law too far. In the first place, it risks conflating two separate, if interlinked, spheres; the "customary law" of the colonial and post-colonial courts, and that which furnishes the everyday lifeworld of Africans. Second, the flavour of novelty, the clean break, which "invention" carries, draws attention *away* from crucial aspects of what seems to me to be happening. The very strength of customary law, the source of its supposedly coercive power, lies in the links it can claim with a past, established, approved state of affairs. Foreign novelties do not lay claim through existing commitments; yet that is what custom does if it does anything. So rather than novelty we should be looking for the exploitation of an existing repertoire, or the artificial sustaining of ancient forms, with detrimental, constraining effects upon the ruled.

The idea of the invented tradition seems to me to imply an impoverished and grossly simplistic understanding of the operation of ideology. It calls up a vision of the manufacture, transmission and assimilation, intact, of some new world view, and the corresponding destruction of existing cognitive and normative foundations of the lifeworld. Much more persuasive is an account of ideology as working with what is already to hand, covertly upon and within an existing lifeworld, transforming without eradicating. . . . But even here we must not neglect the very significant extent to which some cultures are resistant to transformation through co-option. Empirical observations reveal wide and interesting variations in the response of encapsulated groups to the experience of colonial rule.

Nowadays people are more sceptical of the provenance and authenticity of customary law they find in official legal texts.[140] The modern legal order is now openly acknowledged to be a pluralistic one, a series of interrelated normative spheres.[141] It includes the formal legal code, containing a written version of customary law,[142] and of course the common law, both of which are regularly

---

[140] See Gordon op cit n80 41ff.
[141] Allott & Woodman op cit n15 2.
[142] See Woodman in Morse & Woodman *Indigenous Law and the State* 181ff regarding Ghana and Nigeria.

applied in the official courts and in the state bureaucracy. Then there is a version of customary law that has been recorded by anthropologists and lawyers. This is used in more informal contexts and for teaching purposes. And finally there is the customary law that is actually lived out by the people and applied in various traditional and informal tribunals.[143] These legal orders are not unconnected, nor should it be assumed that the people concerned are unaware of how to manipulate the resources offered them by legal pluralism.[144]

---

[143] Sanders (1987) 20 *CILSA* 405ff.
[144] Roberts (1981) 2 *Jahrbuch Afrikanisches Recht* 99.

CHAPTER 2

The Courts

I RULES vs PROCESSES; ADJUDICATION vs RECONCILIATION

Study of the mechanisms of dispute settlement is a relatively recent concern of legal anthropology. Lawyers have never had more than a professional interest in court procedures and anthropologists have concentrated their energies on the normative order of society.[1] For both disciplines, rules and their supposed result, social harmony, had a supreme value.[2] Anthropology during the colonial era thus complemented positivist jurisprudence and at the same time met the colonial governments' requirement for codes and compilations of customary law.

Few scholars today, however, would accept the transcendental value of rules and social order. Sociologists have shown convincingly that conflict is a normal feature of social life and that it can function positively in society to promote

---

[1] Abel (1973) 8 *Law & Soc R* 221–32; Roberts *Order and Dispute* 17ff; Comaroff & Roberts *Rules and Processes* 5–17.

[2] Bohannan 69 and *Law and Warfare* 44–6.

much needed change and development. The emphasis on order and peace is an ethnocentric value,[3] a product of western culture.[4]

[13] BOHANNAN *JUSTICE AND JUDGMENT AMONG THE TIV* 208–13

We found that two folk systems are operative in Tivland: one is the systemization of jural phenomena by the Tiv themselves in their own language; the other is the systemization in English of roughly the same phenomena by administrative officers. The English folk system occupies an unduly large place in the social field because the ultimate political power in the colonial society is thought by all to lie with the British. . . . The folk system of the British covers two sorts of tribunals, which they term respectively native (or Native Authority) courts and magistrates' courts. The folk system of the Tiv also covers two sorts of tribunals, both of which they call *jir*. One type of *jir* is the same institution as the Native Authority courts, seen from a different angle. The other is what we have described in this book as the moot. . . .

In examining the ways in which the *jir* entered into the other institutions and hence into Tiv daily life, we found that the *jir* was a counteraction on the part of society following upon the occurrence of social acts which could be called "breaches of norms". The *jir* is followed by still other social acts which bring about a correction: either re-establishment of the norm or retribution for its breach. We arrived at the series of social acts:

Breach of Norm > Counteraction > Correction

. . .We can see that Tiv organize their jural institutions around a notion which falls squarely into the column of "counteraction". If our own method were similar we should not speak of law, but of "the court". "Law", if it be reducible to so simple an analytical scheme, would certainly demand a different one: law is primarily the rules and the body of rules which are broken; it falls in the first column, not the middle one. However, it overlaps into both other columns because it includes notions of procedure and, since the notion of "sanction" is involved, it is concerned with a penal system and other systems of "enforcement" of "decisions". . . . Thus, it seems to me, the European folk system sees the Native Authority tribunal basically as a court which, within established limits, applies "native law and custom". Tiv, in their folk system, see the same organization as a *jir* which arbitrates disputes brought before it. "Native law and custom" as a "corpus" of "law" which can be "sure", is simply not a Tiv idea. Neither is it a Tiv idea that a "court" may have "authority" to carry out its "decisions". Rather, Tiv believe that a right answer exists to all disputes; they take disputes before the *jir* in order to discover that answer, and the principals to the dispute must concur in it when it is discovered.

Tiv see their tribunals, both courts and "moots", with a single set of concepts. The two have different internal structuring, but in the long run both are *jir* and the purpose of both is to "repair the *tar*" [lineage territory], to make the community run smoothly and peacefully. The elders of the moot also repair the *tar* ceremonially. Tiv see the ceremony and the *jir* as two aspects of the single task of repairing the *tar*: what we might call the government aspect and the religious aspect of social welfare.

Because of its tremendous field of assumption and undefined premiss, "law" probably has one of the most extensive foundations of ethnocentric metaphysic of any discipline. The anthropologist cannot let this field of assumption stand without recognition; he must assume that it may not be valid for the material he has gathered from exotic societies. "Law" is not a science; to make it such would be to destroy it as a basis for social action. The comparison of legal systems—comparative jurisprudence—may be a science, for it and sociology, to which it is related, are devices for understanding social action. Law itself is a basis for social action.

---

[3] See Roberts op cit n1 45–7.
[4] This was not appreciated by early scholars: *Law in Culture and Society* 403–4.

Law, no matter how complex its procedure becomes, over-simplifies human relations. In settling disputes, we over-simplify the actualities by fitting them into the procrustean beds of law and precedent. Tiv *jir* and its attendant concepts do not over-simplify to the same extent: they have no need to do so. When Tiv over-simplify human relationships, they do it in terms of *tsav*, curses, and fetishes, not in terms of law. Both sets of over-implifications bring the correction of the social order within bounds believed to be accessible to human action. It is the idiom of the conceptualization which is different, and it is this idiom which gives us the key to understanding the differences.

Within western jurisprudence the preoccupation with rules was to some extent corrected by American Realism, which directed attention towards the study of the courts in order to understand the law in action.[5] This opened a new avenue of inquiry: the court as an agent of social control. In turn this led to a new vision of society, one in which *processes* rather than rules predominated.[6] The general concerns of legal anthropology thus shifted from the rule to breach of the rule and its correction; at the same time conflict as a field of study grew in importance.[7]

From a lawyer's point of view, the formal and public hearing of a dispute by way of adjudication is the primary method of resolving disputes. Accordingly, any inquiry tends to become preoccupied with what is done in court, although the trial is probably only a brief phase in the progress of a grievance.[8] From an anthropological perspective, which encompasses conflict in society generally, however, the trial must obviously be examined in a wider context. Hence for analytical purposes three phases are distinguished: the grievance, the conflict, and the dispute. The first implies a circumstance which one person believes to be unjust or a ground for complaint. Whether the grievance escalates or not will depend on the aggrieved party's further action. A conflict irrupts only when the other party joins issue. A fully blown dispute, the third stage, results when the conflict becomes a public confrontation.

> 'No dispute exists unless and until the right claimant, or someone on his behalf, actively raises the initial disagreement from the level of dyadic argument into the public arena, with the express intention of doing something about the desired claim.'[9]

By using what is termed the 'extended case method', legal anthropologists projected their inquiry backwards in time to the beginning of a grievance and forwards to the period after judgment.[10]

Not only is the emphasis on rules a peculiarly western cultural value, so too is the idea that disputes must be settled in courts by a process of adjudication, with a win-or-lose result. The aims and procedures of African tribunals are often quite different. Much of the anthropological work on dispute processing has sought to explain why; and this has involved demonstrating a correlation

---

[5] See above, 11ff.
[6] See above, 15ff.
[7] See the review article: Snyder (1981) 8 *Brit J L & Soc* 141 esp 144–6.
[8] Van Velsen in Epstein *The Craft of Social Anthropology* 129.
[9] Gulliver in Nader op cit n4 14. And generally see: Nader & Todd *The Disputing Process* 14–15.
[10] This method can be used as a general diagnostic tool for studying conflict and social control. See, eg: Turner *Schism and Continuity in an African Society*.

between the mode of processing disputes and certain social, economic, and especially political structures.[11]

Where there is no centralized state and thus no permanent judicial institutions, disputants are free to resolve their differences in any manner they choose. At the most basic level this might lead to interpersonal violence, in which case the relative strengths of the parties will obviously determine the outcome of the conflict.[12] Other bilateral processes include various more or less ritualized duels or contests, and, of course, negotiations. None of these modes favours the use of rules.[13]

Once a third party intervenes, the entire nature of the process changes.[14] A trilateral arrangement usually presupposes some form of centralized political authority that can compel the disputants to submit to its jurisdiction and can enforce its judgments. The actual power available to the third party is obviously a question of degree; where it has relatively less power at its disposal, the third party is more likely to take on the role of mediator/arbitrator.[15] In the case of adjudication, judges have the full backing of the state and are capable of imposing their decisions. (For the parties this is a win-or-lose result, but one which the court, by virtue of its monopoly of power, can force the loser to accept.) In fully developed states, courts are the preserve of the central government[16] and they are a principal means of demonstrating state authority. Yet when wielding power, the courts avoid any accusation of arbitrariness or bias by the impartial application of a fixed code of rules.[17]

If a tribunal lacks the power to impose a judgment, it cannot dictate the manner in which the dispute is to be heard. Instead it must rely upon voluntary submission by the disputants, and the outcome of the case will depend upon the tribunal's success in persuading them to accept a compromise.[18] In most African societies courts tended to mediate or arbitrate the cases brought before them rather than to adjudicate. In these circumstances the preferred solution to disputes was the reconciliation of the litigants.[19] The impartial application of rules was inevitably of less consequence.

> 'Justice, instead of the rational and impartial application of abstract rules of law, then becomes a process of persuasion with the accent on the reasonable behaviour of all concerned in a spirit of give and take. The rules of law hereby serve as a broad and flexible basis for discussion and consideration, but are not inviolable and imperative as we know

---

[11] See Gluckman's account of the Barotse below, [20].

[12] Bohannan's distinction between law and warfare in fact offered two polar forms of conflict resolution: *Law and Warfare* Intro. And see the distinction between fighting and talking: Roberts op cit n1 ch 9. Similarly there is a widely accepted distinction between political and judicial modes of dispute settlement: Gulliver *Social Control in an African Society* 297–301. And see Abel (1981) 9 *Int J Sociology L* 245ff.

[13] Gulliver op cit 297; Fallers *Law without Precedent* 11–12; Moore *Law as Process* ch 6; Gulliver (1973) 7 *Law & Soc R* 667; and Hamnett *Social Anthropology and Law* 15.

[14] See Koch *War and Peace in Jalemo* 27–31.

[15] See Gulliver *Disputes and Negotiations* 271 and op cit n13 667.

[16] One of the great truisms of the sociology of law: Ehrlich *Fundamental Principles of the Sociology of Law* 14.

[17] Rheinstein *Max Weber on Law and Economy in Society* 61–4; Nader & Todd op cit n9 21; Eckhoff in Aubert *Sociology of Law* 175; Roberts op cit n1 175.

[18] Gulliver in Nader op cit n4 17–19 and Gulliver op cit n12.

[19] Compare Gulliver op cit n12 1–4 and Bohannan 61–5 with Roberts op cit n1 ch 8.

our laws to be. The successful end of a trial process is a judgment which both parties formally agree to accept and observe.'[20]

Anthropologists have perhaps over-emphasized reconciliation[21] and have failed to appreciate similar aims in the western judicial process (as in cases of out-of-court settlements and industrial disputes).[22] This was doubtless symptomatic of the assumptions that underlay much of the earlier legal/anthropological research: overriding importance was given to rules and to social stability; conflict was treated as pathological and the successful solution of disputes as essential for the social order. This understanding is implicit both in functionalism[23] and in western legal ideology.[24] Once acknowledged, it follows that resolution of conflict is neither inevitable nor a *transcendent* value, and that reconciliation is an ideal, not an invariable goal of all African courts.[25]

II COLONIAL AND POST-INDEPENDENCE POLICIES

The colonial courts of Africa were the beacons of imperial power. They were intended not only to settle disputes but also to proclaim the reach of government and the values of western civilization. This was especially true of the British possessions because, according to the English way of thinking, fair trial was more important than fair laws.[26] Moreover, it was mainly via the court system, viz recognition of existing tribal courts, that colonial governments could claim to have paid due regard to indigenous culture.[27]

The court systems of all the African territories were in substance the same. Courts of chiefs and headmen were constituted as courts of first instance. Subordinate and higher courts, created in the metropolitan mould, were established alongside them. A third hierarchy comprising tribunals staffed by white officials charged with the general administration of the African population was interposed.

The first problem the European colonial powers had to overcome was the physical control of their territories; and this had to be won at the expense of the indigenous rulers.[28] Hence the early period of colonization was characterized by the restriction of chiefly rule, which sometimes meant depriving chiefs of judicial powers. But once the colonies had been subdued, the advantages of retaining and utilizing tribal leaders soon became apparent.[29] If they could be co-opted to the service of the colonial government, they would bring with them the loyalty of

---

[20] Holleman *Issues in African Law* 18. Emphasis on rules can be counterproductive: see Snyder op cit n7 153–5.

[21] Gluckman *The Judicial Process among the Barotse of Northern Rhodesia* 55.

[22] Van Velsen in Gluckman *Ideas and Procedures in African Customary Law* 137ff.

[23] See above, 51–2.

[24] Which regards the impartial application of rules and the formal equality of the parties as the sine qua non of dispute settlement: Cain & Kulcsar (1981/2) 16 *Law & Soc R* 378–9 (also in *Disputes and the Law* 9–11); and see Kidder (1981) 15 *Law & Soc R* 719.

[25] Roberts op cit n1 167.

[26] Hailey *An African Survey* 303–5.

[27] Another possible method was by way of the conflict of laws: Geertz *Old Societies and New States* 228ff.

[28] Chanock *Law, Custom and Social Order* 48.

[29] Hailey op cit n26 527–9.

their followers, and at the same time the administration could economize on manpower. The latter was a persistent theme: there were few whites available or qualified to perform judicial or any other state functions.[30] What at first had been a matter of expedience, was later vaunted as a considered policy—indirect rule. Shepstone's controversial programme for the settlement of the Zulu in Natal was probably the earliest instance of indirect rule in anglophone Africa. By the 1920s and 30s, however, it had been given its name and fresh impetus by Lord Lugard (in Nigeria) and Sir Donald Cameron (in Tanganyika).[31]

The British colonial governments paid little attention to customary law.[32] They believed that well-trained personnel and fair judicial conduct were the best guarantees of the proper administration of justice.[33] In consequence, their main concerns were with the staffing and procedure of the courts and not with the law to be applied. Tribunals were created that could function cheaply and expeditiously, and in a manner comprehensible to the litigants. These requirements were often in conflict with more high-minded considerations of due process. To accommodate such demands within the limitations imposed by finance and manpower, the colonial governments were continually experimenting with new areas of jurisdiction and strange hybrids of appeal and retrial.

Throughout Africa the judicial role of chiefs was conceived as an aspect of their political status as tribal leaders. Colonial governments thought that the combination of administrative and judicial powers in the same person would conform to traditional African ideas of leadership. The absence of rules and formality was one of the most attractive features of chiefly courts; and they could adjudicate suits in a manner familiar to African litigants. Equally in their favour (especially from the government's point of view) was the low running cost. So, apart from the formal requirement that the chiefs' courts be established by a state warrant, there was little interference with the way in which they operated.

Although the chief was at the bottom of the hierarchy of government offices, his position was a pivotal one. On the one hand, as an agent of the state, he was obliged to carry out colonial policy; on the other hand, he was still the traditional leader of his people. At one and the same time he was expected to perform the often contradictory roles of government bureaucrat and patriarchal leader.[34] By the 1930s, the preservation of chiefly authority was a canon of colonial government, endorsed by the anthropology of the period: one of the axioms of structural-functionalism was that tribal institutions functioned to sustain social harmony. In consequence chiefs were assumed to be entirely

---

[30] Allott *New Essays* 12–13; Morris & Read *Indirect Rule and the Search for Justice* ch 8.

[31] See Elias in Kuper & Kuper *African Law* 187–8; and see Robinson (1949) 1 *J Afr Admin* 162–75 for the East and West African variants of indirect rule. The colonial policies of France and Portugal are normally described as ones of *direct* rule, but this was only because their overseas possessions were formally treated, for legislative and administrative purposes, as parts of the mother country: Hooker *Legal Pluralism* 196–203; Robert (1959) 11 *J Afr Admin* 124. Like the British, they also used tribal leaders as agents of government, and the system of courts that they established closely resembled the tripartite arrangement of the anglophone territories.

[32] Lewin *Studies in African Native Law* ch 9.

[33] Seidman *The State, Law and Development* 43–4.

[34] Discussed by Weinrich *Chiefs and Councils in Rhodesia*.

beneficial adjuncts to colonial rule.[35] No doubt this was correct in so far as
indirect rule worked to contain and divert the growing African discontent with
colonialism. But the eventual effect of state support for the chiefs was to
undermine their prestige and to subvert the basis of the traditional order. Before
colonization, most chiefs had governed, in part at least, with the consent of their
people. This check on any abuse of power was removed when the chiefs'
positions came to depend instead on government subventions.[36]

Immediate control of the chiefs was vested in the 'native' affairs department of
the colonial administration. Alongside the chiefs' courts, this department ran its
own tribunals staffed by white administrative officials (the 'native' commissioners) who, like the chiefs, were general administrative agents of government.
Commissioners were supposed to sit as courts of appeal from the chiefs'
decisions, but they also had concurrent jurisdiction to operate courts of the first
instance. The commissioners were expected to be in close contact with the people
and to have an intimate knowledge of local affairs. Their administrative powers
were varied and loosely defined, and again it was a natural extension of these
broad powers that commissioners should also perform judicial functions.[37] In
most countries they were intended to provide a forum that bridged the
traditional chiefs' courts and the western-style magistrates' courts. In this way
they could cater for the litigant who was caught up in a phase of cultural
transition. Above all, like their chiefly counterparts, the commissioners' courts
were expected to dispense quick, cheap and informal justice.

The magistrates' courts and the High (or Supreme) courts constituted the third
section of the colonial legal systems. These tribunals were designed to administer
criminal and public law to the entire population. They were staffed by
professional lawyers who had been specially trained in the metropolitan system
of law. The high fee tariffs of these courts and their geographic remoteness
tended to preclude African civil litigation; nor was any attempt made to adjust
procedures to cater for African requirements. Accordingly nearly all civil cases,
as well as many petty criminal ones, were confined to the chiefs' and
commissioners' courts.

Until the 1930s no one showed any particular interest in the 'native' courts.
They were administered by the native affairs department and they had little
connection with the ordinary courts of the land.[38] From the 1930s onwards,
however, there was increasing dissatisfaction with this system. It was felt that the
standard of justice dispensed in these courts was of a decidedly inferior quality,
in part because the sought-after qualities of speed and informality did not
measure up to western standards of justice. The legal profession and liberally
minded politicians were the first to voice these objections. Their complaints were
later taken up by African nationalists, who added a call for equality before all
courts and non-racial application of the law.

---

[35] Driberg (1934) 16 *J Comp Leg* 230.
[36] Howard (1985) 7 *Third World Quarterly* 326.
[37] Holleman *Chief, Council and Commissioner* regarding the political and administrative roles of the
commissioner in the then Southern Rhodesia.
[38] Brooke (1954) 6 *J Afr Admin* 68.

As criticism grew, more defects in the system emerged. The African courts had low status; their decisions were seldom, if ever, reported; they were the monopoly of a government department; they were cut off from the general legal system. Although there might be links with other courts in the system by way of appeal, revision or review, these remedies were exercised so infrequently that in practice the three hierarchies of courts operated quite independently.[39] This meant that the department of justice and the High Court could exercise no supervisory or corrective functions over African courts. Three different legal traditions had evolved, as each hierarchy developed at its own pace and in its own direction.[40] To counteract this there was spasmodic appeal to the doctrine of stare decisis, but the keeping of proper records in the lower courts was a continual problem and so uniform decision-making was impossible.[41]

Earlier there had been little concern about the quality of the substantive law administered in the African courts, but again from the 1930s onwards there was a demand for greater and more precise knowledge of customary law.[42] (This happened at a time when colonial governments believed traditional African society to be disintegrating under the pernicious influence of western culture.) It was thought to be quite wrong for the chiefs to apply rules which were little more than social usages. There was similar dissatisfaction with the commissioners' courts, which were criticized for administering an Africanized version of equity. All this betokened a lack of the professionalism that was considered indispensable for the proper administration of justice.

Another problem, stemming directly from the conflict implicit in the dual administrative/judicial roles of the chiefs and commissioners, started to become apparent at the end of the colonial period. Both functionaries often had to act as the agents of more or less unpopular government policies; this meant that the courts they ran stood every chance of being tainted by the dislike felt for the policy. Moreover, although it was obvious that administrative officers could not be expected to display the same skills as professional lawyers, commissioners were upbraided for not performing their judicial duties properly, even though their tribunals were not supposed to be the same as the ordinary courts. In this regard the Bushe Report in 1933[43] roundly condemned the system of indirect rule.[44]

A plank of the African nationalist platform in the 1950s was the call for fair procedures, known laws and a separation of powers. One of the consequences of the political movement for independence was a new respect for customary law,

---

[39] Epstein (1951) 12 *Human Problems* 31.

[40] Robinson op cit n31 162–5.

[41] Generally see Bennett (1975) 15 *Rhod LJ* 146–51.

[42] This could be met only by codification or restatement. See the Pim Report cited by Lewin op cit n32 4–5; Chanock op cit n28 53.

[43] Commission of Inquiry into the Administration of Justice in Kenya, Uganda and Tanganyika Territory in Criminal Matters para 21.

[44] See Morris & Read op cit n30 295–308 and further the Report of the Rhodesia Government Commission of Inquiry into the Administrative and Judicial Functions in the Native Affairs and District Courts Department (1961) (under the chairmanship of V L Robinson) paras 112–19.

which was now deemed comparable and compatible with western law,[45] a national heritage to be protected and nurtured.

The African nationalists demanded unification of their legal systems: a blending of customary and common law and a single hierarchy of courts open to all.[46] Unification was rooted in diverse concerns: improving standards in the administration of justice; attempting to promote national unity through legal unity; seeking to eradicate the racism and class differences implicit in colonialism;[47] and giving expression to the new, tribally heterogeneous urban society.[48] In 1953 a conference of judicial advisers was called at Makerere College in Uganda. Here a principle was adopted that every country should have one body of law and one judicial system applicable and available equally to all persons. This proved to be the point of departure for future African legal development.[49]

Decolonization was the occasion to translate these principles into practice. But immediately ideals had to be compromised. The prospect of unifying the substantive law into a single code was too daunting, and was soon abandoned.[50] Unification of the courts was thought to be a more easily won goal, but even in this regard it soon became evident that any material reform required more than a right of appeal from the inferior African to the superior white courts. New personnel were needed to staff the courts.[51] And the merits of the chiefs' and commissioners' courts (their accessibility and their non-professionalism) began to seem more attractive.[52] In fact, these considerations were to become the dominant themes of the post-colonial period.[53]

The reforming zeal of the newly independent African governments often foundered on the resilience of traditional political institutions. Where local chieftaincies were stable and well organized they were quite capable of withstanding the encroachment of the state.[54] In southern Africa, for example, the chiefs' capacity for resistance has been evident in the special place they continue to occupy in all the contemporary legal systems.[55] This has meant that the ideal of integration has been only partially realized.

Most countries have done little more than remove racial qualifications from the jurisdictional powers of the courts. The reforms undertaken by the independent homelands of South Africa are cases in point. The main concern was to eliminate racist elements in the court system inherited from South Africa; and

---

[45] Chanock op cit n28 53–4; Elias *Nature of African Customary Law* Preface.

[46] Allott (1965) 14 *ICLQ* 366.

[47] See Spalding (1970) 2 *Zambia LJ* 85–98.

[48] Cotran (1963) 1 *J Mod Afr Studies* 214.

[49] Brooke op cit n38 69ff.

[50] Hailey op cit n26 41; Spalding op cit n47 79ff and Opoku (1976) 9 *Verfassung u Recht* 65.

[51] Spalding op cit n47 74, citing Hailey op cit n26 41. This was the finding of the Conference on Local Courts and Customary Law in 1963: Cotran (1965) 4 *J Local Admin Overseas* 128.

[52] Noted by the 1963 Conference and discussed in Spalding op cit n47 76ff.

[53] Detailed descriptions of the court systems can be found in Allott *Judicial and Legal Systems in Africa* ((1960) and (1970)).

[54] Roberts (1979) 17 *Afr L Studies* 37.

[55] Even in Zimbabwe chiefs and traditional leaders have had their judicial powers restored under the Customary Law and Local Courts Act 20 of 1990.

this was achieved simply by abolishing the commissioners' courts and by transferring their judicial functions to magistrates' courts.[56]

The fervour for unification and the optimism of the 1960s, the decade of decolonization and development, have proved to be chimerical. The difficulties of imposing a new, unified regime soon led to disenchantment, and the dualism of the past now appears in a more favourable light. Once all litigants have a de jure status of equality before the courts, the debate can progress to the less tractable problem of access to justice.

> '[This] is achieved only when no person is deterred by financial, psychological, or physical barriers from seeking a legal solution to the assertion of a right, for making a claim, or for defending a civil claim or criminal charge.'[57]

Access to justice has become a serious issue in the developed world where, by various measures, such as legal aid and the creation of more informal tribunals, attempts have been made to improve service efficiency, especially for the benefit of the financially and educationally disadvantaged.

[14] BUSH in CAPPELLETTI *ACCESS TO JUSTICE* IV 261-3

In attempting to understand what "access to justice" might mean and what might practically be required to provide it in a society, a primary question is: access to justice *for whom*—for what constituency, group, class, or segment of society? For in almost every part of the contemporary world, societies and nations are not uniform, homogeneous masses, but heterogeneous aggregations of groups and entities, large and small. Values, needs and social structures differ, often widely, from sector to sector within a single society. In short, it may be said that contemporary societies are generally not unitary or singular, but rather *pluralistic* in values, needs and structures.

This phenomenon of societal or social pluralism has an important bearing on the question of access to justice. The concept of justice itself has often been framed in universal or absolute terms, and this continues to be so in many respects. Fundamental rights of man, constitutional guarantees, these comprise a major part of our juridical culture, perhaps nowhere more so than in the realm of the *procedure* for dispensing justice. Indeed, a guarantee of access to justice is itself generally included in this "constitutional" framework—implicitly or explicitly. Nevertheless, in the context of pluralistic societies, even if access to justice is considered a fundamental and universal right, it must be recognized that there is no fundamental and universally applicable means of satisfying this right in practice—and thus no singular meaning of "access to justice".

Therefore, if implementing the principle of equal access to justice is a desideratum, and if the premise is accepted that contemporary societies tend to be pluralistic in varying degrees, it is necessary to develop a pluralistic understanding of access to justice. This means first of all a recognition that social pluralism calls for institutional pluralism, in the domain of providing justice as elsewhere; otherwise what is called "access to justice" may simply be a one-dimensional response that, in the pluralistic context, is unnecessary, unjust, ineffective, or even "totalitarian". With this recognition, an attempt should be made to explore the range of needs that exists among citizens seeking justice, and the range of action and institutions capable of meeting those needs, from direct government agents to publicly sanctioned, voluntary non-governmental arrangements.

---

[56] See, eg, s 54 of the Transkei Constitution Act 15 of 1976; s 91 of the Bophuthatswana Constitution Act 18 of 1977; s 52 of the Venda Constitution Act 9 of 1979; and s 76 of the Ciskei Constitution Act 20 of 1981. Only in Zimbabwe were more drastic reforms enacted: the Customary Law and Primary Courts Act 6 of 1981. See Bennett 61–2.

[57] Zemans *Perspectives on Legal Aid* 10.

In this exploratory process, much may be learned from the development of the last 16 years in the systems of justice of the nations of Africa. Many commentators have described the fundamental "pluralism" of most modern African societies. In these societies, the colonial experience and the rapid rise of technology and urbanism have left an already pluralistic network of indigenous traditional relationships and attitudes coexisting with yet another system of "modern" commercially oriented relationships. Every African nation, since the attainment of independence from colonial rule and the introduction of national governments with a strong desire for national unity, has faced the question of how to deal with this pluralism. And the area of law in general, and procedure in particular, has been at the center of the attempts to grapple with societal pluralism and "integrate" the traditional and the modern. Of these attempts, one commentator has written,

"The political unity of the societies in question has often been realized before their social unity . . . The result is an obligation for governments (that have attained political unity) to continue to take account of the specific character of the societies they govern (since they have not attained social unity), or else to see a unitary law [and legal system] rendered totally ineffective. . . ."[1]

The "access to justice" developments of the last decade and a half in Africa are thus in great part the result of a tension between the profound desire for a unitary justice based on universal procedural guarantees; and the recognition of the need for, and the value of, a pluralistic structure of justice responsive to the pluralistic character of society.

Note

1. Vanderlinden in Gilissen (ed) *Pluralisme Juridique* 32.

The concern to improve access to the courts can be contrasted with popular justice, which has come to be associated with revolutionary movements, especially in developing countries. The former implies an incremental reform of the existing legal system, while the latter suggests a radical break with the past. Popular justice is rooted in democratic principles, in particular trial by peers in an elected tribunal. So far as possible the tribunal is stripped of legal formality and of any past association with oppressive state institutions. Both these movements have been asserted in recent South African history, access to justice resulting in the creation of small claims courts and popular justice leading to the brief appearance of people's courts.

III COURTS OF CHIEFS AND HEADMEN

(1) Recognition in South Africa

The official policy towards the chiefs' and headmen's courts in this country has changed considerably over the years. In the early nineteenth century, when British rule was being extended into the eastern region of the Cape Colony, chiefs were replaced by white magistrates, who were instructed not to apply customary law. This policy was defended as part of the government's civilizing mission in Africa.[58] It is quite obvious, however, that the policy was part of a

---

[58] Brookes *The History of Native Policy in South Africa* 90 and 93; Burman 'Cape Policies towards African Law in the Cape Tribal Territories 1872–83'. More formally it was justified on the basis of Ord 50 of 1828, which had cancelled all laws in the Colony discriminating against Blacks. See Hailey op cit n26 350.

wider programme to undermine indigenous political authority.[59]

In Natal, by contrast, chiefs were allowed to retain their judicial powers and to apply customary law.[60] The main reason for this decision can be traced to the problem of controlling the large number of displaced persons who had moved back into the territory after British annexation. An early form of indirect rule provided a convenient solution: Africans in the colony would be placed under the jurisdiction of tribal authorities.[61] A formal link to the colonial government was provided by declaring the Lieutenant-Governor of the colony the Supreme Chief of the Zulu people. In 1875, the ordinary courts were separated from the chiefs' courts in civil matters,[62] and in 1878, a system of native administrators' courts, having co-ordinate jurisdiction with the chiefs, was founded.[63]

In the Transvaal a policy similar to that of Natal was adopted.[64] The State President was made a paramount chief and below him a Superintendent of Natives operated a court of appeal from the decisions of the inferior courts in African cases. Lower down in the hierarchy, commissioners and chiefs had concurrent jurisdiction in civil cases.

After Union in 1910, the principal concern of the new government was to impose uniformity.[65] The individual history and the special circumstances of each of the provinces had produced curiously diverse court structures and degrees of recognition of customary law.[66] Underlying the desire for uniformity was another, less overt need to promote tribalism and chiefly authority. In government circles it was believed that a return to traditional institutions could deflect the challenge posed by a growing urbanized African proletariat.[67]

It was not until 1927, however, that the African courts were finally reorganized.[68] The Native Administration Act[69] of that year was a major component of a new policy for the African population. Throughout the country courts of chiefs and headmen were established on the basis of authority given by government warrant. At the same time, commissioners' courts and special courts of appeal were founded. This hierarchy was connected to the ordinary courts by way of an appeal to the Appellate Division of the Supreme Court. The advantages of this structure were proclaimed in the opening session of the new Natal and Transvaal division of the Appeal Court.

---

[59] Bennett 41.
[60] Ord 3 of 1849.
[61] Brookes op cit n58 25 and Hailey op cit n26 357.
[62] Law 26.
[63] Law 21.
[64] Law 4 of 1885.
[65] See Dubow (1986) 12 *JSAS* 217ff regarding the Native Affairs Department.
[66] For example, even within the Cape, there was a range of different approaches. In the Colony itself chiefs' courts were officially denied recognition, whereas in Transkei and British Bechuanaland they operated with varying degrees of autonomy. See the remarks in *Sekelini v Sekelini & others* (1904) 21 SC 118 at 124 and *Roodt v Lake & others* (1906) 23 SC 561 at 564.
[67] Bennett 46.
[68] See Dubow op cit n65 230–4.
[69] No 38.

[15] STUBBS P 1929 NAC (N&T) 3–4

It will thus be appreciated that by the system of judicature here outlined, embodying simple and convenient forms of procedure, stripped as far as possible, of legal niceties and technicalities, designed to meet the needs of the situation, and one of the central ideas of which is to bring the legal machine within easy reach of, and accessible to, the highest as well as to the lowest member of the Native community, there is secured to them an unbroken chain for the remedying of their wrongs in civil matters, with comparatively little expense.

From the Court of their Chief or Headman they may in appeal go to their Native Commissioner, and from their Native Commissioner to this Court of Appeal. That is the great open road by which they may travel in seeking redress of any wrong of a civil nature they may have suffered.

And, in *Motaung v Dube*,[70] Stubbs P said that the legislature had attempted to establish tribunals that would suit the psychology of Africans by recreating the flexibility and informality of the tribal courts to which they were accustomed.[71]

Fifty-nine years later, in 1986, the court structure was reorganized again, following recommendations made by the Hoexter Commission of Inquiry into the Structure and Functioning of the Courts.[72] The only element to be retained of the system established in 1927 was the chiefs' and headmen's courts. The Commission explained why these tribunals had been reprieved:

> 'Although in many respects the chiefs' courts function imperfectly their retention is widely supported both by Blacks and by experts in Black customary law. These courts represent at once an indigenous cultural institution and an important instrument of reconciliation. For these reasons a rural Black will often prefer to have his case heard by the chief's court.'[73]

The Commission's view of these courts was perhaps to be expected, because they are generally considered to be guardians of African tradition. Yet, since there are approximately one and a half thousand chiefs' and headmen's courts operating in all parts of the country, it is impossible to make categorical pronouncements about their contribution to the legal system. Their survival depends to a great extent on the political position of the chiefs and their ability to adapt to the expectations of the people they govern.

Twenty-five years ago, the prognosis for the Transkeian chiefs' courts[74] was pessimistic. It was felt that more commercial activity would demand a far greater knowledge of common law, and that this, together with the increased sophistication of the population, would undermine the chiefs' authority and prestige.[75] Aside from this, the chiefs' long association with indirect rule and then apartheid[76] would connect them, in the minds of most, with an outmoded

---

[70] 1930 NAC (N&T) 12.

[71] Which was in keeping with the Transkei tradition of benevolent paternalism: Dubow op cit n65 221–4 and 228.

[72] *Fifth Report* 1983.

[73] Part I para 3.4.3.8.

[74] Seymour Wood 1966 *Speculum Juris* 21.

[75] And see Labuschagne (1976) 1 *TRW* 66–9; Labuschagne & Swanepoel (1979) 12 *De Jure* 28–30, who also cite Roberts (1972) 16 *JAL* 103.

[76] Via the Black Authorities Act 68 of 1951.

and repressive regime.[77] But there is abundant evidence from all parts of Africa
to show that, given the right circumstances, chiefs can adapt in a progressive
manner to meet new challenges, in a way that more formal tribunals are unable
to do.[78]

(2) Jurisdiction

[16] SECTION 12(1) BLACK ADMINISTRATION ACT 38 OF 1927

The Minister may—

(a) authorize any Black chief or headman recognized or appointed under subsection (7)
    or (8) of section *two* to hear and determine civil claims arising out of Black law and
    custom brought before him by Blacks against Blacks resident within his area of
    jurisdiction;
(b) at the request of any chief upon whom jurisdiction has been conferred in terms of
    paragraph (a), authorize a deputy of such chief to hear and determine civil claims
    arising out of Black law and custom brought before him by Blacks against Blacks
    resident within such chief's area of jurisdiction:

Provided that a Black chief, headman or chief's deputy shall not under this section or any
other law have power to determine any question of nullity, divorce or separation arising
out of a marriage.

Only chiefs and their deputies who have been appointed under this section[79] may
constitute official courts. Consequently any judgment given by a chief who was
not formally installed will be treated as a nullity. But this does not mean that the
judgment cannot be recognized for certain purposes. If, for instance, both
parties accept the judgment and the debtor tenders payment to the chief, the
creditor will be bound and the debtor relieved of liability.[80] Conversely, if an
unwarranted chief were to impose a fine or other punishment, this would in
principle give rise to common-law actions in delict and/or crime.

Section 12(1) speaks only of civil jurisdiction. Under s 20 of the Act chiefs and
headmen may also be empowered to try offences at common or customary law,
other than those specified in the Third Schedule to the Act. Such criminal
jurisdiction is limited by the following two provisions. In the first place, if the
accused (or if one of a group of accused) was not a Black or if the offence was
suffered by a person who was not a Black, a chief has no jurisdiction. In the
second place, the punishment imposed may not involve: death; mutilation;
grievous bodily harm; imprisonment; the imposition of a fine in excess of R40
(or two head of large stock or ten head of small stock); or the imposition of
corporal punishment (except in the case of unmarried males below the apparent
age of 30 years).

It is unlikely that chiefs' courts consistently draw the careful distinction
between criminal and civil matters that they are required to do by the Act and by

[77] In South Africa, the various homeland governments have in general been careful to support
traditional rule, so here chiefs' and headmen's courts have, if anything, been strengthened. And see the
case of Malawi: Howard op cit n36 339–40.
[78] See below, 95–6.
[79] As read with s 2(7) and (8) of the same Act.
[80] *Funwayo v Gidivana* 1933 NAC (C&O) 15.

common law.[81] Strictly speaking, if they acted ultra vires and imposed a criminal penalty when not authorized to do so, they would fall foul of the prescriptions of the common law of crime.[82]

In criminal matters appeal lies from a chief or headman's decision to any magistrate's court which would have had jurisdiction, had the proceedings been instituted there in the first instance.[83] Further appeal lies from the magistrate's court to the Supreme Court.[84]

A chief's *civil* jurisdiction is limited to matters governed by customary law. If a case is taken on appeal to a magistrate's court, and it appears there that the common law should have been applied, the magistrate must begin proceedings afresh in his own court, and the chief's judgment will be set aside as being void for lack of jurisdiction. This limitation on the competence of the courts poses a number of difficulties.

The conflict of laws is a complex matter and even the Appeal Courts did not find it easy to decide when common or customary law should be applied. In *Mkize*,[85] for example, an action was brought to recover damages for defamation; it was held that the words complained of would not give rise to an action in customary law, and accordingly the chief lacked jurisdiction to hear the claim.[86] This assumes, of course, that in the circumstances the common law should have been applied to ensure that the plaintiff got his remedy—an arbitrary basis for choice of law.[87] In a more unusual case, *Nkosi v Mdhladhla*,[88] an action for damages for rape, it was held that customary law would permit only a criminal action, and because there was no corresponding civil claim, the chief had no jurisdiction. In other cases, both systems of law offered remedies and so the jurisdiction of the chiefs was confirmed.[89] But where it was clear that only the common law was applicable, for example in an action for damages for adultery in the case of a Christian marriage, the court held that the chief should not have heard the case.[90] Section 12 assumes that certain matters are naturally suited to customary law and that others are more suited to the common law. But in practice it is extremely difficult to make this distinction, and in principle

---

[81] Holleman op cit n37 92 and the editorial in (1967) 7 *Rhod LJ* 1ff. On criminal jurisdiction: see Labuschagne (1974) 7 *De Jure* 38; Olivier 585–7.

[82] Even more seriously, the running of a court by an unauthorized person could formerly have led to a prosecution under the Emergency Regulations for exerting 'power and authority . . . in specific areas by way of structures purporting to be structures of local government': definition of 'subversive statement', as read with s 5, of the Media Regulations R99 10 June 1988. The activities of people's courts and vigilante groups in the mid-1980s resulted in several prosecutions on these grounds. See below, 104. The Media Regulations were repealed by Proc R18 on 3 February 1990. The state of emergency lapsed in all parts of South Africa, except Natal, on 8 June 1990, and in Natal on 18 October 1990, Proc R186.

[83] Section 12(4), as amended by s 3 of the Schedule to Act 34 of 1986 and s 29A of the Magistrates' Courts Act 32 of 1944. See Labuschagne op cit n81 as to whether this is an appeal or retrial.

[84] *R v Kaleni* 1959 (4) SA 540 (E).

[85] 1948 NAC 39 (NE).

[86] See too *Ntshingili & others v Mncube* 1975 BAC 100 (NE).

[87] See below, 118–19.

[88] 1945 NAC (N&T) 46.

[89] *Cebekulu v Shandu* 1952 NAC 196 (NE); *Mkize v Mnguni* 1952 NAC 242 (NE); *Mazibuko v Nyathi* 1953 NAC 118 (NE).

[90] *Yeni v Jaca* 1953 NAC 31 (NE); *Ngwenya v Mavana* 1975 BAC 75 (S). In addition see *Shabango v Ngabi* 1953 NAC 111 (NE).

technical jurisdictional limitations of this nature are inappropriate for such informal tribunals.

The proviso to s 12(1) excludes from the competence of chiefs and headmen questions of nullity and divorce arising out of civil/Christian marriages.[91] Nevertheless, if the action is one that arises out of customary law, the court does have jurisdiction. In consequence it was held that a claim for bridewealth based on a civil marriage could be heard by a chief's court.[92] The Appeal Courts' assumption here—that customary law automatically applies to such claims—is of course a debatable one. Claims for damages for adultery, on the other hand, cannot be heard in chiefs' courts because the common law is deemed to apply in such matters.[93]

Both parties to any action in a chief or headman's court must be 'Black'. This term is defined in the Act.

[17] SECTION 35 BLACK ADMINISTRATION ACT 38 OF 1927

"Black"—shall include any person who is a member of any aboriginal race or tribe of Africa: provided that any person residing under the same conditions as a Black in a scheduled Black area or a released area, as defined or described in or under the Development Trust and Land Act 18 of 1936, or on any land of which the South African Development Trust is the registered owner, shall be regarded as a Black for the purposes of this Act. . . .

Earlier, the courts used a variety of tests to determine whether a person was African (or 'Black' in the parlance of the Act): physical appearance, parentage, habits, and association.[94] But genetic association with 'any aboriginal race or tribe of Africa' has become the predominant test, and only full-blooded Africans are deemed to fall into this category.[95] 'Aboriginal' has been interpreted to mean indigenous, existing in the land from time immemorial, or at least before the arrival of European colonists.[96]

If there is doubt as to a person's racial descent, i e if he or she had an ancestor who was not a member of one of the indigenous peoples of Africa, then the first proviso to the definition directs the court to consider the place of residence and lifestyle of the litigant.[97] If the person concerned lives in an area set aside as an African reserve (now one of the independent or self-governing territories) in terms of the Black Land Act[98] or the Development Trust and Land Act,[99] and in addition if such person had adopted a distinctively African manner of living, he or she could be deemed an African. This proviso is of no assistance regarding Africans living in urban areas because these areas are not considered to be 'Black

---

[91] The remedy of judicial separation was abolished by s 14 of the Divorce Act 70 of 1979.
[92] *Myandu v Dludla* 1978 AC 64 (NE).
[93] See below, 440–1.
[94] See *Anderson v Green* 1932 NPD 241; *Tarr & others v Estate Tarr* 1940 NAC (N&T) 75 at 77–8 and 1941 NAC (N&T) 82 at 83; *Randall* 1942 NAC (C&O) 63.
[95] *Masholo* 1944 NAC (C&O) 25 and *Khamanga v Matete* 1975 BAC 63 (C).
[96] *Ntlako v Dejasmarch* 1952 NAC 103 (C).
[97] *Wyatt* 1956 NAC 119 (S).
[98] 27 of 1913.
[99] 18 of 1936.

areas' in terms of the Act.[100] If there is no evidence as to the race of the person concerned (and presumably where the place of residence is outside one of the homelands), then appearance and lifestyle become the critical factors.[101] Production of an identity document is not conclusive proof of race for the purposes of the Black Administration Act.[102]

Because of the reliance on the test of racial descent, it follows that if a litigant is an artificial person, such as a company,[103] tribal authority,[104] or regional authority,[105] it would not qualify as African because it could not be racially typed.[106] On the other hand, because a voluntary association has no separate legal personality, it can be treated as if it were an African provided that all members are African.[107] In *Zion Church of Christ v Moraba*,[108] the court made it clear that race should be established with reference to the constitution of the organization. Hence, where membership was restricted to Africans only, the organization would be presumed Black regardless of its actual composition.[109]

The racial limitation on jurisdiction has had the effect of excluding an important class of litigants from the chiefs' courts: commercial corporations. By virtue of their regular appearance to recover contract debts, they are, apart from the state, the most powerful and frequent users of the courts. But businessmen and traders, even if they are African and even if they do not sue in their corporate capacity, are prevented from using chiefs' courts because their claims are governed by common law, not African customary law. The net result of these restrictions is to preserve chiefs' courts for domestic and petty civil disputes and for the prosecution of minor criminal offences.

The final jurisdictional limitation is a residential requirement. It has been held that a chief's jurisdiction is not based on the political allegiance of his subjects. His competence is strictly territorial and is confined to persons resident within his chiefdom regardless of their affiliation to his tribe.[110] In accordance with a well-established tradition in tribal courts, it has been held that only the defendant need be resident;[111] but a non-resident defendant may confer

---

[100] *Masholo* 1944 NAC (C&O) 25.
[101] See, eg, *Nkabinde v Nkabinde & another* 1944 WLD 112 and *Ngqoyi v Da Conciecao* 1946 NAC (N&T) 49.
[102] *Khamanga v Matete* 1975 BAC 63 (C).
[103] *Gumede v Bandhla Vukani Bakithi Ltd* 1950 (4) SA 560 (N) and *Khumalo v Insulezibensi Ubopumuze Swartkop Native Co* 1954 NAC 70 (NE).
[104] *Mcwebeni Tribal Authority v Ndamase* 1962 NAC 53 (S).
[105] *Mda v Fingo Regional Authority* 1969 (1) SA 528 (E).
[106] *Sachs NO & another v Mdhluli* 1956 NAC 43 (C); *Ndebele v Bantu Christian Catholic Church in Zion* 1956 NAC 184 (C); *Zulu Congregational Church v Maseko & another* 1957 NAC 146 (NE); *Christian Apostolic Church of SA v Madonsela* 1970 NAC 21 (NE).
[107] *Mdhluli v Zion Apostolic Church of SA & another* 1945 NAC (N&T) 63; *Korsten African Ratepayers' Association v Petane* 1955 NAC 136 (S).
[108] 1982 AC 337 (C).
[109] There is a second proviso to the definition of 'Black' providing that certain juristic persons, representatives of deceased estates and liquidators of joint estates may be deemed 'Blacks'. But since this definition was applicable only to s 10 of the Act, now repealed by s 2 of Act 34 of 1986, it does not affect the competence of chiefs' or headmen's courts.
[110] *Monete v Setshuba* 1948 NAC (C&O) 22; and see Pospisil (1981) 19 *J Legal Pluralism* 105.
[111] *Monete's* case supra.

jurisdiction on the court by submitting to it.[112]

The term 'resident' is, of course, a technical term in the common law. Because the chiefs' and headmen's courts are not supposed to apply common law, it would seem appropriate that they interpret this connecting factor in accordance with customary ideas of belonging to an area. Somewhat illogically, however, in *Ex parte Minister of Native Affairs*,[113] it was held that residence must be construed according to the common law.

The chiefs' areas of jurisdiction, which were previously part of South Africa, now nearly all fall within the national or the self-governing territories. In so far as these places have retained the relevant provisions of the Black Administration Act, the situation described above still applies. In Transkei, Ciskei, Bophutha-tswana and KwaNdebele, tribal courts were reconstituted along the same lines as the South African model but with occasional changes in jurisdiction and procedure.[114] In Bophuthatswana, legislation was passed empowering the President to authorize a chief, headman or the chairman of a community authority to hear civil claims arising out of customary law.[115] Two points of difference with the South African system should be noted: tribal courts no longer share jurisdiction with magistrates' courts (they have exclusive competence); and their jurisdiction over persons is based on tribal affiliation, regardless of where the litigant happens to live or work.[116] Appeals lie to the magistrates' courts. Transkei has replaced the provisions of the Black Administration Act with its own Chiefs' Courts Act.[117] The main purpose seems to have been to delete the racist language of its precursor; but in addition nine Regional Authority Courts[118] having concurrent jurisdiction with magistrates' courts over any person subject to customary law were created.[119] Similarly, Ciskei has replaced the South African provisions on chiefs' courts with its own Administrative Authorities Act.[120]

(3) Appeals and concurrent jurisdiction

[18] SECTION 12(4) BLACK ADMINISTRATION ACT 38 OF 1927

Any party to a suit in which a Black chief, headman or chief's deputy has given judgment may appeal therefrom to any magistrate's court which would have had jurisdiction had the proceedings in the first instance been instituted in a magistrate's court, and if the appellant has noted his appeal in the manner and within the period prescribed by regulation under sub-section (6), the execution of the judgment shall be suspended until the appeal has been decided (if it was prosecuted at the time and in the manner so

---

[112] *Zulu v Mbata* 1937 NAC (N&T) 6.
[113] 1941 AD 53.
[114] See Bekker 18–26.
[115] Traditional Courts Act 29 of 1979.
[116] Section 5(1).
[117] 6 of 1983.
[118] 13 of 1982.
[119] Section 3.
[120] 37 of 1984. KwaNdebele is the only national state to have used its legislative powers to regulate chiefs' and headmen's courts. By Act 3 of 1984 these courts were freshly constituted, although still along the same lines as their counterparts in South Africa.

prescribed) or until the expiration of the last-mentioned period if the appeal was not prosecuted within that period, or until the appeal has been withdrawn or has lapsed: Provided that no such appeal shall lie in any case where the claim or the value of the matter in dispute is less than R10, unless the court to which the appellant proposes to appeal, has certified after summary enquiry that the issue involves an important principle of law.[121]

Under s 29A(1) of the Magistrates' Courts Act[122] the court, when entertaining an appeal, may hear new evidence. This means that it would be more correct to describe the hearing as a retrial than an appeal.[123] Although provision is made in the Rules of Court[124] for keeping a written record of the proceedings, this does not include a record of the evidence heard, and so it may well happen that the evidence must be called again.

A copy of the written record must be delivered to a local magistrate within two months of the date of judgment, otherwise the judgment will lapse.[125]

It was held that commissioners' courts had no power to review judgments given by chiefs and headmen; they had powers of appeal only.[126] With respect to magistrates' courts, however, this must be regarded as an open question.

Although the appeal court may nullify a chief's judgment where customary law was wrongly applied to a claim sounding in the common law, it is not free to alter the cause of action at will. Hence, as a general rule, the magistrate must continue to apply customary law on appeal.[127]

A magistrate's court is also a court of first instance. Its jurisdiction with regard to person, usually cause of action, and sometimes area may overlap with that of chiefs' and headmen's courts. The implications of concurrent jurisdiction have never been fully explored. It is not certain, for instance, whether principles of lis alibi pendens and res judicata apply in these circumstances.[128] Thus, although it has been held that while proceedings are under way in one court they should not be instituted in another, there is no rule prohibiting this.[129] Similarly, despite a ruling that chiefs' judgments were res judicata in commissioners' courts,[130] it has also been held that *any* chief's judgment is appealable even if it is not final.[131] And, of course, the appeal is not an appeal in the usual sense of the word because it may involve retrial.

There are at least two undesirable consequences of the overlap in jurisdiction. The first is the opportunity allowed for forum-shopping: a plaintiff is free to use the court that gives him or her the most effective remedy, no matter whether this

---

[121] And see Rule 9 of the Rules of Court for Chiefs and Headmen n151 below; Khumalo 42–6.
[122] 32 of 1944.
[123] Compare Swanepoel (1978) 11 *De Jure* 113 and *Kumalo v Mbata* 1969 BAC 48 (NE) with *Gumede v Makhathini* 1978 AC 1 (NE).
[124] Rule 6.
[125] Rule 7(2).
[126] *Bhulose* 1947 NAC (N&T) 5; *Latha v Latha & another* 1969 BAC 45 (NE).
[127] *Ntshingili & others v Mncube* 1975 BAC 100 (NE).
[128] Swanepoel (1977) 10 *De Jure* 350–62 and op cit n123 121–7.
[129] *Mdumane v Mtshakule* 1948 NAC (C&O) 28; *Mduduma v Sitwayi* 1970 BAC 19 (S).
[130] *Tsautsi v Nene & another* 1952 NAC 73 (S).
[131] *Ntsabalala v Piti* 1956 NAC 111 (S).

prejudices the defendant.[132] The second is the possibility that an action initiated in the wrong court may have to be moved to the correct forum, with consequent loss of time and money. In South Africa no provision has been made for this eventuality. Most legal systems in southern Africa authorize the clerk of court to decide in which tribunal an action should be pursued.[133] This is not the best solution to the problem because an unqualified person is given extensive powers that can be exercised before all the facts and legal issues of the case have been disclosed. It would be more appropriate if the clerk's powers were advisory only.

(4) Functioning and procedure

(a) Structure and aim of the trial

In the following extract the trial procedures in a headman's court are described.

[19] HAMMOND-TOOKE *THE BHACA* 214–19

The most outstanding feature of Bhaca court procedure is its informality, in fact the general impression is almost one of nonchalance and, occasionally, chaos. This is superficial, however, and stems largely from our own preoccupation with the niceties of legal procedure. Local cases are heard at the kraal of the location headman. The court is held preferably in the shade of a tree. There is no dock or witness-box, and the vast body of procedural technicalities, so prominent a feature of western courts, is entirely lacking. Cases are usually heard in the late morning, and from about ten o'clock onwards men begin arriving on horseback and on foot, joining those who are already there and are sitting in a large semicircle on the grass in front of the cattle-kraal. When the headman appears all rise to their feet and greet him by his praise name, and remain standing until he takes his seat opposite them, either sitting, like them, on the ground, or on a chair or log. Late comers, as they arrive salute the headman and the court ("Zulu! Nebandla") before sitting down.

After greetings have been exchanged and a short time spent in desultory conversation and banter, the first plaintiff is called. He stands before the court and presents his complaint, which is heard in comparative silence. Now and then someone may chip in with a question, or ask the speaker to speak louder, or repeat a sentence he has not heard clearly. Questions asked are often very much to the point, eg at Mhlotsheni a young girl, plaintiff in a case of attempted rape, was asked whether she had cried out or not, but, on the other hand, much irrelevant evidence is admitted. . . . In a small community personality conflicts and jealousies are well known, as well as the personal characteristics of the litigants, and much information, considered irrelevant in our impersonalized courts, has a most practical bearing on the point at issue. If a member of the court, by his questions, shows that he has not grasped the significance of a point, he is enlightened by his neighbours, and it sometimes happens that a heated argument is carried on by two men, perhaps at opposite ends of the semicircle, even while evidence is being led. A general shout for them to keep quiet is not an unusual occurrence. After the plaintiff has stated his case the defendant presents his defence, and any witnesses are called. No attempt is made to segregate the witnesses from each other or to prevent collusion. After all the

---

[132] An empirical study done in an African township in Harare against the background of a similar court system confirmed a decidedly opportunistic attitude to the court structure: Stopforth *Two Aspects of Social Change*.

[133] See s 16 of the Swaziland Magistrates Courts Act Proc 66 of 1938; s 16 of the Botswana Subordinate Courts Proc 51 of 1938 and s 31A of the Subordinate Courts (Amendment) Act 23 of 1969; s 8(2) of the Lesotho Subordinate Courts Proc 5 of 1964.

evidence has been heard conversation becomes general, all features of the case are thoroughly discussed, and witnesses are questioned on any point which may need clarifying. No written evidence is taken and no woman may be a member of the court, although she may give evidence and obtain justice through it. In the latter case she must be assisted by a male relative. Members of the court come and go as they please; late arrivals unselfconsciously interrupt proceedings by going up to the headman and kissing his hand in salute; now and then a man will get up from his place and go behind the cattle-kraal to relieve himself. In questioning the witnesses and accused, some stand, the better to be heard, but the majority remain seated and shout their observations to the court in general—although ostensibly to the headman. If the noise is too great for the witnesses to be heard he will warn them to be quiet.

The composition of the court is very flexible. Theoretically all adult members of the location may attend and take part in the discussions: even young men of 23 or 24 attend and sometimes play a prominent part, but much depends on a man's personality or eloquence as to the extent of his influence in discussion and the weight of his opinion. After a lengthy, and often discursive, discussion the headman sums up the general feeling of the court and, if necessary, quotes precedent in support of the findings. Sometimes, indeed, no formal verdict is given, particularly if a verdict is not accepted by one of the parties and the court is divided on the issue. This is distinctly rare, and the parties usually know who is morally in the wrong and public opinion forces eventual submission. In clear-cut issues the headman's decision is final. To a large extent justice depends on the character of the presiding headman—although he may be forced by the weight of the court's opinion. . . .

Evidence is also given in the form of exhibits—a torn dress, axe, weapons, etc.—but it is doubtful whether or not this is a western innovation. Procedure is not fixed. At one case, where someone objected to the fact that the principal witness for the defence was not present, another chipped in with, "This is the headman's court, not the office where there must be a plaintiff, defendant and witnesses".

When satisfaction cannot be obtained at the headman's court, the dissatisfied party has recourse to the court of the chief. One day a week is set aside at Lugangeni for the hearing of appeal cases from the various locations (cases involving members of the Lugangeni location are heard at the court of the location headman). Formerly cases were heard in the *inkundla* (courtyard) of the Great Place, but today a mud-brick courthouse has been erected. When cases are to be heard, long wooden forms are placed in the courtroom, and a table is placed at the head of the room with a chair for the chief. His secretary sits on his left, for all evidence is taken down, with carbon copies, in a notebook, although no oath is administered. Here the procedure is more formal, modelled to some degree on the commissioner's court at Mount Frere. An important departure from indigenous custom is the fact that witnesses in a case are heard separately so that they will not be influenced by other evidence. The case is heard *de novo* as no written evidence is taken at the headman's court level. The statements of both plaintiff and defendant are recorded by the secretary, while the chief himself makes notes on a pad. Questions are asked almost exclusively by the chief, or his secretary, and occasionally by the chief's *indvuna*—although other members of the court may ask pertinent questions if authorized to do so by a nod from the chief. Despite this relative sophistication, directly attributable to contact, there is still a far greater degree of informality than is permissible in western courts; people may come and go as long as they do so quietly; a man may go outside for a stone to put underneath a rickety bench, and the attempts of the accused, or witnesses, to get out of a tight corner are met with laughter. Proceedings are obviously enjoyed by all. Not only old men ask questions and state their views, and there is an increasing tendency for the more educated younger men to take part.

After all the evidence has been heard the chief confers with his secretary and *indvuna* as to the appropriate judgment, whether to find for or against the accused, or whether to call for further witnesses. Whatever the verdict is, the chief sums up the evidence and gives the reason for his decision, his points being received with affirmatory gestures and nods by the court or with dissentient voices. If the chief cannot come to a decision himself he throws the matter open to the court while the principals and witnesses go out, in the hope that out of the discussion some agreement might emerge. After a decision has been given the winner of the case goes up to the chief and kisses his hand while the loser is formally asked whether he wishes to give notice of appeal to the court of the commissioner. It should be noticed, however, that the procedure of the chief's court just described is a new development, showing strong western influence. Formerly, it seems certain that the chief's court was identical in character to that of a headman and possessed its informal quality. The commissioner's court also acts as a court of appeal from that of the chief, although evidence is led *de novo*. The court of a location headman is a court of first instance for the people of that location, and disputes between people of the various neighbourhood units are brought to him for settlement. If the case is too "heavy" or complicated to be satisfactorily settled at the headman's court, or concerns homicide or treason, it will be taken to that of the chief, and, if necessary, to that of the commissioner. Under the present system of administration (but to be changed under the Bantu Authorities system) it is possible to sidestep completely both the minor courts and go straight to the commissioner, a course increasingly taken by the more sophisticated school people.[1] The two disaffected locations of Mhlotsheni and Lutateni, for instance, refused to take cases from their headman to Chief Makhaula, and took appeals straight to Mount Frere. Thus is the authority of the chief undermined and the pattern of political power inexorably changed.

A factor encouraging the compounding of disputes privately is the levying of court fees. Today a fee of £1 (R2) (formerly a goat or sheep) is charged to "open" a case at the chief's court. Informants stated that it is never paid in kind nowadays. . . . All damages must be paid at the Great Place of the location headman, or, if imposed by the chief, at the capital, and, if paid in cattle, one is retained by the court as a fee. This is comparable to the Mpondo *unthethelelo*, or beast given to a chief as a thank-offering for giving a favourable judgment. Informants stated that there was often much difficulty in enforcing decisions. Today the chief cannot enforce his decisions as formerly, by force of arms, and at no time was self-help permitted among the Bhaca.

Generally, enforcement of a decision is left to the parties concerned, and the withdrawal of the use of force since annexation has led to a serious diminution of the prestige of the tribal courts.

Formerly the penalty in civil cases was always a fine in cattle, sheep or goats, which were attached, if necessary, by a special messenger of the chief. This was the *unsila*, who derived his name from the tail of a leopard which he carried as a badge of office (*unsila*, a tail). It was a serious offence to resist or obstruct the *unsila* in the execution of his duty, and was punishable by the payment of a fine of a goat. Nowadays the chief has, in fact, little power to enforce his decisions, and much must be left to public opinion and the compulsion of internalized attitudes of respect and obedience. In extreme cases, however, where the messenger considers that he is unable to effect the seizure of the property without a breach of the peace, he may report to the judgment creditor who can apply to the commissioner for a process in aid. If this is granted the messenger of the court will act as if the judgment were that of the commissioner's court. This procedure has become necessary due to the virtual emasculation of the chief's compulsive powers formerly resident in his control over the tribal army. In the olden days any tribesman who refused to act on an order from the chief's court would be "eaten up", his stock confiscated and his crops destroyed. Today, after almost a century of White rule, the chief has virtually no organized force at his disposal.

Note

1. Denoting educated, Christian and notionally 'westernized' people.

Gluckman pioneered the study of dispute processing in Africa. His work on the Barotse[134] involved many searching questions, including the role of law in settling disputes, the value of western legal concepts for cross-cultural studies, and the dynamics of trial processes. One of Gluckman's main concerns was to show how particular socio-political structures influence the modes of settling disputes. He revealed that Barotse society, which he called 'tribal', ie dominated by 'multiplex' relationships, would tend to stress the value of reconciliation, which in turn would determine the way that facts are proved and rules applied.

[20] GLUCKMAN *THE IDEAS IN BAROTSE JURISPRUDENCE* 7–11

Since most people in any tribe live in a complex of social relations of this kind, a large number of the disputes arising over both property and the fulfilment of obligations are between kinsmen, or at least between persons in a quasi-kinship with one another. These disputes are therefore inevitably very entangled. What appears to be a trifling dispute, to cite an example from my own experience, over the neglect of a woman to give her father a cup of beer may bring to a head a long record of festering troubles and produce recitals by both parties of grievances exacerbated by smoldering irritations over points of fact. . . .

But it is specifically the interplay of social relations, focused temporarily on some dispute, which is required to illuminate the full mechanism of social control in so small a society. Judgments on the administration of law can go sadly astray in the absence of such information. And it is information on this interplay that is also left out in historical records of judgments, once writing comes into use—especially after writing also begins to restrict pleadings so that these pare down the elements that come before a tribunal. . . .

During each dispute kin who are ostensibly outside the quarrel at issue side with one or the other litigant, and the way in which they take sides is influenced by degrees of kinship, by factional alignments within villages, by past records of friendships and hostilities, and also—this is most important—by ideas of justice, judgments on which of the parties is in the right and which in the wrong. Resentment is provoked to breed further disputes by the manner in which persons align themselves in each quarrel. The festering troubles are exacerbated because in these societies it is believed that one's fellows are responsible not only for injuries patently inflicted on one, but maybe also for mishaps that we would describe as "natural misfortunes". Sickness, crop failure, the illness of cattle, bad luck at fishing, death within the kin grouping, any of these may be ascribed to the witchcraft or sorcery of another. Breach of a taboo or omission of some appropriate offering to the spirits may cause affliction to someone other than the wrong-doer, or even to the community as a whole. A natural misfortune, so to speak, founds an action in tort. In this sort of situation, only the surface eruption out of a factional struggle bred by an increase in numbers of the kin grouping, which produces pressure on resources and competition for power, may be all that is before the court.

I shall consider later how the law of wrongs is influenced by this background. Here I want to emphasize how difficult a task it lays upon those whose duty it is to settle disputes between kinsfolk. Many writers have discussed the process of law in tribal societies in such phrases as restoring the social balance or equilibrium, securing the agreement of both parties to a compromise judgment and, above all, reconciling the parties. This is the main aim of Barotse judges in all cases that arise between kin, for it is a dominant value of the society that villages should not break up and that kin should remain united.

In order to bring out all the facts that are relevant to this kind of dispute, the judges allow each party to recite the full tale of his grievances. The judges, who at the capital may number a score or more, helped by anyone else attending the session, cross-examine the

---

[134] *Judicial Process among the Barotse of Northern Rhodesia.* See further Koch et al (1976) 10 *Law & Soc R* 443.

parties as well as the witnesses these have brought. They may call for further evidence. There is no paring down of the facts in advance for presentation to court, and any judge who knows the parties may contribute that knowledge; the fiction of judicial ignorance is missing in all respects. Nor does a judge recuse himself if he is related to the parties; in fact if he is related to a wrongdoer he should emphasize the wrongdoing. But if he is a party to a case, he cannot sit as a judge.

Although the judges listen to all kinds of statements of fact, they do classify evidence as interested and disinterested, and direct or circumstantial or hearsay. They prefer disinterested and direct evidence, and may advise parties and witnesses not to repeat hearsay, particularly in cases not involving kinsmen. They look for corroboration, and they weigh evidence by several tests. Among the Barotse magical tests are used only in charges of witchcraft and sorcery that can be settled in no other way. Ordeals, like licking the red-hot blade of a hoe or picking pebbles out of a pot of boiling water, were ordered in the past if the verdict on theft or adultery was "almost certainly guilty but not proven". In modern times, charges of witchcraft are not tried in officially established Barotse courts, and ordeals and torture are never used at capitals; if employed at district courts they are usually detected and punished.

After they have heard the evidence, the judges give judgment on the issue: they proceed in order from the most junior to the head of the court. This last, and not a majority of judgments, is what counts, but it is subject to the king's confirmation if the trial be at the capital.

Since the aim is to reconcile the litigants, the Barotse consider a judge to lack forensic wisdom if he rushes straight to the point at issue either in cross-examination or in judgment. The wise and skilful judge inquires into all the grievances that are brought up; he tries to bring into the open the whole record of quarrels and breaches of obligation on both sides. Yet a striking feature of this procedure is that judges during this cross-examination already begin to pass both legal and moral opinions on the actions of the parties and on the sentiments and motives that may be reasonably deduced to explain those actions. For though the judges are trying to reconcile the parties, in the hope that the threatened relationship may endure, they have to defend the law. Hence they state the law and attack any departure from its standards. Above all, in cross-examination the judges try to get the litigants themselves to admit where they have erred, by showing them how the evidence—either their own or that of witnesses—convicts them of breach.

Since Barotse is, or was, a homogeneous society, all of whose members accept the same standards of rightdoing and wrongdoing as the judges, litigants always cast their own stories in terms of these standards. This assists the judges to bring home to them their misdemeanours. Usually by the time the judgment begins, the judges have already made clear where they stand. As the Barotse and other tribes do not have lawyers to represent parties and to cross-examine opponents, this task falls on the judges. Questions in cross-examination are generally framed on the assumption that a person is lying, and it has therefore been incorrectly alleged that in African courts an accused is assumed by the judges to be guilty and must prove his innocence. In fact, in Barotse and all other African courts I know, guilt must be demonstrated. It seems to me that we can understand in similar terms an allegation made by some Anglo-Saxon lawyers, who are used to the judge as an umpire in the juridical contest between counsel, that the French court assumes guilt which the accused must rebut. Like the Barotse judge, the French judge is under a duty to find out the truth himself and therefore he himself conducts much of the cross-examination, with the apparent implication that the accused is lying. . . .

Similarly, Barotse judges not only have to try to reconcile the immediately disputing parties but also, since they are (as they themselves state) "the law" (*Mulao*), they affirm that law against all parties and witnesses wherever the evidence shows default. Therefore they express strong approval or disapproval over many matters raised by the litigants. But they can give decisions that a person be punished or make restitution only on certain limited issues with which they are empowered to deal by accepted rule, and the issue before the court must be one over which the court has power. Occasionally, therefore, an aggrieved person who has been seriously affronted or neglected in terms of general moral norms by a kinsman or in-law, but lacks an issue on which he can sue, will himself commit an offence that forces the defaulter to prosecute him. He goes to court secure in the knowledge that though he may lose the case, the judges will publicly upbraid his opponent for all the latter's breaches of moral obligation.

Holleman is one of the many anthropologists to document trials heard by tribal courts.[135] One such case, considered a model of its kind, concerned a long-standing conflict in a Shona chieftaincy between a father and his son. Although, in that society, there was general reluctance to air family disputes in public,[136] the aggrieved father precipitated a public hearing of his complaints by committing a series of conspicuous offences, some of which, because of their impact on community resources, were quite serious 'criminal' acts. Holleman showed that in simple societies, such as the one he was studying, grievances amongst kinfolk were quite likely to erupt into this type of public display because great importance was vested in family relationships. In contrast, in complex industrialized societies, personal conflict is excluded from the public arena. This means that a troubled relationship, like the one in Holleman's case study, would not be deemed a *legal* issue and hence would not be brought to court. Instead, it would be handled by a social worker, priest or psychologist.[137]

All the ethnographic accounts of dispute processing in tribal courts highlight the role of the community. In order to give this proper emphasis Holleman eschewed the usual dialectical model of the trial process—plaintiff's statement of claim (thesis), counter argument by defendant (antithesis), and judgment by the court (synthesis)—in favour of the following. In the opening phase, both parties state their cases and call their witnesses; in the second stage, the issue is thrown open to the public for debate; and in the third phase, the case is summed up and judgment is pronounced.[138] In terms of this structure it became apparent that the litigants had to persuade not only the judge but also the audience. Further, the judge, who lacked independent means to impose his will on the parties, also had to appropriate community sentiment as a sanction to back up his judgment.[139]

Where the principal aim of the trial is to reconcile the parties, there is obviously no need to dwell on any rules that might be involved in the dispute. Similarly, the immediate ('legal') issues that might have precipitated the case have little significance for the eventual result.[140] By implication there is no strictly formulated concept of legal relevance, in the sense of needing to extract certain

---

[135] Holleman op cit n20 16–47. See further: Holleman *African Interlude* 86–94; Bourdillon 147–67; Mönnig 310–28.

[136] Schapera 283–4; Myburgh & Prinsloo *Indigenous Public Law in KwaNdebele* 111–12; Griffiths in Allott & Woodman *People's Law and State Law* 218; cf Roberts (1971) 15 *JAL* 73ff.

[137] This confirms the view that the definition of disputes should take account of the social systems in which they are embedded: Cain & Kulcsar op cit n24 377–8. And see: Friedman & Percival (1976) 10 *Law & Soc R* 267; Merry (1979) 13 *Law & Soc R* 919–20. The results of these studies show that only divorce actions come before western-style courts.

[138] Holleman op cit n20 46–7; cf the model suggested by Von Benda-Beckmann in Allott & Woodman op cit n136 78–9.

[139] Public opinion is the principal source of coercion in acephalous societies: Peters in Gluckman *The Allocation of Responsibility* 157.

[140] See Von Benda-Beckmann in Allott & Woodman op cit n136 91.

key issues from the complex of facts that constitute the dispute. Such a requirement would detract from the overall aim, because to achieve reconciliation, the whole relationship of the parties over an indefinite period of time must be considered.[141] The dispute is seen in terms of the parties' relationship, not in terms of predetermined, normative categories.[142]

(b) Facts

In the typical family or neighbourhood dispute, the verity of the facts is seldom in issue, and then only in certain predictable types of case (such as adultery, seduction, theft and witchcraft). This means that witnesses do not have an especially productive role. They seldom add new information nor do they elucidate existing testimonies; their main function is the rhetorical one of strengthening their principals' arguments. There are no customary-law rules regulating what type of evidence is admissible. And formal oath-taking is ad hoc and infrequent.[143] All this is to be expected in instances where the dispute involves kinfolk or neighbours, because the matter is usually public knowledge before it comes to court.

Contradictory versions of what happened obviously place the facts in contention, and this is likely to occur when the dispute did not arise from a public incident or when its very nature (such as seduction or adultery) precludes notoriety. In such circumstances, Gluckman showed how the courts assess the credibility of the parties and their witnesses. They do this by skilful cross-examination aimed at catching out the deponent in departures from an agreed norm of reasonable behaviour. Factual truth is never disentangled from observance of norms.

> 'The judicial establishment of "truth" is not always simply finding that "such-and-such is what happened". Legal truth involves the assessment of what happened in terms of both legal and moral norms. For the judges have to find out who has conformed with the law, and who has broken it. Indeed, the statements of the parties are usually cast so that they seem to have conformed with these norms, and it is by these norms that the judges examine and attack evidence.'[144]

Both the complainant and defendant try to vindicate their behaviour 'at the bar of right conduct'.

> 'But in thus seeking to exculpate themselves, the litigants themselves provide a standard against which their behaviour may be measured. . . . They assert in effect that their behaviour is not governed by caprice or sheer wilfulness.'[145]

In order to select the most plausible of competing accounts, a court may go one step further and use a presumption. This is an estimate of probability based

---

[141] Holleman in Fortes & Patterson *Studies in African Social Anthropology* 77.

[142] Cf Weber's legal rationality above, 9–10.

[143] Allott in Cotran & Rubin *Readings in African Law* v1 83ff; and see: Holleman in Fortes & Patterson op cit n141 75ff and Myburgh & Prinsloo op cit n136 136–43.

[144] Gluckman op cit n21 82.

[145] Epstein *Juridical Techniques and the Judicial Process* 8. Gluckman's and Epstein's claims about the use of the 'reasonable man' in customary law have been much discussed and criticized: Diamond (1956) 5 *ICLQ* 627–8; Hoebel (1961) 13 *Stanford LR* 437. See Gluckman's reply in Kuper & Kuper op cit n31 120ff and the 'Reappraisal' in *Judicial Process* 2ed n21. See too: Epstein (1972) 7 *Law & Soc R* 643. There is of course nothing peculiar about the African courts' use of the concept of reasonableness; it is a technical judicial device the world over: Moore op cit n13 226.

on notionally rational motivations for what might otherwise be inexplicable behaviour.[146] Presumptions are drawn from conventional wisdom. They are 'rooted deep in customary patterns of behaviour, values and attitudes'.[147] A presumption is not always explicitly incorporated into the law as a distinct rule; rather it may underlie other rules, whether of substance or procedure. Especially when an offence is necessarily secret—theft, illicit sexual liaisons, and witchcraft are examples—there is unlikely to be any direct evidence of commission, and the only way of discovering what happened is for the court to presume the existence of certain facts. So, in cases of seduction or adultery, customary law has a procedural rule in the form of a presumption, that women never lie about the identity of their lovers.[148] If the offence has a supernatural dimension, the court may appeal to a mystical means for discovering the truth: the process of divination or the ordeal.[149]

(c) Rules

The significance of rules in the trial procedure can be explained by referring to the purpose of the trial (ie reconciliation or adjudication) or more indirectly to criteria altogether extrinsic to the dispute, such as the absence of centralized political structures.[150] In the following extract, however, a new perspective was opened on this question: the internal dynamics of the trial process may decide the relevance of rules.

[21] COMAROFF & ROBERTS in HAMNETT *SOCIAL ANTHROPOLOGY AND LAW* 78, 83–109

[I]s there any systematic pattern underlying the invocation, manipulation and application of stated norms in Tswana processes of dispute settlement? . . . This brief review of the literature indicates that existing explanations of cross-cultural variation in patterns of norm invocation and utilization are largely unconvincing. The common feature of these explanations is that they begin with the assumption that factors extrinsic to the actual conduct of disputes (such as the political organisation of the society and the structure of its dispute settlement agencies) determine the underlying pattern.

Without denying the importance of explanations of this kind, we argue here that much more has got to be known about the internal detail of individual systems before such explanations can be successfully pursued on a cross-cultural level. In other words, intrinsic features have got to be more fully explored and understood before it is worth considering those of an extrinsic character.

It is in this light that we reconsider the invocation and utilization of norms in the Tswana dispute settlement process. . . .

The Batswana perceive the regularities of their everyday lives as being governed by a body of norms collectively described as *melao le mekgwa wa Setswana*, a phrase which has generally been translated as "Tswana law and custom". These norms also furnish the criteria and standards whereby any dispute should be settled. However, the blanket description "Tswana law and custom" covers a wide repertoire of different norms, and

---

[146] Epstein *Juridical Techniques* 12.
[147] Epstein op cit 15.
[148] Epstein op cit 14.
[149] Bennett & Scholtz (1979) 12 *CILSA* 297; Vansina in Kuper & Kuper op cit n31 113–14.
[150] See above, 54.

those that are of critical importance in dispute settlement do not form a separate or identifiable sub-system.

Thus the repertoire embraces a range of precepts commencing with rules of etiquette and polite behaviour, extending through norms enjoying broad social acceptance, and concluding with mandatory injunctions issued in legislative form by the tribal authorities. Related to this continuum, it should be observed that even among those norms which are most important in dispute settlement specificity varies greatly. Thus, precise substantive prescriptions (e.g. that the youngest son should inherit his mother's homestead) shade into precepts of a more general character (e.g. *lentswe la moswi ga letlolwe*, "the voice of a dead man is not transgressed"), and lastly, into maxims and principles of a broad abstract kind (e.g. that agnates should live in harmony with one another). Norms of differing degrees of specificity may, of course, be adduced in such a way as to conflict, the normative level at which argument proceeds may change during a dispute, and the participants may attempt to impose competing normative definitions upon the issue under debate.

We will show that, in presenting a case, Tswana disputants construct and rely upon a "paradigm of argument": that is, they attempt to convey a coherent picture of relevant events and actions *in terms of one or more (implicit or explicit) normative referents*. Any such "paradigm of argument" is sited in the requirements of a particular case, and is not fixed or pre-determined. Its degree of elaboration and integration depends upon several factors, such as the oratorical ability of the disputant, his expectations concerning the strategies of his opponent and his own strategic intentions. Moreover, the construction of the paradigm may vary over a number of hearings of the same dispute before different agencies, since the perceptions, expectations and strategies of the opposing parties may change or become progressively refined. The important point to note is that the complainant, who speaks first, establishes such a paradigm by ordering facts around normative referents which may or may not be made explicit. The defendant, in replying, may accept these normative referents, and hence the paradigm itself; under these circumstances he will argue over the facts *within the paradigm*. Alternatively, he may assert a competing paradigm by introducing different normative referents, in which case he may not contest the facts at all. At the higher levels, where the mode of settlement becomes one of adjudication, the third party responsible for adjudication (a headman or the chief) may order his decision within the agreed paradigm, choose between competing paradigms, or impose a fresh paradigm upon the issues under dispute. We will attempt to demonstrate that the isolation of such paradigms of argument, and the dynamics of their interaction, is crucial if we are to account for the invocation and utilization of norms in the dispute settlement process. . . .

Drawing these observations together, it seems that norms are explicitly invoked by a disputant only when he wishes to question the paradigm of argument elaborated by his opponent, and tries to assert control over (or change) the terms in which debate is proceeding. The complainant has no need to do this in the normal course of events, because the very manner in which he presents the alleged facts establishes his paradigm. Although it did not occur in either of the cases reported above, a Tswana complainant appears to enunciate a norm (or set of norms) only when he anticipates an effort on part of the defendant to question his construction of the dispute itself. . . . Thus, while norms are expressly invoked most frequently by defendants, a complainant may also do so when he wishes to erode his opponent's prospective paradigm in advance. . . .

The second dimension of norm invocation concerns the specificity or generality of the norms employed in dispute settlement. . . . [G]eneralised normative invocations (both implicit and explicit) are associated with arguments in which the relationships themselves are at issue, while substantive, precise ones tend to be a feature of disputes in which the conflict over a right or value is primarily emphasized. In many cases, of course, debate involves both the relationship and the value, and normative invocations reflect this in that both substantive and generalised references are made. Moreover, when disputants appeal to different orders of norm in opposition to one another, we would expect them to state, and argue over, the priority which they assign to competing norms.

In a later work the same authors constructed a model to explain the invocation of norms in Tswana courts.

[22] COMAROFF & ROBERTS *RULES AND PROCESSES* 115–17

[The model describes] respectively, the quality of the social link between the two parties and the nature of their intentions. . . . As this model indicates, the two dimensions intersect in such a manner as to generate four possible situational complexes: (1) that in which dispute over a specific value arises between persons involved in an essentially determinate relationship; (2) that in which confrontation over a specific value occurs in the context of a generalized bond; (3) that in which determinately linked persons contest the nature of their relationship; and (4) that in which the nature and quality of a generalized bond itself becomes the object of conflict between litigants.

MODEL OF PROCESSUAL FORMS

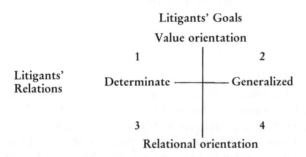

These four complexes may be linearly arranged as follows:
$$1 \rightarrow 2 \rightarrow 3 \rightarrow 4$$
This progression in turn describes the systematic variation of dispute processes in terms of a number of closely related features that underlie their form and content.

 Thus complex 1 would be typified by a contractual relationship in terms of which the dispute would be about a specific object; 2 might concern a dispute regarding inheritance; 3 a neighbourhood dispute and 4 a dispute regarding the general relations of kinfolk. Procedural flexibility increases consistently in the direction of 1 to 4; so too, will concern with the prior history and circumstantial factors of the dispute; the object of the dispute will become more generalized from 1 to 4; moreover, the linear progression from 1 to 4 also implies the increasing possibility that the disputants will differ over the definition of the nature of the dispute and hence may engage in competing efforts to impose their own *paradigms of argument* upon the case.

(d) *Procedure and execution of judgments*

Procedure in the chiefs' and headmen's courts is subject to only minimal regulation.[151] Although the rules of court are supposed not to change the customary modes of procedure,[152] common-law innovations have been

---

[151] The rules are contained in GN R2082 *Reg Gaz* 887 29 December 1967. For detailed commentary see Khumalo 37ff. See further the account by Myburgh & Prinsloo op cit n136 119–35.

[152] Rule 1. This principle has been retained in the national and independent states: Bekker 18–26.

introduced here and there; default judgment is a notable instance.[153] The scale of fees is determined by customary law, but failing any precise rule on this, the fees are prescribed.[154]

Rule 5 prohibits representation by legal practitioners. This prescription was designed to preserve procedural informality and to ensure that neither litigant would be given an unfair advantage by being allowed to engage counsel to argue the case. While this is a defensible policy with regard to the domestic and neighbourhood disputes which tribal courts are normally expected to hear, it is questionable in criminal matters. When a tribesman faces potential sanctions as extreme as banishment or dispossession of land, it is arguable that the procedural right of audi alteram partem should include a right of representation.[155]

Execution of judgment is in general terms governed by customary law except for cases where the judgment has to be executed outside the chief's area of jurisdiction or where the judgment debtor resists with a show of force. In such instances the chief's messenger must inform the judgment creditor, who may then have the judgment enforced through the offices of the local magistrate's court.[156]

IV COMMISSIONERS AND MAGISTRATES

(1) Commissioners' courts

The court system established in 1927 by the Black Administration Act included special courts staffed and organized by the Department of Native Affairs. These were the commissioners' courts, relatively informal and inexpensive tribunals, set up for the purpose of settling civil disputes amongst Africans. The functionaries presiding over them were supposed to be 'specially versed in native law',[157] and under 11(1) of the Act, they were given a discretion to apply either common law or customary law as appeared appropriate in the circumstances of the case. Customary law did not have to be specially proved; commissioners could take judicial notice of it, but where necessary they could call for the assistance of assessors.[158]

Although under s 16 of the Act the parties were entitled to be represented in court, the presiding officer was under a duty to assist any person without an attorney in order to prevent undue prejudice.[159]

The creation of these tribunals was part of the government's new policy of racial segregation. This meant that commissioners' courts were to be kept strictly separate from courts catering for whites. Under s 17(4) of the Act, once a

---

[153] Rule 2.

[154] Rule 13(2).

[155] Cf *S v Mukwevho*; *S v Ramukhuba* 1983 (3) SA 498 (V).

[156] Rule 8 refers to commissioners' courts, but since their abolition this must now presumably be read to mean magistrates' courts.

[157] *House of Assembly* Debates 28 April 1927 col 2907.

[158] Section 19(1) of the Act.

[159] *Sitole* 1940 NAC (N&T) 115; *Qubu v Jaca* 1973 BAC 352 (C) at 361. See Suttner's study of the attitude of the profession to litigation in commissioners' courts: University of Natal *Legal Aid in South Africa* 191–6.

commissioner's court had been constituted, the magistrate's court in the same area lost its civil jurisdiction over Africans. Only the Supreme Court retained concurrent jurisdiction, but of course it could not take judicial notice of customary law, and the fees and costs there were higher.[160]

In keeping with the policy of segregation, special courts had to be created to hear appeals from the commissioners' decisions.[161] In 1928 two appellate divisions were established, one for the Cape and Orange Free State, and the other for Natal and the Transvaal. In 1948 the areas of jurisdiction were delimited anew to create three divisions: Central, Southern, and North-Eastern. Under ss 14 and 18 of the Act, a further appeal could in certain very limited circumstances be lodged with the Appellate Division. This was the only point of connection between the ordinary courts and the African courts.

The performance of the commissioners' courts was criticized on many grounds[162] but their exercise of criminal jurisdiction earned them the most damning censure. In 1957 commissioners were empowered to hear prosecutions for offences committed by Blacks.[163] Although magistrates retained concurrent jurisdiction (and appeals lay to the Supreme Court),[164] the commissioners in practice soon assumed sole responsibility for the prosecution of more minor crimes, especially the notorious pass and influx control laws.[165] Eventually it became evident that the procedures being applied in the commissioners' courts had subjected Africans to a far lower standard of justice than practised elsewhere.[166]

[23] COMMISSION OF INQUIRY INTO THE STRUCTURE AND FUNCTIONING OF THE COURTS *FIFTH REPORT* PART V

6.1 Having considered all the relevant facts the Commission is satisfied that since the establishment of special courts for Blacks, Blacks have undergone a fundamental change as regards their standard of living, life-style, family life and education. It is particularly the urban Black that is subject to South African common law and statute law in his commercial transactions. Restricting urban Blacks under the present dispensation to the commissioners' courts in their civil litigation is unrealistic and unreasonable. That inhabitants of the same country should purely on the grounds of race be criminally prosecuted in separate courts for any offence whatever is, in the Commission's view, by any civilised standard, unnecessary, humiliating and repugnant. The Commission is satisfied that with the exception of courts of chiefs and headmen the policy of separate courts for Blacks is outmoded and obsolete. In the Commission's opinion it is essential that, without delay and in accordance with the guide-lines set forth in the paragraphs below, the separate courts for Blacks be amalgamated with the ordinary courts. . . .

---

[160] *Mbelle* 1947 (1) SA 782 (W). And see *Sigcau* 1941 CPD 71.

[161] Section 13 of the Black Administration Act.

[162] See Suttner (1968) 75 *SALJ* 443–5 and see Bekker (1975) 8 *De Jure* 157 regarding the Appeal Courts.

[163] Section 9 of the Black Administration Act.

[164] *Mfulwane & others v Matabane* 1959 (1) SA 145 (T). Regarding interdepartmental rivalry see the Hoexter Commission of Inquiry into the Structure and Functioning of the Courts *Fifth Report* Part V 3.5–3.20.

[165] Blacks (Urban Areas) Consolidation Act 25 of 1945 and Blacks (Abolition of Passes and Co-ordination of Documents) Act 67 of 1952.

[166] Monama *Is This Justice?* 56ff and West (1982) 81 *African Affairs* 468–73.

6.4 The amalgamation of the special courts for Blacks with the ordinary lower and superior courts poses the question whether the prescribed maximum tariffs for services rendered by practitioners in these courts should still apply under the new dispensation. These tariffs are lower than the similar tariffs that apply in the ordinary lower courts. The evidence before the Commission is that these tariffs are unrealistically low, so much so that legal representatives do not adhere to them. The practice is for costs which cannot be recovered on a party-and-party basis simply to be charged to a client on an attorney-and-client basis. The successful litigant suffers because he has to pay legal costs which should actually have been borne by the loser. In the light of this, the Commission can see no justification for the determination of special tariffs for actions based on Black law between Blacks only.

(2) Magistrates' courts

As a result of these recommendations, both the commissioners' courts and their courts of appeal were abolished.[167] The commissioners' judicial functions were taken over by the magistrates' courts.[168] In so far as this represented an attempt to ensure equality in the administration of justice, it must be applauded. Yet the reform of the South African court system rested on an assumption that magistrates' courts could provide services suitable for an educationally and financially deprived section of society, and in addition one with distinctive cultural expectations. With the abolition of the commissioners' courts, the benefits of lower fee tariffs and relative informality have been lost. Litigants are now expected to prosecute their cases on equal terms with legally represented adversaries, and they can no longer assume that the courts will take account of their special circumstances, such as indigence or lack of education.

Only one adjustment was made to meet the requirements of African civil litigants: magistrates were given the power to take judicial notice of customary law.[169] This amendment was subsequently repealed[170] and now *all* courts in the country may apply customary law.[171] Unfortunately these new powers were not complemented by the intimate knowledge of African affairs which gave commissioners their special expertise in African litigation.

In the circumstances, magistrates' courts cannot be described as 'accessible' to African litigants. A study undertaken in Kenya of a similar change in court structure confirms this impression.[172] From 1930 to 1969 the indigenous courts were progressively assimilated to western-style courts through changes in structure and procedure. While the number of civil cases they heard steadily declined, the number of criminal prosecutions increased. This happened mostly

---

[167] Act 34 of 1986. See the commentary by Prinsloo (1987) 20 *De Jure* 68ff.

[168] The same was true of the independent states: s 54 of the Transkei Constitution Act 15 of 1976; s 91 of Bophuthatswana Act 18 of 1977; s 52(1)(a) of Venda Act 9 of 1979 and s 76 of Ciskei Act 20 of 1981. Bekker 31 says that commissioners' courts in the self-governing territories were abolished by the Special Courts for Blacks Abolition Act 34 of 1986. He adds that (unlike South Africa) there is no appeal from chiefs' courts to magistrates' courts because, apart from Qwaqwa (Act 7 of 1988), these territories have not legislated on the matter. But, to the contrary, certain territories have specially legislated on this matter: Lebowa Act 5 of 1973 and Gazankulu Act 9 of 1973.

[169] Section 54A was inserted into the Magistrates' Courts Act 32 of 1944.

[170] Section 2 of Act 45 of 1988.

[171] See below, [32].

[172] Abel in Burman & Harrell-Bond *The Imposition of Law* 167.

in the rural areas; in the cities the overall litigation rate remained constant or it increased. But then, the author argued, western courts had special attractions for a heterogeneous urban population. Disputants there were not likely to be linked with one another in enduring social relationships. The win-or-lose approach of the courts was of no consequence to the parties because they had no need to preserve their association. A major hindrance to litigation was the high cost of obtaining professional representation, although it was also clear that the social and/or cultural distance between the people and the courts was another disincentive to suing. Even the content of civil litigation changed. While, due to demographic and social changes, there were fewer cases concerning family disputes and intentional delicts,[173] there were more contractual and economic claims. These, of course, were the monopoly of large corporations. The final outcome of this transformation is described below.

[24] ABEL in BURMAN & HARRELL-BOND *THE IMPOSITION OF LAW* 196–8

Two major trends in litigation are discernible as social and institutional variables are changed. First, tribal social structures and modern courts are incompatible; the introduction of the latter into the former leads to a decline in tribal litigation. This should be a matter of some concern, regardless of one's views concerning the relative worth of tribal and modern society. Tribal social relations can be found in all societies, irrespective of their level of technological development or mode of political organization. We are constantly rediscovering multiplex, enduring, affective relationships in economic life, in the extended family, within large institutions, in residential groupings, even between criminals and their victims. Tribal litigation is integrative; it preserves and even strengthens those relationships. If courts are modernized, one forum for tribal litigation is removed. Furthermore, the mere availability of modern courts seems to undermine tribal dispute processing elsewhere in the society. Many commentators recently have deplored the absence of tribal modes of dispute processing in contemporary western society.[1]

The second trend complements the first. Modern social structures and modern courts are compatible; the rate of modern litigation will rise in modern courts in urban areas, and only there. And modern litigation contributes to the development and maintenance of modern social structures in much the same fashion that tribal litigation integrated tribal society. In its ideal form litigants, who are strangers to each other aside from the focus of the dispute and are equals in resources and competence, assert competing claims in terms of a law that favors neither before an impartial judge who unilaterally pronounces and enforces an all-or-nothing judgment. There have certainly been times and places when actual litigation approximated this ideal type, though it is not clear from my data that litigation in contemporary urban Africa does so, or ever will. But the predictable enforcement of contractual obligations, the predication of tort liability upon fault, the free alienation of, and development of security interests in, property, even the greater freedom to form and dissolve family relationships—all can be found in the recent history of western legal systems. And this contribution of litigation to modern society can be valued on grounds that command a broad consensus. Modern litigation is an expression of liberal political and economic theory. The individual litigant, in seeking to maximize his self-interest under clearly defined rules, is seen by classical economics as competing in a free market and thus furthering the most efficient allocation of resources. Similarly, the modern litigant, in freeing himself from traditional social constraints and asserting his political rights, is achieving maximum self-realization of his individuality. Thus the introduction of modern courts into modernizing societies does foster liberal values.

---

[173] Such as the case presented by Holleman op cit n20 22; and see above, [20] and 75.

But this chapter, like other recent analyses,[2] also suggests that these attributes of litigation under liberal capitalism are short-lived, no more than a brief, transitional way station on the road toward patterns of litigation that offend against all the values of the rule of law. Three deviations from the ideal type of modern litigation are already visible in contemporary Africa. First, there is a decline in the accessibility of the court to individual litigants, and warning of a much more radical curtailment in the future, as primary courts are thoroughly professionalized. In modern society, where much interaction occurs between strangers who are not bound together by any relationship, individual disputants confronted with an increasingly inaccessible tribunal will simply terminate the relationship—they will "lump it".[3] Second, there is growing dominance of the court by criminal prosecution, and especially by administrative offenses, which renders it less attractive to potential litigants. Third, adjudication in modern courts, whether civil or criminal, becomes increasingly superficial—a rubber-stamping of decisions reached elsewhere.

In addition to the accentuation of the trends just described, three other developments have been reported by students of litigation in western society, and are clearly incipient in non-western societies as well. Civil litigation is increasingly dominated by large corporate entities, generally private, in much the same way that state prosecutions dominate the entire court structure. These large entities, "repeat players" in Galanter's terminology,[4] find that they can use the civil process efficiently and successfully to extract money from or compel actions by, individual, one-shot defendants. Their total dominance of such litigation transforms it from adjudication into a form of administration. Second, these large entities find that they can extend their control outside the courtroom, structuring their behavior and the behavior of those with whom they transact business in such a way as to ensure a favorable outcome in any future litigation; thus even what appears to be adjudication is in fact administration, when viewed from a larger perspective. Finally, the costliness of adjudication, even to large entities, leads to the development of specialized administrative tribunals that handle an increasing proportion of disputes—and are even more readily dominated by repeat players than are the courts.

The displacement of modern litigation by administration, like the displacement of tribal disputing by modern litigation, should also be a source of concern. Liberal values are subverted. Because litigation no longer takes place between equals, but rather between large entities and individuals who differ enormously in strength, we can expect resources to be misallocated and social and political freedom to be frustrated. And because the courts are shunned, both by individuals and by institutions, the rule of law, which depends on adjudication, is nullified. The significant rules of behavior are legislated by large entities, not by a democratic government. The model of post-liberal society consists of an oligarchy of corporate entities whose size, organization, and resources give them overwhelming advantages in political, social, and economic life. Individuals relate, if at all, only as co-members of the same entity. Litigation is merely a relatively unimportant mechanism by which those entities exercise control, and is almost totally irrelevant to individuals except as they are controlled by it. This dismal picture suggests that efforts to fiddle with litigation in post-modern society—to restore it to the ideal-typical model of liberal adjudication, for example, by extending legal representation or by creating new adjudicative institutions—are misguided. Rather, the issue is how to regain democratic control over the large entities themselves, which dominate the legal system just as they dominate the rest of society.

Notes

1. R Danzig (1973) 26 *Stanford LR* 1; R Danzig & M J Lowy (1975) 9 *Law & Soc R* 675; L Nader & L R Singer (1976) 51 *Calif State Bar J* 281.
2. M Galanter (1974) 9 *Law & Soc R* 95; R M Unger *Law in Modern Society*.
3. W L F Felstiner (1974) 9 *Law & Soc R* 63.
4. Galanter op cit.

V DIVORCE COURTS

[25] SECTION 10 ACT 9 OF 1929

(1) Notwithstanding anything in any other law contained, the [State President] may by proclamation in the *Gazette* establish Divorce Courts which shall be empowered to have jurisdiction to hear and determine suits of nullity, divorce and separation between blacks domiciled within their respective areas of jurisdiction in respect of marriage and to decide any question arising therefrom: provided that the Matrimonial Causes Jurisdiction Act 39 (Act 22 of 1939) shall *mutatis mutandis* apply with reference to the powers and jurisdiction of such courts. . . .

(5) An appeal from the judgment of a divorce court shall lie to the provincial or local division of the Supreme Court having jurisdiction.

Many unnecessary restrictions were imposed on the jurisdictional competence of these courts. The first was the rule, although this was not statutorily expressed, that they can apply only the common law, as modified of course by enactments such as the Divorce Act.[174] This assumed the need to maintain the legal purity of civil/Christian marriages, an ideal which in practice is contradicted by the routine linking of bridewealth agreements to such marriages.

In the second place, the courts' jurisdiction over persons was limited to Blacks only. Since the abolition of the Prohibition of Mixed Marriages Act,[175] interracial marriages are now possible in South Africa, but they may not be dissolved in these courts.

Thirdly, jurisdiction over causes of action is limited to cases of nullity and divorce[176] in respect of civil/Christian marriages[177] and 'any question arising' therefrom. More precision is given to the latter phrase by s 1 of the Divorce Act, where a 'divorce action' is defined to include, inter alia: an application pendente lite for an interdict or for the interim custody of (or access to) a minor child of the marriage or the payment of maintenance and an application for a contribution towards costs. Apart from this, as a matter of practice, the Divorce Courts regularly decide questions of custody, maintenance and matrimonial property. Certain closely related issues, however, are excluded;[178] foremost amongst these are claims for refund of bridewealth. It is still not clear whether the Divorce Courts may entertain claims for damages for adultery. In *Lutu v Lutu & another*[179] it was held that they did have jurisdiction, but in *Nyembezi*[180] and *Mahase v Mahase & another*[181] it was held that they did not.[182] Happily, in terms of s 8 of the Divorce Act as read with the definition of 'court' in s 1, orders of maintenance, custody, guardianship or access in respect of a child may be

---

[174] 70 of 1979.

[175] 72 of 1985.

[176] The remedy of judicial separation was abolished by s 14 of the Divorce Act 70 of 1979.

[177] Customary marriages are excluded in terms of the definition of 'marriage' in s 35 of the Black Administration Act.

[178] *Mtiyane* 1952 NAC 229 (NE).

[179] 1955 NAC 101 (C).

[180] 1955 NAC 66 (S).

[181] 1961 NAC 25 (S).

[182] See Labuschagne & Swanepoel op cit n75 27–8.

rescinded, varied or suspended by another division of the Divorce Courts or by the Supreme Court.

The Supreme Court has retained concurrent jurisdiction in questions of divorce and all allied claims, but of course subject to a higher scale of costs.[183]

Fourthly, with regard to area, under s 10 of the Act the husband must be domiciled within the court's area of jurisdiction.[184] This requirement could prove irksome for large numbers of people who are caught up in the system of migratory labour. Formerly, because of influx control regulations, and today because of the acute shortage of urban accommodation, migrant men are unable to secure permanent, lawful residence[185] in South Africa, which is a prerequisite for obtaining domicile.[186] In consequence the forum domicilii would often be in one of the independent homelands.

The common-law ground for divorce jurisdiction, ie the husband's domicile, has been supplemented by statutory grounds under s 2 of the Divorce Act. This section allows a court to assume jurisdiction if the wife is plaintiff and was ordinarily resident in the area of jurisdiction on the date that the action was instituted and had been so resident in the Republic for one year prior to that date. In addition, the wife would have to show that she was domiciled in South Africa before cohabitation ceased or that she was a South African citizen or domiciliary prior to her marriage. This amendment does not assist African women so much as white women, whose needs were clearly in mind when it was drafted. A large number of African women are domiciled in the independent homelands; they are unlikely to be South African citizens or domiciliaries (before or after marriage) even if they can fulfil the requirement of legal residence in South Africa for one year prior to the marriage.

The Divorce Courts were devised with a view to providing a cheap forum with flexible procedures[187] where litigants could feel that the best possible solution in the circumstances of a divorce was achieved.[188] The findings of an empirical study of the Southern division, however, yielded a generally negative assessment of the court's performance. As regards costs: although the cost of an action was approximately half of what it would be in the Supreme Court, it was nevertheless very high in proportion to an average litigant's income. Concerning flexibility: about one third of the cases heard within the year of study (1981–2) did not involve an attorney. The president of the court had a heavy burden (which he bore without the assistance of social workers or other members of the legal profession) to ensure that any unrepresented parties would not be unduly prejudiced. The overall impression was that cases were being dispatched too quickly.

---

[183] *Maimane* 1931 WLD 99; *Mbelle* 1947 (1) SA 782 (W).

[184] For the definition of domicile see: Forsyth ch 5.

[185] Forsyth 121–2.

[186] And there is a presumption that a man is domiciled where his wife lives; ubi uxor ibi domus: *Webber* 1915 AD 239 at 246.

[187] The rules of court are contained in GN R2726 *GG* 8486 24 December 1982. See Khumalo 235–70 and Kloppers & Coertze *Bantu Divorce Courts*.

[188] Burman 1983 *AJ* 171.

The Hoexter Commission recommended retention of the Divorce Courts, pending the creation of family courts in South Africa. The only change it proposed was the transfer of these courts to the administrative control of the Department of Justice.[189]

VI SMALL CLAIMS COURTS

Imperfect access to justice is a problem that pervades all legal systems. The poorly educated and financially disadvantaged have grave difficulty in successfully prosecuting or defending claims before state courts. Their difficulties are exacerbated by an adversarial system of procedure because the outcome of the trial is weighted in favour of the person who has professional representation, which in turn of course depends upon the resources of the litigant. All these problems are believed to be most acute in the case of small claims.[190]

[26] NADER *NO ACCESS TO LAW* 5

Ours is a nation of strangers, a country where the greatest number of potential abuses occurs between people who are strangers to each other. Parties that buy and sell are often strangers to each other; production is centralized; and large organizations control information, condition the terms of purchase, and shape perceptions through advertising. These forces have culminated in increased dependency, which has brought with it a redistribution of power in our society; most product and service complaints are between people of greatly unequal power.

The direction of law seems to be evolving in similar ways worldwide, although with different consequences in places where the social and cultural structures are different. When nation-state law begins to predominate, as it does in industrial states, extrajudicial processes and social-control mechanisms are replaced. At the same time most actual and potential disputes are those between strangers; the true plaintiff becomes only secondarily important, and the courts decline in personnel relative to population growth and need. Court functions shift away from dispute settlement; access to courts decreases; the function of law as power equalizer diminishes, and law decreases in its role relative to issues that affect the quality of everyday life. Then we return full circle: Extrajudicial processes begin to develop in direct response to these trends, and with them the struggle between the legal system and the litigant for control or influence over the extrajudicial processes that are evolving as a result of the failure of law.

Access to justice was one of the problems addressed by the Hoexter Commission of Inquiry into the Structure and Functioning of the Courts.[191] The Commission recommended the creation of small claims courts in South Africa on an experimental basis. It was hoped that they would obviate various difficulties: the high cost of engaging lawyers (a necessity in cases involving complex questions of law); delays; the psychological barrier many litigants experience when appearing in formal tribunals; and barriers caused by poverty, ignorance and feelings of alienation.[192] The Commission felt that small claims courts should

---

[189] Paragraphs 7.3.1 and 2 of the *Fifth Report*. See further below, 443–4.
[190] Ison (1972) 35 *MLR* 18 and see Cappelletti *Access to Justice* v1 72.
[191] In its *Fourth Interim Report* RP52 of 1982.
[192] Paragraph 2.1–7 of the *Report*.

operate in an informal manner; that they should attempt to reconcile the parties; and that the judges should play a more active inquisitorial role.[193]

These recommendations were translated into law by the Small Claims Courts Act.[194] As the title of the Act suggests, the competence of the courts is restricted to the hearing of small claims which, in terms of s 15 of the Act, are principally causes of action not exceeding R1 500 in value. Certain matters, which previously would have fallen within the jurisdiction of commissioners' courts, are specifically excluded from the competence of small claims courts: the dissolution of customary-law marriages; the validity and interpretation of wills; certain claims for specific performance; and actions for damages for seduction, defamation and breach of promise to marry. All such claims will have to be heard in magistrates' courts, with the consequent disadvantages of higher costs and greater formality.

The requirements of informality[195] and low costs[196] are realized in a variety of provisions in the Act. The officers presiding over the courts ('commissioners' in the parlance of the Act) are advocates, attorneys or magistrates.[197] Except in the case of minors or other persons lacking locus standi, no legal representation is permitted.[198] The laws of evidence are not applicable,[199] and questioning of witnesses may be on an inquisitorial basis.[200]

A major defect of the American small claims court system was avoided by the South African Act: s 7(1) provides that although juristic persons may be summoned to appear as defendants only natural persons may institute actions. In the United States it was found that large corporations and governmental agencies had tended to dominate litigation and, as regular plaintiffs,[201] they had far better chances of defeating individual, first-time litigants.[202]

Apart from allowing the application of customary law, the Hoexter Commission did not specifically consider the circumstances of African litigants in its Fourth Report. Section 14(3) of the Act provides that a court may hear an action between Blacks[203] and that it may apply customary law 'as may be proved'. The latter condition, if interpreted literally, would make the application of customary law impracticable because it means that each rule of customary law must be proved in every action in which the rule occurs. A more tenable construction is that the litigants must prove only those rules which are not yet in a written form, and normally this would imply rules that had not yet been incorporated into a code or precedent.[204]

---

[193] Paragraph 13.6.
[194] 61 of 1984.
[195] Paragraph 13.11 of the *Report*.
[196] Paragraph 13.9.
[197] Section 9(2).
[198] Section 7(2).
[199] Section 26.
[200] Section 26(3).
[201] So-called 'repeat players': Galanter (1974) 9 *Law & Soc R* 95.
[202] Yngvesson & Hennessey (1974–5) 9 *Law & Soc R* 255 and 262.
[203] As contemplated in s 10 of the Black Administration Act. See above, [17].
[204] Kerr (1984) 101 *SALJ* 726.

One of the most serious psychological obstacles to easy access is language, and the Small Claims Courts Act does not attempt to improve upon the situation in magistrates' courts. Section 5(1) provides that either of the official languages of the Republic may be used; subsection (2) provides that if evidence is given in a language with which one of the parties is not sufficiently conversant, a competent interpreter shall be called by the court. Yet, despite the permissive wording of s 5(1), the Legislature does not seem to have envisaged the trial being held in an African language.

There is no requirement in the Act that the commissioners should be able to speak an African language or that they should be proficient in customary law, although it is argued that a commissioner's failure to know and apply customary law might constitute a 'gross irregularity' in terms of s 46(c), warranting review by the Supreme Court.[205] It is unlikely, however, that the type of litigant for whom such courts were designed will have the time, education or initiative to challenge the court's decision.

Two assumptions regarding the nature of the claims brought to the small claims courts appear to be unfounded. First, as the title of the Act says, the courts were created with *claims* in mind, not defences. This implies a bias in favour of plaintiffs, and in an economic system such as ours, this can result in a consistent preference for the claims of shopkeepers, landlords and the like, ie those who are in an economically dominant position relative to the defendant.[206] Secondly, the Act presupposed that small claims were necessarily simple claims which could be settled without the bother of lawyers, legal documents and complex procedures. This assumption is untrue, at least in so far as a case might involve the conflict of laws.[207]

Although the primary function of the small claims courts is adjudication,[208] the Hoexter Commission hoped that an informal atmosphere would encourage commissioners to arbitrate claims, thereby conciliating the parties.[209] This goal is common to most of the movements promoting access to justice in the western world. It is assumed that formal adjudication is costly and cumbersome (and therefore unnecessary for solving minor disputes) and that long-term relationships, such as husband–wife, employer–employee and landlord–tenant, will inevitably be further damaged by adjudication, with its accent on win-or-lose outcomes. Informality, conciliation and arbitration are closely related ideas, which it is believed will succeed in yielding socially more satisfactory results.

Whether these courts can achieve all that is expected of them remains to be seen. The opinion on similar informal tribunals in the United States was not especially encouraging. Abel, for instance, believes that precapitalist legal institutions cannot be used as a model for constructing informal tribunals in modern capitalist societies.

'The effort to do so is inevitably stillborn because it attempts to crossbreed distinct

---

[205] Kerr op cit 729.
[206] Abel *The Politics of Informal Justice* v1 295.
[207] See *Ex parte Minister of Native Affairs: In re Yako v Beyi* 1948 (1) SA 388 (A) at 398.
[208] Paragraph 13.8 of the *Report*.
[209] Paragraph 13.6.

species—formality and informality—to produce offspring endowed with characteristics that are inherently contradictory. . . . Where the parties are relatively equal and bound together by strong enduring ties, they find the process created or sponsored by the state too formal in comparison with two party negotiation, mediation by kin, and perhaps professional therapy. Where the parties are unequal, whichever has the law on its side prefers to appeal to formal authority, seeking enforcement of rights rather than conciliation.'[210]

Unfortunately, now that commissioners' courts have been abolished, a relatively cheap and informal forum has been lost. And, for cases not amenable to the jurisdiction of the chiefs' courts, there is no alternative but small claims courts, which go only part of the way to meeting the requirements of the disadvantaged litigant. The danger now exists that the poorer litigant, who cannot afford the advantages of professional representation, will be encapsulated in a self-contained system of courts with lower standards of justice,[211] the very evil that was to be remedied by abolition of the commissioners' courts.

VII UNOFFICIAL TRIBUNALS

(1) Before the Emergency

The new interest in dispute processing in the 1960s led to a discovery that many, if not most, disputes were being dealt with by unofficial tribunals to the apparent satisfaction of the parties concerned. And during the 1970s it became evident that in the urban areas of South Africa an amazing variety of tribunals was flourishing alongside the state courts. Their proliferation could be attributed to the state's failure to provide adequate law enforcement facilities in the overcrowded and crime-ridden African townships, and to a loss of confidence in the official courts, especially in the commissioners' courts. Before the state of emergency was declared in 1985, opinions about these unofficial tribunals (widely known as makgotla) were divided. Some of the punishments they meted out had attracted shocked condemnation, but certain people saw in them an opportunity for the community to take the initiative in crime control.[212]

The following was the first comprehensive study of unofficial tribunals in South Africa. It was carried out in Mamelodi, a Pretoria township.

[27] HUND & KOTU-RAMMOPO (1983) 16 *CILSA* 179–94

Introduction

Throughout South Africa, urban blacks live in segregated residential areas generally known as "locations" or "townships". The growth of large, modern towns in South Africa represents one of the major aspects of the revolutionary changes now overtaking all African society. Yet despite the need for it, there has been remarkably little research on problems of justice in African urban areas. As a field of study it is still largely virgin territory in which much preliminary spadework has yet to be done. So the present study, which was confined to Mamelodi township outside of Pretoria in the Republic of South Africa, is essentially exploratory in nature. We have tried to set out some of the salient

---

[210] Op cit n206 v2 4–5.
[211] Yngvesson & Hennessey op cit n202 225–6.
[212] Ndaki in Sanders *Southern Africa in Need of Law Reform* 176.

ideas which have emerged from our findings which may, we hope, be relevant to the general understanding of the social organisation of justice in urban African communities.

In this pilot study we have found that there are different and competing subterranean systems of dispute-settlement and peace-keeping at work in Mamelodi. . . .

There are *Makgotla* (singular: *Lekgotla*) or unofficial "people's courts" in Mamelodi which operate under the authority of tribal or homeland representatives who are appointed by chiefs or headmen in the rural areas still governed by indigenous law and custom. There are also informal courts and vigilante groups which have been set up as adjuncts to local ward committees which form part of the community council system. In addition to this, informal networks of neighbours regularly come into and go out of existence as bands for the protection of private property. Cultural movements also exist in the township, and some of these have taken over as part of their function peace-keeping and dispute-settlement activities. Gangs also exist, and they also have their own perceptions of justice and their own ways of achieving it.

In the township, the police and the formal court structure provide between them the fixed points in the official framework for the administration of justice. But for the rest, which is to say for the most, the social system for the administration of justice presents the appearance of continuous flux in which new groups and associations are constantly springing up and often vying with one another. Often they are ephemeral and die away as quickly as they come into being. . . .

[When the Commissioners' Courts, Appeal Courts and Black Divorce Courts] were set up it appears that the South African government hoped to create a simple and inexpensive apparatus for settling disputes between blacks. It was also visualised that the litigants would have their cases tried by experts in indigenous law and custom, and that procedures employed would be simple enough to be comprehended by the average rural black. In theory the Commissioners' Courts were designed to serve the requirements of justice in the townships admirably, but in practice they seem to have failed dismally. . . . [F]ew urban blacks take their grievances to the Commissioners' Courts or to the police. Of the estimated quarter-million blacks under the jurisdiction of the Pretoria Commissioner's Court, one commissioner estimated that less than 2 percent brought their estate problems in for settlement. Although we have no reliable survey data on the matter, it seems clear that the vast majority of blacks living in townships do not turn to the official court structure for help in processing their claims or for redressing their grievances. They turn instead to unofficial agencies of justice such as *makgotla* and also, perhaps increasingly, to other more drastic forms of self-help and violence.

Makgotla

The term "makgotla" reflects the popular usage of the man in the street of the township and the South African media to describe the so-called "people's courts" that have sprung up (most notoriously) in Soweto and other townships throughout South Africa. The expression is misleading because it is often used to refer to a variety of phenomena ranging from the actions of angry mobs, vigilante groups, and even gang warfare to the more legitimate dispute-settlement procedures that exist in conjunction with ward committees of the community council system. The expression is even used to refer to the counselling services of some welfare organisations. The existence of *makgotla* groups in the townships has become a topic of lively debate but, indeed, much of the controversy may result from the careless usage of the term "makgotla" itself.

A definition given by Blaine of *lekgotla* is: "open tribunals following unwritten law and custom having for precedents the judgements of past chiefs. . . ."[1] Comaroff and Roberts define *lekgotla* as a body of "all advisors and headmen" which meets periodically to consider affairs of policy and administration, but which has as a part of its function the settlement of disputes. "The procedure tends to be quite flexible: the chief makes opening and closing statements. Free speech is encouraged, and the chiefly decisions, announced at the end, are expected to reflect the weight of manifest opinion."[2]. . .

The Ward Four makgotla in Mamelodi

There are a dozen "wards" in Mamelodi, each consisting of several "sections" or residential areas occupied by a mixture of ethnic groupings. For each of these wards a community councillor is elected, and he then appoints a dozen or so deputies who, along with himself, form the ward committee. The ward committee is responsible for documenting new residents, issuing residence permits, making sure that rent and utilities are paid, and for sorting out housing and residential difficulties. The committees meet periodically so that neighbourhood grievances can be aired and, in some cases, they have taken over the matter of settling neighbourhood disputes and exercising peace-keeping activities. This is what happened in Ward Four of Mamelodi where a *lekgotla* was created to function as a court and a vigilante organisation ancillary to the ward committee.

The history of the Ward Four *lekgotla* began in 1977. As the story was told to us, a young woman was assaulted in the ward by a young man who was later apprehended by citizens and taken to the police station in Mamelodi. As it turned out, the girl was seriously injured, and the offender was released on his own recognizance by the police and, in the end, was never prosecuted. This incident raised such a howl of protest that many angered residents of Ward Four came together to form a crime prevention unit. Calling themselves the "Volunteers" they identified themselves by the distinctive use of whistles with a special code for rapidly mobilizing vigilante units. Because of a large tree nursery and a park adjacent to the ward which was said to be a shelter for roving gangs in the area, Ward Four was especially plagued at this time by a spate of muggings, knifings, assaults of various kinds, robberies and gang warfare. There was also a truancy problem in the area and as a result "gigs" or non-stop parties which lasted for weeks, attracted an undesireable element and placed the residents of Ward Four at the mercy of bands of delinquents.

The Volunteers met regularly to settle neighbourhood disputes and to administer "sjambokkings" or floggings to recalcitrant youths over whom parents of the ward had lost control. They formed a regular vigilante patrol for policing the ward and during this time it was said that the amount of violent crime in the ward dropped dramatically. In 1979, however, the Volunteers ran afoul of the formal legal system. While they were administering their own brand of justice in the ward, they were also, from the point of view of the police, taking the law into their own hands. The "then and there" justice administered by the Volunteers did not meet the formal law requirements of due process. First the Community Council and then the Minister of the Department of Cooperation and Development warned them to stop their activities. Finally, one of the victims of a sjambokking took his case to the magistrate's court where the Volunteers were fined R1 500. This lawsuit and the publicity it attracted effectively emasculated the Volunteers by depriving them of sanctions with which to back up the moral force of their judgments and policing activities. They were reduced to the use of their whistles alone and the only coercive means they had at their disposal were those originally vested in the ward committee, namely, the revocation of residence permits or writing letters of complaint to the superintendent of the Administration Board. While these sanctions were effective in controlling those in Ward Four who had something to lose (like permits) by Administration Board action, those in the area who were most in need of control were often unregistered transients, non-rent-paying adolescents or others who had nothing to fear by openly flouting the authority of the Administration Board and thus the Ward Four makgotla. . . .

The operation of the court

The limited data we have regarding the decisions taken by these assemblies do not permit any statement of a comprehensive, systematic body of legal "rules" enforced by the Ward Four *makgotla*. But our observations suggest, in any case, that "rules" as such are not fundamental to the system of justice administered by it. The familiar formal law model of linking "facts" to "rules" to deductively arrive at a legal decision does not necessarily seem to apply here. Rather, decisions regarding rights which should be enforced on behalf of any party seem to rest heavily on judgments of individual character derived from participants' knowledge and impressions of a person's behaviour and attitudes. . . .

The emphasis in the Ward Four *makgotla*, then, is on the individual and not the alleged crime as such. The central aim of the Ward Four court process is to prevent the breaking of relationships and to make it possible for parties to live together amicably in the future. Obviously this does not apply in every case, but it was true of a large number that we observed, and it was present in some degree in almost every case. Therefore the court tends to be conciliating. It strives to effect a compromise acceptable to, and accepted by, all the parties and everyone in the audience. This is the main task of the judges. . . .

Makgotla associated with tribal or homeland representatives in the township

Aside from the *makgotla* which form part of the community council ward committees such as the one we investigated in Ward Four of Mamelodi, there exist in many black urban locations *makgotla* which are associated with the homeland representatives there. According to the unpublished research report by Labuschagne and Swanepoel, these courts have many functions other than legal. They educate, serve to acquaint people with the law, integrate and organise public opinion and criticism and serve other social functions as well. In Mamelodi these courts have names: "the Council for the Brothers of the Chiefs" (Pedi), "Mamelodi Venda Urban Representatives Board" (Venda), and "Inkatha Yesizwe" (Zulu). These councils are part of the urban representatives boards and have connections with the black homelands, or with certain chiefs. Because of the emphasis on chieftainship, it seems clear that those who submit themselves to the voluntary jurisdiction of these unofficial courts do so out of respect for traditional patterns and customs of the chiefdoms with which they identify. . . .

Although there are no statistics available on the matter, it seems that those availing themselves of the services of the *makgotla* associated with the homeland representatives must constitute a distinct minority of the entire urban population. Customary forms of authority (including parental authority) are likely to be ignored by many younger generation blacks who, having been born in the township, no longer see themselves as belonging to the homelands, and for whom there is no chiefly authority. These young blacks are not likely to see themselves as citizens of Bophuthatswana or Venda or KwaZulu, for example, but as citizens of South Africa, or perhaps even "Africa" itself. Here, doctrines of "pan-Africanism" prevail. A recent survey estimated that support for the banned African National Congress in the urban areas of Johannesburg, Durban and Cape Town was 47 percent, 37 percent and 28 percent respectively. The Buthelezi Commission found that three to four out of ten black South Africans favoured doctrines of the ANC. These figures, though crude, give a rough idea of the percentage of those who reject the concept of tribalism. Secondly, the emerging black middle class, with its emphasis on Western outlook and modernism often regard tribalism as outdated and reactionary, concerned with shoring up a homeland system which they find difficult to accept. We were told, in fact, that many of those taking their problems to the *makgotla* associated with the tribal authorities probably consisted of the lowest socio-economic class in the township: the *lumpenproletariat*, contract workers living in the hostels, and others fresh from the rural areas. . . .

The Vukani Vulimehlo People's Party

An organisation that is described by the *makgotla* people of Ward Four as "our enemies" is the cultural movement, and the *makgotla* associated with it, of the so-called VVPP (Vukani Vulimehlo People's Party). Although our information is sketchy, it is said that there are now more than 20 000 card-carrying members of this grass roots organisation in Mamelodi, with members in other townships as well. The leader of this organisation is a self-styled "president for life". The organisation is not so much anti-establishment as a mirror of the normal pecking-order. Like a gang, the VVPP is a brotherhood for survival in an insecure and violent environment. Organised in a command or military fashion, it has a constitution, articles and a manifesto to which all members of the organisation subscribe. . . .

According to reports the VVPP has existed for a year or so. The vigilante or law-enforcement arm of the organisation is known to accept anyone, even those with criminal records, just so long as they have sworn allegiance to the group. We heard stories of individuals who had been fined and flogged at the *makgotla* associated with the organisation. We were told that Ndlazi welcomed tsotsis in the VVPP so long as they submitted to the discipline of the para-military organisation. Ndlazi told us that he was himself a fighter and an ex-tsotsi. It is true that Ndlazi's organisation keeps the peace in Ward Seven, but it is also well-known that it offers its protection to operators of shebeens there. Ndlazi has, in fact, been characterised by members of the Volunteers as a "shebeen-supporter". There is no doubt that much good has come from the VVPP, such as social services for single parents and the establishment of a regime of law and order in Ward Seven, but brute force is the main factor behind its *makgotla* and the tyranny of the organisation lies in the autocratic rule of its leader. By setting himself up as president for life under the VVPP charter, Ndlazi has established himself as what one person called a "mini-führer". He has created a para-military infrastructure based on an adherence to discipline and obedience which effectively controls those subject to his command.

We were able to witness a few cases decided by Ndlazi's *makgotla*. Although our observations are incomplete, we did not notice any large, open or public meetings similar to the ones we saw in Ward Four. Instead, the proceedings were semi-private and conducted along the lines of an *in camera* model. The group dispensing the justice was an intimidating sight. The judge-interrogator was, in fact, known by the nickname of "satan". In contrast to the Volunteers' meetings where every effort was taken to give the proceedings a dignified air of judicial decorum, the VVPP *makgotla* that we observed had an inquisitorial air and undercurrent of coercion that could hardly escape our notice. . . .

Other forms of control

Some residents of Mamelodi form their own informal neighbourhood networks for protection of private property. Often these alliances are based on earlier gang or schoolgroup affiliations. They come into and go out of existence as the perceived need for them increases or diminishes. Some local businessmen in the township employ "strong men" who are Baqu and Xhosa (from as far away as the Transkei) to protect their business interests. The owner of a discotheque in the township told us he employed about twenty Xhosa "bouncers". He used these men because, he said, they are "good with knobkerries", and "don't ask questions".

They patrol not only the property of the dance hall, but also the entire block in which it is situated so as to protect the area used by patrons for parking. Thus, we find small "private armies" patrolling sections of the business area at weekends. At this stage we have no means of knowing what form of "justice" they administer. . . .

Gangs and makgotla

It is well-known that gangs exist in Mamelodi, such as the notorious X–R 5s and the Scorpions. But there are other less well-known gangs there as well. It may be said that "gangs" form no part of the social organisation of justice and are thus no proper object of comparison with *makgotla*, but it must be remembered that members of these gangs are often outcasts from the larger society and they have their own perceptions of justice by their own in-group standards. Although we have no formal data on the matter at this point, gangs must surely form a large part of the social scene in Mamelodi, as in other townships. As we have already said, informal estimates put the dropout and truancy rate amongst adolescents at about 35 to 40 percent. The unemployment rate is very high, and it is not unreasonable to suppose that many of these aimless young people obtain their living from illicit pursuits. Some of them may be quite harmless, but muggings, assaults and intimidation are the order of the day in the township, although official police statistics do not reflect this. Virtually everyone we interviewed stated that crime in Mamelodi was collective rather than individual. Gang-related crime seems, indeed, to be the greatest cause of fear in the township.

Notes

1. Cited by Ndaki in A J G M Sanders *Southern Africa in Need of Law Reform* 176.
2. *Rules and Processes* 26.

A useful analysis of urban courts is Epstein's account of the tribunals created by the Northern Rhodesian government in 1938 to serve the Copperbelt. They were staffed by tribal elders drawn from chieftaincies in the rural areas. Epstein isolated three particular problems in the running of these courts, which invites comparison with urban tribunals in South Africa.

In the first place, the administration had difficulty in selecting chiefs who would not provoke accusations of ethnic bias by the heterogeneous population of the Copperbelt.[213] Secondly, the courts had to abandon the traditional mode of hearing cases, ie prolonged discussion by concerned kinfolk and neighbours, which led to the following criticism: 'We trust a judgment which has been given by a collection of people, not by one man alone. How can one man decide a case? With us a case is a public affair.'[214] Thirdly, the diverse ethnic backgrounds of the litigants and the staff running the courts, and the demands of a large caseload, soon meant that cases were being decided on the basis of a rough and ready common sense. Precedents were not applied and naturally there was difficulty in knowing which system of customary law to apply.

Some of these difficulties stemmed from policies fostered by the administration.[215] It had deliberately selected conservative people from the country to staff the courts, so it was no surprise that these judges were ill-prepared to cope with the problems they encountered, such as the variety of claims unfamiliar to customary law.[216] Epstein believed that while the courts were capable of evolving a 'Copperbelt practice' to deal with such problems, their development was impeded by a widening social gap between the chiefs and the urban dwellers. This manifested itself in the litigants' frequent appeal to norms that were irreconcilably opposed to traditional customary law. A consequence was a general suspicion that the administration of 'law' had become arbitrary.[217]

To be compared with this generally unfavourable assessment is the more optimistic study of urban courts in Northern Nigeria.[218] The author maintained that both customary law and African courts were well adapted 'to meeting many of the critical problems of adjustment that arise in the transition from rural to urban environment'. For instance, the formal conflict of laws problems, such as those experienced in the Copperbelt courts, could in principle be resolved by the

---

[213] *Administration of Justice and the Urban African* 12.
[214] Op cit 15.
[215] Epstein *Politics in an Urban African Community*.
[216] The large number of assault cases, eg, was unusual: Epstein op cit n145 *Juridical Technique* 4.
[217] See *Administration of Justice* n213 95. Regarding the problem of which law to apply, see Epstein (1951) 12 *Human Problems* 28ff.
[218] Smith (1972) 20 *Am J Comp L* 223.

courts' tendency to seek solutions to problems without recourse to a fixed code of rules.[219] Similarly, a project on Kenyan courts demonstrated how they had continued to function effectively, albeit in a predominantly rural environment, during an era of rapid socio-economic change.[220] Both these studies maintained that the informality and flexibility characteristic of African courts could prove to be their major advantage in easing the urban dweller's transition from the old to the new world.

The urban–rural dichotomy is not, of course, as simple or as clear-cut as it is popularly supposed to be, and for this reason alone we should be less concerned with the geographic location of the courts than with their functionaries. Conservative/traditionalist judges will no doubt satisfy the needs of a particular class of urban dweller: a person rooted in rural tradition and unable to respond progressively to the problems of a new social milieu.[221] Yet, as the Copperbelt and Nigerian studies implied, forward-looking and accommodating judges could successfully cater for people who were no longer bound by tradition. This suggests that successful judges must have some standing in the communities they serve, which in turn presupposes something often overlooked—the importance of their political role.

In South Africa in the 1970s, when the makgotla had captured public attention, there was considerable debate about whether these tribunals should be incorporated into the state judicial system.[222] Further speculation was pre-empted when the government introduced chiefs' courts into the cities under the aegis of its new constitutional scheme of community councils.

[28] SECTION 1 ACT 94 OF 1980; SECTION 21A BLACK ADMINISTRATION ACT 38 OF 1927

(1) The Minister may, after consultation with any community council established under section 2(1) of the Community Councils Act, 1977 (Act 125 of 1977) confer on a Black in respect of the area of such council or of such portion of such area as the Minister may determine, the same judicial power as in terms of ss 12 and 20 of this Act may be conferred on a Black chief or headman.

The key enactment in the programme for the future government of Africans outside the homelands was the Community Councils Act,[223] in terms of which semi-autonomous black local authorities were established.[224] By s 2 of the Act the Minister of Constitutional Development, after consultation with the appropriate administration board, urban black council or black advisory board, could constitute a council for a defined residential urban area. The jurisdiction of

---

[219] Op cit 239.
[220] Saltman in Cappelletti op cit n190 v3 311ff. See further the suggestion that Liberian-style moots be introduced in America: Danzig (1973) 26 *Stanford LR* 1.
[221] Perlman *The Myth of Marginality* ch 1.
[222] *House of Assembly* Debates 10 June 1980 col 8673–4.
[223] 25 of 1977.
[224] On use of the term 'community' see Thornton & Ramphele in Boonzaier & Sharp *South African Keywords* 29ff.

community councils, subject to the control of the Minister (usually via the local development board), covered a wide range of activities, from the allocation of housing to the management of 'community guards'. Members of the community councils were elected, but the government aim of popular representation miscarried when elections were boycotted. In order to improve the councils' image, they were upgraded by the Black Local Authorities Act[225] to the status of town councils.[226]

The political odium of collaboration that tainted members of the community councils did much to rob their courts of local support. A report from Mamelodi and Soweto reveals that council tribunals and their staff were used for self-seeking purposes: to evict rent defaulters, to protect council property, and to enforce council decisions.[227] Many such tribunals were identified with a species of makgotla run by opportunistic and power-seeking 'big men'.

(2) During the Emergency

The activities of council courts were eclipsed by a new type of tribunal that emerged from the political crisis that erupted in 1985: the people's courts.

[29] SCHÄRF in CORDER *DEMOCRACY AND THE JUDICIARY* 169–81

People's courts in South Africa
Although the idea of people's courts and street committees is not a new one in South Africa or in other countries in a state of conflict, they became a prominent feature of the political scene from the beginning of 1985 until they, and most news and views about them, were silenced by the June 1986 Emergency Regulations.[1]

They sprang up with remarkable rapidity in many African townships throughout the country as part of a community initiative to combat the growing crime rate caused by marginalized members of the township who were exploiting political turmoil. This was further aggravated by the police diverting their energies to fight the political challenge to the state, thereby leaving a gap in conventional policing. Another impetus to the creation of people's courts was that the political movements decided to create disciplinary structures for other reasons too. The consumer boycotts, which had begun in the Eastern Cape during the first few months of 1985, needed to be policed, and the UDF and its affiliates could, of course, not resort to state courts and the police forces to do so. There was also a desire among political movements to demonstrate to the township residents that the movements were capable of running most aspects of township life, including the administration of justice. Creating and participating in people's courts thus became a way of educating township residents politically and strengthening their dignity and feeling of self-reliance.

"People's courts", or "street committees" as they were known in most areas (not to be confused with the non-political street committees in Cape Town, which had the same name) served as both courts and places at which the moral values of a future South Africa were passed on to the residents. They were also a way of involving all residents in political structures. In short, the people's courts were an attempt to experiment with prefiguring the lowest rungs of a post-apartheid adjudicative infrastructure. Being fledgling

---

[225] 102 of 1982.
[226] See Venter 1984 *AJ* 17ff.
[227] Motshekga *Alternative Legal Institutions in Southern Africa* 26–7.

structures in an experimental phase, there were obviously some differences in their structures from region to region, and there were predictably some deviations from the ideals of justice to which they aspired. This can be said equally of the lower rungs of the formal courts. Moreover, they were vulnerable to being side-tracked by power groups in regions where the political organizations were not strong enough to gain or keep control of them.

In order to demonstrate the features of people's courts that bear consideration in the process of democratising the courts, two types of courts that have been researched will be described. . . .

Comparison of two systems of people's courts

. . . Each system is to some extent representative of experiences in some other regions, and can be usefully compared to highlight the positive and negative attributes of people's justice.

1. *Cape Town—The Nyanga East Youth Brigade People's Court*

This court came into being during July 1985 as a result of several converging developments. The first was the escalating exploitation by marginalized youths of the confusion and conflict on the streets of the townships. They exploited the situation for their own material gain and the police were seemingly unable or unwilling to do anything about it, as they were concentrating on policing political activities. Township residents were being robbed, assaulted, raped, and having their houses broken into and their goods stolen by these "hooligans", as they were labelled by the founders of the Youth Brigade court. When the hooligans caused a power failure by sawing off electricity poles, snipping the copper wire and selling the metals to scrap metal merchants, some youths who were negatively affected by these crimes set up a patrol to catch and punish the hooligans.

The second incentive to the establishment of this court was the growing number of people's courts which had already been established in other parts of the country, notably the Eastern Cape. Some of the founders of the Youth Brigade court wanted to introduce into Cape Town the same political agenda which these courts represented.

The third catalyst which led to the establishment of the court was the realization among extra-parliamentary political youth movements that they needed to recruit followers to their organizations and to educate the youth of the townships politically. The people's court was a useful forum in which to combine these three aims.

They first commenced by launching street patrols, as the adults had done before them whenever the township streets became too treacherous for comfort.[2] Through these patrols they succeeded in reducing opportunistic crime somewhat, but the solitary patrol, consisting of about 15 youths, could not cover their whole area of Nyanga East all the time. Complaints were brought to them by victims and witnesses, and they had to establish the soundness of the allegations. As a result, they began running a court as well as a patrol.

The principles in terms of which the court operated were initially aimed at promoting the concepts of collective justice and a caring community. The court was composed of members of the Youth Brigade, who elected four office-bearers: the chairperson, the clerk (who was in charge of the record), a keeper of the complaints book, and an orderly. The chairperson regulated each hearing as one would any meeting, and he (this was an all-male initiative) had no voting rights.

A complainant initially had the gist of the complaint recorded in the complaints book, and efforts were then made to bring the defendants to the court. Depending on the circumstances, the complainant was either asked to bring the defendant to court on the designated day, or given a letter from the Youth Brigade to hand to the defendant instructing him or her to appear. Alternatively, the Youth Brigade would send its patrol, the "pick-up team" to bring the defendant to court.

Once both parties were present, the complainant was given the opportunity to speak, after which any member of the Youth Brigade could ask questions. The defendant was also allowed to put questions to the complainant. Then the defendant was asked to explain his or her position and was again open to questioning by members of the court and the complainant.

Questions of guilt and punishment were settled by means of a democratic vote by all members of the Youth Brigade present. Proposers of certain punishments had to justify them, after which the proposals were voted upon. The intention of the punishment process was to alert the wrongdoers to the consequences of their action, especially the damage they were doing to the liberation struggle and community solidarity. Punishment was usually accompanied by a lecture on how the ideal comrade of a future, apartheid-free South Africa was expected to behave. Punishments were consciously devised not to be impersonal and alienating, and were designed to demonstrate to the wrongdoer that a caring community awaited him or her once the punishment was completed. During the initial phase of the court's existence, a phase that lasted a month or so, punishments were not excessive and there was a focus on community service, such as cleaning out someone's yard, helping old people, and distributing pamphlets for political organizations, as well as handing back stolen goods and performing a service for the victim. When the crime warranted physical punishment, this was administered not by an individual but by several members of the Youth Brigade so that it was seen to be collective punishment. A sentence of fifteen lashes with a sjambok (a quirt) was not generally considered excessive despite the maximum number of lashes in the formal courts being seven. This was pronounced as five-by-three, which meant that three members of the Youth Brigade administered five lashes each.

Once the punishment was complete, the defendant was invited to join the Youth Brigade and become a member of the court. The idea behind this process was that the former deviant was expected to learn to be responsible under the tutelage of more senior members of the Youth Brigade. They held evening review sessions in which the day's cases were discussed and the desired punishment philosophy explained. Members of the Youth Brigade who had called for overly punitive sentences during that day were castigated during these reviews.

Most of the defendants brought to the Youth Brigade court were youths, and it was considered appropriate that an all-youth court could pass judgment on them. Cases that involved adult matters, over which the youths had no jurisdiction, were referred to adult structures, usually street committees or "civics". The adults in the community initially expressed their support for the court, as it was considered responsible for the substantial drop in the crime rate in the area.

... [However] this court became increasingly unpopular in the community during its later phases until it was forced to close by the police, who arrested its core members. Several developments contributed to its loss of popular support. The first was that its membership was made up of youths coming from different ideological tendencies and this resulted in conflict over punishment philosophies. The tendency which favoured a more punitive policy won greater support from the growing number of formerly marginalized youths, whose incorporation into the membership of the court had tilted the balance towards the numerical superiority of less educated members. Within four months the membership of the Youth Brigade had grown from about 50 to 300 and the level of supervision and discipline that the activist leaders were able to give the new recruits who still needed to be politically educated, was clearly inadequate. The democratic voting practice was increasingly abused by a punitive clique that began to express its views more forcefully.... Their domination of the voting procedure made a mockery of the democratic process and resulted in an extraordinarily high conviction rate. Hardly any defendants were acquitted. The virtual certainty of a successful complaint caused some township residents to use the court to punish people they disliked. Sentences escalated to levels where they were no longer considered fair: 100 lashes were administered in extreme cases. Support for the court consequently dropped considerably.

The second factor contributing to the court's loss of legitimacy was the tendency to take on adult-related cases. Given the value system in the townships, it was considered utterly unacceptable to the older generation that youths should arrogate to themselves the right to pass judgment over them. It evoked considerable anger among the older generation, who withdrew their support.

A third reason for the court's loss of popularity was that it was not attached to any single political movement and thus saw itself as accountable to the broad cause of crime control but not to any particular constituency. There were thus no organizations whose admonitions the court members would heed about the deteriorating legitimacy of the court. The relationship between political youth movements and the adult structures in Cape Town's black townships was very tense at the time. The youth movements were loath to abide by directions from adult structures, particularly if these emanated from the squatter areas, whose leadership they considered an impediment to mass democratic mobilization. Moreover, although some of the members of the Youth Brigade court belonged to youth movements of UDF-affiliates, they were not mandated by their organizations to join the Youth Brigade and in several instances interviewees conceded that they had received considerable criticism from their organizations for their continuing involvement in the Youth Brigade. As a result, there was at the time no township group that could curb the Youth Brigade. Yet the political organizations were blamed for the excesses of these self-styled "comrades", a term initially reserved for political activists. The youths of the Youth Brigade called themselves comrades but lacked many of the attributes such as accountability and discipline that usually accompanied the term.

... By June 1986 [the Youth Brigade court] ceased to operate. Other people's courts sprang up in sectors of the townships and in the KTC squatter area. ... By and large their existence was characterised by conflicting claims about their legitimacy, and allegations about abuses. The latter half of 1985 was an extremely turbulent phase in the struggle and it would be very surprising if courts could remain unaffected by the pervasive violence and militant rhetoric throughout that time. The track record of the Youth Brigade court in Cape Town did little to endear the concept of people's courts to the inhabitants, who remember the Youth Brigade court for its latter phase rather than for the initial, more idealistic period.

2. The Southern Cape experience: an integrated adjudicative hierarchy

In the African township of a town that will remain unnamed ... a very different set of structures was created by the inhabitants. There was, as in the Western Cape, a vacuum in conventional policing when the national uprising spread to most parts of the country. Crime and hooliganism escalated, and the people's court set up there was part of a broader initiative to organize the population politically, develop a sense of self-reliance, and shun the apartheid order. The court was formed at the same time that the civic organization, a UDF-affiliate, was created. The adjudicative hierarchy consisted of three tiers. The civic organization was the highest body, which itself was made up of its constituent organizations (parents', women's and youth organizations). It was both a body of first instance for general political matters and a body of appeal from the lower structures. The executive committee of the civic served as the appeal body.

The second tier was especially created by the civic to deal with dispute-settlement. This was the people's court, which consisted of eight people. Four were office-bearers and the other four were representatives from women's, parents' and youth organizations (one for youth under 23 and another for older "youth" up to approximately 30). However, the composition of this people's court at any hearing depended on the type of case that was being heard. If a case involved adults, then it was felt that there was no need for youth representatives to be present, as they were not considered entitled to adjudicate adult matters. The people's court also developed the practice of co-opting members to sit on it for particular cases, if their expertise or insight was necessary. The people's court served as the body of first instance in general matters, and as a body of appeal from the youth, women's and parents' organizations that constituted part of the third tier. Another part of the third tier was the street committees that, apart from many other functions, also themselves solved minor problems arising in their domain.[3] An appeal also lay from these street committees to the people's court. One of the central ideas behind the people's court was, we were told, "to reduce the crime rate ourselves in a more educative way—more than just by punishing people". . . .

This idea was demonstrated by the way in which cases were conducted. In the people's court the litigants were seated amongst those forming the semi-circle that faced the chairperson and the secretary. According to one member "we just wanted the people to feel that they were part and parcel of the solution which was to be reached in that particular discussion". . . .

Procedure was commonsensical and accessible: the defendant was handed a letter by the secretary of the people's court and requested to appear on a certain day. The complainant and his or her witnesses were then asked to state their problem and were open to being questioned. Similarly the defendant and his or her witnesses were asked to proceed. Hearsay evidence was not usually permitted. The decisions about guilt and punishment were discussed at length and then voted on democratically. Sentences emphasized restitution and conciliation. When goods were stolen or damaged, then the fine which constituted the sentence was paid to the people's court which handed it to the complainant to replace or repair the goods. Corporal punishment was limited to six lashes. Punishments of this nature were executed by members of the people's court behind closed doors. There was no general access of the public to the people's court although all township organizations and interest groups had delegates on the court when a matter affected their interests, and they were expected to report back to their organizations. The street committees were open to all the members of their constituency and usually had a member of the people's court present to act as adviser.

The type of cases they heard included a whole range of problems: theft, assault, robbery, housebreaking, unruly or disrespectful children, accusations of witchcraft, disputes between dagga dealers, defamation, and posturing as a "comrade" or misusing the name of the struggle for selfish acts. Serious cases such as rape and murder were not dealt with. Complainants were referred to the police for these matters. Difficult cases such as the trial of suspected informers were handled by the civic's executive at general meetings. In one case where the allegation of spying was unsubstantiated, the complainant was severely admonished and required to apologise publicly. In another case, where there was considerable corroborative evidence to support the allegation, the defendant was banished from the township.

The network of adjudicative structures and political bodies set up in this township was a conscious effort to prefigure a post-apartheid, democratic form of governing the townships. Continuous efforts were made to educate residents through these structures as to their rights and duties. Members of the people's court were convinced that, if there was an accessible and respected set of courts that could effectively solve community and individual problems, then people would resort less to taking it upon themselves to solve problems violently. Residents were thus urged to use the collective structures, through which a rights culture in the township was being established.

Although it may be premature to make an assessment, as the research has not yet probed deeply, the quality of justice offered by the court did not seem to deteriorate in the same way as that of the Cape Town Youth Brigade court. The court's demise was occasioned by the detention in June 1986 of most of its members, when the second recent State of Emergency came into effect.

Evaluation of the two different styles of people's courts

When evaluating community-initiated courts and comparing them to formal state structures, one is constantly reminded of the value-laden nature of our Western legal education. The way in which authority and power are constructed in the two contexts is very different. In the formal system, the efficacy of the judicial system and its source of legitimation are attributed to its separation from the more overtly political executive arm of government. In the informal system no attempt is made to disguise the fact that the people's courts express the morality and values of the most powerful faction within that particular community. If the court does not in fact embody those values, then rival courts are likely to emerge to give expression and effect to a competing set of norms and values, and potential litigants can choose which forum suits their particular cause best. The danger of trying to pose as an "objective" unaffiliated court, as in the Cape Town example, lay precisely in the fact that it was not accountable to any credible local political structure that could both lend it legitimacy and intervene when the gap between ideals and practice widened. The shortcomings of the Cape Town court consisted in its unrepresentative composition, its lack of accountability to a credible organization and enforcement of values that were not supported by the majority of residents.

This raises the important question of what type of rules are enforced in the formal and informal systems. The fear amongst those who are used to Western models of adjudication is that informal courts will operate in terms of specific norms of the dominant faction in a particular locality. If this were allowed to proliferate nationally, then justice would not be the same throughout the country. National legislation on the other hand imposes uniformity. . . .

Looking closely at the type of norms and values enforced by the people's courts, it is clear that, apart from those issues that dealt with the liberation struggle (such as consumer boycott violations and police informers) there was considerable overlap with the norms of the formal system. However, the way of enforcing them was different, and it is here (particularly in the more educative, inclusionary aspects of adjudication) that the formal system may be able to learn something from the people's courts.

Another potential problem relating to the lack of uniformity is that a situation may develop where different power groups in a township or locality set up very different, and competing, courts. . . . The danger here is that adjudicative structures simply become the enforcement arms of political or commercial factions, and that people who choose to use them are not choosing "justice" but a very particular form of enforcement. That is undeniably so. Whenever and wherever there is a choice of structures, individuals will choose the options that will provide them with their favoured remedy. . . .

There are many other problems and dangers that would have to be addressed if one were to think of formalizing the existing informal structures in a post-apartheid adjudicative infrastructure. Does formalizing rob them of their spontaneity and adaptability? Does the commitment and attitude of the volunteers change once they become civil servants? Is it at all possible for a state to stimulate as much community participation as communities themselves do in phases of political struggle? What controls, checks and balances can become real protections against abuses of power of incumbents in "informal" state structures? Is incorporation of informal, politically-linked structures into a post-apartheid adjudicative infrastructure possible in a multi-party state?

Notes

1. Proc R109 of 1986.
2. S Burman & W Schärf (1990) 24 *Law & Soc R* 693.
3. Cf Burman in H Corder *Democracy and the Judiciary* 151ff.

According to the police, at the height of the unrest over four hundred such courts were in operation in all parts of South Africa.[228] It was alleged that they had been mandated by the ANC to undermine the authority of the state.[229] In

---

[228] Sadly much of the work on people's courts has not yet been published. There is an empirical study of Mamelodi by Bapela *People's Courts in a Customary Law Perspective* and a brief survey by Seekings (1989) 5 *SA Review* 119ff. Detailed empirical studies were also made of courts in the Western Cape: Burman & Schärf (1990) 24 *Law & Soc R* 693 and *Informal Justice and People's Courts in a Changing South Africa*; Schärf & Ngcokoto in Manganyi & Du Toit *Political Violence and the Struggle in South Africa* 341; and Schärf 1989 *AJ* 228–34.

[229] Evidence given during the Mayekiso trial: *S v Mayekiso* 1988 (4) SA 738 (W), cited by Schärf op cit 229 and Seekings op cit 123.

the battle-torn townships courts were used as fora for the exposition of political creeds, as devices for the demonstration of power and as testing places for group loyalties. Most were closely identified with resistance to the state and it is no coincidence that this type of tribunal emerges during times of political upheaval.

'In a revolutionary crisis the question of legality becomes one of the most pervasive social questions. This is so, first, because the crisis itself originates through an action that is illegal from the point of view of the former regime. . . . Furthermore in a period of acutely intensified class struggle the several classes and class fractions will offer different, and sometimes antagonistic, conceptions of legality . . . and no one class or class fraction is powerful enough to impose its own conception upon the others.'[230]

Subsequent investigations in South Africa make it doubtful whether all the people's courts can be so unequivocally connected with political upheavals.[231] Initially, like the makgotla before them, they sprang from a breakdown in the formal policing of the townships. The attention of the police had been diverted to containing protest marches and illegal gatherings, to searching for and detaining activists, and they had no time for conventional policing duties. These circumstances provided the opportunity for criminals and other marginalized members of the townships to prey on others in the community.[232] People's courts found an immediate task in the prevention and prosecution of crime.[233] Their jurisdiction then sometimes extended to regulating political campaigns and to maintaining party obedience; and sometimes it reached even further into mediating domestic and neighbourhood disputes.[234]

Crime control provided the immediate occasion for furthering political objectives.[235] To this end, both street patrols and courts were used to discipline the rent and consumer boycotts that had been instituted in defiance of the state. Yet not all tribunals had such overtly political objectives. While in the Eastern Cape and Mamelodi the people's courts were integrated into UDF political structures to such an extent that the appeal ladder coincided with the alternative civil authorities set up in the townships,[236] in Alexandra, Cape Town and Beaufort West, the courts had no particular political alignment.[237]

Popular justice was seen as the aim of many of the courts. Although this concept has no universally accepted meaning, certain characteristics are readily identifiable. Foremost is the democratic election of members of the court, who are then implicitly accountable to the community. Sanctions are not supposed to be punitive; rather re-education, community service and rehabilitation are the main tenets of sentencing.[238] Reconciliation is often held up as a prime goal; violence and punishment are associated with the state system.[239] Simplicity and

---

[230] Santos in Abel op cit n206 v2 251–2.

[231] Schärf op cit n228 229–30.

[232] Schärf & Ngcokoto op cit n228 346–7.

[233] Seekings op cit n228 123ff and Van Niekerk (1988) 21 *De Jure* 295.

[234] Seekings op cit n228 127–8.

[235] Seekings op cit n228 129ff; cf the Cape Town courts: Schärf & Ngcokoto op cit n228 365.

[236] Bapela op cit n228 8–10.

[237] Schärf & Ngcokoto op cit n228 347–8. Political affiliations apparently influenced the composition, objectives and procedures of the courts. See Schärf op cit n228 229–30.

[238] Bapela op cit n228 15.

[239] Van Niekerk op cit n233 296.

informality (often described as a 'common-sense' approach) are the keynotes of the trial procedures.[240] No effort is made to distinguish law and morals: instead the judgments usually restate any principles that might have been infringed in the case.[241]

In so far as the people's courts were linked with popular justice, they repeated the experiences of many other post-revolutionary societies, such as Zimbabwe[242] and Mozambique. In the latter country, although this was ostensibly a reaction to elitism, it was also a realistic response to the flight of legal practitioners and academics when Portuguese personnel withdrew shortly after independence had been attained.[243] At the time it seemed likely that the country would slip back into a customary-law regime administered by chiefs and headmen. This was opposed by the younger members of Frelimo and certain peasants, who regarded such a regime as an obstacle to the revolution.[244] The alternative—continued enforcement of the former colonial law—was entirely unacceptable to the government. So instead Frelimo decided to establish popular tribunals designed to solve any problems brought before them in a common-sense manner.[245] These courts were intended to manifest a new national unity, freed from the class elements that had disfigured the previous colonial order, and to promote the social revolution.[246]

The people's courts in South Africa elevated avoidance of the state system from the pragmatic to the principal reason for their existence.[247] The state perceived this as a serious threat and responded by criminalizing their activities. Accusations of sedition and subversion[248] were brought against persons who purported to run what in effect were alternative state institutions.[249] By 1988 the people's courts had been suppressed or abandoned. Most of their functionaries had been detained and charged with crimes under the Emergency Regulations,[250] but in certain cases the courts had lost popular backing. In some instances in Cape Town, for example, the assumption of jurisdiction over adults proved to be a critical excess of power (because it was a serious breach of the customary norm of deference to seniority) that cost the courts their support.[251]

Given their different aims and backgrounds, it is difficult to generalize about the people's courts, but they should not be dismissed as a transitory phenomenon. They have been applauded for the work they did in crime control

---

[240] The formal system of justice, with its apparently incomprehensible technicality, necessarily implies a uniform central administration run by the state; this in turn is bound to lead to the monopoly of power by a particular class: Santos (1984) 28 *JAL* 95–7.

[241] Schärf op cit n228 231.

[242] See Van Niekerk op cit n233 300; Ladley (1982) 26 *JAL* 101.

[243] Sachs (1985) 13 *Int J Sociology L* 146.

[244] Isaacmans in Abel op cit n206 v2 294 and see generally: Santos op cit n240 94ff.

[245] They might apply the more progressive aspects of customary law, cleansed of its sexist and undemocratic elements: Isaacmans in Abel op cit n206 297.

[246] Sachs (1984) 28 *JAL* 99ff.

[247] See Van Niekerk op cit n233 295.

[248] Under s 54(2) of the Internal Security Act 74 of 1982.

[249] *S v Zwane & others (1)* 1987 (4) SA 369 (W) and *S v Mayekiso* 1988 (4) SA 738 (W).

[250] Proc R109 12 June 1986; Schärf op cit n228 233–4.

[251] Schärf & Ngcokoto op cit n228 358–9. And see Bapela op cit n228 12.

and for responding to the unmet legal need of the poor.[252] In spite of their excesses, they demonstrated an ability to supply a far more comprehensible and satisfactory form of justice for this section of society. Because they sprang from the communities they served, they were adaptable and potentially responsive to the needs around them. As such they can provide a useful model for tribunals in a post-apartheid society.

People's courts should be distinguished from the makgotla which preceded them, and in most cases coexisted with them. Some of the makgotla were identified with the community councils[253] and most had a conservative or a non-political stance.[254] Political allegiance aside, the makgotla never claimed validity or recognition beyond the communities in which they operated, whereas, at least according to the police, this was an implicit ideal of the people's courts. Makgotla in consequence tend to complement state structures rather than to challenge them.[255]

From 1984–88, as political discontent intensified and violence escalated, media reports revealed a new pattern of conflict, this time perpetrated by so-called vigilantes (also known as mabangalala).

> 'In the context of South African townships, "vigilantism" has come to refer not to popular crime-prevention campaigns but to the sinister and violent paramilitary groups based around some township conservatives. And some Makgotla in the period before 1983 seem to have been the antecedents not of people's courts but rather of these violent vigilante groups.'[256]

Like the people's courts, the social and political origins of the vigilantes varied considerably, as did their motives and methods, but they had one common feature: they were opposed to the anti-government political campaigns of the UDF and affiliated people's courts.[257] There were indications that in some instances the vigilantes were associated with makgotla[258] and with the community council courts.[259] More disquieting was the connection between the state security forces and the vigilantes: the use of local organizations like these had obvious tactical advantages for the police and army in environments which they found dangerous and hostile.[260]

As the political conflict waned, so did the activities of the vigilantes. Now it seems that the tribunals operating in the townships before the Emergency, such as the street committees, makgotla and courts run by local 'big men', have resurfaced.[261] But dispute processing institutions of this nature are a worldwide feature of concentrations of poor and ill-educated people who fall beyond the reach of the state system. Questions posed for the future are: should such

---

[252] Van Niekerk op cit n233 301 and Bapela op cit n228 21ff.
[253] Seekings op cit n228 131ff and Bapela op cit n228 6.
[254] Schärf op cit n228 232.
[255] Santos in Fine et al *Capitalism and the Rule of Law* 162.
[256] Seekings op cit n228 132.
[257] Haysom *Mabangalala* 2.
[258] Haysom op cit 4.
[259] Haysom op cit 8 and 12ff.
[260] Haysom op cit 7.
[261] See the study of the street committees by Burman in Corder *Democracy and the Judiciary* 151 and Schärf op cit n228 234.

tribunals be co-opted by the state into the formal legal system? Is it possible for them to survive uncontaminated by contact with the official regime? Can they be controlled?[262]

VIII REFORM: AN OPPORTUNITY LOST?

The changes following the Report of the Hoexter Commission were supposed to effect major improvements in the South African court structure. Yet neither the Report nor the ensuing legislation showed much understanding of the plight of African litigants. The perspective of the reformers could best be described as 'top-down', ie one that disregarded the daily realities endured by the majority of the population.[263] A different view, the African litigants', would have

> 'throw[n] new light on the interaction between legal institutions and society. The disputant's choice of a forum immediately affects both his adversary and himself, for each forum will have its own substantive and procedural rules, which influence the outcome of the dispute and the subsequent relations of the parties to each other and to the society. Disputant choice will also affect the dispute institutions, for the cumulation of these choices will determine the number of cases a forum hears, the characteristics and relationships of the parties who appear before it, the subject matter of the dispute it handles, the participation of intermediaries (such as lawyers), and the involvement of the general public. . . .'[264]

The reformers' approach was bounded by two assumptions. The first was that justice is a state monopoly and hence only the state's point of view is acceptable.[265] (A corollary of this was that all disputes should be heard in professional ('legal') institutions external to the social setting from which they originated.) The second assumption—probably more accurately described as an anxiety—was that the courts' already heavy caseload would become excessive if the public were given easier access to justice. The result of these preoccupations was a failure to consider any tribunals outside the state system.

No attempt was made to measure the 'unmet legal need' in South Africa,[266] although this concept is vital for determining the nature of any improvement in justice facilities. In this regard the wealth of anthropological/sociological literature on dispute processing, which has been used extensively in the reform programmes of developed nations,[267] could have provided valuable insights. For instance, it has been shown that legal needs cannot be simply quantified in terms of suits denied access to state courts. In all societies there are strong inducements for people to shun dispute. Where the potential gain from suing is too low and the costs of pursuing the matter too high, an aggrieved party may decide to take no further action, ie (colloquially) to 'lump it'. The issue which gave rise to the

---

[262] South Africa should obviously take care to avoid repeating the mistakes made elsewhere. India is a notable case in point. Here a concerted effort was made in the 1950s to recreate a traditional type of tribunal—the *nyaya panchayat*—or village council. This has not been an unmitigated success. See Hayden (1984) 22 *J Legal Pluralism* 43 and Meschievitz & Galanter in Abel op cit n206 v2 47.

[263] Roberts *Law and the Family in Africa* 8.

[264] Abel in Burman & Harrell-Bond op cit n172 169.

[265] Galanter (1981) 19 *J Legal Pluralism* 1 and in Allott & Woodman op cit n136 67.

[266] Elusive though it is: Felstiner (1974) 9 *Law & Soc R* 76.

[267] Snyder op cit n7 149.

grievance is then ignored and the relationship with the offending party is continued.[268] A related tactic is 'avoidance', which implies limiting the relationship with an offending party to minimize the repercussions of any grievance.[269] In a multiplex relationship, such as husband-wife or parent-child, the aggrieved person may be forced to play down a conflict for the sake of preserving the relationship. On the other hand, where the relationship consists of a single interest, such as a contract, the aggrieved party may simply 'exit', ie withdraw from the situation and terminate the relationship completely.[270]

It is obviously difficult to estimate the frequency of resorting to such methods of coping with conflict because they have no form of public display; but they can be *structurally* predicted. Hence it may be safely supposed that an aggrieved person who lacks the financial means or the skills necessary to pursue a grievance further in the state courts will probably avoid the conflict, 'lump it', or exit.

The character and accessibility of local dispute settlement institutions[271] have a critical bearing on any decision to prosecute a grievance.[272] The mere availability of state courts does not guarantee their use, and conversely the creation of state courts does not suffice to extinguish existing unofficial tribunals.[273] It has been shown, mainly in anthropological studies, that the poor and powerless prefer to air their complaints in their own tribunals.[274] They have neither the technical knowledge nor the money to utilize state courts[275] and so they litigate in tribunals that for linguistic, kinship and cultural reasons are more congenial.[276] Even if litigants are capable of litigating in formal tribunals, the mere act of initiating a suit might have the effect of escalating an otherwise tolerable grievance and threatening to rupture long-term, close relationships.[277] Conversely, the litigant who is in an unequal bargaining position might be tempted to resort to the state courts in order to balance the power ratio with the other party; but this short-term gain must be weighed against the consequent possibility of social ostracism from the community.[278]

---

[268] Felstiner op cit n266 81; Danzig & Lowy (1975) 9 *Law & Soc R* 675.

[269] Felstiner op cit n266 70.

[270] Again, if the costs of ending a relationship are too high, and most multiplex relationships fall into this category, 'exiting' may not be a feasible alternative: Felstiner op cit n266 79 and 84. An important variable in deciding which option to take is the value of any object that may happen to be in contention. If it is a scarce resource it may be ranked higher in value than the parties' relationship and this might be a compelling reason not to go to court. In this respect it must be appreciated that resources are not necessarily material; they may include such intangibles as honour or sexual rights: Nader & Todd op cit n9 18.

[271] Nader & Todd op cit n9 17.

[272] See, eg, Collier's work on Mexican Indians *Law and Social Change in Zinacantan* 244 and Starr *Dispute Settlement in Rural Turkey*, regarding the role of brokers in channelling individual choices so as to mediate between different cultures. See further Perry in Hamnett op cit n13 189.

[273] Holleman (1979) 17 *Afr L Studies* 5.

[274] See Von Benda-Beckmann (1981) 19 *J Legal Pluralism* 117 and in Allott & Woodman op cit n136 187ff.

[275] See, eg, Witty in Nader & Todd op cit n9 281.

[276] Canter in Nader & Todd op cit n9 247.

[277] See Rufini in Nader & Todd op cit n9 209.

[278] Todd in Nader & Todd op cit n9 86.

The law reform measures in South Africa paid no regard to the various unofficial methods that already existed for handling disputes. If, for example, due consideration had been paid to the tribunals operating in the townships, the legislature might have considered incorporating them into the state system, rather than creating a new and wholly experimental system of small claims courts. It might also have been an appropriate time to rein in the makgotla and to evaluate the performance of the community council courts.[279]

This does not imply that all unofficial tribunals should be incorporated into the state system without careful consideration. In a broad assessment of the informal justice movement (mainly in America), Abel examined critically the arguments usually advanced in favour of it.[280] First, the movement is said to be a necessary response to overcrowded courtrooms and ever-increasing rates of litigation. Yet, as Abel observes, even if the truth of this were conceded, it need not dictate the solution. Other possibilities are an increase of the existing services, or the exclusion of the corporate litigants currently clogging the machinery of justice. Secondly, it is argued that people want informality, meaning cheap, expeditious and approachable courts. To the contrary, however, there is a considerable body of evidence that people want not so much informality as authority. And the inevitable result of creating separate, informal tribunals is differential justice: better services offered to the rich, and inferior services offered to the poor.

Abel concludes that much of the rhetoric surrounding the claims for informalism disguises divisions of wealth and power implicit in all aspects of our society.[281] Attempts to promote informal justice do not eradicate these divisions, nor can informal justice promote a sense of community, with its associated virtues of reconciliation and social harmony.

> 'If it is true that informal institutions express and can help build community, then it is critically important to investigate the qualities of the community they foster. . . . What kind of community should we be striving for in advanced capitalism? Should it be based upon residential neighbourhoods, ethnic enclaves, class solidarity, ideological homogeneity? And how should we view the authority exercised by informal institutions?'[282]

It is clear that one of the main goals of the informal justice movement—reconciliation of the parties—is tied to a particular type of socio-political structure. Where courts have at their disposal the necessary machinery of state to enforce judgments, it is unlikely that they will take the time and trouble that is necessary to persuade litigants to compromise their differences. Nor should it be assumed that the parties will see any benefit in reconciliation. The reason litigants bring court actions is to secure the help of a third party in equalizing

---

[279] Instead the Commission chose to segregate its Report, treating African litigation as a separate category (dealt with in the *Fifth Report*) and thereby precluding certain useful comparisons, such as that between chiefs' and small claims courts.

[280] Op cit n206 v1 7ff.

[281] See his analysis of the contradictions in informal justice: op cit n206 267ff.

[282] Abel op cit n206 11.

power imbalances. And reconciliation is predicated on long-term, multifaceted relationships. Few urban tribunals operate in this type of social milieu. They may hear claims arising between people who happen to be involved in long-term relationships, such as landlord–tenant, but these relationships tend to be specific to particular interests; they are not the same as the generalized relationships of kinfolk or spouses.[283]

---

[283] Radical critics of legal reform in developed countries regard the informal justice movement as a further extension of state control, not a diminution, as is claimed by its advocates: Santos in Abel op cit n206 v1 262 and Snyder op cit n7 151. Further studies aimed at demystifying the process of informal justice are Abel and Galanter in Blankenburg et al *Alternative Rechtsformen und Alternativen zum Recht* Jahrbuch für Rechtssoziologie und Rechtstheorie Band VI 11 and 27 respectively; Abel op cit n12 245ff; Santos (1980) 8 *Int J Sociology L* 379.

CHAPTER 3

Application and Ascertainment of Customary Law

I APPLICATION OF CUSTOMARY LAW: THE CONFLICT OF LAWS

(1) Recognition of customary law: the problem of dualism

In this chapter we consider the problem of choice of law. When a country recognizes two different legal systems, to whom and in what circumstances will the laws be applied? This issue is known either as the conflict of 'personal' laws (ie law conceived in terms of its applicability to persons, instead of territory), or the 'internal' conflict of laws (which emphasizes the recognition of two or more legal systems within a unitary state).

In practice the application of personal law depends on the availability of specialized courts that are competent to apply it. South Africa is no exception: the history of customary law here is inseparable from the history of the courts administering it.[1] This resulted in suppression of conflict problems, because once it had been decided that only a particular court had jurisdiction to hear a matter, it followed that that court could apply only the law it was empowered to apply. In this way the colonial governments could forestall any problem of choice of law. Admittedly some courts were permitted to apply more than one legal system, but there were few rules prescribing how the appropriate law was to be selected; this was left to the courts to solve by themselves on a case-by-case basis.

The recognition of customary law in South Africa has had a chequered history. As European settlement spread out from the Western Cape, the colonial administrations experimented with a variety of different approaches, ranging

---

[1] This was a hallmark of British colonial policy in general: Lewin *Studies in African Native Law* ch 9 and see above, 56ff.

from outright refusal to recognize customary law (in Kaffraria) to an almost unlimited recognition (in British Bechuanaland).[2]

[30] BENNETT *THE APPLICATION OF CUSTOMARY LAW IN SOUTHERN AFRICA* 40–7

When the British occupied the Cape in 1795, Roman-Dutch law was maintained as the general law of the Colony because it was deemed to be a "civilized" system. No account was taken of any other system of law. The British administration then became responsible for founding a consistent policy of refusal to recognize and enforce customary law. Apart from the ethnocentric attitude of the white settlers, the origins of this policy can, perhaps, be explained by the peculiar conditions prevailing in the Cape. The Khoisan peoples living there were, by that stage, few in number and dispersed over a wide area. Their own social and political institutions had disintegrated. The Khoi had succumbed to Dutch rule completely. They had sold off their lands and cattle; some drifted away into the interior and others entered employment on Dutch farms. The San were either hunted down and exterminated or they moved away into the interior. Without the vigour of a living society to sustain it, there was no indigenous system of law to recognize. In time a campaign was mounted in Britain to improve the lot of the black people in the Cape. This culminated in Ord 50 of 1828 which guaranteed equality of treatment for all within the Colony. For southern Africa this was a remarkable enactment, it aimed at "improving the conditions of Hottentots and other free persons of colour at the Cape" and, of course, ultimately, at freeing the slaves. The latter goal was achieved in 1833. In terms of colonial policy, civil equality had been secured and there was no more to be done.

Although the policy of non-recognition might have been tolerable in the western Cape region, it was completely unrealistic on the eastern borders. As the whites advanced further east they came into contact with large numbers of Bantu-speaking peoples in an area which was to become the separate dependency of British Kaffraria. When Sir George Grey became governor, he introduced a new policy for Kaffraria directed at converting Africans to British notions of "civilization" and to Christianity. This scheme was implemented on two levels. In 1855 the administration began gradually to replace the chiefs with white magistrates and, at the same time, to undermine the chiefly authority by the more subtle measure of changing them into government stipendiaries. The fines and payments from judicial work which customarily accrued to the tribal authorities were to be made up by a government stipend. Within a few years the existing chiefs' courts had been eliminated. But the magistrates who replaced them were now in a quandary as to what law they should apply in disputes between Africans. The Law Department in Cape Town refused to consider allowing customary law to be applied; the magistrates on the spot realized that this policy was simply untenable and they had no option but to bow to the views of the litigants and so, de facto, customary law was applied. In 1864 some small concession was made by officialdom when the Native Succession Act was passed.[1] This directed the application of customary law in cases of intestate succession to Africans.

In 1865 British Kaffraria was incorporated into the Cape Colony. It formally became subject to the prevailing policy of non-recognition. This attitude was now justified, in part, on the basis of Ord 50 of 1828, whereby any laws differentiating against Blacks in the Cape were cancelled. All inhabitants of the Colony were deemed to be equal before the law

---

[2] A general overview of this topic can be found in Hahlo & Kahn *South Africa* 319–34 and Hailey *African Survey* ch 7. The South African policies are considered in Rogers *Native Administration in the Union of South Africa* and Brookes *The History of Native Policy in South Africa* chs 9 and 10. In addition see the more detailed accounts of policies in the Cape and Natal: Burman 'Cape Policies towards African Law in Cape Tribal Territories 1872–1883' (also in (1976) 3 *Brit J L & Soc* 204) and Welsh *The Roots of Segregation*. Suttner 'African customary law—its social and ideological function in South Africa' and (1985) 11 *Social Dynamics* 49 provides a critical, structuralist analysis of the place of customary law in the South African legal system prior to 1986.

and this was now construed to mean suppression of a personal law at variance with the received Roman-Dutch law. The white opinion of customary law was a low one and it was argued that if everyone in the Colony were compelled to abide by the laws of the more civilized section of society, those of the lower station would be forced to reach the higher standards. Although this policy was frequently criticized, it was retained until 1927.

There was a complete reversal of the policy of non-recognition when the Transkeian territories were brought under British dominion during the period 1877–94. Prior to this, in 1871, the Cape had become responsible for administering Basutoland. Basutoland was not incorporated into the Cape Colony (as had been the case with Kaffraria) but had been treated as a separate entity. The policy of non-recognition, therefore, did not automatically apply and the Cape Government could take a fresh approach to customary law.[2] Aside from its experience in Basutoland, the Cape had learned something from Shepstone's rule of Natal. So when it came to deal with the Transkei, the Cape Government was armed with a reconsidered policy, described as "progressive . . . adapting itself to the various stages of advancing civilization".[3] Like Basutoland, the Transkei was remote from the centres of power. It had very few whites and a large, well-organized African population. The people had not been completely subjugated nor had they been demoralized by white rule. Customary law was no longer ignored but the colonial conscience could not allow its unqualified application. Certain institutions, such as levirate unions, initiation dances and witchcraft, were prohibited, and recognition of customary law was subject to an overriding proviso that it must be "compatible with the general principles of humanity observed throughout the civilized world". The annexation decrees claimed that the inhabitants of the Transkeian territories were "not sufficiently advanced in civilization and social progress to be admitted to the full responsibility granted and imposed respectively by the ordinary laws of the Colony".[4] This more carefully considered approach to customary law was reflected in the influential Report of the Cape Native Laws and Customs Commission of 1883. Considerable information was collected about customary law, and the opinions formulated by the Commission had a lasting effect on official attitudes in South Africa.

Bechuanaland like Basutoland and Transkei, also had close links with the Cape Colony. British interest in what was then called Bechuanaland was stimulated by fear of expansion from the Transvaal. In 1885 a Protectorate was declared over northern Bechuanaland. The southern portion was constituted the Crown Colony of British Bechuanaland (and ten years later this was annexed to the Cape). It was made clear to the Tswana chiefs that Britain's interest was limited to preventing foreign encroachment. The population of the region was sparse and, apart from the importance of the trade route to central Africa, white settlers had no concern with the empty expanse of the Kalahari. Hence Britain was quite content to accede to the wishes of the Tswana chiefs and leave them to rule over their own people. Policy was formally expressed in Proc 2 of 1885, in which chiefs were given exclusive civil jurisdiction and, apart from some serious crimes, criminal jurisdiction as well, over their subjects. An Order in Council was passed on 10 June 1891, creating courts for the white settlers, a Resident Commissioner's court with assistant commissioners in the southern and northern sections of the Protectorate. Section 8 gave these courts jurisdiction over Africans only "in the interests of peace, or for the prevention or punishment of acts of violence to persons or property". Four years later, in 1895, British Bechuanaland was annexed to the Cape. But no attempt was made to impose the Cape policy of non-recognition of customary law. It seems that the commissioners' courts had very little to do with litigation involving Africans. The chiefs' courts handled the bulk of these cases. There was no contact between the two systems of courts; not even an appeal was allowed from the chiefs' courts until 1924. It was only in 1927 that the anomalous situation of British Bechuanaland was changed to bring it into harmony with the rest of the country.

Now it is necessary to go back in time and look at the position in Natal. In 1843 Natal was annexed by the British who, following the Cape policy, initially introduced Roman-Dutch law as the legal system for the entire population of the Colony. But the policy ultimately developed diverged widely from that of the Cape. The new administration found that there were approximately 100 000 displaced Africans in Natal—victims of Zulu empire-building and the Boer invasion. The most pressing issue was their future government. There was no question of treating these people as the rightful inhabitants of Natal because to have done so would have meant handing back white farmlands. Instead, they were treated as homeless refugees. The Natal Native Commission of 1846–7 recommended that the "refugees" be placed in locations to be governed by superintendents appointed by the Governor. The funds and manpower necessary to pursue this project, however, were simply not available. The seemingly insoluble problem was resolved by a scheme proposed by Theophilus Shepstone.

This scheme provided the basis for the distinctive character of Natal's African policy thereafter. To achieve the necessary control over a large, restive African population, Shepstone decided to use the tribal leaders to govern. This idea was a radical departure from colonial policy in Africa (and it predated Lord Lugard's policy of indirect rule by many years). To revive the political system of an only recently subjugated people was seen as a risky venture and it was not popular with the settlers; but Shepstone weathered the storm. With the restoration of traditional leadership came recognition of customary law. In Ord 3 of 1849 customary law was reinstated in its entirety except in "so far as it was not repugnant to the general principles of humanity observed throughout the civilized world". This, too, was a bold move to make against an established tradition of white prejudice. The chiefs were to exercise judicial functions (as was consonant with their position as officers of government), although the extent of their jurisdiction was not specified. Some check on their powers was maintained through a general control exercised by magistrates (later to be known as "administrators of native law").[5] In 1850 chiefly authority was integrated with the colonial government through the extraordinary measure of declaring the Lieutenant-Governor of Natal to be the Supreme Chief of the African people of the Colony. He now replaced the former Zulu monarch and, in this role, operated a court of appeal from decisions of chiefs and magistrates.

The criticism that Shepstone's policy did nothing to encourage the advancement of Africans—which was what the Cape policy aimed at doing—was met by the introduction of a system of exemptions from customary law in 1864.[6] It was felt that Africans who had become "detribalized" should not be subject to the rule of a chief. Such people could petition the Governor for exemption, stating particulars of family, property, local chief and so on, and furnishing proof of an ability to read and write.

The next landmark in the development of Natal's policy was the codification of customary law. This project had its origins in a law in 1869[7] when much of the customary law relating to marriage and divorce was reduced to a written code and changed here and there to meet government requirements: for instance, a limitation was placed on the amount of bridewealth that could be stipulated for marriage; female consent was made an essential for a valid union and all marriages had to be registered. In 1875 the Board of Native Administration was asked to draw up a complete code of customary law for the guidance of the courts. This was published in 1878. It was not legally binding in Natal but, by Proc 2 of 1887, it was made law for Zululand. The Natal code was revised in 1888 and, finally, in 1891 the amended code was made law by legislative Act.[8] The code was concerned mainly with family law and succession but it contained provisions on public law and procedure as well. Inevitably, given the preconceptions and unscientific approach of the codification team, customary law was distorted; it was also thought to be a good opportunity to amend customary law and so the legislation of 1869 was incorporated. Predictably, the code has been out of touch with African practice and opinion but the courts are bound by its provisions.

A firm and lasting policy regarding customary law in the Transvaal dates from Law 4 of 1885. The principal object of this enactment was to bring Africans under the control of the government. But, in addition, it was provided that all civil disputes between Africans should be dealt with in accordance with customary law. The State President was made a paramount chief—an echo of Natal policy—and, below him, a post of Superintendent of

Natives was created. The Superintendent was the chief executive officer of the administration and he acted as a court of appeal from the decisions of inferior courts in African cases. The State President was empowered to appoint native commissioners in areas where they were needed because of a large African population; where no commissioners had been appointed, the existing landdrosten became native commissioners ex officio. Apart from the native commissioners' courts, provision was made for the appointment of chiefs with primary jurisdiction in all civil cases, concurrent with that of the commissioners and landdrosten. In fact, no chiefs were appointed until well after Union but, as a special proviso to Law 4, the extant powers of the chiefs were retained pending official appointment.

Section 2 of Law 4 provided that the laws, habits and customs observed by Africans should continue to remain in force except in so far as they were inconsistent with the general principles of civilization recognized throughout the civilized world. The recognition formula was similar to Natal but in the Transvaal the courts refused to take cognizance of customary marriages and bridewealth agreements. Polygyny and what was considered to be bride-purchase were deemed to be inconsistent with the civilized conscience.[9] Taken to its logical conclusion the refusal to enforce customary marriages amounted to a refusal to recognize most of the institutions of customary law. The court in *Meesadoosa v Links*[10] spelt out the implications:

> "If the decision of this Court not to recognise marriages contracted according to native custom is to be extended to its logical conclusion . . . we might as well sweep overboard all the native customs . . . insofar as they affect the status of members of that family . . . and the ownership and disposal of property belonging to the different members of the family. The consequence would be that it would strike at the foundation of the custom which prevails among natives as to the family system."

Few changes were made to the system established in 1885. The review functions of the executive and the Superintendent were abolished in 1907 and appeal was allowed from the civil judgment of a native commissioner or chief to the Supreme Court.[11] In 1924 the chiefs' courts were subordinated to the native commissioners' courts in that appeals were permitted from the former to the latter.[12] At all times, the chiefs and the commissioners were competent to apply only customary law. If a litigant wanted the common law, he had to go to a magistrate or the Supreme Court.

The Orange Free State cannot be said to have evolved any policy towards customary law. In the Thaba 'Nchu Reserve specific recognition was given to customary marriages[13] but elsewhere it was not until 1899 that such marriages were formally recognized.[14] In the small Witzieshoek Reserve the chief was given minor civil jurisdiction according to customary law and appeal lay to the Commandant of the Reserve.[15] Apart from these two reserves there were no areas of concentrated African population in the territory which would demand a considered policy.

After Union in 1910 the striking diversity in the approaches to customary law demanded reform. The differences were dramatic. In British Bechuanaland the chiefs had largely unfettered jurisdiction and regularly applied customary law. In the Transkei chiefs' courts operated alongside magistrates' courts and both applied customary law except for important modifications introduced by proclamation. In Natal there was a codified system of customary law and indirect rule. In the Cape customary law was not recognized at all. And in the Transvaal there was the refusal to countenance the fundamental institutions of African family law. Granted that these distinctive approaches were the product of different historical experiences, they were unsuited to the newly unified state of South Africa. The uncertainty and complexity of the law prompted the Supreme Court to call for a change in "this chaotic state of affairs" and a re-organization of the "curious jumble" of proclamations and colonial Acts.[16] At the turn of the century there were other signs of a more profound import. The tribal structures which formerly had posed a threat to the security of the white conquest had been eroded and finally extinguished in the Zulu rebellion. Africans now formed a sizeable urban proletariat; many were educated and

African political associations had emerged. The threat posed by these developments to white hegemony was met by a distinct shift in government policy: the revival of traditional institutions. In this way the energies of an increasingly competitive class of people, who were beginning to challenge whites on their own terms, could be deflected. The merit of "tribalism" in the eyes of the government was that it facilitated racial segregation and thus guaranteed continued white political and economic control. The multifaceted programme of apartheid was given its name and new impetus in 1948, but it had been evolving from the basis of a series of enactments passed long before.

In 1913 the Native Land Act[17] prohibited Africans from buying or leasing land outside certain "scheduled" areas (which at that time comprised less than 8 per cent of the area of the country). This restriction translated into statutory terms a recommendation of the South African Native Affairs Commission of 1903–5[18] that territorial segregation was necessary to safeguard the interests of whites. The Native Trust and Land Act of 1936[19] released more land for the settlement of Africans and tightened up on measures to eliminate African tenancies on white-owned farms. From the lands demarcated in these two Acts the Bantustans (later called "homelands" and now "national states") developed in the period after 1948. The vestiges of political competition were eradicated in 1936 when the Representation of Natives Act[20] removed Africans from the common voters' roll. Prior to this the Native Affairs Act of 1920[21] had provided for the formation of local councils in the African reserves. Thus Africans were excluded from central government and allowed only local government in restricted areas. What emerged was a division between African rural homelands, where Africans were supposed to get on with their own development, and the white-controlled urban areas and farmlands which would be the basis for the real economic and political life of the country. Latterly, the apartheid ideal has been cloaked with the principle of self-determination or free pursuit of a cultural identity. In reality this has meant a sharp separation of the economically impoverished homelands and the ever-expanding industrial centres. Entry by Africans into the urban areas has been controlled by influx control measures: Africans are considered necessary only as a labour force; able-bodied men are welcome in the urban areas for short periods of time on a contract basis. The homelands have become the domain of women, children and the elderly.

A vital piece of legislation responsible for creating the legal dualism that was based on the social and economic dualism was the Native Administration Act of 1927.[22] This enactment provided for a uniform approach to the recognition of customary law and the creation of separate courts to settle disputes between Africans. The Transkei formula for the recognition of customary law was adopted, as was the Natal formula for the organization of the courts. The concern was to build up an African tradition. The Minister of Native Affairs blamed the British (and especially Sir George Grey) for past mistakes. He maintained that the neglect of African laws and customs had undermined the authority of the chiefs and had deprived them of the power to restrain the young.[23] Parliament was now exhorted to be tolerant of customary marriage, polygyny and bridewealth.[24]

Customary law was to be given full recognition in chiefs' courts and, in commissioners' courts in terms of s 11 of the Act, the application of customary law was to be within the discretion of commissioners provided that it had not been repealed or modified and provided that it was not contrary to natural justice or public policy.

Notes

1. Act 10 (British Kaffraria) and Act 18 (Cape).
2. S B Burman *Chiefdom, Politics and Alien Law—Basutoland under Cape Rule 1871–1884* 37–8.
3. E H Brookes *The History of Native Policy in South Africa* 108.
4. Hailey *African Survey* 350.
5. Under Ord 3 of 1849.
6. Law 11 of 1864, as amended by Law 28 of 1865.
7. Law 1.
8. Law 19 of 1891.
9. *R v Mboko* 1910 TPD 445 at 447 and *Kaba v Ntela* 1910 TPD 964 at 969 respectively.

10. 1915 TPD 357 at 361.
11. Act 29 of 1907.
12. Act 7 of 1924.
13. Wetboek van die Oranje Vrystaat IV 1.
14. Law 26 of 1899.
15. Hahlo & Kahn *South Africa* 327.
16. *Roodt v Lake & others* (1906) 23 SC 561 at 564 and *Sekelini v Sekelini & others* (1904) 21 SC 118 at 124 respectively.
17. Act 27.
18. *Report* para 193.
19. Act 18.
20. Act 12.
21. Act 23.
22. Act 38.
23. *House of Assembly* Debates 28 April 1927 col 2907–8, 2914–18.
24. *House of Assembly* ibid col 2918; 2 May 1927 col 3047.

Initially the legal system of South Africa, in common with other colonial territories, was thoroughly dualist in character: common and customary law were treated as personal laws attaching to the two racial groups that constituted colonial society. A strictly enforced social 'colour bar' precluded uncontrolled selection of one law or the other. There has been remarkably little change to this system, although latterly the criterion for application of customary law seems tacitly to have been altered from one of race to one of culture. Now a person is deemed to be subject to customary law if he or she has a predominantly African cultural orientation.[3] A more imaginative use of the conflict of laws, however, could have provided a serviceable method of articulating social change.

[31] SUTTNER (1970) 19 *ICLQ* 134–45

In any colonial or colonial-type situation we find what is known as a conflict of laws: two or more systems of law are potentially applicable to a particular problem and the court has to choose between them. . . .

Because the colonial situation involves a clash of two social systems, this conflict of laws is merely a reflection of a deeper interaction—between the traditional tribal society and the new world. The withdrawal of colonial powers does not resolve this conflict. They leave behind them their law just as they have left their language and political institutions. Whereas the Roman law and the English law, for example, developed to a large extent without outside influence, the growth of African customary law has been interrupted by the introduction of European law to deal with many of the new situations to which the customary law may later have evolved an answer. . . .

It was possibly with a view to future changes in the African social structure that parliament chose the flexible formula: allowing a discretion to apply tribal law, rather than compelling its application or detailed regulations prescribing its use. In addition, the phrase "questions of customs followed by Bantu,"[1] it is submitted, was intended to be interpreted flexibly so as to cater for modifications in African custom and their way of life.

Even at the time of the Act, and at a greater momentum ever since, the traditional society and African behavioural patterns have undergone fundamental alteration. As a result of participation in economic activities outside the traditional framework, a class of Africans has emerged which cannot be suitably governed, in part or as a whole, by tribal rules. . . .

---

[3] This is now widely treated as an aspect of self-determination and minority protection. See generally, with regard to Australia, Canada and the United States: Morse & Woodman *Indigenous Law and the State*.

Clearly the courts face serious problems in adjusting law to meet a situation which has changed and continues to change considerably. Whilst retaining certainty, the law must be sufficiently flexible to encompass the needs of people at varying stages of cultural transition. In this situation one visualises the development of a system of creative judicial administration, where the special courts would fulfil a dynamic role similar to that of the United States Supreme Court. Unfortunately the legislature has not taken adequate steps to ensure that the judges of these courts are adequately trained for their task. Neither Bantu law nor a knowledge of an African language is a compulsory requirement for their minimum qualification—the lower civil service law examination. I realise that in practice very few men are appointed as Commissioners without a knowledge of Bantu law, and that some have had experience in the Bantu Administration Department. But, as I have already indicated, mere knowledge of the substantive nature of Bantu law is not sufficient. Administrators must be able to relate it to its social context.

People charged with the administration of a discretion to apply Bantu law have a great responsibility—in fact "greater than that generally borne by courts of law".[2] It is submitted that adequate exercise of this function requires a systematic training and an appreciation of the effect of social change on law. . . .

In the debate preceding the passing of the Act, the Minister of Native Affairs stressed the creative role of the Bantu Affairs Commissioners: "Certain institutions get obsolete and it is this elasticity which makes a law sound in a nation, especially a young nation like the natives."[3] Yet the courts have generally refused to fulfil a reforming role, to alleviate hardships caused by the application of aspects of traditional law unsuited to the new society. In one case[4] the court refused an application for divorce of a customary marriage despite the fact that the husband had assaulted his wife on a number of occasions, threatened to stab her, told her to go away, and said that he would kill her if she returned. The court declared that he had not intended to drive her away "in the legal sense". The courts have a mandate to reject rules of tribal law when they fall short of natural justice or public policy. It is clear that in cases such as these the court has applied a rule which falls well short of universally accepted standards of justice.

Not only do Commissioners have such a duty of exclusion. It is also submitted that they have the right to adapt rules of indigenous law to make them more suitable for application today. African custom is not static. The "Bantu Custom" out of which the law Commissioners are entitled to apply, arises, is constantly changing. The African's contact with Western institutions, carrying the main burden of South Africa's industrialisation, has caused a splintering of the traditional social order. It "ceased long ago to operate as a complete, distinct entity. Its elements—the subsistence economy, joint families, an elaborate network of kinship ties, devotion to ancestors, hereditary chieftainship—withered away or blended with elements of the alien culture".[5]

The extent to which individual Africans retain elements of or have broken with their culture has, however, varied. Not all, in fact not many, can find complete satisfaction from the Roman-Dutch common law. This means that if the law is to be at all effective it will have to be modified and applied after thorough investigation of the social circumstances of the litigants.

There cannot be one Bantu law uniformly applied to all Africans who do not fall under the common law. Indeed the custom followed by and accepted by African communities varies according to age-group and area of residence. While the old traditional law may be of greater relevance to the conservative peasant in the reserves (though even here it requires fairly extensive modification), courts might have to recognise the creation of "new custom" in the urban areas and amongst the younger generation who often revolt against the vast restraints which the traditional law imposes on their personal lives.

In this century we see social conditions inconceivable in the old society: widows, spinsters and female family heads were unheard of, yet they are commonly found today. Not unexpectedly the traditional law, particularly the stereotyped conception of it which the special courts have created, can only supply a grotesque answer to these problems.

A rigid adherence to *stare decisis*, especially where many decisions are of dubious merit, is of little assistance where the law hopes to offer an answer to the people it serves.

Courts and legislatures have not been totally averse to modification of indigenous law. Unfortunately what alterations they have made have generally been retrogressive, and particularly adverse in their effect on the rights of women, who suffer severe disabilities.

Notes

1. As used in s 11(1) of the Black Administration Act 38 of 1927, replaced by s 1(1) of Act 45 of 1988. See below, [32].
2. *Ex parte Minister of Native Affairs: In re Yako v Beyi* 1948 (1) SA 388 (A) at 399.
3. *House of Assembly* Debates 28 April 1927, col 2909.
4. *Mokoena v Mofokeng* 1945 NAC (C&O) 89.
5. Simons *African Women* 9.

The author speaks of changing customary law to reflect the 'needs of people at varying stages of cultural transition'. The conflict of laws offers a simple solution: rather than change the substance of the law (with the implication that all persons are bound by the changes regardless of their personal predilections), customary law may in individual cases be excluded in favour of the common law. In this way effect can be given to social change on a particular, case-by-case basis,[4] instead of a nation-wide, general basis.[5]

(2) An exercise of discretion

Formerly, application of customary law was regulated by s 11(1) of the Black Administration Act where it was provided that commissioners' courts had a discretion to apply customary law

> 'in all suits or proceedings between Blacks involving questions of customs followed by Blacks . . . except in so far as it [had] been repealed or modified'.

This section was repealed in 1986[6] and re-enacted as s 54A(1) of the Magistrates' Courts Act.[7] The scope of application of customary law was broadened somewhat to include criminal matters,[8] but significantly such law remained limited to 'Blacks'.[9] The abstruse requirement that the suit or proceeding must involve 'questions of customs followed by Blacks' was unfortunately retained. It has never been clear what 'custom' meant in this context: a norm that was not yet a legal norm or a pattern of behaviour having concrete existence? In any event the courts have paid little attention to this stipulation. They have simply assumed that it meant actions in which customary law offered applicable rules.[10]

This implied the existence of 'gaps' in customary law, and on this assumption a rule was contrived that customary law could be applied to a claim only when

---

[4] A measure entailing a degree of artificiality since, in experience, attitudes and beliefs are not held in any coherent or monolithic form. In actual situations culture 'does not function as a whole but in bits': Van Doorne (1981) 21 *Cahiers d'Études Africaines* 482.

[5] Bennett (1980) 18 *J Mod Afr Studies* 127ff.

[6] Section 2 of Act 34.

[7] 32 of 1944.

[8] Cf *R v Swaartbooi* 1916 EDL 170.

[9] As defined in s 35 of the Black Administration Act 38 of 1927. See above, [17] 66ff.

[10] *Nzalo v Maseko* 1931 NAC (N&T) 41; *Magadla v Hams* 1936 NAC (C&O) 56; *Mkize v Mnguni* 1952 NAC 242 (NE). And see *Ex parte Minister of Native Affairs: In re Yako v Beyi* 1948 (1) SA 388 (A).

it could offer a remedy.[11] So persistent was this contention that it survived two Appellate Division decisions[12] in which Schreiner JA held that the circumstances of the case might dictate that justice would better be served by applying customary law even if it did not contain a remedy.[13] In principle, of course, any choice of law rule predicated on the existence or absence of remedies is bound to be arbitrary,[14] and for that reason at least cannot be supported.

In 1988 s 54A(1) of the Magistrates' Courts Act was repealed. The following provision took its place.

[32] SECTION 1 LAW OF EVIDENCE AMENDMENT ACT 45 OF 1988

(1) Any court may take judicial notice of the law of a foreign state and of indigenous law in so far as such law can be ascertained readily and with sufficient certainty: Provided that indigenous law shall not be opposed to the principles of public policy or natural justice: Provided further that it shall not be lawful for any court to declare that the custom of lobola or bogadi or other similar custom is repugnant to such principles.

(2) The provisions of subsection (1) shall not preclude any party from adducing evidence of the substance of a legal rule contemplated in that subsection which is in issue at the proceedings concerned. . . .

(4) For the purposes of this section "indigenous law" means the Black law or customs as applied by the Black tribes in the Republic or in territories which formerly formed part of the Republic.

This enactment, together with the repeal of s 54A(1), had far-reaching implications for the application of customary law. In the first place, the racial limitations were removed, so it is now possible for a white person to be subjected to customary law. Secondly, the confusing qualification that the case should involve questions of customs followed by Blacks was omitted. Thirdly, the caveat that customary law may be applied only in so far as it had not been repealed or modified was dropped. It was in fact otiose, since any law in the country must be read subject to prevailing legislation unless a special exception has been made.[15] Fourthly, customary law may now be applied in *any* court in South Africa. Prior to 1986, both the magistrates' courts and the Supreme Court could apply customary law, but they had to treat it as if it were the custom of common law or a foreign law; in other words it had to be specially proved for each case. This is no longer necessary.

The courts' general authorization to apply customary law is subject to two provisos and one qualification. The latter affects proof and ascertainment: a court may take judicial notice of customary law only if it 'can be ascertained readily and with sufficient certainty'. If the law is not immediately discoverable,

---

[11] *Nkwana v Nonqanaba* 1 NAC 79 (1904); *Tumana v Smayile & another* 1 NAC 207 (1908); *Muguboya v Mutato* 1929 NAC (N&T) 73 at 76; *Ntsabelle v Poolo* 1930 NAC (N&T) 13; *Nqanoyi v Njombeni* 1930 NAC (C&O) 13; *Magidela v Sawintshi* 1943 NAC (C&O) 52 at 53; *Mtolo v Poswa* 1950 NAC 253 (S); *Sibanda v Sitole* 1951 NAC 347 (NE).

[12] *Ex parte Minister of Native Affairs: In re Yako v Beyi* 1948 (1) SA 388 (A) at 399 and *Umvovo* 1953 (1) SA 195 (A) at 201.

[13] And see *Mahashe* 1955 NAC 149 (S) and *Togo v Molatoli* 1976 BAC 20 (C).

[14] Bennett (1979) 96 *SALJ* 413–14.

[15] Bennett (1981) 30 *ICLQ* 86–7 and Allott *New Essays* 179.

it must be proved according to the rules specified for custom (and formerly foreign law). For this purpose s 1(2) of the Act allows the parties to lead evidence of the substance of any legal rule in contention.[16]

The two provisos are of less practical importance. The first is a general reservation in favour of public policy and natural justice, which is considered in detail below. The second proviso excepts bridewealth from the purview of the first. It was a special dispensation intended originally to reverse the practice of the Transvaal courts which, long before 1927, had decreed that bridewealth transactions could not be enforced because they were 'uncivilized'.[17]

Former legislation expressly provided that the courts had a discretion to apply customary law. Although any mention of discretion has now been omitted, it would still follow from the absence of an explicit provision controlling the application of customary law that all courts have a discretionary power to apply it. Earlier, the courts held that this discretion was a judicial one, and if exercised capriciously, arbitrarily or without substantial reason, the decision could be upset on appeal.[18] On this basis the Appeal Courts elaborated a complex set of guides to choice of law.

By making the application of customary law a discretionary matter the legislature actually defeated its own avowed purpose, which was to ensure uniformity of application throughout the country. For some time after the passing of the Native Administration Act in 1927, the Appeal Courts of the Natal and Transvaal division on the one hand, and the Cape and the Orange Free State division on the other, continued to approach the problem in accordance with traditions established before the Act. Thus the Cape division construed s 11(1) to mean that common law was primarily applicable and customary law only in matters which were 'peculiar to Native Customs falling outside the principles of Roman-Dutch law'.[19] The other division of the court took the opposite view: *customary* law was primarily applicable, and it was only as a matter of exception that the common law could be applied.[20] The President of this division of the Court, McLoughlin, was a champion of legal segregation. He maintained that Parliament had disapproved of the Cape's assimilationist policy,[21] and he persisted in holding that customary law was generally applicable to cases involving Africans because it was 'the basic and primary' system of law practised by them. It was 'the system familiar to them, and unquestionably the only system they contemplate and follow in their daily dealings'.[22]

The obdurate refusal of the courts to change their approaches finally prompted the Minister of Native Affairs to seek a definitive interpretation of s 11(1) from the Appellate Division.

---

[16] See below, 141ff.
[17] *Kaba v Ntela* 1910 TPD 964 at 969.
[18] *Umvovo* 1950 NAC 190 (S) and *Mtolo v Poswa* 1950 NAC 253 (S).
[19] *Nqanoyi v Njombeni* 1930 NAC (C&O) 13.
[20] *Matsheng v Dhlamini & another* 1937 NAC (N&T) 89 at 92 and *Kaula v Mtimkulu & another* 1938 NAC (N&T) 68 at 71.
[21] *Yako v Beyi* 1944 NAC (C&O) 72 at 77.
[22] *Yako's* case supra at 76.

[33] *EX PARTE MINISTER OF NATIVE AFFAIRS: IN RE YAKO v BEYI* 1948 (1)
SA 388 (A) at 396–401

Coming now more directly to the nature of the discretion given by the sub-section, assuming that the conditions for its exercise exist, there would seem to be three possible views. The first would be that the native commissioner has an entirely free choice, without being required, in cases where he is in doubt, to prefer the one system of law to the other. The second view would be that common law is to be applied unless the native commissioner is satisfied that native law should be used; and the third would be the converse of the second, namely, that native law should be used save where it was, in the native commissioner's opinion, unsuited to the proceedings. In the two main judgments in question in the present proceedings the president who delivered them appears to have taken the third view, that native law is what he calls the primary system of law applicable in cases between natives and that it should always be applied where possible. It is only, I gather, where native law can provide no answer at all that resort may, in his opinion, be had to common law. In support of his opinion the president adduces a number of arguments, most of which appear to bear rather on controversial matters relating to the supposed advantages of applying native law in native cases than on the question for decision, namely, the meaning to be given to sec 11(1). It may well be that both before and after the passing of Act 38 of 1927 different views have been held by persons having claims to be considered expert in such matters as to the proper place to be accorded to native law and common law in suits between natives; and it may also well be that in different parts of the Union different opinions on the subject have predominated and have changed from time to time. But these considerations appear to me to be of little assistance in arriving at the meaning to be given to the sub-section. No doubt when colonisation takes place among a people having their own customary law, and when the law of the colonists becomes the law of the land, difficult questions of policy are likely to arise as to the proper extent of recognition and use, at any particular period, of the customary law of the native inhabitants; and presumably South Africa has not been exceptional in this respect. Faced by such difficulties, Parliament, in enacting sec 11(1) appears to have used a device which may have been expected to permit of some elasticity and provide scope for development, so as to achieve the primary desideratum of an equitable decision between the parties without laying down any hard and fast rule as to the system of law to be used to attain that end.

I can find no support in the language of Act 38 of 1927 for the president's view that native law should be treated as *prima facie* applicable in cases between natives. On the contrary, the indications are rather that common law was intended to be applied unless the native commissioner in his discretion saw fit in a proper case to apply native law. That view is supported by the general shape of the sub-section, which does not provide that the native commissioner shall have a discretion to apply common law or even that he shall have a discretion to apply common law or native law. Framed as it is, it appears to me that the sub-section assumes that the native commissioner should in general apply common law and on that assumption empowers him in a proper case to apply native law. But I do not find it necessary for the purpose of deciding the present matter to hold that such a *prima facie* preference for the use of common law exists; and as there are various factors which the native commissioner would in one case or another have to take into account and which would ordinarily outweigh any such preference I think that I should assume, what leads for present purposes to the same result, that the native commissioner should exercise his discretion without regarding either of the systems of law as *prima facie* applicable. In each case he has at some stage to determine which system of law it would be fairest to apply in deciding the case between the parties. I think that he should only finally decide which system of law he is going to apply after considering all the evidence and argument as part of his eventual decision on the case; but it would probably be convenient in many cases for him to indicate at an earlier stage, and possibly even at the commencement of the trial, what law he would provisionally regard as applicable.

In this connection reference may be made to a feature that bulks largely in the two judgments under review. The president speaks with disapproval of the plaintiff's having recourse to common law to obtain a greater benefit than would be allowed under native law. By seeking a remedy at common law, where only a less favourable one, or possibly even where none at all, would be obtainable under native law, the president considers that the plaintiff is trying to enrich himself or herself unjustly at the expense of the defendant. It may have been found convenient for a native plaintiff to indicate in his statement of claim on which system of law he relies, but I cannot think that it should be necessary for him to do so. Apart from any rule of Court that may have been introduced in this connection it would seem that the plaintiff should only be required to allege, and later to prove, the facts which he claims entitle him to relief. It is for the native commissioner to decide what relief, if any, the plaintiff should receive, and in order to arrive at that decision he will generally, or at least often, have to decide which system of law to apply. But it is not a question of the plaintiff's forcing his action into a European mould, or ignoring the system of law peculiar to himself to the detriment of his adversary or compelling the Court to deviate from that system by the mere form of his claim—to quote some of the expressions used by the president. This language seems to me to lose sight of the fact that it is the native commissioner's duty to give judgment for that one of the litigants who is in the right according to the legal system which, in the exercise of his discretion, the native commissioner decides to apply in the case. The litigants are entitled to the due exercise of that discretion and neither of them can be criticised because he claims, or claims successfully, that the discretion should be exercised in the manner most favourable to his action or his defence.

It is not necessary for the decision of this matter that this Court should lay down, or even indicate on general lines, the factors that should be taken into account by the native commissioner in exercising his discretion. But I think that I should express my disagreement with a suggestion made by the president that if a native commissioner were to decide to apply common law in a particular case because the parties or either of them were educated, civilised, urbanised or detribalised, to mention some of the expressions used in this connection, he would be giving effect improperly to class distinctions. I cannot agree with this suggestion. No doubt the discretion to decide which system of law to apply in a case carries with it a great responsibility—greater than that generally borne by Courts of Law. And, in particular, the discretion to award damages according to different scales to persons of different social or economic groups has obviously to be employed with circumspection, for generally speaking justice favours equality of treatment. But in actions for damages arising out of an *injuria* it is often only possible to do justice by taking into account the whole personality of the person injured, including his or her social standards. It may well carry more disastrous consequences for a native school teacher in an urban area if she is seduced than for a woman whose life has been spent in the rustic seclusion of a reserve. There may be different kinds of public opinion on the subject in the different localities and the teacher may suffer a sense of shame or downfall that the kraal dweller, despite the existence of tribal sanctions, may not feel. Naturally these environmental factors are not the only ones to be considered and the apparent sensitiveness of the individual may in particular cases be of greater importance in assessing damages in such cases than her walk in life. But it would be quite wrong to apply sec. 11(1) without regard to the circumstances of particular cases. It would not be a proper exercise of the discretion given by that sub-section for a native commissioner to hold that all cases of seduction should be dealt with as if the parties were living under primitive tribal conditions. In this connection reference should be made to a passage in the president's judgment in *Mashego v Ntombela* in which he says:

> "There are no criteria for ascertaining when a native is detribalised, and exemption from Native Law has not been accorded by the Courts on this basis. It can only be definitely applied on the basis of formal exemption from the operation of Native Law."

If by this the president intended to convey that the exercise of his discretion by the native commissioner must be decisively controlled by the fact that the plaintiff or the defendant is, or that both parties are unexempted, I must express my disagreement with this view. The non-exemption of either or both of the parties is only one of the factors to be taken into account by the native commissioner in exercising his discretion.

It is, however, right I think, to point out that it would not necessarily and in all cases lead to a juster result to apply the system of law which alone gives the plaintiff a remedy or which gives him or her the more adequate remedy. Generally, no doubt, if a remedy exists under one of the two systems but not under the other this would be a reason for applying the former, since the existence of a remedy, especially under the more advanced system of law, itself provides some ground for believing that its general application would probably be in the interests of justice. But in some cases it may seem to be preferable to give effect to a defence that the defendant has under the one system and not under the other. For instance in the particular kind of case with which we are here concerned if the woman has already received adequate damages at common law from her seducer it might be thought to establish a fairer balance between the parties if, when he is thereafter sued by the woman's guardian, the latter were non-suited because his case should also, in view of the previous judgment in favour of the woman, be adjudged at common law, which, I assume, would not accord him a right of action. On the other hand if the defendant had failed to implement the former judgment it might be thought to be fairer to award the guardian a further judgment under native law. Or, indeed, the proper conclusion might be that there is no good reason in any case for not allowing both the woman and the guardian to recover in full, each under the legal system that favours her or his case. I mention these possibilities not to express any opinion on them but only to indicate the undesirability of restricting by an unduly rigid practice the discretion which the Legislature has designedly placed in the hands of native commissioners.

In this connection reference may be made to the question how far native commissioners should regard themselves as being bound to follow the decisions of the Native Appeal Courts in relation to the exercise of the discretion vested in them. The discretion is, of course, a judicial one and where a point on which its exercise would naturally depend has already been unequivocally decided in the Native Appeal Court for the area in which the native commissioner's court is situated, or even in the other Native Appeal Court, it would, I think, be the proper course for the native commissioner to follow the decision. For even in matters where discretion operates, the rule of *stare decisis* should in general be observed. This is illustrated by the fact that Judges are accustomed to have regard to previous decisions in making orders as to costs, which are usually discretionary. But the native commissioner must of course pay principal regard to the facts of the case before him since the dominant consideration is his own reasoned view as to the best system of law to apply in order to reach a just decision between the parties.

While this case corrected the dogmatic assertions of the Natal and Transvaal division and clarified the choice of law *process*, it did not prescribe any rules for choosing the appropriate law. Schreiner JA merely alluded to certain factors which could be used to select the applicable law. These 'connecting factors' exist within the complex of facts that constitutes the issue before the court. They serve to link the case to a particular legal system. The discernment and application of the relevant connecting factors lies at the heart of the conflict process: they are the signposts to the appropriate law.

The overall choice of law process is designed to select the legal system which the parties might reasonably have been expected to apply in the context of the case.[23]

---

[23] Bennett 105–6.

(a) Agreement and intention

If the court's goal is to gratify the expectations of the litigants, then it can do no better than give effect to an agreement they may have concluded that a particular law should apply. Such an agreement might be express or it might be inferred from the parties' behaviour. In the majority of cases it is apparent from the face of the plaintiff's summons (viz the nature of the remedy, or the type or quantum of damages sought) that he or she has opted for a particular legal system as the basis of the suit.[24] If the defendant does nothing to contest the choice of this law, the court may infer acquiescence in the plaintiff's selection.

In private international law there has been some disquiet about allowing the parties complete freedom to choose their legal system. It has been argued that they ought not be allowed to contract out of certain mandatory rules which would otherwise bind them. And it was apparent from the wording of the former s 11(1) of the Black Administration Act that the decision whether or not to apply customary law lay within the discretion of the court (a discretion jealously guarded by the commissioners). By implication this meant that the parties, or one party, could not usurp that discretion.[25]

Aside from the possibility of perpetrating a fraud on third persons, however, there seems to be no good reason for inhibiting the parties' selection of a law that is convenient for their purposes. Indeed, people subject to customary law have always been free to apply for exemption from it, and they may use any of the forms and institutions of the common law, such as wills and contracts.[26] It is only where there happens to be a mandatory *choice of law* rule, such as the ones contained in ss 22 and 23 of the Black Administration Act, that the parties are prevented from choosing their legal system.

(b) Nature of a prior transaction

If the court seeks to give effect to the law intended by the parties, it must discover from their words and deeds what legal system they contemplated. In the following case the plaintiff claimed a considerable sum of money representing arrear maintenance for his sister's three minor children. The defendant had been married to the plaintiff's sister, but when she had died the children had been left in the plaintiff's care. He indicated that he was bringing his claim under the common law; if customary law were applied he would be entitled to only three head of cattle as isondlo.

[34] *SIBANDA v SITOLE* 1951 NAC 347 (NE) at 350

The obligation sought to be enforced in the present case is of a contractual nature, i.e. it is based on an implied contract, in respect of which both systems of law provide a remedy; this Court must therefore ascertain and give effect to the intention of the parties. If it is

---

[24] *Mbaza v Tshewula NO* 1947 NAC (C&O) 72.

[25] *Lebona v Ramokone* 1946 NAC (C&O) 14 at 16.

[26] In Botswana by s 4(a) of the Customary Law (Application and Ascertainment) Act 51 of 1969 and in Zimbabwe by s 3(1)(a)(i) of the Customary Law and Primary Courts Act 6 of 1981, special provision is made for express choice of law by the parties.

clear that the parties contemplated Native Law, that law should be applied, otherwise the Common Law obtains.

The parties to the present action are not living under primitive tribal conditions but it is clear from the record of the proceedings in this case that they not only observed Native Law in the matter at issue and in closely allied matters, but also that the matter at issue had its origin in their observance of that system of law.

That this is so, is evidenced by the following factors:

1. Defendant's union with plaintiff's sister, Elizabeth, *was a customary one and not a marriage according to Common Law*. . . .
2. According to plaintiff's evidence, he maintained the children concerned and his sister, Elizabeth, up to her death, *as defendant had not paid lobolo for her but only the "vulamlomo"* fee, which makes it obvious that such maintenance was dictated by Native Law and Custom.
3. Plaintiff stated in his evidence—"defendant never asked me for the children before the last case. I've always been prepared to give him the children since the last case. I've waited for him to bring the balance of the lobolo and fetch the children. Even before the last case I was not refusing with the children but I wanted the balance of the lobolo. I claimed 12 cattle balance at that time. The Court held that the balance of lobolo was only £4. 5s. After the last case defendant did not tender me £4. 5s. and request the children.". . . The retention of a wife and children by her father or other person who would be her guardian if she had not contracted a customary union to secure payment of lobolo outstanding for her by such children's father or other person is also a custom peculiar to Native Law which is known as "teleka" or "ukuteleka".
4. It is clear from the evidence that the amount which was to be paid by defendant to plaintiff for the maintenance of his three children by the latter was neither discussed nor agreed upon by them, which would be an altogether extraordinary mode of dealing if the parties contemplated Common Law, particularly if regard is had to the very lengthy period for which plaintiff maintained the children, viz., from 1st June 1938, until the issue of the summons in the present case on the 20th September, 1950; but which would be the normal procedure under Native Law which provides for the payment of "isondhlo" (maintenance) in such cases at the rate of one head of cattle per child irrespective of the period of maintenance.
5. Plaintiff made no claim for the maintenance of defendant's wife, i.e. of plaintiff's sister, Elizabeth, which is a significant feature in that no such claim lies in Native Law.
6. Plaintiff made no claim for the maintenance of the children over a period of years and only eventually made such claim after having been ordered by the Court in the previous action to return them to defendant, which is a practice much more in keeping with Native Law than Common Law.
7. According to the evidence, plaintiff's mother who took care of the children concerned whilst the former maintained them, received the "vulamlomo" beast and arranged for the customary union of the eldest girl child and did so with plaintiff's knowledge, thus signifying adherence to Native Law.
8. The relationship of the parties coupled with the fact that no sum for the maintenance of the children was discussed or agreed upon by them over a period of years and no claim therefor made for years also lends colour to the view that the parties had Native Law in mind rather than Common Law in the matter at issue.

If a common intention cannot be inferred at the time that the issues are joined, it may be inferred from behaviour out of which the immediate claim arises. It is doubtful whether the court should have treated the claim in *Sibanda's* case as an implied contract, but for purposes of the conflict of laws a clear principle was established: from prior transactions a choice of law may be inferred. Bilateral transactions commonly associated with an African way of life, like bridewealth and loans of cattle, unequivocally point to customary law; and the court is usually safe in imputing to the parties an intention to deal in terms of that system.[27]

(c) Subject-matter and environment of transactions

Where a juristic act or transaction is not culturally marked in any way, and is therefore known to both systems of law, the courts have delved deeper into the case in an attempt to discover its cultural orientation. This they discern from the purpose, subject-matter, or environment of the transaction.

In the following case (a claim arising out of a money loan) it was argued that, because cash was originally unknown in Africa, the common law should be applied. On this basis interest on the loan was claimed.

[35] *MHLONGO* 1937 NAC (N&T) 124 at 125–6

In order to give effect to the intention of the parties the Native Commissioner is bound to ascertain the nature of the contract concluded by them. He cannot, as in the present case, arbitrarily rule that, *ex facie* the summons, a money transaction is obviously unknown to them. This reasoning is illogical since money is in itself only a token and among Natives other articles served as tokens before contact was made with Europeans, e.g. ivory, brass rings, hoes, etc. . . .

The nature of the transaction should be the test. If for instance a lobolo is paid in money as is frequently done nowadays, the transaction remains a contract in Native law and enforceable as such. Obviously too a plea of prescription cannot hold good in such a case.

Now the contract of loan is one which the Natives have practised from time immemorial—it includes the well-known custom of "sisa" otherwise known as "nqoma" or "mafisha" and a loan of a beast or other equivalent for lobolo is also well known and frequently practised. If it should happen that under this custom one man advances a sum of money to another to enable him to complete a lobolo being paid in money it is difficult to contend that the transaction has thereby lost its original nature, viz., a loan under Native custom.

On the other hand it is known that Natives practise commerce and engage in transactions in contracts which are purely every day Common law dealings. Such undoubtedly would fall under the statutory rules of prescription.

The purpose of a transaction has also been relevant in finding an association with a particular legal system.[28] And in the following action the geographical environment of the contract became important.

[36] *SAWINTSHI v MAGIDELA* 1944 NAC (C&O) 47

This is a sequel to the case reported in 1943 NAC (C&O) 52. The evidence showed that the parties were tribal Natives living in the reserve, the one selling certain mealies to the other.

The matter is one common to both systems of law, Native and European.

The parties are reserve Natives contracting in the reserve in home grown products. Unless the contrary be shown they must be taken to have contracted as Natives under the law familiar and peculiar to them, i.e., Native law. There is nothing to show that they did not do so. Had the seller been a licensed dealer in produce, or a trader, and the transaction

---

[27] *Nxumalo v Ngubane* 1932 NAC (N&T) 34. See, eg, bridewealth transactions: *Peme v Gwele* 1941 NAC (C&O) 3 and *Fuzile v Ntloko* 1944 NAC (C&O) 2. Conversely commercial contracts warrant application of the common law: *Dhlamini v Nhlapo* 1942 NAC (N&T) 62 and *Maholo v Mate* 1945 NAC (C&O) 63.

[28] See *Mpikakane v Kunene* 1940 NAC (N&T) 10 and *Warosi v Zotimba* 1942 NAC (C&O) 55.

was in the ordinary course of business, it could be a fair presumption that he was acting under common law and subject to that law. But that is not so here.

Consequently the Native Commissioner's ruling that "Native law will apply and that prescription does not apply with costs" must be upheld and the appeal be dismissed with costs.

Rider by President

I respectfully differ from the dictum in the first judgment of this Court that in cases of doubt common law must prevail. . . . "If both systems are applicable, it is common sense and natural to expect the Natives, who are parties, to think and act under their system rather than the European, whose pitfalls are unknown to them and, therefore, not in contemplation."

(d) Form of a transaction

Where a transaction is known to both legal systems, the parties' use of a form peculiar to one may be decisive in evincing an intent to abide by that system. In these circumstances the courts infer intent from the use of certain culturally specific practices. For instance, if the parties married in church or a civil registry office, the form of the ceremony establishes the applicability of common law to matters as diverse as capacity to marry, the consequences of the marriage, and any divorce action. Similarly, if a person has disposed of property mortis causa by a document duly signed and witnessed, this may be treated as a will, with the result that its terms and the devolution of the estate are governed by the common law. In both examples the form of the juristic act is considered vital for the choice of law.

(e) Lifestyle of the parties

Many cases, notably delictual actions and claims arising out of family obligations, do not involve a prior transaction. In these matters especially, the overall cultural orientation of the parties' lifestyles has had a strong influence on the choice of law. People who adhere to a notionally traditional, African way of life have been deemed subject to customary law, while those who have become acculturated to a western lifestyle have been deemed subject to the common law. By gauging a prevalent lifestyle, the courts have sought to impute a cultural orientation and thus a legal system to the parties.[29] In two well-known cases from Lesotho—*Mokorosi v Mokorosi & others*[30] and *Hoohlo*[31]—for instance, the courts undertook a detailed investigation of the parties' lifestyles, paying close attention to the following factors: place of residence; occupation; religion; the parties' education and the education they gave to their children; style of dress, eating and sleeping habits; use of bank accounts; preparation of wills; consultation with attorneys.[32]

The following South African case demonstrates a similar approach. The plaintiff claimed damages for seduction and for expenses resulting from the birth

---

[29] In Zimbabwe this has been incorporated into the statutory choice of law rules: s 3(2)(*a*) of the Customary Law and Primary Courts Act 6 of 1981.

[30] 1967–70 LLR 1.

[31] 1967–70 LLR 318.

[32] Poulter *Legal Dualism in Lesotho* 24–8.

and maintenance of a child. The defendant objected that the damages should have been awarded in terms of customary law. The Appeal Court held that the court a quo had rightly applied the common law.

[37] *RAMOTHATA v MAKHOTHE* 1934 NAC (N&T) 74 at 76–7

The Plaintiff is a Native farmer on a considerable scale in the Rustenburg district. In addition he owns considerable property in the Alexandra township near Johannesburg. He and his wife were married not under Native law and custom but according to civil rites. He himself was educated at Lovedale and he is a preacher and elder of the Presbyterian Church. He has displayed the greatest care to ensure that his children will receive a good education according to European ideas and not only sent his daughter Motselisi to Lovedale but after she had completed her studies there sent her to Johannesburg for the express purpose of learning music. Above everything else, the letter which the Plaintiff addressed to the Defendant on the 24th October, 1933, in regard to the seduction of Motselisi, clearly indicates that he is an enlightened Native who has become detribalised and has adopted European sentiments and ideas.

The Defendant himself is a tailor by profession and apparently carries on business on a fairly large scale in the Alexandra township. He is a married man, his marriage was contracted according to Christian rites and he is a member of the Lutheran Church.

The court was fortunate in this case that both parties had the same lifestyle; the issue would have been far more difficult to solve if the plaintiff had had one lifestyle and the defendant a different one. Most courts confronted with this type of problem have arbitrarily applied the law associated with one of the parties, most often the defendant. This decision is compelled by an unspecified value judgment in the sense that one party is implicitly deemed more important for legal purposes than the other—a specious reason for choice of law.[33] A more reasoned choice could be made by considering the parties' lifestyles in conjunction with other connecting factors, such as the general environment of the claim.[34]

(f) Exemption from customary law

It was considered to be part of the civilizing mission of the imperial powers to allow fully acculturated Africans exemption from customary law in favour of what was thought the more advanced systems of metropolitan law.[35] This policy was first implemented in Natal,[36] and was continued in terms of s 31 of the Black Administration Act. The discretion to grant exemption is vested in the State President,[37] which is now presumably delegated to the Minister of Education and Development Aid. The procedure has never been popular in Africa, however, and very few people have made use of it.[38]

---

[33] Wengler (1961 III) 104 *Recueil des Cours* 94.

[34] Bennett 110.

[35] Salacuse *An Introduction to Law in French-speaking Africa* 449; Robert (1959) 11 *J Afr Admin* 124–31.

[36] Law 11 of 1864.

[37] See GN 1233 of 1936.

[38] But see Visser in Van der Westhuizen et al *Huldigingsbundel Paul van Warmelo* 258 regarding the free choice of law in the former Dutch East Indies.

The effect of exemption from customary law is uncertain. It is clear that the person exempted is not simply to be treated as though he or she were a white. For example, exempted persons used to remain subject to the jurisdiction of commissioners' courts[39] and they were bound by customary-law transactions they had entered into before exemption.[40] (Despite these decisions, the courts never evolved an acquired rights doctrine to protect the interests of other parties from the exemption procedure.) From the courts' general approach it is apparent that exemption was not treated as a complete change of personal law; rather it was assumed to be an express choice of lifestyle and hence only one factor, albeit an influential one, that could be taken into account in the choice of law process.

(g) *Estoppel and unifying techniques*

Choice of law has been simplified by use of the principles of estoppel and res judicata. It has been held that where the plaintiff invoked a particular system of law in his claim he may not object to the defendant raising defences under the same system.[41] Conversely, if the defendant relied on a defence known to only one system of law, he is estopped from objecting to the plaintiff's reliance on the same system.[42] There is a variation of this argument involving the principle of res judicata. If a litigant sues unsuccessfully under one system of law, he may not later sue again relying on a different system of law. The matter will be treated as res judicata.[43]

The choice of law process has been unified by treating all aspects of an action as subject to one legal system: defences must be governed by the same system of law that was applied to the main claim; damages must be quantified in accordance with the law applied to the cause of action;[44] and likewise questions of locus standi in judicio and the contractual/delictual capacity of the parties are governed by the law applicable to the main claim.[45]

(h) *The 'repugnancy' proviso*

The application of customary law is subject to a so-called 'repugnancy' proviso, namely, a proviso that customary law may not be applied if it is contrary to natural justice or public policy. This was a general limitation imposed on the recognition of customary law in colonial Africa. It was felt that official tolerance should not be compromised by recognition of such barbarous practices as female circumcision, slavery, trial by ordeal, witchcraft, and even polygyny and bridewealth.

---

[39] *Mahludi v Rex* (1905) 26 NLR 298 at 315; *Mdhlalose v Mabaso* 1931 NAC (N&T) 24.

[40] *Kaula v Mtimkulu & another* 1938 NAC (N&T) 68 and *Ngcobo v Dhlamini* 1943 NAC (N&T) 13. But see *Miya v Nene* 1947 NAC (N&T) 3.

[41] *Warosi v Zotimba* 1942 NAC (C&O) 55 at 57.

[42] *Goba v Mtwalo* 1932 NAC (N&T) 58.

[43] *Mahaye v Mabaso* 1951 NAC 280 (NE); *Kabe & another v Inganga* 1954 NAC 220 (C); and see *Booi v Xozwa* 4 NAC 310 (1921).

[44] *Buthelezi v Msimang* 1964 BAC 105 (S).

[45] Section 11(3) of the Black Administration Act 38 of 1927; and see Bennett 112–17.

[38] PEART 1982 *ACTA JURIDICA* 105–10

The application of the repugnancy clause raises three preliminary questions. First, section 11(1) of the Black Administration Act provides that the court has a discretion to apply customary law, except where that system of law is contrary to the principles of public policy or natural justice. In other words, the function of the repugnancy clause is to ensure that customary law will not be applied if it is repugnant. This means that the clause may be invoked by a court only when it has decided, in terms of the conflict of law rules, to apply customary law to the dispute; the court then has a particular rule before it which must be evaluated in the light of public policy and natural justice. The repugnancy proviso should not be construed as a choice of law rule, as has happened at times.[1]

Secondly, should the repugnancy proviso be used to strike down a rule of customary law in the abstract or a rule as applicable to the facts of a particular case? On a literal reading of section 11(1), it seems that the legislature intended the rule to be examined in the abstract. The section provides that "such Black law" must not be opposed to the principles of public policy or natural justice. Clearly, this provision does not empower the courts to consider the application of a rule in the context of a particular dispute but rather to determine, in general, the acceptability of a rule of customary law. On the one hand, this interpretation avoids the risk of applying customary law in an arbitrary manner, ie, if a rule of customary law were struck down only in relation to a particular set of facts, the application of customary law would become ever more uncertain. On the other hand, considering a rule in the abstract ensures that the repugnancy clause is not used merely to avoid hard cases.[2]

Thirdly, should the court regard the terms "natural justice" and "public policy" separately or jointly? The wording of the repugnancy clause suggests that the terms should be considered separately. If that is the case, then what do the terms mean? It is not altogether clear what natural justice means, since it has never been exhaustively defined. From a reading of the South African cases, it appears that natural justice is, nowadays, usually identified with the basic requirements of the law of procedure, such as the *audi alteram partem* rule and other principles of fairness which a court of law should observe. But this is not the only meaning of the term. . . . [A]s used in the repugnancy clause, [it] implies more than that[3] because it is substantive customary law which must not be contrary to the principles of natural justice. In this context, natural justice should be understood to mean natural law, because it is from natural law that principles of natural justice have evolved.

While natural justice, in its modern, narrow sense, refers to matters of procedure, public policy is usually involved in relation to substantive law. The concept was developed in the common law to serve the practical needs of a particular society. Unlike natural justice, it is neither universal nor eternal nor does it, necessarily, propose an ideal standard to which all law ought to conform; rather, it is a principle which can be invoked from time to time, as circumstances demand, to override a particular law. . . . That there is a difference between the two concepts is not always evident from the approach of the courts in South Africa. They have often used a variety of non-specific terms to indicate repugnancy.

Notes

1. *Mbuli v Mehlomakulu* 1961 NAC 68 (S). And see R D Leslie 1977 *AJ* 117.
2. *Maguga v Scotch* 1931 NAC (N&T) 54; *Mdutywa v Mvingwa* 1940 NAC (C&O) 34.
3. Natural justice was applied in its procedural sense in *Phiri v Nkosi* 1941 NAC (N&T) 94 at 98 and *S v Mukwevho; S v Ramukhuba* 1983 (3) SA 498 (V) at 502.

Despite use of the term 'natural justice', which might suggest a culture-free criterion, the courts have assumed that the standards set by western civilization are sufficient in themselves.[46] This might have led to a narrowly ethnocentric

---

[46] See *Gwao bin Kilimo v Kisunda bin Ifuti* (1938) TLR 403 at 405.

approach, but in practice the courts have been remarkably restrained in their application of the repugnancy clause. In this context, the Zimbabwe case *Chiduku v Chidano*[47] is often quoted: the court will invoke the repugnancy clause only with regard 'to such customs as inherently impress us with some abhorrence or are obviously immoral in their incidence'.[48]

When the courts refuse to apply customary law, their reasons are often not given. It might be because the rule was repugnant to public policy; the rule had not been proved to the court's satisfaction; or because a particular *transaction*, not a rule, was in issue. In the following case a husband (the plaintiff) had paid the defendant bridewealth in order to contract a valid marriage. Shortly after the wedding the bride died. The defendant then sent the plaintiff a sister of the deceased (a girl under the age of puberty) as a substitute wife. The young girl refused to remain with the plaintiff who accordingly claimed return of the girl or return of his bridewealth. Both claims were refused by the Appeal Court.

[39] *GIDJA v YINGWANE* 1944 NAC (N&T) 4 at 5–6

The parties to the suit are Shangaans. The Native Commissioner refers to certain authorities on Shangaan custom, according to whom it is a well recognised custom that when a wife dies childless early in marriage, the guardian must, when requested by the husband, provide a substitute wife, or, if unable and unwilling to do so, must refund the lobolo received for the deceased wife. He says that it is unnecessary to decide whether the girl, Ingona, was promised to plaintiff as a substitute wife or not as defendant has definitely refused to agree to allow her to be taken by plaintiff, and that in any case it would be contrary to public policy to recognise plaintiff's claim on this point as the girl has not yet attained puberty.

. . . Section 11 of Act No. 38 of 1927 gives Native Commissioners discretion to decide questions of customs followed by Natives according to Native law applying to such customs, provided that such law is not opposed to the principles of public policy or natural justice.

Whatever then may be the custom in a particular tribe, the Courts will not sanction it if satisfied that it is in conflict with justice or public policy, although the Legislature may not have expressly forbidden it.

Our modern civilization recognises that a girl has full liberty of choice in the matter of marriage and that this freedom is the prerogative of all women of whatever colour or race. A father cannot be allowed to pledge his daughter as a man's prospective wife. The promise said to have been made by the defendant is contrary to public policy and natural justice and cannot be considered for a moment even if substantiated. It is a matter for surprise that plaintiff's attorney has embodied in the summons a claim that Ingona, the pledged girl, should be delivered to his client. That part of the claim is wholly untenable.

The alternative claim is for a refund of the lobolo paid for Gobasi. The Native Commissioner, relying on writings of certain authors, is satisfied that lobolo must be refunded however long a customary union has subsisted if the deceased wife has not born children. That is said to be the Shangaan custom.

In Natal a refund of a portion of the lobolo, not exceeding one half, may be claimed if the wife dies childless within a year after marriage [section 94(1) of the Native Code].[1] No such claim can be brought if death occurs after a year.

In the case of *Peter Mfingo v Willie Dlamini*,[2] which was heard by the Transkei Appeal Court in 1921, the Native Assessors who were consulted stated that in a case where a wife

---

[47] 1922 SR 55 at 58.
[48] See too *Matiyenga & another v Chinamura & others* 1958 SRN 829 at 831.

dies within one month of marriage, more than half the dowry is returnable. The Court accepted that opinion as correct native custom in that Province.

Soshangane, the founder of the Shangaan nation, was a Zulu from Zululand and his army which helped him to conquer the tribes inhabiting what is now Portuguese East Africa, was composed of Zulus. Whether he imposed Zulu law and customs in all their details on the conquered tribes or compromised on the subject is difficult to say after the lapse of so long a time. Possibly, or even more probably, the Shangaan customs of his time have changed to some degree, for even in Natal where the Code was established, many years ago, Natives have invented practices which have no foundation in true native law. It may be that the Shangaan custom referred to is not of ancient origin. It does not appear to be a just custom. To hold that all lobolo cattle must be refunded if a woman dies without having born children, although she may have been a good and faithful wife for many years, does seem unjust. Surely her services to her husband and the marital privileges which he has enjoyed merit recognition. It is not always in the best interests of the natives themselves to give the Court's sanction to all their present day alleged customs. It is one of the functions of this Court to interpret native law and custom in conformity with civilised ideas of what is fair and just.

In my opinion the custom followed by the Zulus and also it seems by the Transkei tribes should be applied to the Shangaans and other tribes who fall within the jurisdiction of this Court.

Notes

1. Now s 66(3).
2. 4 NAC 87 (1921).

At least one of the reasons for the court's decision in this case was the refusal, on grounds of policy, to enforce a particular agreement (or to countenance a particular practice). This seems at first to overlap with the repugnancy proviso but it should in fact be distinguished. The repugnancy clause was included in the legislation affording recognition to customary law in order to prevent the enforcement of certain institutions that happened to fall foul of western moral standards. Such institutions were to be removed from customary law for all time. Hence it was the *rule* in abstract which was to be assessed in light of the proviso, not the particular activity in contention. The courts have always had a residual discretion to refuse to countenance transactions and practices (even if associated with the common law) which run counter to the principles of public policy.[49]

In many cases it is difficult to decide whether the courts disapproved of a rule of customary law in the abstract or in the context of a particular set of facts, although a literal reading of s 1(1) of the Law of Evidence Amendment Act[50] suggests that only the former interpretation is permissible. In *Mokhesi v Nkenjane*,[51] for instance, a man persuaded a woman to run away with him and to marry him according to civil rites. The woman was under the age of 21. Her guardian sued the man under customary law for abducting his daughter and marrying her without paying bridewealth. The court held that this conduct was sanctioned by the common law and that to apply customary law and to hold that the conduct amounted to abduction was repugnant to the principles of public

---

[49] *Nowamba v Nomabetshe* 1906 NHC 39 and *Matiwane v Bottomani* 1932 NAC (C&O) 18 illustrate this point. See Bennett 84–5 and *Masango v Ngcobo* 1938 NAC (N&T) 155 at 157.
[50] 45 of 1988.
[51] 1962 NAC 70 (S).

policy; in addition it would penalize conduct which was permitted by the common law. (One wonders what the court's decision would have been if the girl had been over the age of 21.) Again a proper construction of s 1(1) of the Law of Evidence Amendment Act suggests that only customary-law rules in abstract fall to be considered under the repugnancy proviso. If application of the proviso varied depending on the facts of each case, the enforcement of customary law could easily become confused and arbitrary.

The courts have been remarkably restrained in their use of the repugnancy clause. They have limited it to a handful of situations where customary law: interfered with the right to liberty;[52] rendered people illegitimate;[53] encouraged sexual immorality;[54] favoured the right of an illegitimate child to succession;[55] or simply appeared unjust. The latter is a residual category that accommodates various anomalous cases such as the following: bridewealth must be returned in full if a customary marriage is terminated by the wife's premature death;[56] a replacement beast must be given for a cow that had been loaned, if the cow died and the death was not reported to the owner.[57]

During the last forty years the repugnancy proviso has been invoked hardly at all, suggesting that it is now irrelevant to the further development of customary law. It remains on the statute book as a reminder of the demeaning position of customary law in the colonial period. Doubtless for this reason, the proviso was deleted from the legislation regulating application of customary law in most of the southern African states. Only Botswana has retained the clause[58] as a general restraint on the application of customary law in all courts. In Lesotho[59] and Swaziland[60] it is applicable in the courts of chiefs and headmen. This might be a salutary check on the parochial development of deviant practices that happen to be antithetical to prevailing national policies. But *chiefs* are unlikely to assess new rules of customary law in these terms; it is only the higher courts that will do so. It is now argued that the proviso has outlived its usefulness and that it is up to the legislature, not the courts, to assume responsibility for effecting changes in customary law.[61]

(3) Conflict between different systems of customary law

There is, of course, no single, unified system of customary law in South Africa. It follows that a court may be confronted with a conflict between two or more different systems of customary law. Choice of law rules are provided in the section below.

---

[52] *Gidja v Yingwane* 1944 NAC (N&T) 4.
[53] *Tshiliza v Ntshongweni* 1908 NHC 10.
[54] *Palamahashi v Tshamane* 1947 NAC (C&O) 93; *Linda v Shoba* 1959 NAC 22 (NE).
[55] *Dumalitshona v Mraji* 5 NAC 168 (1927); *Madyibi v Nguva* 1944 NAC (C&O) 36; *Qakamba & another v Qakamba* 1964 BAC 20 (S).
[56] *Gidja v Yingwane* 1944 NAC (N&T) 4 at 7.
[57] *Mcitakali v Nkosiyaboni* 1951 NAC 298 (S).
[58] Section 2 of Act 51 of 1969.
[59] Section 9 of Proc 62 of 1938.
[60] Section 11(a) of Act 80 of 1950.
[61] Peart 1982 *AJ* 116.

[40] SECTION 1 LAW OF EVIDENCE AMENDMENT ACT 45 OF 1988

(3) In any suit or proceedings between Blacks who do not belong to the same tribe, the court shall not in the absence of any agreement between them with regard to the particular system of indigenous law to be applied in such suit or proceedings, apply any system of indigenous law other than that which is in operation at the place where the defendant or respondent resides or carries on business or is employed, or if two or more different systems are in operation at that place (not being within a tribal area), the court shall not apply any such system unless it is the law of the tribe (if any) to which the defendant or respondent belongs.

This provision implies a hierarchy of choice of law rules. The court is directed in the first instance to apply the law agreed upon by the parties. No mention is made of express or implicit agreements, and so it would seem that the courts are free to impute an agreement to the parties by reason of their conduct, the nature or form of any transaction they concluded, the environment of the case and the parties' lifestyles.[62] In other words, the court may utilize the connecting factors listed above, and from these infer an agreement.[63] In most cases this would obviate further reference to the choice of law rules contained in s 1(3) and it would greatly simplify the choice of law process—a considerable advantage because the subsequent rules are obscurely worded and difficult to apply.

In the absence of any agreement, the court must apply the law of the place where the defendant resides, carries on business or is employed,[64] provided that there is only one system of law prevalent in that area. The concept of residence is to be interpreted according to the common law.[65] If there is more than one system of law applicable in the area and if the place of residence etc is not within a tribal area (meaning presumably an urban area), and further provided that the defendant's tribal law is one of those systems applicable within the area, the court is directed to apply the law of the defendant's tribe.[66]

Particular problems arise regarding the Natal and KwaZulu Codes. Both purport to apply to the Zulu *people*, but in *territorial* terms, ie the scope of application is limited by the borders of Natal and KwaZulu respectively. In terms of the conflict of laws, of course, restrictions based on territory and person are contradictory. None the less, there are decisions stating that the Natal Code prevails over other systems of personal law in Natal.[67] Accordingly, where Sotho people had settled in Natal, they were deemed to be subject to the provisions of the Code, and it was held that the only way in which they could guarantee the continued application of their personal law would be to enter into an agreement to that effect. It was not made clear whether mere residence within Natal or something more permanent was necessary before the Code became applicable. But because this is a conflict of *personal* laws and because the purpose of the subject is to give expression to such laws, regardless where the litigants happen

---

[62] *Mahlaba v Mdladlamba* 1946 NAC (C&O) 51 and *Govuzela v Ngavu* 1949 NAC 156 (S).

[63] Bennett 122.

[64] *Govuzela's* case supra; *Rubushe v Jiyane* 1952 NAC 69 (S).

[65] *Ex parte Minister of Native Affairs* 1941 AD 53. See further *Madhlala v Mbata* 1939 NAC (N&T) 141.

[66] See Bennett 121–6; Forsyth (1979) 96 *SALJ* 418; Bekker 64–5; Lewin (1944) 61 *SALJ* 269.

[67] *Molife* 1934 NAC (N&T) 33; *Ndhlovu v Molife* 1936 NAC (N&T) 33.

to be, an inflexible application of the Codes on territorial principles should whenever possible be avoided.

The converse problem arises where people from Natal move to other parts of South Africa. There are dicta stating that the Natal Code does not apply outside the borders of the province,[68] but there is no definite decision indicating whether people subject to the Code within Natal should continue to be bound by it when they go to other parts of South Africa. Nor is it clear whether they should be domiciliaries of Natal or simply members of the 'Zulu tribe'.

The concept of 'tribe' is fundamental to the application of s 1(3). It is a pity that the Legislature continued to use it when the term had long ago been abandoned by anthropologists on the ground of its vagueness.[69] Apart from this, tribal structures have been greatly altered by the attempts of successive South African governments to divide and reconstitute African populations in ways amenable to their policies.[70] All of this means that the modern 'tribes' of South Africa are to a large extent artificial creations. There is no indication how the courts are to determine tribal affiliation nor how they are to check the authenticity of the various systems of tribal law they are supposed to apply.

(4) Conflict between foreign and domestic systems of law

A phenomenon without precedent in the South African courts is a conflict between a local and a foreign system of customary law. In this case, 'foreign' implies a different country. The same 'tribal' law may be involved but the parties concerned might be domiciliaries (and/or nationals) of different states. The applicable system of customary law might have been altered or repealed by legislation in one country and not in the other. For instance, both parties might be Tswana, although one is domiciled in South Africa and the other in Botswana. In such circumstances, which system of law should a South African court apply: the local, unmodified form of customary law or the amended Botswana system? And what rules should be used to select that system?

In principle, whenever the law of a foreign state is involved, the court should employ choice of law rules provided by private international law.[71] These are designed to cater for conflicts conceived in territorial terms.[72]

[41] BENNETT *THE APPLICATION OF CUSTOMARY LAW IN SOUTHERN AFRICA* 134–5

[T]here is difficulty inherent in the use of private international law: how would the court know whether the system of foreign law conflicts with its domestic common law or a domestic system of customary law? This is, in essence, a matter of determining the type of conflict in issue. The problem can best be analysed in terms of a hypothetical case. A person domiciled in Zimbabwe and subject to Shona law comes to South Africa; while

---

[68] *Zwana v Zwana & another* 1945 NAC (N&T) 59; *Mashapo & another v Sisane* 1945 NAC (N&T) 57.

[69] Hammond-Tooke *Bantu-speaking Peoples* xv; Gulliver *Tradition and Transition in East Africa* 7–35. And see generally 34 above.

[70] Mafeje (1971) 9 *J Mod Afr Studies* 253.

[71] See *Chirwa v Mandah* 1956 NAC 209 (C).

[72] Bennett (1980) 43 *THRHR* 28.

in the country, he enters into an agreement with a person subject to Sotho law. Subsequently the South African defaults on the agreement. An action is brought in a South African court. The conflict could be perceived in one of two ways:

(i) If the court decided that the issue concerned a choice between Shona and Sotho customary law, it might decide to apply the choice of law rules contained in its domestic legislation, ie s 11(2) of the Black Administration Act,[1] the rules regulating conflicts between domestic systems of customary law. . . . Alternatively the problem could be solved by use of private international law.

(ii) If, on the other hand, the court decided that the conflict was between Shona customary law and South African common law, the choice of law rules might be found in s 11(1) of the Black Administration Act[2] or, again, private international law. Reference to s 11(1) and the South African case law in point might indicate the applicability of South African common law or a domestic system of customary law. (Although it would not indicate which system of customary law was applicable.) Conversely, if the private international law choice of law rules were used, they might point to the application of South African law or Zimbabwe law. In the latter case a further question would arise: which system of Zimbabwe law should apply, customary law or the common law? And if customary law were chosen, which system of customary law? In any event, the court would probably arrive at a completely different conclusion to that reached by use of s 11(2). . . .

There is, in a sense, a "double" conflict involved. This means that when two territorially defined systems of law appear to be applicable to the solution of a case and both recognize personal systems of law, the court must address a preliminary question: which of its own systems of law is involved? No rules have ever been formulated to solve this problem. It is submitted that the preliminary conflict question must be settled by the choice of law rules supplied by the lex fori; these are the only rules available. In the hypothetical case given above, s 11(1) of the South African Black Administration Act should be referred to first. This will decide whether there is a conflict between a foreign system of law and South African common law or between the foreign law and a South African system of customary law.

This does not complete the classification of the conflict problem, however. Once the court has ascertained that South African customary law is to apply, it must then discover which system of customary law is involved. Section 11(1) of the Black Administration Act does not offer any guidelines in this regard. No doubt, in the South African context, the court will apply a notional lex tribus, the law of the litigant's tribe. In the hypothetical case this would be Sotho law. But it would be more appropriate to look to the rules governing conflict between domestic systems of customary law. In the case of South Africa this would be s 11(2) of the Black Administration Act.

Notes

1. Now s 1(3) of Act 45 of 1988.
2. Giving the court a discretion to apply customary or common law.

In any case involving a foreign legal system in which two or more personal laws are recognized and enforced, the type of problem alluded to above will be encountered. In other words, there is a preliminary question of which set of conflict rules to apply. The court must first, via private international law, locate the issue in the appropriate territorial system, and then, by reference to whatever internal conflict rules are available in that system, decide which system of personal law to choose.

II PROOF AND ASCERTAINMENT OF CUSTOMARY LAW

The rules of customary law are inherently volatile. If customary law is acknowledged to be rooted in the communities to which it applies, then it follows that if the courts are to administer an authentic version, they must take account of changes in social practice and attitude. But such is the diversity of the social groups subject to this type of legal regime that the full range of rules cannot possibly be accessible to a court at any one time.

This, of course, is a predicament peculiar to tribunals of the western, adjudicatory type, where legal certainty is a sine qua non of justice.[73] Informal tribunals that arbitrate or mediate claims can afford to be much more tolerant of uncertainty in the rules they apply.[74] Once customary law is enforced by state-recognized courts, the demand for certainty will naturally tend to assert itself, and so it is not surprising that these courts see lack of precision as one of its principal shortcomings.[75] This problem is compounded by the alienation of the courts from the communities they serve. South African magistrates and judges are white; because they are socially segregated, customary law becomes for them a foreign system, and they tend to be unaware of shifts in attitude and behaviour in the African population. In South Africa this is a legacy of apartheid, but elsewhere the same tendency emerges whenever the judiciary is profession-alized and separated from the society it serves.

In South Africa, save for chiefs and headmen, the courts' knowledge of customary law is necessarily second-hand. At best an individual might have acquired knowledge through detailed study or personal acquaintance with a local community (this was supposed to have been the job of commissioners, at least when the office was first instituted). In the Supreme Court and in magistrates' courts, for reasons of practicality as much as legal policy, a rule was devised that judicial notice could not be taken of customary law.[76] If a question of customary law did happen to arise, it would have to be treated as a matter of fact, which would mean that it would have to be proved by calling witnesses. For various reasons, however, the high cost of litigating being one,[77] customary law was seldom brought into issue in these forums. It was partly to avoid the difficulties that would arise from requiring proof of each rule of customary law that the commissioners' courts were first established in South Africa by the Black Administration Act.[78] But the problem was not completely overcome. Commissioners were still a partially professional judiciary subject to transfer, and in many other ways they were socially detached from the communities they served.

The South African courts were ill-prepared for the restructuring that occurred in 1986, when the commissioners' courts were abolished and their jurisdiction

---

[73] See generally: Woodman in Allott & Woodman *People's Law and State Law* 145ff.
[74] See above, 54–5 and 75.
[75] Allott *Future of Customary Law in Africa* 14–17.
[76] *Tabata* (1887) 5 SC 328; Kerr (1957) 74 *SALJ* 313ff.
[77] See *Bantu Reformed Apostolic Church v Ninow & another* 1947 (1) SA 187 (W); *Sibasa v Ratsialingwa & Hartman NO* 1947 (4) SA 369 (T).
[78] 38 of 1927.

transferred to magistrates' courts.[79] No provision had been made for acquainting the courts with the special problems and requirements associated with African civil litigation. The Supreme Court used to treat customary law as if it were the same as the common-law custom,[80] a perfectly reasonable equation since both were deemed to originate in a community's acceptance of certain standards of behaviour.[81] But custom is an exception to the general law of the land; and it must satisfy certain objective requirements (uniformity, certainty, and observance for a long period of time) before it can be accepted as binding.[82] This means that the court's role is inevitably ambiguous: it prospectively *constitutes* the custom as a binding rule while at the same time it retrospectively *declares* that the custom was binding.[83]

This theoretical quibble is of marginal importance compared with the practical difficulties caused by applying the tests of acceptance. Even in the Supreme Court it was conceded that insistence on the satisfaction of these tests would make the application of customary law so time-consuming and laborious that cases could not be effectively adjudicated.[84] Nevertheless, the equation of custom and customary law was at least an indirect acknowledgement by the Supreme Court that it had no competence to pronounce on rules generated by community practice.

In order to avoid having to prove each rule of customary law as and when it arose, the Supreme Court invoked the aid of two exceptions to the rule regarding custom.[85] The first allowed the courts to take judicial notice of a custom that had been incorporated into a statute. The prime example of this exception is the code of Zulu law.[86]

Codification may serve many purposes, including the general social aim of bringing the law closer to the layman.[87] It is clear, however, that the Code in Natal (and more recently in KwaZulu) was supposed to make customary law more certain and amenable to the requirements of the judiciary and administration.[88] The first version of the Natal Code was produced in 1878; it was a compilation of various administrative measures and the more important institutions of customary law, suitably modified to meet colonial policies. It was revised several times, in 1891, 1932, and 1967; the current version was promulgated in 1987.[89] In 1981 the partially autonomous self-governing

---

[79] Section 1 of the Special Courts for Blacks Abolition Act 34 of 1986.
[80] *Ex parte Minister of Native Affairs: In re Yako v Beyi* 1948 (1) SA 388 (A) at 394–5; *Mosii v Motseoakhumo* 1954 (3) SA 919 (A) at 930; *Masenya v Seleka Tribal Authority & another* 1981 (1) SA 522 (T) at 524.
[81] See, eg, Allott op cit n75 3 and (1958) 2 *JAL* 101.
[82] See the tests laid down in *Van Breda & others v Jacobs & others* 1921 AD 330.
[83] Van Niekerk (1968) 85 *SALJ* 282.
[84] *Ngcobo* 1929 AD 233 at 236 and see: Bekker (1976) 39 *THRHR* 359.
[85] Kerr op cit n76 313.
[86] *Mcunu* 1918 AD 323 at 328.
[87] Stone (1955) 29 *Tulane LR* 307.
[88] Kerr (1958) 2 *JAL* 82.
[89] R151 *Reg Gaz* 4136 9 October 1987.

territory, KwaZulu, issued its own code of Zulu law.[90] This prompted the South African government to reformulate the Natal Code in order to harmonize the laws applicable in the province. Neither Code pretends to be a comprehensive written version of all extant Zulu law. Rather they are statutes, inspired by customary law, but including many legislative innovations and seeking to impose a uniform legal regime on all Africans in Natal.[91]

The Natal Code demonstrates an important difference between customary and common law: the Code embodies the ideas and rules of the period in which it was drafted, with the result that it always lags behind contemporary attitudes and practice. No sooner has a code been promulgated than it needs revision.[92] To obviate this problem, several African countries have opted for restatements of customary law. These are no more than written descriptions of previously unwritten rules. A restatement does not have the binding quality of a code[93] but it does provide a readily accessible source of customary law. In Botswana, for instance, there is special legislative provision for restatements which are to be treated as prima facie evidence of customary law.[94] Despite the obvious advantages that restatements have over codes, it must be appreciated that even a restatement, by virtue of being a written document, imposes a rigidity and precision on customary law that it would not otherwise have had.[95]

The second exception to the rule requiring proof of custom allows a court to take judicial notice of a custom that has been captured in precedent. Accordingly a rule of customary law that has been proved in one case may be invoked in a later, similar case on the ground that the court is bound by the earlier precedent.[96] This exception has benefited mainly the Appeal Courts; over the years they have amassed a large body of precedents, a process which has been encouraged by the doctrine of stare decisis. It is perhaps somewhat anomalous to require application of this principle to customary law—a fluctuating, ever-changing repertoire of norms—but the Appeal Courts have insisted on it.[97]

The effect has been to create, albeit in an incremental fashion, a rigid and out-of-date set of rules, in fact, a type of code. There is always room for judicial manoeuvre (by use of the technique of distinguishing facts), and potentially the courts have been well placed to respond to changes in social practice. Yet the South African courts have declared on many occasions that they are not prepared

---

[90] Act 6; subsequently amended by Act 13 of 1984 and then revised and reissued: KwaZulu GN 36 of 1985.

[91] In other words the Code overrides any other system of customary law in Natal: *Molife* 1934 NAC (N&T) 33; *Ndhlovu v Molife* 1936 NAC (N&T) 33. For the scope of application of the Codes, see Bennett 125–6.

[92] Stone op cit n87 309; Hahlo (1967) 30 *MLR* 250–2.

[93] Cf Keuning in Ife University *Integration of Customary Law* 69–70.

[94] Section 12 of the Customary Law (Application and Ascertainment) Act 51 of 1969. And see Allott op cit n75 27–30.

[95] Bennett & Vermeulen (1980) 24 *JAL* 206.

[96] *R v Mpanza* 1946 AD 763 at 771. See too: *Angu v Attah* (1916) PC '74-'28 43 at 44 and Allott *New Essays* 259–65.

[97] *Fuzile v Ntloko* 1944 NAC (C&O) 2. And see Kludze in Allott & Woodman op cit n73 97ff.

to engage in law-making. They see their task as one of applying law.[98] At the most the courts might have applied common law in the place of customary law where application of the strict rules of customary law seemed inappropriate, but even this they were reluctant to do.[99] The commissioners' courts

'succumbed to the temptation of relying on the authority of past precedents and out-of-date ethnographies. The impression gained from the case reports is of a rurally based, traditional system of customary law that is more in keeping with a social formation of a hundred years ago. Social lag is a problem with all legal systems; it is accentuated in the case of customary law. The courts find it easier to apply the customary law which is certain and accessible than to undertake the admittedly laborious task of ascertaining changes.'[100]

Since the abolition of the commissioners' courts and their Courts of Appeal, African civil litigation has become the responsibility of the magistrates' courts and the Supreme Court.[101] The decisions of magistrates' courts are not, of course, reported and the cost of appeals means that few civil cases involving customary law will ever reach the Supreme Court. The overall effect will be the loss of a source of customary law. Any opportunity that the courts might have had in the past for the progressive development of customary law has now been forfeited. Access to customary law, as it changes and emerges from its community origins, will either be via commission of inquiry or anthropological/ sociological research.

In South Africa customary law is presently contained in precedents, codes and textbooks. Such is the need for readily accessible material, that this law will inevitably continue to be accepted and applied as current law, regardless of the discrepancies between the rules and social reality.

When a court is uncertain what rule to apply or whether the rule before it is an authentic representation of customary law, its approach should, in principle, be that outlined by the court in *R v Dumezweni*:[102]

'Where there is a dispute as to the existence or nature of a law or custom, it would either not be well established or well-known, or one of the parties would in honest or pretended ignorance or misunderstanding be contesting what is in fact well-established and well-known. In the former case the native commissioner would have to hear evidence. In the latter he may, where the law or custom is clear, decide without hearing evidence, relying on his own knowledge, but in such a case it would be necessary, for purposes of the record, and in giving reasons in an appeal from his decision, to note the contention of the parties and his reasons for not hearing evidence.'

Special legislative provision has now been made for the first instance: in terms of s 1(2) of the Law of Evidence Amendment Act[103] a party may adduce evidence to establish a rule of customary law which is in doubt.

In the past, under s 19(1) of the Black Administration Act, a commissioner's court could call to its assistance one or more assessors to give advice on matters of customary law. This alleviated the court's problems of determining the

---

[98] *Maguga v Scotch* 1931 NAC (N&T) 54; *Matsheng v Dhlamini & another* 1937 NAC (N&T) 89 at 93.
[99] Bennett 24 and 66–7.
[100] Bennett 23; and Akanki (1970) 4 *Nigerian LJ* 31.
[101] Following from s 3(b) of Act 34 of 1986.
[102] 1961 (2) SA 751 (A) at 756–7.
[103] 45 of 1988.

credibility of a party's allegations. Yet the role of the assessors was always somewhat ambiguous;[104] in certain respects they functioned as expert witnesses, in others they were adjudicators. They could give useful opinions on customary law, but as it happened they were invariably selected from the ranks of chiefs and headmen, and so tended to be conservative. Latterly they were seldom (if ever) called,[105] and now there is no statutory provision for them.

The usual way of establishing a controverted issue of customary law was for an interested party simply to call evidence in the form of witnesses, or to argue the matter on the basis of written authority, such as ethnographies, precedents or statutes. In principle it should be possible to endorse all law by reference to texts, but customary law is different: because it is deemed to originate in social practice, it can be treated as law *or* fact. If it is treated as fact, witnesses should be called. There are no rules concerning the number or the qualifications of these witnesses nor has their role ever been clearly specified: are they before the court to give an *expert* opinion as to the existence of a rule of customary law, or do they attest to its existence as a matter of fact?[106] The South African courts have tended to prefer as witnesses persons actively engaged in customary law. In *Sibasa v Ratsialingwa & Hartman NO*,[107] as an exception, the court was prepared to accept evidence from the government ethnographer, but only with reluctance. The courts' preferences are quite unfounded; an anthropologist who has conducted a careful study of customary law would be able to give an opinion at least as reliable as that of a chief or headman, if not more so.

If customary law is deemed to be law, rules may be authenticated by reference to texts. The question then arises as to the type of text that should be used. Obviously the courts will prefer the familiar legal forms of statute and precedent; the writings of jurists and anthropologists will inevitably be subsidiary sources. But there is no good reason for this approach. A rule of customary law may have been accepted in a particular decision as the result of an idiosyncratic opinion; it may have been adduced by a single witness; the court may have accepted the rule on the ground that there was insufficient evidence (on a balance of probabilities) to contradict the other party's assertion. No anthropologist would accept as sufficient the assertion of a single person, and any reputable ethnography is prepared on the basis of data collected by careful observation, recording of local court cases and extensive interviews over a long period of time. This would offer a far better guarantee of accuracy than the isolated opinions of witnesses or assessors. Conversely, of course, there needs to be some assurance that the work satisfies these criteria before it is accepted by the court, and in this regard it might be necessary to call the author to give evidence.[108]

The general rule of evidence is that he who alleges must prove. The onus therefore is on the person alleging a rule of customary law to prove it.[109] And,

---

[104] Allott *New Essays* 266–9.
[105] Khumalo 60.
[106] Allott *New Essays* 262–4.
[107] 1947 (3) SA 369 (T) at 378.
[108] See Akanki op cit n100 27.
[109] *Maqovuka v Madidi* 1911 NHC 132; *Mosii v Motseoakhumo* 1954 (3) SA 919 (A) at 930.

despite intimations to the contrary,[110] the test is on a balance of probabilities.[111] But what if a person alleges a rule of customary law and fails to produce satisfactory proof? Presumably the court will take for granted an already existing corpus of customary law, contained in precedents and codes, which will be deemed applicable in the absence of proof of a contrary rule.

The problems of proving customary law in the courts are considerable. Aside from the question of change, there is the matter of local variation. Customary law is not a single corpus of rules uniformly applicable throughout the land. There is no reason why any particular community should not evolve its own rules, which in principle would then be binding on members of that community only. It is quite likely that such rules will never be recorded or given a judicial stamp of authority. In the following case the court was confronted with this type of problem. The question was whether a twin could succeed to his brother, in other words, whether twins should be treated as one person (which is what one of the parties alleged to be the custom of his area) or two people. The issue was an entirely novel one for the court. It resolved the problem by relying on certain general principles which it claimed were generally observed in the country.

[42] *MAZIBUKO* 1930 NAC (N&T) 143 at 143–6

STUBBS P: May I at once say this case raises novel and intriguing points of law: the rival claims of a surviving male twin to his deceased twin brother's property and the eldest brother of the "house"....

The Native Commissioner in discussing the issue cogently observes: "The question at issue therefore was whether this custom regarding the property of twins was a valid one and whether it could nullify or qualify the ancient custom of primogeniture. Chapters 25 and 38 of the book of Genesis deal with notable twins in the time of Moses but do not give them the right to succeed to each other but only give seniority to the first-born twin. In no law can I find any authority that gives a twin the right to succeed to the property of his deceased twin brother of such twins. Is the alleged custom ... one that can be regarded as a well-established custom having the authority of law? Van der Linden on *Custom* says: 1. It must be based upon sound reason; 2. It must be satisfactorily proved (a) by a great number of witnesses, (b) by an unbroken chain of decisions based upon the custom, (c) by long usage. Holland in his *Elements of Jurisprudence* says of custom, as a source of law: 'Its characteristic is that it is a long and generally observed course of conduct....' Does the custom relied on by defendant comply with any of these requirements? It does not; and moreover as the effect of accepting it as a valid custom would be to qualify or abrogate succession by the law of primogeniture it cannot be accepted as it only originated within the last 50 or 60 years while the law of primogeniture has been observed by the natives from time immemorial. Great stress has been laid by the defendant in what he calls plaintiff's acquiescence in the custom, but as most of plaintiff's actions are those that an elder brother does for a younger who is not one of twins, no weight should be given to these actions of plaintiff, e.g., the giving of the girl to the surviving brother of her intended husband is frequently done to my knowledge where no question of twins arises and the giving of the cattle by an elder brother for a younger frequently occurs. The present acknowledged custom of rearing twins in separate kraals seems to me to negative the fiction of one entity for the two persons."

This view is challenged on a variety of grounds the essential one of which is that the weight of evidence establishes that the custom of one twin succeeding to the property of

---

[110] *Dumalisile* 1948 NAC 7 (S); *Nomantunga v Ngangana* 1951 NAC 342 (S).
[111] *Gecelo* 1957 NAC 161 (S).

another twin on the death of the latter without issue to the exclusion of the eldest brother (General Heir) has prevailed for 50 or 60 years amongst the Natives of the district of Estcourt, isolated instances of which are given, has the force of law and in so far at any rate as that district is concerned qualifies or abrogates the succession by the law of primogeniture which from time immemorial has been of universal application. There can of course be no doubt that a number of witnesses of standing notably the Chief Peni Mabaso and Induna Mpukane Mbata have been called to prove that similar instances of twin succession of the description in point have occurred in the Estcourt district but it would indeed be a dangerous doctrine to hold that because such is the modern development within a tribal entity in a given area, a law which has its genesis in the ancient polity of the founders of the race and has been universally recognised and generally applied down through the ages to present times, a law which is embodied and receives its further sanction and reaffirmation in the Code of Native Law, secs. 101, 106 and 115, is ousted thereby. To me the argument against such a proposition is irresistible. . . .

The contention that the succession of a twin to the property of a deceased twin in circumstances which amount to a negation of the fundamental rule of primogeniture does not, apart from any other considerations, seem to be borne out by historical fact because among certain leading tribes the custom has always been to kill the twins soon after birth. . . .

I have drawn an outline of the disabilities of twins in the general make up of Native family life to emphasise that the comparatively modern innovation among a section of the Zulu in the district of Estcourt by which it is sought to override a custom which goes to the root of succession and inheritance is one which should be closely scrutinised and weighed before accepting it as having definitely a place in the customary jurisprudence of these people. I think I have said sufficient to show that whether the case be that of twins or individuals more fortunately circumstanced in Native life it does not lie with this Court to allow these attempts at impingement upon institutions of law entrenched.

The courts act as the final arbiters of customary law, and there is an irresistible tendency for them to arrogate to themselves a knowledge which might in fact be imperfect or fragmentary.[112] The courts cannot presume to know all customary law, yet they have been given a general discretion to apply it. One of the ways in which this discretion may be exercised is in deciding when and in what manner rules of customary law need to be established. The discretion does not authorize a court to make a private investigation[113] because the general principle of procedural fairness should be observed: in any case of doubt the parties must be informed so that they can call witnesses of their own if they choose to do so. Conversely, in order to decide a controversial issue, the court may call its own witnesses.[114] It was also held that if a commissioner decided to rely on his specialized knowledge to reach a finding, he should indicate this on the record,[115] which at least will alert any interested party to the possibility of contention.

---

[112] Morris & Read *Indirect Rule and the Search for Justice* 188.
[113] *Rowe v Assistant Magistrate, Pretoria & another* 1925 TPD 361 at 369–70.
[114] *Morake v Dubedube* 1928 TPD 625 at 631.
[115] *S v Sihlani & another* 1966 (3) SA 148 (E).

CHAPTER 4

Customary Marriage

I THE FAMILY AND MARRIAGE

(1) Law and reality

The family is a basic unit of social organization. It defines the people with
hom we are permitted to mate[1] and it prescribes a field of domestic
responsibilities within which we can find material and psychological support.[2]
The ties of blood are such that kinfolk can always rely on the generosity and
affection of their relatives.[3] Even more is expected of the African family. In
societies where there are no state institutions to attend to the education of the

---

[1] Fox *Kinship and Marriage* 27.
[2] Radcliffe-Brown *Structure and Function in Primitive Society* 52–3; Radcliffe-Brown & Forde 11–13.
And in stateless societies kin groups have political functions too: Evans-Pritchard *The Nuer* 5 and 117 and
Fortes *The Dynamics of Clanship among the Tallensi* ch 7.
[3] Actual or supposed: Fortes *Kinship and the Social Order* 233–4.

young or to care for the sick and the needy, and where there is no social welfare system to guarantee financial security, kinfolk are obliged both to socialize the individual and to support him or her from birth to death.

In western legal systems the relationship between law and the family is acknowledged to be a complex and sensitive issue. Initially, the family was considered a private domain, a refuge from legal intrusion.[4] The law-maker's role, after observing a decent interval of time, was merely to express changes in social mores. Legal intervention was permitted only to facilitate the settlement of disputes on the breakdown of marriage. More recently, legislative action has been taken to protect the more vulnerable family members, ie women and children. Latterly governments have come to appreciate the financial significance of the family; they have been able to justify cuts in welfare budgets by referring the indigent to their families as the primary units of support. For this reason, in the last two decades the family has achieved a new prominence in political and legal debates.[5]

In Western Europe, from the end of the nineteenth century (when marriage assumed its modern characteristics as a consensual partnership of individuals),[6] the nuclear family was taken to be both a social norm and an ideal.[7] Some writers went so far as to claim that it was a *universal necessity* because it was the only institution capable of performing certain essential social functions.[8] It comes as no surprise then that systems of western family law have 'been predicated on the basis of a husband wage-earner, a wife homemaker and a little over two dependent children' despite the fact that only ten per cent of families comply with this stereotype.[9]

Customary law is mainly about the family. We would therefore be justified in expecting it to reflect, in some measure at least, any changes that may have occurred in the African family structure and function. Yet in South Africa customary law is disturbingly out of harmony with social reality. This is because the state's attitude to intervention in African family affairs was (and still is) quite different to what it was in the case of European families.

When the colonial venture began, the settlers believed that they had a Christian duty to eliminate the polygynous family, which was thought to be immoral and degrading. But, as nineteenth-century prejudices faded, so too did this missionary zeal. In South Africa it was replaced by indifference. The colonial courts modified customary law here and there—the most notable change was the rule requiring free choice of marriage partner—but they drew back at the prospect of any thorough-going reform. In any event it seemed pointless: the general belief was that there was a natural, evolutionary progression from the extended African family (the remnant of an earlier, less

---

[4] Rheinstein & König (1972) 4 *IECL* ch 1 paras 5 and 6.
[5] Bottomley in Burns *The Family in the Modern World* 13; and see Viljoen in Steyn *Marriage and Family Life in South Africa* 3–5.
[6] Rheinstein & König op cit n4 para 15.
[7] Rheinstein & König op cit n4 para 67.
[8] Murdoch *Social Structure* and see Viljoen in Steyn op cit n5 5ff.
[9] Freeman 1985 *Current Legal Problems* 165.

civilized age) to the nuclear European family (a product of advancement and industrialization).[10] Legislation could not alter this predetermined course; it could simply encourage it.[11]

By the mid-twentieth century, it was obvious that the African family was not what it had been at the time of colonial conquest, and that legal reforms were urgently needed to ameliorate the position of women and children. Yet the courts, and at least until 1985 the legislature, clung to their policy of non-intervention. This long period of inactivity could in formal terms be justified by the government's scruples about interfering with matters of African culture, which was supposed to be the preserve of the independent and self-governing territories. There was a further danger of making 'paper laws', ones that would be resisted by an uninformed, conservative, and possibly hostile population. And for their part, the courts have always relied on the time-worn adage of legal positivism: their job is to apply the law not to make it.[12] But the most probable explanation for the inertia is political disenfranchisement; it leads to an unbridgeable social gulf between the law-maker and the legal subject[13] with a consequent insensitivity to the latter's problems.

If and when the government decides to act, it will be confronted with profoundly difficult policy decisions. Is an antique version of customary law to be preserved as a mark of cultural identity, or should it be modified by common law? Should customary law be changed to take account of new international standards of personal freedom, especially those guaranteeing the status of women and children? Whose interests are to be furthered: men's or women's, the family's or the individual's, the parents' or the child's? Should law act as a beacon for social development or should it merely reflect contemporary mores? To find answers, reliable information is going to be needed: what do people think about the family, how it is structured, and how it is reacting to present social, economic and political forces?

(2) The extended family

The stereotypical African family has always been taken to be 'extended'. In anthropological terms this implies an augmentation of the nuclear unit (father, mother and their children) by vertical extensions (including people from the ascending and descending generations), and/or by horizontal extensions (linking a series of conjugal units by polygynous marriages). Families extended vertically are often described as clans, that is to say groups of descendants who believe themselves to be related to a common ancestor, although their exact genealogical links can no longer be traced. Clans normally segment into more intimate units—lineages—the members of which can actually trace connections with their relatives.[14] Eponymous patrilineal clans are found throughout southern

---

[10] Murray (1980) 6 *JSAS* 148–52.

[11] See Goode *World Revolution and Family Patterns* 8–10.

[12] Assisted here by the 'jural' approach to customary law: Hund *Legal Ideology and Politics in South Africa* ch 2.

[13] See Burman (1985) 14 *Quarderni Fiorentini* 175.

[14] Radcliffe-Brown & Forde 14ff.

Africa, but their only practical significance today is the rule of exogamy: clan members may not marry one another. Of greater day-to-day importance is the lineage, which is normally only four to six generations deep. The lineage has provided the model of the African family: a large household, comprising a patriarch, his wives, children and grandchildren, dependent brothers and sisters, and any others who choose to attach themselves to him.[15]

Family members are ranked vis-à-vis one another, each rank (or status) carrying with it certain distinguishing rights, powers, duties and privileges. Three criteria are used to differentiate status: sex, age, and generation. These criteria may be combined, as happens in Africa, to yield a patriarchal family structure, one where only senior males are accorded full powers and authority; all women and junior men are subordinate.[16]

Status is indicated by the terms used to address kin and to refer to them.[17] In Africa a classificatory system of terminology prevails. This means that a large number of relatives is included under the same term of identification, implying a common type of relationship. Thus, if A and B are related to one another, and X stands in a certain relationship to A, he/she is regarded as standing in the same relationship to B. Relatives are divided into a few broad categories, and so instead of one's father's brother being called 'uncle', he is called 'father', and once subsumed under the general category of father, he is treated as such.[18] 'The effect of this system is in general to bring within your mental grasp a much greater number of your kindred than is possible under the [descriptive] system.'[19]

Early ethnographers extolled the extended family for the support and protection it afforded its members. The kinship ethic was said to foster a spirit of collectivism (widely regarded as a species of socialism), an obligation of co-operation whereby the whole force of the community could be used to defend the individual against the outside world.[20] And yet, although this family form was regarded as the norm of African society, the reality, even forty years ago, was different.

[43] WILSON *KEISKAMMAHOEK RURAL SURVEY* V 3 *SOCIAL STRUCTURE* 4–8, 46–50

A—LOCAL GROUPS
Each of the fifteen villages in Keiskammahoek District has its own land, and its own headman and village council, and is politically independent of all other villages, but under the direct authority of the Native Commissioner, the local representative of the Union

---

[15] James (1985) 44 *Afr Studies* 160–1.
[16] See below, 301ff.
[17] The determinative effect of nomenclature is examined by Kuper *South Africa and the Anthropologist* 83ff.
[18] Radcliffe-Brown & Forde 6–7.
[19] Which is characteristic of cognatic kinship systems: Maine *Lectures on the Early History of Institutions* 214. See further on kinship nomenclature: Radcliffe-Brown & Forde 170 and 172 (Zulu), 101 (Swazi) and 146–9 (Tswana).
[20] Kidd *Kafir Socialism* 3; Westermann *The African Today and Tomorrow* 147. The individual sacrificed freedom for the security of the group; see Goode *The Family* 50–3.

Government. Each village is sub-divided into sections under sub-headmen, and the sections are further divided into hamlets. A hamlet consists of a group of "kraals" or homesteads, which are separated from other such groups by a stream or gully, or a stretch of unoccupied land. A homestead (*umzi*)[1] consists of several huts clustered around a cattle byre, and occupied by a kinship group—traditionally, and ideally, by a man with his wife or wives, their unmarried children, and married sons with their wives and children, but nowadays often only by a single elementary family, or a widow with her children. Each homestead has its recognised head, who is the senior male member or, if he is dead, his widow. He (or she) organises the economic activities of the members and they all go to him for advice and direction; nothing which affects them should be done without his permission.

Villages vary in size from 330 to 1,700 members actually living in them, and in addition there are members who are away working in town.

Though each village is established on its own land, the form of tenure varies, and this affects the social structure very considerably. Each village has a commonage on which its members pasture their cattle but, in some, arable land is held on freehold tenure, in others on quitrent tenure, in others on "communal tenure", and in seven villages certain areas are held directly from the South African Native Trust.

Where there is freehold or quitrent tenure, families and lineages are the land-owning groups and inheritance of land within the family or lineage is secure; on the other hand, in a "communal" village, it is the village which is the land-owning group and acquisition of a field depends upon the support of fellow villagers, more especially of the village headman and subheadmen. Tenure on "Trust" land is much like that in a communal village, though holders are subject to more restrictions regarding their use of the land.

In a communal village access to land depends first and foremost on having been born in the village, and though a third of the married men have no fields, each has a chance of acquiring one if he waits long enough, paying his taxes and returning each year to the village; but in the freehold villages there are two classes, the landowners and the "squatters". In the early days, some of the freeholders and quitrenters owned more land than they could use. They brought in relatives to settle on their land, or share cropped, rented or lent portions of it to settlers who built their homesteads on the commonage; or else they permitted "wanderers" from the European farms to build on and use a portion of their landholdings in return for services. . . .

Although people in communal villages regard themselves as superior to the people of the Trust because they have long had land rights, they are nevertheless referred to derogatorily by freeholders and quitrenters. On the other hand, the people in communal villages have a strongly developed sense of community and neighbourliness, and they in their turn tend to regard landowners as rude and anti-social in their individualism. Much of the superior attitude of land-owners derives, however, not only from their sense of freedom from authority, engendered by their security of tenure, but also from their rather better standard of living. In the past, those who owned land could borrow money and buy more stock, becoming the wealthiest in stock with the social status which that conferred. Today, freeholders and quitrenters tend to have better housing, many having European style square houses with iron roofs, and they are on the whole more progressive and better educated, with more children going on to secondary school, or training as teachers, than the people in communal villages. . . .

Homesteads vary somewhat in size and composition, with the type of tenure. The average number of members, for the district as a whole, is seven, but it ranges from an average of nine persons on freehold land to six in a communal village. Homesteads on freehold land are larger, partly because holdings are larger, and partly because the acquisition of land by a married man before his father's death is very difficult and therefore he cannot set up a separate homestead. The number and identity of people actually living in a homestead varies very much in the course of a year, because migrant bread-winners circulate between country and town and their dependants often stay with relatives during their absence.

When a married man lives in his parents' home he has his own hut, but if he has no land of his own he and his family will "eat from the same pot" as his parents. This is the usual arrangement in areas of private land ownership, but in a communal village a man more often has his own allocation of land, and then he will have his own storage arrangements and his wife will cook a separate pot. He no longer forms an integral part of his parents' home, but creates a more or less separate homestead alongside the parental establishment, the main bond between them being the common use of the cattle byre. Only if a son acquires land at a distance does he establish his homestead quite apart, near his field.

While homesteads are not so far apart as among other Nguni, there are no continuous large residential settlements in the district, and left to themselves the people choose to scatter. . . .

B—KINSHIP GROUPS

The basic form of kinship grouping in the village is the monogamous family, consisting of a husband, a wife and their unmarried child or children, either their own or adopted. Polygynous families in which one husband marries more than one wife, each of whom, together with her children, forms a separate unit in the homestead, are very rare today. The homestead (*umzi*) in which the family lives forms the nucleus of the local or territorial grouping.

The monogamous family when it coincides with the homestead is the simplest form of domestic family. Very rarely, however, does an elementary family live alone in a homestead. Traditionally, the people lived in patrilineal kinship groups (*imzi*), and in the days when danger from marauders made concentration necessary for defence, a number of married men, together with their wives and children, would live together in one *umizi*. Although brothers or sons are never ordered to leave a homestead unless they or their wives are repeatedly quarrelsome or are believed to be witches, nevertheless the tendency now is towards the breaking up of *imizi* very soon after the brothers or sons get married. Fission may arise because of friction between wives and brothers, but it is chiefly influenced at the present time by the sense of economic individualism acquired by the younger generation in the course of their labour migration experiences, wives being particularly anxious to have their own homesteads in order to be free of a mother-in-law's tutelage.

On the other hand, two major factors, both of them economic and inter-related, work against the breaking up process and cause families to live gregariously in the one homestead. There is too little arable land in the district relative to the population. Not only are married men unable, therefore, to acquire landholdings and to establish independent homesteads as they would wish, but the agricultural produce of the area is inadequate to feed the population. Remunerative employment outside the district is therefore imperative in order to meet the subsistence requirements of the family. . . .

A son or brother who leaves the homestead peacefully usually prefers to establish his new homestead near his close paternal relatives; in villages of freehold and quitrent tenure he is, in any case, confined nowadays to the land belonging to his lineage group. Consequently, the homesteads of male members of one agnatic group are usually found in the same locality. The lineage group consists of all the surviving agnatic kinsmen with whom relationship can be traced through a common grandfather, great-grandfather, or great-great-grandfather, but they are seldom all found residing in the locality; some members of the lineage group are living in other districts or in urban centres, either having emigrated from Keiskammahoek or else having remained in their districts of origin while a few of their paternal relatives came to settle in the Keiskammahoek District.

. . . While each group of kinsmen is itself patrilineally constituted, affinal links are created between two groups on the marriage of a man and woman. The behaviour of a wife at her father-in-law's homestead is characterised by elaborate verbal (*ukuhlonipha*) and spatial (*ukuceza*) avoidances, observed as a mark of respect. Relations between a man and his mother-in-law and also between parents-in-law are similarly characterised by mutual respect and avoidance. . . .

The children born of a marriage belong to the husband's lineage group, but they are especially honoured guests at the homesteads of their maternal uncles. . . . Although women customarily go to live with their husbands' families on marriage, they may return to the parental, brothers' or other relatives' homes on the death or desertion of a husband, after divorce, or for any such reason as dissatisfaction with their marriages, failure of their husbands to support them, or because they are accused by their husband's family of witchcraft or sorcery. Their children normally remain with the husband's family but may accompany their mother, particularly if they are small and she is returning to her people because she was widowed early, or was deserted, or not supported by her husband. Nevertheless, such children, even though they live with the maternal kinship group, remain members of their paternal kinship group and retain their paternal surname. Illegitimate children, on the other hand, usually live with and are absorbed by the maternal group, adopting the surname of their mother's father.

Members of various lineage groups who claim to be descended from a common paternal ancestor constitute the patrilineal clan (*isiduko*). The lineal connection with the clan founder is remembered in varying depth; usually it cannot be traced more than four or five generations above the senior survivor; in some cases an additional eight to ten ancestors on the ascending plane are remembered. But while members of lineages of the clan can trace ancestry in varying depth to the clan founder, they have in the course of lineage sub-division lost the point of connection one with the other; therefore the links which each lineage traces with the clan founder form a chain isolated from those of other lineages. Members of a clan describe themselves as "people of the same blood", "people derived from the same stem", and the name of their common ancestor, the clan founder, constitutes the clan name by which the members of the various lineages recognise their clan relationship. While women retain their clan identity on marriage, they cannot transmit their clan name or the legal affiliation it implies to their children. However, illegitimate children absorbed into their maternal lineage group adopt its clan name. . . .

Thus, among all the people in the district, the locally concentrated kinship group is the lineage, or more often that part only of the lineage, namely the lineage remnant, actually domiciled in the district; members of the lineage group represented in the district are usually concentrated in one village. As domestic families, however, these agnatic kinship groups are split up among various independently established homesteads.

Note

1. Umzi is the word used for the patrilineal kinship group which lives together in the one homestead. The word umzi is also commonly used for the homestead itself, the cluster of one to five huts facing onto the cattle byre and overlooking the arable fields belonging to or registered in the name of the head of the umzi.

(3) Factors of change

The belief that the extended family is the norm in southern Africa persists. In reality, however, family structures have been so attenuated that it would be misleading to regard the extended family as representative. As one writer says, although there might be

'evidence of a relatively stable agnatic structure which endures through several generations [there is also] evidence of high rates of individual mobility, conjugal instability, illegitimacy, desertion and the break-up of families'.[21]

The disintegration of the extended family confirms evolutionist ideas about the progress of civilization. Maine, for instance, contended that 'the unit of an ancient society was the Family, of a modern society the Individual'.[22] And,

---

[21] Murray *Families Divided* 112.
[22] *Ancient Law* 74 and 99; and see Goode op cit n11 3–4.

although evolutionist thinking may have been discredited, it lingers on to inform popular ideas about the goals of social change and development. Individualism (the principle on which modern European family law was fashioned) is widely accepted as an ideal, and some countries—Ivory Coast is a notable example— have legislated with the express purpose of destroying extended family networks, because kinfolk were believed to be parasites discouraging individual initiative.[23] Yet individualism and the nuclear family are not the inevitable result of bio-social evolution. In Europe there is convincing evidence that they are the product of the competing forces of the Church and the state.[24]

Anthropologists working in southern Africa have been hard pressed to find acceptable criteria for defining the family as a discrete unit.[25] To some extent they have been able to explain variation in family composition by paying more careful attention to the developmental cycle, a process often overlooked in early ethnographies, but one that has a marked effect on the size and structure of the family.[26] This gives only a partial explanation; more is needed for a complete account of the actual composition of a household.[27] Such is the extraordinary diversity in modern family structure, however, that anthropologists have had to acknowledge that there is no uniform type in South Africa that can be designated 'the norm'.[28]

There have been many different forces at work on the African family. Probably the first extraneous influence was Christian teaching.[29] This demanded that the faithful be monogamous.[30] Less conspicuous perhaps, but even more profound, was the effect of labour migrancy.[31] Worldwide, since the eighteenth century, capitalist enterprise has required a constant supply of ready labour, and the development of mining and manufacture exerted a demand for able-bodied workers from the country. The position of the family was an awkward one. On the one hand the family was the principal source of material support for urban workers (and of course it continued to be the unit of reproduction); but its actual presence at the site of employment was unnecessary.

---

[23] Rheinstein & König op cit n4 para 74; Abitbol (1966) 10 *JAL* 141.

[24] Goody *The Development of the Family* ch 6; Glendon *State, Law and Family* ch 7.

[25] Use of kinship terminology is unfortunately not a reliable guide because it is both descriptive and constitutive: cf Wilson & Mafeje *Langa* 86–90 and Reynolds in Burman & Reynolds *Growing up in a Divided Society* 308ff regarding changes in terms used in a Cape Town squatter camp.

[26] Initially, a domestic group is composed of a young man and woman. When they produce children, the group expands; later, as the children marry and move away, the group contracts: Fortes in Goody *The Developmental Cycle in Domestic Groups* Introduction 4ff; Spiegel in Mayer *Black Villagers in an Industrial Society* 117–21.

[27] Other factors, such as commensality (eating together) and coparency (income sharing) must be considered. See, eg, Sharp & Spiegel (1985) 55 *Africa* 137ff and Spiegel (1986) 45 *Afr Studies* 17ff; and further: Simkins in Burman & Reynolds op cit n25 19.

[28] See the eclectic approach of Webster *Family and Household in KwaDapha, KwaZulu* 7–14.

[29] Segalen *Historical Anthropology of the Family* 31–2.

[30] See, eg, Vilakazi *Zulu Transformations* and Campbell (1970) 3 *CILSA* 213–14.

[31] Schapera *Migrant Labour and Tribal Life*; Wilson *Keiskammahoek Rural Survey* v3 111–12; Murray op cit n10 139ff.

In southern Africa, as labour requirements intensified with the opening of mines and supporting industries,[32] African workers were discouraged from bringing their families to the nascent urban areas. One reason for depriving labourers of domestic support was the need to preserve the rural economy.[33] Employers could then keep wages at a level low enough to meet only the individual worker's requirements while he was actually employed. In the meantime his family continued to support itself, and when the worker returned home it resumed responsibility for him too. This was the origin of the system of oscillating labour migration. By fiscal measures workers were compelled to seek employment in white mines, factories and farms, but at the same time they had to maintain connection with their rurally based families, which ministered to them when they were sick, disabled, or out of work.

Urbanization was the physical manifestation of these social and economic forces. Sociologists regarded urban industrialism and the nuclear family as natural complements.[34] They reasoned that the extended family could survive only while it had the land or wealth to support its non-productive members. Once the material base shrank, without commensurate increase in political patronage or jobs, family members would be forced to disperse.[35] Some people welcomed urbanization in the belief that newcomers to the towns would be freed from the encumbrance of their families. It was thought that when emancipated the city dweller could progress economically and become acculturated more quickly.[36] But the general opinion was much less positive. It is a commonplace that city life corrupts; it is supposed to be the cause of sexual immorality, loss of parental control and juvenile delinquency.[37] The decline in moral standards was attributed to the absence of a prevailing public opinion, itself the result of a collapse in the tribal and family cohesiveness that typified country life.[38]

The rural/urban drift has long been taken to be the mainspring of social change in Africa: people who moved to town became more 'westernized' or less 'tribal' because of their contact with the notionally more advanced white culture.[39] Yet the problem of specifying what was meant by 'urbanized'[40] should have warned of the inadvisability of attributing all change to this factor. Work, residence, and other such factors do dictate a degree of conformity to a lifestyle that can be described as 'urban'. But there is a concomitant influence on people living in the

---

[32] Farmers' demands for labour were met by various legislative devices, notably the hut and poll taxes: Welsh *Roots of Segregation* 23. This forced Africans out of their traditional economy onto the labour market. Cf Harries in Marks & Rathbone *Industrialization and Social Change in South Africa* 142 who shows how obligations of kinship provided the conditions precedent for migration.

[33] Wolpe (1972) 1 *Economy & Society* 425; cf Martin in Smith *Households and the World Economy* 151ff.

[34] Goode op cit n11 10–18; Parsons (1943) 45 *Am Anthropologist* 22.

[35] Goode op cit n20 53.

[36] Phillips *The Bantu in the City* 73–4.

[37] 1903 South African Native Affairs Commission *Report* para 269–81; Krige (1936) 9 *Africa* 5; Hunter (1932) 29 *SA J of Science* 681.

[38] Shropshire *Primitive Marriage and European Law* 26; Janisch (1941) 15 *Bantu Studies* 11; Kidd op cit n20 41; Phillips op cit n36 90ff.

[39] This cultural distinction predicates several ethnographies; eg Coertze in Eloff & Coertze *Etnografiese Studies in Suidelike Afrika* 291ff.

[40] Mayer 4ff.

country,[41] and some urban dwellers show a marked commitment to pre-existing social networks in the country: the phenomenon of encapsulation.[42]

[44] PAUW *THE SECOND GENERATION* 194–6

Our main findings may be summarized in terms of the "triangle of forces"—Western culture, traditional Xhosa culture, and urbanization—referred to at the outset. In terms of the contrast between "Western" and "traditional" we may say that the culture of the urban Xhosa of East London is predominantly orientated to Western cultural patterns. In the economic and technological field patterns are almost completely Western. For their means of livelihood the urban Xhosa rely almost exclusively on Western forms of occupation such as wage labour in industry and commerce or domestic service, white-collar employment, trading, or returns from investment of capital in property. In respect of material culture one may point to housing, furniture, clothing and transport, all of which follow Western patterns, although houses and furniture are often of a very simple nature. Formal education in schools on Western patterns is "normal" and a large proportion of town Bantu have a real connexion with a Christian denomination, while many of the rest claim allegiance to one. Western medicine is generally accepted. Diverse forms of Western sport, concerts, the cinema, ballroom dancing and jiving, and vocal groups represent large-scale westernization in the recreational field. Visiting and drinking are more or less "neutral" in this respect. Fah-fee is of oriental origin but reflects the cosmopolitan nature of the Western urban pattern.

In respect of marriage and values connected with the family it is more difficult to decide whether Western patterns predominate. Love-making is obviously influenced by present-day Western ideas, but patterns of pre-marital relations as such can hardly be classified as either Western or traditional, although lip-service is paid to traditional sex norms. Where marriage does take place it is usually legalized by church or civil rites, but this is often accompanied by the customary negotiations through intermediaries on behalf of the parents, and giving of *lobolo*. In *amabhaso* parties and wedding receptions there is a merging of tradition and patterns of Western origin. Conjugal relations are closer than they used to be, but the traditional patriarchal patterns are still valued and continue to influence relations between husband and wife. In some white-collar families, however, Western "middle-class" values are consciously fostered.

In the political field there is a desire to participate in a system based on Western democratic patterns in concert with non-Xhosa peoples, but the traditional chiefs are still respected by many, and people attach a positive value to clan and tribal identity.

There are, however, significant instances of the persistence of behaviour patterns orientated to traditional Xhosa culture. We have already referred to *lobolo*, which is almost universal where marriage does take place. Male initiation is also very widely adhered to and is probably the "purest" example of a traditional institution persisting in town. Witchcraft beliefs and other traditional beliefs relating to the causation of illness and other forms of misfortune are common, and continue to influence the behaviour of many townspeople. Beliefs relating to the ancestor cult are still held by many people, and are occasionally given concrete expression in ritual.

The general orientation towards Western culture is not the result merely of urban living, because the process of westernization started long ago during the time of the present townspeople's rural ancestors. Most of the parents who moved to town, and even the majority of grandparents, already belonged to the category of School people, the acceptors of church and Western education and of "civilization" generally. Even in the rural areas, School people are orientated to Western patterns in much of their material culture, religion, education, norms of cleanliness and in their relative readiness to accept

---

[41] Manona (1988) 47 *Afr Studies* 4.
[42] Emerging from Mayer's study 90ff; and Reader *The Black Man's Portion* 13–14. Cf Mair in Phillips 20–8 (regarding rural) and 28–45 (regarding urban family life).

innovations on Western lines where possible. Migrant labour in urban areas has of course contributed its share towards the westernization of the rural School Xhosa, but it is largely the result of "agents" and institutions acting directly within the rural environment, such as missions, schools, government agencies and white traders. The School migrant coming to town has found there the opportunities for greater fulfilment of those Western-orientated ideals fostered by his School background in the country. Urban living has therefore merely contributed to a process of westernization which started within the rural environment, and it is difficult to distinguish cultural characteristics of the urban Bantu which are the result specifically of being born and brought up in town.

In the case of the small proportion of townspeople whose parents were Red, the degree of westernization they have attained is more closely related to urbanization. They themselves often connect their departure from Red behaviour patterns with urban living. However, they are often less westernized than the children of School immigrants, some of them being what we have termed "semi-Red".

When one is viewing urban Bantu society from the angle of structure it is easier to distinguish changes which are specifically related to urbanization. The rural structure has, of course, been affected by westernizing influences. The emergence of the Red–School division and the relative weakening of patrilineal kinship ties and paternal authority on the School side illustrate the point. However, patrilineal kinship ties still dominate the rural structure, mobility within the rural community is restricted, status is largely ascriptive—in short the social network remains essentially close-knit. Moreover, although the rural Xhosa have been drawn into the administrative and legal machinery of the South African state, the latter tends to be superimposed on a system of chiefs, headmen and councils reflecting traditional patterns.

In the urban situation, however, traditional patrilineal patterns have lost much of their significance for the structure and growth of domestic groups, and have largely had to make way for distinct matrifocal tendencies, to the extent of families becoming extended in the matriline much more commonly than in the patriline. Although kinship ties and clan membership are valued, larger kinship groups cannot be regarded as important categories of interaction in day-to-day relations. Group activity takes place according to the principle of association rather than kinship. Seniority in terms of patrilineal descent is still significant when rites and ceremonies are performed, but is less important in the urban status system than the emerging distinctions in terms of education and wealth. Political authority is exercised by government and municipal officials appointed according to principles totally different from seniority in terms of patrilineal descent. In spite of the presence of a tribal council in town, and the connexion that some prominent townspeople have with this, it has little relevance for the daily life of the average townsman as compared to officials and police.

Immigration to town has had a direct effect on social networks, resulting in the loosening of individuals' networks. But with prolonged urban living of town-born persons, networks seem to be becoming less loose-knit for members of the lower social stratum. De-segregation of conjugal roles also seems to be related to urbanization, although other westernizing influences cannot be ruled out.

(4) Apartheid

The processes described above were, to a greater or lesser extent, common to all countries in Africa. In South Africa the same processes were intensified by at least seventy years of a policy of apartheid. The immediate concerns of this doctrine—white dominance and racial segregation—were predicated on the physical separation of Whites and Blacks into different living areas. This generated a 'contradiction between the economic and social pull of the urban areas and the government's policy of creating rural "homelands" for Africans'.[43] None the less, a sharp distinction was drawn between the urban centres (where the industrial/mining economy was located) and the rural areas (which rapidly degenerated into an economic and political periphery).[44]

Although the origins of apartheid are detectable as early as the seventeenth century, it did not become a considered political doctrine until the Report of the Native Affairs Commission in 1903–5, which recommended political and territorial segregation of the nation. In 1913, this proposal was implemented in the rural areas by the Natives Land Act:[45] existing African reserves were set aside as 'scheduled areas', places where Africans only were permitted to own or occupy land. In 1936, this Act was supplemented by the Native Trust and Land Act[46] in terms of which a Trust was established to purchase more land on behalf of Africans (so-called 'released land').[47]

The consequent impact of these enactments on rural life, however, was minor compared with the shifts in population caused by the expansion of mining and industry in the 1930s and 1940s. While the general economy improved after the Depression, the African reserves became ever poorer and overpopulated. They could no longer provide a secure material base for urban workers, and after the Second World War the earnings of migrant labourers were no longer used solely for individual support; they had become a vital source of income for the entire family.[48] Poverty drove more and more people out of the reserves into the towns and on to white farms. It was ostensibly to solve problems of crime and disease in the overcrowded townships that the government was called upon to restrict the rural-urban migration.

Before 1910 the residence of Africans in towns was subject to the separate control of each municipality, but throughout South Africa a fairly uniform pattern had developed. Africans were confined to separate zones; their presence in white areas was regulated by curfews; 'passes' had to be carried at all times; trading was controlled; and brewing of liquor was strictly forbidden. After Union, the administration of the urban African population became the responsibility of the newly established Department of Native Affairs. In 1922 the Report of the Transvaal Local Government (Stallard) Commission established a principle that urban areas were the white man's creation and that Africans were

---

[43] Burman in Hirschon *Women and Property/Women as Property* 117; Holleman (1960) 11 *J Racial Affairs* 82ff.
[44] Wolpe op cit n33 425; Legassick in Palmer & Parsons *The Roots of Rural Poverty in Central and Southern Africa* 175ff.
[45] No 27. At this time the reserves amounted to little more than 7,3 per cent of the total land area of the country.
[46] No 18.
[47] In 1932 the Native Economic (Holloway) Commission 46ff reported that urgent land husbandry measures were necessary to check rampant soil erosion in the reserves. This led to the establishment of 'betterment areas' (Betterment Proc 31 of 1939), a series of decrees stipulating the grouping of previously scattered rural homesteads into villages, and the division of land into residential, agricultural and pastoral sections. See Letsoalo *Land Reform in South Africa* 51–6.
[48] See Rich (1980) 7 *J Afr Studies* 70ff.

to be allowed there only on sufferance. From this premise flowed the ideas that shaped the key enactment for the future—the Natives (Urban Areas) Act of 1923.[49]

This Act was concerned with diverse issues, and although frequently amended and once consolidated,[50] it remained until 1986 the principal statutory instrument controlling Africans in urban areas. Local authorities, assisted by 'native advisory councils', were empowered to establish locations and to erect single-sex hostels for Africans.[51] Non-Africans could not acquire land rights in the locations and, conversely, Africans were not permitted to live outside these locations. In 1937, an amendment to the Act[52] prohibited Africans from entering urban areas to look for work. Only those who had approved employment were entitled to be in the cities; persons deemed to be 'idle, dissolute or disorderly' could be repatriated to their reserves or sent to work colonies.[53]

The Nationalist Party victory in 1948, which gave the name and further impetus to the policy of apartheid, led to an even stricter regime of influx control. The entire system rested on race classification. Paradoxically, however, this was not implemented uniformly. Section 5(1) of the Population Registration Act[54] required the division of the South African population into white, black and coloured categories; but it was not the only legislation that racially typed people.[55] Different statutes used different criteria (such as appearance, social acceptance and parentage) for specific purposes, confusing an already problematic definition.

Control of movement was facilitated by the obligation, imposed on all African males over the age of 16 (and later extended to females),[56] to carry a reference book or 'pass'.[57] The Bantu Labour Act of 1964[58] placed a further brake on movement into the urban areas by providing that Africans were not permitted to leave the area of a labour bureau (ie a reserve) in order to seek employment.[59] Only licensed persons and labour bureaux were authorized to recruit black labour.

In 1952, by amendment to the Urban Areas Act,[60] every African who wished to stay in an urban area had to prove an entitlement in terms of the following section.

[45] SECTION 10 NATIVES (URBAN AREAS) CONSOLIDATION ACT 25 OF 1945, AS AMENDED BY SECTION 16 ACT 42 OF 1964.

(1) No Black shall remain for more than seventy-two hours in a prescribed area unless he produces proof in the manner prescribed that—

---

[49] No 20.
[50] 25 of 1945.
[51] They could also require employers to provide accommodation.
[52] No 46.
[53] Section 17, later s 29 of the Consolidation Act.
[54] 30 of 1950.
[55] See above, 66ff.
[56] See below, 315.
[57] Sections 13 and 15 of the Natives (Abolition of Passes and Co-ordination of Documents) Act 67 of 1952.
[58] No 67.
[59] Chaskalson 1984 *AJ* 33ff.
[60] No 54.

(a) he has, since birth, resided continuously in such area; or

(b) he has worked continuously in such area for one employer for a period of not less than ten years or has lawfully resided continuously in such area for a period of not less than fifteen years, and has thereafter continued to reside in such area and is not employed outside such area and has not during either period or thereafter been sentenced to a fine exceeding five hundred rand or to imprisonment for a period exceeding six months; or

(c) such Black is the wife, unmarried daughter, or the son under the age of eighteen years, of any Black mentioned in paragraph *(a)* or *(b)* of this sub-section and after lawful entry into such prescribed area, ordinarily resides with that Black in such area.

Housing regulations were of critical importance to securing urban residence.[61] Persons holding s 10(1)*(a)* or *(b)* rights were given priority in obtaining accommodation in the locations.

[46] BURMAN 1984 *ACTA JURIDICA* 96–9

In terms of the Group Areas Act 41 of 1950 Africans may not live in a white group area. However, this Act, together with Proc 5 of 1968, exempts domestic servants from the provisions relating to the occupation of premises in a group area by disqualified persons, provided that they live on the premises of their employers and, in the case of Africans, the requirements laid down in the Blacks (Urban Areas) Consolidation Act 25 of 1945 are complied with. Under this dispensation, *only* domestic servants may live in the white Group Area. Their spouses may not spend the night with them on those premises, and their children, even if babies, may not live on the premises. The penalties for breach of these regulations are fines of up to R500 for the employer for the first offence (with a minimum fine of R500 for second and subsequent offences), which is usually more than adequate incentive to the employers to ensure that the law is observed. Since this is the only alternative housing available to Africans in urban areas outside African group areas, housing in the townships is of paramount importance.

African housing in Cape Town is acknowledged by the government to be in extremely short supply, as it is in all urban areas in South Africa. In 1983 the figures for Cape Town's official African population and housing stock, when juxtaposed after allowing for hostel beds, gave a hypothetical occupancy rate of 146 people per house, and that was without allowing for the illegal population.[1] As a concomitant of the Coloured Labour Preference Area policy, there is no freehold for Africans in Cape Town, and at the time of writing only one very small development with 30-year leasehold, sponsored by the Urban Foundation. All other housing is owned by the Department of Co-operation and Development and controlled by the Western Cape Development Board. Informants interviewed for the study had sometimes waited 10 or 12 years for a house, and a housing official interviewed stated that the biggest houses (four rooms, including the kitchen) were classified as overcrowded only when they contained 30 or more inhabitants. Officially, it is illegal to build a shack in the backyard of a township house. Since a man with s 10(1)*(b)* rights may not bring his rural wife to town until he gets a house of his own, it is virtually impossible for such a family to be united legally in Cape Town. Where a house *is* acquired, extreme measures will be taken to retain it if necessary.

This is manifested in a number of ways which have a striking impact on the operation of family law. Houses are always registered in the man's name, unless on divorce the wife gets custody of minor children, in which case the house may be transferred to her if she

---

[61] GN R1036 14 June 1968; see Corder 1984 *AJ* 57–8 and Olivier (1988) 3 *SA Public L* 26–9. The size and permanence of housing had repercussions on family size and structure: where houses were built out of temporary materials they could be altered at will to accommodate whoever wanted to live there. In this way the group could determine the size of the building, not vice versa: Goody 28 cited in Segalen op cit n29 39.

has urban residence rights. Every time the Southern Divorce Court comes on circuit to Cape Town, it is the scene of extremely bitter fights over custody, although there is an abundance of evidence from social workers, lawyers and subsequent custody variation cases that many children in the custody of fathers in the townships are particularly poorly cared for. Lawyers interviewed were unanimous that the main reason that so many more African fathers contest custody than those in other sections of the population, and so bitterly, is to prevent the loss of the house, although the customary-law attitudes imported with lobola payments would also seem to reinforce two other reasons present in all sections of the South African population, namely a dislike of paying maintenance and a belief that the child "belongs" first and foremost to the father's family. In the Supreme Court and Southern Divorce Court case samples drawn for this study, 21,7 per cent of African fathers obtained custody of their children in the Southern Divorce Court, as against 9,5 per cent of white fathers and 6,3 per cent of coloured fathers in the Supreme Court. This occurred despite the finding in interviews with the judicial officers in the Southern Divorce Court indicating that they had a stronger preference for maternal custody than those in the Supreme Court. Apart from the higher number of fathers contesting custody, the awards may be partially explained by the phenomenon of fewer mothers contesting custody than in other population groups. Reasons for this include the inability of mothers with only s 10(1)(c) rights to retain urban rights for their children, as described above, or to be able to support their children adequately in either the rural areas when endorsed out, or illegally in town.

Where the father loses the custody dispute, he may still retain the house if he can show good cause why it should go to him rather than to his ex-wife. The existence of dependants who will live with him is considered a valid reason for retaining the house, and both lawyers and social workers told of men who remarried immediately in order to be able to show dependants to the housing authorities. Where this occurs, the wife with custody must somehow find lodgings for herself and her family. If this proves impossible in Cape Town, she has only two alternatives if she and the children are not to lose their s 10 rights, and both entail dissolution of even the attenuated family unit. Either she can send the children to family, friends or a boarding-school in the country during the school year (though this does not solve the problem of school holidays). Or alternatively, she may find someone to care for them in the urban area, while she obtains accommodation by becoming a live-in domestic servant in a non-African group area. As indicated above, it is illegal for any child to live with her there.

Apart from divorcees and widows with s 10 rights and the custody of minors, only married couples are at present officially allocated housing, and at present in Cape Town this is interpreted as being those married by civil law or those whose customary unions were registered and who had documentary proof of this fact. This in effect presents yet another bar to a s 10(1)(b) man bringing a customary-law wife to town, since most customary unions are not registered and in such situations he cannot hope to acquire a house, even in the long term, by waiting his turn on the housing list. His only hope of *ever* bringing such a wife to town is to have a house and other dependants already, for example, from a prior marriage. These facts are widely known in the townships and urban African legislation is therefore in practice reinforcing an already existing urban trend towards the disappearance of customary unions. Civil-law marriage is increasingly the first choice of most couples, or else it is subsequently resorted to and supersedes an existing customary-law union. However, the continued and flourishing existence of the institution of lobola imports many customary-law attitudes (of both the couple and their families), and related practices, into civil-law marriages, most frequently to the detriment of the wife and her family.

The housing regulations dealt with above, when coupled with the inability of men with s 10(1)(b) rights to bring customary-law wives to town, the extreme unpleasantness of single quarters in the townships, and the men's reluctance to remain in town without another wife, leads many men with customary union partners to enter into a second, urban marriage, usually by civil law. Not only does this increase the African birth-rate, contrary to the aims of government policy, but it also greatly increases the number of families that are victims of the dual family-law system—namely, customary-law families where the unions are summarily dissolved by the men's civil-law marriages.[2] Interviews indicate that in practice the customary unions are frequently not treated as dissolved when the men visit the rural areas (leading to a further increase in the African population), but the added strain on a man's finances of a second, town family very frequently leaves the rural woman with no support from him. Given the almost complete dearth of rural employment, the gross inadequacy of the state welfare system for Africans, and the decay of the lobola system as a means of social security, the rural family is left in dire straits. Interviews in the squatter camps indicated that many women there were rural wives who, in desperation, had come in search of non-supporting customary-law husbands, only to find them with another wife.

Notes

1. SA Institute of Race Relations *Survey of Race Relations in South Africa* (1983) No 37 277.
2. Cf s 1 of Act 3 of 1988.

The logical consequence of the government's decision to segregate the population was forced resettlement. The immediate reasons and statutory authorizations for this were diverse. In white farming areas, unwanted farm labourers, squatters and labour tenants were moved on an individual basis. In the reserves, removals were en masse, justified as the consolidation of a homeland or as 'ethnic rationalization'. Other removals were the result of 'betterment planning' schemes for the more efficient use of rural lands.[62] In urban areas, the removals were based on proclamations under the Group Areas Act;[63] these were aimed at separating the races and clearing squatter settlements. All in all, since 1960, an estimated 2,8 million people have been forced to leave their homes.[64]

The grand apartheid programme culminated in the denationalization of a substantial portion of South Africa's African population.[65] By s 3 of the National States Citizenship Act[66] the citizenship of one of the homelands (formerly styled 'reserves', then 'bantustans', and then 'national states') was ascribed to all Africans; but they remained South Africans. Once independence had been granted to a homeland, however, these people forfeited South African citizenship, and by this means about nine million Africans were denationalized.[67] South African authorities were afforded a new measure of influx control: the deportation of unwanted 'aliens'. Moreover, s 12 of the Urban Areas Act provided that no person who was a foreigner (although formerly a South African citizen) might ever acquire s 10 rights. The overall effect was to deprive the children of people holding s 10(1)(a) and (b) rights of any chance of ever acquiring South African nationality.[68]

---

[62] See below, 271ff.

[63] 36 of 1966.

[64] Platzky & Walker *The Surplus People* 10; see too Olmesdahl in Rycroft *Race and the Law in South Africa* 101–4.

[65] Rycroft op cit 209ff.

[66] 26 of 1970.

[67] Dugard (1980) 10 *Denver J Int L & Policy* 16; Dean (1978) 11 *CILSA* 66. Certain categories of people acquired South African nationality again under Act 73 of 1986.

[68] Budlender (1985) 1 *SAJHR* 5.

In the late 1970s, internal unrest, economic sanctions, and growing international protest compelled a degree of forbearance. The broader political and territorial design of apartheid was maintained (it was to be transformed into 'orderly urbanization')[69] but the de facto presence of township dwellers was now in some small measure legally acknowledged.[70] Later, following the declaration of a State of Emergency, a package of reform statutes was passed in 1986: the Restoration of South African Citizenship Act,[71] which allowed certain categories of people to re-acquire South African citizenship; the Abolition of Influx Control Act,[72] which repealed most of the Urban Areas Act including s 10; the Identification Act,[73] which repealed the Blacks (Abolition of Passes and Co-ordination of Documents) Act.[74] These enactments were supposed to give effect to the government's new policy of eliminating racial discrimination, extending equal opportunities to all South Africans, and abolishing legal controls on urbanization. The reforms did little to allay political discontent, and sceptics doubted whether material change would occur.[75]

In any event the old system of influx control had become impossible to enforce, and the earlier self-assurance of the government had disappeared. As one writer remarked:

'research, far from showing a monolithic government manipulating policy to its own ends, disclosed a legislature unable to cope with the intricacies of the society it wished to control.'[76]

Legal efficacy aside, the statutory entitlements needed by the state to regulate freedom of movement could now be found in other legislation, much of it predating the influx control measures, and all of it having the advantage of being apparently non-racial in application.[77]

(5) The modern family

The following account of Lovedu marriage covers a timespan of approximately a hundred years. In it various influences can be observed. They can be categorized chronologically: first, a period of missionary activity when Christian beliefs were introduced to the area; secondly (a period lasting from the turn of the century until the end of the Second World War), a time of labour migrancy and the introduction of new agricultural methods; thirdly, large-scale white investment in the economy and the full implementation of influx control, resulting in overcrowding and dependency on wage labour. Key institutions, such as the preference for cross-cousin unions and bridewealth, were altered, and

[69] 'Riekert' Commission of Inquiry into Legislation Affecting the Utilization of Manpower 1979.
[70] Accordingly, in 1978 a 99-year leasehold scheme was introduced (Act 97) to benefit s 10 right-holders.
[71] No 73.
[72] No 68.
[73] No 72.
[74] 67 of 1952.
[75] Robertson in Rycroftop cit n64 107–118; Schoombee & Davis (1986) 2 *SAJHR* 208; Hindson (1985) 25 *Cahiers d'Études Africaines* 401.
[76] Burman 1984 *AJ* 101.
[77] Prevention of Illegal Squatting Act 52 of 1951, as amended by Act 68 of 1986; Trespass Act 6 of 1959; Slums Act 76 of 1979; and the Aliens Act 1 of 1937. See Robinson in Rycroft op cit n64 112.

marriages were seriously destabilized, as evidenced by a sharp increase in incidences of adultery and desertion.

[47] KRIGE in KRIGE & COMAROFF *ESSAYS ON AFRICAN MARRIAGE IN SOUTHERN AFRICA* 150–6

Since the coming of Rev. Reuter, the first white missionary to settle in the North-Eastern Transvaal Lowveld, Lovedu marriage has been subjected to attack on three main fronts—ideological, administrative and economic. . . . Christianity as taught by the missionary was opposed to polygyny and the levirate. It stressed marriage as an arrangement based on the free choice of individuals, not between families; discouraged the extended family by requiring a newly-married couple to build and occupy a home of their own, away from their parents; opposed bridewealth; regarded cross-cousin marriage as incest, an idea still propagated in schools today, and, by disallowing this form of marriage among Christians, undermined the position of the father's sister and her control in family life in this group. Christianity thus posed a threat to the whole character of Lovedu marriage. The bridegroom's mother, traditionally a partner in the marriage of her son, with rights to control over the bride, had no place in Christian marriage. Neither had the husband's sister, since bridewealth was outlawed. With the abolition of polygyny and bridewealth, there was no need in Christian marriage to protect the house property of each wife. The husband simply took over all control over property. Furthermore, the present-day problem of illegitimacy amongst schoolgirls, and the difficulties this places in the way of their marriage, derives from Christian innovation: the abolition for converts of the girls' puberty ceremonies, which formed the traditional preparation for marriage; the delay in marriage resulting from going to school; and the policy of co-education.

Christianity and education also created new material needs: clothes had to be worn and laundered; school-fees to be paid; utensils and furniture to be obtained for a westernized mode of life. For all this, money was essential. By 1936, Christian men commanded all the most highly paid jobs by virtue of their education, while their women in the Lovedu area had applied themselves to moneymaking activities—dressmaking, baking, making pots on a large scale to be hawked by ox-wagon on neighbouring farms and Reserves.

Yet the new faith made slow progress. By 1936 Christians still formed less than 5 % of the population. And it is only since World War II and the mushrooming of schools resulting from new economic opportunities and promises of self-government (for which education would be essential in modern conditions), that the new Western, individualistic attitudes to marriage have been gaining any ground.

Of the economic forces operating to undermine the Lovedu system of marriage, the first to make itself felt was migrant labour.

The system of migrant labour as we know it today among the Lovedu came . . . with the imposition of a poll-tax payable by men from the age of 18. To pay a tax in money in a subsistence economy involved working for the white man. The rinderpest of 1896, followed by unprecedented drought and starvation, also contributed towards forcing people into the labour market. Hence by 1936–8, when we made our first study of the Lovedu, 37 % of males over c.15–18 years of age were absent at any one time at the labour centres, chiefly the Witwatersrand and Pretoria. Today the percentage of migrants absent at any one time is 65 % and higher. At that period (1936–8), owing to a self-sufficient subsistence economy, the character of Lovedu migrant labour was different from what it has become today. Men usually went to work to achieve limited objectives—money for poll-tax, for bridewealth, to buy a plough, clothes and other European goods (eg a bicycle or a wagon). When their objective had been achieved they returned home. Their periods of absence tended, however, to grow longer as time went on. As a result of the absence of a large proportion of men there had come to be by 1936–8 a good deal of dislocation at home. This was expressed in an increase in adultery and in desertion of their wives on the part of men who disappeared in town never to return, or who married townswomen.

Heirs to district headmanship holding good jobs sometimes refused to return to take up their responsibilities at home, where life had become dull and uninteresting to some.

On the other hand, the disrupting effects of migrant labour at that time were offset by a number of factors that had a cushioning effect. Important among these was the introduction of the plough, which greatly increased the number and size of fields that could be cultivated. This enabled the women, who had not yet begun to go out to work for wages, to carry on at home during the absence of the men and to produce sufficient to feed their families, albeit on a less well-balanced diet. For the land available for cultivation was still adequate for the needs of the people, except in periods of drought.

Important also in counteracting the dislocating effects of migrant labour was the character of Lovedu marriage itself. The fact that most marriage partners were "born for" one another; that all first marriages were arranged by parents; and the rights and control exercised by women in marriage and home affairs, all made it possible for marriage and family life to continue with less disturbance than might otherwise have been the case. Girls could go over in marriage to their relatives-in-law in a normal manner even during the prolonged absence of the men they were marrying. If a son with a wife in town refused to accept his cross-cousin his mother could, and often did, marry the girl herself and install her at home. Even the desertion of the husband working in town did not break up the marriage. Polygyny made young men more ready to accept wives chosen and married on their behalf in their absence than they otherwise might have been, while the extended family made it possible to arrange for at least one man to remain at home while others went out to work. In this way control could be maintained.

A further factor which offset the effects of migrant labour was the position of women in the society, their power in decision-making in family affairs, the possibility of their holding political office, and, in general, rule by a queen whose ritual seclusion kept the capital free for a long time from the corrupting, materialistic values and undermining effects of Western contacts.

Thus, a self-sufficient economy based on adequate land, the introduction of the plough, the sporadic nature of migrant labour and, above all, the traditional Lovedu system of marriage and the place of women in the society, together served to cushion the dislocating effects of migrant labour on marriage and family life in the period before World War II.

During the 1930s, when marital dislocation as a result of migrant labour was beginning to make itself felt, differences in outlook on the part of the White administration on questions such as wife-beating began to cause problems and confusion in the settlement of disputes. A change in rules regarding divorce, usually attributed by the Lovedu to the native commissioner at that time and based probably on practices of peoples further to the south, came into operation. In the case of malicious desertion on the part of the wife (and soon almost all cases of divorce became interpreted in Lovedu courts as due to malicious desertion), the husband, instead of receiving only the bridewealth, was to be awarded both return of bridewealth and the right to the children. Seeing in the new ruling some hope of counteracting the new tendency of wives to run away to male compounds on nearby farms and citrus estates, the counsellors composing the queen's court did not oppose this change, and few people nowadays remember the original rules governing divorce. Yet this new rule runs counter to basic concepts underlying Lovedu marriage: the strong ties uniting the triad of bridegroom, his mother and his sister, with their rights and obligations in the marriage; the son's right to benefit by his mother's claim to her brother's daughter in marriage; the whole principle of enjoined cross-cousin marriage. It runs counter also to deep feelings about the close ties of children of the house with the mother's kin. Whereas orphans are never allowed to be reared by a co-wife of their deceased mother, unless she happens to be also their mother's sister, the new divorce arrangements required just that. As a result, children often and repeatedly run away to their mother, especially if she has not re-married, and usually end up by remaining with her. Where a divorced father has received bridewealth for his daughter, her mother often creates endless trouble for him by persuading her daughter to desert and break up her marriage. For these reasons some men refuse custody of their children. In some cases women do seek to return to their husbands rather than be separated from their children, very often just at the point when son or daughter becomes marriageable, so strong is their feeling that no other woman should benefit from the services of their son's wife. . . .

The end of World War II ushered in momentous changes in the North-Eastern Transvaal Lowveld. Up to that time the area had remained relatively isolated and poorly developed because of its unhealthy climate. The cessation of hostilities had given an impetus the world over to large scale agricultural schemes and aerial spraying for the eradication not only of pests but also of certain human diseases. Such was the success in combating malaria in the Northern Transvaal Lowveld that, by the late fifties, this disease had been almost completely eliminated. This opened the way to full economic exploitation by whites of an area which was rich both agriculturally and in mineral wealth, and brought to an end the relative isolation of its people from the mainstream of South African development. Rapid growth took place in farming in tropical fruits and vegetables, canneries and other light industries made their appearance, and the Phalaborwa mining complex was put into operation. The opening up of new roads and communications brought into being a new trend in migrant labour; viz., week-end commuting between the Reserves and the estates, plantations, canneries and sawmills, where people worked during the week. This was of great advantage in diverting to the family in the reserve more and more resources that might otherwise have been squandered in town. It also gave a great fillip to the interest of life in the Reserve. But it also has an unsettling effect: week-ends have become periods of heavy drinking and the prosecution of love affairs between migrants and married women at home.

The stamping out of malaria and general improvement in environmental services occurred just at a time when rationalization in farming, influx control in urban areas and the "back to the Reserves" policies of the Nationalist Party were causing a strong movement of the population away from European farms and industrial centres into the African Reserves and Trust Areas. The result of this was an unprecedented population explosion in the Lovedu Reserve. In 1936, the density of population in one of the most thickly populated parts of the Lovedu Reserve had been 180 per square mile. Less than 40 years later, according to the 1970 census, the average density of population in the Reserve had risen to over 400 per square mile. Running parallel to this increase of population was an economic revolution: the change from a subsistence economy to reliance on wage labour and bought food, necessitated by sheer shortage of land and the inadequacy of existing Lovedu methods of cultivation. By 1970, the Lovedu family had become dependent for its staple food on bought maize produced by the white farmer.

This change took place in spite of the fact that, between c.1927 and c.1945, the Lovedu had more than doubled the size of their Reserve by buying from the Government a number of unoccupied farms in the hitherto unhealthy, low-lying area to the north and east. This eased some of the congestion for a time. After 1960, the queen's jurisdiction was greatly increased by the addition also of new Trust farms to the north. But these Trust lands were immediately occupied also by large numbers of outsiders of diverse origins from European farms and urban areas.

Reliance on wages and bought food is undermining the economic basis of Lovedu marriage and the position of women in the indigenous economy. No longer is the traditionalist wife the economic mainstay of the family, providing food for her children and husband by cultivating her fields. Owing to shortage of fields for cultivation, women have had to seek new ways of earning income, chief among which is the sale of distilled spirits and home-brewed beer, made mostly with grain issued on credit and paid for with the proceeds. A ready market for these is at hand in the form of week-end commuters. By 1970 a new word had entered the Lovedu vocabulary and found its way into Lovedu courts: "sahport", the concept that it is the duty of a husband to shoulder the responsibility of supplying his wife and children with bought mealie meal.

Another development resulting from reliance on wage labour is a new attitude to levirate. Christians have always been opposed to the levirate, but land shortage is making it unpopular also among traditionalists. It is resented by wives because of the extra drain imposed on the husband's slender resources in the absence of adequate land for the widow to cultivate for food for her children.

Wage levels today still manifest to some extent the influence of conditions and conceptions holding earlier this century when wages of migrant labourers supplemented a subsistence economy based on adequate land for each family in the rural Reserves. Even at its best, the western-type wage system is no substitute for the security of land to a Lovedu tribesman. For wage levels in a western economy are based upon a domestic unit composed of the elementary family and income is supplemented by a system of state-provided welfare services, where necessary. Neither of these conditions holds in the case of the Lovedu. According to a census taken in three representative areas in 1967, one of which had an unusually high proportion of Christians, only 10 % of Lovedu domestic groups were found to be elementary families, 75 % being extended families and compound families (husband plus two or more wives and children), while welfare services for Africans in Reserves are minimal.

At a time when Lovedu women were seeking ways in which to acquire money a ready solution to their problems began to make its appearance. From 1950, developments in vegetable- and fruit-farming and the growth of light industry created a new demand for female migrant labour for picking tomatoes and tea, sorting oranges and de-barking eucalyptus poles to be trucked to the Witwatersrand mines. Many farmers send lorries daily to pick up these labourers in the mornings on the road near their homes, taking them home again in the afternoons. Some estates run compounds for women with a crèche for young children. The number of Lovedu women employed in migrant labour of this kind is not yet great; but the new trend will have far-reaching consequences for Lovedu marriage and family life, more especially because many women migrants form liaisons with male workers and children are born.

Who are the women that go out to work? It is primarily widows, divorced or deserted wives with children to support and women with illegitimate children who, at present, are taking advantage of these job opportunities. This trend provides a measure of the failure of Lovedu marriage to afford adequate security against the exigencies of life under the new conditions.

Before World War II, the major problem arising from migrant labour was the desertion by Lovedu husbands of their wives. Today a reverse process, in the form of a high incidence of desertion on the part of married women, has become evident. This has arisen as a result of improved transport, in particular the Modjadji Bus Services set up by the Lovedu themselves. No longer need a neglected or disgruntled wife remain at home with her mother-in-law. For a small fare she can catch a bus that will take her out of the Reserve to a lover or friend at a compound for male migrants on a fruit estate or factory. Here she will be welcomed as a temporary wife and installed in the married quarters by any man anxious for home comforts. The increase in desertion of wives and in divorce has become a major problem. . . .

Despite all the factors at work in the direction of change in the marriage system of the Lovedu, the traditional norms still hold for the bulk of the population (probably over 80 %). Cross-cousin marriage is meeting with challenges and its incidence is decreasing; nevertheless, it remains the foundation of the Lovedu system of marriage. Polygyny is still common—in a census of four districts in 1967, 40 % of married men were found to have more than one wife. Moreover, the extended family still predominates—75 % of all domestic units in the same census were extended families. The significance of such figures for family security and stability under conditions of migrant labour emerges from the discussion which follows.

As we have indicated, bridewealth among Lovedu traditionalists, even today when usually paid in money, forms a closed circuit of exchange and must not be used to satisfy consumer needs, except in cases of hunger or distress. In keeping with the character of the Lovedu marriage contract, such money is usually hoarded by the bride's mother, whose future security is bound up with it, to be used for the marriage of her son and for maintaining links of cross-cousin marriage with her natal family. Among Christians, however, bridewealth has undergone a basic change. Carried out as a private transaction, because not fully approved by the church, the passing of bridewealth is regarded as compensation for nurture and varies according to the standard of education of the bride. No limitations are placed upon how it is used and it is not earmarked for the brother of the bride, as among traditionalists. Divorce and desertion are common today but concubinage (*ho gaula*), known of old in Lovedu society, is still uncommon in the Reserve, though it occurs frequently in the married quarters of compounds attached to estates and factories.

Commentators on modern marriage have remarked on the abandonment of the old rituals and the preference for civil and Christian forms. They have noted a marked increase in casual unions, and the neglect of formal divorce proceedings when couples want to separate. The mediating influence of the extended family has waned and even parents have little say in their children's marriages. Many traditions, such as the rule that the new bride starts married life by living under the watchful eye of her mother-in-law or that a wife must return to her own family to bear her first child, are now ignored.[78]

Spousal relations are often fraught with tension, partly because of the new roles that have been thrust upon husbands and wives, and partly because of the prolonged absences required by migrant labour. Although the known or the traditional always serves as a basis for action, religious, economic and other factors generate pressures to conform to new patterns; and the anonymity of the urban setting allows people to flout the strictures of tradition. The causes and implications of all this are not necessarily comprehended by the people involved, who in any event seldom have any legal or educational guidance in how they should respond.[79]

[48] HELLMANN in ADAM *SOUTH AFRICA: SOCIOLOGICAL PERSPECTIVES* 162–76

The traditional pattern in a strongly patrilineal society was one of male domination, female subordination, and rigid segregation of conjugal roles. Despite the changed economic role of women—roughly one-third of married women are gainfully employed—their increased responsibilities for home and budget management and for the rearing and education of the children, and the greater interdependence of the members of the smaller urban family, many men maintain their traditional attitudes and patterns of behaviour. In some families women have likewise retained their attitudes of traditional society, particularly more recent immigrants from the country and women of little or no formal education. In others wives are acutely resentful of their husbands' lack of co-operation and claim the right to greater equality of treatment. In a number of families, notably among the professional and higher-income groups where the spouses both have attained a higher standard of education, patterns of companionship, joint consultation, and shared responsibility are emerging. To the majority of women this represents the ideal to which Africans should aspire—an ideal which they have largely taken over from white society and which many seem to believe is the white norm. Men do not to the same extent accept this democratic pattern as a goal. Even many modern, sophisticated men view the dawning emancipation of women as a threat which will destroy the patriarchal authority they have been conditioned to regard as their right. . . . Marriage is no longer a contract

---

[78] Phillips 28ff.
[79] See further Mayer 216–17; Marwick in Argyle & Preston-Whyte *Social System and Tradition in Southern Africa* 36–54.

between two groups of kin, with personal preferences being regarded as a minor consideration. The selection of a marriage partner is today determined by individual choice based on mutual attraction and congeniality. But *lobolo*—the traditional transfer of cattle from the family of the bridegroom to the family of the bride which validated the right of the groom's family to the children the bride would bear—is still paid in the overwhelming majority of marriages, whatever their legal form. . . .

Although monogamy is practically the only form of marriage in towns—three of 151 marriages in a recent (unpublished) Soweto survey were polygynous and in no case was more than one wife present in the town—polygynous attitudes based on the attitude that a man is entitled to have access to a number of women persists, and polygyny is being replaced by an informal system of concubinage and by extra-marital liaisons. There is much talk in the townships of the extent of marital infidelity, and the incidence of separations—even if not of legal divorces, though these, too, are increasing—appears to be high. . . .

I am of the opinion that broken families form a larger proportion than any broad-based survey would reveal because of the regulations which govern the right to occupy houses in the townships. Only married men who are qualified to live in the town and who are permitted to have their wives with them can become registered occupiers of a house. If this permission is refused, the inducement for a man to contract a customary union with one of the many women as anxious to obtain a house as he is must be great.

. . . [T]he general direction of cultural development is, I submit, clear. Pauw says, "The culture of the urban Xhosa of East London is predominantly orientated to Western cultural patterns."[1] Wilson found that in Langa "a community has emerged with characteristics very similar to those of urban communities in other countries and radically different from the traditional tribal societies of the Nguni peoples".[2] I, for myself, do not doubt that the future of South Africa must be envisaged in terms of a dominant Western culture within which there will be sub-cultures sharing the same basic institutions but differing in peripheral cultural traits.

Notes

   1. *Second Generation* 194.
   2. M Wilson & A Mafeje *Langa* 76–9.

Whatever reform measures are now envisaged for customary law, it is unlikely that the family can be reconstituted in either an extended or even a nuclear form.[80] Previous networks of kin have been permanently disrupted. Many working males are absent from rural households for prolonged periods.[81] Unemployment and the decline in agricultural production have led to ever greater poverty, which has inevitably eroded the material foundation of the kinship ethic. Income can no longer be shared amongst members of the extended family; it must be concentrated in the earner's household.[82] This has the effect of asserting the identity of that unit at the expense of more remote relatives. And, if the income becomes too meagre, dependants must be dispersed[83] for the sake of the survival of remaining family members.[84] Family management and child-rearing have become female responsibilities. The young and able-bodied have attained an economic independence that allows them considerable freedom.

---

  [80] Cf James op cit n15 162.
  [81] See the account of Lesotho: Spiegel in Verryn *Church and Marriage in Modern Africa* 435ff.
  [82] Lye & Murray *Transformations on the Highveld* 108–12.
  [83] Sometimes under cover of 'fostering': Spiegel op cit n27 23–31.
  [84] Sharp & Spiegel op cit n27 133.

Formerly the balance of authority was weighted firmly on the side of senior men; gradually it is coming down on the side of women and juniors.

While it is no doubt true that forces of cultural conservation are always at work[85] and that industrial urbanization does not necessarily destroy the extended family, it is clear from both statistical evidence and from ethnographic studies that extended families are in no sense a norm. Nuclear families are now much more common,[86] and female-headed households are ubiquitous.[87]

II THE NATURE AND RECOGNITION OF CUSTOMARY MARRIAGE

'Marriage is fundamental to any society. Biologically it is the means by which the group is replenished and enabled to persist in time; socially it forges bonds which link the otherwise insulated in-groups of the family and lineage to other, similar groups, adding the bonds of kinship to the unifying mechanisms of language, culture, economic co-operation and political allegiance.'[88]

As this quotation suggests, marriage is a universal institution. Yet as a cultural artifact its incidents are bound to vary; and the distinctive characteristics[89] of customary marriages have provided the occasion for a persistent policy of discrimination.

[49] PHILLIPS *SURVEY OF AFRICAN MARRIAGE AND FAMILY LIFE* xi–xvii

If . . . we seek to identify the main distinguishing features of African customary marriage, as compared with "European marriage", there will no doubt be general agreement that the most obvious of such features is the toleration, and even approval, accorded to polygamy. Almost universally, a marriage according to native law and custom is potentially polygamous in the sense that there is during its subsistence no legal impediment to the contracting of another marriage (or of an unlimited number of other marriages) by the husband. Any suggestion of compulsory monogamy as an indigenous institution must be interpreted as having reference only to exceptional cases—e.g. to the restriction imposed on the husband of a female chief—or to quite unrepresentative tribes (such as possibly the Galla). In general, monogamy is either a self-denying ordinance, in the sense that a man voluntarily renounces or abstains from polygamy, or it is dictated by inability to afford more than one wife. Where the traditional outlook still prevails, the possession of a number of wives is normally a mark of importance and success in life, and—for this among other reasons—is something which the average African man would gladly achieve if he could: in other words, monogamy is, for the majority who are in fact monogamists, a matter of necessity rather than of choice.

It is this polygamous element which most radically differentiates African marriage (though not African marriage alone) from European marriage. It constitutes, moreover, the point of greatest resistance to the teaching of Christian missions concerning marriage. It may be added that it reflects, and at the same time intensifies, the fundamental inequality between the sexes which appears to be typical of African social systems, even in

---

[85] Kuper op cit n17 ch 10.

[86] Simkins in Burman & Reynolds op cit n25 38; supported by Pendleton *Katutura* 139; Nzimande in Steyn op cit n5 38; Hellmann in Adam *South Africa: Sociological Perspectives* 162.

[87] Marwick in Argyle & Preston-Whyte op cit n79 46 and Preston-Whyte ibid 54ff.

[88] Hammond-Tooke 91; and see Schapera 125.

[89] For descriptions of which see: Mönnig 193–4; Holleman 128–45; Van Tromp 40ff; Schapera 130–8; Hammond-Tooke 102–5; Reader 174–84; Whooley in Verryn op cit n81 245ff and Krige 120–3. For comparative materials see: Elias *The Nature of African Customary Law* 145–8 and Obi *Modern Family Law in Southern Nigeria* 155–6.

matrilineal societies. Whatever may be said as to the material advantages accruing to a wife as a result of having co-wives to share her duties, it can hardly be denied that the institution of polygamy is normally associated with a social system in which there is unchallenged male dominance.

Another outstanding feature of African customary marriage is the institution commonly called "bride-price". There are few African tribes in which it is not found in one form or another. To quote Professor Radcliffe-Brown: In most African marriages ... the making of a payment of goods or services by the bridegroom to the bride's kin is an essential part of the establishment of "legality".[1] Within the wide limits of the institution as so defined there is a great diversity of custom. The payment may be in livestock, in other chattels (e.g. hoes, brass rods, or lengths of cloth), or in money. Its value may be great or small. The total amount may be required on the handing-over of the bride, or it may be payable by deferred instalments. Differing (and sometimes elaborate) rules govern the repayment of bride-price in the event of death or divorce. . . .

It is sometimes implied, if not stated expressly, that the possibility of easy dissolution is characteristic of African customary marriage. But as a generalization this appears to be too sweeping. It is true that in very many tribes (probably in the great majority) a marriage can be dissolved by inter-family arrangement, without the necessity for any judicial pronouncement. But it does not follow that a divorce can be easily obtained at the mere wish of husband or wife (or even of both of them) in the absence of substantial grounds. Native law frequently requires that the wife's relatives should refund the bride-price (in part, at least) as an essential condition of the validity of the divorce; and this requirement tends to have an obstructive effect. Another possible deterrent is the prospect of losing the right to the children. Attention may be drawn, on the other hand, to the fact that in some tribes a union does not acquire the strictly binding quality of marriage until it has been in existence for a number of years; and doubtless other examples could be cited in support of the view that African marriage is easily dissoluble. On the whole, however, it would seem that no very definite conclusions can be drawn from a comparison between African and European marriage in the matter of dissolubility. It must be remembered that divorce by mutual consent is not unknown in European secular law; and that while in some African tribes divorce is exceedingly common,[2] there are others in which (to quote Professor Gluckman's account of the position in Zululand) it is "almost unknown"[3]—in practice, at any rate, and occasionally, it seems, even in law.

In seeking to identify the outstanding characteristics of African customary marriage, we may justifiably include a reference to the collective aspect of the marriage transaction and relationship. There is a considerable weight of authority for the statement that, from the point of view of indigenous law and custom, a marriage is to be regarded primarily as an alliance between two kinship groups and only in a secondary aspect as a union between two individual persons. Such a formula can easily be pressed too far; nevertheless, it does appear to embody a principle of great importance—viz. that the indigenous institution of marriage can only be understood if it is viewed as an integral part of the kinship system as a whole. It is here, for example, that we find the key to certain customs which obviously presuppose a conception of marriage as a transaction giving rise to reciprocal rights and obligations between two groups of kinsmen and binding those groups together in a relationship which remains effective beyond the lifetime of the original individual spouses. This principle of a continuing relationship is closely connected with the institution of bride-price; and it finds expression in, for example, the levirate (or the somewhat different custom of "widow-inheritance"), under which a widow is expected to co-habit with one of her deceased husband's kinsmen; and in the sororate, which imposes on the kinsmen of a barren or deceased wife an obligation to provide another woman to make good the deficiency or loss. Among the consequences of the operation of these and similar customs is inevitably a curtailment of the woman's freedom of choice. The interests of the group are in such cases regarded by traditional law and opinion as overriding the personal wishes of the individual.

... Before concluding this brief sketch of the main distinctive features of African customary marriage, we must not omit to mention the emphasis laid on procreation as the chief end of marriage. Dr. Mair points out that "the importance of securing legitimate descendants accounts for the most characteristic features of African marriage law".[4] This tendency to concentrate attention on the procreative aspect of marriage seems to be the key to the understanding of much that would otherwise be puzzling to a European observer and it is illustrated by the fact that in a very large proportion of the disputes involving customary marriage law the crucial issue concerns the determination of the question, To which kinship group shall the children belong? Although there are great differences between patrilineal and matrilineal descent systems, the importance attached to the procreation and "ownership" of children seems to be common to both.

Notes

1. Radcliffe-Brown & Forde 46.
2. D Forde *Marriage and the Family among the Yakö of South-Eastern Nigeria* 75, where it was estimated that not less than 30 percent of the women are divorced at least once in their married lives.
3. Gluckman in Radcliffe-Brown & Forde 180. For other examples see: J G Peristiany *Social Institutions of the Kipsigis* 87–9; Ashton 85–6.
4. Mair in Phillips 1.

Some features regarded as unique to marriage in Africa in fact have parallels in medieval European marriage. The English union, for instance, was

'a compact between two bodies of persons, the kin of the woman who agree to wed their daughter to the man, and his kinsmen who pledge themselves that the terms of the agreement will be carried out. The bridegroom and his kinsmen must promise to make a payment . . . to her father or other legal guardian.'[90]

The medieval marriage (like its African counterpart) was a privately negotiated arrangement, that could best be described as a *process*. The spouses' status did not change absolutely or immediately; instead, their relationship developed and strengthened over the years, gaining definition with the birth of children and payment of dowry or bridewealth. But, as first the Church and then the state began to assert authority, family control over this process was displaced, until eventually a valid union could be contracted only by fiat of a priest or marriage officer.[91] (Conversely, it could be dissolved inter vivos only by judicial or ecclesiastical order.)[92] The Church and the state had the occasion to impose whatever requirements for marriage they thought necessary, which meant that it lost its informal character and was demarcated with far greater precision.

Colonists in Africa either ignored or overlooked the features common to both European and African marriages. Instead, differences were stressed, no doubt to emphasize the distinction between ruler and subject. Three requirements were thought indispensable for any true marriage: monogamy, the free consent of the spouses, and indissolubility.[93] Hence the essence of mid-nineteenth century

---

[90] Radcliffe-Brown & Forde 44; and see Hahlo & Kahn *The South African Legal System and its Background* 345–6 for parallels in Germanic marriage.
[91] A similar development has occurred in a Tswana chiefdom: Campbell op cit n30 218 and 221–3.
[92] Radcliffe-Brown & Forde 45.
[93] See Goody op cit n24 204ff.

marriage was expressed as follows: 'the voluntary union for life of one man and one woman to the exclusion of all others.'[94]

The legitimacy of imperialism depended heavily on the sanction of the Church; and the quid pro quo was state support for ecclesiastical policy in the colonies. Both Church and state regarded African marriage with distaste. All manner of social and moral evils were attributed to it. The 1852–3 Natal Commission, for example, reported that bridewealth was the price paid for women, whom men then treated like slave labourers. Polygyny was supposed to free men from the need to work so that they could idle away their days in sensual indulgence.[95] One colonist maintained that polygyny:

> 'destroys all love between man and wife—it encourages war as a means of procuring cattle to pay for the panders to their lust and idleness; and by a fearful destruction of life, brings about an inequality of the sexes'.[96]

Sixty years later, at a World Missionary Conference, African marriages were still being condemned because they were 'at variance with the instinctive feelings of natural morality'. Polygyny was branded 'one of the gross evils of heathen society which, like habitual murder or slavery, must at all costs be ended'.[97]

Not surprisingly Africans were unmoved by this moral outrage; and some degree of compromise was required if missionaries were to make any headway in evangelizing the population.[98] The lesser of the two evils—bridewealth—was to be tolerated. And those with greater insight and more experience of Africa could even commend it, partly because of the protection it supposedly offered the wife,[99] and partly because of its stabilizing influence on marriage.[100] But there could be no compromise with polygyny.

These were the opinions that mediated the more general recognition of customary law.[101] In 1883, the Cape Government commissioned a full investigation of Native Laws and Customs from recognized experts in the field.[102] Although many of the people who gave evidence to the Commission were critical of customary marriage, and their goal was to mould customary law 'into some shape that would conform more closely to civilized law and . . . [to] secure the sanctity of marriage and the rightful place of woman', the ultimate Report was for the times remarkably enlightened.

---

[94] *Hyde v Hyde & another* (1866) LR 1 PD 130 at 133. This decision was adopted into South African law by Innes CJ in the leading case, *Seedat's Executors v The Master (Natal)* 1917 AD 302 at 307–8, where the court held that no country was under an obligation to recognize a legal relationship that was 'repugnant to the moral principles of its people'. See generally: Dlamini 1982 *De Rebus* 593.

[95] In view of these prejudices, it is perhaps understandable that the Commission recommended prohibition of both polygyny and bridewealth: pp 37–8.

[96] Cited by Welsh op cit n32 69; see too Simons 1961 *AJ* 17–19.

[97] Cited by Hastings *Christian Marriage in Africa* 15. Fifty years later even Reuter *Native Marriages in South Africa* 313 claimed that polygyny was contrary to the natural law.

[98] Junod (1941) 15 *Bantu Studies* 30–1.

[99] Soga 263ff.

[100] Junod 279.

[101] Simons *African Women* 22, 30–33 and 37–40 and 1960 *AJ* 314.

[102] See Kerr 1986 *Transkei LJ* 11ff.

[50] SECTION 84(b) 1883 CAPE COMMISSION REPORT ON NATIVE LAW AND CUSTOM

Dealing with the question of marriage in its broadest aspect, we cannot accept the view extensively held, that in dealing with a people among whom civilization and Christian law have but lately come, marriage can only be recognised and regarded as legal and valid when such marriage has been performed according to the rites of civilized or Christian countries and has been duly registered. We recognise the essential element of marriage to be a contract between a man and a woman, into the celebration of which a certain defined social, or civil, or religious ceremony enters, while at the same time we hold that the Christian law of marriage sets forth the truest and purest idea of such a union, and fixes what should obtain amongst those who have accepted Christianity as a religion, or in States ruled by Christian law. But we cannot on this ground hold that marriages celebrated in this or in other countries where Christianity has not been established, or where the civilization is not Christian, are not in reality marriages, whether such marriages are monogamous or not, so long as certain essential conditions are fairly fulfilled, viz., mutual life, fidelity, mutual support, and recognition of certain duties to the offspring of such unions or marriages; for were this not recognised, at least two-thirds of the entire population of the globe would be in the position of being illegally married, and therefore without any of the rights of marriage or responsibilities to children which belong to marriage, and the children without their just and natural rights.

The Commission was prepared to accept bridewealth on the ground of its beneficial social function, but only as a contractual accessory to marriage. And, with regard to polygyny, it distinguished those practices that were repugnant to humanity and justice, such as infanticide and suttee, and those that were contrary to the Christian code of behaviour. It felt that matters falling into the last category, such as polygyny, could not be legally proscribed merely because they were unchristian.

The more tolerant views of the Cape Commission were echoed in the Report of the 1903 South African Native Affairs Commission. The provisions on bridewealth were adopted in their entirety,[103] and this time even polygyny found some favour,[104] although the Commission had no wish to defend it. The custom was considered 'essentially material and unchristian' and the Commission looked forward to the time when it would pass into oblivion.[105]

Abhorrence of customary marriage was deeply rooted and neither of the Commissions brought about a change in legal policy. A mere twenty years ago the Law Revision Committee reiterated the refusal to recognize customary marriage for fear that it might encourage a taste for polygyny amongst Whites.[106] The implication is that Africans do not have a true form of marriage.

[51] *GUMA* 4 NAC 220 (1919)

Here it is necessary to guard against the assumption that, because the single term "marriage" is used to describe the conjugal relationships established under both the

---

[103] Paragraphs 302–3.

[104] It was said to have originally been a product of war, which causes an imbalance in the sex ratio. The palpable decline in the incidence of polygyny was thus attributable to peace and a correction of this imbalance: para 290. Cf Clignet *Many Wives, Many Powers* 16ff.

[105] Paragraph 296.

[106] Kahn (1964) 81 *SALJ* 103. And see *Ismail* 1983 (1) SA 1006 (A) at 1024–6, where the court reconsidered the grounds for withholding recognition of polygynous marriages, albeit in casu Islamic marriages.

common law of the country and Native law, they are one and the same thing. They have indeed so much in common, that each form regularises sexual union and the status of offspring, but in other respects the two institutions are fundamentally different in nature and the law governing them. While a common law marriage implies a contract on both sides of exclusive cohabitation terminable only on death or the decree of the Courts, a Native marriage is essentially casual and one sided, allows polygyny, and may be dissolved by the action of either party: it is moreover subject to the doctrine of "no cattle no wife" . . . .

Within the sphere of its own origins and the present conditions of its existence, it is doubtless a suitable form of relationship, but to project it into the whole field of South African Common Law as something identical with civil marriage would need the clearest reasons and the weightiest authority for its support. . . .

The simple fact is that the Native customary relationship can be identified as a marriage only by reference to its surroundings: its recognition is strictly limited and local: and to separate the custom from its associations, universalise its recognition, and judge of its significance in every issue of South African Law by the tests of a civil marriage must inevitably lead to confusion and chaos. Whatever it may be a marriage by Native Law is not equivalent to a marriage by common law.

In 1927, the Black Administration Act[107] finally accorded customary marriages partial recognition[108] and at the same time shielded bridewealth from further attack under the repugnancy proviso. 'Marriage' and 'customary union', however, were defined in such a way as to limit recognition of the latter to the newly established commissioners' and chiefs' courts.

[52] SECTION 35 BLACK ADMINISTRATION ACT 38 OF 1927, AS AMENDED BY SECTION 9 ACT 9 OF 1929

"Customary union" means the association of a man and a woman in a conjugal relationship according to Black law and custom, where neither the man nor the woman is party to a subsisting marriage;

"marriage" means the union of one man with one woman in accordance with any law for the time being in force in any Province governing marriages, but does not include any union contracted under Black law and custom or any union recognized as a marriage in Black law under the provisions of section *one hundred and forty-seven* of the Code of Black Law contained in the Schedule to Law No. 19 of 1891 (Natal) or any amendment thereof or any other law.

The anomaly ensued that, so far as the common law of South Africa was concerned, customary marriages were not considered completely valid. For special purposes, in certain statutes, they might be recognized,[109] but generally they had no currency in the magistrates' courts and the Supreme Court. One of the many bizarre consequences of this rule was the overriding effect given to a civil/Christian marriage: such a union could nullify any prior customary marriage that either of the spouses might have contracted.[110] Naturally, this

---

[107] No 38.
[108] Simons *African Women* 54–5.
[109] Section 5(6) of the Maintenance Act 23 of 1963; s 4(3) of the Workmen's Compensation Act 30 of 1941; s 1 of the Income Tax Act 58 of 1962; s 1 of the Group Areas Act 36 of 1966. See further Hahlo 32–5.
[110] See below, 455ff.

tended to undermine the value of traditional marriage.[111]

The refusal to recognize customary marriages was brought into dramatic focus by dependants' suits for damages caused by the death of a breadwinner.[112] If the action were initiated in a commissioner's court, the marriage was fully recognized and the claim might succeed;[113] but much depended on the accident of jurisdiction. In *Mokwena v Laub*,[114] the defendant happened to be 'White' and so not amenable to the jurisdiction of commissioners' courts and hence not subject to customary law. The plaintiff's action accordingly had to fail. *Mokwena's* case was later confirmed in an Appellate Division decision: *Santam v Fondo*.[115] Eventually, in 1963 the patent absurdity and injustice of the situation provoked legislative intervention.[116]

[53] SECTION 31 BLACK LAWS AMENDMENT ACT 76 OF 1963

(1) A partner to a customary union as defined in section *thirty-five* of the Black Administration Act, 1927 (Act No 38 of 1927), shall, subject to the provisions of this section, be entitled to claim damages for loss of support from any person who unlawfully causes the death of the other partner to such union or is legally liable in respect thereof, provided such partner or such other partner is not at the time of such death a party to a subsisting marriage.

(2) No such claim for damages shall be enforceable by any person who claims to be a partner to a customary union with such deceased partner unless—

(a) such person produces a certificate issued by a Commissioner stating the name of the partner, or in the case of a union with more than one woman, the names of the partners, with whom the deceased partner had entered into a customary union which was still in existence at the time of death of the deceased partner; and

(b) such person's name appears on such certificate.

(2A) A certificate referred to in subsection (2) shall be accepted as conclusive proof of the existence of a customary union of the deceased partner and the partner or, in the case of a union with more than one woman, the partners whose name or names appear on such certificate.

Far from enabling widows to prosecute their actions, the technical requirements of this section have frustrated many otherwise unassailable claims.[117] In *Makgae v Sentraboer (Koöperatief) Bpk*,[118] it was held that the certificate specified in s 31(2) was a condition precedent to the enforceability of the action,[119] and in *Dlikilili v Federated Insurance Co Ltd*,[120] the court held that the document

---

[111] Peskin in Verryn op cit n81 395.

[112] Kerr (1956) 73 *SALJ* 402–8.

[113] *Ngqongqozi & another v Nyalambisa & others* 4 NAC 32 (1919); *Kanyile v Mbeje* 1939 NAC (N&T) 25; *Zitulele v Mangquza* 1950 NAC 249 (S).

[114] 1943 (2) PH K64 (W).

[115] 1960 (2) SA 467 (A) at 470–4; Kahn (1960) 77 *SALJ* 279–84.

[116] See discussion by Van der Vyver (1964) 27 *THRHR* 94ff.

[117] *Mayeki v Shield Insurance Co Ltd* 1975 (4) SA 370 (C) at 373.

[118] 1981 (4) SA 239 (T) at 247.

[119] This case thus overruled *Pasela v Rondalia Versekeringskorporasie van SA Bpk* 1967 (1) SA 339 (W) —see Kerr (1982) 45 *THRHR* 83—but in its turn was criticized by *Hlela v Commercial Union Assurance Co of SA* 1990 (2) SA 503 (N), where s 31(2) was held to be principally evidential in nature.

[120] 1983 (2) SA 275 (C) at 283.

required must be 'a certificate of an extract from a formal register', ie a 'record [of] a *registered* customary union';[121] other forms of proof would not suffice.

As the remaining prejudices of colonialism were eliminated in other parts of southern Africa,[122] the obdurate refusal to recognize polygynous forms of marriage in South Africa began to appear less tenable. More importantly perhaps, polygyny is practised by so few that it has now ceased to be a relevant social issue.[123] Proposals for reform finally came in 1985, when the Law Commission published a working paper on African marriage.[124] Three years later limited remedial legislation was passed[125] rescuing customary marriage from the damaging effects of a concurrent civil/Christian marriage.[126] Unfortunately the impetus for further reform seems to have dissipated.

III CAPACITY

(1) Age

Customary marriage is a group, not an individual concern. Family heads are therefore free to choose whichever family member seems the most suitable to make a good alliance. It follows that any predetermined rules prescribing the capacities of the future spouses would be a hindrance. There seems to be only one exception: because the purpose of most unions is procreation, the spouses should be over the age of puberty.

In all systems of customary law this is the single most important rule. The attainment of puberty, however, varies from person to person, and in a preliterate society where ages cannot be fixed with precision, the usual practice was to wait until the spouses were physically mature.[127]

More specific rules governing capacity are imposed when the community or state begins to take an interest in marriages. Thus, it was formerly the case amongst most of the peoples of southern Africa, that a person could not marry until he or she had been initiated. This conferred a socially approved status of adulthood and with it marriageability.[128] More overt intervention is evident in the Zulu kingdom, and the Pedi and Tswana chiefdoms where initiation ceremonies were assimilated to service in military regiments. It was only after

---

[121] Dlamini (1984) 101 *SALJ* 34–9; Kerr (1984) 101 *SALJ* 224–7.

[122] For example, s 6(1) of the Customary Law and Primary Courts Act 6 of 1981 in Zimbabwe and s 3(1) of the Marriage Act 21 of 1978 in Transkei (where *all* forms of marriage are now potentially polygynous); see generally Bennett & Peart 1983 *AJ* 145ff.

[123] SA Law Commission *Marriage and Customary Unions of Black Persons* para 11.2.6. And see Moller & Welch *Polygamy and Well-being* 60.

[124] Op cit Working Paper 10.

[125] Act 3 of 1988.

[126] See below, [138].

[127] Holleman 72; Van Tromp 35–6; Van Warmelo & Phophi 159; Krige 103; Clerc (1938) 12 *Bantu Studies* 77; Roberts 23; Campbell op cit n30 216–17. In Roman law too there was no fixed age for contracting a valid marriage. Marriageability depended on the attainment of puberty, an age that was finally settled as being 12 for girls and 14 for boys: Gaius *Institutes* 1.196. It is argued that this is still the rule for civil/Christian marriages in South Africa: Erasmus et al *Lee & Honoré: Family, Things and Succession* 24.

[128] Reuter op cit n97 105–10.

completion of this duty that recruits were permitted to marry.[129] Today the regiments have been suppressed, and although initiation is still thought to be an important requirement for men, it is often overlooked in the case of women. Accordingly, the age of puberty should probably be taken as the sole requirement for marriageability in customary law.[130]

(2) Consent

The requirement of spousal consent is the most significant common-law intrusion into customary marriage. This rule originated in Roman and canon law,[131] but it has now been declared a universal human right.[132] In customary law, which regarded marriage as an alliance of kin groups to be negotiated by senior males, the views of the spouses were of no great moment.[133] Moreover, because the bride and the groom had no access to the bridewealth that was necessary to validate the union,[134] they could not marry without the co-operation of their family heads.

Two practices caught the attention of colonial authorities: child betrothals and forced marriages. Child *marriages* were in fact unusual; the pledge of a daughter in marriage, in other words a child *betrothal*, was much more common. Girls might be promised as brides for reasons of lineage politics or kinship amity—motives either venal or expedient. The future union might be negotiated long before the child was even born, and customary gift exchanges would keep the agreement alive until the girl was old enough to be handed over to her groom.[135] Marriage need not even be explicitly stipulated. Where the marital system favoured sororal polygyny, it would be understood by all concerned that a young girl would have to follow the path of her older married sister if the latter were to die young, prove to be barren, or in some other way become incapable of performing her duties as a wife and a mother.[136] In any case a woman's matrimonial destiny would often be determined by the bridewealth that her family had already given to contract other marriages. So it was said: 'Cousin [paternal uncle's child] marry me, that the cattle return to the kraal.'[137]

Somewhat different was forced marriage. In this case a bride, or occasionally a groom,[138] already fully mature and capable of making an independent choice of spouse, was compelled to marry. Such arrangements could never have been common, because an unhappy match would cause domestic discord, which was always something to be avoided.[139] Ideally, marriage was seen as the culmination

---

[129] See Krige 106–17; Schapera 104–17; Roberts 24 and Mönnig 119ff esp 124. See below, 344–5.
[130] Olivier 9; Van Warmelo & Phophi 159.
[131] Hofman 1983 *AJ* 31.
[132] Article 16(2) of the Universal Declaration 1948; and see Nhlapo (1989) 3 *Int J Law & Family* 15–16.
[133] See, eg, Matthews (1940) 13 *Africa* 7ff. Cf changes in the Ngwaketse chiefdom: Campbell op cit n30 219.
[134] Simons *African Women* 93.
[135] Matthews op cit n133 19ff.
[136] Schapera 155; and see further: Torday (1929) 2 *Africa* 285ff; Kuper in Radcliffe-Brown & Forde 99; Marwick 136ff.
[137] Ashton 63; Schapera 128; Krige (1939) 12 *Africa* 406.
[138] Cf *Presenti v Mashalaba* 1941 NAC (C&O) 78.
[139] But see Burman in Hirschon op cit n43 120.

of a youthful romance, sealed by a parental arrangement regarding bridewealth. The elaborate rituals of the courtship and the marriage negotiations normally gave a bride-to-be many opportunities to voice her doubts or preferences. If her father were obdurate, she could appeal to the mediating influence of her uncles or other relatives; or she might elope with a lover.[140] As a last resort she might even ask her chief or headman to intercede.[141]

In a patriarchal society, however, women are expected to be obedient and to make the best of their circumstances. Recalcitrant brides would be forced to submit.[142] By western standards it would not always be easy to judge whether a marriage had been voluntarily contracted; when did a bride's acquiescence mask actual aversion? Aside from the general duty of compliance that predisposed women to accept their lot, modesty discouraged them from displaying great enthusiasm for a suitor.[143] And the tradition of twala[144] (which was available to a frustrated suitor, with or without the connivance of the woman's guardian) gave an appearance of legitimacy to many forced unions.[145]

The colonial governments took immediate measures to correct these practices. When the Transkeian Territories were annexed, forced marriages were prohibited and made criminal offences.[146] In Natal under the Code, an 'official witness', who was obliged to attend all customary weddings, had to ask the wife publicly at the ceremony whether she was marrying of her own free will. If she were silent or demurred, he would be obliged to stop the wedding immediately.[147] If the head of a family were to coerce a woman into an unwanted marriage, he would be guilty of an offence.[148] Elsewhere in South Africa, where there is no specific legislation on this point, the courts have refused to give effect to forced marriages on the ground of policy.[149] But under the common law there is no criminal penalty for forcing a woman to marry against her will unless she had also been compelled to have sexual intercourse.[150]

In other parts of Africa, child betrothal agreements were treated somewhat differently. It was felt that they were not inherently contrary to public policy or natural justice, and provided that the boy or girl had not been persuaded to have

---

[140] See below, [58].

[141] Whitfield 87; Schapera 129; Simons *African Women* 102–3; and see the account given by the court in *Nomatusi v Nompetu* 3 NAC 165 (1915). In a Tswana chiefdom the formalization of the marriage procedure before chiefs and headmen has endorsed the woman's consent: Campbell op cit n30 219–20.

[142] Simons 1958 *AJ* 328–9.

[143] See Phillips & Morris *Marriage Laws in Africa* 99; Wilson in Krige & Comaroff *Essays on African Marriage in Southern Africa* 136.

[144] See below, [59] and [60].

[145] See, eg, *Gebeleiseni v Sakumani* 1947 NAC (C&O) 105; and compare *Mkupeni v Nomungunya* 1936 NAC (C&O) 77.

[146] Sections 30 of Procs 110 and 112 of 1897 and s 29 of Proc 140 of 1885.

[147] Section 42 of the Natal and KwaZulu Codes.

[148] Section 116(1)(b) of the Codes and see Phillips & Morris op cit n143 100.

[149] *Nomatusi v Nompetu* 3 NAC 165 (1915); *Mpangalala & another v Njijwa* 5 NAC 14 (1924); *Gempeza v Ntsizi* 5 NAC 103 (1926); *Mbanga v Sikolake* 1939 NAC (C&O) 31; *Gidja v Yingwane* 1944 NAC (N&T) 4; *Gebeleiseni v Sakumani* 1947 NAC (C&O) 105; *Zimande v Sibeko* 1948 NAC 21 (C) at 23.

[150] *R v Mane* 1948 (1) SA 196 (E); and even here the man's honest intention to marry was treated as an extenuating circumstance.

intercourse before reaching a marriageable age, nothing wrong had been done.[151] In South Africa, however, such agreements were treated in a fashion similar to forced marriages: they were declared to be contrary to public policy and accordingly unenforceable.[152]

[54] *SIBEKO v MALAZA* 1938 NAC (N&T) 117

The plaintiff entered an agreement to marry, although his wife-to-be was evidently a sickly woman; anticipating future problems, he was alleged to have paid to the woman's father five head of cattle to secure the future marital services of another daughter, then one year old. When this woman came of marriageable age, he sued her guardian for specific performance. The Court dismissed the claim partly because it deviated from the Swazi custom of inhlanti and partly because child marriage was forbidden.

The Swazi custom, which appeared to have much in common with that of the Bapedi, Bavenda and other tribes, fragments of which the Swazi incorporated on conquering the country is based on the "sororate" whereby a man having married a woman has a preferent claim to her sister or sisters as, among the Swazi, on completion of a marriage the father-in-law points out a sister who is to be the "inhlanti" of the new wife. The word is used in the sense of "a reserve" in speaking of a supplementary member of a team, the idea on which it is based being that the reproductive power of the wife has been acquired by the lobolo and any defect in the wife in this respect needs to be corrected by her people who implement their contract by supplying another female of the family. In the absence of full or half sisters it is open to the head of the family to point to (kombisa) one of his sons as the "inhlanti", meaning thereby that a daughter born of that son's wife will take the place of her aunt as the accessory wife. It is considered equitable that the inhlanti should come from any house established by the cattle of the man taking a female of the family to wife.

While the pointing out of an inhlanti takes place quite irrespectively of the success or failure of the first marriage, the exercise of the right to marry her is governed largely by the economic factor. If it be established that the wife is barren or is quite unlikely to bear children or that she has died childless, then in either [sic] event no lobolo becomes due for the substituted wife although a beast or two may pass as gifts.

But where these factors do not operate whether there have been children or not, taking of an inhlanti involves payment of a full lobolo. In these circumstances the fact that a marriage is "likely" to prove unfruitful has but slight bearing on the custom. Indeed it is unusual for a Native to marry a sickly younger daughter whose elder sisters have already been taken by other men with an overlapping right of "inhlanti" over the younger sister.

The long delay which must ensue for the taking to wife of a wife's brother's child is also a deterrent to the practice of the custom.

It is moreover a feature of the custom that the inhlanti is merely pointed out and not until the prospective husband has exercised his prerogative does he become liable to pay lobolo. In any event the inhlanti, before becoming the wife of the prospective husband, must go through a marriage ceremony as did her predecessor. . . .

Child marriage is forbidden by the legislature of this Country (Act No 8 of 1935). The custom relied on is perhaps something short of a marriage, but the custom in its ramifications, provides for what may be termed completion rather than consummation of the contract in the case of a very old man, who may not live to enjoy the girl bespoken, by a symbolical sleeping together of the parties under the same blanket—without intercourse, which act converts her into a "wife" of the man so that on attaining puberty she is required even after his death to procreate children for him by an approved male of his family.

---

[151] Phillips & Morris op cit n143 98.
[152] *Butelezi v Ndhlela* 1938 NAC (N&T) 175.

There are other exceedingly undesirable features of the contract which this Court cannot regard without consideration of the qualification imposed by Section 11 that a custom which is contrary to public policy is not to be enforced. . . . Its occurrence locally may not be so frequent as to incur direct legislative action—but the common law forbids the betrothal of girls under 12 years of age (puberty)—van der Keessel, Th 52 and the trend of current legislation is definitely in the direction of extending protection to children and young females.

A custom, therefore, which endangers such protection must necessarily be regarded by this Court as being contrary to public policy and that can readily be said of the present instance.

Although unenforceable, a child betrothal can become a valid marriage if the initial defect of lack of consent is later cured when the person concerned reaches a marriageable age.[153] Until then, on the basis of the pari delicto rule, anything paid over in consequence of the agreement cannot be recovered.[154] Otherwise there is no criminal penalty.[155]

When the rule of spousal consent was first introduced, it was not popular with guardians of the young, who correctly saw it as a major derogation from parental authority.[156] But in fact the courts never realized the potential of its implications. In the first place, they paid no attention to the age at which a proper consent could be formulated. Under the Marriage Act[157] the common-law age for marriage is fixed as 18 for men and 15 for women, but it has always been assumed that this does not apply to persons subject to customary law.[158] Presumably the age of puberty is applicable to them.

In the second place, the individual's freedom to marry is not absolute. In both customary and common law there is a further requirement of parental approval. Historically, in Europe, this was a safeguard against the admission of undesirable members to the family so that the integrity of the group and its estate could be preserved.[159] Today the rule in the common law performs a different function: to cure defects in the judgment of minors.[160] By contrast, in customary law, the courts have construed the requirement of parental approval in such a way that it has nothing to do with the protection of minors. For instance, the consent of a minor *groom's* father is not considered necessary,[161] and provided the child is over the age of puberty, he can contract a valid marriage, apparently even against his father's wishes.[162]

If officialdom has erred on the side of permissiveness in the case of men, it has gone to the other extreme in the case of women. The consent of the bride's

---

[153] Simons op cit n142 330.

[154] *Zulu v Mdhletshe* 1952 NAC 203 (NE); *Mngomezulu v Lukele* 1953 NAC 143 (NE).

[155] Cf Zimbabwe: s 11(2) of the African Marriages Act 23 of 1950 ch 238.

[156] Simons *African Women* 103 and see Cape Commission 1883 Evidence para 517 cited by him.

[157] Section 26 Act 25 of 1961.

[158] See, e g, SA Law Commission *Investigation into the Advancement of the Age of Majority* para 11.1.

[159] In Europe it was only from 1800 onwards that the individual gained a measure of freedom to decide on a spouse of his or her choice: Glendon op cit n24 24–5.

[160] SA Law Commission *Advancement of the Age of Majority* para 3.1.

[161] Except in Natal and KwaZulu: s 38(1)(*b*) of the Codes.

[162] Presumably (although this might now prove to be a false assumption in view of changes in the structure of family authority), his guardian's control over bridewealth is thought sufficient restraint on precipitate and ill-considered matches.

guardian under customary law is indispensable to the validity of a customary marriage.[163] No union results, not even one that is valid until set aside, as would be the case in the common law.[164] This rule applies regardless of the woman's age or de facto capacity. And, to prevent evasion, there used to be a special provision in Natal and the Transvaal that the rule also applied in the case of civil/Christian marriages.[165] Nowadays a woman can escape the stubborn refusal of her guardian's consent only by entering a civil/Christian marriage, but then seemingly only if she has attained the age of majority.[166] In the case of customary marriages there is no way of compelling a guardian to give his consent, no matter how unreasonable or avaricious his motives for withholding it.[167]

The strictures of this rule have been relaxed in Natal and KwaZulu where major women may now contract their own marriages.[168] Here, in any event, a woman's guardian may not unreasonably withhold consent.[169] A district officer may administratively investigate any complaint and may authorize a marriage, making an appropriate order regarding the amount of bridewealth payable.[170]

Sexual relations that have not been authorized by marriage are deemed to be wrongs against the woman's guardian.[171] Hence if a man were to cohabit with a woman without first securing her guardian's approval, he might face an action for damages for seduction. The difference between delict and matrimony rests on the fragile basis of a guardian's acquiescence in his daughter's liaison. It is probably due in part to this tenuous distinction that there are so many cases concerning the *inference* of consent.[172] Acceptance of earnest cattle, acceptance or a promise of bridewealth, failing to object to the spouses' cohabitation, and demanding bridewealth have all been construed as consent to a customary marriage.[173]

(3) Prohibited degrees and preferred marriages

Every kinship system is concerned with rules prohibiting or encouraging marriage between persons who are related to one another.[174] A prohibition,

---

[163] *Gcina v Ntengo* 1935 NAC (C&O) 21; *Dlomo v Mahodi* 1946 NAC (C&O) 61.

[164] Hahlo 93.

[165] Section 22*ter*(1) of the Black Administration Act, inserted by s 2 of Act 23 of 1972. The latter provision was repealed, first in KwaZulu by s 124 of Act 6 of 1981, and later in South Africa generally by Act 91 of 1985.

[166] Under the Age of Majority Act 57 of 1972.

[167] Cf Phillips & Morris op cit n143 102–3. Compare the situation in Zimbabwe under s 5 of the African Marriages Act ch 238.

[168] Without prejudice to the rights of any person normally entitled to bridewealth: s 38(2) and (3) of the Codes. Hlophe (1984) 17 *CILSA* 165–7 claims that the status of majority conferred by s 16 of the Codes entitles women to marry without bridewealth.

[169] Section 38(1)(*a*) of the Code; although, a contrario, under s 38(1)(*b*) the intended *husband's* guardian evidently can.

[170] Section 39.

[171] *Mbongwana v Ngolozela & another* 3 NAC 256 (1912); Schapera *The Bantu-speaking Tribes of South Africa* 205; Simons *African Women* 228.

[172] Simons *African Women* 116 also points to the vicissitudes of completing a customary marriage in the absence of formal wedding rituals.

[173] *Stimela & another v Madolo* 5 NAC 102 (1926); *Mothombeni v Matlou* 1945 NAC (N&T) 123; *Memani v Makaba* 1950 NAC 178 (S); *Ngcongolo v Parkies* 1953 NAC 103 (S).

[174] Radcliffe-Brown & Forde 60–2.

common to all systems of customary law in southern Africa, is against marriage between ascendants and descendants of the same patriline. Technically this is termed a rule of clan exogamy; in other words, two people may not marry if they both belong to the same descent group. The Nguni extend this prohibition to marriage with persons related through any of the four grandparents.[175] By implication levirate and sororate unions are not permitted.[176] Kinship is marked by use of the same clan name; but names are not an infallible guide because, if the blood link has become too tenuous, it is no longer a bar.[177] And, within clans, segments are constantly breaking away to form new clans, and then marriage is allowed.[178] Any scruples about incest can be overcome by purification rituals.[179]

It is not only marriage between persons related within the prohibited degrees that is forbidden, but any form of sexual relation, including intercrural intercourse.[180] Breach of this rule constitutes the crime of incest which (like other offences that are difficult to detect) attracts the special odium normally reserved for witchcraft and crimes of a supernatural dimension.[181]

The Sotho-Tswana regime is different: affinal relatives are not so strictly distinguished from relatives by blood. The basic prohibition against marriage between men and women related in the direct line of descent remains, and marriage is prohibited between a man and his aunts, nieces, stepdaughters, stepsisters and their daughters.[182] Apart from these prescriptions, any relative on the father's or the mother's side is marriageable. Certain unions are positively encouraged; and typical is the preference for cross-cousin marriage.[183]

[55] MÖNNIG *THE PEDI* 198

Discussions on prohibited marriages raise no emotions. It is considered completely unnatural that any man should ever contemplate intercourse with one of his prohibited relatives, and these matters are given no further thought. The importance of the preferred unions to the Pedi is, however, so great that they are frequently discussed at great length and with very strong feeling.

It has been shown that marriage is a union of two groups, rather than of two people, and also that it is not primarily concerned with bringing about a sexual partnership. Marriage is contracted largely to create and perpetuate relations and alliances between groups of people. Such alliances ensure the easier and more equal distribution of *magadi* [bridewealth], and the closer the relationship between such allied groups of people, the greater the satisfaction to all parties concerned regarding the flow of marriage goods. Marriage selection among the Pedi is, therefore, socially organized and controlled.

---

[175] Van Tromp 36; Krige 156 and Hunter 184–6.

[176] Van Tromp 37. But cf s 37 of the Natal and KwaZulu Codes.

[177] *Malinga v Msezane* 1944 NAC (N&T) 13.

[178] Hoernlé in Schapera op cit n171 80.

[179] Holleman 57–9; Junod 256–60; Bryant *The Zulu People* 583–5; Clerc op cit n127 77–9.

[180] Ukumetsha: Hoernlé in Schapera op cit n171 80.

[181] *Mhlanga v Msibi* 1930 NAC (N&T) 80 at 82; *Nyawo* 1936 NAC (N&T) 12; *Mountain v Mandla* 1946 NAC (C&O) 38; Radcliffe-Brown & Forde 70–1. See further: Myburgh *Indigenous Criminal Law in Bophuthatswana* 87–8.

[182] Mönnig 194; Matthews op cit n133 9–12; Campbell op cit n30 218; Poulter 74–5; Schapera 125–7; Coertze 211–19.

[183] See too: Krige & Krige 142–4; Schapera 127–8 and in Radcliffe-Brown & Forde 150–2; Roberts 25–6; Lye & Murray 115ff; Van Warmelo & Phophi Part I 8–61.

The Pedi prefer marriages between a young man and his mother's brother's daughter, his father's brother's daughter or his father's sister's daughter. There is no distinction in kinship terminology or in behaviour pattern between mother's elder or younger brothers, or between father's elder or younger sisters. But a distinction is clearly made between father's elder and younger brothers. The preferential marriages include the daughters of both, so that there are actually four preferred marriages among the Pedi.

The preferred cross-cousin marriage is symmetrical or bilateral, allowing marriage with the daughter of both the mother's brother and the father's sister. The preferred marriage with a parallel cousin is, however, asymmetrical or unilateral, and marriage is allowed only with the ortho-cousins (that is cousins belonging to the same group, which in the patrilineal society include only the daughters of father's elder and younger brothers). Marriage with mother's sister's daughter is prohibited. Apart from these preferred marriages, there are some others which are highly favoured, and in practice more frequently concluded than the actual preferred marriages. These are extensions of the preferred marriages to the daughters of father's half-brothers and half-sisters, and the daughters of mother's half-brothers.

Wherever family bonds have been attenuated, the rules regarding prohibited and preferred marriages tend to be less rigorously enforced.[184]

[56] WILSON & MAFEJE *LANGA* 76

Lineage segments were held together traditionally among the Nguni, partly because the male members lived in one homestead, and partly because they shared a common inheritance in cattle: the fact that members participated in common rituals and observed an absolute taboo on marriage with fellow clansmen also bound them together. In Langa, not only do kinsmen not share a dwelling, but no immovable property can be inherited, for occupiers cannot buy their houses, nor can they build their own, and there is no family herd to pass on. So the control and inheritance of substantial property, on which a lineage organization depends, are absent. Only country ties, with rights over freehold or quitrent land, or a less secure right to inherit a field in a village with "communal tenure", magnify patrilineal descent and the unity of a group of male kin. Thus common residence, and shared rights in inherited property, have disappeared among townsmen, and the rule of exogamy, which forbade marriage within the clan, is questioned. Traditionally clan identity was constantly asserted by the use of the *isiduko*, the clan name, as a polite greeting, and children grew up knowing very well which of their friends and contemporaries fell within the prohibited degrees of marriage and which did not. In the country *iziduko* are still commonly heard in greeting, and conservatives in town, the pagan migrants and elderly people will use it, but among the townees, and younger people generally, *iziduko* are out of fashion. The use of clan names has been largely displaced by the use of surnames which are required in all official contexts, and in dealings with whites. In an earlier generation school families all took a name—usually that of a male ancestor but sometimes that of an admired European—as a surname.

A study of marriage made in Langa sixteen years ago showed only two breaches of clan exogamy, but as identification of clansmen lapses, the rules are weakened, and a number of young men and women expressed the view that they no longer mattered. A country woman of 30 who has been in town for less than ten years, "would never dream of marrying a fellow clansman", but a young man of 19 living in the same house said he would marry a girl of his own clan, "Why should we use clans when whites use none? What is the use of not following their practice since we are following them in our way of life?"...

---

[184] And see Mair in Phillips 12–13 and Pauw 113–14 and 125–6, who notes that in the towns choice of the marriage partners is becoming more individualized.

On the whole, the women questioned were more conservative than the men. A housewife of 31, with ten years' education, who has lived mainly in town, would not consider marrying, or even having a love affair with, a fellow clansman, and a contemporary of similar background said the same. Neither of them inquired about clan names in ordinary contacts, but both said they would withdraw from a love affair immediately if they found a man to be of their own clan. . . .

These samples are sufficient to indicate that the attitude toward clan exogamy is changing; only a statistical study of the clans of recently married husbands and wives, their mothers and grandmothers, would show how far there is a change in practice.

The 1949 Prohibition of Mixed Marriages Act[185] drastically reduced the choice of marriage partners by providing that unions contracted in South Africa between Africans and white persons were void and of no effect.[186] These restrictions were abolished in 1985[187] and provision was made for the retrospective validation of previously void marriages.[188]

IV MARRIAGE NEGOTIATIONS

(1) Negotiations

Although, strictly speaking, marriages were to be arranged by the families of the prospective bride and groom, and great store was set on sexual purity (which was inculcated into youth in their initiation schools),[189] adolescents sought their own matches, which meant that they were inevitably preoccupied with courting and love-making. Experimentation and sex play were usually tolerated by the elders, provided that there were no untoward social consequences.[190] Premarital pregnancies were especially disapproved of,[191] but in this regard intercrural sex (metsha, hlobonga or soma) was safe, and was fully accepted [192] by the Nguni peoples.[193]

Christian missionaries, however, regarded any form of sex play as a moral evil to be discouraged.[194] The courts refused to take their side: they would not allow an action for damages for seduction where the offence complained of was no more than metsha.[195] And in Natal it was held that metsha did not constitute the crime of indecent assault[196] or rape.[197]

Although metsha was condoned by the guardians of youthful morals, if a girl were to be caught spending a night with her lover away from her family, her

---

[185] No 55.

[186] Similarly, a marriage between an African and a White entered into *abroad*, if the man had a South African domicile or citizenship, was void: s 1(2).

[187] Act 72.

[188] See further Simons *African Women* 106.

[189] Cf Ashton 51 and 55; Hammond-Tooke *Bantu-speaking Peoples* 236ff.

[190] Schapera (1933) 6 Africa 68–70.

[191] Schapera *Married Life* 38; MacLean 63.

[192] See Van Tromp 20–2; Kohler *Marriage Customs in Southern Natal* 31–6; Krige 105; Marwick 87; Whitfield 114.

[193] Cf Ashton 39–40; *Moso v Ramabele* 1940 NAC (C&O) 149; *Tsoali v Lebenya* 1940 NAC (C&O) 22.

[194] Hunter 183–4; Reuter op cit n97 111–14 esp n24.

[195] *Qabazayo v Ncoso* 2 NAC 7 (1910); *Nkonze v Moyeni* 1945 NAC (C&O) 19.

[196] *Mpini v Rex* 1905 NHC 147.

[197] *R v Mutati* 1909 NHC 53.

father might demand that the lover pay a fine.[198] So too with the Tswana: the lengthy pre-marriage phase (go ralala) entailed the prospective husband spending each night at his bride's homestead; yet if his father-in-law caught him there in the morning, he risked a fine of one beast.[199] The Transkeian courts jumped to the conclusion that this fine was a payment for sexual favours and they refused to enforce actions to recover it on the ground that it was contra bonos mores.[200]

That standards of sexual morality have changed radically in recent years is a commonplace: 'premarital pregnancy is now so common that no special stigma attaches to it.'[201] The complaint everywhere is that rules and limitations that were previously strictly enforced are now disregarded.[202] This is partly because enforcement institutions such as age grades and initiation schools no longer operate as effectively as they once did, and partly because the supervision of behaviour is not as easy as it used to be in close-knit rural communities. The stereotype of the modern urban dweller is a person living with promiscuous abandon.[203] This is an exaggeration, but it is also true that the traditional restraints, such as those implicit in metsha, are disdained as old-fashioned,[204] and that casual or informal unions (where couples cohabit without any intention of marrying) have become both permissible and common.[205] None of these changes in sexual mores finds expression in the courts' judgments. In actions for damages for seduction, the guardians of females continue to obtain the same favourable terms that they did in the past.[206]

Private courtship, according to the ideal, culminated in a decision by the couple to ratify their relationship with marriage. The boy was then supposed to inform his father, and if his father approved of the match, marriage negotiations could commence. Customary law took no cognizance of a private engagement agreement between the boy and the girl[207] because marriage was legally beyond their control.[208] This meant that only an agreement between their guardians (technically known as an 'affinition' agreement) had legal consequence; and even this was not the same as a common-law engagement. Breach of promise in the common law entitles the injured party to claim damages for hurt feelings and patrimonial loss, an action that is unknown in customary law.[209] It is reported that amongst the Kgatla (a Tswana tribe), however, actions for breach of promise are now permitted in the chiefs' courts. Apparently, private betrothals, on the

---

[198] Called umnyobo: Hunter 182. According to Whitfield 115 this practice is limited to East Griqualand.

[199] Mathews op cit n133 21–2.

[200] *Mayeza v Majayini* 3 NAC 201 (1915); *Palamahashi v Tshamane* 1947 NAC (C&O) 93.

[201] Phillips 23.

[202] Phillips 33–5.

[203] Mayer 253.

[204] Mayer 253ff; Pauw 121ff; Whooley in Verryn op cit n81 324–5. But consider Christian attitudes to extra-marital sex.

[205] See Mayer 256–61. A high rate of illegitimate births has been one result: Pauw 118. And see below, 360–1.

[206] Cf Pauw 120.

[207] Holleman 76ff.

[208] Poulter 77–8.

[209] Raum & De Jager *Transition and Change in a Rural Community* 46–8.

basis of which couples start to cohabit, have become so common that the courts have decided to give a means of redress against the inconstancy of a fickle lover.[210]

Before the marriage negotiations commence, the two families are in a sense socially distanced. (This is particularly evident in the case of the Nguni peoples, whose various rituals often resemble mock battles.) To clinch an agreement this social gulf has to be bridged by careful observance of various formalities.[211] A typical mode of negotiating the affinition agreement is described below.

[57] READER *ZULU TRIBE IN TRANSITION* 179–84

Makhanya marriage, not differing in this respect from the marriage systems of many other societies, is initiated by the efforts of the intending husband and his group. Since they take the initiative, it is necessary for the boy's descent group to make themselves aware of the intended bride's qualities and the material circumstances of her immediate descent group. They will already have had contact with her, for she visits them even during qoma, (choosing a lover) in order to hlonipha (pay respects). The women of the kraal watch her closely, and her female companion also scans them and their ways. The visits are reciprocated by the sisters of the intending bridegroom, who then have a chance to see the girl at work in her home environment. . . .

With matters satisfactorily settled on both sides, and the girl's consent obtained, the young man tells his parents that he wishes to marry her. His mother informs her brothers, the *malumes* of the young man, and the father informs the immediate members of his patrilineal descent group, probably at a weekend beer-drink. The girl meanwhile passes the news to friends of her own age, and tells her mother privately that her sweetheart wishes to speak with her father. In this way the most proximate members of the descent groups concerned become aware of the impending union. If no radical objections are forthcoming, preparations are put in hand to make the beer which will be required in the *ukucela* ceremony. The mother and engaged girl are assisted in this task by a close friend of the latter, normally the one who previously visited with her.

In the meantime the young man's father takes him to the cattle kraal and indicates the beasts which he is prepared to provide towards the lobolo payment. Sitting in council with his brothers he also deliberates upon the choice of an umkhongi (go-between) to act on behalf of the boy in the negotiations between the two descent groups. This man may be one of the father's brothers, but is preferably a malume (mother's brother), for a certain genealogical distance is desirable in one who will have to support all the initial strains of descent-group connection. The ukucela party is then made up by an assistant or escort (umphelekezeli) who is usually a father's brother if the umkhongi is a mother's brother. In this way both sides of the boy's family are represented in the party. The umphelekezeli does not normally speak in the subsequent proceedings except in agreement while the umkhongi is acting. He is, however, empowered to deputize if his principal is sick or unavoidably detained, and most important, he acts as witness on the boy's side to all contracts agreed by the umkhongi. . . .

Early on the appointed day the *umkhongi's* party stand outside the gate of the girl's father's kraal, usually dressed in their best clothes and carrying sticks and dancing shields. Without delay the *umkhongi* calls out their errand in a loud voice, using one of a number of well-worn sequences for the purpose. [He will also call out the beasts he has brought with him.]. . .

From the interior of his hut the kraal head, who has heard all this, tells one of his family to show the party into a prepared hut. A small pot of beer is brought in to make them

---

[210] Especially in favour of women: Roberts 31.

[211] See further: Mönnig 130ff; Raum & De Jager op cit n209 43; Clerc op cit n127 80–4; Junod 101–6; Schapera 129; Holleman 99ff; Krige 126–8; Phillips 35–6 and 39.

welcome. Presently the girl's father comes in, together with his brothers who are going to act as witnesses. One of these has been appointed to speak on behalf of the father, and after a comfortable silence he says: "I have come now. What have you been saying?" The *umkhongi* repeats his words exactly as before, not changing a single beast. He nowadays comes straight to the point, and does not pretend that he has come about some other matter.

The business of *izibizo* (demands) is now initiated. This is an opportunity, while there is a disbalance in the powers of coercion of the two descent groups, for the girl's family to recoup in advance some of the heavy expenditure to which they will be put during the course of the marriage sequence. In most cases that reciprocity which marks the entire sequence is fulfilled: money and goods claimed now will be precisely counterbalanced by gifts made and monies expended by the girl's side later. Occasionally, however, where the girl is particularly attractive or desirable, or the father especially grasping, there is little doubt that advantage is taken at this stage of the proceedings to extort money.

Firstly the spokesman will say that the girl's father refuses to proceed with the matter until he has received a fee of £2 for *imvulamlomo* (the opening of the mouth), which must be produced immediately by the *umkhongi*. When this first instalment of *izibizo* has been paid (and the *umkhongi* comes well provided with money for the purpose), the pressure may temporarily be relaxed and the girls of the kraal will be called in. They have chosen one of their number to speak for, and lead them.

"Do you know these people?" the father's spokesman asks her. "Yes, we know them."

"Did you allow them to come here?" "Yes, *I* did," replies the girls' leader.

"Who is this *I*?" "It is so-and-so" (naming the girl to be married).

The father's spokesman then turns to the *umkhongi* and asks, "Which is the one among these girls?" The *umkhongi* points to where she is standing at the back of the group. The girls are then dismissed. This group ceremony evidently performs the function of identifying one of the terms of the contract before witnesses, a not uncommon procedure in important contracts.

The *izibizo* demands now proceed. The *umnyobo* of £2 to £3 may be called for, an imaginary fine for the alleged fact that the young man has been seen in the girl's hut; the *izindlebe* (the ears—"I can't speak before I hear") of £1; the *ingqaqamazinyo* (teeth-loosener—"to loosen my teeth") of £1 to £2; the *izikhwehlela* (phlegm—"I can't speak before I cough"), a payment of a large fowl or goat; and perhaps many others. If the girl's father is particularly rapacious, his spokesman may call in one of the favourite sons, and he may be asked rhetorically whether he wants a new suit of clothes. The *umkhongi* continues to pay out the money with which he has been entrusted until it is exhausted.

Acid comments and joking may occur during the passage of this money, but on this visit the *umkhongi's* party is not nowadays insulted. The other side have far more to gain than in former times, and the ritual antipathy traditionally proper to this part of the proceedings has lessened. When the money is paid out the *umkhongi* promises to come again, saying that he must return to his principal. The first time of *ukucela* is concluded by the consuming of the beer and food which have been specially prepared for the occasion.

The sanction enforcing *izibizo* demands is that if the money is not sufficiently forthcoming the negotiations will break down; a position which will also ensue if the demands are reported to the Administration or become the subject of civil action. In pagan *ukucela* these *izibizo* added to *lobolo* are therefore ubiquitous, and go largely unchallenged unless the girl herself lends support against them to the young man and his family.

... Apart from ritual antipathy, aggression is also required if the bride's group are to obtain the full money and goods due to them. The boy's representative can only reply meekly by saying that his principal gave him just so much, that it is not his fault that the payments are outstanding; or he may quote the Zulu aphorism, *isithunywa asibulawa* (the messenger is not killed).

Further *ukucela* visits take place until all the *lobolo* beasts have been produced or suitable arrangements have been made for their transfer by instalments, and a satisfactory balance has been reached between the amount of *izibizo* demanded by the girl's side and the amount which the boy's side are prepared to pay. The father of the girl then causes an *imvuma* (agreement) goat to be slaughtered for the *umkhongi*. As representative of the boy's father, the *umkhongi* is sprinkled with the gall, and has the goat's inflated gall bladder tied to his wrist or head. This sacrifice, apart from reporting to the girl's ancestors, marks the conclusion of the initial effort of the boy's group. It indicates that through its representative this descent group is temporarily at rest in relation to the girl's group. The drawing together of the two groups which has been achieved through the transactions to date is shown symbolically in that members of the girl's group proceed to address the *umkhongi* and his assistant both as *nkhwenyana* (brother-in-law). The term is meant not to apply to them directly, but as representatives of a group of people who will soon become relatives-in-law.

The remainder of the *umkhongi's* task is to persuade the parents of the girl to accept a definite wedding date, and to put the ceremony into motion. Little difficulty actually occurs, but the parents may make all kinds of formal obstacles, to which at this stage a largely ritual significance can be attached. They are showing that they value their daughter in her ancestral descent group and do not wish to lose her. The father may suddenly ask for his *umgundandevu* goat (lit. the beardshaver). The mother may demand the *ubikibiki* goat or money which she alleges that she was promised in the initial negotiations. At this stage, too, if not before, the father may emphasize the importance of the contract by demanding the physical transfer in advance of the first beast of the *lobolo*, the *eyokumemeza*, and perhaps of the second accompanying beast too. Sometimes these beasts are called for as early as the second *ukucela* visit, serving to guarantee that the boy really intends to marry the girl. Once transferred, the cattle remain in the prospective father-in-law's kraal, although he does not own them until after the marriage ceremony. He can use their produce and inspan them, but if they have issue before the marriage such increase belongs to whoever supplied the beasts, for they are still his. If, for any reason, the marriage does not take place, these cattle must be returned. The whole of the *izibizo* is similarly returnable to the father of the boy, or whoever provided the money.

Agreement as to the bridewealth, supported by delivery of one or more beasts as earnest,[212] finalizes the affinition agreement. Some of the intimacies associated with married life are then permitted. Metsha, for instance, could be abandoned for full intercourse;[213] the couple could start using the appropriate kinship terms;[214] the matrimonial abode might be prepared;[215] and the future husband could insist that his bride-to-be remain faithful to him.[216]

One of the most important issues arising out of breach of an affinition agreement is the fate of the often substantial pre-marriage gifts and payments.[217] The courts seem to have taken no particular line on this question. There is, of course, authority for the proposition that customary law has no action for breach of promise to marry,[218] in the sense that it does not allow damages for hurt

---

[212] Van Tromp 58–9; Ashton 64ff; Matthews op cit n133 20–1; Schapera 128.
[213] Bryant op cit n179 539.
[214] Schapera 132; Holleman 102.
[215] Roberts 29.
[216] Van Tromp 62; Schapera 130; Roberts 29; cf Poulter 78.
[217] In Natal the many cattle given during marriage negotiations provoked so much litigation that the Code limited the groom's obligations to providing ingquthu and bridewealth: *Mapumulo v Gumede* 1916 NHC 157.
[218] *Jimsoni v Lubaca* 1920 NHC 35; *Ndimande v Mkize* 1943 NAC (N&T) 87.

feelings.[219] But apart from this, claims for a refund of the expenses incurred in the engagement celebrations[220] and the trousseau[221] have also been refused.

At this point two divergent approaches take form. According to the one,[222] *any* cattle paid in anticipation of marriage are deemed to be a deposit,[223] with the result that ownership technically remains in the donor, entitling him to recover what he gave if the marriage does not materialize. (Any increase[224] or loss[225] also accrues to him.) Yet, by treating all payments prior to the marriage as sisa, two quite different things are confused: the earnest (often called the 'engagement' cattle)[226] and advance instalments of bridewealth. If the affinition agreement does not ripen into a marriage, the return of the *earnest* must naturally be determined on the basis of fault: if the man or his guardian breaches the agreement for no good reason, the earnest is forfeit; and conversely, if the woman or her guardian is in breach, it must be returned.[227] But under customary law all *bridewealth* must be returned regardless of fault.[228]

Secondly, in apparent disregard of the rules governing sisa contracts (and probably also customary law itself), the courts have shown a strong inclination to resolve all claims for refund of instalments of bridewealth on a rough-and-ready basis of equity, ie using fault as the main criterion. Hence there is a series of decisions from Transkei,[229] that are alleged to be based on customary law,[230] in which the courts held that if the prospective husband were to break off an engagement without good cause,[231] he would lose any bridewealth he had already paid.[232] In addition it was held that bridewealth had to be returned if the

---

[219] In view of the ethnographic evidence this would seem to be quite correct. See Gluckman *Ideas and Procedures in African Customary Law* 64; cf Schapera in Gluckman op cit 326.

[220] *Ndaba v Mbata* 1939 NAC (N&T) 32; *Mbuyisa v Ntombela* 1939 NAC (N&T) 93; *Cili v Nyatikazi* 1943 NAC (N&T) 14.

[221] *Dilikane v Mazaleni* 2 NAC 103 (1911).

[222] *Palane v Mabanga* 1934 NAC (N&T) 67 at 70; *Magwaza* 1937 NAC (N&T) 3; *Nhlapo v Konondo* 1937 NAC (N&T) 161; *Nene v Xakaza* 1938 NAC (N&T) 96; *Mlangeni v Dhlamini* 1948 NAC 10 (C).

[223] This idea may have originated in the Natal Code, where it was quite arbitrarily provided that such advance payments must be treated as if they were sisa cattle, which is a species of deposit: s 58 of the Natal and KwaZulu Codes. See further: *Msibi v Sibanyoni* 1940 NAC (N&T) 28; *Mtembu v Mngwaba* 1940 NAC (N&T) 67; *Mzimela v Mkwanazi* 1941 NAC (N&T) 12.

[224] *Dyomfana v Klassie* 2 NAC 95 (1910); *Matyesini v Dulo* 3 NAC 102 (1915); *Dlikilili v Salman* 1944 NAC (C&O) 19.

[225] Which in turn means that the woman's guardian is obliged to report any deaths in order to escape liability for replacement: *Tanyana v Tshwane* 3 NAC 101 (1915); *Zinti v Nozikotshi* 3 NAC 188 (1913); *Duma v Sidoyi* 4 NAC 56 (1919); *Ndipane v Luzipo* 1936 NAC (C&O) 34; *Nyamane v Busakwe* 1944 NAC (N&T) 78. Cf *Mcitakali v Nkosiyaboni* 1951 NAC 298 (S).

[226] See Mönnig 132, Van Tromp 42, and Poulter 78–9 on the giving of earnest. Roberts 28–30 speaks of all the gifts given as evidence of betrothal; these are returnable unless the man was at fault.

[227] Van Tromp 59–60; Poulter 79; Schapera 133.

[228] Van Tromp 59–60. And see *Nyamane v Busakwe* 1944 NAC (N&T) 78.

[229] Cf *Mlangeni v Dhlamini* 1948 NAC 10 (C).

[230] *Gqezi v Nzaye* 1 NAC 271 (1909); and see *Kesa v Ndaba* 1935 NAC (C&O) 64.

[231] The corollary is where the prospective bride or her guardian has broken off the engagement; in that case the groom can recover his bridewealth: *Ndlovu v Mradla* 4 NAC 112 (1918); *Qanqiso v Mnqwazi* 4 NAC 109 (1922); *Zombovu v Nowalaza* 5 NAC 54 (1927); *Memani v Makaba* 1950 NAC 178 (S); *Nthebe v Mteung* 1951 NAC 57 (C).

[232] *Nojiwa v Vuba* 1 NAC 57 (1903); *Yapi v Ngayi* 1 NAC 61 (1903); *Tole v Ndumiso* 1 NAC 141 (1907); *Lucani v Mbuzweni* 2 NAC 27 (1910); *Ngcobo v Msululu* 2 NAC 33 (1910); *Ntonga v Dulusela* 4 NAC 80 (1921); *Nampetshwa v Kambula* 1952 NAC 43 (S).

woman died before the marriage.[233]

The reason usually given by the groom-to-be for refusing to go ahead with the marriage is his fiancée's sexual misconduct.[234] When it came to *his* sexual misdemeanours, however, the courts found that they were bound to start introducing western moral standards. Whereas in customary law a man's philandering would not give a woman cause for complaint,[235] the courts now had to allow an action[236] because they could not expect the woman to marry a man she found morally abhorrent.[237] In only one case was any doubt expressed about the authenticity of these rules, and both for this reason and on policy grounds, the court held that bridewealth must always be refunded to the donor

> 'in matters relating to lobola, practices have sprung up which have their origin in greed and are far removed from the true concepts of the lobolo custom. . . . To allow a father of a girl who has been jilted by her lover to keep all the lobolo cattle which have been delivered to him not only would be unjust as it might amount to what in other words is very heavy damages—far heavier than damages paid by a seducer, but would also enrich the girl's father. . . .'[238]

If the courts are going to continue to allow this equitable remedy, then it is arguable that they have not taken it far enough. If the parties are to be penalized for their misconduct, why limit the action to recovery of instalments of bridewealth? On equitable principles there would be merit in extending the action to include compensation for (or return of) the gifts that mark the regular proposal form of marriage. These have become a costly incident of the negotiations, and there is no reason why the fickle suitor should be allowed to resile from his promises with impunity.[239]

The 'regular proposal' marriage presupposes an approach made by the groom's family and the agreement or at least compliance of all the parties involved. Peculiar circumstances may prompt resort to one of the so-called 'irregular' procedures which, despite their name, are hallowed by convention. A 'reverse proposal' marriage, where the girl's family takes the initiative, is perhaps one of the more unusual modes. It is used where the girl is of high rank, but for various reasons has attracted no suitors.[240]

More common are two modes in which either the girl or the man takes the initiative. The former is known amongst Zulu-speakers as baleka and the latter is more generally called twala.[241]

---

[233] *Tiyeka v Sikayi* 5 NAC 47 (1926); cf *Valashiya v Ntoa* 1932 NAC (C&O) 32.

[234] If he condones her transgressions he loses his claim: *Mlakalaka v Bese* 1936 NAC (C&O) 22.

[235] *Fetana v Sinukela* 1 NAC 22 (1897).

[236] *Hebe v Mba* (1897) 12 EDC 6.

[237] *Mehlomakulu v Jikejela* 1942 NAC (C&O) 110.

[238] *Nyamane v Busakwe* 1944 NAC (N&T) 78 at 79.

[239] See Holleman 139–40; Roberts 29–31 and Campbell op cit n30 216. Oddly enough, the courts do not seem to have experienced problems in determining when the engagement was breached or whether there was in fact a breach. In the absence of any clear indication of intent, however, difficulties might have been expected in view of the fact that the formation of marriage is potentially a long process: cf *Tole v Ndumiso* 1 NAC 141 (1907) and *Msibi v Sibanyoni* 1940 NAC (N&T) 28.

[240] Hoernlé in Schapera op cit n171 112.

[241] See further: Bryant op cit n179 538; Krige 128–31; Van Tromp 63–7; Holleman 121–3; Soga 271–2; Reuter op cit n97 142ff.

[58] READER *ZULU TRIBE IN TRANSITION* 185-7

The operative factor to set in motion this escape device [baleka] is urgency. It is resorted to by a girl under one or more of three sets of circumstances:

(a) Fundamentally, and most urgently, when she has already been fully *cela*'d: the cattle having been promised and perhaps some of them delivered, and the *izibizo* having been paid in full; and she meantime falls in love with another man.

(b) When she is in love with someone to whom she is not engaged, and another boy initiates *ukubaleka* negotiations.

(c) When, having failed in *ukubaleka* negotiations, she proceeds to another boy the same night in order to avoid the shame (q.v.).

If the matter is not urgent, as when both sets of parents are opposed to a match desired by the young couple themselves, there is no occasion for *ukubaleka*. The couple merely proceed to have a child, and then the marriage must take place. . . .

When she decides to *baleka*, the girl chooses her best friend to go with her, who in this function is known as the *umhlalisi* (one who sits down with her). Without wearing any distinctive garb which would betray their errand, the two girls steal off to the kraal of the intended husband, arriving after dark so that they will not be seen. . . . This concludes the initial effort of the girl and leaves the onus of response upon the boy's group. What they will do depends upon whether the girl is acceptable or not. . . .

On the day after the girls' arrival a council (*ibandla*) of adult males of the boy's descent group meets under the kraal head in order to set the marriage negotiations in motion. The kraal head informs the meeting that "there is a debt" (*nant'icala*) in the kraal. The girls remain out of sight in their hut. The *ibandla* proceeds to decide how many cattle are available, and they also settle upon an *umkhongi* and his assistant. . . . Arrangements for *izibizo* and *lobolo* otherwise proceed as for normal *ukucela*. Until these arrangements have been completed the girls remain at the kraal of the boy's father. When all is agreed they return home with the *umkhongi* on his final *lobolo* visit, generally with some of the cattle. As usual, the girl's father has been notified of this visit, and is present with all the members of his descent group who care to come, as well as any strangers who happen to have been attracted by the beer. The *umkhongi* receives his *imvuma* goat on this visit, and additional animals may be slaughtered for the assembled company.

Finally, the *umkhongi* arranges the wedding date and is rewarded in the same way as for *ukucela*. A marriage resulting from *ukubaleka* has the same social and legal standing as one following upon orthodox *ukucela*. . . .

[*Ukubaleka* is, however, on the decline.] The course of individualism among the people has recently gone so far . . . that parents and descent groups cannot direct marriage partnerships nearly as much as they formerly could. . . . The only real reason for *baleka* now is that a girl might change her mind after accepting a certain man and when the *ukucela* negotiations were well under way. Another reason for the decline in *baleka* is that whereas formerly if a girl *baleka*'d to a man he had to marry her, this is no longer the case. If such a girl is not wanted, either by the boy himself or by his people, there are two institutionalized ways of indicating the fact. If the boy wants the girl but his parents do not, he must make all the marriage arrangements himself, unless his relatives can be induced to persuade the parents to agree or to give help themselves.

Twala is a form of abduction in which the future husband and his friends carry off the girl with or without the connivance of her own father.[242]

[59] WHITFIELD *SOUTH AFRICAN NATIVE LAW* 115-16

The abduction is carried out by the bridegroom elect with the assistance of a few of his male friends; but it may be performed by his friends without his co-operation. She is seized

---

[242] See further: Van Tromp 63ff; Ashton 65; Simons *African Women* 117-19; Hunter 187-8 and 531-2; Junod 119-20.

when walking abroad, hustled along and taken to the groom's kraal, if his father had previously agreed to the marriage, and in the absence of such consent she is temporarily hidden at the kraal of a relative or friend, whereupon the abduction is reported to the groom's father or guardian. If he approves of the action of his son or ward he orders that the girl be brought to his kraal; but, on the other hand, if he opposes the marriage, he returns the girl to her father or guardian with a beast, which is regarded as a fine. If he approves of the union he immediately advises the girl's people of her presence at [his] kraal, and formally asks for her in marriage. Her people fetch her back to their own kraal, and if the proposal of marriage is acceptable, the groom's people are called upon to pay *lobolo*. Steps are then taken to deliver it, usually in instalments, and until the bride's father intimates that a sufficient number has been paid on account, he continues to inform the payers that "he sees nothing". And so they go on bringing in the instalments until the father signifies that a sufficient number of cattle has been delivered to justify the marriage proceeding. When the girl is returned to her people after her abduction, she is often accompanied by a fine for the abduction.

This method of securing a marriage is used for many reasons: to force the girl's father to give his assent;[243] to avoid the expense of a wedding;[244] to hasten matters where the girl is pregnant; and to persuade or coerce her to marry.[245] If the girl's guardian is amenable, the usual marriage negotiations may proceed. If he rejects the proposal, the girl's suitor may have to pay a fine[246] independently of any liability he may have incurred to pay damages for seduction.[247]

Whatever the personal reasons for this style of marriage, twala has become increasingly popular in recent years.[248]

[60] MANONA in MAYER *BLACK VILLAGERS IN AN INDUSTRIAL SOCIETY* 189–93

Ukuthwala is the most common form of marriage among the immigrants.[1] Yet in spite of its widespread occurrence, this type of marriage has not been accepted as normal. The practice is still termed *ukuthwala*, which literally means "to carry". One who marries in this manner, in addition to the normal *lobola*, is expected to give an extra beast known as *inkomo yokuthwala*. . . .

The marriages by *ukuthwala* which have been increasing from the 1920s have increased even further during the past few decades. Monica Wilson[2] noted that *ukuthwala* marriages increased from 14,6 per cent of all marriages in the 1920s to 18,3 per cent in the 1930s and reached 30,3 per cent in the 1940s. . . . [I]t can be seen that these marriages have increased further and constitute 55,9 per cent of all marriages since 1950. . . .

There are many reasons for the increase in the *ukuthwala* type of marriage in the rural areas. Economic changes make it difficult for most men to fulfil their customary obligations regarding *lobola*. In addition, the preponderance of this informal type of marriage reflects the extent to which traditional sanctions have declined today. In particular, wage earning, which accords economic independence to the young men and women, breaks down traditional relationships. Many parents today have to adjust themselves to a situation in which they have to depend on their adult children for support,

---

[243] *Dhlamini & another v Mkize* 1929 NAC (N&T) 100.
[244] Van Tromp 67–8; Soga 272.
[245] *Shabangu v Nkosi* 1941 NAC (N&T) 118.
[246] Bopha: Xhosa for 'bind or tie'. See: Hunter 188; Van Tromp 66ff; and Simons *African Women* 118.
[247] *Sikemele & another v Bambizulu* 4 NAC 1 (1920); *Nyila v Tsipa* 4 NAC 2 (1922). There is considerable judicial confusion concerning the question whether this fine merges with bridewealth if and when a marriage is concluded: see Simons *African Women* 118 and Van Tromp 66.
[248] Whooley in Verryn op cit n81 295ff.

and in which the young men can provide *lobola* themselves out of their own earnings. Because of the consequent decline in their authority, most parents are no longer in a position to force their children to marry in a manner which they regard as acceptable. Marriage has become more of an individual affair in the sense that parents now have very little influence in the marriages of their children.

The young people themselves play the leading part at every stage in the *ukuthwala* as practised today in Burnshill; it is their decisions which make the marriage come into being. The man and the girl arrange it together, although this is not yet the norm among the immigrants. The present day *ukuthwala* is a form of elopement, and cases of *ukuthwala* by abduction are relatively few. In the few cases of what can still be termed abduction, force is seldom used. Most men marry by *ukuthwala* women with whom they are in love and arranged marriages are extremely rare. The girl's parents are usually notified after the *ukuthwala* when some boys are sent with the message. In most cases the formal negotiations take place only some time after the *ukuthwala*, mainly because many men leave their homes soon after marrying. After the *ukuthwala* the girl remains indoors until the following day when new clothing is bought for her. The attire for the new wife is a long German print dress, a black doek (head-scarf), as well as a neck-scarf, *uxakatho*. Sometimes the husband buys the clothing himself and it is his responsibility to provide the money for it.

In another sense, the increase in the incidence of *ukuthwala* is a direct result of the absence of a large proportion of adult men from their homes for most of the year. As we have already noted, most men are at home only for a month each year. It is during these brief visits home that most of the *ukuthwala* marriages take place. Couples elope and begin to live together because the recognized process of marrying, which entails negotiations, is time-consuming. Eloping is much quicker and more convenient for a migrant who has to return to work soon. As a result, the *ukuthwala* today is an informal form of marriage. It is rarely preceded by the recognized negotiations between the two families (*ukucela*) or by the payment of *lobola*. It is this fact which, in the main, distinguishes the *ukuthwala* from the traditional or customary marriages which were normally preceded by several months of negotiations between the two families. In the present-day cases of *ukuthwala* the negotiations are almost invariably made and *lobola* given only after the marriage. This means that most of these cases of *ukuthwala* are *ukuthwala nje*, i.e. just to elope or abduct, as distinct from *ukuthwala ngokucela*, i.e. to elope or abduct after obtaining the consent of the girl's relatives. In many of these marriages the drinking of the milk ritual is omitted, which in the past was the manner in which an *ukuthwala* marriage was regularized.

On account of these loose forms of marriage, it is now much more difficult to determine the marital status of men and women in the community. In a marriage which follows the accepted pattern, the passage of cattle between the two families is a public act which denotes the marriage. At present it is the dressing of the wife by her mother-in-law (*ukunxityiswa*) which completes the *ukuthwala*. Thereafter the woman assumes her new status as the wife of the *umzi*.

Several marriages of this *ukuthwala* type had been in existence for some years without any *lobola* being given. . . .

There are several other motivations for marrying by *ukuthwala*. These unions, although they come into being by the agreement of the couple, are often "forced marriages" in that they often follow the pregnancy of the woman. A young man would make a girl pregnant before he leaves for work and, on one of his subsequent visits home he might decide to marry her by *ukuhlalisana* to prevent her parents from demanding damages from him. In other instances these unions are treated so lightly that they approach the *ukuhlalisana* (staying together) relationships which are common in town. The union simply becomes a convenient arrangement for the man while he is at home.

Notes

1. People who had moved into the area since 1945, mainly from white-owned farms.
2. *Keiskammahoek Rural Survey* v3 85.

In view of their attitude towards individual liberty and spousal consent, it was to be expected that the courts would be somewhat suspicious of this form of marriage. Technically in common law, twala could amount to abduction or kidnapping,[249] although it might be difficult to discern whether a crime had actually been committed because the romantic charade demands that the girl put up a show of resistance.[250] None the less, in an early decision it was held that twala was no defence to a charge of assault,[251] and later the court refused to 'countenance its use as a cloak for forcing unwelcome attentions on a patently unwilling girl'.[252]

(2) Transfer of the bride and the wedding ceremony

According to all the local kinship systems marriage is patri- or virilocal: in other words, the bride should go to live with her husband, either at his own or his father's homestead.[253] (And with Nguni peoples this was one of the principal determinants of the marriage.) The transfer of the bride is always an affair of some moment, marked by various colourful rituals that enrich and intensify the event,[254] serving simultaneously to ward off evil, to summon the protection of the ancestral spirits, and to express the social solidarity of the two families.

[61] KRIGE in KRIGE & COMAROFF *ESSAYS ON AFRICAN MARRIAGE IN SOUTHERN AFRICA* 185

Bride-removal, accompanied by various rituals, often of a religious nature, marks the transfer of rights over the woman. The husband now becomes responsible for her maintenance (and she for his). He now has rights to her labour and exclusive sexual access, with the right to sue for adultery. Above all, bride-removal marks the establishment in the husband's family of a new house, the smallest and most important social unit, a growing point in the social structure. For a man it opens the door to subsequent economic and political position and influence; for a woman bride-removal means a transition to a new group and the new "house" established provides her with a developing domain in which she gradually assumes responsibility and control. . . . Bride-removal has meaning also for the families of both husband and wife, inaugurating their full association as affines, with mutual responsibilities in the marriage; also for the ancestors to whom the change must be reported and who become responsible now for the protection, fertility and general well-being of the couple.

The rituals accompanying bride-removal take various forms, associated with such aspects as reporting the bride-removal to the lineage (Nguni) and to the ancestors and soliciting their protection and blessings; symbolically incorporating the bride into the group of her husband; uniting the two families in commensality for the first time, etc. There is no necessary order in which these rituals must be carried out, but certain of them take place in association with each other.

There is a marked difference in the degree of elaboration of marriage procedures and rituals, associated with the degree of re-arrangement in the social and religious structure necessitated by the marriage. Where there are strong corporate exogamous localized

---

[249] Labuschagne (1988) 13 *TRW* 33ff.
[250] Hunter 187–8; Holleman 110; Van Tromp 70–1.
[251] *R v Swaartbooi & others* (1916) EDL 170; cf Van Tromp 63ff.
[252] *Mkupeni v Nomungunya* 1936 NAC (C&O) 77. See s 101 of the Natal and KwaZulu Codes.
[253] Preston-Whyte in Hammond-Tooke *Bantu-speaking Peoples* 179.
[254] Ritual is an institutionalized procedure with powerful symbolic and emotional significance. A ritual act resonates with a people's entire belief and social system. See Beattie *Other Cultures* 202ff.

lineages, highly aware of their distinctiveness, the changes are considerable and the ceremonies marking them are carried out with a maximum of publicity, as among the Nguni. Where, as among the Venda and Lovedu, there is no corporate lineage, and bride and groom may be "born for" each other, the two families may have been affinally linked for generations and there are no antagonisms to be overcome; there is here no feasting, no necessary ritual offering and the bride arrives quietly in her new home accompanied by a few companions. Among the Sotho-Tswana, ritual slaughterings associated with bride-removal have died out in many groups.

Changes in social conditions have, in the course of time, become reflected in the rituals, eg the S. Sotho *tlhabiso*, a slaughtering and feast, probably originally associated with bride-removal, when the bride was commended to the care of her ancestors, now confirms and publicizes completion of the transfer of 10 head of cattle or its equivalent, the minimum laid down by Sotho legislation to establish the husband's claims to his children. . . .

[62] NGUBANE in KRIGE & COMAROFF *ESSAYS ON AFRICAN MARRIAGE IN SOUTHERN AFRICA* 84

The word "marriage" is not translatable into Zulu because its indigenous meaning is not that of a contractual union between the spouses as in the case of the English term. A Zulu woman "goes on a long journey" (enda), this action being known as *umendo*. A man, on the other hand, takes or receives a wife into his patrilineal home (thatha) where she is expected to be productive and continue the descent line of her husband's patrilineage. . . . Most rituals during the wedding ceremonies are connected with the bride and her mother-in-law, while the bridegroom plays a rather insignificant part. This is understandable if we consider the fact that it is she who is being transformed from maidenhood to motherhood, and it is she who is being integrated into a different descent group. Indeed, it is she who has "a long way to go" to achieve complete integration into the new group and the house (uterine unit) of her husband's mother, from whom she is going to take over eventually.

The rituals marking the wedding[255] fulfil at least three legal functions. In the first place, they provide evidence of the event; in preliterate societies ritual is a vital memoria technica. In the second place, the ceremony performs the cautionary function of checking inconsiderate or precipitate action. Finally, ritual separates the significant from the mundane;[256] it supplies meaning to otherwise ambiguous acts. Mere cohabitation, for example, is not a marriage (and a 'quiet' wedding would look suspicious),[257] but if cohabitation is accompanied by the appropriate ritual, it is transformed into marriage. By implication customary law need not concern itself with intention (or volition) because it can be assumed that the parties understood the ritual activity in which they participated. In contrast, the common law has shed most of its ritual requirements, although this has meant sacrificing the advantage of absolute certainty that ritual gives juristic acts. (This function has now been taken over by a literate and technically advanced

---

[255] The following descriptions of marriage ceremonies may be consulted: Van Tromp 54–8; Kohler op cit n192 32ff, Krige 134–50; Bryant op cit n179 543–57; Schapera 134–8; Hunter 193–202; Mönnig 135–7; Marwick 101–23; Junod 107–20; Clerc op cit n127 85–7; Hammond-Tooke 105–12; Ashton 66–71; Krige & Krige 154–6. See Kuper *Wives for Cattle* 134–7 for a comparison of Nguni and Sotho-Tswana ceremonies.

[256] Fuller (1941) 41 *Columbia LR* 800–3; Tiersma (1988) 9 *J Legal History* 15–17.

[257] Pauw 100–1.

bureaucracy.) Instead, the common law seeks to give effect to the *intention* of the parties in whatever form this may have been expressed.[258]

The sharp distinction between law and custom that is enjoined by positivism would in the normal course oblige common-law courts to separate the legal (and essential) from the customary (and therefore optional) in marriage ceremonies—something that is extremely difficult to do. When a particular ritual is deeply rooted in tradition, it may become the focus of a wedding, although it has a purely cultural significance. Or a profound religious meaning might be interpreted as legal, as opposed to customary, simply because the participants regarded it as important.[259]

In contrast, customary law was always flexible and pragmatic. Strict adherence to ritual formulae was never absolutely essential in close-knit, rural communities, where certainty was neither a necessity nor a value. So, for instance, the ceremony to celebrate a man's second marriage would normally be simplified;[260] similarly, the wedding might be abbreviated by reason of poverty[261] or the need to expedite matters.[262] Aside from this, indigenous rituals might be supplanted by exotic ones: a wedding ring may now be used in place of the traditional gall bladder of a slaughtered beast[263] and for many a church ceremony has become indispensable.[264]

Insistence on the proper performance of a set wedding ceremony could cure the ambiguity of many formless relationships, but it seems that the use of rituals is waning.[265] In any event the courts have refused to become engaged in the task of deciding what is legal and necessary in wedding rituals. They straight-forwardly rejected *all* the rituals associated with the transfer of the bride, claiming that these were mere customs and in consequence not essential for the validity of the marriage.[266] They decided instead that the *reason* for the ceremony, the handing over of the woman, was the vital ingredient.[267]

By avoiding one problem the courts created for themselves another. How should cohabitation be interpreted when the bride was not in fact transferred to her husband's homestead? There may be many good reasons for not complying with the norm of virilocality. For instance, in cases of twala, the woman is already at her husband's homestead when the bridewealth negotiations start.

---

[258] Tiersma op cit n256 17.

[259] See, eg, Poulter 118–22 regarding the tlhabiso, the slaughtering of an ox, and Murray op cit n21 121–2. Cf *Lebenya v Mosola* 1947 NAC (C&O) 58. Similarly, see Van Tromp 77–9 and Manona in Mayer op cit n26 189 regarding the Southern Nguni ukutyis' amasi (drinking sour milk).

[260] Either because he was a widower or because he was taking a polygynous wife: Schapera *Married Life* 71.

[261] Schapera *Married Life* 72; Van Tromp 57–8.

[262] Because of pregnancy or an elopement: Marwick 121.

[263] Ashton 68.

[264] Ashton 70–1; Schapera 136 and *Married Life* 65ff; Pauw 94. See further: Mair in Phillips 39 and Hunter 220.

[265] See Simons op cit n142 323–5.

[266] *Mpakanyiswa v Ntshangase* 1 NAC 17 (1897); *Faneyana v Mbumane* 1918 NHC 103; *Ntenze v Ntsolo* 1930 NAC (C&O) 30; *Sila & another v Masuku* 1937 NAC (N&T) 121; *Sibiya v Mtembu* 1946 NAC (N&T) 90. In contrast it can be inferred from several references to 'celebration' that rituals are a necessary element under the Natal and KwaZulu Codes. See ss 38(1)(c), 40(3), 42, 43 and 45(1).

[267] Bekker 108.

And, with the Tswana, the husband would be expected to cohabit with his future spouse at her parents' abode for some time before she settled down with him.[268] Bridewealth would be paid and the woman would move to his homestead only after she had given birth to a child.[269] This stage of the spouses' relationship might be described as an affinition agreement, but it would be an unduly technical designation; rather this is part of the process of marriage. To overcome such difficulties in particular cases the courts have used the fiction of a 'constructive' delivery.[270]

This fiction is strained to breaking point today when the exigencies of employment or the shortage of housing prevents the bride from going to live with her husband. After an initial hesitation, during which they refused to countenance any deviation from customary law unless a new rule to the contrary could be proved,[271] the courts relented, and subsequently they have allowed many departures.[272] Yet, in the conditions in which many people find themselves, a rule insisting on transfer of the bride is simply otiose. Apart from the husband's inability to accommodate her in the cramped urban townships, the growing incidence of female-headed households suggests that women are providing the stable residence factor in domestic relationships, not men.

In fact, it seems that the courts have been paying mere lip service to the requirement of bridal transfer. Their main concern has always been with the parties' intention, which can be inferred from cohabitation. This then transfers the gravamen of the inquiry to the attitude of the women's guardian. If he did not object to his ward's relationship (which can be deduced from his acceptance of bridewealth or non-suit for seduction damages), a marriage will be presumed, irrespective of where the matrimonial home happened to be or how the 'spouses' came to be living there.[273]

V BRIDEWEALTH

(1) Meaning and function

Frequent reference has already been made in this book to 'bridewealth', a word that has been chosen to translate numerous vernacular terms, such as lobolo, bogadi, bohali, munywalo, ikhazi, rovoro.[274] Each of these words refers to the transfer of property, usually livestock, by the husband (or his guardian) to the wife's family as part of the process of constituting a marriage.[275] In many parts of Africa, notably the francophone territories (and formerly Transkei),[276] the

---

[268] Go ralala: Matthews op cit n133 21–3.

[269] Schapera 134ff.

[270] *Dlomo v Mahodi* 1946 NAC (C&O) 61; *Ngcongolo v Parkies* 1953 NAC 103 (S).

[271] *Mbalela v Thinane* 1950 NAC 7 (C). In addition see *Ngcangayi v Jwili* 1944 NAC (C&O) 15.

[272] *Mothombeni v Matlou* 1945 NAC (N&T) 123; *Ntabenkomo v Jente & another* 1946 NAC (C&O) 59; *Sefolokele v Thekiso* 1951 NAC 25 (C).

[273] See, eg, *Jama v Sikosana* 1972 BAC 21 (S).

[274] Jeffreys (1951) 10 *Africa* 145–6; Phillips xii n3; Phillips & Morris op cit n143 4 n3.

[275] Cf bridewealth constituted by service of the groom: Holleman 124–8; Radcliffe-Brown & Forde 48.

[276] Koyana *Customary Law in a Changing Society* 3.

term 'dowry' is used.[277] Both bridewealth and dowry involve the transfer of property at marriage, and it has been conjectured that the former might even have evolved into the latter.[278] But the two institutions bear little resemblance to one another. Dowry is a payment by the wife's family to the groom; this property constitutes the nucleus of a conjugal estate,[279] normally providing some form of security for the wife against dissolution of the marriage.[280]

The long-standing debate about the correct English word, like all disputes regarding accurate terminology, bore evidence of a more profound disagreement about meaning and function. The early view, one usually espoused by Christian missionaries, was that bridewealth represented the purchase price for a wife, and as such should best be rendered by the term 'brideprice'.[281] Because of this construction, some governments prohibited the giving of bridewealth,[282] and the courts refused to enforce agreements connected with it.[283] This understanding has been exposed as a complete fallacy: even a superficial knowledge of customary marriage would show that the wife is neither a slave nor a chattel.[284] But the misconception was so strong that even certain chiefs[285] were persuaded to ban the practice.[286]

From the 1920s onwards, structural-functionalism and the more tolerant sentiments of cultural relativism did much to rehabilitate bridewealth in public opinion.[287] In the first place, anthropologists showed that bridewealth functioned as a benign medium of exchange, enabling the husband's family to obtain the reproductive potential of a woman,[288] and the wife's family to replace the daughter they had lost.

---

[277] Dlamini 167.

[278] Goody op cit n24 240–61.

[279] Tambiah in Goody *Bridewealth and Dowry* 61ff.

[280] Dower, ie a portion of a deceased husband's estate which the law assigns to his widow for her life, is another way of providing for the wife: Goody op cit n24 242–3 and *Production and Reproduction* 105–6. Dowry is most common in southern Europe and the Orient, but this does not mean that it is confined to these areas: Radcliffe-Brown & Forde 46; Goody op cit n279 21ff. Amongst the Kgatla, eg, daughters are usually given arable fields which provide the nucleus of a marital estate: Schapera 203; Comaroff *The Meaning of Marriage Payments* 13. And a recent development throughout southern Africa is the substantial marriage payments made by the wife's family, by way of contributions to the new household and to the nuptial ceremonies: Vilakazi op cit n30 63ff; Simons *African Women* 94; Murray (1976) 35 *African Studies* 117. Because of the assumption that dowry does not exist in Africa, no one has paid any attention to this 'reverse bridewealth', and there are no rules governing legal liability in respect of it.

[281] See: Dlamini 90–3; MacLean 68 (Warner's notes); Bryant op cit n179 592; and generally Chigwedere *Lobola—the Pros and Cons*.

[282] For example, the Transvaal: s 24 of Law 3 of 1876.

[283] *Kaba v Ntela* 1910 TPD 964 at 967.

[284] Dlamini 169. See further: Lye & Murray op cit n82 112ff; Hunter 192; Brookes *The History of Native Policy in South Africa* 233 and 235–9; Simons *African Women* 88.

[285] Of the Kgatla and Ngwato: Schapera 145–7.

[286] See, too, Ashton 71 and Reuter op cit n97 237ff who (at 239) concludes that bridewealth should be changed into dowry.

[287] An account of the functions of bridewealth is given by: Nsereko (1975) 23 *Am J Comp L* 693ff and Dlamini 1984 *De Jure* 150–5.

[288] Holleman 148–9; Evans-Pritchard (1947) 6 *Afr Studies* 187.

[63] PRESTON-WHYTE in HAMMOND-TOOKE *THE BANTU-SPEAKING PEOPLES OF SOUTHERN AFRICA* 187–8

The rights over a woman which are transferred to her husband and his agnatic group include rights in her both as a wife (rights *in uxorem*) and as a mother (rights *in genetricem*). Into the first category fall rights of sexual access and to her labour, both domestic and in the fields. Her husband can claim reparation for adultery or any other injury which impairs the fulfilment of these duties. Rights *in uxorem* are, of course, matched by the duties on the part of the groom and his agnates to provide the woman with a "house"—living quarters, fields and lifelong security. The second set of rights transferred on marriage relates to the procreative powers of the woman. Rights *in genetricem* acquire for the husband and his lineage legal control over all children born to a woman unless and until the marriage is dissolved by divorce, which may entail the return of bridewealth. The importance of this aspect of marriage is expressed in the saying found in many of these societies: "Cattle beget children". So complete is the transfer of the childbearing capacities of the woman to her husband and his lineage that, whoever actually fathers her children (their *genitor*), it is the woman's husband who is regarded as their *pater* (social father). It is the facts of the bridewealth transfer that fix a child's social position in society. An impotent man may ask one of his kinsmen to have intercourse with his wife and so give him children and, most important, an heir. Similarly, children of an adulterous union entered into by a married woman belong to the family of her husband. The *genitor* may have to pay a fine for adultery but he cannot, among most Southern Bantu, claim guardianship over his children. In the prolonged absence of a husband, possibly as a migrant labourer, the birth of adulterine children may be welcomed by the husband and lineage as fulfilling one of the major aims of marriage.

Bridewealth interpreted in this way could plausibly be described as 'child price', a term endorsed by the customary-law principle that parental rights are determined by payment of bridewealth.[289] This is captured in maxims such as 'cattle beget children' and 'the children are where the cattle are not'.[290] So even children who are conceived in adulterous liaisons belong to their legal father. Yet the convergence between rights to children and payment of bridewealth is not always exact: the husband's family usually retains rights to the children, even on default of full payment;[291] and, where the woman is barren, her husband may not necessarily reclaim his bridewealth.[292]

Nineteenth-century sceptics were further mollified by two theories showing that bridewealth functioned both to stabilize marriage and, far from degrading women, to protect them. As early as 1883, the Cape Commission defined bridewealth as:

> 'a contract between the father and the intending husband of his daughter, by which the father promises his consent to the marriage of his daughter, and to protect her, in case of necessity, either during or after such marriage.'[293]

The rules regarding return of bridewealth on dissolution of the marriage supported this view: the husband who had neglected or mistreated his wife was penalized. In Soga's emotive words:

---

[289] See too: Mönnig 136–7; Reuter op cit n97 218–22; Mathewson (1959) 10 *J Racial Affairs* 72; Jeffreys op cit n274 145ff.

[290] Radcliffe-Brown and Gluckman in Radcliffe-Brown & Forde 80 and 200 respectively; and see Brandel (1958) 17 *Afr Studies* 34ff.

[291] See below, [95].

[292] See below, 270–1; Dlamini 187.

[293] *Report* para 70.

'The custom, so much the subject of abuse by the well-meaning but uninformed, is, as applied by many tribes, the Bantu woman's charter of liberty.'[294]

Closely associated with this idea was the notion that women actually *needed* bridewealth because it was a public measure of their worth.[295] This view, still current, seemed to be borne out by the inflated sums demanded by guardians, ostensibly to recover the costs of their daughters' upbringing and to reflect the status and virtue of their wards. But it is obviously misleading to say that bridewealth gives women financial or social security. It accrues to a wife's guardian, to be used at his discretion; unlike dowry, the woman has no legal right to it.[296]

Anthropologists also contended that bridewealth discouraged divorce.[297] By comparing a limited range of ethnographic data, Gluckman said that where large payments of bridewealth were the norm (which happened to be a feature of patrilineal societies) the divorce rate was low; conversely, where the amount of bridewealth was relatively insignificant (as happened to be the case in matrilineal societies), the divorce rate was much higher.[298] This theory implied that bridewealth functioned as a mechanism to check marital delinquency. Subsequently, the hypothesis had to be revised in light of further research indicating that high marriage payments depended on the stability of marriage, rather than the other way round.[299] And it was often argued that the payment of large amounts of bridewealth (which could be attributed to the introduction of cash as a medium of exchange) coincided with a high rate of marriage instability.[300]

[64] DLAMINI *A JURIDICAL ANALYSIS AND CRITICAL EVALUATION OF ILOBOLO IN A CHANGING ZULU SOCIETY* 171

Perhaps the one theory which has enjoyed a wide following, in particular among blacks, is that *ilobolo* is a stabilizing factor and a guarantee of good treatment by the husband, and a guarantee of good conduct on the part of the wife, because should he ill-treat his wife, he will forfeit his cattle if the marriage is dissolved, and thus lose both wife and cattle, or alternatively, should the wife misbehave the father would have to return *ilobolo* if the marriage is dissolved through her fault. . . .

This theory ignores the fact that *ilobolo* in early Zulu society was in many cases not delivered by the husband but by the father of the bridegroom, especially for the first wife. This would mean that in the past there should have been a regular breakdown of marriages of the first wives, because in any case the husbands would not care for them which is not true. It is doubtful whether in all cases of unhappy marriages the thought of the father's impending forfeiture of cattle would be sufficient deterrent for the woman. Conversely, there are instances where a woman tolerated a marriage where the husband grossly ill-treated her. If she would only be deterred from deserting him because she was afraid that her father would lose *ilobolo*, then there would be no reason why she would stay because in any case the principle is that should the marriage be dissolved through the husband's misconduct, he forfeits *ilobolo*. . . .

---

[294] Pages 274–5.
[295] See: Dlamini op cit n287 151–2; Hunter 190 and Chinyenze (1983–4) 1/2 *Zimb LR* 241.
[296] See Junod 280.
[297] Evans-Pritchard op cit n288 182ff.
[298] Gluckman in Radcliffe-Brown & Forde 182ff. See further Goody *Kinship* 242.
[299] Gluckman op cit n219 62–3.
[300] Simons *African Women* 95.

[This] theory ... seems to rest on the wrong premise that once *ilobolo* has been delivered, stability is ensured. This is not borne out by the facts. Moreover, this theory places emphasis on economic motives .... Practised ... by people in a society not actuated by economic gain, *ilobolo* cannot easily be said to have its basis in acquisition or loss of property.[1]

Note
  1. Cf Hunter 212.

Gluckman's hypothesis, linking bridewealth, patrilineality and divorce, provoked further speculation on the general relationship between bridewealth and social structure. On the one hand, a correlation was discovered between dowry and cognatic kinship systems, and bridewealth and unilineal kinship systems.[301] On the other hand, a connection was revealed between the amount (and nature) of bridewealth and agricultural or pastoral economies.[302]

Even more complex equations of social causation were involved in Marxist anthropology. Bridewealth was seen as a mechanism for the reproduction of structures of inequality, the dominance of elders over juniors and women. In preindustrial African societies the position of the elders could not be maintained by sheer physical force, nor did it depend on their control over the production process (access to technology, knowledge and the means of production were relatively free to all members of these societies). Instead, it was argued that dominance was facilitated by marital exchanges: juniors could acquire wives only if they were given the means of paying the necessary bridewealth, and it was only through marriage that they could escape the strictures of their status to become, in their turn, elders. Thus:

'Of the goods produced by the community and handed over to the seniors as prestation some will not be redistributed but [will be] kept over at the level of the seniors to sanction access to wives. Possession of these goods will testify to the seniors' status: these objects become the attributes of "social age".'[303]

There is a contradiction implicit in this account. Each payment of bridewealth puts the elders in position where they must sacrifice their authority by allowing subordinate juniors to marry; but if they did not submit, their families would die out or disperse.[304] An argument allowing the reduction of the entire system of bridewealth to the subjective assessment and/or reasonableness of the elders has been described as naive.[305] A better explanation is that the elders are in no

---

[301] Goody op cit n279 17ff and 26. He contends (28–30) that dowry is a feature of stratified societies and hypergamy, whereas bridewealth is a feature of relatively egalitarian societies. Plausible as these theories may be, they have not attracted much of a following, mainly because they were based on overgeneralizations, both of the ethnographic data (Comaroff op cit n280 7–10) and of the political economies of Africa (Kuper op cit n255 166).

[302] Although Kuper concedes that there is no apparent correlation between the size of cattle holdings in a particular society and the quantity of bridewealth paid (Turton in Comaroff op cit n280 67ff), he maintains that there is a connection between agriculture and high bridewealth, as opposed to pastoralism and low bridewealth: Kuper op cit n255 158. In each case the bridewealth goods are valuable commodities in terms of the overall economy.

[303] Meillassoux (1960) 4 *Cahiers d'Études Africaines* 38ff (reproduced in Seddon *Relations of Production* 135–42). See further Terray *Marxism and 'Primitive' Societies* 163ff.

[304] Meillassoux *Anthropologie Économique des Gouro* 223.

[305] Hindess & Hirst *Pre-capitalist Modes of Production* 78.

position to deny marriage or to withhold bridewealth because it is by means of these transactions that their position of dominance is both constituted and confirmed.[306]

Opposed to this economistic approach is another view stressing the ritual/legal significance of bridewealth.[307] Adherents point to societies where bridewealth is withdrawn from the general economy into a closed system of marriage transactions,[308] or where the amount paid is determined solely by the generosity of the donor. With the Tswana, for instance, the husband gives only what he can afford; it would be regarded as bad form to haggle about the amount during the marriage negotiations.[309]

[65] DLAMINI *A JURIDICAL ANALYSIS AND CRITICAL EVALUATION OF ILOBOLO IN A CHANGING ZULU SOCIETY* 191

The original purpose of *ilobolo* among the Zulus ... was in essence not an economic consideration, but a social and spiritual symbol of a bond between the two families. Cattle which were the main means of *ilobolo* were very closely linked with the ancestral spirits and the clan. Besides, *ilobolo* cattle could be used as a means of communicating with the spirits of the ancestors. The treading of the *lobolo* cattle on the premises would be tangible proof to the ancestors that the woman was about to marry. Upon their arrival the father of the woman or the eldest male in the homestead would then say "nina basekuthini nazo-khe izinkomo zomtwana" meaning "there are the cattle of the child, you of so and so". . . . [T]he *lobolo* cattle are a means of securing the father's consent to the marriage and also of bringing about the marriage relationship. The relationship is created by the marriage and the *lobolo* is the only means of creating the marriage. Marriage negotiations would therefore never be commenced without the offer to deliver *ilobolo*. It is in this sense that it was inconceivable for the Zulus that a marriage could take place without *ilobolo*. Even a man who could not afford to offer *ilobolo* had at least to count stones. On failure to get any help from the relatives he would ask his father-in-law to consent to the marriage on the understanding that his eldest daughter would be the source of the *lobolo* for the mother. But even then, at least one beast *eyamadlozi* had to be given. Without *ilobolo* there would be no marriage, even if the parties would stay together, and the children born of such union would be illegitimate. *Ilobolo*, therefore, distinguished a marriage from an illicit union. . . .

In addition *ilobolo* can be regarded as counter-performance by the bridegroom in return for the transfer of the right of guardianship by the father over the woman and his children to him. The right transferred includes her services, sexual privileges and bearing of legitimate issue. It also serves in concrete form to indicate that a marriage is intended. Thus it is obvious that the purpose and function of *ilobolo* is cumulative.

It is indisputable that marriage, children and bridewealth are closely intertwined.[310] Bridewealth is the idiom by which many personal relationships are expressed. It serves to

'transform mating, which in itself may have no intrinsic social value, into a socially meaningful process, and thereby locate it in a universe of relations'.[311]

---

[306] Comaroff op cit n280 25.

[307] Krige op cit n137 403; Van Tromp 49.

[308] See the clear separation noted by Sansom in Kapferer *Transaction and Meaning* 143ff.

[309] Dlamini 177; Matthews op cit 133 13; Schapera 138 and Swanepoel *Die Bogadi Gebruik* 32–4.

[310] See: Marwick 124 and Dlamini op cit n287 149–50.

[311] Comaroff op cit n280 37.

(2) The modern context

The durability of the institution of bridewealth is remarkable. It has survived changes in composition, amount, and mode of payment; it has survived also the onslaught of missionaries, colonial governments and courts. But in order to survive it has had to adapt,[312] and not surprisingly its current form and function bear little relation to those of bridewealth in the past.[313]

With the advent of capitalism in Africa, cattle and other property that had formerly been reserved for marriage transactions, acquired a new value, measurable against the trade goods that were being imported. Simultaneously, exotic imports, because of their rarity and cost, were without difficulty assimilated to the category of elite marriage goods. Cash soon became the predominant medium of exchange and labour acquired a monetary value. Once bridewealth started to lose its special symbolic qualities,[314] there was nothing to stop it functioning as the purchase price for a woman.[315] Yet, at least in the early days of colonialism, the vulgarization of marriage was resisted, and seniors retained their prerogatives. Various linguistic devices, for instance, could be employed to keep the commercial and marital uses of cattle strictly separate.[316] And, if juniors could afford to pay for their own bridewealth by engaging in wage labour, the seniors could set the price even higher to keep control of marriage beyond their reach.[317]

Inexorably, however, marriage was commercialized. Paradoxically this was the very idea that anthropologists had been at pains to quash; but nowadays there seems to be justification for saying that bridewealth contributes to the subordination of women.[318] The general economic milieu is responsible at least in so far as it influences popular thinking. A typical contemporary explanation of bridewealth contends that cash must be given to the bride's family to compensate them for the loss of their daughter; and this gives seniors a legitimate excuse to recoup their expenditure on education.[319] Although in sociological terms this argument does not explain why bridewealth is given in the first place,[320] it gives people a plausible excuse for satisfying their immediate economic needs and justifies the husband's refusal to pay maintenance for his wife and children on breakup of the marriage.[321]

---

[312] Mathewson op cit n289 72–6; Holleman op cit n43 106–9.

[313] Dlamini op cit n287 150ff.

[314] Simons *African Women* 95. And see Lugg (1945) 4 *Afr Studies* 26–7.

[315] Mathewson op cit n289 75.

[316] Sansom in Kapferer op cit n308 143ff; Evans-Pritchard op cit n288 181.

[317] An inevitable consequence was stress in the relationship between seniors and juniors: Meillassoux in Seddon *Relations of Production* 150–3.

[318] See Chinyenze op cit n295 229.

[319] See Brandel op cit n290 34.

[320] Dlamini 179–81; (1985) 18 *CILSA* 365; op cit n287 152–3.

[321] Burman & Berger (1988) 4 *SAJHR* 340.

Levels are set very high in relation to incomes. No doubt there is an element of profiteering in this: the marriage of a daughter is a windfall in many households. But the institution is now arguably dysfunctional, having none of the benefits previously claimed for it.[322] People charge bridewealth for their daughters simply because they themselves had to pay it and, of course, to settle inherited marriage debts.[323] Because it is now paid in cash, bridewealth is dissipated to defray day-to-day expenses instead of being kept as financial security for the divorced or widowed wife. The entire institution of marriage is said to be undermined: men cannot afford to pay the sums asked of them, so they enter into informal unions, which condemns their offspring to a status of illegitimacy.[324]

In a community which is already desperately poor, the continued practice of bridewealth seems irrational and self-destructive. In almost one fifth of households in Lesotho, for example, annual bridewealth transfers (in or out) represented approximately a third of the median household income.[325] Yet a new interpretation of the institution shows that:

> 'far from being a form of "irrational" expenditure, large *bohali* transfers . . . redistribute upwards, from the junior (active migrant) generation to the senior (retired) generation, a proportion of the means of subsistence derived from earnings in South Africa.'[326]

[66] MURRAY *FAMILIES DIVIDED* 146–7

How then are social relations sustained (1) within the rural household which consists of a migrant and his immediate family, and (2) between rural households in the labour reserve? The answers to these questions offer the key to understanding the persistence of bohali in Lesotho at levels at least as high as those prevalent in the nineteenth century. Marital transactions are competitive exchanges. Their moral idiom is the transfer of cattle for rights of paternity. Their practical purpose is to maintain the integrity of the rural household as an effective structure of supports and dependences. Migrant earnings materially sustain significant relationships of kinship and affinity. They also, through their partial disposition in bohali transfers, confer legitimacy upon those relationships. The implications of this point are extremely important. On the one hand, the persistence of bohali must be related to changes that have taken place outside the boundaries of Sesotho "society". On the other hand, this wider framework of analysis requires no less attention to the particular experience of Basotho and to the ways in which they articulate that experience. Accordingly, it is impossible to isolate the material or "economic" aspect of bohali transfers from their ideological or "cultural" aspect, and to ascribe priority to one or the other. Bohali is "cultural" in that Basotho effect resolutions of personal identity with reference to the transactions summarized in the Table below:

---

[322] Cf Dlamini op cit n320 362.

[323] Hlophe op cit n168 169.

[324] Hlophe op cit n168 168–70; Dlamini op cit n287 158. Cf Dlamini op cit n320 365ff who protests against Hlophe's call for abolition or restriction of the practice.

[325] Murray (1977) 21 *JAL* 84.

[326] Murray op cit 80 and op cit n280 99ff. See further: Lye & Murray op cit n82 114; Phillips 36–7; Pauw 129–30; Koyana op cit n276 2ff; Brandel op cit n290 34ff.

Marital transactions: their cumulative significance

From husband's kin	From wife's kin	Significance
sheep of *koae*		to "receive" the wife when she first arrives at husband's home
cattle: either		
6 *matšeliso*		compensation due for eloping with, abducting or "spoiling" a girl
or		
6 *lenyalo*		where there is a previous agreement, this payment is evidence of serious intention to marry
7 *ho supa mohoehali*		to "point at one's mother-in-law" (a gratuitous insult which achieves nothing and shows the husband is "merely playing")
8 *ho thea bohali*		to "lay the foundation" of the marriage
10 *ho phetha hloho*		to "complete a head"; this establishes husband's paternity of children
	ho hlabisa bohali	feast provided by wife's family, to mark receipt of 10 or more *bohali* cattle and to fulfil marriage contract
	sheep of *koae*	to mark first formal visit of husband to wife's natal home
	ho phahlela morali	to "pack for" one's daughter: clothes and household goods for wife from her parents for use in marital home
ho khaola bohali		transfer of such additional cattle as necessary to complete number specified in original agreement

and they also rationalize such resolutions retrospectively. The calculations that they make are constrained by custom and sanctioned by recourse to the courts. *Bohali* is also "economic" in that transfers in livestock and cash are substantial items of income and expenditure in household budgets.

Bohali transfers in Lesotho today, at least in the Lowlands, are derived largely from the earnings of migrants. They are no longer provided in livestock by a variety of agnatic and matrilateral kin on the side of the husband and distributed amongst a similar variety of kin on the side of the wife.[1] They are drawn from and contribute to a general subsistence fund concentrated largely within the household. However, to the extent that *bohali* transfers constitute items of expenditure for migrants and items of income for the heads of women's natal households, they effect a redistribution of income in favour of the senior generation, which thus has a clear interest in continuing to demand high rates of *bohali.* . . .

Migrants also have an interest in substantially fulfilling their *bohali* obligations, for their own long-term security is best assured by establishing access to legitimate dependants within a rural household. Given a high rate of conjugal dissociation, which is a consequence of oscillating migration, the migrant has to balance two considerations. On the one hand, the rationality of investment in the next generation, of the sort that *bohali* transfers represent, is qualified by his initially tenuous attachment to his own dependants. On the other hand, so long as *bohali* remains the idiom in which inter-household competition for the earning capacity of the next generation is rationalized and resolved, such investment remains the only way in which he can legitimately assert his own interests as against those of his affines. It is sensible for the migrant to dispose his resources accordingly: that is, both in maintaining his dependants in a rural household, which is a condition of conjugal stability, and in "buying off" his affines by meeting their bohali demands, in order to validate in jural terms the relations of mutual dependence within his rural household.

Note
1. Ashton 62–87.

Bridewealth remains popular in the sense that few people are prepared to contemplate its abolition.[327] For many its appeal lies in its power as a cultural symbol:

'In a world of rapidly changing conditions, it is not surprising that Blacks do cling to anything which can give them their distinctive cultural identity.'[328]

(3) A legal requirement for marriage?

Section 11(1) of the Black Administration Act[329] provided that

'it shall not be lawful for any court to declare that the custom of lobola or bogadi or other similar custom is repugnant to [public policy or natural justice]'.[330]

The moral outrage of the Church and state is spent; bridewealth is now a protected institution. Persons who enter into a bridewealth transaction can be certain that their agreement will be enforced like any other contract. What implications does this have for customary marriage?

To the people of southern Africa marriage and bridewealth have always gone hand in hand. And from the courts' point of view the giving of cattle or other property is a concrete event that has the merit of injecting certainty into an otherwise amorphous relationship. If for this reason only, bridewealth commended itself as an essential requirement for the validity of marriage.[331] Unfortunately, the courts at the same time defined customary marriage as a contractual relationship between two families,[332] with bridewealth as its object.[333] This was misleading. It ignored the absence of any concept of contract in customary law,[334] and it suppressed important cultural variations: the Nguni

---

[327] Durand *Swartman, Stad en Toekoms* 39 established that 95 per cent of the people questioned were in favour of retaining bridewealth. See too: Dlamini op cit n320 363; Chigwedere op cit n281 52ff.

[328] Dlamini 198. Whooley in Verryn op cit n81 313 puts it thus: 'Lobola . . . is the framework that people use to express and to bring about complicated changes in terms of relationships and deep changes in terms of emotional realities, values, attitudes and concepts. It is also the language that the ancestors understand and bless.'

[329] 38 of 1927.

[330] As amended; now s1(1) of Act 45 of 1988.

[331] See Reuter op cit n97 245–56; Van Tromp 77. This is typical of the jural approach; cf Roberts in *Law and the Family in Africa* 241ff.

[332] Comaroff op cit n280 17–18.

[333] Radcliffe-Brown & Forde 46; Bekker 150.

[334] Jeffreys op cit n274 147–9; Comaroff op cit n280 18 n1; Gluckman *The Ideas in Barotse Jurisprudence* 71; Dlamini 313ff.

emphasize the transfer of the bride as a determinant of marriage, while the Sotho-Tswana emphasize the transfer of bridewealth.[335] At a more abstract level of analysis, this proposition assumed that marriage was logically prior to bridewealth and independent of it, ie that marriage could exist without bridewealth, which by implication would be dependent upon and would facilitate marriage.[336] It was as if 'the primary reason that marriage payments exist is to expedite or regulate proper marriage exchanges'.[337]

So, at the outset, the courts' approach was compromised. On the one hand they held that bridewealth was 'the rock on which the customary marriage is founded'[338] and on the other, that bridewealth was a redundant accessory to the marriage contract.[339]

[67] BLAINE P 1927 NAC (N&T) 4

Lobolo has by this section of the Act been brought to a definite basis of uniformity throughout the Union, and quite rightly so, for, despite the disfavour in which it is held by certain schools of thought, its underlying principle is unquestionably an integral part of the foundation on which the whole fabric of native family life and society rests.

... *Ukolobola (ikazi, bohadi)* may be taken to be a contract between the father and the intended husband of his daughter, by which the father promises his consent to the marriage of the daughter, and to protect her in case of necessity, either during or after such marriage, and by which in return he obtains from the husband valuable consideration, partly for such consent, and partly as a guarantee by the husband of his good conduct towards his daughter as wife. Such a contract does not imply the compulsory marriage of the woman. The "ikazi" may, upon every principle of sound law, be recoverable under such a contract.

It is not a contract of purchase and sale. The terms "buying and selling" are scarcely fair terms to apply in describing the transactions referred to. The property given in the case of marriage amongst these people forms a provision for the widow and family in case of the husband's death which arrangement is held sacred and universally respected.

The interpretation of bridewealth as an accessory to marriage has had the advantage of allowing it to be transposed to novel situations—principally the civil or Christian marriage—subject to a different code of rules. Yet the ethnographic data would not bear out any distinction between marriage and bridewealth. Comaroff, for instance, on the basis of his study of the Tshidi (a Tswana people), has shown that it is bridewealth which determines whether an incomplete union becomes a full marriage.[340] This does not mean that a precise demarcation between marriage and informal or illicit unions (like concubinage) is found in customary law. The gradual fulfilment of the bridewealth obligation by instalments would confound such a notion. Instead, marriage

---

[335] Kuper op cit n255 127.
[336] Reuter op cit n97 232 and Jeffreys op cit n274 153.
[337] Comaroff op cit n280 36. See his case study of the Tshidi 161ff, where he argues that the assumed linear relationship between marriage and affinity, and the clear demarcation between marriage and illicit unions does not hold true.
[338] *Mbanga v Sikolake* 1939 NAC (C&O) 31; Bekker 151.
[339] Jeffreys op cit n274 150ff; Comaroff op cit n280 17–18.
[340] Matthews op cit n133 18.

'is closely associated with the concept of debt; the debt, as the saying goes, is the relationship . . . marriage tends to be viewed as a process of becoming rather than as a state of being'.[341]

The courts' other view—bridewealth constitutes marriage—is also not unproblematic. What is required of persons who wish to contract a customary marriage: physical delivery of bridewealth or mere agreement? With the ever-escalating cost of bridewealth relative to average income, it would be necessary to take account of the parties' actual financial circumstances before pronouncing on the validity of their marriage. A pragmatic approach of this nature would be tolerable in small-scale communities, where personal circumstances and the general economic environment could be taken into account, but the courts' reason for insisting on bridewealth as an essential of marriage was, partly at least, to make the union more certain in the modern context.

In fact, the ruling that 'there can be no marriage if there are no dowry cattle in the kraal of the woman's father'[342] has proved to be an unhelpful overgeneralization that the courts could not implement consistently, especially in situations where full and immediate payment of bridewealth was not the norm. In Transkei, for example, they soon had to abandon a requirement for actual delivery. In *Maxayi v Tukani*[343] it was held that the Pondo marriage is complete when the wife goes to live with her husband, and her guardian consents. Bridewealth may be demanded after this; delivery is not essential. Similarly, in *Ntobole a/b Ceza v Mzanywa & another*,[344] it was held that the union is validated by agreement although no property has changed hands.[345]

Implicit in the bridewealth requirement is an understanding that cattle or other marriage goods will convert mere cohabitation into a legal marriage, in other words, that the transfer of property on marriage has an unambiguous meaning. With the waning of ritual and the conversion of marriage goods into trade goods, this unfortunately is not always the case. Even livestock (which are so closely associated with marriage) have a wider currency for the settlement of other obligations, such as seduction damages. And today, with cash as the universal medium of exchange, a simple payment of money is always a potentially equivocal act.

The social context generally supplies the meaning of payments, but where the context is itself ambiguous the payment becomes doubly uncertain.[346] In customary law cohabitation may be a delict, a marriage, or on the way to becoming a marriage. Payment of cattle or cash signifies either damages for seduction, a pre-marriage gift, bridewealth, or an instalment of bridewealth. If

---

[341] Comaroff op cit n280 38.

[342] *Sipoxo & another v Rwexwana* 4 NAC 205 (1919) at 206.

[343] 1 NAC 99 (1905).

[344] 3 NAC 190 (1914).

[345] The Natal and KwaZulu Codes have gone even further; neither payment nor agreement is essential to create a valid marriage: s 38(1). See *Dhlamini* 1967 BAC 7 (NE).

[346] The problem is exacerbated by the rule that seduction damages may merge into and become part of the bridewealth: *Mothombeni v Matlou* 1945 NAC (N&T) 123; *Mpantsha v Ngolonkulu & another* 1952 NAC 40 (S).

the usual marriage negotiations are missing, and if there has been no wedding ceremony, it becomes extremely difficult to decipher the parties' relationship.[347] Where payment *preceded* cohabitation, it is usually taken to be bridewealth.[348] Otherwise, in the reverse situation, there is nothing to be gleaned from the mere giving of cattle or cash. In such circumstances, the *recipient's* attitude tends to be decisive: did he receive the consideration as bridewealth or as damages?[349] This means that whatever the courts may say about the necessity for giving bridewealth, marriage is actually constituted by the wife's guardian—a proposition that does not fit comfortably with the principle of individual freedom of marriage.

(4) Composition and amount

Because bridewealth goods are supposed to circulate through the society they must be non-perishable.[350] In southern Africa this requirement has been met by use of livestock, especially cattle.[351] Cattle pervade all aspects of African culture. They provide subsistence and a medium to communicate with the ancestral shades.[352] They are the currency of social intercourse, conferring on the holder power and prestige.

While payment of bridewealth in cattle is generally believed to have been the norm, this was not always the case. When stockholdings were affected by disasters (notably the Great Cattle-Killing of 1856–7) substitutes, such as assegais, sheep, horses, hoes, and even mealies, were given instead.[353] And, in the low-lying areas of the eastern Transvaal, the presence of endemic stock diseases, especially trypanosomiasis, has precluded the use of cattle.[354]

The use of a particular type of property for bridewealth can be explained by one of two competing accounts: that the property is a productive resource and as such has intrinsic value to the community concerned,[355] or that the goods acquire value only by virtue of their association with bridewealth transactions.[356] In either case the type of property is critical to the validity of the transaction because, if bridewealth constitutes marriage, then it must be clear to the parties and to the community that whatever property was paid was bridewealth and was not intended for some other purpose. In precapitalist economies it was a relatively simple matter to extract one particular class of goods and to restrict its use to marriage transactions. The scarcity of such property would normally place

---

[347] See *Mpanza v Qonono* 1978 AC 136 (C) at 141–2. Even intermittent payments, which might be construed as a response to theleka, could equally be damages for seduction; see *Gcina v Ntengo* 1935 NAC (C&O) 21.

[348] *Madonsela v Duba* 1942 NAC (N&T) 74; *Matholo v Moquena* 1946 NAC (C&O) 17; *Nyembe v Mafu* 1979 AC 186 (NE).

[349] *Jama v Sikosana* 1972 BAC 21 (S); *Mpanza's* case supra.

[350] Compared with perishable goods, which are normally used to celebrate the marriage and/or set up a new household: Goody op cit n279 11.

[351] See Kuper op cit n255 ch 2 on the semiotics of cattle.

[352] Berglund *Zulu Thought-patterns and Symbolism* 199–209.

[353] Van Tromp 44 and Soga 121ff.

[354] Hoes might be given instead: Junod 108–9.

[355] Kuper op cit n255 167.

[356] Evans-Pritchard op cit n288 182; Krige op cit n137 424.

it beyond the means of juniors and would afford seniors control over the marriage proceedings.[357]

When all property has been subsumed under a market economy,[358] and as the ritual significance of cattle diminishes, marriage goods are bound to lose their distinctive character.[359] Yet a careful study of cattle transactions amongst the Pedi revealed countervailing forces. Ceremony, ritual formulae, and various linguistic taboos were used to suppress the commercial connotations of bridewealth cattle and to reassert their purely social function.[360] And, countrywide, the unique meaning of cattle lingers in a formula that whatever cash is given represents so many head of livestock.[361]

Be that as it may; money is legal tender and the courts cannot deny its currency in marriage transactions, especially when they are deemed ordinary contracts. Accordingly, it has been held that the husband (or his guardian) has the option of paying in cattle or cash,[362] and conversely the wife's guardian may stipulate that cash (or other recognized marriage property) be given.[363] Research in Zululand shows that people there will insist on at least portion of the bridewealth being paid in cattle, regardless of any problems this might occasion the groom.[364] Given the circumstances of the average urban dweller and the principle of freedom of marriage, this seems unreasonable, and it is doubtful whether it could be supported in court.

If bridewealth is to be paid in cattle or any other form of livestock, it must consist of an average, ie a selection of young, old, large and small beasts.[365] Further, where cattle were the original payment, the defendant must return the same beasts if the marriage is dissolved.[366] Where he no longer has the stock, he may pay their cash equivalent.[367]

The use of cash and the possibility of returning bridewealth has exposed the problem of inflation. How much is the woman's guardian obliged to refund on divorce, bearing in mind that the marriage may have been transacted several years previously? The courts have established a general principle that a local average value must be paid,[368] and that this is the market value at the time of the suit, not at the time of the original transaction.[369] Where there is no available standard value of cattle in a particular area, evidence must be called to establish one.[370]

---

[357] Meillassoux in Seddon op cit n317 142–5.
[358] Kuper op cit n255 109.
[359] Murray op cit n280 17.
[360] Sansom in Kapferer op cit n308 143ff.
[361] *Majongile v Mpikeleli* 1950 NAC 260 (S); Brandel op cit n290 35; Van Tromp 43.
[362] *Msimango v Sitole* 1940 NAC (N&T) 33.
[363] *Majongile's* case supra.
[364] Dlamini 226–8.
[365] *Raphuti & another v Mametsi* 1946 NAC (N&T) 19.
[366] *Mdinge v Kotshini* 1951 NAC 270 (S).
[367] *Sigidi v Mfamana & another* 1954 NAC 50 (S).
[368] *Mapango v Zuma* 1 NAC 207 (1908); *Mdinge's* case supra.
[369] *Majongile v Mpikeleli* 1950 NAC 260 (S).
[370] *Makabane v Maluka* 1965 BAC 22 (NE).

Until the 1960s, the courts attributed a standard value of £5/R10 to an average beast.[371] This had the effect of putting to the proof any person who alleged a higher value: evidence would have to be called to establish the allegation.[372] The principle of stare decisis has unfortunately fixed the standard at a level which is now unreasonably low.[373] It is only Natal, by frequent amendment to the Codes, that has kept pace with changing market values.[374] Currently cattle are valued at R100 per head.[375]

The amount of bridewealth to be paid depends on the particular situation, most importantly the economic circumstances of the parties and the qualities of the bride. The general custom of the area, however, provides conventional limits, and in this regard comparative studies have shown that where agriculture is the mainstay of the economy, bridewealth payments tend to be high (the Southern Sotho, Tsonga and Lovedu are usually cited as examples). Conversely, in pastoral economies, bridewealth is relatively low, as with the Tswana.[376] Another influence on the amount is what people believe the proper function of bridewealth to be. Where it is viewed as compensating the wife's family for something they have lost, it tends to reflect the value placed on her services and/or her child-bearing capacity.[377] Moreover, because women's virginity and chastity are prized, these qualities will warrant greater amounts, and so too will the rank of the woman's father.[378]

All of this is legally relevant in at least two respects: in the absence of any evidence as to a specific agreement to pay a certain sum of bridewealth, how do the courts determine the amount? And can the bride's guardian insist on a sum that is unreasonable by local standards, thereby preventing his ward's marriage?

The courts have addressed only the first question. Somewhat arbitrarily, a distinction has been made between tribes that stipulate fixed amounts of bridewealth and all others. In the former case evidence need not be led to establish the quantum because it is presumed to have been predetermined by the conventional scale. The Southern Sotho are a case in point: the bridewealth must comprise twenty head of cattle, plus a horse ('the herdboy'), an ox ('the driver') and ten sheep or goats ('the loincloth').[379] This fixed sum applies only to women who have never been married before or have not yet had children; the bridewealth for a previously married woman must be determined by

---

[371] *Ntsabalala v Piti* 1956 NAC 111 (S) at 115; *Nzuza v Kumalo* 1958 NAC 78 (NE); *Mtuzula v Nkohla* 1964 BAC 41 (S); *Makabane's* case supra; cf *Moni v Ketani* 1961 NAC 58 (S). See further: Sansom in Kapferer op cit n308 159. In *Tikolo v Simanga* 1 NAC 51 (1902) the court established an equation with other forms of livestock: 10 sheep or one horse is the equivalent of one cow.

[372] *Ntsabalala's* case supra; *Mtuzula's* case supra.

[373] Murray op cit n325 79ff and Burman in Hirschson op cit n43 127.

[374] See Dlamini 240ff.

[375] Section 60 of the Natal and KwaZulu Codes.

[376] Kuper op cit n255 158. And see above, 199–200.

[377] Goody op cit n279 3–4.

[378] Goody op cit n279 12 argues that a fixed scale of bridewealth is the mark of an egalitarian society. Given the relatively stratified societies of southern Africa, such as the Swazi and Zulu kingdoms, this contention is perhaps questionable.

[379] Ashton 71–2; Duncan 23; *Mgogo v Jan* 1 NAC 278 (1909).

agreement.[380] Whether this formulation still applies is questionable; modern ethnographic work shows that the fixed quantity is merely an ideal[381] often varied by the parties.[382]

In most systems of customary law there is no fixed amount, but this does not mean that there are no limits. For instance, the Tswana[383] or the Pedi[384] bridegroom in theory need give only what he can afford. The wife's family has no means of compelling payment of more. Underlying this system is a belief that bridewealth is a gesture of thanks to the woman's family for their care in bringing her up.[385] Even so it is customary to give conventional amounts, in particular an even number of beasts;[386] an odd number would signify that the wife's family had leave to ask for more.[387] The Southern Nguni, too, stipulate no definite amount of bridewealth: some is paid at the time of the wedding and thereafter the wife's family may demand a beast at the birth of each child. To this end, the wife may be impounded by her family from time to time to encourage the husband to pay (theleka).[388] The Tsonga,[389] Shona,[390] and Venda[391] favour negotiated or agreed amounts of bridewealth. But again the degree of flexibility is not great and convention has dictated limits, as with the Swazi where the recognized number is ten. The wife's family may bargain for more, but this would be considered sharp practice.[392]

In the final analysis the distinction between fixed and negotiated systems seems artificial.[393] In all cases there is a conventional scale, which may be appealed to in cases of doubt.

In Natal and KwaZulu, a maximum amount of bridewealth is specified in the Codes:[394] ten head for the daughter of a commoner and fifteen head for the daughter of a headman, the son, brother or uncle of a chief. For chiefs' daughters there is no limit. Although in practice most people keep to these amounts, they are the upper limits and less may be agreed upon.[395] (In the case of the marriage of a virgin, an ingquthu beast is payable in addition.)[396] Any attempt to circumvent the provisions of s 61 by charging money instead of cattle could be met by s 60, which provides that for the purposes of any dispute the value of each head shall be regarded as R100. But the Code is not proof against payment

---

[380] *Nyokana v Nkwali* 6 NAC 13 (1928); *Mbuko v Letaka* 1945 NAC (C&O) 61.
[381] Poulter 90–1.
[382] *Mojakisane v Khoapa* 1938 NAC (C&O) 28 at 30; Poulter 95.
[383] Schapera 138 and 140; *Married Life* 77; Swanepoel op cit n309 25 and Coertze 227.
[384] Mönnig 133.
[385] Roberts 35.
[386] Two to six head: Roberts 35; four to ten head: Schapera 140.
[387] Swanepoel op cit n309 30; see Roberts 110 regarding the Tlokwa where amounts are now being negotiated.
[388] Van Tromp 43; Soga 266.
[389] Ramsay 7, 13 and Junod 109.
[390] Holleman 161ff.
[391] Van Warmelo & Phophi 103.
[392] Marwick 125.
[393] Dlamini 240.
[394] Section 61(1).
[395] Dlamini 231.
[396] Section 67 of the Codes.

of bridewealth in forms other than cattle or cash, or against the deliberate inflation of the pre-marriage gifts.[397]

Where both parties, although Zulu, do not *come from* Natal (and such non-technical language must be used because it has never been established whether the relevant connection is domicile, residence or tribal affiliation), the restrictions of the Codes do not apply.[398] Further, if only the bridegroom comes from Natal, the Code is inapplicable.[399]

(5) Payment

(a) The father's duty

By convention a father was obliged to pay bridewealth for his sons' first wives.[400] This was a consequence of the authority structure in extended families: the head of the household had control over all socially significant property and hence the marriages of his junior wards.[401] To some extent this structure has now been subverted by the entry of young men onto the labour market; as the principal source of family income, they have inevitably become responsible for providing their own bridewealth.

Under s 64(1) and (2) of the Natal and KwaZulu Codes the obligation resting on the head of a family is a legal one, if it can be shown that the son contributed towards his house on the understanding that he would be given bridewealth. The same provision obliges an older brother (who is an heir) to provide bridewealth for younger brothers.[402]

Elsewhere the courts have interpreted the father's duty as a moral one only.[403] This implies that a son has no right of action against his father to compel payment of bridewealth.[404] The son's claim is further restricted in three other respects. First, the father may recoup expenditure on his son's bridewealth from the marriage of the son's first daughter;[405] the son is entitled to some of this, but the overall right of apportionment is his father's[406] (and, according to one judgment, he may sue his son for repayment).[407] Secondly, the father must approve his son's match;[408] if he dissociates himself from the union, he cannot be held responsible for paying the bridewealth. Thirdly, the father's liability extends only to his sons' first wives.[409]

---

[397] Dlamini 232.

[398] See, e g, *Mtshali v Nkosi* 1942 NAC (N&T) 44. In addition see *Thela v Nkambule* 1940 NAC (N&T) 113.

[399] *Nzimande v Dhlamini* 1935 NAC (N&T) 18.

[400] Dlamini 277ff; Van Tromp 44; Schapera 140; Marwick 126; Hunter 122–3.

[401] Meillassoux in Seddon op cit n317 135ff.

[402] Dlamini 281–3.

[403] *Mtobhoyi v Nkolongwana* 1914 NHC 190; *Langa* 1931 NAC (N&T) 39. *Jeliza v Nyamende & another* 1945 NAC (C&O) 34 is equivocal, speaking of 'contribution'. But see *Manqele* 1940 NAC (N&T) 71.

[404] *Gungubele v Xolizwe* 2 NAC 65 (1910).

[405] *Mnxaku v Madolo* 3 NAC 67 (1913); *Madolo v Mjonono* 3 NAC 68 (1915).

[406] *Mzileni* 5 NAC 39 (1923).

[407] *Mehlomlungu v Gumasholo* 1960 NAC 60 (S).

[408] *Mboqoka v Sibudu* 1934 NAC (C&O) 3; *Cheche v Nondabula* 1962 NAC 23 (S) at 27.

[409] *Khemane v Ned* 1948 NAC 15 (S).

As they stand, the courts' rulings have had the effect of devaluing the provision of bridewealth relative to the father's other support obligations (especially education). Paying bridewealth could have been assimilated to the parent's general duty of support; instead it has been made optional and accessory.

(b) Customary obligations of contribution

In all parts of southern Africa the amount of bridewealth demanded for marriage is high in relation to the income of the ordinary man. Various more or less institutionalized strategies are available to assist the donor to amass the requisite sum. One of the most common is the linking of uterine brothers and sisters: the brother obtains a right to his 'cattle-linked' sister's bridewealth when she gets married.[410] Where a family has more daughters than sons, the head must make a public declaration that a specific daughter is to be linked to a specific son.[411] The Venda have a similar practice that operates even more extensively: when a woman's bridewealth is paid, her father is obliged to use it for his oldest son's marriage. This son in turn is expected to provide bridewealth for the next son, and so on.[412]

This type of arrangement promotes a discrete system of circulation with a powerful dynamic of its own. Marriage goods are withdrawn from general use and are committed solely to obtaining wives. The extract below shows that amongst the Lovedu the linking of siblings interlocks with the kinship system and is reinforced by the structure of preferred marriages.[413]

[68] KRIGE & KRIGE *THE REALM OF A RAIN-QUEEN* 142–4

The ideal marriage is marriage of a man with his mother's brother's daughter or of a woman with her father's sister's son. This does not mean that all cross-cousins are preferred mates. It is, for instance, considered irregular for a man to marry his father's sister's daughter; that cases of such marriages are found should not surprise us. There are irregularities in every sphere of culture, and the rules of mate selection are particularly liable to be upset because of the complex interrelations that arise in the social system. The fundamental rule is that a man must marry, not the daughter of any brother of his mother, but the daughter of that brother who has used his mother's marriage cattle to obtain a wife for himself. His mother and his mother's brother are cattle-linked sister and brother because, when she married, the cattle that came in were handed to the brother for obtaining a wife: the cattle of the sister are said to "build a hut for her brother". We may thus say that a man must marry a daughter of his cattle-linked maternal uncle, and we may call her his "cattle-linked cross-cousin".

But the Lovedu phrase the matter rather differently and more significantly. They say that the sister has "built the house of her brother" (the cattle-linked brother), that therefore she "has a gate" by which she may enter his house, this gate being "the gate which the cattle seek", and that it is her right to demand from the "house built by her cattle" a daughter who must come to her as her daughter-in-law to stamp and cook for her. . . .

---

[410] See Holleman 169–72; Kuper op cit n255 59ff; Clerc op cit n127 98–9.

[411] See, eg, Marwick 126; *Sonqishe* 1943 NAC (C&O) 6.

[412] Kuper op cit n255 77ff.

[413] Bridewealth in the early 1960s consisted of 5 to 8 head of cattle, some goats and money: Krige in Gray & Gulliver *The Family Estate in Africa* 155ff.

If the demand is not acceded to, whether the reason be that the daughter refuses to go or her parents refuse to fulfil their obligation, the results may be disastrous. The sister (or her husband) may "pull down the house she built at her brother's" by taking back her cattle, and she may give them to some one else who will establish a house that is prepared to fulfil its obligations; or, if the cattle have already passed on, in the chain of exchanges, from the wife of the cattle-linked brother to that wife's brother or, further still, the "roots of the cattle" may be "followed", perhaps involving the snapping of the chain at several points. The whole system of interrelations created by the cattle may, in such a case, be thrown out of gear and the repercussions may be so widespread that the whole country is said "to be spoilt". There are, however, many safety devices and the genius for effecting compromises ensures the isolation of the stresses and strains to manageable limits.

The ideal form of marriage, that of a man with his cattle-linked cross-cousin, turns out to be an inevitable consequence of the whole social system, the ground pattern of which is determined by kinship obligations though the detailed arrangements are regulated by the cattle-linking exchanges. It is conceived of not so much as a cross-cousin marriage as of a niece performing an obligation towards her cattle-linked aunt. The conception of a marriage is not wholly submerged, but it stands out far less boldly than the conception of the duty of a niece to love, cherish, and obey her cattle-linked aunt. The central feature, the pivot upon which the whole system is conceived to turn, is the passing of the cattle from a sister, by whose marriage they come in, to her uterine brother, to be used by him for the purpose of acquiring a wife; and from the wife of the brother they pass on to her uterine brother and so on *ad infinitum*. Brother and sister of the same house are cattle-linked, but each is also linked to a partner by the marriage validated by the cattle. The sister-brother cattle link and the husband-wife marriage-plus-cattle link form a continuous chain from sister to brother to wife of brother to brother of wife of brother and so on, which is doubled and redoubled in the second generation, when the same interlinking takes place and the son of the sister marries the daughter of the brother, the brother receiving cattle and the sister a daughter-in-law, while the son of the brother marries the daughter of the brother of his wife. It will be noticed that the three essential links are those between brother and sister, between husband and wife and between cattle-linked cross-cousins, and these links, as well as the whole network of subsidiary links, arise from the implications of marriage and cattle-linking. The brothers who receive the cattle from the sisters return daughters to them and again receive cattle; the brothers become the nucleus of a group providing brides, and hence, from the point of view of the sisters and their children, they are the brides or parents-in-law (*vamakhulu*), while the sister's husbands are, from the point of view of the brothers and their children, the group supplying bridegrooms (*vatsezi*) or sons-in-law (*vaduhulu*). The *vamakhulu* give brides and receive cattle; the *vaduhulu* give cattle and receive brides.

The courts will not enforce a man's claim to his sister's bridewealth simply on the understanding that the linking of siblings is the usual practice of the area.[414] The claimant must prove that the bridewealth goods were specifically allocated to him.[415] To substantiate this claim he will have to lead evidence of a public announcement at a family meeting[416] or some official documentation.[417]

The allocation does not give the son a real right. He has a mere expectation[418] which means that he may not sue his father for delivery.[419] All property is

---

[414] Cf *Mdhlalose* 1917 NHC 163.
[415] *Mngadi* 1931 NAC (N&T) 53; *Mtembu* 1943 NAC (N&T) 65.
[416] *Sitole* 1943 NAC (N&T) 17.
[417] *Mpungose* 1947 NAC (N&T) 37.
[418] *Nkosi v Tenjekwayo* 1938 NAC (N&T) 94; *Mahlobo* 1947 NAC (N&T) 31.
[419] *Gungubele v Xolizwe* 2 NAC 65 (1910).

presumed to vest in the head of the family to be disposed of at his discretion.[420]. As a result any increase in the bridewealth accrues to the head of the family[421] and his creditors may attach this property in execution of his debts.[422]

Another strategy available to the head of a family, and one particularly suited to polygynous households, is the borrowing of property from a senior house to obtain a wife for a junior house. In Natal this is known as ethula, and it is written into the Codes.[423] An interhouse debt is created that is normally repaid out of the bridewealth obtained from the marriage of the first daughter of the junior house.[424] The obligation is enforceable only if the debt was clearly specified by the head of the family and only where property from one house was used to benefit the son of another.[425]

Most people would regard their patrilineal kin as the first source of assistance for bridewealth. (In fact, the contribution functions in many respects to affirm group identity.) With the Tswana[426] and the Pedi,[427] for example, the bridegroom's relatives, according to a loose order of preference (viz maternal and paternal uncles, paternal aunt, and their respective descendants), are each expected to give what they can. Generally speaking, these intrafamilial contributions are not considered to be recoverable debts, although with the Southern Sotho, the sizeable amount customarily given by the husband's senior maternal uncle may later be reclaimed from the bridewealth of the niece.[428]

No time limit is imposed on claims for repayment. Men may be sued for bridewealth that was borrowed by their grandfathers or great-grandfathers.[429] The debts are commonly secured by the promise of bridewealth to be received from the borrower's first daughter,[430] an arrangement that amongst the Southern Nguni is known as ukwenzelela.[431] If the marriage produces no daughters, the debt may be repaid from the bridegroom's estate when he dies.[432] In this way bridewealth obligations pass from one generation to another.[433] This is a mixed blessing. Debts may be idealized as a source of family solidarity, but they also appear as 'ropes which start from the neck of one and go to the neck of the other'.[434] Today, however, in view of the fragmentation of the extended family

---

[420] *Gumede* 1950 NAC 171 (NE).

[421] *Magwaza* 1937 NAC (N&T) 3.

[422] *Xulu v Langa* 1940 NAC (N&T) 117 at 118–19; *Radebe v Tshapa* 1948 NAC 36 (NE).

[423] Section 1(1).

[424] Cf *Mkwintshi v Nkomidhli* 1917 NHC 170.

[425] Section 65 of the Natal and KwaZulu Codes; *Shandu* 1956 NAC 134 (NE); Dlamini 291ff.

[426] Schapera *Married Life* 77–8.

[427] Mönnig 133.

[428] Poulter 141 and 144–6.

[429] *Ntlokondala v Palele* 1945 NAC (C&O) 21.

[430] *Ndabankulu v Pennington* 4 NAC 171 (1919); *Vatsha v Mfenduna* 1936 NAC (C&O) 39. These promises are not deemed repugnant to natural justice: *Dali v Siyeza* 1914 NHC 197.

[431] *Nobumba v Mfecane* 2 NAC 104 (1911); *Nketshenketshe v Gobo* 1959 NAC 57 (S); Van Tromp 45–6. In *Payi* 1962 NAC 9 (S) this was distinguished from the father's right to claim a refund. The claimant must obviously wait until the girl marries before suing: *Ximba* 1959 NAC 18 (NE).

[432] *Molo NO v Gaga* 1947 NAC (C&O) 80.

[433] Simons *African Women* 94.

[434] Junod 531 and see 282.

and the erosion of the kinship ethic, payment of bridewealth is bound to become an individual responsibility.[435]

(6) The recipient

The bride's guardian, normally her father or his heir, is entitled to receive her bridewealth.[436] He retains this right even if he has not raised his daughter.[437] Where the bride is living under someone else's care, the head of her foster homestead may negotiate her marriage and may receive her bridewealth. But he is deemed to act as an agent for her guardian,[438] to whom he must account in due course.[439]

In principle women are not allowed to receive bridewealth for their daughters.[440] Changes in the composition of the family, due especially to the labour migrancy of males, however, are cause for reconsideration. Women are of necessity becoming more involved in marriage negotiations,[441] and there is no good reason why de facto independent women should not receive their daughters' bridewealth.[442] In respect of legally emancipated women at least, this power has already been incorporated into the Natal and KwaZulu Codes.[443]

Whoever receives the bridewealth may be obliged to share part or all of it with various people having prior claims, such as those who contributed to paying the recipient's own bridewealth.[444]

(7) Ownership and delivery

Because bridewealth may determine the validity of marriage and because of the strong influence of common law (in which property transfers are a significant feature), ownership and delivery have become important and technical issues. In customary law, the transfer of bridewealth would be decided by local custom and private arrangement. The Tswana, for example, used to require full transfer at or before the wedding.[445] In most places it was usual to give bridewealth only when the first child was born.[446] Under the Laws of Lerotholi,[447] part or all of the bridewealth is supposed to be paid at the wedding; but, given the regular practice of deferment and the uncertainty whether bridewealth is a prerequisite of a valid marriage,[448] this requirement seems to be no more than a formality.

---

[435] Dlamini 303–4, eg, reports that ethula is fast disappearing, which is only to be expected with the decline of polygyny and parental authority. See Burman in Hirschon op cit n43 127.

[436] Dlamini 258; Olivier 89ff.

[437] *Ramncwana v Siyotula* 1937 NAC (C&O) 172; *Matomani v Kraai* 1947 NAC (C&O) 18.

[438] *Lutoli v Dyubele* 1940 NAC (C&O) 78. And see *Mdakane v Kumalo* 1938 NAC (N&T) 219.

[439] Dlamini 259–60; Bekker 167–71.

[440] *Mogidi & another v Ngomo* 1948 NAC (N&T) 18. Nor may she be sued for payment: *Ntuli v Mkonza* 1964 NAC 97 (NE).

[441] *Magadla v Gcwabi* 1940 NAC (C&O) 69.

[442] *Mankayi v Qomoyi* 1973 AC 232 (S).

[443] Section 59.

[444] Olivier 89–92; Van Tromp 45–6; Schapera 142.

[445] Schapera 141. It seems that bridewealth is now often paid after the wedding: see Roberts passim.

[446] Ashton 66–7; Olivier 78–80.

[447] Section 34(1)(c).

[448] Poulter 101–5.

Under the Natal and KwaZulu Codes[449] bridewealth must be paid on the day the marriage is celebrated unless there is an agreement to the contrary. Any livestock paid before this date remain in the ownership of the donor. They are treated as a loan or sisa—a 'confusing and artificial' construction[450]—that unfortunately has been extended to other parts of the country, and would now seem to be generally applicable.[451]

Actual physical delivery of the bridewealth is not necessary to transfer ownership.[452] This becomes relevant where the transfer of livestock has been forbidden by destocking or health regulations. In Transkei a practice evolved of accepting transfer by mere description or by word of mouth; the cattle could then remain in the possession of the donor.[453] The courts obligingly treated this as a form of constructive delivery, viz the recipient became owner by a process of constitutum possessorium or traditio longa manu.[454]

Section 58(1) of the Natal and KwaZulu Codes provides that delivery on its own does not transfer ownership. It is the celebration of the marriage which is the critical legal event.[455]

(8) Enforcement

Where bridewealth has been delivered before or at the time of marriage, there is obviously no problem of enforcement. Difficulties arise only when payment has been deferred or where no definite amount was agreed upon (as with the Southern Nguni). Because bridewealth is integral to the marriage, its enforcement by action in court is problematic, and customary law sensibly allowed the threat of losing parental rights to the children to operate as the major inducement to pay timeously. Non-payment does not necessarily imply that the marriage should be terminated. It might mean that the husband was angry with his wife or that he simply lacked the means to pay. But if the courts allowed the father-in-law to sue, the action could disrupt an otherwise tranquil marriage; or if divorce were in fact contemplated, a premature suit might be tactically inadvisable. Hence actions were permitted only in limited circumstances.[456] If the parties had agreed to the payment of a specific amount of bridewealth, or if it was fixed in accordance with a conventional scale, the wife's guardian could sue.[457]

Where the system of customary law involved did not have a fixed amount of bridewealth, the aggrieved party would have to use the customary remedy of

---

[449] Section 58(1).
[450] Dlamini 271.
[451] See above, 187.
[452] For the effect on marriage, see above, 206–7.
[453] *Robo v Madlebe* 4 NAC 213 (1919); *Ngwevenunu v Macasimba* 5 NAC 39 (1923); *Mahlelo & another v Mehlwantsundu* 5 NAC 43 (1925); *Moyeni v Nkuhlu* 1946 NAC (C&O) 2.
[454] *Ngqungiso v Gobo* 1946 NAC (C&O) 10; Vilakazi op cit n30 65.
[455] *Bhulose v Nzimande* 1951 NAC 331 (NE). See Dlamini 265ff esp 267: apparently there was no settled opinion in customary law about when ownership passed.
[456] An action is permitted under the Natal and KwaZulu Codes: s 66(1).
[457] *Mfomdidi v Mdletye* 3 NAC 174 (1915); *Qashilanga v Mtuyedwa* 1936 NAC (C&O) 89; *Ngalimkulu v Mndayi* 1947 NAC (C&O) 65; *Mavuma v Mbebe* 1948 NAC (C&O) 16.

theleka, the impounding of the wife and/or her children. When the husband asked for her return (phuthuma), she would be released only if he made a further payment. If the wife's guardian were to institute an action for bridewealth, the husband could raise the failure to theleka as a defence.[458] (Where it was apparent that the husband had the means to pay but refused to do so, however, the wife's guardian could then in principle take action to dissolve the marriage.)[459] So far as the courts were concerned, this procedure had one disadvantage: it did not accord with the common-law idea of the sanctity of the marital consortium. Hence the guardian's right to theleka was qualified by a proviso that once the husband had paid approximately six head of cattle, further theleka would not be allowed.[460] This had the indirect effect of prescribing a fixed quantum of bridewealth.

VI ESSENTIALS OF CUSTOMARY MARRIAGE: A QUEST FOR CERTAINTY

A group of anthropologists (who coincidentally were all studying the Sotho-Tswana) has convincingly argued that the customary marriage should not be conceived of as a single event, but rather as a developing process.[461] Comaroff's work on the Tshidi showed that a marriage eventuates from (a) a series of negotiations between the two families, which are (b) concluded by the giving of a gift, usually a sheep to the prospective bride's family. (c) The future husband will then be allowed to cohabit with the woman, and for that purpose he takes up residence with her family. (In the past, this period of uxorilocal residence might have lasted a number of years; now it is much shorter.) Thereafter, the woman moves to her husband's homestead. (d) At about this time, the bridewealth should be given, although delivery is often delayed until much later. Finally, (e), Comaroff calls attention to public recognition, a diffuse element permeating all the others. His conclusion is that, with the qualified exception of bridewealth, none of the five factors he enumerates is a definitive element of marriage.[462] It follows that 'in the course of the development of the marriage, the locus of control over the woman and her children may be uncertain'.[463]

Uncertainty does not mean that the Tshidi do not distinguish between marriage and various other types of union, because in fact they do. At one extreme there is the fleeting relationship, to which neither party has a serious commitment. If the relationship becomes an established liaison, it might be thought of as concubinage (bonyatsi). Where the couple set up house together,

---

[458] *Mkohlwa v Mangaliso* 1 NAC 202 (1908); *Monghayelana v Msongelwa* 3 NAC 292 (1913); *Skweyiya v Sixakwe* 1941 NAC (C&O) 126; *Tonya v Matomane* 1949 NAC 138 (S); *Menzi v Matiwane* 1964 NAC 58 (S).

[459] *Zenzile v Roto* 1 NAC 223 (1909).

[460] See *Ndabeni v Tingatinga* 1 NAC 142 (1907); *Ntlekwini v Maqokolo* 4 NAC 345 (1919).

[461] Kuper (1970) 5 *Man* 466ff; Murray op cit n280 99; Roberts op cit n331 241ff; Comaroff & Roberts (1977) 21 *JAL* 97ff.

[462] Op cit n280 168.

[463] Kuper op cit n461 478.

without initiating formal marriage proceedings, they may be described as 'living together';[464] or the union might be described as in the process of becoming a marriage. At the other extreme, there are the mature unions which are indisputably marriages.[465] But there is no precise way of differentiating these relationships.

In close-knit, rural communities certainty does not have an overriding importance.[466] In any event, proof of the existence of a marriage would seldom present a problem. The union is attested by the involvement of go-betweens and the elders of family councils in the complex ceremonies of negotiation and transfer. And the private nature of marriage allows the parties, within limits, to adjust their relationship to suit the exigencies of a particular situation. In more anonymous urban contexts, on the other hand, proof of customary marriage becomes more difficult, a problem compounded by the fact that there are many more occasions when the parties need to prove their marital status.[467]

The routine processing of similar situations by courts and bureaucrats perforce leads to the crystallization of a particular marital relationship as 'the norm'. And this may result in the imposition of features considered characteristic of 'the norm' as criteria essential for recognition. The recognizing authority obviously has considerable discretion. (This is evident in the study of another Tswana chiefdom, that of the Ngwaketse, whose chiefs had formalized the entire marriage procedure.)[468]

The model of marriage imposed by the colonial authorities (one which they mistakenly thought was universal) was a consensual union of the spouses. At the time that the common law was being introduced to southern Africa, this idea had only recently been finalized in European law.[469] The courts implemented it zealously: marriages that had been procured without the volition of one of the parties were deemed 'repugnant to our civilized conscience';[470] and consent became the overriding consideration.

How was consent to be gauged, especially in the case of women? Initially it was felt that:

> 'Something more is required than the mere handing over of a woman to a man as if she were a mere chattel. The occasion should be marked by some sort of ritual. . . . This is very necessary in order to avoid the possibility of coercion.'[471]

But consent is an intangible that can be discovered in an infinite variety of acts and events. On one occasion, for instance, it was inferred from the style of the

---

[464] See, too, Mayer 264 and Pendleton op cit n86 139–43.

[465] Comaroff op cit n280 165.

[466] In *Neku & another v Moni* 1938 NAC (C&O) 61 at 62, eg, the court, in a remark, revealing about its attitude to customary law, said that certainty was a basic principle of a civilized legal system.

[467] For example, to obtain housing, claim insurance, or social welfare benefits.

[468] Although failure to comply with their requirements did not invalidate the union, it did attract criminal penalties: Campbell op cit n30 221–3.

[469] Glendon op cit n24 24.

[470] *Zimande v Sibeko* 1948 NAC 21 (C) at 23. And see: *Zulu v Mdhletshe* 1952 NAC 203 (NE); *Mngomezulu v Lukele* 1953 NAC 143 (NE); but cf *Neku & another v Moni* 1938 NAC (C&O) 61, where the marriage was by the husband's proxy. This would invalidate a civil marriage but it did not influence the court's decision. See too: *Mchunu v Masoka* 1964 BAC 7 (NE).

[471] *Simelane v Sugazie* 1935 NAC (N&T) 45.

wife's dress and her assumption of marital roles.[472] Wedding ceremonies were
certainly not the only possible indicia[473] and they were soon dismissed as 'the
religious element of the proceedings', of no more importance than 'prayer,
music, singing or a wedding reception in a European marriage'.[474] Inevitably,
where the ritual had a pagan association, its fate was sealed.

[69] *KGAPULA v MAPHAI* 1940 NAC (N&T) 108 at 109–10

In the native areas of this Province [Transvaal], the ancient formalities which obtained
before the advent of European civilization, are probably still observed, at least to some
degree, when customary unions are entered into, but in and near to the towns and
industrial centres there is a steadily growing laxity in the observance of native custom.

It is unfortunate that the Courts have no legislative authority to refer to when called
upon to decide such cases as the one before us. Whilst laxity in such matters must be
discouraged as far as possible, the situation which has steadily developed as a result of
natives having become detribalised, and for other reasons due to the influx of civilization,
cannot be ignored. It seems to us that if it can be established that the man and the woman
consent to live together in a customary union, if the parents also consent and if lobolo or
bohadi is paid and all the interested parties regard the union as having been established,
the Courts must hold that it has, in fact, taken place. It is not essential that there should
be a feast and other celebrations before such a union can be recognised. These remarks
apply to the type of native referred to and the parties to this action belong to that
category.

In applying these principles to the present case we find that—
(1) five head of cattle were delivered to the Respondent, and in addition, four sheep were
     promised;
(2) the Appellant and Elizabeth thereafter lived together as man and wife for a period of
     eight years;
(3) no further claim for cattle was made during the period of their cohabitation;
(4) Elizabeth's parents visited her from time to time during that period and were on
     friendly terms with the Appellant;
(5) on her death she was buried in Appellant's father's kraal.

In view of these facts, it appears that all the interested parties regarded the cohabitation
as a valid customary union, although there had been no marriage feast or formal handing
over of the woman by her father. Unless and until the legislature lays down the essentials
which must be observed before a customary union can be recognised in the Transvaal,
each case which comes before the Court must be decided on its merits and in the light in
which the cohabitation of the parties concerned is regarded by both of them and by their
parents.

Long cohabitation raises a strong presumption of marriage, especially when the
woman's father has taken no action indicating that he does not so regard it, although in
a position to raise objections and to take action to terminate it.

The courts have always relied on cohabitation as a significant indication of
intent; but today it is no longer necessarily conclusive.[475] For many reasons men
and women who have no intention of marrying may enter relationships that are
intended to last for shorter or longer periods. In such circumstances the payment
of bridewealth will determine the nature of the relationship (although it is

---

[472] *Neku & another v Moni* 1938 NAC (C&O) 61.
[473] *Ngcongolo v Parkies* 1953 NAC 103 (S).
[474] *Sila & another v Masuku* 1937 NAC (N&T) 121 at 123. And see Simons op cit n142 322–5.
[475] Which was noted by the court in *Ngcongolo v Parkies* 1953 NAC 103 (S) at 105.

evidence of the consent of the groom and his wife's guardian only, not of the bride). Yet the mere transfer of property, without more, is also ambiguous. In *Cele v Radebe*,[476] for instance, it was unclear whether the delivery of livestock by a man to the guardian of the woman with whom he was living constituted damages for seduction or bridewealth.[477] In this case the *length* of the period of cohabitation was decisive: the couple had been living together for 26 years and had had seven children. The court held that such long cohabitation raised a presumption of marriage, and that the delivery of livestock should thus be regarded as bridewealth. The time at which property is transferred may help to clarify its nature; according to the decision in *Nyembe v Mafu*,[478] the presumption of marriage is 'almost irrefutable' if cohabitation is preceded by the handing over of cattle.[479]

The courts' often conflicting decisions regarding the requirements of a customary marriage have been summarized into the following formula: consent of the bride, the groom, and the bride's guardian;[480] payment of or agreement as to bridewealth; and the handing over of the bride.[481] (The last two elements are in fact implicitly treated as physical evidence of the requirement of consent.)[482] In practice, even where one or more of these elements is missing, its existence can be assumed by an inference drawn from the others.

The search for factors constitutive of customary marriage presumes that the marital relationship is both a social norm and a relationship desired by the parties, a view clearly evinced by the presumption in favour of marriage: where two people live together as man and wife for a long period of time they will be deemed to be married.[483] Are these suppositions correct?

In the first place, customary marriage is quite probably not the norm in South Africa; urbanization, apartheid, labour migrancy, forced removals, and many other factors have conspired to devalue and undermine it.[484] In the second place, the courts may be wrong in imputing a desire to be married to people found living together. This widespread phenomenon, while doubtless often a result of economic and social forces beyond the control of the individuals concerned, may also be an indication of personal choice resulting from conscious consideration of the advantages and disadvantages of marriage. A study of marriage in a Windhoek township, for instance, revealed that these informal relationships are preferred, because the partners are free to conduct their private and public lives

[476] 1939 NAC (N&T) 49.
[477] Simons op cit n142 333.
[478] 1979 AC 186 (NE) at 188.
[479] Cf *Mbanga v Sikolake* 1939 NAC (C&O) 31. See also Koyana op cit n276 44–6 and Church in Sanders *Southern Africa in Need of Law Reform* 33, who concludes that bridewealth is not essential to the validity of customary marriage.
[480] Olivier 45–6 adds the groom's guardian.
[481] Olivier 44ff; Bekker 105; and see Clerc op cit n127 94.
[482] Simons op cit n142 327–8.
[483] *Ndaba v Tabete* 1917 NHC 63; *Nyembe v Mafu* 1979 AC 186 (NE).
[484] See above, [47] and 169–71.

as they see fit, without interference from their families and the Church or state. And, of course, no bridewealth need be given.[485]

From a legal point of view, the customary-law marriage offers few, if any, advantages to women and children.[486] Children gain nothing in the way of legal protection, because according to customary law they are always affiliated to a family regardless of their legitimacy.[487] Women actually stand to lose legal capacities when they marry, and their claims to maintenance and custody/guardianship of children are not improved. Rather, it would seem that the major benefit of marriage lies in the social prestige associated with it, a benefit that is diminished by the anonymity of the urban environment.[488] Moreover, the emergence of the female-headed household suggests that many women cope without marriage and may even prefer non-marital relationships.[489]

The state, however, has not suffered the ambiguity of customary marriage and cohabitation gladly. Certainty, by way of readily accessible proof, is needed to enable the spouses to interact with third parties and especially the bureaucracy.[490] The solution throughout Africa has been seen in a requirement that all marriages be formally solemnized and/or registered.[491]

In Natal this has always been necessary. Certain essential requirements are laid down by s 38(1) of the Codes: *(a)* the consent of the father or guardian of the intended wife (which consent may not be withheld unreasonably); *(b)* the consent of the father or family head of the intended husband (should such be legally necessary); *(c)* a declaration in public by the intended wife to an official witness at the celebration of the union that the union is of her own free will and consent.[492] (Bridewealth, it should be noted, is not essential.)[493] Within a month of the celebration, the marriage must be registered.[494] In Transkei too the essentials of customary marriage are statutorily determined[495] and registration is a requirement.[496]

In South Africa at present no formalities are required and registration is neither compulsory nor does it affect the validity of the union. It is merely compellable at the instance of the husband, the wife, or the wife's guardian.[497] A certificate of registration 'shall on its mere production in any court or in any

[485] Pendleton op cit n86 141. And see the attitudes to marriage in Soweto: Peskin in Verryn op cit n81 393ff.
[486] See Peskin in Verryn op cit n81 394.
[487] Offspring of informal unions are disadvantaged (and normally only the eldest son) in case of succession. See below, 371–2.
[488] Shropshire op cit n38 1–26.
[489] Pendleton op cit n86 140 reports that little stigma is attached to couples living together.
[490] Janisch op cit n38 11; Lewin (1941) 15 *Bantu Studies* 23; Shropshire op cit n38 ch 3.
[491] Simons op cit n142 340–1.
[492] Bekker & Coertze 1976 *De Rebus* 601.
[493] Cf Dlamini 346.
[494] Section 45 of the Codes.
[495] Sections 29 and 31 of the Marriage Act 21 of 1978, and see Van Loggerenberg 1981 *Obiter* 5–6.
[496] Sections 33 and 34; and see ss 48 and 49. On registration a woman becomes subject to her husband's guardianship: s 37. Similarly, in Zimbabwe, registration is essential for the validity of marriage but failure to comply does not affect the status of the children: ss 3, 4, 7 and 8 of the African Marriages Act ch 238.
[497] Regulations 7 and 16 of GN R1970 25 October 1968, promulgated under s 22*bis* of the Black Administration Act 38 of 1927. The regulations are reproduced and discussed in Bekker 393–404.

other proceedings be *prima facie* proof of its contents'.[498] The South African Law Commission,[499] however, proposed the following requirements: *(a)* competence of the parties at customary law to marry one another; *(b)* consent of the husband, the wife and legal guardian of either of them if below the age of 21; *(c)* solemnization by a marriage officer. Despite awareness of the 'inertia, distrust, and conservatism' that militate against co-operation,[500] registration is recommended as an essential ingredient of marriage.[501]

Elsewhere it has been shown that the imposition of formal requirements such as these has had the effect of depriving many existing unions of the limited validity they otherwise enjoyed.[502] So, paradoxically, by requiring registration of *all* marriages, the state may sweep away those customary unions which presently hover on the verge of being or becoming full marriages. These are the unions that depend for their validity on the opinion of the neighbourhood,[503] or the as yet unspecified intention of the parties. Under the proposed statutory regime they will be sacrificed for the dubious advantage of giving an admittedly small number of other unions greater certainty.

In other parts of the world, the idea that marriage is central to family law, and society in general, is now being challenged on both legal and pragmatic grounds. First, it seems that in modern legal systems marriage is not an essential relationship for the purpose of attributing rights, duties and powers. The obligations of support, the attribution of domicile and nationality, rights of succession, and so forth need not depend on a prior marriage.[504] Secondly, the belief that marriage is vital to facilitate a range of social functions, in particular socializing children, is now disputed as a product of functionalist theory.[505] These assumptions are considered to be the result of a particular ideology of how families *should* function, and in consequence they are contested, by feminists especially.[506] Thirdly, and most tellingly, the presumed social norms are not reflected in reality, not even in developed countries.[507] Should the law not be adjusted to take account of these challenges?

In the United States the term 'new marriage' was coined to call attention to the revolution in contemporary social relationships, such as the free terminability of marriage and the appearance of de facto unions alongside formal marriages.[508] These new social patterns have rendered many marriage laws anachronistic. Western legislatures, after a brief period of hesitancy, initiated comprehensive reforms affecting taxation, matrimonial property, alimony, and succession. At

---

[498] Regulation 8(4). Conversely, under s 45(3) of the Natal and KwaZulu Codes, registration must be accepted as 'conclusive evidence' of the marriage. See too *Nxumalo v Zulu* 1941 NAC (N&T) 70.

[499] *Marriages and Customary Unions of Black Persons* p194.

[500] Simons op cit n142 341.

[501] Pages 196–7.

[502] Parker (1987) 1 *Int J L & Family* 133ff.

[503] Wilson op cit n31 v3 94 cited by Simons op cit n142 327.

[504] Clive in Eekelaar & Katz *Marriage and Cohabitation* 71ff and see further: Allott & Woodman *People's Law and State Law* 26ff.

[505] Eekelaar *Family Law and Social Policy* 20.

[506] Rowbotham *Women, Resistance and Revolution*; Mitchell *Woman's Estate*.

[507] Freeman op cit n9 165.

[508] Clark (1976) 12 *Willamette LJ* 441 cited by Glendon in Eekelaar & Katz op cit n504 62.

the same time, in the interests of social stability and protection of the vulnerable, informal unions were given legal recognition (especially for purposes of tax and social welfare),[509] and the stigma of 'living together' was gradually removed (by, for example, abolition of the concept of illegitimacy).[510] Should similar adjustments not be contemplated in the case of customary law?

---

[509] See Freeman & Lyon *Cohabitation without Marriage* ch 5.
[510] See Hoggett and Bates in Eekelaar & Katz op cit n504 99–100 and 105–8 respectively.

CHAPTER 5

Consequences of Customary Marriage

I RANKING OF WIVES

Under customary law a man may marry as many wives as he wishes or can afford. Each wife establishes a separate house and the houses are ranked, normally according to the date of marriage. The status of the wives and their houses is physically represented by the arrangement of the homestead, an arrangement that is determined by three fundamental oppositions:[1] right versus left (expressing the order of marriage/seniority, as well as a male/female dichotomy); centre versus side (reflecting the permanence and seniority of kin as opposed to the transience of affines); and up versus down (expressed by the location of the great house in relation to the cattle byre).[2] With the Zulu and the Southern Nguni peoples the left/right opposition is most strongly asserted,[3] and probably as a result it is the one that has been encoded into customary law.[4]

[70] PRESTON-WHYTE in HAMMOND-TOOKE *BANTU-SPEAKING PEOPLES OF SOUTHERN AFRICA* 179–82

Should the husband . . . take subsequent wives during the lifetime of any one spouse, the family takes on a compound nature. In this case it is composed of two or more constituent

---

[1] Kuper (1980) 50 *Africa* 8ff (reproduced in *Wives for Cattle* 140ff).

[2] The latter is also sometimes expressed as west versus east. See further: Holleman (1940) 14 *Bantu Studies* 31ff; Hughes *Land Tenure, Land Rights and Land Communities in Swazi National Law* 69ff. Cf the archaeological record: Hall (1984) 54 *Africa* 76–8.

[3] Hughes op cit 338–9. But of course all of these oppositions are relative to one's spatial orientation to the homestead: Mönnig 212–13.

[4] Not without difficulty: Kerr 169–73.

units each of which centres on one of the co-wives and her children. In many respects it is this unit composed of a woman and her offspring, rather than the family consisting of a man, wife and child, which should be considered the basic structural feature of the kinship systems of many African societies. Certainly in the majority of these societies the independence of the so-called "house" (Nguni: *indlu*; Sotho: *lapa*), formed around a wife and her children, is basic, not only to social and domestic arrangements within the wider family, but also to the development and internal differentiation of the lineage and lineage segment for which the family provides the growth point.

Whether the family has a simple legal or a compound form, each new marriage is seen as establishing the house of the woman concerned. She must be provided eventually with dwellings for herself and her children and with fields, a kitchen and a granary for the provision of food for the unit. Livestock, in particular cattle in the case of the Nguni, may be attached to the house and their issue remains as house property. It is the duty of a polygynist to treat each of his wives with utmost fairness and to allocate property to their houses equally. Once allocated, house property is inviolable and should be used only for the benefit of the children born to that house: it can be inherited by them alone. The Lobedu express this principle in the saying "houses do not eat one another".[1] ...

The principle of the independence of the house and the woman's control over its property puts a wife in an extremely strong position within the domestic group. Although the husband has the final say in any dispute, it is his duty to respect the wishes of his wives and not to impair their house property in any way. In this respect a wife in a compound family is probably in a stronger position than is the wife in a simple legal family where there may not be the same clear division and allocation of property.

The relationship of the constituent houses within the compound family is always formalized. Each wife and her accompanying house is ranked or graded with respect to her co-wives and their houses. The principles underlying the grading of houses vary slightly from society to society and may differ in the case of commoners and aristocrats. Order of marriage is one important factor in deciding a wife's status. Today, among Nguni commoners, it is the first wife married who takes the position of chief or great wife and it is her son who is the main heir and his father's successor in office. She has important ritual duties within the family and homestead and it is in her house that meat from sacrifices may be laid aside for the ancestors. Subsequent wives are ranked in order of their marriages.

Traditionally among the Zulu, it appears that the great wife might have been married only late in life. Certainly, in the case of a chief in many Nguni societies, the great wife is married only after he has assumed office. Theoretically her position and that of her first born son, his heir, are publicly proclaimed by the fact that the bridewealth is collected from the political group as a whole. ...

Ranking of wives may sometimes be affected by the social position of the woman herself. Should a Zulu man marry a woman of an aristocratic lineage she immediately takes precedence over any other wives he may have. Among the Pedi, a woman who is chosen from among the range of kinswomen preferred as mates should be elevated to the position of the great or ritual wife who bears the heir. Among the Lobedu and some other Sotho groups the uterine mother's brother's daughter is always the chief wife and, failing such a marriage, it is the woman acquired with the man's sister's cattle or by cattle provided by the father who assumes this position. Tswana rank wives in order of betrothal rather than on order of actual marriage and in most cases a wife married to replace another assumes the rank of her predecessor.

The grading of co-wives within large Nguni compound families is more complex than in the other Bantu-speaking groups. Wives are not only ranked but are linked together to form definite subsections within the overall family and homestead unit. These divisions are given expression in the physical layout of living quarters. With the exception of the Bhaca, who distinguish merely a great wife,[2] all Cape Nguni divide co-wives into two sections, each occupying its own side of the homestead. In the one are found the dwellings and kitchens of the "great wife"—usually the first wife to have been married by the polygynist. The other side of the homestead is the preserve of the "right-hand" wife, who is usually the second woman to be married. Any further wives are affiliated as "rafters" (Xhosa: *amaqadi*) to the sections of either of these principal wives and their houses are established on the side of the homestead controlled by their principal. Though subordinate to one of the main wives, the houses of women married after them are completely independent as far as house property is concerned. It is possible for a son in a subordinate house to inherit in the house of the main wife should she bear no heir but, unless this crisis occurs, the children of subordinate houses inherit only within their own unit.

Among the Natal Nguni the grading and organization of houses in the compound family are similar to the above except that, in the case of a very large family, three, instead of two, houses may be differentiated. At the top of the homestead opposite the main entrance is the principal dwelling, the *indlunkulu*. The mistress of this and its subsidiary wives and surrounding area is the chief wife. To the right of the *indlunkulu* section (as one looks towards the main entrance of the homestead) is situated the section of the left-hand (*ikhohlo*) wife and the third section, the *inqadi*, may be situated on the other side of the *indlunkulu*. Traditionally, the first wife married was eventually settled in the *ikhohlo* section, when the man took his great wife and established her in the *indlunkulu*. It is to one of these sections that any subsequent wives are attached. The *inqadi* section is really subordinate to the *indlunkulu* and may provide the heir should the great house fail to do so. Among the Nguni the *ikhohlo* section appears to be largely independent and can in fact move out of the main homestead as soon as a son is married and able to take responsibility for a separate unit. The pattern sketched above is seldom achieved today. Reader, writing of the Makhanya of southern Natal, states that the practice of establishing an *inqadi* section had fallen into disuse. The Makhanya spoke of only two houses, "the *indlunkulu* as the right, and strong arm; the *ikhohlo* as the left and weak one", and any further wives were affiliated to one of these houses. As Reader comments: "the *inqadi* ... is an institution which rested upon the economics of times of plenty which are gone, and political power which is no more".[3]

The position of the great wife and the general order of marriage does not necessarily involve a corresponding hierarchy in terms of authority, although it may do so.

E J Krige points out that amongst the Lobedu a chief wife, although she has important ritual and other duties, exercises no control over other wives. If the preferred wife of a man is one of his younger wives and one whom he has married only late in his life after marriage to other wives, she may be completely overshadowed by the more established women.[4] A similar situation obtains amongst the Pedi. In the case of the Nguni there appears to be more likelihood that senior wives will wield authority over junior wives. Among the Lobedu a wife married with cattle belonging to the house of another wife will be subordinate to her and will cook for her "like a daughter-in-law".

The grading of wives within the polygynous family is of great importance since it indicates unambiguously the rights and social position of the children of co-wives. The status of a man in the wider agnatic group may be contingent, furthermore, not only upon the place of his father in this descent group, but also, if his father is a polygynist, upon the status of his mother within the compound family.

Notes

1. Krige & Krige 175.
2. Hammond-Tooke 36.
3. Reader 61.
4. Krige & Krige 174.

Systems of polygyny have been classified into two general types—simple and complex—and the latter is further divisible into Southern Nguni and Zulu variants.[5] Under the simple system, which broadly pertains to the Sotho-Tswana peoples, a man has one main (or great) wife, who would normally be the first woman he married; the second wife is subordinate to her, and each subsequent wife is subordinate to her predecessor.[6]

In the complex system of polygyny, the division of the homestead is given far greater emphasis. According to the Southern Nguni version, a man's first wife is again the great wife, but the second wife establishes a separate section of the homestead, the right-hand side. A third wife is affiliated to the great-house side, a fourth wife to the right-hand side, and so forth.[7] Occasionally, and then only in royal families, a left-hand (xhiba) house may be instituted, but this ranks as an additional support to the great house.[8]

Similar principles are evident in the ranking of Zulu wives, although the actual position of the houses may not be the same because of a different orientation to left and right. The Codes distinguish the households of royalty and commoners. With the latter the first wife establishes a great-house section,[9] the second wife a left-hand (ikhohlo) section, and subsequent wives are affiliated to these two sections in order of marriage.[10] Chiefs may establish a third senior house, the iqadi, or right-hand house.[11] Traditionally, a chief's first wife would be a woman of his own choice. The second wife would be chosen in consultation with the people of the chiefdom, and she would be designated the great wife.[12] Custom determines a wife's rank, but her husband may vary it by a public declaration at the time of the wedding (or even later), provided that he does not upset the status of existing houses.[13]

In expositions of customary law, the polygynous structures described above are so pervasive that it is easy to lose sight of social reality: scarcely any modern households are in fact polygynous.[14] The divergence between law and reality prompts the question: should customary law not be changed to reflect present circumstances?[15] If the law is supposed to be grounded on contemporary social practice, then the monogamous family, the female-headed household, and the phenomenon of 'serial polygyny' (ie successive marriages) would be more

---

[5] Regarding the implications for succession, see below, 401ff. For diagram see: 404.

[6] *Maganu* 1938 NAC (N&T) 14; *Sijila v Masumba* 1940 NAC (C&O) 42; and Bekker 126, who cites Ramsay 9 and 26, claiming that only the Tsonga fall into this category. Bekker 132 claims that the Sotho-Tswana do not structure their homesteads according to a left/right opposition (with the implication that they have a simple system of polygyny). This may be true in individual cases (see, eg, Schapera *Married Life* 88–9) and for purposes of succession the concepts of left/right are not articulated: see below, 401–2. But this opposition is always evident in the layout of the homestead. Cf Mönnig 212ff.

[7] *Mndweza* 1937 NAC (C&O) 142 at 145.

[8] Soga 54; Cook *Social Organizations and Ceremonial Institutions of the Bomvana* 16; Van Tromp 95–7.

[9] Section 69.

[10] Section 68(1)*(b)*.

[11] Section 68(1)*(c)*.

[12] Krige 39. The same is true of the Southern Nguni: *Tyelinzima v Sangqu* 4 NAC 375 (1920) and Kerr 165ff.

[13] *Dungumuzi v Zuya* 1915 NHC 95; *Gcanga v Gcanga & another* 1949 NAC 137 (S); s 70–73 of the Natal and KwaZulu Codes. And see *Ntukwini v Miso* 1918 NHC 216.

[14] See above, 167.

[15] It is questionable whether polygyny was ever the norm. See Wilson in Krige & Comaroff *Essays on African Marriage in Southern Africa* 133–4 and 138–9.

appropriate models for legal development. As it is, the most common forms of social relationship are unregulated and many of the present rules of customary law are redundant, except in so far as some chiefly families and a few wealthy people are concerned.[16] It may be argued that there is nothing injurious in this obsolescent regime; the rules apply only to people who choose polygynous marriage. In other words, this is a matter of personal choice which the law should respect. But the argument overlooks the fact that the choice is the husband's and that polygyny endorses the subordinate position of women.

II THE RIGHTS AND DUTIES OF SPOUSES

The relationship of the spouses, and their relations with their children and families are governed by a complex code of customs, moral standards and beliefs, all of which tend to underwrite the principle of patriarchy.[17]

[71] SCHAPERA *A HANDBOOK OF TSWANA LAW AND CUSTOM* 150-1

Marriage effects a change in the legal and social status of both husband and wife. They form a separate family in the tribe, and in general play the part of full adult members of the community. The husband, as long as he continues to stay with his wife in the home of either his or her parents, is still to a considerable extent under the authority of the household-head. But once he sets up his own household, he is for all practical purposes his own master. The woman, on the other hand, passes from the legal control of her parents into that of her husband, who now becomes her guardian and as such responsible for her actions. He is the official head of the household, while she is regarded as his *motlhanka* (servant). She cannot as a rule sue or be sued except through him (or in certain cases, e.g. divorce proceedings, through her father or his legal representative); while if she does wrong he is generally held liable and must pay any fine or damages incurred. She can acquire property in her own right, but must consult her husband in all her business dealings. She must be in all respects subservient to his will, and must live wherever he chooses to build his home.

But, although a wife is thus under the legal tutelage of her husband, various rights and privileges must be accorded to her. It is his duty to protect her, and to treat her kindly and considerately; to cohabit with her regularly, subject, however, to the special taboos on sexual intercourse between married people; to provide her with a hut, food, clothing, and maintenance generally, and to assign fields, cattle, and other property to her house for her use. It is her duty in return to work for him and be faithful to him, to bear and nourish children for him, to cultivate her fields, and to prepare the food, and generally to occupy herself with the many domestic duties which family life entails. Neglect or refusal on the part of either husband or wife to carry out these duties leads almost invariably to domestic quarrels, and, if carried to an extreme, may give the other grounds for divorce.

The husband's power over his wife is by no means absolute. He may beat her if she has misconducted herself; but her own family's power, to which she can always appeal and flee, is generally an effective check against abuse of this right, while if he carries it to an extreme he may be punished at the *kgotla* [local court].

Customary law remains untouched by controversies (like marital rape and wife-battering) or even by the prosaic issues (like joint decision-making,

---

[16] See Murray *Families Divided* 116–18.
[17] See further Van Tromp 97–109; Mönnig 216–17; Holleman 202–11; Clerc (1938) 12 *Bantu Studies* 94ff; Poulter 167ff; Campbell (1970) 3 *CILSA* 328–31.

property sharing and the wife's freedom of movement) that have been topical in the common law. The only initiative to bring customary law into line with social practice was the Law Commission project of 1985.[18] This yielded two significant proposals: rights to maintenance should be governed by the common law[19] and the wife should be given full proprietary capacity.[20] Neither have yet been translated into legislation.

III PROPRIETARY CONSEQUENCES

[72] SCHAPERA *A HANDBOOK OF TSWANA LAW AND CUSTOM* 152–3

Both husband and wife are expected to take an active part in the economic life of the household. Every family as a rule has its own fields for cultivation, and its own cattle, goats, sheep, and other domestic animals. It is thus able to provide the bulk of its own food supply. The respective tasks of men and women in this connexion are clearly defined by the traditional division of labour between the sexes common to all the Tswana. The men and boys herd and milk the cattle, and also obtain meat by hunting; while the women are largely responsible for the care of the fields. In the olden days the men merely cleared the trees and bushes from the fields; the women then had to break up the soil with their hoes, plant the seed, remove the weeds, keep off the granivorous birds and other pests, and finally reap and thresh the crops. Since the introduction of the plough the men have taken a more considerable part in the work, notably in the ploughing itself, but most of it is still done by the women.

In addition to carrying out these subsistence activities, the members of a household build their own huts, both men and women having specified tasks to perform. The men do all the woodwork and erect the framework of the roof, while the women build the wall, thatch the roof, and smear on the mural decorations which are the pride of every self-respecting housewife. The women further build the homestead walls and granaries, plaster them and the huts with a mixture of earth and cowdung, keep the homestead clean and in good repair, stamp and grind the corn, prepare the food, fetch water and firewood, as well as the raw materials for their building and smearing activities, make conical baskets and the grass aprons of the small girls, mend and wash the clothes of the family, and look after the young children. Clay pots and certain kinds of basket are as a rule made by certain women only, the craft being handed down from mother to daughter in the same family. These women not only supply their own households, but sell their products to others less fortunately situated. The men cut wood and bushes for building and fencing, and for the manufacture of various wooden utensils, make sleds for transport purposes, bring wood and earth from afar for their wives when necessary, make certain kinds of basket, and from the skins of wild and domestic animals make a variety of objects, such as mats, karosses, riems, sandals, milksacks, bags, and (in the olden days) the clothing of the family. Wooden eating-bowls and stamping-blocks are generally made by special craftsmen from whom others must purchase them. So, too, all such iron goods as hoes, spears, and axes were formerly made by specialists, who sold their products for cattle or grain.

Both husband and wife are expected to perform the various tasks on behalf of their household which tribal life still imposes upon them. It is further the special duty of the

---

[18] *Marriages and Customary Unions of Black Persons.*

[19] Thereby allowing a clear substantive right (together with the appropriate procedural safeguards) in place of the vaguely conceived notions of customary law: clause 13 of the Working Paper. See below, 277ff on maintenance. While it is clear from clause 13(2) that this was intended to apply to the maintenance of children, there is nothing expressly excluding spouses from its ambit.

[20] With the implication that her acquisitions would not become house property: clause 7(6). See below, 232ff.

husband to provide his family with the necessities of life, including food, clothing, and household goods and chattels; he must give his wife land to cultivate, and procure cattle for milking and ploughing; and in these days when the range of goods regarded as essential to every decent household has increased so considerably as a result of contact with the Europeans, he must if necessary also go out to work so as to obtain the money with which to purchase them. Failure on his part to do all this, or failure on the part of the wife to carry out her special domestic tasks, almost invariably leads to trouble.

It may be noted here that there is no "community" of property between husband and wife. Any property a woman possesses at marriage, or acquires during the marriage, is never looked upon as part of the husband's estate, but must be looked after separately by him; and the wife has a full right and say in the disposal of such property. If there is a good understanding between husband and wife, he can freely use her cattle, but in doing so he is always bound to recognize that they actually belong to her and not to him. Such property can never be seized to pay the husband's debts. In case of divorce the wife is entitled to take it all back with her.

In the context of customary law, a category of 'proprietary consequences' sounds somewhat contrived. Customary law has (or at least had) no clearly conceived property law[21] and writers of the western legal tradition were hard pressed to find language appropriate to describe this aspect of the marriage relationship. The courts, however, could not afford to temporize. When they had to adjudicate claims put to them, in a typically pragmatic fashion they transposed their familiar common-law institutions, such as ownership, usufruct and trust,[22] on to the structure of the polygynous family. From this basis they elaborated three categories of property: house, family, and personal.[23]

[73] *SIJILA v MASUMBA* 1940 NAC (C&O) 42 at 44–7

The Native Custom of polygyny (plurality of wives), has resulted in at least two forms of establishments, the one, in which there is virtually one only one main wife, the others being all subordinate and subsidiary to her, a grouping which might be termed the "simple" establishment, the other is the "complex" establishment favoured by the Nguni tribes—the Zulu-Xhosa speakers—consisting of two or three main "houses" with ancillary "houses" dependent upon and subordinate to their major houses directly, the whole being under the control of the husband and kraalhead.

Under the "simple" establishment system the control and ownership vests directly in the head and in the son of his major wife on his death. The minor wives and the sons of their "huts" have no rights in the estate, beyond a right of maintenance, and in the case of sons, of lobola for their first wives.

Among the tribes practising this system women have far less share and say in administration of the estate, being themselves regarded as assets and "inherited" by the heir or some other favoured male relative of the deceased, who thereafter has the duty of supporting the women.

The universal heir has the burden of providing for the members of the family, who consequently are not concerned with the protection of personal rights. In a modified manner, a degree of possessory ownership has been created, as the replies of the Assessors in Maganu's estate indicate.

---

[21] This would seem to be the consequence of an economy that originally offered people a relative abundance of land and food for subsistence: Hunter 112ff and see below, 392ff.

[22] Whitfield 259.

[23] Section 1(1) of the Natal and KwaZulu Codes; *Zulu* 1955 NAC 107 (NE). See further: Holleman 211–14; Hunter 65–112; Schapera 214–29; Clerc op cit n17 103–4; Van Tromp 109–23; Poulter 172–5.

Notwithstanding this simplicity of control there is yet considerable restraint on the head of the family in regard to his management of the estate in his lifetime, for Native Law looks on him as a "father" of the family rather than the "owner" of the estate. It is a joint communal possession, containing in some instances ancestral property in which the senior males of the kraalhead's family and indirectly the ancestors are concerned. Hence, though the kraalhead is legal owner of the estate, his ownership is burdened with what we might call personal rights of various types of which maintenance and habitatio are two of the chief, subject to mutual corresponding duties on the part of the beneficiaries.

When we consider the "complex" establishment we find this simple conception complicated by the apportionment of the estate among the chief houses and their subsidiaries; and by a new form of succession and inheritance. The kraals are now not necessarily combined in one locality—indeed, it was the practice in olden days to spread out the kraals on different ridges, localities or even different districts—according to the rank and wealth of the kraalhead.

The immediate consequence of such a division and dispersion is that direct control by the kraalhead of the separate units of the estate is no longer possible, and the prospective heir and the wife of each unit, assuming the care, acquire a sense of proprietorship which tends to crystalise into a claim of ownership even in the lifetime of the kraalhead. (*Mfenqa vs Tshali* 1 NAC 31 (1900)). Until comparatively recently the influence of European conceptions of the rights of wives and widows tended to encourage the growth and recognition of these premature claims (*Mapoloba* 2 NAC 186 (1911); *Sonazi v Nosamana* 3 NAC 297 (1914); *Luke* 4 NAC 133 NAC (1920)). . . .

These decisions are quoted at length for they show more clearly than otherwise the relative power over and control of estate property—the heir is in no better position than his father and if the widow has no final say in affairs after the death of the husband she has no greater right during his life-time. Indeed, as now established, the widow has merely a right of maintenance. She has no property rights in the estate beyond this personal right of maintenance and habitatio. Yet the Courts have held in a series of cases that the husband lacks the right to impoverish one "house" at the expense of another; that if he does use the property appertaining to or apportioned to any house for the direct benefit of another he thereby incurs a debt as between those houses.

This principle has not been clearly evolved in practice. It is more clearly brought out in the Natal Code, but it exists in the Transkeian Territories usually in the instance of taking cattle from one house for the purpose of lobolaing another wife.

It was, however, decided by the Court that the Kraalhead may dispose of the produce of any one kraal for the general benefit of the whole family. (*Tshobo* 4 NAC 140 (1919).)

It is also an accepted principle of Native Law that a husband may use the stock of all or any of the houses to discharge a debt due by him.

Indeed, in regard to dealings with people outside of the family circle, no distinction is recognised, for a writ will be levied against all or any of the property of the kraalhead without the least concern for the claims of any of the individual houses of that kraal. In other words the law draws no distinction in regard to subsidiary rights in the estate of a Native, the kraalhead during his life-time is the person in whom the estate vests and who has control of it and dominium therein. (*Mfenqa v Tshali* 1 NAC 31.)

Coming to consider the subsidiary rights of the wife and her sons, we find that the Courts have recognised a right of action by a wife to restrain her husband from diverting property from her house to another without just cause; similarly the Court will restrain a husband from dissipating the assets of any one house without just cause. . . .

In Mfenqa's case above quoted the Court refused to recognise a right in the son of a house to what amounts to a claim for ownership in the stock apportioned to his mother's house. The view of the Magistrate was rejected that "the Plaintiff (the father), having handed over the stock to the second hut, merely retains his right over it as head of the family, but the part of this right has become vested in the *heirs* of the house". . . .

The whole of the foregoing exposition is, however, qualified by the conception in Native Law that the family is a unit composed of past and present members whose interests are jointly bound up with the family property (stock), and that the stock does not belong outright in individual ownership to the head of the family, but is held in trust by him as the "Head" of the whole family.

In the Native system of procedure it is the elders of the family, i.e. the elders and equals of the husband, who would see to it that the interests of the group are not abused. They would initiate action on behalf of any section of the family not adequately represented, as the assessors state.

It is when recourse is had to European Courts with a procedure foreign to the Native system that complication and confusion results. The European individualistic system regards one man as outright owner, and it is in deference to the principles of that system that the present day idea of personal ownership in a kraalhead has taken root.

Be that as it may, it is perfectly clear in either system that no rights *in rem* vest in an heir, major or minor, to the estate before the death of the father and he cannot seek during the father's life-time to maintain any suit affecting property rights of the house of his mother.

(1) House property

According to the case law, house property includes the following categories.

(a) Gifts to the wife and her earnings

The general view, originating in a Transkei decision *Sixakwe v Nonjoli*,[24] is that

'whatever a woman may earn after her marriage belongs to the husband. This is subject to the condition that he may not divert such earnings from the house to which she belongs or dispose of them in any way without consulting her.'[25]

Only if the husband himself made a gift to his wife, would it become her personal property.[26] An exception to this rule was made in the case of a wife living apart from her husband; it was held in two decisions that her earnings would not accrue to him.[27] In the first case the court distinguished *Sixakwe*, but it avoided an investigation of the wife's property rights by treating the matter as a problem of spoliation.[28] In both instances the separation was apparently indefinite or permanent.[29]

In addition to earnings, the goods or cattle customarily given to a bride by her father when she marries, have been deemed house property.[30] With the Zulu, for example, an important gift is the mbeka beast, a symbol of the woman's family and its ancestors.[31] The Xhosa-speaking peoples have a similar institution, the

---

[24] 1 NAC 11 (1896).

[25] *Nomtwebulo v Ndumndum* 2 NAC 121 (1911); *Tantsi v Tabalaza* 4 NAC 107 (1922); *Fanekiso v Sikade* 5 NAC 178 (1925) at 180; *Mpantsha v Ngolonkulu & another* 1952 NAC 40 (S). Similar rulings emanated from the Transvaal, *Mkwanazi* 1945 NAC (N&T) 112 at 114, and Natal, *Nhlabati v Lubungu* 1907 NHC 52. Cf Mönnig 341 and Poulter 176.

[26] *Monelo v Nole* 1 NAC 102 (1906) and *Mpafa v Sindiwe* 4 NAC 268 (1919).

[27] *Majomboyi & another v Nobeqwa* 2 NAC 63 (1911); *Logose v Yekiwe* 4 NAC 105 (1919).

[28] See further Simons *African Women* 195–8.

[29] The position in Natal and KwaZulu is governed by ss 13, 19, 20 and 78 of the Codes, discussed in: *Masuku v Kunene* 1940 NAC (N&T) 79. See also *Mpungose v Shandu* 1956 NAC 180 (NE) and *Ntombela & another v Ntombela* 1960 NAC 79 (NE).

[30] Section 78 of the Codes.

[31] Krige 137; *Ntamane v Nkosi* 1935 NAC (N&T) 20; *Makikane* 1936 NAC (N&T) 63; *Vilakazi v Nkambule* 1944 NAC (N&T) 57; *Mtshali v Mhlongo* 1944 NAC (N&T) 71; *Mkwanazi* 1945 NAC (N&T) 112; *Butelezi v Mtetwa* 1952 NAC 22 (NE); *Mpungose's* case supra; *Sithole & another v Sithole* 1967 BAC 18 (NE).

ubulunga beast, but for reasons which have never been altogether clear, it was (initially at least) not treated in the same way. Scholarly opinion claimed that this 'beast with its progeny remains the "personal" property of the wife and can never become the property of the husband';[32] but the courts were for some time undecided. In *Siduli v Nopoti*[33] it was held that

'under all circumstances a married woman, whether continuing in bonds of matrimony or a widow, is entitled to possession of the *"ubulungu"* beast. . . . [S]he is entitled to take it with her wherever she may elect to go.'[34]

This view was supported by a decision that the wife's son (not her husband) was entitled to inherit the ubulunga beast when she died.[35] In another decision,[36] however, the court held that on dissolution of marriage the wife's *father* could claim it.[37] The balance of authority eventually came down in favour of the view that the ubulunga beast is the property of the husband. This was established in the following judgment where the previous cases were reviewed.

[74] *MBOLO v NOMANDI* 1930 15 PH R1

In earlier times . . . [t]he woman to whom an "Ubulunga" beast was given at the time or during the subsistence of her marriage or widowhood was entitled to its possession and could take it with her wherever she went. The animal and its progeny remained the property of her father's kraal and the husband did not acquire any ownership in them.

Nowadays, owing to some extent to contact with European civilisation, the custom has lost much of its meaning and sacredness and the Courts acting on the opinions of Native Chiefs and other authorities on Native Custom have decided quite definitely that although the wife to whom an "Ubulunga" beast is given has an interest in it and its progeny, and although the husband cannot divert them from her house to that of another wife without her consent, the *dominium* in them is vested in him, and on his death they form part of his estate and become the property of his heir.

Van Tromp disagreed completely with this decision,[38] questioning the reliability of the expert advice given by the chiefs. But unfortunately *Mbolo's* case has been ratified in many later judgments.[39] The only hope of overruling it

---

[32] Van Tromp 114.

[33] 1 NAC 20 (1897).

[34] *Siwangobuso v Ngindana* 1 NAC 142 (1907); *Tshaka v Buyesweni* 1 NAC 144 (1907); *Jakavula v Melane* 2 NAC 89 (1910) and *Jonas v Mhlekwa* 3 NAC 284 (1916).

[35] *Nomanti v Zangqingqi* 3 NAC 283 (1913).

[36] *Jelani v Mrauli* 2 NAC 54 (1910).

[37] But not its progeny, which the husband could keep: *Joko v Gqirana* 3 NAC 285 (1913); *Tengela v Madi* 1964 BAC 35 (S) at 38.

[38] Page 117.

[39] It was quoted with approval in *Rarabe* 1937 NAC (C&O) 229 at 232 and followed in: *Pasiya v Skade* 1942 NAC (C&O) 116; *Kilasi v Matshaka* 1944 NAC (C&O) 99; *Zilwa v Gagela* 1954 NAC 101 (S). In addition see: *Nomanti v Zangqingqi* 3 NAC 283 (1913); *Malinde v Mpinda* 4 NAC 364 (1918); *Sigogo v Nogaya* 1936 NAC (C&O) 105; Olivier 159–61 and Koyana *Customary Law in a Changing Society* 55–9.

lies in the enactment of the Law Commission proposals on customary marriages.[40]

(b) Acquisitions by other inmates

The general rule is that all property acquired by a minor accrues to the house to which he or she is affiliated. Hence the court, in *Kuzwayo v Khuluse*,[41] held that a minor 'can acquire no personal private rights in that property on obtaining majority or on marriage'.[42] A family head will no doubt allow his son to keep certain goods. But in a case where, in time of need, the son returned what had been given to his father, it was held that this should not be construed as a loan because the property had belonged to the father in the first place.[43]

Translated into common-law terms, this rule means that a minor has no real rights in anything he or she earns or acquires. Dominium vests in the head of the family who may dispose of the property as he sees fit.[44] The Natal and KwaZulu Codes introduced some qualification by requiring the family head to utilize minors' income 'primarily for the maintenance and benefit of the house . . . and for general family purposes'.[45] To this end unreasonable conduct is subject to administrative scrutiny.[46]

(c) Bridewealth received for daughters in a house

Bridewealth received from the marriage of a daughter accrues to the daughter's house. This rule has been incorporated into the Natal and KwaZulu Codes.[47] It is quite likely, however, that incoming bridewealth will immediately have to be disbursed to settle outstanding debts.[48]

(d) Fines and damages

There is plenty of case authority for the proposition that the fines or damages received in respect of unmarried daughters, especially seduction damages, should be treated as house property.[49] It would seem logical to extend this rule to

[40] While clause 7(1) of the Bill appended to the Report on *Marriages and Customary Unions of Black Persons* provided that the legal consequences of a customary marriage should be governed by customary law, clause 7(6) allowed a wife full capacity to acquire, possess and dispose of property in her own name, without her husband's assistance. None of this property would accrue to her house without her consent, and it seems that the ubulunga beast could be subsumed under this provision.

[41] 1951 NAC 321 (NE).

[42] *Mkwanazi v Zulu* 1938 NAC (N&T) 258; *Sitole* 1945 NAC (N&T) 50. This follows the Transkeian ruling in *Mtungata v Qemba* 4 NAC 104 (1919).

[43] *Njeyana v Sekgobela* 1939 NAC (N&T) 83 at 84; cf *Ngqulunga* 1947 NAC (N&T) 84 and Marwick 67. Cf n77 below.

[44] *Mfazwe v Modikayi* 1939 NAC (C&O) 18 at 22. See further *Mofokeng* 1948 NAC (C&O) 20; Mönnig 341; Marwick 47 and 67; and Poulter 174ff.

[45] Section 19.

[46] Section 19(3). See below, 236–7.

[47] By s 1(1) definition of 'house property'; *Tshozi* 1941 NAC (N&T) 92; *Mpungose* 1946 NAC (N&T) 37. See too: Schapera 218; Poulter 173; Marwick 46; Mönnig 341. Cf Venda law: *Maganu* 1938 NAC (N&T) 14 at 15; Bekker 73; Olivier 142.

[48] *Fanekiso v Sikade* 5 NAC 178 (1925) at 180.

[49] Bekker 72–3; *Mbongwana v Ngolozela & another* 3 NAC 256 (1912); *Ngema* 1933 NAC (N&T) 3 at 5; *Phefo v Raikane* 1942 NAC (N&T) 16; *Sikwikwikwi v Ntwakumba* 1948 NAC 23 (S) at 24.

include any damages received for the inmates of a house.[50]

(e) Household effects

Pots, utensils, sleeping mats, and the domestic apparel which a wife brings with her when she marries, are normally deemed to belong to her personally.[51] In certain urban communities this type of property has increased greatly in value and now ideally includes full bedroom and kitchen suites.[52] Any furniture, cooking utensils, crockery etc, which is acquired while the woman is married, however, becomes house property and falls under the control of the husband.[53]

(f) Allotted property

Apart from the property listed above (which accrues to a house automatically), the family head may specifically allot property to a particular house.[54] Rights to agricultural land in the rural areas is a significant item in this category.[55]

(g) Unallotted property

In the usual case this would be family property, but according to the assessors in *Fanekiso v Sikade*,[56] 'all property not otherwise allotted belongs to the Great House'.[57] By implication, among the Southern Nguni at least, there can be no general estate of 'family property' because any property not accounted for accrues to the great house.[58] It is questionable, however, whether this ruling reflects an authentic version of customary law. In *Tshemese*,[59] for example, the court held that the family head is 'entitled and morally bound to make suitable provision for the maintenance of all his houses', and that maintenance is payable from the property found in the great house. Hence

> 'there seems to be a clear distinction between property acquired by the great house from the earnings of inmates and fines and lobolo received for its daughters, and property which accrues to the great house from other sources. The latter type of property is *very near to being family home property*.'[60]

---

[50] See Olivier 142 regarding adultery damages, and Kerr 160.

[51] And in consequence can be reclaimed by her family on dissolution of the marriage. See: Poulter 175–9; Holleman 355; Hunter 119; and *Ngema* 1942 NAC (N&T) 27.

[52] Burman in Hirschon *Women and Property/Women as Property* 128.

[53] *Sechabela v Mahlafuna* 1944 NAC (N&T) 64 at 66. See also Hunter 130 and Mönnig 341.

[54] See the definition of 'house property' in s 1(1) of the Natal and KwaZulu Codes and: *Sivanjana* 3 NAC 27 (1915); *Bulose* 1916 NHC 164; *Fanekiso v Sikade* 5 NAC 178 (1925); *Mguguli* 1966 BAC 53 (S); Schapera 218; Poulter 173.

[55] In *Soni* 1951 NAC 366 (NE) at 368, the court noted that although the concept of 'individual ownership' of land was originally not known in customary law, it has now become generally accepted and is recognized in the Natal Code. Accordingly it was held that immovables can form house property. Also see *Dodo v Sabasaba* 1945 NAC (C&O) 62 and Poulter 173.

[56] 5 NAC 178 (1925) at 180.

[57] *Sivanjana* 3 NAC 27 (1915); *Kapari v Possa* 5 NAC 164 (1926); *Mtsholozi & another v Rivibi* 1932 NAC (C&O) 23.

[58] Bekker 134.

[59] 4 NAC 143 (1921) at 145.

[60] (Italics added) Bekker 74. See generally in this regard: *Mqotyana v Sihange* 4 NAC 134 (1920); *Fanekiso v Sikade* 5 NAC 178 (1925); *Kapari v Possa* 5 NAC 164 (1926); *Masango* 1938 NAC (N&T) 38; *Zamela* 1944 NAC (C&O) 20; *Qwabe* 1945 NAC (N&T) 101; *Magubane* 1948 NAC (N&T) 29; *Mhlungu* 1950 NAC 192 (NE).

House property is supposed to be used for the common good of the family. Accordingly, while individual claims to it might be recognized, the interests of the family as a whole predominate.[61] The principle of patriarchy authorizes the head of the family to articulate these wider interests by giving him powers of administration and control.[62] Section 20 of the Natal and KwaZulu Codes explicitly endows him with 'charge, custody and control of the property attaching to the houses of his several wives'.[63] This means that he may 'in his discretion use the same for his personal wants and necessities, or for general family purposes'.[64] His first obligation is to use house property to maintain the wife and children of the house concerned.[65] In the second instance, it should be used to settle the first wife's bridewealth debt or to provide bridewealth for the oldest son of the house[66] and, thirdly, to furnish a daughter with her trousseau.[67] Fourthly, any damages or fines due in respect of wrongs committed by inmates must be satisfied from this source.[68]

Customary law imposes only one limitation on the family head's powers: he may not divert property from one house to another without creating an obligation upon the recipient household to repay the debt.[69] And before he shifts house property, he is obliged (morally it would seem) to consult the wife of the house affected, together with the oldest son, if he is sufficiently mature.[70] Any breach of these obligations is taken very seriously. It would either provide a good reason for divorce or give the aggrieved wife a right to sue her husband unassisted.[71]

Unfortunately the law has not been developed any further than this. What if the head of the family were to dissipate family property through negligence or incompetence? Only under the Natal and KwaZulu Codes is any provision made for such a situation. Minors (and presumably wives) may initiate an 'administrative enquiry' via a district officer or chief in cases where the family head had acted unreasonably in exercising his powers to dispose of a minor's earnings for purposes of supporting the relevant house. As a result of this hearing, the head of the family head may be ordered to desist; failure to obey

---

[61] Holleman 320 and s 19 of the Natal and KwaZulu Codes.

[62] *Tshobo & another v Tshobo* 4 NAC 142 (1920).

[63] Marwick 46; cf Mönnig 341.

[64] Section 20. See also *Sitole* 1945 NAC (N&T) 50 and *Ngcobo* 1946 NAC (N&T) 14.

[65] *Sekeleni v Sekeleni & others* (1904) 21 SC 118; *Meleni v Mandlangisa* 2 NAC 191 (1911); *Mavayeni* 5 NAC 91 (1927); *Tonose* 1936 NAC (C&O) 103; *Phalane v Lekoane* 1939 NAC (N&T) 132; *Sijila v Masumba* 1940 NAC (C&O) 42; *Mbekushe v Dumiso* 1941 NAC (C&O) 57.

[66] *Tala v Matobane* 1 NAC 149 (1907); *Mti v Mvacane & another* 3 NAC 56 (1915); *Mboqoka v Sibudu* 1934 NAC (C&O) 3; *Jeliza v Nyamende & another* 1945 NAC (C&O) 34; *Khemane v Ned* 1948 NAC 15 (S); *Rubushe v Jiyane* 1952 NAC 69 (S); *Cheche v Nondabula* 1962 NAC 23 (S). See also Hunter 122 and Krige 179.

[67] Bekker 75 and 147; Olivier 138.

[68] *Mlati v Mabale* 1937 NAC (N&T) 86; *Mlanjeni v Macala* 1947 NAC (C&O) 1. See generally Bekker 74–7 and Olivier 151ff.

[69] *Sijila v Masumba* 1940 NAC (C&O) 42 at 45; *Mbuli* 1939 NAC (N&T) 85; and ss 20 and 21 of the Natal and KwaZulu Codes.

[70] *Fanekiso v Sikade* 5 NAC 178 (1925). See also: Holleman 208; Mönnig 216 and 341; Reader 161; Hunter 121; Poulter 174–5. Cf Van Tromp 110.

[71] *Noseki v Fubesi* 1 NAC 36 (1900); *Nosentyi v Makonza* 1 NAC 37 (1900); *Sijila v Masumba* 1940 NAC (C&O) 42; Poulter 175.

would be deemed a criminal offence.[72] Section 30(1) has an even broader provision: if a family head were to act 'foolishly or prodigally' in respect of family/house property, and if after an administrative enquiry by a district officer he were found unfit for his position, he might be suspended. A complaint can be made by any person with an interest in the matter.[73]

The main issue that needs to be addressed in South Africa is whether the remedies—removal from office or divorce—are not too drastic. Would it not be advisable to augment them by allowing family members real rights in house property? This would entail the use of proprietary actions in customary law which have advantages over the cruder remedies of family law: an aggrieved person could recover his/her property without (possibly permanently) rupturing domestic relations. If this proposal were accepted, a problematic implication would be the type of rights that the individual should be allowed. Full-scale dominium would undermine the family interest in property. But no doubt there are lesser rights that are, much like those elaborated in West Africa, more in harmony with the African family ethic. These include rights to pro rata shares in produce, rights of ingress to and egress from land, and the right to be consulted when alienation of family property is proposed.[74]

(2) Family property/general estate
The following property falls into this category.

(a) Acquisitions of the family head
The earnings, or property bought with the earnings[75] of the family head, together with his inheritances,[76] accrue to the general estate. This rule follows from his position in the household: he is not an inmate of a particular house and so his property does not fall into a house. Conversely, gifts by the family head to inmates are considered to be house property, subject, while he is alive, to his control. On his death, the gift forms part of the estate of the son to whom it was given.[77]

(b) Property in an heirless house
While the head of the family is alive, any property acquired by a house is generally deemed to be house property. When he dies, property in a house without an heir becomes family property, to be inherited by the general heir.[78]

---

[72] Section 19(3).
[73] Section 30(2). Ghanaian customary law also used to entertain only one remedy against the head of a family; aside from a petition to have him removed from office, he was immune from suit. This rule can be traced to Sarbah *Fanti Customary Laws* 90; it was taken up by the courts in *Abude & others v Onane & others* (1946) 12 WACA 102 at 104. The rule was only recently repealed by the Head of the Family Accountability Law of 1985. See Daniels (1987) 31 *JAL* 103ff and Kludze (1987) 31 *JAL* 107ff.
[74] See Obi *Modern Family Law in Southern Nigeria* 57ff.
[75] *Ndayimana v Nkunzini* 1913 (1) NHC 151.
[76] *Butelezi* 1942 NAC (N&T) 74.
[77] *Mhlungu* 1950 NAC 192 (NE).
[78] *Mvundhla* 1940 NAC (N&T) 72; *Radebe* 1943 NAC (N&T) 54; *Vundla* 1960 NAC 47 (NE).

(c) Bridewealth

The Venda regard bridewealth received for daughters as family property because it does not accrue to a particular house.[79]

Under the influence of English law, and with implicit reference to the common-law concept of the corporation,[80] the courts in Ghana and Nigeria have done much to develop the concept of family property. This has involved detailed consideration of the following issues: the creation and termination of family estates; the person(s) entitled to object to the alienation of family property; when and how objections may be brought; the consequences of leaving the family; and the standards expected of those in positions of control. The result has been a clear delimitation of individual rights in relation to the family interest. In view of increased commercial dealing in capital assets (especially land), and the enhanced earning power of family members, direct judicial intervention of this nature has made a valuable contribution to the advancement of customary law. By contrast, in South Africa conceptual categories were fixed at the turn of the century and the courts have not seriously contemplated the creative development of customary law since then. The category of family property was formulated in opposition to house property with one major purpose in mind: to ensure the separation of heritable estates. The consequence of this conservative approach has been the suppression of individual rights in favour of an unmitigated regime of patriarchy.

(3) Personal property

In customary law, as a general rule, property of an intimate nature, which would serve the interests of the individual only, was deemed to be personal property. It could be used and disposed of without reference to the needs of anyone else. Given the economic circumstances of most societies in preconquest southern Africa, there was little opportunity (or indeed inclination) to amass such property. The most important items were wearing apparel, adornments, tools and weapons.[81] Productive property, especially large livestock, inevitably attracted the interest of others, and so was assimilated to the categories of house or family property. This tendency found expression in a legal presumption that 'ownership in all cattle within the kraal vests in the kraalhead' until the contrary is proved.[82]

The use or function of property provides a prima facie basis for its classification as family/house property on the one hand, or personal property on the other. The reasons for giving certain items furnish additional clues. For

[79] *Maganu* 1938 NAC (N&T) 14. Moreover, according to Olivier 144, bridewealth returned to the husband's family on dissolution of the marriage also falls into the general estate. They refer to *Tabeta & another v Mabuza* 1937 NAC (N&T) 87 in support of this proposition, but in this case there was only one wife and so the question whether the refunded cattle were house property or not was not in issue.

[80] Lloyd *Yoruba Land Law* 76ff; Kasunmu & James *Alienation of Family Property in Southern Nigeria* 3; Coker *Family Property among the Yorubas* chs 1 and 2.

[81] Holleman 320. So far as the wife is concerned, this rule is supported in: *Yimba* 1940 NAC (N&T) 35; *R v Njokweni* 1946 NPD 400; *Xakaxa v Mkize* 1947 NAC (N&T) 85; *Mpungose v Shandu* 1956 NAC 180 (NE); *Dhlamini* 1967 BAC 7 (NE). The wedding outfit, surprisingly, does not belong to the bride; this is her husband's property: *Mokoena v Mofokeng* 1945 NAC (C&O) 89 at 90. As regards other members of the family, see: Hunter 119; Poulter 175 and Marwick 67.

[82] *Cili* 1935 NAC (N&T) 32 at 33 and see Cook op cit n8 153–4.

example, there is a widespread convention that a bridegroom must give his mother-in-law a beast (in Zulu known as the ngquthu beast) when he consummates his marriage. This is a tribute to her and the female shades of her family.[83] Not surprisingly, the courts have subsumed this under the category of personal property,[84] to be used as the woman sees fit.[85] Similarly, the Transkeian courts have spoken of a 'calabash beast', which was defined as 'an animal given from the dowry of a daughter to the girl's mother'; the woman was accorded full rights in this beast and its progeny during her lifetime.[86]

Gifts and allocations of property made by those in positions of authority as marks of their favour or patronage or in order to assist juniors to establish their independence are more difficult to categorize.

[75] SCHAPERA *A HANDBOOK OF TSWANA LAW AND CUSTOM* 216–21

The acquisition of cattle by gift is fairly common. Every man should, during his lifetime, under the *go tshwaisa* custom, allocate to his unmarried sons cattle and other livestock as their own property. A wealthy man will give his sons many cattle, the eldest receiving proportionately most, the others according to their order of seniority; but commoners, if they can manage it, generally set aside a heifer for each of their sons, which with its offspring then belongs to that son. The allocation must be formally made before witnesses, so that there shall be no subsequent doubt as to the ownership of these cattle. Chiefs and other prominent men often hand over one or more servants to a son; this carries with it the implication that the cattle these servants are herding now belong to that son. Among the Kgatla a man may also set aside a field for one of his immature sons, and use some of its corn to purchase cattle; these are then regarded as belonging to that son. Should a father not provide in such ways for his son, he is expected when the latter marries to give him one or more heifers to start a herd of his own.

Daughters may be given cattle in the same way as sons, but this is not often done. More usually daughters, if they receive anything at all, will be given goats, with whose offspring cattle may afterwards be purchased for them. But, among the Ngwato and Kgatla, a woman on marriage commonly receives from her father, if he can afford it, one or more heifers as *ketêêtsô* or *serotwana*. She may subsequently be given other cattle of her own by her husband; and she also receives one beast from the *bogadi* paid for her daughter. An unmarried woman who is a concubine may likewise be presented with cattle by her lover.

A man can obtain cattle by gift from other people besides his parents. Formerly, when a boy came out of the initiation ceremony, his maternal uncle and other relatives were expected to give him cattle *go mo alosa*, to welcome him back. They can ... make him similar gifts at any other time if they wish. . . .

The cattle owned by a married woman are kept at the cattle post of her husband or guardian. They do not form part of his general estate, but are inherited by her own children. She has, however, much less control over her cattle than a man has over his. She cannot dispose of them without her husband's permission and through his agency, since they are kept at his cattle post and he looks after them. If she wants anything, she must therefore ask him to sell an ox for her. He may refuse to do so, but if his refusal is

---

[83] See Krige 391 (regarding terminology); Berglund *Zulu Thought-patterns and Symbolism* 206–9; Holleman 182.

[84] *Mpongo v Mandlela & another* 3 NAC 34 (1913); s 67(2) of the Natal and KwaZulu Codes. In addition see *Mohlakula v Elizabeth* 1 NAC 56 (1902).

[85] Therefore it does not become house property: *Qulo* 1940 NAC (N&T) 4 at 5; *Mpungose v Shandu* 1956 NAC 180 (NE); *Mbanjwa* 1964 BAC 122 (NE); *Khanyile d/a v Zulu* 1966 BAC 35 (NE); *Ndebele* 1971 BAC 70 (NE); *Mbutho v Cele d/a* 1975 BAC 247 (NE); *Mpungose v Zulu* 1981 AC 50 (NE).

[86] *Mkwenkwana v Teyisi* 3 NAC 35 (1912). And under Gcaleka custom it was heritable by her second son.

unreasonable she can appeal to other members of the family or to the headman of the ward. The money obtained from the sale of this beast belongs to her, but she should give some of it to her husband. The husband, in turn, may not dispose of his wife's cattle without her consent, although if there is a good understanding between them he can use the cattle pretty freely.

A divorced wife takes her own cattle back to her parental home. Her husband, however, is generally entitled to keep back any cattle he has himself given her, both for the use of her house and as her private property (*mphô*, gift); while if she has any children she must leave her cattle behind to be inherited by them. But cattle given by a man to his concubine (*nyatsi*) are her absolute property, and he cannot take them back even if she deserts him.

Any cattle belonging to an unmarried son or daughter remain under the father's control. The child has no right to give away, sell, lend, or otherwise dispose of them without his consent. Should the child require anything, he may ask his father to sell an ox for him, but the latter may refuse if he thinks it unnecessary for the animal to be used in this way. The father, on the other hand, may use the cattle as he thinks fit on behalf of the child. But should he dispose of them for his own ends he is expected to replace them. Once a son is married, and sets up his own household, he obtains full control of his cattle and can do with them as he likes.

Among the Ngwaketse, it was formerly the rule that no young member of the tribe could own separately an animal acquired as the result of his labours. Tribal custom decreed that it belonged to his father. The discipline of the tribe has been largely destroyed by the stopping of the initiation schools, and the younger members found themselves with a new outlook, wanting to own cattle, but not under the control of their fathers or elder brothers. As a result of being unable to own cattle they spent their wages earned at the diamond mines, or at the Rand, on "swagger" suits, watches, or other articles of little use to them. The Chief (Seepapitso) saw the effect of these changes and had a law passed making it possible for any one to hold cattle in separate ownership.

Wage labour has obviously had a profound impact on the economic relations of the family, tending to 'personalize' property in the sense that it encourages the individual to retain what he or she has earned.[87] Until recently, however, there was scarcely any ethnographic evidence of its effects on domestic relations in South Africa. The following gives a very brief account.

[76] MÖNNIG *THE PEDI* 342

The whole conception of personal property and the right to enter into contracts with regard to such property has been altered by the introduction of money into the economic system of the Pedi. It has influenced not so much the position of married women as of minor children. Any money obtained by a married woman through her earnings or by exchange which is brought into the household is considered to be household property over which the husband has control. But the individualistic conception is seen in the fact that women earning money may spend at least a portion of this at their own discretion on receiving their earnings and before returning to the homestead. Minor children, who, under basic Pedi law had no contractual ability, may use at least a portion of their earnings, and any modern commodities that they buy in this manner are regarded as their personal property, which they may dispose of without consulting their father. But once such money earned by children is brought into the homestead, or has been converted into traditional commodities, or particularly if it has been exchanged for cattle, the father again obtains control.

Courts in the 1930s and 1940s were reluctant to give effect to these social changes. They thought that if they interfered with the family head's control over

---

[87] Holleman 322–3.

property it might have the effect of depriving minors of 'that valuable asset in Native Law of Communal support, especially in the provision of a wife'.[88] Hence they were careful not to detract from patriarchal privileges.

[77] *MLANJENI V MACALA* 1947 NAC (C&O) 1–2

The Assessors further stated that if a son buys stock and earmarks them for himself or if the father earmarks stock for his son, the father can, during his lifetime and while the son is living at his kraal, use the stock for his own purposes against the wish of the son and without incurring any liability to replace them; but if the son establishes his own kraal, he can compel the father to deliver to him such stock as may still be in existence, although the father is not obliged to replace stock he has disposed of.

There can be no doubt that this statement of Pondo Law is correct and apparently it is also the law of other Native tribes in the Transkeian Territories, where the basic principles of Native Law in general regard the family as a collective unit with joint responsibilities and assets. All property accruing to members of the family goes into a common pool and is administered by the kraalhead; liabilities incurred by members of the kraal are satisfied from such property. The family unit thus resembles a partnership of which the head of the kraal is the manager. The difference is that in a partnership the relationship between the partners is based on agreement, whereas in the family unit the relationship is based on Native custom. It is usual for a son to send his earnings home for the general support of the family, but sometimes the father or head of the kraal is asked to buy stock for the son. The father is not obliged to do so, but if he does, such stock will generally be earmarked for the son, or the father may earmark some of his own stock for the son. In Native Law this does not mean that the ownership of such stock vests in the son; the right to dispose of such stock still remains with the father; all the son acquires is a special interest in such stock, for although the concept of individual ownership is unknown in basic Native Law, a special interest in property allotted to or acquired by an inmate of a kraal is recognised. It is customary for the head to consult the major inmates of his kraal before property is alienated. If the head and the inmates cannot agree, the will of the head prevails. If an inmate still resists the head, he will most probably be given the stock and be expelled from the kraal, but few Natives care to incur such displeasure. The result is that the inmates generally accept the proposals of the kraalhead, especially so as provision is generally made for the replacement of specially earmarked stock out of the dowries of daughters or otherwise. [See *Sandlana v Mdibaniso* 1939 NAC (C&O) 146.]

As the law stands at present, women are allowed outright ownership only in property that is customarily given for ritual purposes[89] and a man acquires full proprietary capacity (and hence the potential of amassing property of his own) only when he establishes an independent homestead. The courts have done nothing more to expand the category of personal property relative to house or family property. Instead, full legal capacity has been taken to be the qualification for acquiring property rights, and in so far as women and junior men lack full capacity, they have been denied real rights.

When the Transkeian Territories were annexed,[90] it was provided that all persons over the age of 21 would become majors. The same provision was later enacted in the Age of Majority Act[91] and the Natal and KwaZulu

---

[88] *Mfazwe v Modikayi* 1939 NAC (C&O) 18. And see: *Ngqulunga* 1947 NAC (N&T) 84. See below, [114].

[89] See *Malaza v Mndaweni* 1975 BAC 45 (C) at 62.

[90] Section 39 of Procs 110 and 112 of 1879 and s 38 of Proc 140 of 1885.

[91] 57 of 1972.

Codes.[92] In *Mlanjeni v Macala*,[93] the court held that the concept of the age of majority introduced 'individual ownership of property as opposed to family ownership',[94] a debatable conclusion. Majority gives family members the *power* to hold property; it does not confer on them *rights* opposable against the head of the family. In other words, the law of persons cannot cure the deficiencies of the law of property. At best, this type of reform can liberate people to engage in commercial and other dealings outside the family; it cannot protect their acquisitions from other family members.

Because individuals have no real rights to the property they earn or acquire, they must claim their support from the head of the family. In the result, a person's material needs must be satisfied by a claim for maintenance, a right operable in personam. If he or she were given real rights in any property acquired, this would take account of changed economic relationships in the family, especially the tendency towards greater individualism.[95]

---

[92] Section 14, as read with the definition of 'personal property' (included in the definition of 'family property' in s 1(1)). See too *Dhlamini* 1960 NAC 49 (NE).

[93] 1947 NAC (C&O) 1.

[94] *Ndema* 1936 NAC (C&O) 15.

[95] See below, 394–5.

CHAPTER 6

Dissolution of Marriage

I DIVORCE AND THE STABILITY OF MARRIAGE

For all practical purposes, divorce is the only time that matrimonial rights and duties need to be defined. While relationships are not under threat, there is no need for definition; but 'the moment one or other interested party seeks to dissolve a particular union prior to its natural end' the distribution of rights and duties becomes a critical issue.[1] Then, through competing constructions, each of the parties tries to achieve the most favourable settlement.

Most works on customary law avoid using the word 'divorce' in order not to confuse customary and common law;[2] they use instead a less culturally specific term, 'dissolution'. Unfortunately, this is a generic term that does not distinguish two separate situations: where the marriage is ended through causes outside the parties' control and where the parties themselves put an end to their relationship. For the latter situation, divorce remains a useful descriptive term.

Nevertheless, common- and customary-law divorce processes should not be confused. There are at least three distinguishing features. First, unlike a civil or Christian marriage, the customary marriage can be prolonged beyond the death

---

[1] Comaroff & Roberts (1977) 21 *JAL* 114–15.
[2] Cotran & Rubin *Readings in African Law* v2 209.

of one of the spouses by levirate and sororate unions. Secondly, the common-law marriage may be terminated inter vivos only by decree of the state, acting through a court. It follows that a couple may dissolve their union de jure only on terms prescribed by the state. In principle, divorce is not a private, consensual arrangement,[3] although it must be conceded that the courts are often circumvented in certain important issues (such as the division of the estate, maintenance, and child custody) which are arranged by pre-trial contracts between the spouses. The courts ratify these as a mere formality[4] by implication allowing the rules regarding division of the estate and custody/guardianship to be contractually waived.

In customary law, by way of contrast, the termination of marriage can be negotiated by the spouses and their families. They are free to settle on any terms they choose and reference to a court is necessary only if they cannot agree. Freedom of manoeuvre is somewhat restricted by the possibility of having to refund bridewealth, which is partly determined by considerations of fault. Hence although there are no *grounds* for divorce in customary law, the *reasons* are pertinent to arguments for and against the return of bridewealth.

Thirdly, the principal issues in a common-law divorce action, namely, maintenance, distribution of the matrimonial estate and custody of the children, are of little account in customary law.[5] This system assumes that when a wife leaves her husband she will be absorbed into her own family, and that the children will either remain with their father or will move to their mother's family, depending upon whether bridewealth was paid. The continued support of the wife and children did not pose social or legal problems. The common law, on the other hand, being predicated on a nuclear family, takes it as axiomatic that the husband will be a full-time worker and that the mother will raise the children; neither of the spouses can rely on the assistance of an extended family. This means that the husband must continue to maintain his former wife and children by making over some fraction of the matrimonial estate or by giving them regular cash payments. Hence the paradox in western legal systems that although the ostensible purpose of divorce is to put an end to marriage, it in fact perpetuates certain marital rights and duties. For this reason divorce is now acknowledged to be a long-term process,[6] continuing until the spouses are capable of providing for themselves.

[78] RAUM & DE JAGER *TRANSITION AND CHANGE IN A RURAL COMMUNITY* 79–80

Many informants clearly revealed that divorce in the sense used in European courts of law does not exist for them. There is no public denouncement, or ritual or legal act to establish the divorce. After we had explained the concept of divorce to our traditionalist

---

[3] The common law was changed, of course, by the Divorce Act 70 of 1979, which now permits divorce on the ground of irretrievable breakdown of the marriage. But the spouses are still not allowed to end their relationship by private agreement: there must be proof acceptable to a court that continued cohabitation has become impossible.

[4] Mnookin & Kornhauser (1979) 32 *Current Legal Problems* 65ff.

[5] See Phillips & Morris *Marriage Laws in Africa* 126.

[6] Rheinstein & König (1972) 4 *IECL* ch 1 para 104.

informants, they insisted that nothing similar exists, or has ever existed, in their society. Complete dissolution of a marriage is very rare and they claim that in their society there is no need for such a procedure. Separation, often only temporary, is the nearest they would concede. When we pointed out to them the existence of the necessary procedure in Bantu law they merely stated that very few people ever make use of it, as the matter is settled by the lineage elders and the two families concerned. Traditionalists described dissolution of marriage in their society as separation of the spouses, which is seldom permanent, and results in little change in the status of husband and wife. It is actually more an interruption of marital life, which may occur on several occasions in the married life of a couple.

Other ethnographers have made the same observation;[7] and it has been noted that while informal divorce is recognized, it is rare and socially frowned upon.[8]

The rising divorce rate has been a preoccupation of western legal systems for at least the past fifty years. The problem has been ascribed to many causes, one of them being the ease with which divorce may be obtained. In comparison, customary marriages seemed to be more durable, a virtue that was popularly attributed to the stabilizing effect of bridewealth.[9] Gluckman said that Zulu marriage conceded 'neither jural divorce, nor breach of conjugal (domestic) relations'[10] (and there are similar reports from other parts of southern Africa).[11] He claimed that there was a correlation between this phenomenon, patrilineality, and high bridewealth payments.[12]

A later refinement of Gluckman's argument paid closer attention to the rights involved. All marriages are concerned with the domestic and sexual services of the wife (uxorial rights) and with parental rights to the children (genetricial rights); but in patrilineal societies, as with the Zulu, the lineage as a whole acquires genetricial rights, while uxorial rights vest in the husband alone. By contrast, in a matrilineal society, like that of the Lozi, the genetricial rights are retained by the mother's family while the husband acquires only uxorial rights. This, it is argued, makes the marriage more easily terminable; marital stability is promoted when the family as a group acquires genetricial rights.[13]

This line of argument has been criticized[14] on three grounds. First, it presupposed that marriage and the person or family entitled to parental rights could be precisely defined, whereas in reality customary marriage is a cumulative process during which the locus of control over the wife and children is bound to be uncertain. Secondly, a particular transaction such as bridewealth does not

---

[7] For example, Van Tromp 151.
[8] Marwick 133; Schapera 159; Holleman 267. Mönnig 334 says that among the Pedi a fine is levied on any person wishing to divorce.
[9] See, eg: Bekker 151; Hunter 212–13; and the argument above, 197ff. Cf Simons 1958 *AJ* 335–6.
[10] (1953) 53 *Man* 141.
[11] Weinrich *African Marriage in Zimbabwe and the Impact of Christianity* 160ff; Ashton 85–7; Schapera 159.
[12] See above, 199. But more plausibly it seems that whenever property is given to constitute a marriage, the dissolution is made more difficult because the recipient will be reluctant to return what was given: Rheinstein & König op cit n6 para 98. Thus they contend that informal cohabitation is more prevalent in the non-propertied classes: para 101.
[13] Mitchell in Southall *Social Change in Modern Africa* 316ff; Huber *Marriage and the Family in Rural Bukwaya* 180; Mair *Marriage* 189–91.
[14] Murray *Families Divided* 142ff.

unequivocally determine uxorial/parental rights. They are called into issue only when the marriage breaks down, and in practice the payment of bridewealth is not the only relevant factor. Thirdly, Gluckman's vision of the Zulu was of a society relatively unaffected by the political and economic forces sweeping through southern Africa. He paid little attention to the destabilizing effect that extrinsic factors (notably labour migration) were having on marriage.[15]

It is in fact impossible to make a categorical pronouncement on the divorce rate in customary law because we have very little statistical information,[16] but even if an empirical study were undertaken, how would the situation be assessed, given the difficulty of defining basic concepts? Divorce implies the existence of a marriage[17] and the definition of customary marriages is notoriously difficult.[18] Apart from this, informal unions have become much more common and they are obviously not dissolved by formal divorce procedures. Furthermore, even established marriages may be ended informally by the spouses; and with no reference to the courts (or even the families) it is impossible to determine whether the marriage is actually at an end.

This should not be taken to imply that customary marriage is a stable institution in South Africa. Migrant labour, apartheid, forced resettlements, unemployment, crime, and the acute shortage of urban housing are all factors that tend to undermine domestic relationships.[19]

When a marriage is terminated, the wife and children, for social and economic reasons examined below, are in a vulnerable position. An unregulated divorce settlement, lacking special procedures to protect their interests, can work to their disadvantage. This makes the intervention of a disinterested third party, which is characteristic of the western legal systems, a desirable feature for all divorce actions. The goal of safeguarding the weaker members of a family cannot be achieved, however, if there are no legally recognized relationships. The social circumstances of developed countries are now such that their legal systems are prepared to take cognizance of stable de facto unions, especially where children are involved.[20] It is felt that although individuals might want to escape the duties associated with the formal institution of marriage, long-term cohabitation and parenthood entail responsibilities that cannot be shirked. In South Africa, the prospect of introducing such enlightened policies seems remote, especially in view of the refusal to recognize even fully fledged customary marriages.

II SUBSTANCE AND PROCEDURE

(1) The reasons

In customary law there is no such thing as 'grounds for divorce', in the sense that there are conditions which must be satisfied before the parties can be released from their marital obligations.

---

[15] Murray (1977) 21 *JAL* 79.
[16] Cf Weinrich op cit n11 160ff and ethnographic studies by Hunter 212 and Mönnig 334.
[17] See *Chokoe v Mashiwane* 1940 NAC (N&T) 96.
[18] See Comaroff & Roberts op cit n1 113–14.
[19] Burman (1987) 1 *Int J L & Family* 210.
[20] Evatt et al in Eekelaar & Katz *Marriage and Cohabitation in Contemporary Societies* 298ff.

'One can only speak of grounds of divorce in that sense where a divorce requires the formal sanction of judicial authorities. . . . Otherwise one cannot go beyond recording typical arguments which . . . have been held to justify a wife in leaving her husband or a husband in driving away his wife.'[21]

Yet because refund of bridewealth is the principal issue when a customary marriage is dissolved, and because this depends partly at least on the relative fault of the parties, the *reasons* for divorce are always important, and in this regard, observance of the correct procedure is assumed to demonstrate an underlying moral probity.

Divorce involves careful tactical manoeuvre. If the parties cannot agree on the refund of bridewealth, appeal to a third party is necessary, and when in a public forum, arguments must be marshalled to show that one party acted in a blameworthy fashion according to accepted standards of marital behaviour. Even husbands, who are not strictly obliged to justify their acts, will encounter problems when claiming return of bridewealth if they had no good cause for rejecting their wives. A wife especially must be in a position to allege plausible reasons. She must either convince her guardian to support her in the divorce action, or if she cannot win him over and she has to plead her case alone in court, she must be able to show good cause for wanting the marriage ended. Women can normally rely on two reasons: that their husbands did not support them, or that their husbands exceeded the right of moderate chastisement.[22]

[79] ROBERTS *BOTSWANA: TSWANA FAMILY LAW* 50

As indicated in the previous section, the agencies for settling matrimonial disputes are chiefly concerned to promote reconciliation and do not lay great emphasis upon individual instances of misconduct. There are no "grounds" upon which a divorce will automatically be granted, but merely a number of matters which the court will regard as powerful indications that the marriage has broken down, should efforts at reconciliation fail.

(i) *Justifications available to both sexes*
(a) Refusal to render conjugal rights over a long period without reasonable cause.
(b) The practice of sorcery intended to harm the other spouse.
(c) Desertion. Either party may obtain a divorce on the basis of desertion where the other has been absent from the home for a long period and has failed to carry out his or her matrimonial duties. Such divorce is seldom granted until the absent party has been away for at least two years.
(d) Physical cruelty. This must normally be of a very severe quality, when it is remembered that a husband is entitled to subject his wife to reasonable physical correction.

(ii) *Justifications available to the husband*
(a) Persistent failure by the wife to carry out her household duties.
(b) Adultery by the wife.
Comment. Some informants insist that adultery by a wife is a ground upon which the Chief's Court must grant a divorce on demand, but the Court records lend no support to this view.

---

[21] Mair op cit n13 182.
[22] Mair op cit n13 187–8.

(iii) *Justifications available to the wife*
(a) Failure on the part of the husband to provide reasonable maintenance for the wife and children; this includes failure to provide adequate accommodation;
(b) Persistent adultery by the husband, where this is coupled with failure to have normal sexual relations with the wife.

Failure to perform any of the duties of a spouse, if sufficiently serious, will be considered culpable.[23] Sexual misconduct (always a prime cause of marital dissension) is, notwithstanding, not always a good reason for divorce. An affaire by the wife, for instance, is on its own not considered a sufficient reason;[24] and if in spite of this the husband chooses to repudiate his spouse, he may lose his bridewealth.[25]

[80] *MSHWESHWE* 1945 NAC (C&O) 9–10

In regard to the first ground of appeal, it is true that adultery is not a ground for the dissolution of a customary union unless the wife persists in her misconduct, in which case the husband is entitled to the return of the dowry paid for her (see *Ngawana v Makuzeni* 1 NAC 220 and *Gomfi v Mdenduluka* 3 NAC 21). But this is not a case in which plaintiff seeks to recover the dowry, and it has been held on a number of occasions (see e g *Mbono v Sifuba* 1 NAC 137 and *Fuzile v Ntloko* 1944 NAC (C&O) at 6) that where the husband is prepared to forfeit the dowry paid for his customary wife he is entitled to reject her and dissolve the union without assigning any reason whatsoever. It is clear, however, that he must act reasonably and must comply with custom. By custom he is required to consult his male relatives, to report the rejection to the headman or other official and to take or send his wife with messengers to her people. He cannot discard her and leave her stranded on the veld (*Meleni v Mandlangisa* 2 NAC 191) and such action on his part will not have the effect of dissolving the union. In *Sila & another v Masuku* (1937 NAC (N&T) 121), it was stated that in Native Law a customary union is a contract, not only between the parties to the union, but also between the family groups. It follows, therefore, that until the dowry holder has been informed of the rejection and while the dowry still remains with him, the union legally remains in existence....

The statement in *Meleni's* case, *supra*, that the husband must show "good and reasonable cause" for repudiating his wife, goes perhaps too far, for it goes without saying that a husband is not likely to repudiate his wife for no reason whatsoever. In any case, she is entitled to go to her dowry holder, who is under an obligation to support her. But the decision in the case clearly indicates that in driving his wife away he must comply fully with the customary procedure, and until he has complied with custom the wife is entitled to all the privileges of her house and can refuse to recognise the dissolution of the union.

If a wife commits adultery, the aggrieved husband may demand that her guardian discipline her, in addition to which he has an action for damages against her lover. But if he brings this action, he loses his right to proceed with the divorce because he is deemed to have condoned his wife's behaviour.[26] In effect the husband is put to the choice; he may sue for divorce or for damages, but not for both.[27]

---

[23] See Campbell (1970) 3 *CILSA* 334–7.
[24] *Bungane v Nongwadi* 1931 NAC (C&O) 43; *Gulwa v Jim* 1945 NAC (C&O) 58; *Mokhantso & another v Chochane* 1947 NAC (C&O) 15; *Am v Kuse* 1957 NAC 92 (S).
[25] *Ngxala* 3 NAC 165 (1917).
[26] *Tetani v Mnukwa* 1 NAC 38 (1900).
[27] *Mayile v Makawula* 1953 NAC 262 (S); *Mfazwe v Mfikili* 1957 NAC 33 (S) 34.

Adultery becomes a sufficient ground for divorce where it is persistent,[28] incestuous,[29] where the wife actually goes to live with her lover,[30] or where she (or her guardian) obstructs the husband in his action against the lover.[31] If the wife goes so far as to attempt to marry the other man, this too could provide a good reason.[32]

The wife's prenuptial pregnancy entitles the husband (if he were not the father) to reject her and to reclaim his bridewealth.[33] But he must act quickly, because condonation of his wife's condition compromises his position in the divorce action.[34]

The husband's impotence is deemed a good reason to end the marriage.[35] (Although generally sickness does not provide a good ground for divorce in customary law.)[36]

Accusations of witchcraft by the husband against his wife, if persistent[37] or formally prosecuted by 'smelling out',[38] give the wife good reason to leave him. The matter must be serious, and calculated by the husband to result in his wife's desertion.[39] Actual practice of witchcraft by one spouse would clearly also be a good reason to end the marriage; but the Witchcraft Suppression Act[40] probably accounts for the dearth of reported cases on this issue.

(2) The method and signification

Because dissolution of a customary marriage is in principle a private affair, a party to the union cannot obtain divorce by approaching the court with a request for a divorce order. And the courts have disclaimed any general authority to dissolve marriages.[41] They will intervene only when it is clear that one party is determined on the divorce and that his or her intention has already been communicated to the other party.

[81] BOURDILLON *THE SHONA PEOPLES* 153–7

The most common type of case to come before the chiefs' courts are marriage cases, whether between a quarrelling husband and wife or, less frequently, between father-in-law and son-in-law over marriage payments. Divorce has always been possible in Shona society, but the dissolution of a marriage contract normally involves the return of a proportion of the bride-price. The exact amount that is to be returned depends on how

---

[28] *Mshweshwe* 1946 NAC (C&O) 9.
[29] *Mangaliso v Fekade & another* 5 NAC 5 (1926).
[30] *N'guaje v Nkosa* 1937 NAC (N&T) 98.
[31] *Ngawana v Makuzeni* 1 NAC 220 (1908); *Ndabeni v Mangunza* 2 NAC 48 (1910); *Mhlangaba v Dyalvani* 2 NAC 139 (1911).
[32] *Nkuna v Kazamula* 1941 NAC (N&T) 128.
[33] *Gweni v Mhlalo & another* 3 NAC 179 (1913); *Am v Kuse* 1957 NAC 92 (S).
[34] *Mtshakaza v Zwelendaba* 1978 AC 93 (S).
[35] *Ndatambi v Ntozake* 1 NAC 3 (1895).
[36] *Magandela v Nyangweni* 1 NAC 14 (1896).
[37] *Mathupa v Mahupye* 1933 NAC (N&T) 6.
[38] *Links v Mdyobeli* 1947 NAC (C&O) 96; *Nyamekwangi v Maduntswana* 1951 NAC 313 (S).
[39] *Mqitsane v Panya* 1951 NAC 354 (S).
[40] 3 of 1957.
[41] In the Transvaal at least: *Saulos v Sebeko & another* 1947 NAC (N&T) 25 and *Duba v Nkosi* 1948 NAC 7 (NE).

long the couple have lived together, on how many children the wife has born to her husband and marginally on who is to blame for the dissolution of the marriage. If the marriage was of long standing, the court may decide that nothing is to be returned even if no children were born, whereas if the marriage was of brief duration and unfruitful, and especially if the wife appears responsible for its failure, the court may decide that everything should be returned to the husband, including gifts he had made to his wife. The birth of children always results in some of the roora[1] being retained by the wife's family, and rutsambo[2] payments are rarely returnable once the couple have begun to live together. If the husband is deemed responsible for the failure of the marriage, the terms of the return of the agreed portion of the bride-price may be unfavourable to him: he may, for example, have to wait until his wife is remarried before receiving his due.

Since the marriage contract is between families rather than between the spouses, proceedings for the dissolution of the contract may be necessary on the death of one of the spouses. If the wife dies soon after the marriage (and the same applies if she proves to be barren), it is the duty of her family to provide her husband with a younger sister as a second wife with no further payments, and it is the duty of the groom's family to accept the girl that is offered to them. Should the husband die, it is the duty of his family to see that the wife is cared for by his successor or by some other man in the family (and care here includes all the obligations due to a wife) and it is the duty of the wife to accept a successor (often the man of her choice) as her husband. Should either party fail in their duties, the other family may demand the dissolution of the marriage contract.

Initially, the purpose of the court is to save the marriage if at all possible, and the kinsmen of the two parties together with the elders of the court try to arrange a compromise solution. The wife's family especially have a vested interest in preserving the marriage since otherwise they have to return some of the bride-price they have received, which may already have been dissipated on other marriages in the family or on expensive consumer goods. The husband's family have a smaller financial interest in effecting a compromise, but a blatantly unreasonable man, as an unreasonable woman, is bad for the reputation of the family and the husband's kinsmen normally put pressure on him to accept a reasonable compromise. Some chiefs may refuse to allow the dissolution of a marriage when the case first comes before the court, demanding instead that a compromise be attempted for some months to see if the marriage can be salvaged. In such a case, it is important for the court to delve deeply into the grievances of each side and to try to expose the root cause of the quarrel.

But often the break-up of the home is established before the case comes before the court and, especially if the case has been before the court previously, only the terms of the dissolution of the contract need to be decided. In such a case the debate and the tactics centre on which is the "guilty" party and which party "refuses" to continue the marriage: to lay "guilt" and "refusal" or either one of these as far as possible on the other party increases the chances of a favourable decision on the return of bride-price. In this context, "guilt" implies any action or omission which gives the other party a potential cause to seek the dissolution of marriage. It includes on the part of the wife barrenness, desertion, serious failure as a housewife, repeated unfaithfulness, the practice of witchcraft, and so on; on the part of the husband, "guilt" can mean, for example, maltreatment of the wife (for which she should show bruises in evidence) or failure to pay the agreed bride-price. "Refusal" may simply be obstinate "guilt" when one spouse persists in a repudiation or desertion of the other without just cause; but it may also be the refusal of the innocent party to continue marriage relations when the guilty party makes an apparent effort to save the marriage—an attitude which tends to impair the innocent party's ability to obtain a favourable ruling from the court. For this reason, a categorical rejection is avoided as far as possible by each party to the case.

Neither "guilt" nor "refusal" necessarily imply moral culpability. In fact a certain amount of provocation, such as veiled threats or accusations of witchcraft by the husband or slipshod work by the wife, may take place in order to make the other party responsible for the apparent "guilt" or ultimate "refusal". These provocations are often naively ignored by traditional courts which tend to judge a divorce case by apparent and evident facts rather than by motives which require explanation.

Quite clearly in such cases the courts become legalistic in their approach, concerning themselves with applying recognised laws or customs rather than finding out the root of the trouble. In cases involving the dissolution of a marriage contract, the disputing parties are not kinsmen and not usually close neighbours, and hence they are not likely to be involved together in communal activities. When there is a chance of saving a marriage and keeping the families together, discussions in the courts may take several hours to cover all aspects of the relations between husband and wife in an attempt to expose the root cause of the conflict. When the families involved in a divorce case are close neighbours, the courts attempt to get the disputing families to reach an agreement even though the marriage is terminated. But in most marriage cases, the failure of the marriage is an established fact, and the disputing families neither need nor intend to have any further relations with each other. Yet the marriage is not finally dissolved until an agreement is reached on the return of the bride-price or a portion of it to the husband's family, and until this happens reconciliation is theoretically possible—hence the tactics of trying to put the other party in the wrong. In practice, the dispute brought before the court is not so much a conflict within the local community that needs to be resolved as a wrangle between distant families about the portion of bride-price to be returned and the terms of its return.

Notes

1. Bridewealth.
2. A substantial pre-marriage gift given by the groom or his family.

The physical expression of divorce is the reversal of marriage. Hence where the marriage had been informally contracted, the divorce is likewise a relatively casual affair involving separation of the spouses based on a breakdown of their relationship; where marriage was constituted by the giving of property, divorce is signified by its return.[42] But while clear evidence of a divorce can usually be found in refund of bridewealth, the return of the wife to her family (or at least her departure from her husband's house)[43] is an equivocal act. It might imply that her relationship with her husband had temporarily deteriorated (but not to an extent justifying dissolution of the union), or that the woman had gone home to bear a child or to incite further payment of bridewealth. Thus the wife's unilateral act of desertion is legally ineffective.[44]

Observance of certain conventional procedures clarifies this otherwise ambiguous situation. If the wife wants to divorce her husband, she should declare her intention by reporting to her headman.[45] When the husband accepts his wife's desertion, which is normally evinced by his claiming (or abandoning) bridewealth, the marriage will be deemed to be dissolved.[46] Conversely, if the

---

[42] Stephens *The Family in Cross-Cultural Perspective* 232; Gibbs (1963) 65 *Am Anthropologist* 552; Rheinstein & König op cit n6 para 96. But, as Rheinstein & König para 97 say, 'The emphasis on legal procedure grows with the growing importance of property'.

[43] Kuper 19; Schapera 161–2; Van Warmelo & Phophi 453, 519 and 531.

[44] *Ponya v Sitate* 1944 NAC (C&O) 13.

[45] *Mxonya v Moyeni* 1940 NAC (C&O) 87.

[46] *Nkabinde v Mlangeni & another* 1942 NAC (N&T) 89; *Kosane v Molotya* 1945 NAC (N&T) 70.

husband wishes to divorce his wife, he should escort her to her family and report the matter to a headman.[47]

[82] *BOBOTYANE v JACK* 1944 NAC (C&O) 9 at 11

Native Law does not recognise a dissolution of the union by mere desertion of the wife or husband, by abandonment, or even by bare repudiation, for these are all eventualities provided for by the lobolo cattle; the wife can always claim support from their holder, and the husband can always "putuma" his wife after any length of absence; the wife or widow can always return to her husband's kraal or more usually to that of her son, his heir (after his death), and resume her former status.

All these indicate that Native Law requires something more than a mere private unilateral act or repudiation to terminate the union.

On the part of the husband, he has the right to repudiate the wife, with forfeiture of his lobolo if the act be unjustified in Native Law, but before the wife can act on such repudiation and re-marry it is necessary either to return all or some of the lobolo, or to take the matter before the headman or chief and obtain a public repudiation by the husband.

On the part of the wife, a repudiation can become effective only by restoration of the lobolo or part thereof, for there is no corresponding practice known to Native Law which gives the wife a right similar to the husband's of public repudiation with resultant forfeiture of lobolo.

It may happen that a father or his representative may decline to restore the lobolo and frustrate the woman's desire to terminate a customary union. Custom apparently pictured her driving back her dowry herself, but our Courts have come to vest a fuller ownership in those cattle in the dowry holder than did Native Law. Hence she is to-day compelled to seek the aid of the Court for an order compelling the dowry holder to make proper refund and the Native Commissioner's Court is bound to grant her such order in a proper case, her husband being joined in the action to dissolve the union.

Return of the bridewealth is a less ambiguous act than departure of the wife, and the courts have relied heavily on it as evidence of an intention to divorce. Where the bridewealth had already been refunded, the court held that the marriage had ipso facto been dissolved;[48] and even tender was considered sufficient, whether or not the husband had accepted it.[49] Otherwise, a court order to refund bridewealth has been held to operate in the same way as a divorce order.[50]

It is a short step from using return of bridewealth as an indication of intent, to making it an unvarying rule.[51] In certain early Transkeian decisions, for instance, the courts insisted on return of at least one beast to mark dissolution.[52] This approach can easily degenerate into sterile formalism, especially today when the ritual significance of bridewealth in constituting marriage has diminished. More importantly perhaps, an inflexible rule might have the effect of deterring the wife's guardian from supporting her divorce action, since there is every

---

[47] Mere eviction of the wife does not suffice to end the marriage: *Mshweshwe* 1946 NAC (C&O) 9 and *Jack v Zenani* 1962 NAC 40 (S).

[48] *Nonafu v Pike* 1 NAC 120 (1906); *Novungwana v Zabo* 1957 NAC 114 (S).

[49] *Mfazwe v Mfikili* 1957 NAC 33 (S).

[50] *Sibiya v Mbata* 1942 NAC (N&T) 71; *Kabi v Putumani* 1954 NAC 210 (S).

[51] See, eg, *Zibeni v Bangani* 1974 BAC 445 (S).

[52] Regardless of the number of cattle that the wife's guardian would ordinarily be entitled to retain: *Njikazi v Ngawu* 3 NAC 66 (1912); *Gqedeyi v Makati & another* 3 NAC 180 (1913); *Mabani v Jekemani* 3 NAC 182 (1915).

likelihood that he will have expended the bridewealth on family subsistence or the settlement of his own marriage debts. Given the policy that the power to create or terminate the marriage is the spouses', it is in principle wrong to make the dissolution of marriage depend on the financial circumstances of one of the parties.

By and large, the courts have not fallen into this trap. Their major concern has been to discover the parties' intention, and important as bridewealth may be in this regard, they have been quite prepared to consider other factors. For example, if the wife, with the connivance of her guardian, contracts a second marriage, this reveals a clear rejection of the first union,[53] given the customary-law prohibition on polyandry. (Exceptionally, if the husband were unwilling to let his wife go, the second marriage might simply be regarded as void.)[54] Similarly, separation of the spouses might be long enough to permit an inference that the marriage had ended.[55] A period of 11 years' separation[56] or 10 years and the husband's failure to seek his wife's return[57] were held to be sufficient to mark dissolution.[58] Mere ill-treatment[59] or failure to support a wife,[60] on the other hand, do not per se suffice to end the marriage because neither of these factors necessarily shows the requisite intent to dissolve the union.

(3) The position of the parties

(a) The wife

[83] VAN TROMP *XHOSA LAW OF PERSONS* 151–6

If life at the umzi becomes unbearable as a result of the wife's misbehaviour, her husband can either send her home or force her to go to her people. He may leave her there as long as he wants to and may, if he wishes fetch her back one day should she then wish to return. The usual procedure for her husband under such circumstances is to leave her with her own people indefinitely if her character is such that she would make life at the umzi unbearable. Under these circumstances the marriage is not dissolved and any children born to his wife are still considered as his. If adultery has been committed and the adulterer is known to the husband the latter may institute a claim against him, but there can be no dissolution of the marriage for that reason. The adulterer can lay no claim to such children resulting from his adulterous intercourse with another man's wife. The lawful husband of the woman may come forward at any time and claim both his wife and the children borne by her.

If the woman refuses to return to her husband her father may on her account send back part of the ikhazi handed to him by the woman's lawful husband, thereby indicating that

---

[53] *Gijana & another v Mangali* 1946 NAC (C&O) 60.

[54] *Matshiki v Klaas* 4 NAC 62 (1921), and the bridewealth paid in respect of it as forfeit to the husband.

[55] *Didi v Maxwele* 4 NAC 198 (1921), although any such inference is not lightly drawn.

[56] *Speelman* 1944 NAC (N&T) 53.

[57] *Mhlanga v Hleta & another* 1944 NAC (N&T) 40.

[58] Even so, the courts have sometimes required return of bridewealth as an added guarantee that the parties really intended divorce: *Mbana v Dilayi* 1940 NAC (C&O) 73. And see *Gulwa v Jim* 1945 NAC (C&O) 58.

[59] *Mokoena v Mofokeng* 1945 NAC (C&O) 89; cf *Stolleh v Mtwalo & another* 1947 NAC (C&O) 33.

[60] *Ngqoqo v Nobatyeli* 1947 NAC (C&O) 44; *Gatebe v Mlangeni* 1947 NAC (C&O) 76.

the woman does not wish to return to him, and the marriage is dissolved. . . . I was told by many old amaXhosa that it was not unusual formerly for the woman herself to drive these cattle back to her lawful husband, thereby showing that the marriage was dissolved. When she did this she acted in silence and was almost naked. This indicated in a most formal and perceptible manner her contemptuous repudiation of all marriage ties; the full implication of her behaviour was made sufficiently clear to her husband when he saw her driving these cattle into his ubuhlanti. The matter was settled.

Once this is done the woman may again marry and the children will be those of her second husband.

If the husband of the woman, on the other hand, persists in ill-treating his wife and in making her life at the umzi strained and unbearable she may take advantage of the first opportunity to return home to her own people.

Her husband can, after some time, either follow or pursue his wife or leave her at the umzi of her father. If he does not follow or pursue her the position is the same as when the woman leaves her husband, as in the case already described.

When the husband traces his wife under such circumstances, and he nearly always does if he is the cause of her leaving him, the *Ukuteleko* custom is brought into operation. If the husband of the woman does not hand over the beast claimed under the ukuteleko custom he cannot sue the father of the woman for the return of his wife.

The parents of the woman may even prevent her from returning to her husband until such time as he has fulfilled his obligation under this custom, and he has no remedy. He cannot dissolve the marriage, but has to hand over to her people the fine imposed upon him. Should the husband never comply with the requirements under this custom, the woman may never return to him and he will never get back his ikhazi or part thereof. But if the family of the woman is convinced, after the parties have had an opportunity of stating their side of the question in the family court, that a reprimand is sufficient to dispose of the case, they will reprimand the husband and send the woman back. Should the woman have left her husband without sufficient cause she will receive a scolding and be sent back to him. Where she absolutely refuses to return to her lawful husband, her father and family are obliged to return part of the ikhazi and thus dissolve the marriage. For, according to Xhosa Law, the marriage can only be dissolved by the return of at least a portion of the ikhazi, according to the circumstances. . . .

Should his daughter refuse to return to her husband, after exhortations from her family, it is usual for the father, before the matter ends in the Chief's Court, to return of his own accord a part of the ikhazi and thus formally to dissolve the marriage. If the father of the woman refuses to tender part of the ikhazi to her husband who does not follow his wife, she need not return to him but may remain at the umzi of her own people, who must maintain and care for her while she must work for them in return. They may not drive her back to her husband if he does not care for her or if she is reluctant to return to him.

Should the father or lawful guardian of the woman refuse to comply with her wish to dissolve the marriage by the return of part of the ikhazi she will appeal to her paternal uncles. If, after the matter has been discussed in the family court and her father still refuses, the matter may finally be decided in the Chief's Court. Should the Chief be convinced of the wife's case he will order the father to return part of the ikhazi and thereby dissolve the marriage. The father or lawful guardian of the woman will then obey the order of the Chief and restore part of the ikhazi to the husband of the woman. . . .

When a portion of the ikhazi is restored to him, the husband has no other choice but to accept these cattle and to consider the marriage dissolved. The husband may object to the number of cattle the father of the woman tenders, but he will not object to the dissolution of the marriage, for if he does, he has no remedy. . . . A court, not even the Chief's Court, can or does dissolve a marriage, much less grant a "divorce". A marriage is dissolved by the wife assisted by her family, and a court may only point out the legal duties of the parties involved to attain this end; or a court may settle disputes in connection with it, e.g. the woman's father returns one head of cattle, whereas the husband claims that three head shall be restored. . . .

Dissolution of marriage therefore is in substance always a bilaterial transaction: from the side of the husband's family the wife returns home, and from the side of the wife's family at least a part of the ikhazi is returned; although ultimately the dissolution of the marriage depends upon the wish of the woman and her family. The husband can drive away his wife, cause her to leave him, but he cannot one-sidedly dissolve the marriage. Neither can the desertion of the wife alone, whether as a result of ill-treatment by her husband or as a result of being forced by her husband to leave on account of her misbehaviour, cause the dissolution. The return of at least part of the ikhazi is in either case essential. . . .

The amaXhosa state that normally there can be no second or subsequent marriage of a woman who was once married, meaning, that unless part of the ikhazi, according to the circumstances of the case, is returned and the existing marriage rescinded, there cannot be a second marriage for the former one still subsists.

Because customary marriage is a union of two families, it follows that dissolution must be negotiated by the representatives of those families. This means that the wife has no power to end her marriage; she did not negotiate the bridewealth and she may not tender its return.[61] She is totally dependent on her guardian to prosecute the divorce on her behalf,[62] a situation that may easily work to her disadvantage.

The colonial courts in Transkei, however, were dedicated to improving the position of women, so they were prepared to allow wives free rein in prosecuting their own divorce actions. It was held that a wife might: sue on her own account by returning the bridewealth;[63] bring the action in court either unassisted[64] or assisted by her guardian;[65] or, with her guardian's consent, tender return of bridewealth.[66] Shortly after the establishment of the Appeal Court in 1927, this liberal policy was reversed.[67]

[84] *NQAMBI* 1939 NAC (C&O) 57 at 59

The Native Assessors are emphatic in their view that Native Law does not give a wife the right to dissolve the union without the restoration of some of the dowry.

They contend that a wife can compel a dowry-holder to "keta" (i.e. refund) some of her dowry to obtain dissolution by complaint to the Chief who will order the restoration to dissolve the union.

This view conflicts with what this Court has, hitherto, regarded as an equitable right of the wife to dissolve the marriage at her option in the same manner as is apparently permitted the husband.

The decisions of the Court to this effect are clearly actuated by misplaced sentiment which entirely ignores the basic principles of a Native union, that there are not two but at least three contracting parties, and that the basis of the union is not the mere consent of the spouses, as in our law, but it is the dowry (ikazi) which forms the bond. The Courts have consistently recognised this principle in dealing with a husband's action for dissolution of a customary union by requiring him to sue the dowry-holder for the return

---

[61] *Sweleni v Moni* 1944 NAC (C&O) 31; *Mokgatle* 1946 NAC (N&T) 82; *Nhlabati v Lushaba* 1958 NAC 18 (NE); cf Duncan 38 for Lesotho.

[62] *Nhlabati's* case supra.

[63] *Noenjini v Nteta* 2 NAC 106 (1911).

[64] *Noklam v Qanda* 4 NAC 202 (1920).

[65] *Qeya v Latyabuka* 4 NAC 203 (1920).

[66] *Mayo v Nomhlaba* 3 NAC 172 (1912).

[67] Cf Koyana *Customary Law in a Changing Society* 24ff.

of a deserting wife, or in default for restoration of the dowry. The wife is never sued
directly or personally for a divorce.

Any practice which allows a woman to sue her husband on the basis of a bilateral
consensual contract, for dissolution of a customary union is thus obviously in conflict
with sound Native Law and Custom. It is not, as is stressed in the decisions, a matter of
majority in the woman for that alone does not create a right to sue in all and every cause
even among Europeans; nor is it a question of reciprocal rights for the husband, though
apparently acting capriciously in driving away a wife, does so with the safeguard of
knowledge of the resulting forfeiture of his dowry cattle. A wife acting alone is not subject
to even this restraint if allowed to sue without the dowry-holder.

In this respect Native Custom wisely retains an important stabilising effect in Native
marriage and social conditions as does the Common Law in European communities. There
is thus no question here of any conflict of Native custom with public policy to justify
abandonment of the Native system.

Nor can it be contended that it is inequitable to require a wife to join her dowry-holder
in any action for dissolution. An unwilling dowry-holder can be brought before the Court
either singly or in conjunction with the husband, when, on good cause shown, she may
obtain an order of Court for dissolution of her marriage by restoration of some portion
of her dowry, or should the circumstances justify that course in Native Law, with an order
of forfeiture of the dowry by the husband, the costs of the action being awarded against
the husband or dowry-holder or both, according to the demerits of their defence or
opposition to the action.

The Transvaal and Natal division did not regard the early Transkeian approach
as authentic customary law nor did it consider itself bound to follow the
Transkeian decisions. And so, albeit reluctantly, this division of the court held
that the wife was not a party to the divorce action. Her position was discussed
in the following case.[68]

[85] *PHIRI v NKOSI* 1941 NAC (N&T) at 94–5 and 97–8

Gane (Member):

I am in entire agreement with the findings on fact arrived at by the learned President. In
regard, however, to the procedure proposed in dealing with cases of divorce such as this,
while I am in private accord with the views expressed by the President that the woman
should be cited as one of the parties to the case, I hesitate to assent thereto in view of
possible repercussions. The fact must not be lost sight of that while in the towns natives
have to a considerable extent departed from Native Custom, there are still large tribes
living in the Transvaal under tribal conditions and the result of a ruling such as that
indicated may have far-reaching effects.

It is the policy of the legislature to recognise native custom, and in the present instance
the custom in reference deals with the position of the native woman living under tribal
conditions. Women have no *locus standi* in native Courts and cannot, save under very
exceptional circumstances, appear in the Civil Courts without the assistance of their legal
guardian according to tribal custom.

In all matters connected with native marriage disputes it is the invariable practice
(except in Natal where special legislation has been passed) for the party to whom lobolo
has been paid (or his heir) to be cited alone and service of notice on such party is for all
practical purposes regarded as service on the woman. The dowry (lobolo) holder is looked

---

[68] In which the husband had been the plaintiff. Simons *African Women* 129–35 and op cit n9 334–8
gives a critical commentary of this case.

to to restore the woman to her husband, and if he is unable to do this, he is required by custom to restore such portion of the lobolo or dowry, which falls to be refunded.

A ruling requiring the woman to be cited, while advisable in urban areas, might well be looked upon with disfavour by the natives living under tribal conditions as it might be regarded as emancipating the women and taking them out of the control of their guardians, thereby leading to laxity in married life and the possible, if not probable, refusal by the guardian to support wives who have been discarded by their husbands on the grounds that the women being cited personally are no longer subject to their control. . . .

Braatvedt, P. (dissentiente):

Where a native chooses to bring an action in the Court of a Native Commissioner, and asks for an order dissolving a customary union and awarding him a refund of the lobolo which he paid for her, he should, I think, cite the woman, duly assisted by her protector (i.e. her father, brother or other natural guardian), and also her protector. The grounds upon which a dissolution of the union is claimed, should be clearly set out in the summons which should also state the number of cattle which are claimed from her protector by way of refund of lobolo. That is the practice obtaining in Natal and I can see no reason why it should not be adopted in the Transvaal, but many reasons why it should be adopted.

The woman in such a case is the person most vitally concerned. The Court is asked to declare that her marriage (for that is what a customary union really is) be dissolved. Such an order affects her whole future, her status and sometimes her relationship to her children. It is a fundamental principle of law that no judgment should be given against a person who is not a party to the action and I cannot conceive of any reasons why that principle should be departed from just because the parties are natives. It may be argued that the procedure suggested is unknown to Native Custom and Court practice in the Transvaal, but the dissolution of customary unions by Courts of Law was unknown in all Native Custom and yet the Courts now do entertain such cases. The Courts do try to decide cases in accordance with Native Custom where such custom is not opposed to the principles of natural justice. I am of opinion that to order dissolution of a customary union without citing the party against whom such an order is sought, is opposed to the principle of natural justice. Native Customs must be evolved in conformity with our concepts of what is right or just. We are not bound to conform with them when they are obviously harsh and unjust.

The customs of Natal natives in regard to the dissolution of unions were very much the same as those still obtaining in the Transvaal, but there the Legislature, realising that the position was unsatisfactory, regularised the position and provided safeguards by means of the Native Code, against the possibility of inflicting injustice on an innocent party, for a woman may be entirely innocent although her husband may allege that she has deserted him. She should be given an opportunity of being heard.

There is far too much slackness in the Transvaal in regard to both the manner in which customary unions are contracted and in which they are dissolved.

There is no finality in an order for the return of a woman or alternatively for a dissolution of the union. No time limit for her return is fixed by the Courts as far as my experience goes. When then does the dissolution take place? And why should her father be called upon to return her? She may have been married many years and her father have lost all control over her. When she leaves her husband she may go to another man and not to her father.

For all these reasons I feel that the time has arrived when this Court should definitely hold that the procedure as practised in Natal should be adopted in the Transvaal.

Despite this ruling,[69] two principles are clear: a woman cannot be compelled to abide by a marriage that she no longer wants, and her guardian may not dissolve

---

[69] See further *Tyobeka v Madlewa* 1943 NAC (N&T) 60 and Olivier 179.

her marriage without her approval.[70] Both principles complement the woman's power to contract her own marriage and the prohibition on forced marriages. Thus, even if the wife's guardian refused to prosecute her divorce, she should be entitled to do so herself.

The wife's procedural incapacity can be cured by the appointment of a curator ad litem.[71] In this event, because her guardian is not acting as plaintiff in the action, he must be joined as a co-defendant with the husband. The summons would then have to allege the grounds on which the divorce is claimed, a prayer for dissolution (directed against the husband), and a prayer for return of bridewealth (directed against the guardian).[72] On the other hand, if the woman's guardian is prepared to assist her in obtaining a divorce, he and his ward must be joined as co-plaintiffs in the action.[73] Otherwise the wife has no formal role to play in divorce proceedings.[74] Her presence in court is necessary only when the custody of her children is in issue,[75] but even this is not considered a legal requirement.[76]

(b)   The guardians

In view of the above, it seems paradoxical that the court will not accede to a prayer by the wife's guardian for an order of dissolution of the marriage. It is only the wife who may claim this.[77] But, acting on behalf of his ward, the guardian may end her marriage extra-curially. This is usually done simply by tendering return of the bridewealth (less any deductions to which he would be entitled), a procedure known as keta in Xhosa.[78] If the husband contests the amount offered, he would be obliged to sue in court for the balance.[79]

The husband's guardian has no role to play in the divorce action. Despite two early decisions that he might sue for return of bridewealth where he had originally provided the cattle in question,[80] it was subsequently held that he had no locus standi.[81]

---

[70] *Marawu v Mzima* 3 NAC 171 (1915); *Jubele v Sobijase* 5 NAC 56 (1924).

[71] *Mokgatle* 1946 NAC (N&T) 82.

[72] *Mokgatle's* case supra.

[73] *Nhlabati v Lushaba* 1958 NAC 18 (C) at 20. The guardian is a full party to the action; he does not merely cure the wife's procedural incapacity: *Mnyandu v Dludla* 1978 AC 64 (NE).

[74] She is not considered to be a party to the action: *Mpilo v Tshabalala* 1948 NAC 24 (C); *Mpantsha v Ngolonkulu & another* 1952 NAC 40 (S).

[75] *Sibiya v Mbata* 1942 NAC (N&T) 71.

[76] *Nkabinde v Mlangeni & another* 1942 NAC (N&T) 89.

[77] *Matumba v Rangaza* 1948 NAC 29 (C).

[78] The husband's acceptance is not necessary to terminate the marriage. Mere tender is enough: *Mendziwe v Lubalule* 3 NAC 170 (1913); *Mayile v Makawula* 1953 NAC 262 (S).

[79] Alternatively, although this is an unusual procedure, the wife's guardian may demand that the husband formally repudiate his wife before a chief or headman: *Mxonya v Moyeni* 1940 NAC (C&O) 87; *Novungwana v Zabo* 1957 NAC 114 (S).

[80] *Mzama v Xekana* 1 NAC 61 (1903); *Tyozo v Mtshula* 3 NAC 80 (1915).

[81] *Mtimunye v Mabena* 1939 NAC (N&T) 129; *Majola v Ndhlovu* 1942 NAC (N&T) 43; *Mahasoane v Dhlamini* 1944 NAC (C&O) 24.

(c) The husband

If the husband has decided to dissolve his marriage, he should escort his wife back to her family where he can formally announce his intention to end the union.[82]

The husband should be punctilious in his observance of correct form. For example, where a man told his wife to go back to her own family and to take lovers if she wanted to, it was held that, although this amounted to repudiation of the union, the husband's bridewealth was forfeit.[83] The court felt that if the husband had had good cause to end his marriage he would not have acted so unceremoniously. Observance of form lends an assumption of blamelessness,[84] which is critical to the strategy of divorce, because the husband who is thought to have acted arbitrarily or capriciously is penalized.[85]

A claim for return of bridewealth is construed as a clear statement of intent to dissolve the marriage.[86] (And at the same time it may imply that the wife was at fault.) The husband's action should be directed against the woman's guardian,[87] although where the bridewealth had been paid to someone else, the action should be brought against whoever actually received it. If that person did not transfer the bridewealth to the wife's guardian, as he is supposed to do, he is personally liable.[88]

Where the wife had provoked the divorce by deserting her husband,[89] the courts have held that he must then sue the wife's guardian for her return, failing which, return of the bridewealth.[90] Unless she is actually under the control of her husband, the woman's guardian is fully responsible for her;[91] accordingly, the action does not lie against some third person who might be harbouring the wife.[92]

Careful attention must be paid to the details of the pleadings. The husband should not sue simply for dissolution of his marriage.[93] If he does so, his claim will be dismissed, because the courts do not see their role as essential for dissolution of the marriage. Conversely, if he sues for divorce merely by

---

[82] Were he merely to drive the woman out of his house, this would not signify divorce; the intention must be made explicit: *Ngcongolo v Parkies* 1953 NAC 103 (S).

[83] *Doni & another v Nkebese* 1943 NAC (C&O) 51.

[84] As well as making the intention to divorce manifest: *Mlingisi v Ngqotso* 1949 NAC 141 (S). And see: *Bobotyane v Jack* 1944 NAC (C&O) 9; *Mkwanazi* 1945 NAC (N&T) 112. Cf *Doni's* case supra.

[85] *Kos v Lephaila* 1945 NAC (C&O) 4.

[86] *Xanase v Tunce* 1939 NAC (C&O) 36; *Kosane v Molotya* 1945 NAC (N&T) 70.

[87] *Masuku v Masuku & another* 1968 BAC 20 (NE), with reference to s 83(c) of the Natal Code (now 54(b)).

[88] *Mayekiso v Quwe* 1942 NAC (C&D) 38; *Mkekana v Langasiki* 1942 NAC (C&O) 51. Hence, if he wishes to escape liability, he will have to prove (*Dumezweni v Monye* 1962 NAC 81 (S)) that he handed the bridewealth over to the rightful guardian: *Mantshupa v Kwebi* 1938 NAC (C&O) 37; *Dlumti v Sikade* 1947 NAC (C&O) 47; *Mpilo v Tshabalala* 1948 NAC 24 (C).

[89] See *Mathupa v Maupye* 1933 NAC (N&T) 6.

[90] *Mbenyane v Hlatshwayo* 1933 NAC 284 (NE); *Lucas v Namba* 1940 NAC (C&O) 37; *Kosane v Molotya* 1945 NAC (N&T) 70; *Saulos v Sebeko & another* 1947 NAC (N&T) 25; *Machiae v Jacobs* 1957 NAC 97 (C); *Khoza v Nkosi* 1980 AC 82 (NE). See generally: Bekker 187ff; Olivier 179ff; Simons op cit n9 335.

[91] *Apleni v Njeke* 5 NAC 35 (1923).

[92] *Ngamani v Sitsaka* 5 NAC 58 (1927).

[93] *Maseko v Mhlongo* 1953 NAC 40 (C).

claiming return of his bridewealth, the case will also be dismissed, as disclosing no cause of action.[94] (In addition it will be presumed that he rejected his wife, and so should be penalized in the return of bridewealth.)[95] Should he wish simply to claim refund of bridewealth, he must allege that his wife and/or her guardian have already repudiated the marriage,[96] which can be substantiated by showing that the wife had eloped with another man.[97] Where there is no such clear evidence (the wife's desertion in particular is inconclusive) the husband should sue for her return and, *in the alternative*, for refund of bridewealth.

The woman who wished to escape from an unwanted marriage generally had only two options available to her. She could go back to her own family or run away to another man. If she chose the latter course, her husband could not immediately sue her guardian for her return; he was first obliged to look for her.[98] The guardian had to help in the search;[99] any deliberate obstruction would probably be construed as an attempt to end the marriage. Once the wife had been found, she had to return to her own family.[100] Conversely, if she had been traced to her family, her husband's responsibility ended,[101] and she fell under her guardian's control. This meant that he had a duty to persuade her to return to her husband.[102] In principle he could not compel her to act against her will,[103] and so, if he were unsuccessful, he would have to refund the bridewealth.

Where the court has ordered the guardian to return his ward to her husband, the wife's refusal to go back is tantamount to dissolution of the marriage.[104] The purpose of the court order is to secure the permanent cohabitation of the spouses[105] and so return for only a brief period of time is not considered to be compliance. Several decisions have hinged on the question of what constituted a proper return. Where the wife remained with her husband for two months before leaving him again, it was held that the judgment had been discharged.[106] By implication, he had to sue for her return afresh if he wanted her back.[107] Where the wife arrived with none of the clothing or household utensils her husband had given her, it was clear that she did not intend to stay.[108] Similarly,

---

[94] *Nyembe v Zwane* 1946 NAC (N&T) 2; *Matlala v Tompa* 1951 NAC 404 (NE).
[95] *Sirabele v Kwelekwele* 1944 NAC (C&O) 11.
[96] *Mahloane v Mohale* 1947 NAC (C&O) 95.
[97] *Mzwakali v Monwabisi* 1930 NAC (C&O) 59.
[98] *Mampeyi v Rarai* 1937 NAC (C&O) 148; *Qalindaba v Mjilana* 1942 NAC (C&O) 93; *Willie v Skyman* 1943 NAC (C&O) 61; *Sibovana v Dlokova* 1951 NAC 281 (S); *Nkonzo v Jim* 1951 NAC 341 (S).
[99] *Willie* and *Nkonzo*'s cases supra.
[100] *Qalindaba v Mjilana* 1942 NAC (C&O) 93.
[101] *Mdunana v Ntsuntswana* 1953 NAC 271 (S).
[102] *Qalindaba*'s case supra; *Sibovana v Dlokova* 1951 NAC 281 (S).
[103] *Josi v Makamba* 1951 NAC 335 (S).
[104] *Ndlanya v Mhashe* 1 NAC 112 (1906); *Manamela v Kekana* 1944 NAC (N&T) 35; *Kabi v Punge* 1956 NAC 7 (S) at 12.
[105] *Mangceza v Dlangani* 1 NAC 125 (1906).
[106] And had become res judicata: *Zabulana v Mpandla* 4 NAC 103 (1921).
[107] *Mcitwa v Debeza* 1933 NAC (C&O) 6; cf *Mdizeni v Ngqolosi* 1960 NAC 20 (S).
[108] *Zondeka v Konono* 1930 NAC (C&O) 32.

if it was obvious that the husband did not want her back, and when she did not in fact stay, it was held that there had not been a proper return.[109]

Another problem has been the period of time within which the guardian must comply with the order to return his ward. In the interests of certainty it has been held that the court should specify a date in its judgment,[110] otherwise the husband will not know when he should claim return of his bridewealth.[111]

A court order requiring a wife's guardian to return his adult ward to her husband lies uneasily alongside such basic human rights as freedom of movement.[112] And there is nothing in the case law to intimate that the guardian is obliged to take into account the wife's safety or general welfare.[113] He has the option of refunding a portion of the bridewealth instead (which will unequivocally establish the fact of divorce)[114] but the choice lies entirely within his discretion.

If the wife has deserted, the husband should formally demand her return before taking any further action. With the Southern Nguni this convention is known as phuthuma.[115] By dovetailing with the guardian's power to theleka his ward, it provides a way of protesting against maltreatment by the husband and/or a device for prompting further payment of bridewealth.[116] Phuthuma functions either to correct matrimonial misdemeanors or as a prelude to divorce.[117]

Where this is the local custom, the courts have held that the husband *must* phuthuma his wife before he can sue for her return or for refund of bridewealth.[118] It follows that failure to do so can be used as a defence to an action for return of the woman.[119] More importantly, in the overall tactics of the divorce, phuthuma operates to shift the blame for ending the marriage onto the husband. If he does not phuthuma, he will be deemed to have repudiated his wife, with consequent penalty when it comes to refund of bridewealth.[120] The husband is put to the test: either he makes phuthuma of his wife and suffers an

---

[109] *Piti v Gona* 1945 NAC (C&O) 39.

[110] *Shongwe v Mhlongo* 1953 NAC 201 (NE).

[111] *Mdinwa v Maqakamba* 1953 NAC 131 (S).

[112] There seems to be only one procedural safeguard in her favour: the husband may not forcibly remove his spouse from her family. To do so would give her guardian an action for damages: *Mbata & others v Kubeka* 1964 BAC 103 (NE).

[113] The reasonableness of insisting on the wife's return was called into issue in only two cases. In the one, the guardian raised the fact that the husband had ill-treated his wife as a defence to the husband's claim for return of the woman. The argument was unsuccessful: *Debeza v Mcitwa* 1934 NAC (C&O) 56. See too *Seme & another v Radebe* 1946 NAC (N&T) 75. In neither case were the principles involved fully debated.

[114] *Mdinwa v Maqakamba* 1953 NAC 131 (S).

[115] Olivier 192–3; Koyana op cit n67 18ff.

[116] *Mlingisi v Ngqotso* 1949 NAC 141 (S).

[117] It conveniently allows for settlement of the wife's grievances and/or punishment of the husband, who may have to pay a fine to the wife's guardian. See *Jas v Mpunga & another* 1946 NAC (C&O) (5).

[118] *Nkonzo v Jim* 1951 NAC 341 (S); *Zondela v Mpayi* 1952 NAC 92 (S); *Gova v Gushu* 1953 NAC 261 (S).

[119] And see *Mlingisi v Ngqotso* 1949 NAC 141 (S).

[120] *Mzwakali v Monwabisi* 1930 NAC (C&O) 59; *Nkosi v Tshapa* 1950 NAC 5 (C); cf *Mrolo v Bokleni* 1948 NAC 2 (S).

investigation of his behaviour (with the possibility of having to pay a fine for ill-treating her), or he stays away and forfeits bridewealth.[121]

How long does the guardian have to wait for the husband to phuthuma, before he may initiate divorce proceedings? And does a long delay by the husband affect the amount of bridewealth he may reclaim? Although in principle the status of the marriage should not be left uncertain indefinitely, the courts have not given any clear answers to these questions. In three cases the husband lost his bridewealth because he procrastinated for too long;[122] in one case he obtained return of the full amount;[123] in another, after 22 years, he was obliged to pay three beasts as a fine and was then allowed to reclaim his wife.[124]

One further question: if the husband has successfully made phuthuma, but his wife does not remain with him, is he obliged to repeat the process before he can sue for her return or repayment of bridewealth? In *Sijako v Nontshebedu*[125] it was held that where the wife had stayed with her husband for only one week, he was not obliged to phuthuma her again. But in *Mdizeni v Ngqolosi*,[126] where the husband had made phuthuma several times before she finally consented to return, the court held that he was obliged to phuthuma her again when she left after five months.

(4) Reform: Natal, KwaZulu and Transkei

Procedural fairness is of particular importance in the context of divorce. In relation to husbands, wives and children are at an economic and social disadvantage, and unless special provision is made to protect them, these disadvantages are perpetuated in divorce settlements. Because customary law is steeped in the principle of patriarchy it now compares unfavourably with standards set by other legal systems.[127]

Historically, in western legal systems, divorce procedures were aimed at achieving four goals.[128] The first, chronologically, was preservation of marriage. But once marriage had been secularized and the religious prohibition on divorce had been abandoned, this goal was eschewed in favour of the second: the maintenance of the prevailing moral code and the resolution of marital conflict. The first part of this formula is clearly reflected in Roman-Dutch common law, while the current South African Divorce Act[129] is committed to achieving the second part. When no-fault divorce was introduced, the focus of the proceedings inevitably shifted from upholding standards set by the Church/state to the

---

[121] If he can show that he did not ill-treat his wife, his phuthuma will oblige the wife's guardian to persuade her to return or to refund the bridewealth: *Ndzondza v Willem* 1952 NAC 231 (S).
[122] In *Maseti v Meme* 1 NAC 119 (1906) there was a 19 year delay and one head was returned as a symbolic mark of divorce. See further: *Mzwakali v Monwabisi* 1930 NAC (C&O) 59 and *Nkosi v Tshapa* 1950 NAC 5 (C).
[123] *Mtuyedwa v Tshisa* 1 NAC 122 (1906).
[124] *Mfomdidi v Mdletye* 3 NAC 174 (1915).
[125] 1960 NAC 17 (S).
[126] 1960 NAC 20 (S).
[127] See Rheinstein & König op cit n6 para 109.
[128] Andrup in Eekelaar & Katz *The Resolution of Family Conflict* 163ff.
[129] 70 of 1979.

interests of the individual. And in principle, once divorce became a private concern, the spouses could part company on any terms they liked. In consequence, more recent common-law divorce actions were concerned mainly with what were previously considered ancillary issues: maintenance and custody/guardianship. And this led to the third goal: safeguarding any children of the marriage. Once their interests were involved, the courts intervened, claiming a protective jurisdiction over minors.[130] The typical divorce thus became a settlement, in the first instance negotiated by the spouses' lawyers, and then formally approved by a court.

The final goal, one that is now pursued in nearly all western legal systems, is to assist and restructure broken families. This has entailed the progressive delegalization of divorce, mainly by co-opting the help of private and state welfare agencies, but also by freely accepting the spouses' private agreements in place of adjudicated settlements. This in turn has encouraged a movement away from adjudication of divorce disputes to mediation or conciliation. It has been openly recognized that legal mechanisms are unable to stem the rising divorce rate or to solve the multifarious problems caused by the breakup of marriage.[131]

The adversarial system of adjudication, with its win-or-lose approach and its tendency to favour the party wealthy enough to afford counsel, bears particularly harshly on women and children, and does nothing to encourage post-divorce harmony.[132] In common-law courts these problems have been alleviated by providing legal aid,[133] insisting on the representation of children, and involving social welfare agencies. The Hoexter Commission of Inquiry into the Structure and Functioning of the Courts[134] went further. It recommended the establishment of family courts with an inquisitorial procedure,[135] in the hope that a therapeutic approach would be fostered by a tribunal specializing in domestic conflicts.[136] Unfortunately these proposals have not yet been implemented.

Customary law (which favours reconciliation of the parties, ostensibly no-fault divorce, and private settlements) would in principle seem to be amenable to the reception of modern developments in western divorce law. But, apart from introducing the common-law guideline of the 'child's best interests', the courts have done nothing to safeguard the interests of women or children. Instead they have allowed the husband and the wife's guardian to dominate divorce proceedings. It is difficult to assess the customary-law divorce procedures in South Africa with any precision, mainly because of the variety of different tribunals that can hear divorce (and related) actions, and also because of

---

[130] As these goals changed, so did the functions of the courts. When it became unnecessary for a court to decide whether the marital relationship was such that divorce ought to be granted, its main purpose changed to providing a forum in which the terms of settlement could be decided.

[131] See Weitzman *The Divorce Revolution* 1–51 for a history of divorce law.

[132] Schäfer 1983 *AJ* 193; Eekelaar in Bates *The Child and the Law* v1 97–9.

[133] See Burman 1983 *AJ* 174–5 regarding the obstacles to obtaining legal aid in South Africa.

[134] *Fifth Report* RP78 of 1983 Part VII; cf SA Law Commission *Report on the Law of Divorce* RP57 of 1978 para 18.7.

[135] Paragraph 8.9.3. And see Schäfer op cit n132 199.

[136] Encouraged by informal procedures and easy accessibility: para 2.8.

the paucity of empirical data.[137] To the credit of customary law are the rules that the wife be assisted by her guardian or a curator ad litem[138] and, formerly, that the commissioners' courts assist unrepresented litigants. But a serious deficiency is the rule that customary divorces may be arranged without recourse to a court at all. And now, with the abolition of commissioners' courts and the transfer of their jurisdiction to magistrates' courts, women and children are likely to find themselves in an even more vulnerable position than before.[139]

The only material reforms to have been implemented were in Natal, and latterly in KwaZulu and Transkei. Unfortunately, the exemplar in all cases was pre-Divorce Act Roman-Dutch law, which was not the best model for progressive development since it was predicated on adversarial procedures and fault-based divorce. The most significant innovation was to grant the wife locus standi to prosecute her own divorce.[140] This is linked to her guardian's duty to reconcile her with the husband, presumably an attempt to reproduce the customary-law preference for reconciliation.

[86] SECTION 50 NATAL AND KWAZULU CODES

(1) A wife who seeks divorce shall on leaving her husband's family home forthwith inform the person who received *lobolo* for her, if any, or his successor in title, and upon her declaring her refusal to live with her husband and her intention to seek divorce such person shall as soon as practicable attempt to reconcile the partners and should he fail to effect a reconciliation the wife may institute proceedings for a divorce in a magistrate's court.

(2) A husband who seeks divorce must notify his intention to the person who received *lobolo* for the wife, or his successor in title, which person shall as soon as practicable attempt to reconcile the partners and should he fail to effect a reconciliation the husband may institute proceedings for a divorce in a magistrate's court.

To demand of an individual that, regardless of his sentiments or capacities, he must reconcile his ward and her husband is pointless. And, as a mandatory procedure for all divorces, conciliation is otiose. It is clearly absurd where it would be dangerous or impossible for the wife to return to her husband.[141] Moreover, if conciliation is going to work, it should occur at an early stage of marital conflict,[142] both parties should seek it,[143] and both must be committed to dealing with one another in the future.[144] Notwithstanding these reservations,

---

[137] The only two studies concerned the Black Divorce Courts. They yielded quite different assessments: Sinclair in Eekelaar & Katz op cit n128 146 and Burman op cit n133 175–6.

[138] In chiefs' courts no representation is permitted.

[139] See Rwezaura (1983–4) 1/2 *Zimb LR* 91–2 for Tanzania.

[140] Section 48(1). And see *Tshelembe v Nhlapo* 1944 NAC (N&T) 17.

[141] In one case it was held that where the wife had disappeared, conciliation was obviously unnecessary: *Kambula & another v Kambula* 1946 NAC (N&T) 7. The requirement is arguably too vague to be enforced, since there is no indication what the guardian is expected to do.

[142] See the Hoexter Commission *Report* para 3.6.

[143] Where it is imposed, it is unlikely to be accepted, and may end up being counter-productive in dissipating marital discord: Silberman & Schepard (1986) 14 *NY Univ R Law & Social Change* 743.

[144] And some measure of coercion, notably social pressure, is necessary to make them abide by the settlement. Given the effects of migrant labour and the anonymity of the urban environment, neither of these conditions is likely to be realized in South Africa. See Merry in Abel *The Politics of Informal Justice* v2 40.

the courts have made it clear that reconciliation is an essential preliminary to the divorce action[145] not an empty formality.[146]

Elsewhere conciliation/mediation has come to be regarded as the panacea of matrimonial ills, and it is now a familiar feature of divorce legislation in diverse jurisdictions.[147] Enthusiasts claim that a mediated settlement can take much of the bitterness out of the divorce proceedings and that it encourages the spouses to find compromise solutions of long-term benefit to themselves and their children.[148] On the other hand, there are disadvantages: more particularly, where the parties started with unequal bargaining positions, the ultimate settlement continues to reflect their inequality.[149] This finding emerged from research in Botswana, where it was discovered that traditional conciliation procedures in a chief's court reinforced patriarchy.[150] Where a person had to rely on his or her skills of persuasion and negotiation and where the members of the tribunal were committed to upholding African traditions, women were almost bound to be disadvantaged.[151] Hence the inequality of the spouses' positions, which can be exacerbated by an adversarial procedure, will not necessarily be cured by conciliation.

In Natal and KwaZulu the wife has been made a full party to the divorce action. But what of her guardian? Because he retains an interest in the bridewealth, he cannot be ignored, and care is taken to protect his position.

[87] SECTIONS 51 AND 52 NATAL AND KWAZULU CODES

51. Notwithstanding anything contained in section 54, no order for the return or forfeiture of *lobolo* shall be granted in any action for the dissolution of a customary marriage unless the person who received *lobolo* for the wife, or his successor in title, is cited as a party to the action.

52. The dissolution of a customary marriage by divorce, except when decreed at the suit of a wife by reason of the wrongful acts, misdeeds or omissions of the husband, shall be accompanied by the return to the husband of at least one beast or its equivalent by the

---

[145] *Ngubane* 1937 NAC (N&T) 27. See Bekker (1976) 9 *CILSA* 354.

[146] On at least two occasions it was held that the attempt to reconcile may be made at any time prior to judgment: *Cele & another v Cele* 1957 NAC 144 (NE); and see *Mkize v Nqulunga* 1941 NAC (N&T) 25.

[147] Under s 4(3) of the South African Divorce Act 70 of 1979, eg, the court may recommend conciliation, and under the Mediation in Certain Divorce Matters Act 24 of 1987 a family advocate may be appointed. In Ghana, s 9 of the Matrimonial Causes Act No 367 of 1971 introduced the option of informal conciliation. The 1968 Kenyan Commission on Marriage and Divorce recommended that divorce be granted by a court only if the parties produced evidence that reconciliation had been attempted before a marriage tribunal and had failed. See Read (1969) 5 *East African LJ* 134. This recommendation was finally incorporated into s 106(2) of the Tanzania Law of Marriage Act 5 of 1971. See Read (1972) 16 *JAL* 34.

[148] Mediation is also cheaper and quicker than adjudication. See Scott-Mcnab (1988) 105 *SALJ* 709ff for a positive assessment; and further: Parkinson (1983) 13 *Family L* 22–5 and 183ff; Roberts (1983) 46 *MLR* 537 and Silberman & Schepard op cit n143 745ff.

[149] See Merry in Abel op cit n144 39.

[150] Griffiths (1986) 14 *Int J Sociology L* 359ff.

[151] A study in Tanzania, regarding a statutorily imposed conciliation procedure, revealed that women favoured non-traditional courts (especially when claims for division of the estate or maintenance were concerned) because they had a better chance of obtaining fair settlement there: Rwezaura in Abel op cit n144 65 and see further on Tanzania: Rwezaura & Wanitzek (1988) 2 *Int J Law & Family* 20–1.

person who received *lobolo* for the wife, or his successor in title, where he has been cited as provided for in section 51.

This means that a court may not make an order for return of bridewealth[152] unless the wife's guardian is cited as a party.[153] (Conversely, where the action concerns only the return of bridewealth, the wife need not be cited.)[154] When ss 51 and 52 are read together, however, it appears that the wife's guardian need not be a party if the husband's misdemeanours were the cause of the action.[155] The court in *Dhlamini v Kuluse*[156] gave an extended interpretation to the word 'cite' in s 51 holding that if the woman's guardian was named as assisting her, and if he was present and gave evidence at the trial, he would be bound by the court's judgment. This construction has not been followed.[157] If the order for return of bridewealth is to be effective, the wife's guardian must be an actual party to the action.[158]

[88] SECTIONS 53 AND 54 NATAL AND KWAZULU CODES

53. Upon the dissolution of any customary marriage the court may make such order as to the custody and maintenance of the minor children born out of such marriage as may be just and expedient.

54. When granting any decree of divorce the court shall give clear and explicit orders and directions as to the following matters—

(a) subject to the provisions of section 27(5), the custody of the minor children of the marriage, and any necessary provision for their maintenance;

(b) The number of cattle, if any, to be returned to the husband by the person who received *lobolo* for the wife, or his successor in title, if such person has been cited as a party in terms of section 51.

The court's obligation to make a specific order about custody and maintenance of children brings customary law into line with s 6(1) of the Divorce Act.[159] Section 27(5), mentioned in s 54(a) (which is out of place in the context of custody), introduces a radical departure from customary law: it allows the court to grant the *mother* sole guardianship of any minor children of the marriage. Otherwise, s 54(a) reflects the main concern of customary law, the refund of bridewealth.[160]

---

[152] Section 52 assumes that at least one beast must be returned to the husband to signify dissolution of the marriage. This would seem to be an unnecessary technicality. The section itself acknowledges that where the wife is suing for divorce on the basis of her husband's misdeeds, bridewealth need not be returned. This reflects the general principle of customary law. See *Mosina v Ndebele* 1943 NAC (N&T) 2 and *Mhlanga v Hleta & another* 1944 NAC (N&T) 40.

[153] In the language of the Codes 'the person who received *lobolo*' for her: *Ngcobo v Mabaso* 1935 NAC (N&T) 40 and *Xulu v Mtetwa* 1947 NAC (N&T) 32.

[154] *Masoka v Mcunu* 1951 NAC 327 (NE).

[155] *Qwabe* 1953 NAC 211 (NE).

[156] 1937 NAC (N&T) 147.

[157] Stafford & Franklin 138.

[158] *Mkize* 1951 NAC 360 (NE). But, as Stafford & Franklin 137–8 say, this seems unnecessary as, eg, where the guardian is absent or cannot be found.

[159] 70 of 1979.

[160] Subject to the usual deductions based on: the number of children born of the marriage and fault (*Masoka v Mcunu* 1951 NAC 327 (NE)); the length of time that the marriage lasted; and the likelihood of the wife's remarriage (*Mahaye v Lutuli* 1952 NAC 279 (NE)).

With regard to grounds for divorce, the Codes impose an outdated version of the common law, reflecting the rules applicable in South Africa before the Divorce Act[161] was passed.[162]

[89] SECTION 48 NATAL AND KWAZULU CODES

(1) An action for divorce in respect of a customary union may be maintained by either partner on any of the following grounds—
(a) adultery on the part of the other partner;
(b) continued refusal on the part of the other partner to render conjugal rights;
(c) wilful or malicious desertion on the part of the other partner;
(d) continued gross misconduct on the part of the other partner;
(e) that the other partner is undergoing a term of imprisonment of not less than five years;
(f) that conditions are such as to render the continuous living together of the partners insupportable or dangerous.
(2) The wife, by customary marriage may in addition maintain a suit for divorce from her husband by reason of—
(a) gross cruelty or ill-treatment on the part of the husband;
(b) accusations of witchcraft or other serious allegations made against her by the husband.

As opposed to enumerating these grounds for divorce, it would have been simpler if the Codes had incorporated the breakdown principle, which is more in keeping with the spirit of customary law. None the less, paragraphs (d) and (f) of s 48(1), which allow an unspecified variety of facts to be alleged in support of a prayer for divorce, bear close resemblance to the breakdown principle.[163]

The most important departure from customary law is the requirement, implicit in this section, that the marriage be dissolved by a court, ie private divorces are not countenanced.[164] It follows that if the court does not consider the plaintiff's grounds for suit sufficient, it may refuse the petition.[165]

Section 48 of the Transkei Marriage Act[166] provides that courts *may* grant divorce decrees. As read with s 37, this implies that extra-judicial divorce is still permissible. The grounds upon which a court may grant a divorce are laid down in s 43 and they are in essence the same as the grounds pertaining in South Africa prior to the Divorce Act. In Transkei, however, particular provision was made for customary law in that the court may order divorce 'on any ground which shall, in accordance with the customary law which applied to the consummation of such customary marriage, be sufficient for a decree of divorce'.[167]

---

[161] 70 of 1979.
[162] See Stafford & Franklin 126–31 and Bekker op cit n145 347–54.
[163] From disobedience and destructive character—*Mdukuza v Malibase* 1913 (2) NHC 100—to incurable disease—*Mbhata* 1940 NAC (N&T) 41. See Bekker op cit n145 352–3.
[164] *Mlaba v Myeni* 1942 NAC (N&T) 6.
[165] See, eg, *Nyaka & another v Nyaka* 1947 NAC (N&T) 16.
[166] 21 of 1978.
[167] Section 48(b).

III NULLITY

The concepts of nullity and judicial separation[168] originated in canon law.[169] Both provided ways of ending the cohabitation of the spouses without impugning the sanctity and indissolubility of marriage. As such, they were the result of Christianity's prohibition on divorce. Once the influence of religion over marriage had abated, and divorce was permitted, marriage could be terminated in one of two ways. In the case of divorce the union was dissolved on the basis of grounds existing at the time that the action arose; in the case of nullity the grounds existed at the time that the parties purported to marry one another. A decree of divorce operates prospectively, ie from the time that it was granted; a decree of nullity declares that there had never been a marriage, and so, in effect, the union is terminated retroactively.

Nullity was introduced into customary law by the Natal Code. It was the inevitable consequence of state intervention in marriage. When the formation of marriage requires state (or Church) approval, rules are prescribed to determine when the union comes into existence.[170] It follows from this that breach of the rules results in a void marriage, which may in turn necessitate a declaration of nullity.[171]

[90] SECTION 49 NATAL AND KWAZULU CODES

A declaration of nullity in respect of a customary marriage may be applied for and obtained by or on behalf of either partner on any of the following grounds—
(a) insanity of the other partner at the time of the celebration of the marriage;
(b) impotence or other permanent physical defect on the part of the other partner preventing consummation of the marriage;
(c) the absence of any of the essentials of a customary marriage as set forth in section 38(1);
(d) the fact that the woman was, at the time of the celebration of the marriage, the wife of another man by civil or customary marriage; or
(e) the fact that the man was the husband of another wife by civil marriage:

Provided that a declaration of nullity in respect of a customary marriage on the ground of the insanity of one of the partners shall not be obtainable unless the fact of such insanity was unknown to the other partner at the time of celebration of the marriage and unless the action be instituted within a reasonable time after the celebration of the marriage.

Section 49 of the Transkei Marriage Act[172] also provides that any party to a customary marriage may apply for a declaration of nullity on one of the following grounds: *(a)* the other party was insane at the time of marriage; *(b)* the woman was already married by customary or civil rites; *(c)* 'any other ground which shall, in accordance with the customary law which applied to the consummation of such customary marriage, be sufficient for a declaration of nullity'.[173]

---

[168] The latter now abolished in South Africa by s 14 of the Divorce Act 70 of 1979.
[169] Roberts *Law and the Family in Africa* 241ff.
[170] See above, 169.
[171] See Stafford & Franklin 131–3.
[172] 21 of 1978.
[173] Section 49*(b)*.

The sanction which the common law invokes for failure to comply with the requirements for creating a marriage—nullity—is seemingly non-existent in customary law. If the relevant rules were not observed (and no doubt there would need to be an element of wilful refusal), the marriage would probably be dissolved in the ordinary way.

> 'This does not mean that African law ignores 'no-marriages'. Obviously a relationship between a man and a woman living in concubinage would not produce effects of a marriage if their pretensions force a court to decide that indeed they are not married. As such, in a sense, African law recognizes 'non-existence of marriage' especially in cases where the formal requirements of the law of marriage are not complied with. This means only that individuals are not able to pretend that they are married if no marriage has taken place.'[174]

The retention of nullity in African marriage legislation seems, on reflection, to have been shortsighted.[175] Its retroactive effect is fictive, in the sense that it does not reflect the fact that the parties might have been living together as husband and wife for a long period of time. This means that theoretically at least a nullity decree, unlike a divorce decree, does not authorize orders of maintenance or guardianship and might result in rendering the children illegitimate.[176] For these reasons European legislators have tended to abandon nullity by assimilating it to divorce.[177]

To some small extent these concerns have been addressed. Section 55 of the Codes provides that when a court grants a nullity decree it must order return of the bridewealth paid, including any increase. It may also make an order for the refund of the expenses incurred in connection with the union, which might include the ngquthu beast. Under s 50 of the Transkei Marriage Act,[178] the court is obliged to make orders regarding custody and maintenance of the children and return of bridewealth.

The Codes obliquely introduced a distinction between void and voidable marriages. Failure to comply with the *essentials* of the marriage (as laid down in s 38 of the Codes) renders the union void ab initio and not merely voidable, which is the consequence of a marriage flawed by any of the factors specified in s 49.[179]

IV RETURN OF BRIDEWEALTH

In customary law the central issue in divorce proceedings is refund of bridewealth,[180] an obligation taken so literally[181] that the husband could demand

---

[174] Pauwels in Roberts op cit n169 231.
[175] Pauwels in Roberts op cit n169 237.
[176] Cf s 6 of the Children's Status Act 82 of 1987.
[177] Cf Hahlo 107 and 116–17.
[178] 21 of 1978.
[179] *Mdhlalose v Kaba* 1938 NAC (N&T) 43; *Mlete* 1940 NAC (C&O) 105.
[180] Physical delivery would seem to be essential: *Mbiza v Devete d/a* 1963 NAC 88 (S). This confounds the argument that the reason for giving bridewealth was to provide support for the wife if she returned home.
[181] In Transkei there used to be a rule that in all cases at least one beast had to be given to the husband, regardless of whether the wife's guardian's deductions equalled or exceeded the total number of cattle paid: *Gqedeyi v Makati & another* 3 NAC 180 (1913); *Mfesi v Maxayi* 4 NAC 199 (1919); *Nkonkile v Ngqono* 4 NAC 98 (1920); cf *Ntsodo v Dlangana* 1950 NAC 195 (S). See n52.

return of the same cattle he had originally given.[182] If they had died in the interim, the defendant could settle the claim with a cash equivalent.[183]

The courts' present approach has been fashioned by a tendency to generalize rules from particular instances, subject to an overriding requirement of equity.[184] So, for example, the rule amongst the Ndebele[185] that if the wife repudiated the marriage, her guardian must forfeit the full amount of bridewealth, was extended to all the peoples in the Transvaal.[186] The relative fault of the spouses in causing the breakdown of the marriage was introduced as the major equitable factor. It was held, for instance, that if the husband acted unreasonably in repudiating his wife, this would be a ground entitling her guardian to retain portion of the bridewealth.[187] Other grounds justifying retention are that the husband was impotent,[188] that he assaulted his wife,[189] or that he abandoned her.[190]

The birth of children is a convenient yardstick for measuring the fulfilment of the wife's marital obligations. Thus the general rule is that the wife's guardian is entitled to retain one head of cattle for every child born of the union.[191] In *Mekoa v Masemola*[192] the court went so far as to say that this was an expression of natural justice. The rule even holds good in respect of a child fathered by a man other than the husband, ie an adulterine child,[193] because the husband has parental rights over it. Further, the wife's guardian may retain one head of cattle in respect of a miscarriage[194] unless this occurred within the first three months of pregnancy.[195]

The courts' approach to deductions for the wife's services during marriage is less consistent. The guardian was allowed to retain a beast or two under Pondo law,[196] and in a case from Natal,[197] a deduction of two head for eleven years of marriage was permitted. But it was held that retentions of this type were not recognized in Bhaca law[198] or elsewhere in Transkei.[199] Equitable principles seem to have been responsible for the refusal of claims where the spouses had been

---

[182] *Mbombo v Ncapayi* 4 NAC 57 (1919); *Ntloni v Tyako* 1947 NAC (C&O) 5.

[183] *Danti v Mbuzo* 3 NAC 79 (1913); *Mdunana v Ntsuntswana* 1953 NAC 271 (S).

[184] Duncan 40–1, eg, says that disposition of bridewealth is based on equity.

[185] *Mogidi & another v Ngomo* 1948 NAC (N&T) 18.

[186] Allowing for deductions representing the children born of the union: *Mekoa v Masemola* 1939 NAC (N&T) 61.

[187] *Gunqashi v Cunu* 2 NAC 93 (1910). To establish fault the husband's tactics in provoking his wife's desertion will be carefully scrutinized: *Kele v Keti* 1 NAC 171 (1908).

[188] *Ndatambi v Ntozake* 1 NAC 3 (1895); *Ncose v Nandile* 4 NAC 197 (1920).

[189] *Xakata v Kupuka* 2 NAC 62 (1910).

[190] *Shabangu v Masilela* 1939 NAC (N&T) 86.

[191] *Gaga v Dyaba* 1931 NAC (C&O) 4; *Tusi v Cekwaan & another* 1939 NAC (N&T) 63; *Nkuna v Kazamula* 1941 NAC (N&T) 128; *Manjezi v Sirunu* 1950 NAC 252 (S).

[192] 1939 NAC (N&T) 61.

[193] *Gqozi v Mtengwane* 1960 NAC 26 (S); *Ng'cobo v Zulu* 1964 BAC 116 (NE).

[194] *Mayeki v Kwababa* 4 NAC 193 (1918).

[195] In *Jelani v Mrauli* 2 NAC 54 (1910) this was said to be a rule of Tembu law.

[196] *Tusi v Cekwaan & another* 1939 NAC (N&T) 63; *Sihoyo v Mandobe* 1941 NAC (C&O) 5; *Novungwana v Zabo* 1957 NAC 114 (S). And see Hunter 210.

[197] *Ng'cobo v Zulu* 1964 BAC 116 (NE).

[198] *Mzizi v Pamla* 1953 NAC 71 (S).

[199] *Ntwanani v Tuba* 3 NAC 65 (1916).

married for only two months[200] and where the wife was very young and soon after her divorce remarried.[201]

According to Pondo law the wife's guardian may retain a beast in respect of the wife's wedding outfit;[202] but this deduction is not permitted in other parts of Transkei.[203] A further deduction is permitted for the wife's personal use when she returns to her family.[204]

Although the return of bridewealth is in theory a necessary reversal of the process of creating a marriage, it is questionable whether in practice it can still be realized today without seriously prejudicing the wife and/or her family. As marriage goods become assimilated to the general economy, they are used to defray day-to-day expenses and so cannot be repaid without occasioning the wife's family hardship. Moreover, where the recipient has had to expend the bridewealth on the settlement of his own marriage debts, he will not be in a position to refund it. Such circumstances discourage divorce, and although this may be conducive to marriage stability the person who is likely to suffer as a result is the wife.

V PROPERTY CONSEQUENCES

(1) Post-divorce support systems

In former times, a person was dependent for economic survival on the support of kinfolk and to a lesser extent on neighbours and chiefly rulers. Today, individuals are expected to earn their own livelihoods from wage-labour, although with the spread of social welfare systems, the indigent may supplement their incomes with state allowances.[205]

Customary law is still predicated on the assumption that the individual's primary source of support is the extended family. The feasibility of this should be assessed in terms of the following account, which is a comparison of the economic situation in two rural villages. The fictitious name 'Polelo' was given to a 'betterment village' created in 1977 in the Matatiele district of Transkei, as part of a general programme to rationalize the use of land.[206] The name Kgano is used for a 'closer settlement' village in Qwaqwa, which was established in 1974 to accommodate the people who had been removed from areas within South Africa, notably farms in the Orange Free State.[207] Land in this village had been set aside for residential purposes only and the population density was very high. In both villages the economic support system of the family had been either destroyed or seriously disrupted.

---

[200] *Tshuze v Qobosha* 3 NAC 90 (1912).

[201] *Nkuna v Kazamula* 1941 NAC (N&T) 128.

[202] *Mkanzi v Masoka* 1949 NAC 145 (S).

[203] *Gobo v Mgqitywa* 3 NAC 296 (1914); *Mzizi v Pamla* 1953 NAC 71 (S).

[204] *Mfazwe v Tetana* 2 NAC 40 (1910). It should be noted that the husband may not keep the nquthu beast: *Magwanya v Mtambeka* 1 NAC 42 (1901). Nor may he claim any increase in the cattle given to the wife's guardian: *Dliwako v Makonco* 1 NAC 93 (1905).

[205] See: Glendon and Sen in Meulders-Klein & Eekelaar *Family, State and Individual Economic Security* v1 3ff and 70ff respectively; Land in Freeman *The State, the Law and the Family* 25.

[206] See above, 155 n47 regarding betterment planning.

[207] See above, 159 regarding forced removals.

[91] SHARP & SPIEGEL (1985) 55 *AFRICA* 142–6

[The individual case studies completed by the authors] indicate the crucial importance for domestic groups of a reliable source of cash income as the main shield against impoverishment. We find, however, that, as in the Lesotho cases, access to a reliable cash income is by no means evenly distributed within our sample populations.

There are two sets of factors which affect the likelihood of access by domestic groups to a reliable cash income. The first relates to the size and composition of a given household; the second concerns the degree of experience of members of domestic groups in the wage-labour market.

The size of a given household does not itself determine the likelihood that its members will have reliable sources of cash income. What is important, however, is the relationship between size and the particular composition of a given group. Our own material confirms Murray's finding[1] that small households can be at a severe disadvantage if they lack members of an age suitable to be in wage employment. Murray also showed that small female-headed households were at a particular disadvantage, given the difficulties women have in finding a reliable job. On the other hand, large households with several adult members who are potential wage-earners are likely to be relatively well-off, provided the adults can find employment.

We found one important variation from the situation in Lesotho. Civil pensions—set both in the Transkei and in Qwaqwa at R98, paid bi-monthly in 1982–83—are available to the aged in the Bantustans (even though many have difficulty in getting them); Lesotho cannot provide this. It means that old people in the Bantustans need not depend to the same extent on younger kin as do those in Lesotho; indeed, we find that households comprising only old people with pensions are among the least insecure in both research areas. In Qwaqwa particularly the isolation of such people can be a positive advantage by limiting the number of those who can make a claim on the person.

Many people in Polelo have had considerable experience of participation in migrant wage labour. This extends back over three or four generations, even though the experience may not all have been acquired in Matatiele itself. Despite the variation within Polelo in this respect, people in the village generally know ways of entering the market—either through formal recruitment procedures or through the use of personal contacts in various centres of employment. The *de jure* population of Polelo in fact includes several people who have permanent residence rights (section 10(1)(a), (b) and (c)) in prescribed urban areas: these are people who choose to maintain a rural home.

Kgano's population, on the other hand, has a highly varied migrant wage-labour experience. Most people moved into the village between 1974 and 1978, having been relocated from white-owned Orange Free State farms. People were not necessarily isolated on these farms, and many men had intermittent experiences of migrant labour from the farms. But the constraints on finding employment in Qwaqwa differed from those with which they had been familiar, and late arrivals in particular had not been in the Bantustan long enough to find out how to work the system. This was much more important as a barrier to securing a reliable cash income through contract employment than was the fact of the extremely low educational levels of an ex-farm labouring population. In neither Kgano nor Polelo was there, in fact, any noticeable correlation between level of educational experience and likelihood of gaining contract employment.

In addition the scale of Qwaqwa is such that most people are socially and physically removed from sources of information regarding job opportunities. People often expressed the view to us that, in these circumstances, getting a job seemed similar to winning in a game of dice. This high degree of impersonality was not observed in Polelo, where people had the opportunity of face-to-face, regular contact with influential people such as government officials living in the village. The latter passed on information about contracts on offer and where to get them.

Differences between Matatiele and Qwaqwa

One must not overemphasize the apparent contrast between Matatiele and Qwaqwa. It would not be true to say that impoverishment has not been occurring in Matatiele, precisely because conditions in the regional periphery generally are a direct consequence of accumulation processes in South Africa. These processes result in an overall tendency towards growing impoverishment which can be demonstrated empirically. Historical material on this issue is abundant.[2] Our own observation shows it to be a continuing process; in Matatiele, for instance, we have witnessed the most recent stages in the transformation of a freehold farm into a squatter camp providing residential sites and limited pasturage to several thousand people in the space of the last ten years. Many of these are people who have been forced to leave overcrowded locations in the district or have lost contact with their natal homes during extended periods of employment on white-owned farms in the vicinity.

This . . . suggests that the present limited availability of agricultural resources in an area such as Matatiele must be seen as a factor which can do no more than arrest the process of impoverishment temporarily, certainly as far as most of the inhabitants are concerned. Furthermore, access to these particular resources has become unevenly distributed, so that many are now highly vulnerable.

It has been estimated that one-third of the total population of the South African Bantustans lived in closer settlements by 1980, whereas "the great majority of rural people in the homelands had land rights of some kind in 1960".[3] More and more people have, therefore, come in the relatively recent past to experience the kind of conditions described for Kgano in Qwaqwa.

The dependence of Kgano residents on access to a reliable cash income is acute . . . . This is not simply because agricultural land is denied to them, but also because the scope for other income-generating activities is severely limited by the overall local situation. People in Kgano cannot "compensate" in some way for their lack of agricultural resources by increasing the scope of other petty production or retailing activities. The presence of more people in a given area does not of itself create a larger market for local goods and services. The various local income-generating possibilities in the rural periphery are not alternatives: each depends on the possibility of others being practised, and all depend together on access to reliable cash incomes.

One informant in Kgano, by no means exceptional, had been without reliable wage employment for four of the five years since his arrival from an Orange Free State farm. He had, he said, spent a very significant proportion of the four "wasted years" (as he called them) queueing fruitlessly at one or other of the Labour Bureaus in Qwaqwa. A couple of "piece jobs" had come his way: he had cleared the grounds of the university for three months in 1981 and had worked for a large South African construction company engaged in a project for the local authorities for four months in 1982. In no sense, he emphasized, could this latter job be construed as "real work": he had had no contract, had been paid a starvation wage (R30 per month) and had been made redundant, with many others, at a day's notice. He had tried his hand at local retailing by hawking vegetables. . . . But . . . he found it necessary to spend most of his time waiting at the Labour Bureaus. There were, he said explicitly, two reasons for this. Hawking required a cash input, which he often lacked, before selling could begin; and, as he put it, "All of us can't all sell things all the time—someone's got to buy vegetables rather than sell them, and there are just too many of us trying to sell and not enough able to buy."

Kgano residents are made even more vulnerable by the fact that the processes of long-distance relocation and arbitrary assignment to residential sites destroy a range of existing relationships between people. Taken together, relocation, arbitrary site allocation and acute dependence on access to scarce secure wage employment make it difficult for people to establish viable alternatives to the relationships which have been destroyed.

[Two case studies] provide illustrations of the way in which these several factors hang together. In each case the residents of the site had lost all access to reliable cash income. Their vulnerability was compounded, moreover, by the fact that they were socially isolated from people beyond their respective site boundaries. Two limiting factors were in operation here. In each case the site residents had lost all contact with kin as a result of relocation. In addition, however, most other people in their respective neighbourhoods within the village were themselves entirely dependent on access to wage earnings.

This particular dependence meant that the neighbours around the sites in question had no resources upon which to base any long-term offer of material assistance to the affected site residents. For the latter this double isolation—from direct access to secure wage earnings and from other people—led also to the rapid disintegration of the fundamental links of kinship among the population of the sites. In [one] case this process of disintegration was already far advanced by July 1983. The parents on the site expressed to us their anxiety for and guilt about their children. They had, they said repeatedly, failed as parents. "I cannot sleep at night any longer," said M.S.'s wife, "because my son was so ill when he last came home (at Easter). But I sent him back to work (in Welkom, 300 km away) because his is the only income we have. I am being forced to kill one child in order to feed the others."

Our observations suggest that neighbourliness is an important relationship in people's lives in Kgano. Residents of nearby sites do attempt to construct networks of neighbourliness and to express these relationships in the idiom of kinship. But such networks are based on short-term reciprocity rather (than) on any long-term commitment. Loss of access to reliable sources of cash income condemns most households to dropping out of the networks of reciprocity at precisely the point when those networks are needed most urgently. This is what happened to the residents of M.S.'s site. . . . Neighbours to whom we spoke conceded M.S.'s claim that he had exhausted the possibility of begging or borrowing from them; but they also explained that they were appalled and ashamed by the sight of his household literally starving to death in front of them while they could do no more to help.

Social life in Kgano is forced into a Hobbesian mould. As one of the areas of closest settlement in Qwaqwa it is notorious for an appalling rate of serious and petty crime. Residents recognize that this results from the density of habitation, the high rate of un- and underemployment and the lack of other income-generating resources. Migrants returning home with wages know that the walk home from the bus stop is a risky business; people keep to their own sites after dark to avoid roaming gangs of *tsotsis* (thugs), and they know that the *tsotsis* are, in fact, their own children and those of their neighbours. Attempts to build networks of neighbourliness are in part a direct response to this menace: people who can be persuaded to address one as "father" or "brother" by day are less likely, perhaps, to harass by night.

But people recognize that use of the idiom of kinship in these circumstances creates no more than an "as if" relationship. People cannot expect too much of their relationships with neighbours, because the long-term commitment of generalized reciprocity cannot exist under the conditions experienced in Kgano.

It is clear that people in the areas studied in both Matatiele and Qwaqwa appeared to attach primacy to relationships with kin as resources for sustenance and social support. Where kin were near by people did turn to them first for assistance if it was needed. Where kin were not present, people explicitly lamented their absence. People were prepared and anxious to define kinship as widely as possible, for the purpose of giving and receiving, because the vagaries of relocation and betterment often brought only the most distant kin together.

People were also forced to recognize the "as if" nature of relationships with neighbours: despite use of the idiom of kinship here, long-term commitment to these relationships was rendered impossible by circumstances. It follows that people were making an implicit distinction between kinship and the "as if" relationship with neighbours. The fact that this distinction was being made is significant, and the significance is not diminished by the fact that the distinction was ambiguous (which it must be in a situation where people use clanship as a means of social identification). The interesting question is why people bother to make the distinction at all in the circumstances of closer settlement villages in the rural periphery.

The question arises not simply because of the inherent ambiguity of the distinction. It arises because the structural conditions referred to above (relocation, arbitrary site allocation, dependence on remittances, the absence of other income-generating resources) would seem set eventually to turn all relationships of kinship into the "as if" variety. This tendency results, in other words, from the impossibility of long-term commitments in relationships both across and, most devastatingly, within site boundaries in areas such as Kgano.

Even if one's father, brother or sister lives on the very next site there can be no assurance, given the conditions people face, that long-term material assistance will be forthcoming from them if it is needed. The question of whether they want to help or not becomes largely irrelevant. In Matatiele it is still possible for kin or neighbours who have a reliable source of cash income and access to agricultural land, for instance, to offer to employ one or more residents of a vulnerable site to work on the land or to herd animals in return for board, lodging and even a small cash wage. . . . But given the absence, for most, of any local income-generating activity in Kgano, help extended to others simply adds to the pool of consumers for particular cash incomes: any offer of labour by the others cannot be utilized, and they cannot repay in kind. The social and material base of even close relationships of kinship is being eroded.

An answer to the question of why people in areas such as Kgano still appear to find kinship significant as an idiom of relationship, and as a basis for giving and obtaining social and material support, must lie in their own past experience rather than in some quality inherent in kinship itself. In the case of Kgano people almost all the adults have experienced conditions on white-owned farms in the Orange Free State and Transvaal. On those farms the standard unit of employment was the extended family. This meant that members of that unit co-operated in activities to generate a joint income and were frequently co-resident in homesteads on the farms where they were employed. Ideas derived from this experience are likely to have been carried over by the first generation of people relocated to Qwaqwa.

In the case of people in Polelo, the continuing experience of the efficacy of kinship links provides for a sustained commitment to the idiom of kinship in structuring social relationships. Because of the uninterrupted, albeit changed, agrarian circumstances, betterment in Polelo did not disrupt existing forms of relationships. But the more disruptive effects of betterment are apparent on nearby freehold "squatter" farms to which surplus people have relocated.

Notes

1. *Families Divided* 55.
2. C Bundy *The Rise and Decline of the South African Peasantry*; W Beinart *The Political Economy of Pondoland 1860–1930*.
3. C E W Simkins in South African Institute for Race Relations *Resettlement: Papers* 25.

According to orthodox customary law the economic maintenance of the wife and children on dissolution of marriage was of little consequence. The children would remain with their father's family and the wife would be absorbed by her own family.[208] Women were not expected to engage in wage labour; they were the responsibility of their guardians.

Poverty and the attenuation of family ties, however, have the potential of transforming women and children into economic burdens, and on the breakup of marriage women especially are likely to find themselves at a serious

---

[208] The giving of bridewealth was seen as the provision of security for this eventuality. See above, 197–9.

disadvantage. Their employment opportunities are far worse than men's and their pay is lower.[209] Yet sex roles dictate that mothers must raise children which means that they will support both themselves and their offspring. In consequence, their working lives are dogged by the problem of finding child-care centres. To complete the scenario, there is a likelihood that the wife will lose accommodation provided by local authorities once she is divorced, because it remains registered in her ex-husband's name. Remarriage is one of the best survival strategies available, but even in this regard women are statistically less likely to find a new spouse than men are.[210]

In Western Europe the legal response to the social problems posed by divorced women[211] was twofold: to extend the husband's liability to maintain his wife and children beyond the termination of the marriage, and/or to allow the wife a share of the matrimonial estate.[212] The latter, which has been dubbed a 'property' approach, is retrospective, founded on proprietary rights established automatically (or by contract) at the time of marriage. Financial issues arising on divorce are resolved by dividing the assets amassed by the parties while they were married. This approach works best in relatively affluent societies and it complements an extended notion of property.[213] The former, a so-called 'support' approach, assumes that the spouses have a perpetual duty to support one another.

> 'Marriage was viewed implicitly as a contractual exchange of the husband's support for the wife's services, the consideration offered to the wife being lifelong provision by the husband of the necessaries of a comfortable existence.'[214]

The frequency of divorce was responsible for the introduction of alimony or spousal maintenance in order to augment the wife's share of the marital estate.[215] But today, many western, and all socialist, legal systems have either partially or wholly abandoned the support approach in favour of the property approach. One reason was the difficulty of enforcing maintenance orders; another was the likelihood of the husband's remarriage and his inability to support two families.[216] More generally, as women have attained a greater degree of financial security through better job opportunities and the policy of equalizing pay, the continuation of the husband's support obligation became redundant.

(2) Matrimonial property

In order to make provision for the divorced wife and children, it would in theory be possible to develop customary law so as to create a matrimonial property

---

[209] And African women in South Africa have felt the effects of apartheid most keenly: Burman & Barry *Divorce and Deprivation in Apartheid South Africa* 6–8.
[210] All these issues are explored in Burman op cit n19 210–11.
[211] Gray *Reallocation of Property on Divorce* 6–7 and Smart (1982) 10 *Int J Sociology L* 133.
[212] Burman & Barry op cit n209 2–5.
[213] Cf the 'new' property below, 395–6; Burman op cit n19 212; Gray op cit 290.
[214] Gray op cit 282.
[215] See generally Rheinstein & Glendon (1975) 4 *IECL* ch 4 paras 29–51 and Glendon *State, Law and Family* 135–6.
[216] See generally O'Donovan (1982) 45 *MLR* 424; and, eg, Van Houtte & De Vocht (1981–2) 16 *Law & Soc R* 321ff.

system. But this would require drastic changes to the present legal regime,[217] according to which nearly all the property acquired by a wife becomes house property, which is deemed to belong to the husband.[218] The result is that on divorce the wife leaves home empty-handed.[219] Certain specific objects, whose distinct character was denoted by mystical sanctions and associations with a wife's child-bearing functions, are deemed to be the woman's.[220] But these isolated instances do not amount to a matrimonial property system that affords the wife meaningful protection when her marriage ends.[221]

A study undertaken in a Tswana chiefdom shows that customary law can in some small measure be developed to cater for women. Here, where the husband had no good reason for initiating a divorce, household property (with the exception of land and cattle) would be divided between the spouses.[222] Similar research in Zambia revealed that chiefs' courts there had modified customary law with a view to improving the lot of women. But their decisions were regularly overruled by the subordinate courts, ironically, because they were contrary to 'customary law'![223]

(3) Maintenance

If the former wife cannot expect a share of the matrimonial estate, the other solution would be to oblige her spouse to make regular payments of maintenance.[224] Under customary law, however, where the purpose of divorce was to end all connection between the two families,[225] this idea was either unknown or at best undeveloped.[226]

In general terms, customary law had little concern with the regulation of relationships between individuals. Rights and duties vested in the family to be exercised by the most senior male, and by comparison the interests of family members inter se were only dimly conceived. In particular, customary law had little to say about the obligations of the head of a family towards members of the

---

[217] Compare the reforms introduced in Zimbabwe; under s 7(1) of the Matrimonial Causes Act 33 of 1985, the court may order a division of the matrimonial estate, paying due regard to such matters as the contributions made 'by looking after the home and caring for the family': s 7(3)(e). See Ncube in Armstrong *Women and Law in Southern Africa* 9 and 12ff. These reforms were made applicable to customary marriages: s 16 of the Act.

[218] *Nomtwebulo v Ndumndum* 2 NAC 121 (1911); *Mkwanazi* 1945 NAC (N&T) 112; *Mokoena v Mofokeng* 1945 NAC (C&O) 89; *Mpantsha v Ngolonkulu & another* 1952 NAC 40 (S); *Malaza v Mndaweni* 1975 BAC 45 (C) at 62. See generally Simons *African Women* 196–8.

[219] See Rwezaura op cit n139 93–4 and Rwezaura & Wanitzek op cit n151 11–12 and 16–18 for reforms in Tanzania.

[220] See Van Warmelo & Phophi part 3 633–9; cf Duncan 41–2.

[221] Ncube and Nhlapo in Armstrong op cit n217 11 and 45 respectively. And see above, 236–7.

[222] Fault is a critical factor, signified by payment of a fine of five head by the wrongdoer: Campbell op cit n23 333–4.

[223] Himonga in Armstrong op cit n217 56ff.

[224] Such orders may be made for the benefit of the spouse or for the children, but the requirements of both are normally so closely related that any income goes to their support as a unit. In any event spousal maintenance in low-income divorces is very unusual: Burman op cit n19 214 and Burman & Berger (1988) 4 *SAJHR* 197.

[225] Mönnig 335.

[226] The position used to be the same in English Law: Eekelaar (1986) 6 *Oxford J Legal Studies* 165; and see Eekelaar & Maclean *Maintenance After Divorce* ch 1.

group. A telling indication of this was the absence of defined procedures for protecting the rights of children, which is essential if such rights are to be effectively enforced.[227] Instead, emphasis lay on the family head's responsibility for the acts of subordinates and his rights of guardianship over them.

The common law in this regard is much more fully developed. The substantive rights and duties of support are derived from the Roman-Dutch authorities but they are now statutorily enforced.[228] The Maintenance Act[229] established special courts that were empowered, upon complaint, to investigate a parent's means for the purpose of making an order[230] to pay either future or arrear maintenance.[231] Failure to obey was made criminally punishable in terms of the same Act.[232]

The emphasis on procedure is a necessary consequence of social conditions. If a society is such that a child cannot expect as a matter of course to receive care and protection, then some means must be found to compel responsible persons to fulfil their duties. With this aim in view, the common law has designated the courts upper guardian of all minor children so that a child has the authority of the state rather than the 'natural affection' of parents as a guarantee of its support. To activate the courts' protective jurisdiction, the Maintenance Act allows an actio popularis.

> 'It is no longer a party who is *dominus litis* and who launches the action or application. It seems that any interested person including of course a former husband or wife, may lay a complaint with a maintenance officer concerning the failure to pay maintenance for another person or himself or herself. Such maintenance officer having investigated the complaint may then institute an enquiry in a maintenance court.'[233]

Once the action for support can be initiated by a third party, the care of children is removed from the exclusive domain of the family.

Customary law has an institution which superficially resembles maintenance: the payment of isondlo.[234] This can be claimed by any person who has raised a child (whether legitimate or illegitimate) on demand of custody by the parent. It is limited to an amount of one beast. Isondlo is a gift or reward for the successful rearing of the child and is a tangible token of the transfer of parental rights to the donor.[235] Isondlo bears no relationship to the common-law conception of

---

[227] See Bennett 1980 *AJ* 115ff.

[228] The analogy with the development of Roman law is compelling. The law relating to children showed a clear trend whereby the interests of the paterfamilias were gradually suppressed in favour of the child: Beinart 1958 *AJ* 98 and Nicholas *Introduction to Roman Law* 90.

[229] 23 of 1963.

[230] Sections 4 and 5.

[231] See Boberg 252 and 258. It was declared trite law in *Oberholzer* 1947 (3) SA 294 (O) at 298 that claims for arrear maintenance were barred by the principle in praeteritum non vivitur, but this is no longer so in respect of maintenance claims for children: *Woodhead* 1955 (3) SA 138 (SR) at 140. The commissioners' courts, however, followed the view expressed in *Oberholzer's* case: *Mbongwa* 1951 NAC 338 (NE); *Ngwane v Vakalisa* 1960 NAC 30 (S); and *Yokwana v Bolsiki* 1963 NAC 41 (S).

[232] Section 11(1). Note that the Act does not create substantive rights and duties: Boberg 292.

[233] *Buch* 1967 (3) SA 83 (T) at 86–7, cited by the court in *Hlabathi v Nkosi* 1970 BAC 51 (C).

[234] Van Tromp 139–42; or dikotlo in Tswana: Schapera 166 and 172. See too Duncan 8–9.

[235] Cf the Shona institution of maputiro: Holleman 93.

maintenance[236] because the right to payment does not vest in the child nor is the donor obliged to pay ex lege. Further, isondlo does not signify reimbursement for past maintenance nor is it a contribution to future maintenance.[237] Despite these differences, isondlo has been confounded with maintenance,[238] sometimes inadvertently and sometimes deliberately in an effort to update customary law to meet modern conditions.

The following is a rare example of judicial law-making in the Black Appeal Courts. The mother of a child, born of a customary union, was deserted by her husband. The child was left in the care of its maternal grandfather (the plaintiff) who demanded the sum of R8 per month as maintenance until the child was 18 years old or self-supporting, whichever occurred first. The father (the defendant) refused to accept the arrangement, tendering instead one beast as isondlo. The child's grandfather rejected this offer and the court agreed that it was not nearly sufficient.

[92] *HLENGWA v MAPHUMULO* 1972 BAC 58 (NE)

Plaintiff is dissatisfied because defendant never did anything to maintain the child Buka. Seeing that defendant had paid *lobolo* I cannot see why defendant left the child with plaintiff. The fact that he did so is an indication that he had agreed that his father-in-law should keep the child—at least *pro tem*. It also strengthens plaintiff's averment, on a balance of probabilities, that defendant had offered to pay maintenance. Later when defendant sued plaintiff before the Chief's court for the return of the cattle the plaintiff pleaded that he offered the child to defendant and that the latter refused to take it. Defendant on the other hand stated in his plea before the Bantu Affairs Commissioner that he offered *isondhlo* to plaintiff and that the latter refused to take the *isondhlo* beast.

One can understand why the *isondhlo* beast was refused. One beast can certainly not be a *quid pro quo* in modern times for the care of a child and all the expenses connected with it. . . .

Plaintiff then resorted to the only other remedy he thought he had and that is to issue summons for maintenance at R8 per month.

The Bantu Affairs Commissioner did not indicate (as is so often the case) which system of law he applied. Although summons was issued for a monetary payment I feel that the Bantu Affairs Commissioner should have applied Bantu (Zulu) Law.

It is clear that the parties are still thinking in terms of tribal law. The association of defendant and Bafunani was one which led to the payment of *lobolo* and the establishment of a customary union. Defendant did not sue before the Bantu Affairs Commissioner for the return of his cattle but before the Chief's court—a court which can only hear claims under Bantu Law. There is nothing against a party bringing a claim for maintenance under Bantu Law before the court of the Bantu Affairs Commissioner. The only point in doubt is whether such a claim is limited to the value of the *isondhlo* beast.

It seems to me that this is a case where the principles of the customary law should be examined to see if they can be made to meet the demands of modern life. No-one can rear a child on the proceeds of one beast. If the beast were a cow it might be argued that this could be done but there is no mention by the authorities that the beast should necessarily be a cow or heifer. It is apt, at this stage, to examine certain changes in another field of the family customary law. I refer to *lobolo*. The payment of *lobolo* has undergone a material

---

[236] *Cele* 1947 NAC (N&T) 2 at 3: ['it] is not payment for moneys, etc, disbursed, it is a gift and reward for the successful rearing of those wards.' See too *Mbata v Zungu* 1949 NAC 72 (NE) and especially *Sibanda v Sitole* 1951 NAC 347 (NE) above, [34].

[237] See the assessor's description in *Gatyelwa v Ntsebeza* 1940 NAC (C&O) 89.

[238] *Mafanya v Maqizana* 3 NAC 158 (1914); *Mtetwa v Nkala* 1937 NAC (N&T) 157.

change during the last 30 years—a change which is today recognised by the Courts. Today *lobolo* need no longer be paid in cattle. It is in fact frequently paid in money and more often than not (as in the present case) in money and cattle. In all such cases the money is referred to as "cattle". This development was dictated by the ever changing demands of a modern economy and the standards of modern living. The change in payment has, however, not affected the principles underlying the whole idea of *lobolo*.

Similarly the principle of *isondhlo* is not necessarily violated if the *isondhlo* is paid, not in cattle, but in money and in the amount commensurate with the demands of modern life.

I am of the opinion therefore that plaintiff's claim for maintenance is a valid one also under Bantu Law and that it need not be restricted to the payment by defendant of an *isondhlo* beast only.

This case put isondlo into an uncertain position. Does it still entail payment of only one beast, and if not, in what circumstances can more than one beast (or cash equivalent) be demanded?[239] Alternatively, can *both* maintenance and isondlo now be claimed? If isondlo is now equivalent to maintenance, can anyone bring a claim for it on behalf of the child? Although *Hlengwa's* case was applauded as a rare example of judicial law-making,[240] it would have been much simpler to exclude customary law altogether in favour of the common law.

The exclusion of customary law is technically justifiable in three situations: where legislation has overruled it; where common law must be applied in terms of the conflict of laws; because of the repugnancy proviso. First, all customary law must be read subject to any legislation in point. The relevant statutes in this regard are the Deserted Wives and Children Protection Acts and Ordinances, which were passed in the four provinces at the end of the last and the beginning of this century.[241] In 1943 these enactments were incorporated into the Black Administration Act[242] by s 10*bis*.[243] This section was later repealed by the Maintenance Act, 'except in so far as it may impose any liability upon any person to maintain any other person'. On this fragile link all statutory claims under the Maintenance Act must be based, unless the child has a right to maintenance under the common law.[244]

In order to establish that an African father is legally liable to maintain his child in terms of these enactments, it must be proved that the child: is under 15 years of age; is that of the person who was summoned; has been deserted without adequate means of support; and that the father can afford to maintain it. The requirement of desertion is, of course, unduly restrictive. What of situations where the father did not 'desert', but none the less neglected his children, a

---

[239] The cash equivalent of cattle need not approximate market value: Burman & Berger op cit n224 199.

[240] Dlamini (1984) 101 *SALJ* 355.

[241] Section 2 of Act 7 of 1895 (Cape); s 2 of Act 20 of 1896 (Natal); s 2 of Ord 44 of 1903 (Transvaal) and Ord 51 of 1903 (Orange Free State). See *R v Rantsoane* 1952 (3) SA 281 (T) at 285; *R v Kumalo* 1952 (4) SA 638 (O); *Mabanga v Msidi* 1953 NAC 82 (C); *Sekgabi v Mahlangu* 1954 NAC 164 (NE); *Kabe & another v Inganga* 1954 NAC 220 (NE) at 224; *Ngcobo v Dhlamini* 1970 BAC 86 (NE) at 88. Cf *R v Mofokeng* 1954 (1) SA 487 (O), where the court stated that an African father is legally obliged to maintain his illegitimate child under common law.

[242] 38 of 1927.

[243] Section 4 of Act 21.

[244] Which the court in *R v Mofokeng* 1954 (1) SA 487 (O) held to be the position. See the case note by Hahlo (1954) 71 *SALJ* 119–20.

particular problem in view of the system of labour migration? Moreover, unlike the common law, liability extends only to the child's parents, not to more remote members of the family.

Section 4(1) of the Maintenance Act provides the machinery for enforcing the substantive rights:

> 'Whenever a complaint on oath is made to a maintenance officer to the effect that—
> (*a*) any person legally liable to maintain any other person fails to maintain such other person . . . the maintenance officer may . . . institute an enquiry in a maintenance court.'

The phrase 'legally liable' in this section must be determined by the provincial enactments or by the common law because the Maintenance Act does not create *substantive* rights.[245]

It is clearly to the advantage of an African child if an action for support is brought under the common law. This is possible in terms of the conflict of laws. In *Sibanda v Sitole*,[246] for instance, the person who had raised the children in question was precluded from claiming £422 as reimbursement for his expenses. The court held that where the parties contemplated customary law in their dealings, that system of law should be applied. Instead the plaintiff was allowed to claim only three beasts as isondlo. The conflict of laws is used more commonly to determine maintenance when the child's parents were married by civil or Christian rites. The formalities of the marriage, together with the consequences and rights and duties on divorce, are then governed by common law.[247]

A conflict of laws approach has a commendable degree of flexibility, allowing a sensitive assessment of the parties' cultural orientation in each case. Yet this very flexibility could jeopardize the position of the wife or children. While the choice of law is the court's, the decision to apply one or other legal system is, in the final analysis, determined by the attitudes of the litigants. In *Sibanda's* case, for instance, it was the attitudes of the plaintiff and defendant, not the children involved, which determined choice of customary law. The ultimate policy objective of ensuring a child's right to support may thus be defeated by permitting the litigants to choose a system of law that does not contain such a right. Apart from this, the conflict of laws assumes that both customary and common law are separate and different legal systems. It does not envisage a modification of customary law that has assimilated it to the common law. If, for example, isondlo were to be transformed into maintenance, as suggested in

---

[245] Boberg 292; *Dhlamini v Mabuza* 1960 NAC 62 (NE) distinguished between liability under the ordinance and liability under the common law. Cf *Yokwana v Bolsiki* 1963 NAC 41 (S) where this distinction was not clearly drawn, and *Mofokeng's* case supra.

[246] 1951 NAC 347 (NE). The conflict approach appears also to have been used in: *Mafanya v Maqizana* 3 NAC 158 (1914); *Gatyelwa v Ntsebeza* 1940 NAC (C&O) 89; *Nzimande v Phungula* 1951 NAC 386 (NE); *Maluleka v Thipe* 1953 NAC 62 (C). The last two cases were concerned with the locus standi of the mother.

[247] This includes both the husband–wife (*Mabuntana* 1948 NAC (C&O) 26) and the parent–child relationships: *Xaba* 1971 BAC 127 (C); *Lesejane* 1972 BAC 167 (C); *Maneli* 1972 BAC 198 (C). In the latter three cases liability under the Maintenance Act was dealt with under the common law without comment by the courts.

Hlengwa's case, there would no longer be a conflict situation because the two laws would be the same.

Potentially, as a matter of public policy or natural justice, customary law may be excluded if it lacks rules necessary to provide children with maintenance. Previously the repugnancy proviso[248] has been invoked with respect to the custody of children[249] and there is no reason why it cannot be used to secure rights to maintenance.

Any legal uncertainty alluded to above may now be a thing of the past. Decisions made in the last years of the Appeal Courts indicated that the common law was being regularly applied to maintenance claims. The judgments unfortunately did not examine the issue in as much detail as one would have liked but there were dicta in two cases[250] stating that liability is governed by common law. And in a third case[251] the court held that under s 5(6) of the Maintenance Act the husband of a customary marriage is the legal guardian of children born of the union and is thus responsible for their maintenance under *either* customary *or* common law,[252] both during the marriage and on divorce.[253] It should also be remembered that under s 53 of the Natal and Kwazulu Codes a court, when granting a decree of divorce, is empowered to make an order regarding the maintenance of minor children as may be 'just and expedient'.

The South African Law Commission[254] sought to put liability for maintenance beyond doubt. It recommended that the common law should be applied 'provided that any provision that has been made at customary law for the support of another should be taken into account in determining the extent of the duty to support'.[255]

In the common law spousal maintenance is now governed by s 7 of the Divorce Act,[256] which allows the court to make an order of maintenance or to confirm a private agreement between the spouses. The Law Commission recommended that a statutory provision, modelled closely on this, be made applicable to customary marriages.[257]

[93] CLAUSE 9(9) OF THE BILL APPENDED TO THE WORKING PAPER ON *MARRIAGE AND CUSTOMARY UNIONS OF BLACK PERSONS* 1985

A court granting an order of dissolution of a customary marriage may, having regard to the existing or prospective means of each of the parties, their respective earning capacities, financial needs and obligations, the age of each of the parties, the duration of the customary marriage, the standard of living of the parties prior to the dissolution of the

---

[248] Contained in s 1(1) of the Law of Evidence Amendment Act 45 of 1988. See above, 129ff.

[249] *Mbuli v Mehlomakulu* 1961 NAC 68 (S) at 71.

[250] *Gcumisa* 1981 AC 1 (NE) and *Ngcobo v Nene* 1982 AC 342 (NE) at 348.

[251] *Muru* 1980 AC 39 (S).

[252] But not both. See Burman & Berger op cit n224 199.

[253] Similarly, the court in *Lekwakwe v Diale* 1979 AC 299 (C) assumed that both parents of a customary marriage had a duty to support children.

[254] *Marriages and Customary Unions of Black Persons* para 11.5.1.

[255] And see clause 9(5) of the Bill appended to the Report.

[256] 70 of 1979, the successor to s 10 of the Matrimonial Affairs Act 37 of 1953.

[257] See Sinclair (1981) 98 *SALJ* 474ff regarding s 7(2) of the Divorce Act. Compare the position in Zimbabwe: Ncube in Armstrong op cit n217 12ff.

customary marriage, their conduct in so far as it may be relevant to the break-down of the customary marriage, and any other factor which in the opinion of the court should be taken into account, make an order which the court deems just in respect of the payment of maintenance by the one party to the other for any period until the death or remarriage of the party in whose favour the order is made, whichever event may first occur.

There are three notable omissions in this clause. First, no mention is made of the court's power to make a written agreement between the parties regarding division of the estate or payment of maintenance an order of court. Such agreements derive from the common law,[258] and there is no reason why they should not be made part of the customary divorce process.[259] Secondly, nothing is said about the wife's contribution as homemaker. Thirdly, no provision is made for any prospective benefits arising out of the marriage, such as pensions and retirement annuities.[260] An undesirable inclusion in the Bill is a reference to the parties' conduct. In so far as this reintroduces fault as a factor influencing distribution of property, it is to be regretted.[261]

Clause 9(9) was indirectly inspired by s 25(1) of the English Matrimonial Causes Act of 1973.[262] The purpose of this Act was to place the spouses 'in the financial position in which they would have been if the marriage had not broken down'.[263] Before this principle is implemented in South Africa, however, it must be carefully examined to ensure its suitability in the context of local needs; and this is a complex issue.

The proprietary consequences of divorce are closely connected with other issues, such as custody and accommodation. This is often not appreciated by the courts, whose views do not always coincide with those of the poor; housing rights and citizenship, for example, are usually critically important in South Africa, yet they are not formally alluded to in the divorce settlement.[264]

[94] BURMAN in HIRSCHON *WOMEN AND PROPERTY/WOMEN AS PROPERTY* 130–4

There is a strong tendency for lawyers and laymen other than Africans to assume that, because Africans are by far the poorest section of the South African population, property plays no significant part in the issues arising for Africans on divorce. It is certainly true that many of the problems faced by Africans are very different from those which arise among the wealthier sections of the population, but it is the very uniqueness of their property and property institutions which creates the most serious problems. For African women the situation is further complicated by the tendency of both the customary law and, on occasion, the South African State, to treat them and their children as the property of their men.

---

[258] Hahlo 355 n14.

[259] Although the wife's lack of contractual capacity and locus standi must be noted as potential obstacles.

[260] See Hahlo & Sinclair (1981) 98 *SALJ* 476–8. The common law in this regard has already been amended: Act 7 of 1989.

[261] This no longer reflects the policy underlying the Divorce Act, which is to minimize guilt in favour of the breakdown principle.

[262] See Eekelaar *Family Law and Social Policy* 171 for a comparative account.

[263] The 'principle of minimal loss': Eekelaar op cit 173. And see Eekelaar 1979 *LQR* 253ff.

[264] Burman op cit n19 212.

Probably the most important rights in property for an African in Cape Town are those in the marital house, even though no African owns a house in the city: all housing is owned by the State. However, even if the man himself has the right to permanent residence in Cape Town, without being allocated a house, he cannot legally bring his wife and family to the urban area. With the length of the housing waiting list, the loss of the marital house loses an African far more than merely a roof over his or her head. In the system that the Administration Board uses to control the urban African population, the complications arising from the possession or loss of a house are both far-reaching and serious.

Houses are normally registered in the husband's name and if a woman has no children, on the breakdown of her marriage she will either have to move out into lodgings or stay on at the house, with all the unpleasantness that may entail. There is a widespread problem of violence by husbands, who may periodically assault their wives and/or their children. Both drink and customary law sanction of "chastisement" by the husband appear to play a role in this, as well as overcrowding. Informants of all population groups confirmed that the police were extremely loath to intervene in what had been defined as marital violence. For Africans the problem is complicated by the great housing shortage, which has resulted in many estranged couples being forced to live under the same roof, though not as man and wife, thus rendering the wife particularly vulnerable to assault. Several women asserted that a desire to be safe from their husbands' violence in such a situation was the major reason for their instituting divorce proceedings. Fortunately for them, they could do so at civil law, (whereas in customary law only their guardians could institute divorce proceedings) and with the increasing breakdown in urban areas of the return of *lobola*, they were more likely to be free of family pressure to return to their husbands.

If a wife has young children, her position is better. Custody of young children is now usually given to the wife, and in the last few years the Administration Board, which controls housing for Africans, has tended to give the house to the custodial parent, but only on sight of the divorce decree. This means that a husband with young children and an erring wife who has not abandoned them may well think twice before instituting divorce proceedings which will probably result in his being obliged to move out of the house to single quarters and to go to the bottom of the waiting list for a house. Since the house is not owned by the parties, the divorce court will not intervene in its allocation and the wife may well find herself eventually in possession and in control of the most valuable asset she is likely to have in the city.

Possession of the house may, however, threaten an equally crucial asset—her pass (or permit to be in an urban area), if it is issued under section 10(1)(c) of the Black (Urban Areas) Consolidation Act of 1945.[1] This gives her rights to be in the urban area only while married to a man with permanent rights of residence. . . .

Custody of Children and Maintenance

The combination of state policy, African men's attitudes generated by the customary law, and, above all, the housing shortages result in far more contested African divorces than among other "population groups", mainly extremely bitter fights over the custody of children. African divorces of civil law marriages are heard usually in a special court [the Southern Divorce Court], where unrepresented plaintiffs are common, so that legal costs are not a deterrent to lengthy court disputes and lawyers have not had an opportunity to reach a settlement. Widespread attitudes among men dictate that payment of *lobola* should give the husband custody of at least the older children and should preclude the payment of maintenance, since the children are his. This reluctance to relinquish custody to the mother and to pay maintenance is reinforced by the economic difficulties of paying maintenance out of a usually very low wage when maintaining the second family he is likely to acquire. Above all, his desire for custody is reinforced by the spectre of losing his house to the custodial mother.

The primary criterion of the court in awarding custody is the welfare of the child, with the assumption that with young children and with girls the mother is *prima facie* the best custodian. A great deal of mud-slinging is therefore usually involved in the attempt to prove the other parent is less suitable, and parents have to show that, if they work, someone suitable is available to care for the children. Since African wives very seldom receive maintenance for themselves in the Southern Divorce Court,[2] and since maintenance for children is usually perforce very low as a result of the husband's other commitments, both parents will work in virtually all cases where work can be obtained. But child care provisions are minimal and most alternatives (such as help from relatives imported into the city for that purpose or sending children to rural areas) result in serious problems, especially for women who have little income or security when divorced. Throughout most sections of South Africa women's wages are lower than men's (there are no equal pay provisions) and African women are largely excluded from the more skilled or semi-skilled lucrative work and are, as outlined above, frequently in occupations particularly vulnerable to economic fluctuations. The result is that divorced African wives, more than any other section of South African society, are forced to rely on unpaid family and communal assistance for minding their children, ironically while they themselves are in many cases employed as nursemaids for white children. While a woman's affection for her children obviously plays a major role in her decision to fight for custody of them, the fact that she is "subject" enough under civil law (in contrast with customary law), to become a custodian at all is again a somewhat mixed blessing.

Moreover, since the *lobola* system generally no longer operates to provide for an abandoned wife, the wife will probably have to go to the Maintenance Court to obtain a court order for child maintenance. A man unwilling to pay can, however, considerably delay the order, and make enforcement difficult or impossible after it is made. If he is unemployed, no order can be made against him, although theoretically he can be jailed if it can be shown he is refusing to work. However, this is difficult, as even allowing for those who choose not to work, the rate of unemployment among urban Africans with a right to be in Cape Town is very high; from a survey it was estimated as 13 per cent for only the three established townships in 1981 at the height of the economic boom in South Africa. And though many men earn some money in the informal sector, these earnings are usually difficult for the ex-wife to prove.

Even when he is employed, the amount a husband may be ordered to pay will depend on his income and other obligations. A number of men in this position have a customary union wife and family in the "homelands", and the maintenance courts in practice will take these into account (including the customary union wife) when dividing his income to allow for dependants, though there is no guarantee that the money allowed for them is necessarily sent to them. As with other South African men, though more frequently, given the attitudes and pressures described above, an African man may also have a new wife and family, so that a higher number of men than in other South African population categories are in the position of having support obligations to not two but *three* families. Often, too, money must be sent to parents, since African pensions are very low (R89 every second month) and elderly parents in the "homelands" or city often rely on their children for assistance, while attitudes within the society make refusal of such demands difficult. Given the mores of urban African society, it is also not uncommon for a man to be paying maintenance for one or more children of ex-girlfriends. Thus an exceptionally heavy number of support demands fall on the population category with the lowest salaries in South Africa. Several women informants said that with all these likely scenarios in mind, they had decided it was not worth pursuing a claim for maintenance, but where they do it seems likely that it is the customary wife who will be the ultimate loser.

There are small state child-maintenance grants for African women with two or more children if their incomes are below a certain (very low) level and if their husbands have completely disappeared.[3] Non-payment by the husband whose whereabouts is known, however, will not qualify a woman for child maintenance, and an African woman with one child or none is most unlikely to obtain maintenance.

As has been noted above, urban claims for the refund of *lobola* are fairly rare, and informants indicated that in general such claims were considered a waste of time, as the money was usually spent before the divorce occurred. This at least partially relieved women of the urgings of their families to return to their husbands, unless there was still a possibility of further *lobola* payments. However, a frequent ploy in African marriage quarrels has always been for the woman to return to her family until a further payment is made, whether of or in addition to the original *lobola*. This is taken as an indication of how much the husband wants her back and an earnest of his good intentions. As a result, since the finality of a quarrel is not usually clear, families may urge a woman to return if the husband offers a further payment. Many informants relied on their families for financial assistance to pay for their divorces, and family pressure to return to the husband may result in this assistance being withheld. It may also result in the withholding of financial support by a family able to provide it, being in receipt of *lobola* which was meant to ensure support for the wife in the event of marriage breakdown. Thus the uses of property under civil and customary law may converge to leave the woman in need of more financial assistance than under the customary law, but subjected to all the pressures generated by the *lobola* system to act against her will.

Notes

1. Now abolished by Act 68 of 1986. Despite this, the situation has not been radically changed: cf H Schoombie & D Davis (1986) 2 *SAJHR* 208.
2. The Southern Divorce Court is loath to go into questions of maintenance, which are usually referred to the (commissioner's) maintenance court. But South African law provides that a woman may obtain maintenance for herself only if it is awarded at the divorce hearing. As the Southern Divorce Court is so loath to consider maintenance questions, it is extremely rare for women to obtain it, unless it has already been agreed between the parties' lawyers and embodied in a consent paper, which the court will then make an order of court when granting the divorce—a fairly rare phenomenon.
3. See the section on state maintenance below, 288ff.

Aside from her own earning capacity, the woman's main source of income on divorce is likely to be maintenance. The current criteria for determining the amount vary widely, to include the ex-husband's support obligations towards new wives, parents in the homelands, and illegitimate children. In such circumstances it is understandable that the sums awarded are very low. Nevertheless, any award is still likely to be a relatively large proportion of the divorced wife's income.[265] A question of policy now awaits the South African courts: whether to encourage the support approach or to change to the property approach, or to strike out in a new direction altogether. At the outset it must be appreciated that the property approach (not provided for in clause 9(9) in any event) would be difficult to implement in view of the material poverty of the great majority of people in South Africa and the undeveloped nature of customary property law.[266] But the support approach is equally problematic.

During the past decade, the English courts steadily decreased maintenance awards. The main reasons given were that the wife was able to become a separate wage earner; the husband normally remarried and was therefore unable to support two families on one income; and permanent maintenance perpetuated women's inequality and their dependence on men. To some extent regular maintenance payments have been replaced by so-called 'rehabilitative alimony' (awards for a specific period of time while the wife is finding work or retraining)

---

[265] Burman op cit n19 220.
[266] See above, 276–7.

and a 'clean break' policy whereby the problem of spousal support is solved once and for all by a single property transfer at the time of the divorce.[267]

There are further disadvantages with the support approach that are peculiar to Africa. First, the strongly entrenched division of labour along gender lines means that the wife will almost inevitably be left to care for the children of the marriage, while the husband retains guardianship (with its attendant benefits). Secondly, the high value placed on procreation, together with the tradition of polygyny, makes it almost certain that the husband will remarry or contract an informal union of some sort. He is thus unlikely to be able to fulfil maintenance obligations arising out of his first marriage. Thirdly, because the support approach requires an investigation of the circumstances of each case, it encourages litigation. This is a serious hindrance (for women in particular) to the realization of rights.[268]

Fourthly, there is the endemic problem of enforcing maintenance orders. Evidence from a survey undertaken in Cape Town[269] and reports from elsewhere show a very low level of compliance.[270] And in South Africa[271] procedural delays in the maintenance courts and bureaucratic inefficiency are additional problems. Research has revealed the probability that the father would be unemployed and a high rate of default. Although criminal prosecutions and garnishee orders are possible enforcement devices,[272] these are very difficult for the woman to procure and are not easy to execute.[273]

Fifthly, there is the technical problem of enforcing maintenance orders in one of the many independent[274] or neighbouring states ringing South Africa. These legal complexities have been obviated to some extent by the Reciprocal Enforcement of Maintenance Orders Act.[275] This provides for the automatic registration (and thus recognition) of a local maintenance order in a foreign maintenance court, provided that the foreign country concerned has been proclaimed as one to which the Act applies and that the proper diplomatic channels have been used to transfer a certified copy of the order to the proclaimed country from the Minister of Justice and thence to a maintenance court.[276] Once the order has been registered it is deemed to be a local maintenance order.[277]

---

[267] In effect this is a return to the 'property' approach. See generally Eekelaar & Maclean op cit n226 ch 3.

[268] Ncube in Armstrong op cit n217 26.

[269] Burman & Berger op cit n224 339–41.

[270] Glendon op cit n215 275 for the United States and Eekelaar op cit n262 190 citing evidence collected by the Finer Commissioner in England and evidence from Australia and Canada.

[271] Burman & Barry op cit n209 19–21 and Burman & Berger op cit n224 350–1.

[272] Section 11 of the Maintenance Act 23 of 1963.

[273] Burman op cit n19 215 and 221–2 and Burman & Berger op cit n224 205. In England the problem of enforcement led to greater state involvement in the collection process, whereby the state assumed responsibility for the enforcement of maintenance orders through the agency of the Supplementary Benefits Commission: Glendon op cit n215 276–7. There is also doubt whether criminal sanctions should be used to enforce family obligations: Finer Commission (1974) v1 para 4.170.

[274] Burman & Berger op cit n224 198.

[275] 80 of 1963. See Forsyth 364–5.

[276] Sections 2 and 3.

[277] Section 6.

Finally, the single greatest obstacle to be confronted is the problem of poverty. A maintenance order, even if it can be enforced, is worthless if the person obliged has no income or a very low one.

(4) State support

As a result of the decay of family support systems and the prospect of unemployment, increasing numbers of African women have turned to the state for help.[278] By contrast, in developed countries assistance from this quarter is now being questioned on two different grounds.[279] Why should the state assume the individual's burden of familial support (usually in fact the husband's)? This should continue to be a personal responsibility.[280] A more general objection is that increased state intervention in family life promotes paternalism, which ultimately erodes individual freedoms.[281]

Whatever the arguments against giving state maintenance, the consequences of refusing it in South Africa at present seem indefensibly harsh. During the marriage, the family is often supported by both spouses; on divorce the remnant family faces a drastic fall in income relative to its needs (which remain at a fairly high level). The burden of satisfying these needs then falls on the least qualified and most poorly paid spouse.[282]

Unfortunately, the welfare system in South Africa has not yet reached a stage where the regular award of state maintenance can be debated as a question of principle. The amounts given are so small and the awards are so infrequent that they do not nearly meet the needs of the indigent.[283] *Spousal* maintenance awards are unlikely to be made in the case of low income groups, and in the case of *child* maintenance, the amounts are clearly inadequate to meet subsistence demands.[284] Different state departments deal with provision of welfare depending on the race of the applicant.[285] They all stipulate that only single women with at least one minor child qualify for maintenance grants.[286]

Maintenance will normally be awarded to a woman only if she has been divorced or has been deserted or separated from her husband for more than three months.[287] Because in principle the father is expected to support his own children, the woman must seek an order from a maintenance court before she

---

[278] This is so even in countries espousing more progressive social policies, such as equal pay: Eekelaar op cit n262 166. And see Glendon op cit n215 279 and Gray op cit n211 325ff.

[279] See, eg, the decisions cited by Smart *The Ties That Bind* 117.

[280] Although, because husbands remarry, they can no longer afford to discharge their duties. See Gray op cit n211 327–8.

[281] And one direct cause of this is the lack of accountability of welfare and judicial authorities: Murch *Justice and Welfare in Divorce* 214.

[282] See Davis et al (1983) 13 *Family L* 217ff.

[283] Burman & Barry op cit n209 10 and Burman & Berger op cit n224 197.

[284] Burman op cit n19 229–30 and Burman & Berger op cit n224 347–8.

[285] And women from the independent homelands may be expected to claim there: Burman op cit n19 228.

[286] In practice two children: Burman op cit n19 227.

[287] Alternatively, the woman might allege that the father of her children had disappeared (in which case the police must certify that he cannot be traced), was dead, or had been imprisoned for more than three months.

approaches the Department. If the whereabouts of the man are known, the woman is most unlikely to receive a state grant, and even if he persistently refuses to obtain work or ignores a court order, the woman will not receive state aid in the interim. Assuming that no assistance is forthcoming from the maintenance court, the following conditions must be fulfilled before the woman can finally qualify:

(a) if she is of working age, she will not be given aid if she is unemployed, unless she can show that she is medically unfit (in the case of an African woman, the fact that she has a baby to care for will not exempt her);

(b) she must be unmarried and must not be cohabiting with a man;

(c) she must have at least two children to support (but the grant will cover a maximum number of four children);

(d) the child or children must be under the age of 16 (when it is assumed that children will begin work; exceptionally the grant will be extended until a child turns 18) and must be attending school;

(e) under the means test the woman's income is set at an extremely low level.[288]

The grant is reviewed annually.[289] The combined effect of these provisions is to ensure that 'the most disadvantaged families in the most disadvantaged section of the community may receive no regular assistance at all from the state'.[290]

VI CUSTODY AND GUARDIANSHIP OF CHILDREN

In customary law the husband and his family have full parental rights to any children born to the wife during the marriage, provided that they have fulfilled their obligations under the bridewealth agreement. Yet, because marriage is a private agreement between the two families, there is in principle nothing to prevent them from making another arrangement if they wished. This flexibility is apparent in the following extract.[291]

[95] HOLLEMAN *SHONA CUSTOMARY LAW* 296–7, 306–7, 314

Under Shona law a tribal court has the power to make an order regarding the custody of and parental rights to the children born of the marriage, but it will not do so unless this question is actually disputed by the parties. Normally it is taken for granted that all children remain under the control of their paternal family, unless they are very young, in which case the mother or maternal family may take care of them until they are big enough to return to the father. Since the latter arrangement, when it is expected to last for a number of years, may give rise to a claim for maintenance (*marero, uredzwa*) against the paternal family, the parties may ask the court to make a ruling on this point. The court may then lay down that the child or children concerned are to be returned to the custody of the father at a certain age, with or without compensation of maintenance. The question

---

[288] See Burman op cit n19 224–5 and Burman & Berger op cit n224 347–8.

[289] As Burman & Barry op cit n209 30 say, the African woman who has four children and is employed will receive children's maintenance of R56 per month to add to her own income; but if she is to pass the means test, her income must be less than R42,08. This can be contrasted with the Primary Household Subsistence Level for Africans which was calculated in 1983 to be R191,69 for a similar family unit resident in Cape Town.

[290] Burman & Barry op cit n209 32.

[291] See further: Simons *African Women* ch 21; Schapera 161; Van Warmelo & Phophi part 3 589ff.

of maintenance is often influenced by the terms upon which the marriage is to be liquidated. If, for instance, the court considers these terms to be comparatively favourable to the *vatezwara*,[1] it may deny them the right to claim maintenance. . . .

Sometimes a marriage is terminated without the customary refund of *rovoro* cattle because the small amount of marriage compensation paid so far by the husband does not warrant such a refund. In such cases usually no third party is involved in the dispute, and the marriage is dissolved either because of the failure of the *vakuwasha*[2] to complete their *rovoro* payments, or because the wife has died and the *vatezwara* do not wish to provide a substitute in view of the poor performance of the *vakuwasha* in paying their *rovoro* dues. When there are children of the marriage and a number of *rovoro* cattle have been paid so far, the *vatezwara* may agree to leave the children with the *vakuwasha* and retain the cattle as a compensation which is then referred to as *maputiro*[3] (*kuputira mwana*, to cover a child). The inference of the term *maputiro*, when used in this connexion, is peculiar. The relationship between the families is considered to have been terminated, but since there has been no question of a division of cattle (*kugura rovoro*)—which is normally considered essential before a marriage can be legally dissolved—there is, strictly speaking, no question of a dissolution of a *marriage*. On the other hand, it cannot be denied that the original relationship between the parties constituted a perfectly valid marriage, in spite of the fact that the marriage contract was as yet "incomplete", pending the fulfilment of the *rovoro* obligation. Shona informants were unable to reconcile these obviously conflicting legal views. They argued that the *tezwara* is entitled to rescind the marriage agreement because the failure of the *mukuwasha* to complete his *rovoro* obligation constitutes a breach of contract; that the position of the *mukuwasha* is now to some extent comparable to that of a person who, by paying *maputiro* to the maternal family, acquires parental rights to the child he has unlawfully raised with an unmarried woman. This fiction circumvents the question of marriage, but as far as the children are concerned the analogy can be safely drawn because legitimacy can be established without marriage by the payment of cattle. The informants' statement at any rate faithfully reflects the Shona point of view that the right to the children and its compensation is the dominant issue under the circumstances; the change-over from *rovoro* cattle to *maputiro* erroneously implies that the marital union between the parents was unlawful, but this is no longer of importance to either of the parties.

In these cases, as in other cases of dissolution of marriage, the basic idea is that the cattle retained by the *vatezwara* should substantially compensate for the children retained by the *vakuwasha*, but again, there is no fixed ratio between children and cattle. . . . Neither is it customary to base the compensation for any one child upon the usual amount of *maputiro* payable in cases of pre-marital children.

Sometimes, when the amount of *rovoro* given so far does not nearly compensate for the number of children born of the marriage, the *tezwara* may decide to assume control of one or more children for a number of years and then allow the father to resume control against payment of a few head of cattle, which are ostensibly a compensation for maintenance (*marero, uredzwa*), but really a bid to rectify the unfavourable *rovoro* balance. If, therefore, such a compensation exceeds the amount normally payable for maintenance (which is usually not higher than one head) it can more correctly be regarded as an additional *maputiro*, or even as an outstanding *rovoro* instalment.

When only a very small portion of the marriage compensation has been paid by the husband (e.g., only a cash amount as *rutsambo*), the *vatezwara* will assume control of all children born of the marriage. The *vatezwara* may then return whatever payments the *vakuwasha* have made in connexion with the marriage, and such a refund is then regarded as an indication that the *vatezwara* wish to terminate the marriage, to wipe out all traces of the existing relationship between the families, and that they do not intend to relinquish their right to the children even if the *vakuwasha* should later wish to offer cattle in order to resume parental control. But to deprive a *mukuwasha* in this manner of the possibility of claiming his children, is regarded as sharp practice. Normally it remains open to a father to re-establish parental rights over his children if he is able to give adequate compensation to the *vatezwara*. . . .

Although the dissolution of the marriage terminates all legal obligations arising from the marriage contract as such, it may sometimes establish new obligations between the families. In all cases in which the maternal family assume custody of a child or children for the time being, either because insufficient *rovoro* has been paid by the father, or merely because their paternal relatives cannot provide adequate care for them, a new set of obligations is created. The maternal family is responsible for the well-being of the children in their custody, but the father is expected to contribute food and clothing when necessary. If he fails in this, the custodians may refuse to hand over the children to him until he has reimbursed their actual out-of-pocket expenses. Normally one or two head of cattle are payable as *marero* or *uredzwa* (maintenance) when the children have stayed with their maternal kin for a considerable number of years. The question of payment may be settled at the time of the liquidation of the marriage, when the *mukuwasha* leaves one or two head of cattle with the *tezwara* when the refund of *rovoro* is made. Often, however, the matter is left in abeyance until such time as the father claims custody of his children. In this event the maternal family can refuse to hand the children over until a reasonable compensation has been paid.

Notes

1. The party who receives bridewealth.
2. The party who gives bridewealth.
3. Cf isondlo.

The indeterminate nature of customary unions inevitably has an effect on rights to children: if marriage is only gradually established as the requisite marriage payments are made, parental rights are bound to be uncertain. In Lesotho, for instance, the standard amount of bridewealth is twenty head of cattle, ten small stock, and a horse—an amount clearly beyond the means of the average household—which means that payments have to be made in instalments over a period of ten to twenty years. Where a man has paid six head of cattle or less, he has no claim whatsoever to his children; but if he has paid ten head, his wife's family cannot dispute his right. Uncertainty creeps in where the number is between six and ten head. Claims are then resolved according to individual circumstances. Influential factors are the degree of intimacy between the families and the tactics of divorce procedure.[292]

While the courts have not discounted the significance of bridewealth in determining rights to children,[293] they none the less give overriding effect to principles of the common law. In the first place, they have assumed a protective jurisdiction as upper guardian of all minor children, which they exercise at any time when: a child is without a guardian, the guardian has neglected his or her duty, or the natural guardians cannot agree on what is best for the child.[294] In the second place, the welfare of the child is deemed to be of paramount importance.[295] In divorce suits both these principles become operative because it

---

[292] Murray (1976) 35 *Afr Studies* 104–5.
[293] See, e g, *Radoyi v Ncetezo* 2 NAC 174 (1911) and *Matsupelele v Nombakuse* 1937 NAC (C&O) 163.
[294] *Coetzee v Meintjies* 1976 (1) SA 257 (T) at 261.
[295] The court's protective jurisdiction is medieval in origin (Hahlo & Kahn *South African Legal System* 386), whereas the welfare principle is a nineteenth-century innovation: Stoljar (1971) 4 *IECL* ch 7 paras 8–10.

is assumed that whenever its parents separate a child is put at risk, and it then needs the protection of a disinterested third party.[296]

The child-welfare principle has no specific content.[297] This indeterminacy has allowed the courts to give expression to whatever views were current on proper child-rearing. In nineteenth century Europe, for instance, patriarchal values encouraged the belief that the child's best interests would be served by giving the father custody. Later, the child's interests were considered best served by awarding custody to the innocent party in the divorce action. More recently new insights gained from child psychology and changed conceptions of female roles have led to an almost automatic assumption that children should be placed in the custody of their mothers.[298] Today some experts are sceptical of the belief that a child of divorced parents is necessarily at risk. There is also doubt whether the welfare of the child should be central to the divorce proceedings;[299] and it is now being questioned whether the state should intervene at all.[300] Empirical studies have shown that in practice the courts rarely upset existing custody arrangements[301] apparently without doing any harm to the children concerned.[302]

During the subsistence of a marriage full expression is given to the principle of patriarchy: the father is considered to be the natural guardian with plenary rights to his children. On this point common law[303] and customary law[304] are agreed. When the marriage is dissolved by divorce, this principle no longer applies. In common law both the father and mother are deemed to have equal rights to the children.[305] Consequently, *custody* is awarded to the parent who is most likely to serve the best interests of the child,[306] and in the ordinary course the father is allowed to retain the right of *guardianship* unless there is some good reason to deprive him of it.[307]

It is not altogether clear whether the welfare rule has been incorporated into customary law,[308] or whether customary law has simply been excluded in favour of the common law on the basis of public policy and natural justice. In either

---

[296] Maidment *Child Custody and Divorce* 18. The development of children's rights has been closely associated with the emancipation of women and the feminist movement: cf Brophy (1982) 10 *Int J Sociology L* 149ff. Once both parents were given equal rights to their children, a criterion had to be found to evaluate competing claims: Maidment op cit 107. This gave rise to the welfare principle and, as adjudicator in these suits, the state acquired the power to intervene in what was previously a reserved, domestic domain.

[297] Initially it was not conceived to be in the exclusive interests of the child; rather it was introduced to serve society as a whole: Eekelaar op cit n226 168.

[298] Maidment op cit n296 3–6.

[299] Maidment op cit n296 74–5.

[300] Goldstein et al *Before the Best Interests of the Child* 11–12.

[301] If the mother already has custody of a child at the inception of the divorce action, the courts tend to confirm the status quo: Eekelaar & Clive *Custody After Divorce* para 13.25; Maidment (1976) 6 *Fam Law* 236 and 238.

[302] Eekelaar in Baxter & Eberts *The Child and the Courts* 5ff.

[303] *Calitz* 1939 AD 56 at 62.

[304] *Mokoena v Mofokeng* 1945 NAC (C&O) 89; *Kabe & another v Inganga* 1954 NAC 220 (C). And see s 27(1) of the Natal and Kwazulu Codes.

[305] *Fletcher* 1948 (1) SA 130 (A) at 135.

[306] Sornarajah (1973) 90 *SALJ* 133–6.

[307] Boberg 420; Hahlo 394.

[308] *Mkize* 1951 NAC 336 (NE); *Msiza & another v Msiza* 1980 AC 185 (C) at 191.

event the cultural orientation of the parents is given no direct expression in custody suits.

[96] *MBULI v MEHLOMAKULU* 1961 NAC 68 (S)

This is an appeal from the judgment of a Native Commissioner's Court declaring the plaintiff to be the guardian of her child, Lumbulelo and entitled to its custody and the delivery of the Post Office Savings Bank book in respect of the funds standing to the child's credit, in an action which the plaintiff brought against her father, the defendant, in these respects.

The defendant pleaded specially that the plaintiff's summons did not disclose a cause of action in that she was not in law entitled to claim the guardianship and custody of the child.

The grounds of appeal resolve themselves to this that the Native Commissioner erred in applying common law in deciding the case and should have applied Native law instead.

It is not disputed that the plaintiff is the defendant's daughter by a civil marriage, that she is a teacher by profession, that the child is her illegitimate daughter by one, Lerotoli, that the plaintiff had, subsequent to the birth of the child entered into a civil marriage with another man who had paid dowry to the defendant for her, that Lerotoli paid six head of cattle to the defendant as damages in accordance with Native law and custom in respect of the plaintiff's seduction and pregnancy which resulted in the child's birth, after the defendant had brought an action against him, that Lerotoli had never taken any interest in the child and that the plaintiff had given to the child from her savings the R440 standing to its credit in the Post Office Savings Bank.

The Native Commissioner based his decision to apply common law on his finding that the parties had aligned themselves to this the more advanced legal system as evidenced by these facts, viz., that the plaintiff was the defendant's daughter not by a customary union but by a civil marriage, that she was a teacher by profession and had contributed very substantially towards the material welfare of the child, that the child had been baptised in church and that the plaintiff had also entered into a civil marriage. The Native Commissioner also took into account the interest and welfare of the child. In this connection he pointed out that the plaintiff was a devoted mother, that she possessed adequate means to provide for her child and that she was comparatively well educated and in a position to care for and provide for the education of the child whereas the defendant on the other hand was quite willing to allow the child to go to strange surroundings in Basutoland should it be claimed by its natural father who lived there and had not seen the child or made any contribution towards its support or welfare. . . .

As we are here concerned with the custody of a child, it seems to me that the question of the application of common law or Native law and custom falls to be decided not solely on the basis of which legal system it would in all the circumstances of the case be fairest to give effect to as between the parties but that the dictates of public policy fall to be borne in mind in the light of the first proviso to section 11 (1) of the Native Administration Act, 1927,[1] which precludes the application of Native law where it is contrary to the principles of public policy or natural justice. This aspect gives rise to the question whether it would be in the best interests of the child to award its guardianship and custody to the plaintiff or to the defendant.

There are factors favouring the defendant's claim on this basis, viz., that the child has been with the defendant before the plaintiff's marriage in 1952 except for two years i.e. 1956 and 1957, when she had it, and the defendant appears to have looked after the child properly and is in a position to provide for it; for in general it is undesirable to uproot a child from a suitable environment. There are, however, weighty counter-considerations, viz., that the child, a girl of eleven years, would if its guardianship and custody are awarded to the plaintiff be going to its mother who has shown her close attachment to it as evidenced by the generous provision she made for it in the Post Office Savings Bank book from her savings and generally from the way she provided and cared for its welfare which together with her evidence as a whole make it manifest that she wants to have the child because of her love for it as a mother and not for any ulterior motive; further, her husband is agreeable to her having the child and they are in a position to provide for it, including its education, adequately.

To my mind, however, the paramount consideration here is that by awarding the guardianship and custody of the child to the plaintiff its future would be assured whereas the position would be otherwise if the award were made to the defendant as in that event the latter could not, as was conceded by him in the course of his evidence, resist a claim under Native law and custom by the natural father for the child's custody regard being had to the fact that the defendant could not rely on the common law as all his rights to the child flow from Native law and custom and bearing in mind that the natural father of the child paid the full damages for the plaintiff's seduction and pregnancy which, in Native law, entitles him to claim the child at any time notwithstanding that he has shown no interest whatsoever in it; and in the event of his death it is competent for his heir to make the same claim. On the other hand if the plaintiff obtains the guardianship and custody of the child, a judgment awarding the child to its natural father in an action brought by him against the defendant would not be binding on her unless she had been joined therein; and in that event it would be open to her to rely on common law, this being the system by which her rights to the child are governed and in support of her contention that this legal system should be applied she could rely on the fact that the natural father of the child had taken no interest in it over a lengthy period so that her contention could hardly fail. This fact could not of course be relied upon by the defendant in that it is not relevant in Native law and custom under which it is competent for the natural father or his heir to claim a child at any time irrespective of what may be in the child's interests provided he has paid the full damages for the seduction and pregnancy of the child's mother and he pays the *isondlo* beast.

It follows that the Native Commissioner cannot be said to have erred in having applied common law in deciding the case and the appeal should accordingly be dismissed, with costs.

Note

1. Substituted by s 1(1) of the Law of Evidence Amendment Act 45 of 1988.

By implication, the concepts of custody and guardianship must now be distinguished: guardianship is decided by customary law and custody by the child's best interests. In common law, custody refers to the day-to-day control of the child, and it includes decisions about education, religious instruction, and where the child is to live. Guardianship implies administration of the child's property, payment of its debts, and liability for its obligations, together with the power to appear in court on the child's behalf.[309] Any *benefits* that might accrue to the parents are largely affective. In customary law, by comparison, the economic benefits would be substantial. And there is a well established rule that a guardian has the right to the bridewealth of a daughter.[310]

The commissioners' courts assumed that the father would retain full parental rights to a child on divorce. This meant that there was an onus on any person alleging that it would be in the child's best interests to remain in the custody of

---

[309] Hahlo 394–6.
[310] See: *Mdinda v Pahlana* 1917 NAC 133; *Mpisana d/a Tshutsha v Mpisana* 1942 NAC (N&T) 48; *Nkabinde v Mlangeni & another* 1942 NAC (N&T) 89 at 91; *Mokoena v Mofokeng* 1945 NAC (C&O) 89. But in cases where custody and guardianship have been separated, there is as yet no decision specifying the beneficiary of a child's earnings.

the mother to prove that the father was not a fit and proper person.[311] Conversely, the courts assumed that the mother would be best suited to look after young children, and that she should have custody of them until they were old enough to fend for themselves.[312] No specific age for the transfer of a child to the father has been fixed, but it is normally taken to be about 7 or 8 years.[313] So it happened that, in the case of *young* children, the onus was cast on the father: if the mother was to be deprived of the custody of the child, he had to show that she was not a fit and proper person to look after it,[314] or that the conditions in which she lived were likely to cause the child physical or moral harm.[315]

Although the courts are prepared to grant the mother custody of her children, this does not imply that they are willing to equate her rights with those of the father.[316] Following the strict logic of customary law, she has no parental rights at all since she was not a party to the marriage. If, for example, bridewealth had not been paid, the children would go to the wife's *guardian*, not to the wife. The courts' reluctance to accord women rights is apparent from a series of decisions concerning the wife's position in custody cases. It was held in *Nkosi v Dhlamini*[317] that the mother had no locus standi in a custody suit; the action had to be brought by her guardian. All the courts require is the wife's presence during the custody action.[318] It is evident that this concession was not a matter of law but of expedience to allow the woman to give evidence of what would be in the child's interests.[319]

In Natal and KwaZulu the Codes have improved the wife's position considerably. Under s 27(5) the mother may be awarded sole guardianship of her children on divorce.[320]

It may be that under customary law at present the custody of children can be settled by an agreement between the parties to the divorce action (although it is

---

[311] See *Tshabalala & another v Tshabalala* 1944 NAC (N&T) 35; *Gumede* 1955 NAC 85 (NE); *Mahlangu v Nhlapo* 1968 BAC 35 (C). In Zimbabwe the courts regularly assumed it to be in the child's best interests to allow the father custody, because he would determine the child's marriage: Maboreke in Armstrong op cit n217 143.

[312] *Manamela v Kekana* 1944 NAC (N&T) 35; *Kambu* 1950 NAC 26 (C); *Mkize* 1951 NAC 336 (NE); *Muru* 1980 AC 39 (S); *Motloung v Mokaka & another* 1980 AC 159 (C). Customary and common Law are the same on this point: Ashton 87; Roberts 52; *Meyers v Leviton* 1949 (1) SA 203 (T) at 204.

[313] *Maruping* 1947 NAC (N&T) 129.

[314] *Maruping*'s case supra.

[315] *Mohapi v Masha* 1939 NAC (N&T) 154. In *Motloung*'s case supra at 164 the court held that there was no onus on the *woman* to show that it would be in the best interests of the child to remain with her. The court did not approve of the technical term 'onus' in the context of custody disputes, because it was for the court to decide the issue after consideration of all the circumstances of the case.

[316] Simons *African Women* 211–15.

[317] 1955 NAC 27 (C). See further *Tshabalala v Gracy & another* 1943 NAC (C&O) 60.

[318] *Mbenyane v Hlatshwayo* 1953 NAC 284 (NE); *Ngakane v Maalaphi* 1955 NAC 123 (C); *Mpete & another v Boikanyo* 1962 NAC 3 (C). In *Sekupa v Jonkman* 1966 BAC 20 (C) 23 this was based on natural justice. Bekker 201 fn182 says that these decisions should have based their deviance from customary law on grounds of public policy.

[319] *Nkabinde v Mlangeni & another* 1942 NAC (N&T) 89 at 92.

[320] The South African Law Commission has proposed formal recognition of a mother's parental right to her children: *Marriages and Customary Unions of Black Persons* para 11.6.1 and clause 9(6), as read with clause 14(1)(c), of the bill attached.

not clear whether the wife would have the right or power to make such an agreement).[321] The courts will naturally uphold such agreements only if they are in the child's best interests. Accordingly it was held that an agreement implying the sale of children will not be enforced;[322] and in *Ntsendwana v Maseti*,[323] where the husband had relinquished his claim to the children in consideration for the wife's father returning excess bridewealth, the arrangement was held to be contra bonos mores and thus invalid.

Children are generally believed to be unable to formulate a decision as to what would best serve their interests. As a result the courts must make 'some kind of imaginative leap and guess what a child might retrospectively have wanted once it reaches a position of maturity'.[324] Contemporary common-law assumptions about proper child-care patterns are evident in the courts' judgments awarding mothers custody of young children and fathers guardianship.[325] African cultural expectations have been overruled and western social mores predominate. This is the theory. Economic imperatives dictate a completely different arrangement in practice. Although a court might have awarded custody to the mother, there is always the possibility that she will be forced to send the child to its grandparents or other relatives in a rural area.[326] The consequence has been the reproduction of the structures of apartheid and various extraneous factors, some positively detrimental to the child, influence de facto child-rearing. The following extract shows how availability of housing in urban areas influences custody arrangements.

[97] BURMAN & FUCHS *CUSTODY ON DIVORCE IN APARTHEID SOUTH AFRICA* 11–15

In the case of Blacks, both customary law considerations and the results of apartheid legislation lead to demands for father custody. Among the Black population, almost all men give bridewealth (termed *lobola* among the Xhosa, the predominant "tribe" in the Cape), even where a civil law marriage takes place. In customary law, which continues to govern bridewealth transactions, the giving of *lobola* transfers the children born of the union into the man's family, and there can be no question of the mother then obtaining custody if the marriage breaks down, except on a short-term basis if the baby is very young. For the same reason, a Xhosa man will not pay child maintenance under customary law, except a set amount of one cow in certain circumstances.[1] The attitudes concomitant with *lobola* lead many men to express great indignation when confronted with a civil law which awards the custody of children to the mother and forces the father to pay maintenance for them, especially as African men frequently have an unusually large number of support obligations and considerably smaller incomes than the men of any other population group in South Africa. To this must be added the consideration that,

---

[321] This possibility emerges from *Mathebe d/a Mathebe v Katima* 1944 NAC (N&T) 69, where it was assumed that the father had full parental rights and was thus custodian, unless there was evidence of an agreement to the contrary.

[322] See, eg, *Kubayi v Ngobeni* 1939 NAC (N&T) 52.

[323] 3 NAC 39 (1914).

[324] Eekelaar op cit n226 170.

[325] Cynics have remarked that the principle of the child's best interests has operated as a piece of legal rhetoric into which judges can write their prejudices: King (1987) 17 *Family L* 186.

[326] Grandmothers in particular bear a heavy burden rearing young children. See Izzard (1985) 11 *JSAS* 258 regarding Botswana and Murray op cit n14 110–12 regarding Lesotho.

despite fixed customary law to the contrary, many custodian mothers who were interviewed expressed great determination that their ex-husbands should not receive any of the *lobola* paid for the daughters of the dissolved marriages when the girls in turn married. *Lobola* payments are often equal to several months' pay—amounts which it would take years to save—and many fathers are reluctant to forfeit or jeopardize them.

An additional and very important factor operates for Coloureds, Asians and, above all, Blacks. In South Africa the Group Areas Act, No. 41 of 1950, obliges different population groups to live in separate areas. As a result, in the urban area of Cape Town, council housing is in short supply for Coloureds, very short supply for Asians, and is almost unobtainable for Blacks. As a result of the Coloured Labour Preference Policy of the Government, Blacks are not allowed to own any fixed property in the Western Cape and can obtain houses only by renting them from the Western Cape Administration Board. Black interviewees told of waiting ten years or more for houses. Houses are registered in the husband's name but, if a marriage breaks down, the wife may be able to get the house transferred to her if she has a divorce certificate showing that custody has been awarded to her. Loss of a house by a man means going to the bottom of the housing list. The policy of Black influx control to the cities prevents any Black without urban residence rights from living in an urban area, and a woman from a rural area cannot obtain urban rights unless her husband has a house in which they can live. Thus, if a Black man loses custody of his children, and thereby loses his house, should he subsequently marry a woman without urban rights, he will not be able to bring her to live in the urban area until he can get another house. They may not become lodgers. The incentive to contest custody, not for the sake of the children but to retain the house, is therefore strong.

For all these reasons, it is not surprising that the Black divorce court is the scene every session of bitter custody fights and that our sample showed 21.7% of Black fathers obtaining custody.

The group areas policy gives rise to even stronger reasons for paternal custody claims in the case of marriages between different population groups, particularly between Blacks and Coloureds. Our one-year sample included 20 such marriages, in all but one of which the wife was Coloured. In the case of such marriages, the couple must live in a Black township and their children will be classified as Black unless the mother has been able to obtain Coloured classification for them, which is very difficult. (Coloured classification carries many economic and other benefits, compared to Black classification, and is therefore much sought after in such cases.) Should the marriage break up, children classified as Black cannot live in a Coloured group area. Nor can they attend a school in a Coloured area. Thus, if, as is frequently the case, the wife in such marriages is coloured and the children are classified as Black, the children must remain with the father. Their mother as a divorced woman cannot obtain any house (including the marital home) or lodger's permit in a Black area, and the children cannot live with her in her Coloured area. Nor are children who are not White allowed to live with a parent who is a live-in domestic servant in a White group area. Lawyers and social workers told of distraught women clients finding themselves trapped by the law. It is therefore not surprising that almost half our sample of fathers in this type of marriage obtained custody of their children.

Mothers' surrender of custody

Similarly, a variety of factors unique to South Africa may cause a woman to surrender her custody claim. . . . Among the poorer sections of the community, many women cannot afford to support their children on their own. There is no equal pay legislation in South Africa, and the disparity between women's and men's pay exists at all income levels except, to some extent, the professional, with the greatest disparities in Cape Town found between Black men's and women's pay. As a result of the Coloured Labour Preference Area policy, most Black women with jobs in Cape Town work as domestic servants. Live-in jobs are easier to find but do not permit children to live with their mothers. Live-out jobs frequently involve very long hours. In either case, the problems of obtaining and paying for child-care are manifold. In addition, South Africa's welfare system is both rudimentary and racially graded, providing very little assistance for divorced Black mothers, and none where the mother is able-bodied but unemployed. Maintenance payments from husbands, where awarded and actually paid, are usually minimal. For such a woman ... without a second household income to shorten her work hours or help pay expensive boarding school fees, the two most common alternatives are equally distasteful. Her children may roam the streets in gangs constantly involved in petty crime ... or may be sent back to their grandparents or other family in the rural areas. In the latter case they will probably be better supervised and it is cheaper to support them there, but their mother will not see them for long periods and the rural solution frequently involves loss of urban rights for the Black children, a problem discussed in more detail below. Both divorce records and interviews produced cases where women were unable to contest custody because they felt unable to care for and provide for their children in the circumstances they faced.

...[F]or Black women there is the consideration of preserving their children's rights to urban residence.[2] As there was large-scale malnutrition, an absence of employment opportunities, and a high child mortality rate in many of the rural areas even before the present disastrous drought, urban rights are exceptionally valuable. Many women hold urban rights only by virtue of being the wife of a man who qualified for them in the past through birth, ten years' legal residence or fifteen years' legal employment in an urban area. On divorce they lose these rights and are endorsed out to a rural area. Should they obtain custody of the children, the children must accompany them. Residence away from the urban area for more than a few months results in loss of existing urban rights, even where acquired by virtue of birth in an urban area. Rather than deprive their children of urban rights in this way, some women may choose not to contest custody.

Given all these considerations, it seems likely that the high number of fathers gaining custody of their children is the result both of more fathers requesting it and more women surrendering it. In other words, despite government pronouncements and legal expectations to the contrary, local conditions, legal procedure, attitudes engendered by religious and customary laws, and apartheid policy produce an unusually high proportion of children who are not brought up by their mothers.

The reality of custody allocation in South Africa

Even the above figures of non-maternal custody are far from reflecting the degree of non-maternal care for many children after divorce. The implications for the children of a custody allocation will depend very much on what arrangements are made for their care after the divorce, which in turn will depend on the childcare and incomes available, as well as family patterns.

As noted above, the Supreme Court and Southern Divorce Court devote very little time to investigating exact arrangements for the children after divorce, and one President of the Southern Divorce Court specifically stated that it was not the Court's business to do so. That Court is unable to reallocate the crucially important urban house, for example (this is done by an administrative committee) and so is unable to ensure that the mother will in fact obtain it. If she does not, she may be unable to claim the children in practice, even after winning custody, and cases of this type were encountered. As indicated above as well, for many Cape Town children, custody allocation to mothers who are forced to work long hours means that the children receive very little maternal care in practice. One divorced social worker who had herself been a domestic worker described their situation as "sometimes going to work, leaving not a piece of bread in the house and not knowing who will look after the children after school".

Much the same may apply if the father is granted custody, though the evidence indicates that more frequently the lack of care is due to interests outside the home rather than extreme economic pressure. A President of the Southern Divorce Court who spoke of the difficulty of distinguishing in court which men wished to obtain custody of their children merely to avoid paying maintenance, described the result of allocation to such fathers: If he gets custody, he doesn't pay anything and he doesn't feed them either—he just leaves them to themselves. That's why you find perhaps dozens of them, perhaps thousands of them—I don't know—roaming the streets, looking for food, stealing. They're hungry. And not because they're orphans; they have parents, but . . . they're in the care of the father, who doesn't care.

Non-parental care in either case, if provided at all, is often from busy relatives, friends, or other children.

Because of childcare difficulties, financial problems, and traditional Black extended family patterns, Black parents who obtain custody of their children (and to a lesser extent, Coloured parents) frequently send their children to live with grandparents or family in either urban or rural areas. Even our small Southern Divorce Court sample showed that, to the Court's knowledge, children in a third of the cases were being reared by grandparents or other family members without the presence of the parents. Moreover, the disruption of family life has led not only to a high divorce rate among the Black and Coloured population groups, but also to a very high rate of illegitimacy (by any system of law). As a result, interviews frequently revealed grandparents bringing up the offspring of several of their children. In other words, a number of cousins were being reared together. However, unlike earlier rural extended families, these households did not contain the young children's parents. Black children, particularly, appeared to be moved between parents and various relatives several times as they grew up, as circumstances necessitated. Stories of child neglect, especially where parents failed to send money, were encountered from divorcees, doctors, and social workers on a number of occasions. Despite the resemblance to the extended family of the past, a new form of extended family appears to be taking shape, with children frequently seeing very little of their parents and often cared for by poverty-stricken relatives who sometimes provide most inferior care.

Notes
  1. Isondlo.
  2. Influx control legislation was abolished by Act 68 of 1986.

It is questionable whether the present legal regime, despite its protestations, can in fact serve the interests of the child.[327] Divorce is a private affair in customary law and so there is no guarantee that the position of the child will be judicially scrutinized. In reality custody is determined by private arrangements. This is quite usual in western legal systems and there is weighty scholarly support for it on the ground that parents are in the best position to evaluate the relative advantages.[328] Moreover, because

'a child's social and psychological relationships with both parents ordinarily continue after the divorce, a process that leads to agreement between the parents is preferable to one that necessarily has a winner and a loser'.[329]

But the problem remains that privately ordered settlements leave the way open to exploitation of the vulnerable parties.[330]

In South African circumstances it is difficult to know what the courts are to do other than to accept such arrangements. They have a generously described power to intervene directly to protect children, and customary law may be overruled to achieve this end, but judges need information about the child's immediate situation and the social milieu in which it will be raised. The tribunals in which customary divorces are litigated,[331] however, are not designed to provide

---

[327] Long-term interests at least.
[328] Goldstein et al *Beyond the Best Interests of the Child* 49ff.
[329] Mnookin & Kornhauser op cit n4 70.
[330] Freeman *The Rights and the Wrongs of Children* 198–9.
[331] Now chiefs' and magistrates' courts.

objective or professionally assessed information. Of the parties who are able to provide information, the mother is allowed in court only to give evidence; otherwise it is her guardian (who has a mercenary interest in any decision) who will prosecute a custody case. The realities of this country make it impossible to predict the results of child-rearing arrangements when the society is chronically beset by political dissension, is marked by grave inequalities of wealth and power, and is often lacking basic medical or educational facilities for the poor.

A technical factor that complicates custody cases in southern Africa, is the likelihood that a South African court order may have to be performed in one of the independent or neighbouring states. This involves a problem of private international law: to what extent is the foreign state bound to recognize and enforce decisions of a South African court and vice versa?[332] In principle, orders of the parties' forum domicilii must be recognized, but there is every indication that local courts may act independently by reason of their protective jurisdiction to ensure the welfare of the child.

VII STATUS

It seems that divorce has no effect on the status of the wife: she reverts to the guardianship of her father.[333] Bekker[334] says that in the Cape Province all persons become majors when they attain the age of majority and that women are emancipated on divorce. He bases his argument on a series of cases concerned with widows and 'kraal' inmates, all of which were influenced by the age of majority proclamations passed in Transkei.[335] These decisions are of dubious authority. It would be better to argue that the Age of Majority Act[336] now applies, and in terms of this women acquire full capacity when they turn 21.

If the wife has born children, the divorce will not affect the status of the house she established in her husband's homestead. He may keep the house alive by introducing a substitute wife and by placing her in the house.[337]

---

[332] See Forsyth 366.
[333] *Mhlongo & another v Sibeko* 1937 NAC (N&T) 34 at 36–7 states the law for the Transvaal. In Natal and KwaZulu the position is governed by ss 14 of the Codes.
[334] Page 230.
[335] See, eg, *Maqula* 1950 NAC 202 (S).
[336] 57 of 1972.
[337] Bekker 198. See s 71 of the Natal and KwaZulu Codes.

CHAPTER 7

Women

I PATRIARCHY

In sub-Saharan Africa male dominance and respect for age were (and still are) the norm. All available positions of authority, whether in households, village communities or government offices, were occupied by senior men. Early European observers thought that these patterns of male superiority were universal and therefore a natural phenomenon. In 1861, Maine in *Ancient Law*,[1] for instance, claimed that patriarchy was the original condition of mankind. In the same year, the Swiss jurist Bachofen published his book, *Das Mutterrecht*, which argued for the primordial supremacy of matriarchy, and even gynocracy, yet this was a primacy that was subsequently overturned by the principle of patriarchy.[2] The social order of both ancient and contemporary societies was the same: men were dominant.

It was Margaret Mead who began the counterargument. She showed that attitudes to gender were in fact cultural constructs.

> 'If those temperamental attitudes which have traditionally been regarded as feminine—such as passivity, responsiveness, and a willingness to cherish children—can so easily be set up as the masculine pattern in one tribe, and, in another, be outlawed for the majority of women as for the majority of men, we no longer have any basis for regarding aspects of such behaviour as sex linked.'[3]

Later anthropologists amassed an impressive range of evidence to show how arbitrary gender roles can be. In one society only men are permitted to trade and hunt; in another these might be exclusively female activities.

It cannot be denied, of course, that every society takes cognizance of the physical differences of the sexes, and through various diacritics (typically dress, manners and speech) these differences are elaborated into complex codes of

---

[1] Page 119.
[2] There is, in fact, no evidence of a primordial state of matriarchy. This thesis is based on myths: Coontz & Henderson *Women's Work, Men's Property* 26.
[3] *Sex and Temperament in Three Primitive Societies* 279–80.

behaviour. What is striking about these codes is not that they exist, but that male activities are given overriding value and importance.[4] Mead also noted this:

> '[W]hatever the arrangement in regard to descent or ownership of property, and even if these formal outward arrangements are reflected in the temperamental relations between the sexes, the prestige values attach to the activities of men.'[5]

In southern Africa, for example, it is usual for men to herd cattle and to hunt; women garden and gather roots, berries and similar wild produce. Yet meat is the food reserved for feast occasions, while the vegetables and food produced by women, even though it might be the staple, is regarded as everyday fare.

The attitudes and expectations organized on this basis rank men above women, providing a social structure that gives men authority.[6] This does not necessarily mean that women are materially disadvantaged or ill-treated. Nor should it be assumed that individual women lack *power*: through various devices, notably gossip, magic, and withholding services, women have always contrived to mitigate male authority. But these devices are usually considered illegitimate; they are trivialized, or stigmatized as positively dangerous, and are thus made punishable. Again, female power may have considerably systematic effect.[7] In certain societies, such as the Yoruba, women control trade and commerce; in others, such as the Lovedu, they may occupy positions of political authority; in still others, individual women may gain power via occupations as diviners or priestesses. But although women may wield great influence, the social structure keeps the balance of authority in favour of men.

The many reasons that have been given for the asymmetry in gender relations[8] may be grouped into two broad categories: those attributing patriarchy to the biological differences between men and women, and those attributing it to social causes. Most theories have this in common—a gender-based division of labour. According to biological theories, because women give birth to and nurse children, their economic and political life must be more circumscribed than that of men. Simmel, for instance, claimed that woman,

> 'because of her peculiar functions was relegated to activities within the limits of her home, confined to devote herself to a single individual, and prevented from transcending the group-relations established by marriage, family [and] social life'.[9]

Any argument that 'biology is destiny', however, is unlikely to be given credence in feminist studies, if only because it would accept the inferior position of women as unchangeable. This aside, the theory has weak explanatory power. Physical differences do not have inevitable social entailments; in particular they cannot explain why man, as a category opposed to woman, is given primary

---

[4] Rosaldo in Rosaldo & Lamphere *Woman, Culture and Society* 19.
[5] Op cit n3 302.
[6] Namely, a legitimate form of power or the right to demand obedience and compliance. Patriarchy is widespread and Millett *Sexual Politics*, for one, argues that it is universal. See further McDonough et al in Kuhn & Wolpe *Feminism and Materialism* 11 and 42.
[7] May *Zimbabwean Women in Customary and Colonial Law* 15–21.
[8] See Schlegel *Sexual Stratification* 22–34; Coontz & Henderson op cit n2 Intro.
[9] *Conflict (and) The Web of Group-Affiliations* 180.

value and social worth.[10] Nor can biological theory resolve a paradox central to many systems of patriarchy: men are esteemed despite the fact that women perform the most important productive work. It was not appreciated until recently, for instance, that African women bear the primary responsibility for food production.[11] This oversight was no doubt due in part to the pervasive western assumption that only men work to feed and support their families. But in addition men overshadow women because they wield control over economically valued items, such as cattle, as well as engaging in all prestigious activities, such as hunting, arguing court cases, and performing religious rites.

[98] MARWICK *THE SWAZI* 60–3

In the economic life there is a rigid differentiation between the sexes and all work is performed according to traditional rules. Labour is divided. The Swazis are pastoralists and horticulturists.

Cattle tending is exclusively a male occupation and females are rigidly excluded. The cattle are herded by boys and milked by them or the men. The cattle kraals are erected and maintained by males. It is interesting to note that with the advent of the plough a greater proportion of tilling passed to the men, since it was necessary to use oxen. Ploughing is slowly displacing hand-hoeing, which is principally the work of women. . . .

Men perform the heavier horticultural work also, eg stumping and removing stones from gardens. Other spheres of male activity are hunting, making the framework of huts and leather working. The men exclusively are the hunters whether they hunt singly or in organized groups. . . .

The exclusive sphere of the woman is that of domestic duties. The woman is responsible for the provision of food for her family, for keeping her hut and its surroundings in a clean and tidy state, for tending the children and for providing herself with household utensils.

In the traditional economic life of the people there was little overlapping in the work performed by the two sexes. Contact with European civilization has modified this, and it is now not uncommon to see girls herding cattle because the men have been forced to leave their homes to find employment to earn money to pay their taxes to the Government, and to provide the wherewithal to satisfy a multiplicity of new wants. . . .

Among the woman's chief duties is beer making—a task which every woman must know thoroughly.

At the present time all women do not make their own utensils, such as pots and mats. There are women who have acquired a special skill at the work, and to whom all the local women will go to get their supplies. They will barter crops or pay money for their requirements. Even though this is so now, all girls are taught how to perform all these tasks, though the tendency to specialize is becoming more and more hardened.

Grass cutting is seasonal and takes place in mid-winter. Thereafter women will be seen plaiting grass into ropes on their way from one place to another, and at odd moments during the performance of their other duties. The main purpose of grass cutting is for new huts or for the repair of old ones.

The women's part in hut making is to cut the grass and then to bind it up into endless rolls. . . .

The floor of the hut is put in by the women. It consists of stamped and hardened earth polished (*ukuyila*) with smooth stones. The women repeat the process off and on to keep

---

[10] See Coontz & Henderson op cit n2 1ff for a summary. Contemporary biological theorists have a more sophisticated approach. They regard physical make-up as no more than a 'script' for behaviour: Sanday *Female Power and Male Dominance*.

[11] Boserup *Women's Role in Economic Development* ch 1 was the first to concentrate on this. See, too, Paulme *Women of Tropical Africa* 75ff.

the floor in good order. It is also smeared with cattle dung to keep it clean and sweet smelling. . . .

With regard to the men the advent of European civilization has had a marked effect on their economic life. They play a greater part in the agricultural activities since they now do the major part of the ploughing and sowing, owing to the use of ploughs instead of hand-hoes. There being no warfare the necessity for going to serve in one of the regiments for long periods does not arise, and their chief concern is to find money to pay their taxes. Consequently they enter the employment of Europeans as domestic servants, agricultural workers, or go off to the gold and coal mines and to the wattle and sugar plantations. The proportion of women who leave their homes to seek employment is still low but is increasing.

The broad outline of this account holds true for all parts of southern Africa. Everywhere the work of women is the same: longer, more monotonous, and often more arduous than that of men.[12] Yet although it is vital, it lacks social recognition.[13]

The incongruity of male authority and female productivity finds its most convincing explanation in the second category of theories on gender relations. For these it is axiomatic that patriarchy is socially constructed; and in this regard, because Marxist theory pays close attention to the division of labour and the element of exploitation implicit in gender relations, it is frequently appealed to.[14] Engels' work *Origin of the Family, Private Property and the State* (1891) has exerted a strong influence on feminist studies. In it he described an historical process whereby women were transformed from the free and equal partners of men to subordinate and dependent wives or wards. According to Engels the cause of this transformation was the emergence of private property and the family, both terms taking on a specific meaning in the context of his work.

In the primordial society Engels posited, food had to be collected and prepared daily. Production was for use only, to meet subsistence needs, and there was no surplus that could be accumulated and used for exchange. The 'household' was the basic social and economic unit. It was communistic in the sense that all food stores were held in common, and all work was done for the benefit of the household rather than for particular members. Decision-making involved equal participation of all members, men and women; and the absence of private property made men's productive work and women's household work of equal social significance.

Women's status was transformed from one of equality to one of subordination by the appearance of valuable productive resources (for Engels 'private property' meant only goods or resources with *productive* potential, which would exclude personal or individual goods), viz domesticated animals and land.[15] Animals especially were a qualitatively new kind of commodity, because apart from meeting subsistence needs, they reproduced themselves, thereby yielding a

---

[12] See, eg, Ashton 88–90; Schapera 152–3; and Krige 184–5.

[13] In consequence women find it difficult to exploit their economic position to their own advantage: Whitehead in Hirschon *Women and Property/Women as Property* 176 and 189.

[14] Coontz & Henderson op cit n2 35; Leacock *Myths of Male Dominance*.

[15] This became possible only when technological development and natural resources facilitated the development of skills needed to domesticate animals and/or invest labour in land, so that its productivity lasted for an appreciable length of time. Enduring productivity led to enduring private ownership. See further below, 385–6.

surplus. (Engels assumed that they were owned by men.) Once property fell under private control, the communal economy of the household was broken and the 'family' arose, soon to overshadow the household as the key economic and decision-making group. Unlike the household, it was an hierarchical structure, comprising property-owning senior males and their dependants.

The new wealth meant that there was a surplus of goods available for exchange between productive units. With time, production by men (specifically for exchange purposes) expanded and eclipsed work in the household. Male labour too acquired an exchange value, ie it became 'valuable' for survival in the cash economy. The woman's work became correspondingly less important; it had only use value. Female status and independence declined accordingly.[16] Under industrial capitalism production takes place almost exclusively outside the household; this is the realm of men. Women work in the sphere of the family for husbands and children; their labour is necessary but socially subordinate.[17]

The premise of the egalitarian, primordial society has perhaps been the most problematic element in Engels' thesis. Anthropologists have been able to confirm that in some societies, before they were transformed by forces of colonialism and capitalism, women had considerable power and autonomy.[18] And it may be that this finding is valid for all precapitalist societies: feminists have revealed the bias of male informants and male anthropologists in producing many of the early ethnographies;[19] they also point to the inability of Westerners to perceive egalitarian structures characteristic of these societies.[20] But it remains difficult to prove the details of a social formation that originated in theoretical conjecture. More accessible to contemporary research is the period between the communal and capitalist modes of production.[21] Here at least Engels' thesis has been corroborated in so far as it has been convincingly demonstrated that with the penetration of capitalism female status declines markedly.[22]

Nearly all studies of gender relations take for granted a social dichotomy between domestic and public spheres of activity.[23] A person's status as a male, for instance, is achieved by performance in the public sphere. As a child, he is taken from the domestic domain in which he was raised, and by a series of rituals he is taught to seek his manhood outside the home. So, for a boy to become an adult man, he must prove himself by a series of achievements amongst his peers. Women, by contrast, become women simply by staying at home and following

---

[16] See Saffioti *Women in Class Society* 35–52.
[17] See Sacks in Rosaldo & Lamphere op cit n4 207–11; and cf Bozzoli (1983) 9 *JSAS* 146ff who argues that precapitalist modes of production had already provided the necessary structure of female subordination before colonial conquest.
[18] Leacock op cit n14 157–8 and see: Mullings in Hafkin & Bay *Women in Africa* 240ff; cf Bozzoli op cit 139ff.
[19] Quinn (1977) 6 *Annual R of Anthrop* 186.
[20] Coontz & Henderson op cit n2 24.
[21] Coontz & Henderson op cit n2 35.
[22] Boserup op cit n11 53; Young in Kuhn & Wolpe op cit n6 124ff; Cock *Maids and Madams* 241ff; Etienne & Leacock *Women and Colonization* 17ff and Mbilinyi (1972) 10 *J Mod Afr Studies* 57.
[23] An analytical framework recommended by Rosaldo in Rosaldo & Lamphere op cit n4 23ff. Cf Lebeuf in Paulme op cit n11 93ff, who claims that this dichotomy is typical of the western way of thinking and has succeeded in distorting perceptions of African society.

in their mothers' footsteps. The criteria for male achievement are generally culturally constructed, having little to do with the natural world. A woman, on the other hand, has an ascribed status: she is 'naturally' what she is. Any praise she acquires comes to her for doing what she was 'naturally' destined to do.[24]

From this it follows that the male world is the world of culture (the man-made systems of human experience), whereas the female world is embedded in nature.

> 'They must care for children, feed and clean them, and perform the messy chores. Their social interaction is more difficult for them to structure, being intimate and subject to variation in their own and their children's moods. Women's lives are marked by neither privacy nor distance. They are embedded in, and subject to, the demands of immediate interaction.'[25]

Women's lives thus appear more spontaneous and irrational in comparison with men's.[26] Women are individual and particularist, an anomaly in the ordered world of men; women are to be cared for and controlled.

In functional terms the various behaviour patterns expected of women are designed to confine them to a compliant life in the domestic sphere. An example of the life of a Pondo woman is described in detail below.

[99] HUNTER *REACTION TO CONQUEST* 32–47

Between father and daughter there is often the same affection and familiarity in early childhood that there is between father and son. As a girl grows older she is more and more with her mother, but she is never segregated from the menfolk of her *umzi*, her father and brothers, and need observe no taboos towards them except when menstruating. As a small girl before puberty she may even run in and out of the cattle kraal. . . .

A father owes his daughter protection and support both before and after her marriage. If he receives her *ikhazi* he is obliged to provide her with a wedding outfit, and to dress her all her life. He is responsible also for providing her from time to time with gifts for in-laws, and with articles of household furniture which require replacement. If she leaves her husband he is responsible for her support. A father is responsible for providing the beasts necessary for ritual killings for his daughter and for carrying out the ceremonial before her marriage and when he has received her *ikhazi*, also after her marriage. He summons her to any feasts he makes. He is responsible for burying her if she dies in his *umzi*.

A father usually stands by his daughter if she has quarrelled with her husband's people, giving her shelter if she is "smelt out" for witchcraft at her *umzi* and refusing to admit the accusation. Very rarely is a daughter or sister of the head of the *umzi* accused of witchcraft. If a daughter returns home complaining that she has been ill treated, the father, if he thinks she has ground for complaint, will scold the husband and probably demand a beast (*uswazi*) in compensation.

Own brothers and sisters play much together as small children, and although from about six years, when the boys go out to herd, and both boys and girls begin to go about in gangs with those of their own age and sex from other *imizi*, they do not see so much of each other; nevertheless, they live on intimate terms in the *umzi*. Often I have seen a small sister snuggling up to an older brother, keeping warm under a corner of his blanket and getting tit-bits from his plate. Even when grown up sisters will sit and chat with their brothers near the kraal. To an elder brother, who in time may be in the place of her father, a girl should show respect, but "a younger brother does not matter".

---

[24] Rosaldo in Rosaldo & Lamphere op cit n4 28–30.
[25] Rosaldo in Rosaldo & Lamphere op cit n4 27–8.
[26] Cf Strathern in MacCormack & Strathern *Nature, Culture and Gender* 174ff.

Very often a girl's brother receives her *ikhazi* instead of her father, and then he has the responsibilities of a father towards her.

From the wives of all her brothers a woman may take what personal possessions in the way of clothing and household utensils she likes. She shares in the gifts brought by her brother's bride. . . .

Wives of her younger brother must treat a woman with great respect, calling her *ndodakazi* (lit. female husband) or *nina ka-* (mother of-). When she comes to visit her brother they must wait upon her, and make no complaint. A sister visiting her brother usually assists his wives in housework, or field work, because "the wives do not like that there should be one lying down doing nothing", but this is of grace. It is her prerogative to be waited upon.

When visiting an *umzi* it is always possible to pick out sisters or daughters of the head of the *umzi* by their bearing. They speak to visitors much more readily than do wives. . . .

By her brother's children a woman is treated with respect. It is her particular duty to hand the special piece of meat, *intsonyama*, of the beast killed ritually for the initiation of her brother's daughter. She becomes an *ithongo* (ancestral spirit) to her brother's child. When she is an *idikazi* (woman living at the *umzi* of her father or brother) the behaviour towards a father's sister (*udade bobawo*) approximates to that towards the father's brother's wife. She is another woman of the *umzi*, who helps to provide the children with food and with whom they are in intimate daily contact. I have seen a woman being very tender with the child of a brother in whose *umzi* she lived, cooking a special dish for it when it was ill, feeding it, and cuddling it, but normally she lives in another *umzi* and is only seen occasionally. A phrase applied to a child who is slow and stupid is *"Abathanga dade bobawo!"* (She does not reflect her father's sister.) . . .

Own sisters grow up together like brothers, but after marriage live in different *imizi* and have no common economic obligations. Very probably their children belong to different clans. Sisters visit one another, and may meet when visiting father or brother. Often a young married woman "borrows" a younger sister to live with her, and act as nurse to her children. But sisters do not normally see very much of one another after marriage. There is nothing but the affective tie to hold them together.

Elder sisters make younger sisters fag for them, but there is no sharp distinction between junior and senior, buttressed by a special economic relationship, and linguistic terms, as there is between brothers. *Udade wethu* or *umnt'akwethu* is used for both younger and older sister.

A man has no special rights over his wife's sister and has to give full *ikhazi* if he marries her, but the idea that sisters are to some extent social equivalents is shown by the fact that a woman, when visiting her sister's married home, observes avoidance taboos towards her sister's husband's father, as does her sister, but does not avoid the men's side of her sister's own hut, as she ordinarily does in the hut of a clan other than her own. . . .

Behaviour of a wife

The position of a wife in an *umzi* is very different from that of a daughter or a sister. The first virtue demanded of a bride is that she should be *khuthele* (diligent, eager). She rises at dawn, before any one else, and goes to fetch water. "If the people are not up when she comes back she must not go to sleep again, but exert herself and sweep before she goes to the fields." Every day she should go to fetch wood, and it is she who in winter goes to gather wild spinach from the distant fields. She does the heavy end of grinding and cooking, and helps in garden work, mudding and repairing of huts. She must care for her husband's comfort. "What is a wife for if she is not there to pick the fleas off your blanket, and put your mat in the sun so that you sleep without being bitten?"

A bride must show respect (*ukuhlonipha*) towards all senior relatives of her husband, particularly his male relatives. Her respect is expressed in avoidances of parts of the *umzi* frequented by men, of personal names and words like them, and if she is a junior wife of the owner of the *umzi*, of the right of the great hut, because she must respect the spears and milk sacks in the great hut. "If dogs are eating meat, or pigs rooting in the mealies on the men's side she can only throw things at them." Children, when their mothers threaten to beat them, fly to the men's side of a hut of a senior relative of their father and are safe. Often one sees the right half of a hut unswept or unsmeared because the bride doing the work could not cross to the men's side. She must never go near the cattle kraal in which her husband's father or grandfather is buried, and avoids the *inkundla* (courtyard between huts and kraal) in which men sit. When entering a hut of a senior relative of her husband, male or female, she must turn sharply to left and circle round the back, so as to avoid the men's side (*ukuceza*).

Women agree that *ukuceza* is one of the trials of life. It adds enormously to the work of the bride, and skirts get wet trailing through long grass. Once a man cut a path for his wife to *ukuceza* by, but every one said he was not in his right mind. At night no one *ukuceza*, "we even walk across the *inkundla* then, but we cover our heads", says a young wife. . . .

A bride avoids the name, and words, of which a principal syllable is similar to the principal syllable of the name of her husband's father, his brothers, her husband's elder brothers, and his father's father, whether they are living or dead. She also avoids the personal names of her husband's mother, paternal aunts, and elder sisters, but does not avoid words similar to them. When she arrives she is told (by her husband's sister, or a co-wife) what words are avoided in the *umzi*.

For the first few days after her arrival she wears a handkerchief tied low on her forehead. She can never bare her head, or until she has a child to feed, her breasts, in the presence of a senior relative of her husband, male or female. When I wore a hat I was asked, "Whom do you, an unmarried girl, avoid that you wear that thing on your head?" Often I have seen women, wishing to take the handkerchief from their heads to tie up a bundle, twist a wisp of grass round their heads that they might not be guilty of going bare-headed before in-laws. . . .

Gradually the avoidances of a bride become less strict. After a few days the handkerchief which she wears low over her forehead is raised by some old person of the *umzi*. She gives gifts to her husband's mother that she may eat with her, and gifts to her husband's father that she may hand him food. "After about a month she will give her husband's mother a gift, perhaps a three-penny bit, and then she may eat with her mother-in-law, or she may put before her mother-in-law even two shillings, and then ask her for snuff." After that she may receive things directly from her mother-in-law. "After a year she goes home, gets a new dish, and a new eating-mat. She brews some beer, and with the gifts hands it to her father-in-law. After that she can hand anything to him directly and may ask him for snuff." A goat is killed, after which she may work in a field on the site of an old *umzi* of her husband's family, and eat maize or snuff tobacco grown on it. The circles she makes behind the huts grow less wide as she grows older, and when senior relatives of her husband die, or he builds an *umzi* for himself, he becomes owner of an *umzi*. Then there is no hut of which she must avoid the men's side, and she walks straight across the *inkundla* when passing from hut to hut. Sooner or later a ritual killing is made, after which she may drink the milk of her husband's cattle except when she is ritually impure, but avoids instead milk of her father's cattle. After a year she can eat parts of any beast killed, except one killed ritually for a person who is ill. The meat of a beast so killed is again sometimes "stolen", but a wife must not eat it in the presence of a senior male relative of her husband. A wife should never eat of the meat of a beast killed ritually for her husband's father, but in practice it, too, is sometimes "stolen". . . .

A bride does not attend any social gatherings except an occasional girl's initiation dance unless they happen to be actually at her own *umzi*. She is fully occupied with her work and it is not considered suitable that she should gad about. Once she is married she cannot go to the dances which she attended as an unmarried girl, and she does not yet accompany her mother-in-law and the older wives of the *umzi* to beer drinks and feasts. After she has been married about four years, some say "when she has two children", she begins to go to meat feasts. "Her mother-in-law keeps on asking her to go, but she refuses; then her mother-in-law says, 'I am not going to ask you to go any more, go when you like.' Then she goes." She begins to go to beer drinks after she has attended meat feasts, and only spends the daylight hours at them, while old women may sleep there. . . .

But even a young wife gets home to visit her people, and asks for clothing and household utensils. A bride usually returns home after four or five months to ask for clothing, and most wives visit their homes two or three times a year, staying a fortnight or more each time. If they live close they go oftener, and do not stay so long. . . .

So long as she lives in her mother-in-law's *umzi* a wife, no matter how long she has been married, is responsible to her mother-in-law, even more than to her husband. "If I want to get permission to go home I ask my mother, and then tell my husband that my mother says I may go," says one young woman. Impoliteness to a mother-in-law may result in a bride being sent back to her own people. . . .

Nevertheless, a mother-in-law is expected to be an *ihlathi* (bush, shelter) to her daughter-in-law against her husband. A son respects his mother's hut, and if a wife is beaten she may fly for refuge there. . . .

Even, however, when a woman becomes the *inkosikazi* of an *umzi*, she remains subject to her husband. (*Inkosikazi*—lit. female chief.) Wife beating is common, and in certain circumstances considered quite justifiable. If a woman does not have food properly prepared for her husband when he comes home in the evening, or if she returns late or drunk from beer parties, or gives her husband cause for jealousy, and is beaten, her neighbours will think that she has only got her deserts. . . .

There is a double standard of sexual morality, and most of the quarrels between husband and wife turn on this. Premarital conception is forbidden by custom, and a married woman is forbidden relations with any except her own husband. A man may have as many wives and *amadikazi* (loose women) as he chooses or can afford. In actual practice very many of the married women have lovers, but adultery is not condoned by their husbands, who make every effort to catch and prosecute the adulterer. Many husbands keep a jealous watch on their wives, though some allow them great freedom. . . .

Marriage being exogamous a wife is necessarily of another clan and responsible to other ancestral spirits than her husband, and in the new group she is also something of an outsider, and therefore dangerous. After her marriage she comes under the control of her husband's ancestral spirits, although still remaining responsible to her own, and after a ritual killing has been made she drinks the milk of her husband's cattle, avoiding that of the cattle of her own clan. The longer she is married the more closely she is assimilated to the new clan; in time even the restrictions on her behaviour are gradually relaxed and she becomes an *ithongo* (ancestral spirit) to her children who belong to her husband's clan, but she is never completely assimilated. The feeling that the wife is a stranger and dangerous is expressed in the accusations of witchcraft and of bringing into the *umzi* an *ithinzi*, an emanation of her ancestral spirits which harms the *umzi* to which it is brought, and such accusations are lodged even against wives who have long been married.

But despite this conflict husband and wife are closely bound together by common economic obligations and interests. The wife is punished if she does not fulfil her duties of cooking and cultivating, but the husband has reciprocal duties in ploughing, hut building, and providing cattle. Their common concern is to increase the property of the house and provide adequately for their children. The husband cannot dispose of property allotted to a wife's house without consulting her. He is expected to consult her in all important matters, but, said Geza, "Men don't consult women, they just tell them what they are going to do".

Husband and wife seldom go about together. When they attend the same beer drink or festival the man usually goes with the other men of the *umzi* or men neighbours, the wife with the other women of the *umzi*, but they live in intimate contact within their own *umzi*. The men sometimes sit apart near the kraal to gossip and eat, but very often they eat with the women indoors, or sit with them just outside the huts. In a small *umzi* where there are few adults their relations are necessarily intimate. That there is sometimes real

affection between husband and wife is proved by the fact that a husband sometimes stands
by his wife when she is accused of witchcraft, and leaves his own family rather than leave
her.

The sanction for behaviour is primarily public opinion. Custom lays down very
definitely what the behaviour of a wife should be, and a breach of the code would be a sign
of bad breeding. On her arrival at her *umzi* a bride is told what words she must avoid, and
she makes every endeavour to do so correctly. "A bride talks little and listens to the old
women." Women laugh and say that they "make mistakes at first, but if the in-laws are
kind they overlook them". A girl before her marriage has some practice in avoidance, for
she avoids the names of the parents of her sweetheart as if they were in-laws, and for a
week after initiation she behaves as a bride in her own home. The avoidance taboo is
strengthened by the threat, "You will go bald if you say your father's name", but
although this is a threat commonly spoken of, it is not generally believed that it will
happen. A more effective sanction is *ukuconozisa*.

When a wife has refused to fulfil some duty, or angered a member of her *umzi*, any
member of the *umzi* ("even a child") may say to her," *Ngu bawo lo*", "That is father", ie
"You have said your father-in-law's name". *Maconini* is an expression also used as
equivalent of *ngubawo lo*. Some say that if a bride has made a slip in verbal avoidance and
been overheard, she will consider herself *ukuconozisa*, even though nothing is said. When
one wife is *ukuconozisa* all the wives on that *umzi*, including the culprit's husband's
brothers' wives, must go to their own homes and fetch some gift. The culprit brings a goat
or sheep or £1 or 10s, the others a goat or 10s or 5s each. The gifts go to the owner of the
umzi, who on the women's return kills a goat or sheep (not one they brought) "to make
peace". . . .

Ukuconozisa is regarded as a disgrace (*ihlazo*) to an *umzi* and is not common. "People
with evil minds do it." Some women maintain that it is "just a device to get money", and
a woman is usually *ukuconozisa* by her sisters-in-law, who have come home in need of
something.

If a woman really behaves badly she is either told to go home, or life is made so
unpleasant for her that she does so of her own accord, and the marriage is dissolved.

Umlaza

Women's taboos are bound up with the concept of *umlaza* (ritual impurity). A woman
has *umlaza* during her periods until she washes after the flow ceases, after a miscarriage,
or the death of a husband or child, for about a month, and after sexual connexion until
she washes. A man has *umlaza* for a month after the death of wife or child, and after sexual
connexion until he washes. Meat of an animal which has died, pork, and honey infect those
who eat them with *umlaza* until they wash.

People with *umlaza* are dangerous to cattle and to all stock except pigs and poultry.
A man with *umlaza* cannot enter the cattle kraal or milk. A woman may ordinarily walk
through a herd of cattle on the veld, but when she has *umlaza* she circles round it.
A daughter of the *umzi* avoids crossing the *inkundla* or going near the cattle kraal when
menstruating. A woman may never step over ox-yokes and chain. One informant
volunteered that this taboo used only to apply when they were menstruating. "But the
men did not always know when they were menstruating, so they forbade them all
together."

No one with *umlaza* may drink milk. . . .

Umlaza negatives the value of medicines. A person with *umlaza* touching a medicine
makes it useless, and more must be gathered, hence a woman doctor will get some one else
to pick her medicines during her menses. . . .

Besides "killing" medicine *umlaza* is dangerous to sick persons themselves, aggravating
any pain. Persons with *umlaza* cannot go near an *umkhwetha* (novice diviner) or let their
shadows fall upon her, or warm themselves at her fire, or eat the remains on her plate.
From fear of *umlaza* a novice does not go about freely, is always cooked for separately, or
dished up for first, never shakes hands, and often sits apart behind a screen. A novice is

supposed to remain chaste. Circumcised boys, *abakhwetha*, are protected from *umlaza* until they come out of the lodge. A man who had had sexual intercourse would wash before going near the boys.

Umlaza has a bad effect on weapons and warriors, making them soft (*thambekile*). . . .

A wife may never walk in her husband's spoor. If he goes straight out of the door she must go out at an angle. To tread on his spoor would make him *thambekile* (soft) in war. A sister or daughter treading on a man's spoor does not matter except when she is menstruating. When menstruating a daughter of the umzi will not go to the men's side of the hut of which she is free at other times.

II WOMEN IN THE CITY

For some women the anonymity of cities has provided a welcome release from the strictures of a traditional life in the country.[27] The processes of urbanization and acculturation are held to account for the considerable changes that mark the status of city women.

[100] MAYER *TOWNSMEN OR TRIBESMEN* 233–5, 244–9

Town can be expected to attract people who have little to lose in the country. If this applies to certain categories of men—dispossessed farm servants, drought-stricken peasants, unhappy or deviant personalities—it tends to apply even more widely among women, whose disabilities in the rural social system are more pervasive and general. Even the most fortunate rural woman has to go through a long period of subjection to men and to older women; the least fortunate, such as widows and unmarried mothers, may suffer deprived status permanently. Many Xhosa women seem to use East London as a semi-permanent escape. Most agree that it is a place "to be free", "to be independent", "to get away from the rule of the people at home". In different terminology, women have reason to like this new environment where status depends less on ascription and more on achievement.

That females *can* be more independent in town all Xhosa, both male and female, both Red and School,[1] seem to agree: but how this independence is valued remains another question. Neither Red nor conservative School men like the idea of an emancipated woman, other than the senior woman who is acting head of a homestead. It is realized that when girls and women can "run away to town" the whole structure of the patriarchal family and the maintenance of its basic values is threatened.

That women and girls can keep their own economic and social footing, not by virtue of their relations to men, but in their own right—this of course is one of the great novelties of town life as compared with the Xhosa countryside. Living in the country means, both for Red and for School people, living in a domestic unit that is defined patriarchally. The woman's right to live in an *umzi* (homestead) depends upon her relationship to some man, alive or dead. The definition of her household duties also depends on this indirectly, in so far as this determines her seniority relative to the other females of the homestead. Moving to town frees her from both the men and the senior women. Age and sex distinctions, without ceasing to be relevant in interpersonal relations, lie much lighter as a whole. At least money may be earned, lodgings hired and property acquired, regardless of sex, seniority or marital status.

Prima facie one might expect many Xhosa women to break away from rural society permanently, but it must be considered how to define the break, to identify the "real home" of a husbandless woman. Property-rights in the country, which are a good index of country-rootedness in the case of men, hardly apply. Under communal tenure women cannot inherit land, though widows may retain the use of their deceased husbands' fields.

---

[27] See too: Obbo *African Women* ch 5 regarding the motives prompting migration to urban areas in Tanzania; Epstein *Urbanization and Kinship* 309ff; and Schapera *Married Life* 299–307 and 311ff.

The transfer of land to unmarried women, e.g. daughters with illegitimate children, is frowned upon by the authorities. On quitrent land there is theoretically no legislation to prevent a woman from acquiring land by purchase, but it has been official policy to prevent such acquisition. Town, in fact, is the only place where women can acquire real property. A woman can earn money which, though it could not buy her an *umzi*, can buy her a location house or shack.

In judging whether a woman is giving up her country-rootedness, perhaps one should regard her "residence right" as the closest parallel to a man's property right. As men can hope to inherit or acquire an *umzi*, women can hope to marry into one, or else remain acceptable in the parental one. The question of whether a woman hopes or aspires to become the "wife of a homestead" is therefore relevant, and also the question what close kin she has in the country and how much effort she makes to keep a "home" open with them. A younger woman or girl would, for example, have to send a proportion of her earnings home, instead of spending them for personal gratification; to obey the senior kin whenever they may require her to go back home; to avoid attachments to people who would involve her too closely in town life, including would-be lovers or husbands; to be willing to send children home so that they can be brought up by the grandparents and lend a hand in the homestead.

As a woman grows older her closest ties in the country are less likely to be with her parents, more likely with siblings or her own children. Her closest ties in town, at any time, are likely to be with the most regular lover or husband-substitute, and/or her children.

By such tests as these, relatively few of the women in East London appeared to be country-rooted exclusively. . . .

In one way or another, then, most women and girls who come to town feel they have "more future there than in the country". To this extent they have the strongest motives for staying and making good. It is true that a return to rural life would usually be less difficult for a woman than for a man. If he is ever to go back to the country, a man needs a right to the use of land, whereas a woman needs only some kin who are willing to receive and befriend her. Some women, defeated by town, do go back to relatives in the country; some are pulled back by the thought of the children they have left there. But going back again means embarrassment, and the necessity to take up again a kind of life that was found irksome before.

The women's tendency to become town-rooted (or at least doubly rooted) was particularly noticeable in the Red section because of its contrast with the men's attitude. Whereas the average Red man spoke longingly of "going home" and hoped to bring his retirement as near as possible, the Red woman often expressed herself as perfectly content with a life in town. "Why should I be anxious to go home?" asked a Red unmarried mother of 32, who works as a pineapple packer. "I am a woman, a mother, but I am not married. I have no homestead of my own. If I went home I would be under orders from my brother or his wife. Here in East London I am free. I do as I please. I have my own room. My lover is at liberty to come and sleep with me at my room, or I can go and sleep with him at his. You cannot find such freedom in the country. There, your lover will have to walk on his toes if he visits you at night."

Town has been seen to confer two new freedoms on a woman—to earn money, and to consort freely with lovers. Both these freedoms have to be discussed with reference to their bearing on urbanization; but first the earning of money.

A woman can earn money in East London either by accepting employment in the White-dominated economy (as a domestic servant or in some industrial or commercial undertaking) or else by carrying on a business enterprise within the locations. Both these ways of earning seem to have a tendency to "urbanize" women, in one sense or another, more effectively than the men's jobs are likely to "urbanize" men. To make a broad generalization, one may say that the women's paid employment is very often of a kind (domestic service) which fosters new cultural aspirations; while their self-employment within the location is very often of a kind whose rewards are substantial enough to constitute a strong town-located interest.

Employment and urbanization

Red and School girls compete for domestic and factory work, but School girls have some additional openings. A girl who is literate in English and/or Afrikaans may become, say, a waitress in a White café or boarding house, or a shop assistant in the poor North End district. Such jobs are rated somewhat higher than domestic service, though they do not necessarily pay better in terms of real wages. There are two particular occupations which rate much higher still and also pay far better, namely teaching and nursing, but both of these are restricted to a small, highly educated fraction of the School female population.

With the exception of factory work, the common run of women's employments are such as to develop or encourage town-style personal habits and wants. . . .

Some women entrepreneurs liked to contrast their own independence with the dependence of the employed woman: "The business is your own, the profit is your own, there is nobody to say to you 'Hurry up!' Stand on your own feet, I say, do not be like a suckling baby!" "Holding a hawker's licence, as I do, is better than being in the employ of anybody. I am satisfied. I feel that my *amawethu* (ancestral spirits) have been with me." It was characteristic that several middle-aged women had something positive to say about life in East London which scarcely any Red man ever said, namely, "If you are ambitious there are chances here to get rich". Vegetable hawking, and the making and selling of fatcakes or the kind of bun called *irostile*, are common enterprises mainly in the hands of women, both Red and School. Some other businesses are mostly run by School women, e.g. dressmaking, sewing and mending, peddling secondhand clothes, and hawking meat and offal. There is general agreement, however, that to make "real money" and make it quickly there is no better way than by selling liquor, and this is a woman's business too. School women are no less involved than Red women. . . .

All these types of women's enterprises serve their necessary functions in the economic life of the locations but the brewing business has a special social importance of its own. As has been seen, the entire social life of the Red migrants in town depends on beer, while School people also need their liquor suppliers who know how to observe the School convention of secrecy. Some women brew on a small scale and mainly for their own lovers with their *iseti*, but others build up a large clientele. Everyone seems to agree that in this business "the competition is very strong compared with competition for jobs in town". Success requires strong personality.

Women brewers have to cope with their customers, rough, half-drunk men; with their competitors; and last but not least (since the business is strictly illegal) with the police. Some are bold: "I do not worry too much about the police. I am getting used to them. In order to be successful one has to be careful not to be arrested; but at the same time bold and undaunted." . . .

But the businesses of the self-employed women, whether small or large, are hardly of a kind in which accumulated savings can well be reinvested. Because of this, and because of the necessarily precarious nature of illegal enterprise, nearly all self-employed women have the ambition to buy a wood-and-iron house as soon as they have saved enough. Owning a house in her own name may give a country-bred woman a very special satisfaction as well as an assured income. "A house here is the best possession for an unmarried mother like myself. The property is registered in my own name and it is I who collect the rentals. There is no fear of a brother who, in the country, could claim anything that belonged to his unmarried sister. Here I can do what I like." (Red woman, aged 32.) . . .

Some mature women referred to the comfort and convenience of town compared with the drudgery of a country homestead. "Life is much easier here for a woman in my position", said a semi-invalid widow in her late 50's. "I do not have to go and collect firewood, for I use paraffin to cook my food. I do not have to carry water from the river—the tap is only a few steps from my door. The dairies are near by too: 'Milk, milk!' I hear the milk boy shouting very early in the morning." Many more emphasized their pleasure in "being independent". This was not only a point scored off the domestic servant in town—it was, and more importantly, a point scored off the women of similar age and status who stay at home in the country: "In my hut at East London I am both the head and the wife. I do as I like. I have nobody to consult." "I do not like the idea of being under somebody else's rule. That is why I only go to visit my brother's family at Tshabo, and do not live there permanently."

Note

1. 'Red' referring to conservative traditionalists; 'School' referring to more westernized, frequently more educated, and Christianized people.

The urbanization of women in southern, as opposed to other parts of Africa, has certain distinctive features attributable to the peculiar constraints of apartheid.[28] This regime required the separation of families: wives and children had to remain in rural homelands while breadwinners found work in urban areas. In this way women underwrote the low wages paid in mines and factories.[29] The social consequence was that women in the rural areas had to assume responsibility for running households.[30] Where they had access to land and other necessary resources, they could adapt to subsistence farming,[31] although in southern Africa this was not easy because of the customary-law rule that land could be allocated only to men.[32]

As the economy of the homelands deteriorated, the families of migrants found it impossible to survive on agriculture and herding. Women perforce became dependent on the remittances of their husbands and kinsmen,[33] and when the reserve economies eventually collapsed, women too were driven into the towns to make a living for themselves and their children.[34]

Not all women had the guarantee of a permanent right of return to their rural bases; hence unlike male migrants, when they came to the city, they came to stay.[35] And yet, as urban newcomers, their situation was much more precarious than that of men. In the first place, the occupations available to women were marginal and subject to economic fluctuation. Usually the only jobs they could find were in domestic service,[36] and many women had to engage in illicit activities, such as brewing and prostitution. In the second place, it was more difficult for women to gain a permanent and a legal presence in urban areas. Influx control legislation was their major obstacle.

The two statutes mainly responsible for inhibiting free movement were the Blacks (Urban Areas) Consolidation Act[37] and the Blacks (Abolition of Passes

---

[28] Also see above, 154ff.

[29] Wolpe (1972) 1 *Economy & Society* 425. See above, 155. A similar residential pattern is found elsewhere in Africa: Okeyo in Etienne & Leacock op cit n22 202; Epstein op cit n27 308–9. And see Mbilinyi (1988) 16 *Int J Sociology L* 1ff.

[30] See Showers (1980) 6 *SA Labour Bulletin* 54.

[31] As in Ghana (Bukh *The Village Woman in Ghana*) and Kenya (Okeyo in Etienne & Leacock op cit n22 201).

[32] Boddington 1979 *Africa Perspective* 21 and James (1988) 14 *Social Dynamics* 46.

[33] Murray (1980) 6 *SA Labour Bulletin* 21.

[34] Yawitch *Tightening the Noose* 13.

[35] Preston-Whyte in Argyle & Preston-Whyte *Social System and Tradition in Southern Africa* 77.

[36] Cock op cit n22 307ff.

[37] 25 of 1949.

Social Context

and Co-ordination of Documents) Act.[38] The latter act, by obliging African women to carry passes, subjected them to the legal regime that had been prescribed for men. Prior to this, because women did not have to carry passes, they could move at will through the country.[39] In 1952 an amendment to the Urban Areas Act[40] provided that no African could remain for longer than 72 hours in a prescribed (ie urban) area unless he or she could prove an entitlement to be there.[41] Very few women qualified.[42]

Further restriction.

The Black Labour Act[43] further restricted the woman's right of entry to urban areas. In practice the bureaux responsible for recruiting labour excluded women, and when they were prepared to make an exception, they required the consent of the woman's guardian.[44] Urban housing served as yet another inhibition on the woman's freedom of movement. She would be regarded as lawfully resident in a city and could thereby qualify under the Blacks (Urban Areas) Consolidation Act, only if she were included on her husband's lodger permit. If no housing was available, she obviously could not acquire urban residence rights. In 1983 the figures for housing available for the *official* African population in Cape Town revealed a hypothetical occupancy rate of 146 people per house. This meant that it was virtually impossible for a family to be legally united in the city.[45] It is now evident that housing allocation was used to reinforce influx control legislation. In 1968, the government stopped spending on urban accommodation, a ban lasting for ten years, during which the housing problem grew to crisis proportions. In 1978 the policy was reversed, and even African women were allowed to buy houses in their own right or to rent them if they could show that they had children to support.[46] But it proved impossible to overcome the backlog; thousands of people were driven to hiring illegal accommodation in backyard shacks, to living as unlisted lodgers (without appearing on lodgers' permits) or as squatters.[47]

③

---

[38] 67 of 1952. See above, 156.

[39] Wells in Hay & Wright *African Women and the Law* 125.

[40] Section 27 of Act 54.

[41] Under s 10(1)*(a)–(c)* or unless he or she had a permit to seek work in the area: s 10(1)*(d)*. See above, [45].

[42] A few had s 10(1)*(a)* rights because they had been born in an urban area and had lived there continuously since birth. A somewhat larger number had s 10(1)*(c)* rights because they were the wives or unmarried daughters (under the age of 18) of men who qualified under s 10(1)*(a)* or *(b)*.

[43] 67 of 1964. It prohibited the recruitment of Africans for employment by anyone who did not hold an employer's recruitment licence. All black males, at the age of 15, were obliged to register at a labour bureau serving the area in which they lived. (An African living in the area of a labour bureau could not leave the area in order to look for work.) Women were exempt from compliance with this provision, but if they wanted work in an urban area, they also had to be registered.

[44] Paragraph 13(1)*(h)* of the Labour Bureaux Regulations Proc R74 1968 *GG* 2029 29 March 1968. See generally: Chaskalson 1984 *AJ* 33ff.

[45] Burman 1984 *AJ* 97.

[46] See s 11A of the Black Administration Act 38 of 1927 below, 334–5.

[47] The long-term disadvantage for such people was that they could not obtain s 10(1)*(b)* rights because they failed the test of 15 years' legal residence in an urban area: Yawitch op cit n34 9. For a brief period the de jure situation was improved by the courts in: *Komani NO v Bantu Affairs Administration Board, Peninsula Area* 1980 (4) SA 448 (A) and *Oos-Randse Administrasieraad en 'n ander v Rikhoto* 1983 (3) SA 595 (A). But in 1983 these decisions were overruled by Act 102, inserting s 10(1A) of the Urban Areas Act. See Corder 1984 *AJ* 43–4.

Emancipation of woman.

From a survey of population figures over a thirty-year period, it is evident that apartheid legislation had a considerable measure of success in reversing the flow of women to urban areas.[48] By dividing families and making it more difficult for husbands to exercise the authority that is the prerogative of the African man, apartheid has undoubtedly contributed to the de facto emancipation of women.[49] The composition of urban households tends to confirm this. Pauw's study of an East London township,[50] conducted in the early 1970s, revealed that 42 per cent of the households had female heads.[51] In this he discerned a tendency to matrifocalism; in other words he said that the father/husband was either completely absent from the family or had become a marginal figure. Whereas males previously had had critical functions, principally as links with chiefly authority (and thereby rights to arable land), and as sources of cattle and wealth, Pauw claimed that they had now become dispensable. He found that although the assistance of males might occasionally be necessary (to negotiate housing rights for instance), many households functioned quite satisfactorily without them. He concluded that the husband/father role had lost its significance in urban areas. Case studies in Durban led to a similar conclusion.[52] Here female-headed households usually consisted of women who were uterine kin; the relationships amongst these women were the most enduring and functionally the most important.

Authors have long been remarking on the startling increase of female-headed households[53] and this includes households in rural areas. Well-known in this regard is Schapera's 1934 study of a Kgatla ward in Mochudi, in Botswana.[54] Forty years later Roberts used the same study as the basis of a temporal comparison.[55] He found that the percentage of marriageable, but unmarried, women had increased dramatically—from 23 to 55 per cent—and that the proportion of such women who had borne children had increased slightly from 65 to 77 per cent. The tendency in Mochudi was reflected in other parts of Botswana, where the 1971 census revealed that one third of all households in the country were constituted by unmarried women with their dependent children.[56] In Lesotho too[57] the three-generation household, based on an unmarried

---

[48] In 1950 46,7 % of African women were living in the reserves; in 1960 the figure was 44 %; in 1970 52 %; and in 1980 57 %: Simkins *Four Essays on the Past, Present and Possible Future Distribution of the Black Population of South Africa* 57. Cf Wells in Hay & Wright op cit n39 126 who argues that the pass laws were a matter of political expediency rather than an effective means of controlling urbanization. Compare the situation in Tanzania: Swantz *Women in Development* 141.

[49] At what cost? See Lapchick & Urdang *Oppression and Resistance* 16–39 describing the plight of women in urban and rural areas, and Monica Wilson's foreboding predictions in *Changing Status of African Women*.

[50] Pages 141–63.

[51] Page 147.

[52] Preston-Whyte in Argyle & Preston-Whyte op cit n35 55ff.

[53] See: Hunter (1932) *SA J of Science* 681ff; Hellmann *Rooiyard*; Hellmann in Adam *South Africa: Sociological Perspectives* 12; Roberts in *Law and the Family in Africa* 241ff.

[54] Together with an Ngwato ward in Serowe: (1935) 9 *Bantu Studies* 203ff.

[55] Schapera & Roberts (1975) 45 *Africa* 258ff.

[56] See Peters (1983) 10 *JSAS* 105–6.

[57] Murray *Families Divided* 110 and Lye & Murray *Transformations on the Highveld* 107–9.

daughter and her children, has become relatively common.[58]

How is this phenomenon to be interpreted and what are the implications for the legal status of women? At the outset it should be appreciated that the definition of marriage is critical to determining whether in fact women should be deemed single. Yet this is impossible to fix with precision in customary law.[59] Furthermore, it is not settled whether female-headed households should be described as a trend towards matrifocalism,[60] a term that is in any event ambiguous.[61] The mere absence of men does not always mean that men have become redundant. In contrast to Pauw's findings in East London, for example, Murray discovered that in Lesotho, despite migrant labour and a high rate of marriage breakdown, agnatic structures were sustained by virilocal residence patterns. Wives continued to reside with their husbands' families and likewise divorcées and widows returned to their natal homes rather than create new homesteads.[62]

The social significance of household composition remains ambiguous. The gender and marital status of a household head are not *conclusive* indications of authority structures within the household or of its relationships with the outside world (although these are the very issues that must be answered in order to assess the social significance of the female family head).[63] Families are not entirely self-regulating. The attitude and perceptions of society, in particular the bureaucracy, are vital in this regard. For instance, if local administrations regard men as the only legitimate heads of families, then men retain their connections with authority and thus their importance within the family.[64] For these reasons, if a stand is to be taken on improving women's status, it should be argued as a matter of principle and not only on the basis of changes in family structure.

III | LEGAL CAPACITY OF MARRIED WOMEN

(1) Female status

Status is the condition of belonging to a group or category of people, to which is ascribed a set of rights, duties, powers, liabilities, privileges, and disabilities. Unlike contractual rights and duties, which in principle are voluntarily chosen, the rights and duties associated with status are imposed ex lege.[65] So, although a person may by an act of volition, such as marriage, acquire a status, the rights and duties attached to it are ascribed and are not (except sometimes within prescribed limits) variable.

---

[58] See too above, 165–6.
[59] Peters op cit n56 111.
[60] Such suggestive labelling for a study of family structure in KwaZulu, eg, was rejected: Webster *Family and Household in KwaDapha, KwaZulu* 36.
[61] See Smith in Goody *The Character of Kinship* 121ff. Matrifocalism implies: the cultural value placed on the mother-role; the internal structure or composition of households; the socio-economic marginality of husband/fathers; or a combination of all three.
[62] Murray op cit n57 110.
[63] Peters op cit n56.
[64] For example, men were vital for obtaining urban residence rights under s 10(1) of the Blacks (Urban Areas) Consolidation Act 25 of 1945 and they alone have access to rural land.
[65] Paton *A Textbook of Jurisprudence* 398.

A person's status flows from membership of a category of people. The most common criteria for constituting these categories are age, gender, and marriage.[66] One status is always relative to another: the status of father is relative to child, woman is relative to man, minor is relative to major, and so forth. In consequence, the rights attributed to a status must find their correlative duties expressed in a complementary category.[67]

Small-scale or precapitalist societies are frequently described as 'status dominated' because nearly all a person's rights and duties were imposed by virtue of belonging to a certain category of people. In contrast, the rights and duties derived from contract were of peripheral importance.[68] This observation was the basis of Maine's famous aphorism: 'the movement of progressive societies has hitherto been a movement from Status to Contract.'[69] In status dominated societies a pattern of interrelated statuses, determined mainly by the kinship system, provided a social structure to realize the imperatives of material support and reproduction.

For legal purposes,[70] status implies a person's capacity. In consequence, three related concepts must be distinguished: status (a condition); capacity (a power to acquire and exercise rights); and the rights themselves.[71]

An effective method of confining women to a domestic sphere of activity was to deprive them of any competence to deal with people in the outside world: all 'public' acts would be treated as nullities. Western legal systems, for example, in common with others supporting patriarchy, formerly denied women four legal capacities that are essential to facilitate transactions in the market place and other public contexts. These were contractual, delictual, and proprietary capacity, and locus standi in judicio. The ostensible reason for doing so was woman's intellectual immaturity and lack of judgment. On this understanding they were assimilated to the category of children and were subjected to the control of a 'guardian', ie a senior male.

The code of rules governing the status of wives in customary law is described in the following extract.[72]

---

[66] Paton op cit 399.

[67] On the relativity of status see Beattie *Other Cultures* 36.

[68] Gluckman *The Ideas in Barotse Jurisprudence* 171ff.

[69] *Ancient Law* 100.

[70] According to the definition current in the social sciences, status defines the identity of social actors (the persons between whom a relationship exists); and it includes their roles or what they are expected to do. This accounts for Talcott Parsons' use of the omnibus term 'status-role': *Essays in Sociological Theory* 42.

[71] Allen *Legal Duties* 47. Afrikaans writers have criticized English texts for indiscriminate use of the term 'legal capacity'. They claim that two concepts must be separated: the capacity to *perform* juristic acts, and the capacity to *have* rights and duties. There is a clear example in the case of minors: because they are deemed to lack the requisite judgment, they are incapable of incurring contractual obligations, but they may none the less acquire contractual rights. See Boberg 37ff for a summary. More precise terminology was elaborated by Hohfeld *Fundamental Legal Conceptions*.

[72] See further: Schapera 82; Mönnig 268; Reader 160–2; Reuter *Native Marriages in South Africa* 160–1; Duncan 4–7; Van Tromp 97–109; Coertze 246–77. The status of unmarried women is considered in the chapter on Children below, 338ff and widows in the chapter on Succession below, 410ff.

[101] SCHAPERA *MARRIED LIFE IN AN AFRICAN TRIBE* 91–5

Where the couple form a part of a larger household, their behaviour towards each other is governed by the fact that they are both still subject to its head. As long as the wife lives in her parents' home, she remains under the immediate authority of her father, to whom she must answer for her conduct. She works together with the other women of her home, and has little to do with her relatives-in-law. Her husband generally comes merely to sleep with her, and so cannot control her by day; but even if he spends most of his time with her, and by helping his parents-in-law contributes to her keep, any attempt on his part to bully her is immediately resisted by them. They are actually entitled to claim an ox or goat from him as damages if he thrashes her while she is still under their roof. In a patrilocal marriage his authority is greater, for she is more directly under his supervision and protection. But he is himself still dependent upon his father, whom he must inform of all his movements and consult in all his business affairs; and should he neglect or ill-treat her, his parents will at once rebuke and correct him. A wife's lot, nevertheless, is notoriously difficult while she is living with her parents-in-law; she must attend humbly and submissively upon them, is given all the more unpleasant or monotonous tasks to do, and becomes in effect the general servant of the household. She must prove that she is a worthy addition to the family—and the standards set can sometimes be very exacting.

It is not until they have moved into their own compound that the relationship between husband and wife appears in its proper perspective. The change is reflected mainly in their respective legal positions. The husband is now for all practical purposes his own master. Although still tied to his father or eldest brother by obligations of deference, obedience and service, he has far greater freedom in running his home and managing his other affairs. He has attained to the dignified status of head of his own household, and with it becomes not only responsible for all his own actions, but also the full guardian of his wife and children. The wife is always legally dependent upon her husband. She cannot as a rule resort to the tribal courts except through him as her representative, and if she does wrong or falls into debt he is liable for any payments that must be made. She cannot bind herself to any contracts without his approval, she must live wherever he chooses to build his home, and she must obey all his commands. In spite of her legal subjection, however, her status too is improved by the establishment of their own household, for she now becomes its mistress and acquires a new authority in domestic affairs. She is responsible for the care of the compound, she can entertain friends and visitors more freely than ever before, and in time she will have her children and other dependants to work under her own supervision.

Both husband and wife contribute to the economic maintenance of their household. The wife must see to the building and care of the compound itself, the preparation of food and other forms of housework, and the cultivation of the fields; the husband helps in the building and ploughing, but his principal activities are to supervise the care of the livestock and to hunt. As long as they are dependent members of another household, they work with the rest for the common benefit. But once they have established their own home, the burden of maintaining it falls largely upon themselves alone. The husband, especially, is obliged to provide his wife with a dwelling, clothing, food and similar forms of support; he must clear one or more fields for her to cultivate, and procure cattle and other livestock to furnish her and her children with milk and occasionally meat. Nowadays, when the range of goods considered essential to every decent home has increased so greatly through contact with Europeans, he must also, if necessary, and if young enough, go abroad to work for the money with which to purchase them. As he grows older, he relies upon his sons to do so instead.

Property a husband sets aside for the use of his wife he cannot afterwards alienate without her consent, and when she dies it is normally inherited by her own children. She looks after the huts, the produce from her fields, the fowls and all the ordinary household utensils and implements; she decides how they are to be used and she can at her discretion sell some of the crops, fowls and common utensils, in order to supply other wants. In case of divorce she is entitled not only to her personal belongings, such as clothes, but to most of the household utensils and to half the corn in her granaries. She cannot however, dispose of her husband's personal belongings, guns, wagons, and similar objects used exclusively by men, and the produce of any fields not specially assigned to her so, too, the cattle and fields allotted to her by her husband remain under his authority, subject to the qualification noted above, and if she is divorced she has no claim over them. . . .

A wife may also have property in her own right. As we have seen, her parents at marriage gave her a few household utensils, and occasionally also a field and a heifer or two. She may afterwards acquire property as part of the *bogadi* received when her daughters get married, or by outright gift from her husband, or by inheritance from her mother and nowadays also from her father. Moreover, she can earn money by making and selling beer, pots, baskets and similar commodities, or by the practice of dressmaking or magic. Her earnings are at her own disposal, but a good wife will share them with her husband. Any property a woman thus possesses at marriage, or subsequently acquires, is never looked upon as part of her husband's estate; he cannot use it without her authority, it cannot be attached to pay his debts, and, in case of divorce, she takes it away with her.

In addition to all this, marriage imposes sexual obligations upon husband and wife. She must always be ready to gratify his sexual desires, except on the occasions when intercourse between them is specially prohibited. Moreover, she is expected to be faithful to him. If she commits adultery, he can beat or otherwise punish her, and can claim damages from her lover; but he will not usually divorce her, unless she persists in this conduct. He himself, on the other hand, is not required to be as faithful to her. Even if he has no other wives with whom she must share his attentions, he frequently has concubines, and normally she can take no action against them at court. It is only in Christian marriages that the ideal of a husband's fidelity is now sometimes met, and here, too, adultery by either spouse is accepted in court as a ground for divorce. Usually, however, a wife does not complain about her husband's love-affairs, so long as he cohabits with her regularly, and so gives her a reasonable opportunity of bearing him children. No marriage is considered really complete unless it produces offspring; and a barren woman is regarded with some contempt by her neighbours, and with scarce-concealed disappointment and even hostility by her husband's relatives. Under tribal law he is entitled to divorce her merely for this and to recover his *bogadi*, although she may instead bring another woman from her home to bear him children in her place. The children of a marriage always belong to the husband and his people, once *bogadi* has been paid. They never go with their mother in case of divorce, unless they are still young, when she may receive custody of them until they are old enough to return to their father.

The wife's inferior status evident enough from what has already been said, is further reflected in the behaviour demanded of her in everyday life. She should pay formal deference to her husband, speaking to him respectfully, waiting upon him, serving him first with food, walking before him in the street, and not going about, especially at night, without his knowledge and permission; she sits on the floor, whereas he has his stool or chair; and if strangers come to the compound she must refer them to him and wait in the background while they are talking together. But despite these and many other discriminations against her, her position is by no means humiliating. She and her husband often eat together, speak to each other by their personal names or by the conventional terms "father" and "mother" used between all adults, sit together when entertaining visitors, go about together to beer-drinks and other festivities, and, above all, consult together in matters of domestic importance. She has her recognized place in the wider family councils, and is particularly influential when the marriages of her children are being considered.

The formalities of guardianship may be waived where the woman is mature and when circumstances demand.

[102] ROBERTS *RESTATEMENT OF AFRICAN LAW, BOTSWANA, TSWANA FAMILY LAW* 18

While women still remain, in theory, subject to guardianship throughout their lives, the practical effects of this state are now very limited in some situations. Once a woman's husband is dead, even though she remains technically subject to guardianship, the control formerly exercised over her is greatly relaxed. Often she effectively takes over the management of her own property, with her guardian looking after her cattle in accordance with her directions. Older married women and widows similarly manage their own property and even conduct their own litigation. It is again increasingly common for a young unmarried woman or a woman separated from her husband to leave her group in search of employment and ultimately to set up a homestead of her own with any children who may have been born to her, breaking off all associations with the group from which her guardian would traditionally have been drawn and effectively managing her own property and maintaining her household.

The woman's position, as depicted by Schapera, although subordinate, allowed her a fair measure of security and protection. But these benefits would depend on the disposition of her husband or her family. For instance, although it is generally conceded that women had a claim to support, customary law allowed only imperfect methods of enforcement; and it is in a procedural sense that the woman's vulnerability becomes most apparent. A husband's duties were of a moral or conventional nature; if he neglected them or abused his authority, his wife had no direct action against him. She was expected to appeal to her own father for protection; and his obligation was also nebulously conceived in morals and custom.[73] As a last resort, the woman might appeal to her headman, but even in this instance she depended upon a man for her protection.[74]

(2) The courts' response

— *Interpretation of A C law.*

The colonial governments were initially sympathetic to African women, whom they perceived as living in virtual bondage. This did not accord with the ideals of female emancipation that were gradually gathering impetus in nineteenth-century Europe. But feelings were ambivalent:

'What was in process of liberation was the concept of human individuality and its pre-eminence over all considerations of birth and fortune . . . but many people saw the application of this concept to women's status as a threat to marital happiness and to the whole basis of relationships between male and female.'[75]

Both bridewealth and polygyny were thought to degrade women and were discouraged;[76] forced marriages were prohibited.[77] But it was by the introduction of the common-law concept of the age of majority that women were to receive their greatest measure of protection.

---

[73] *Ngwenya & another v Zwane* 1959 NAC 28 (NE).

[74] If women's rights were so poorly expressed and if women, because of their reproductive potential, were deemed to be the equivalent of bridewealth (Holleman 319) it would follow that they could be regarded as legal objects rather than subjects: Strathern in Hirschon op cit n13 158.

[75] Oakley *Sex, Gender and Society* 13–14.

[76] Welsh *The Roots of Segregation* 69–70.

[77] Welsh op cit 84–5.

A major was automatically released from the incapacities imposed on the category of children, and so it was thought that by similarly empowering women they would be enabled to interact with society, which would lead to an overall improvement of their situation. This goal was founded on two implicit assumptions: that legal reform should precede social and economic reform, and that women would be eager to avail themselves of these new opportunities.

In the Cape, because customary law was not recognized, all persons, Africans included, attained majority at a predetermined age.[78] The same rule was extended to the Transkeian Territories,[79] and so it was claimed that women had been withdrawn from male tutelage.[80] On this understanding the courts held that when widowed a woman attained full capacity,[81] entitling her to ownership of property acquired after her husband's death[82] and even during her marriage.[83] Yet the granting of these powers was clearly premature. Predictably, African men were hostile to the reforms.[84] Most women were unaware of their new status, and the few that were, seldom tried to act upon it.[85] Had they enforced their rights, there was every likelihood that they would have been ostracized by their kin and social circle.[86]

In Natal, where customary law was given wider recognition, female incapacities were retained. Section 27 of the Code provided that a male became a major on marriage (either civil or customary) or on attaining the age of 21, but that a female was deemed to be a perpetual minor unless she was specifically emancipated. Section 28 of the Code allowed unmarried women, widows or divorcées to apply to commissioners' courts for orders of emancipation. Provided that the applicants could fulfil the strenuous criteria laid down in the Code, they could escape some of the more irksome aspects of customary law.[87] So few women applied for exemption, however, that in practice the exemption procedure was a dead letter.[88]

Elsewhere the courts were prepared, grudgingly it must be admitted, to free African women from some of the constraints of customary law on the basis of a conflict of laws, namely if they had abandoned a 'tribal' way of life. In the following case, for example, a woman sued in her own name for seduction damages and for maintenance of her child. The action was allowed because the common law, not customary law, was applied.

---

[78] 21 under Ord 62 of 1929.
[79] By ss 39 of Procs 110 and 112 of 1879 and by s 38 of Proc 140 of 1885.
[80] *Nbono v Monoxoweni* (1891) 6 EDC 62.
[81] *Nolanti v Sintenteni* 1 NAC 43 (1901); *Nosaiti v Xangati* 1 NAC 50 (1902).
[82] *Xolo* 1931 NAC (C&O) 23.
[83] *Nobulawa v Joyi* 5 NAC 159 (1926); *Ndema* 1936 NAC (C&O) 15.
[84] Reuter op cit n72 161–2.
[85] Simons *African Women* 188.
[86] See the case study by Mann in Hay & Wright op cit n39 151 regarding the predicament of a wife married by Christian rites in Lagos. There is an interesting comparison with similar reforms in the Muslim regions of the Soviet Union: Massel (1968) 2 *Law & Soc R* 179ff.
[87] See Simons *African Women* ch 20.
[88] Shropshire *The Bantu Woman under the Natal Code of Native Law* 22.

[103] *MONAHENG v KONUPI* 1930 NAC (N&T) 89 at 90–3

The parties are apparently detribalised and their place of residence is the Native Township, Evaton and Johannesburg, respectively. . . .

It seems fairly obvious from his reasons for judgment that the Native Commissioner considered that the parties to the suit had abandoned Native customs and modes of life and were living as Europeans; he therefore elected to decide this matter under the common law and eschewed Native law. We must therefore deal with it as a matter falling under the former system.

That being so . . . we must first consider whether plaintiff in that Court was competent to sue as a femme sole.

In South Africa and under Roman-Dutch law a girl who, having been a virgin, is seduced is herself entitled to sue for damages as for an injury to herself personally, without the intervention of her parents unless, of course, she is a minor, when she must be assisted, so far as the mere institution of the action is concerned in the same way as other plaintiffs who are minors, though the injury is one to herself personally.

In the case before us it is not stated on the Record whether or not the plaintiff has attained her majority, but it is assumed she is a major. It need not be alleged that the party is a femme sole: the law does not presume incapacity.

If this action had been maintained at Native law the respondent would be out of Court because it is the almost invariable unwritten rule among the Bantu that the action is brought by the girl's parents or guardian, but in the circumstances of these people living in a large industrial centre as they do and having become detribalised and adopted standards of living and outlook of the more enlightened classes it seems to me . . . that we are bound to regard them in a light wholly different to the primitive order of society of the kraal. I, however, take this view most reluctantly because the moment we break away from established institutions of Native customary law in these matters, we find ourselves confronted with innumerable fine distinctions and complications. . . . Many other distinctions calculated to confuse and perplex a people less enlightened than ourselves could be enumerated, but I think by indicating the above two I have sufficiently shown how desirable it is in cases of this nature to avoid, as far as possible, getting away from a system of law, whatever its shortcomings may be from our standpoint, that is more in harmony with Native standards and their conceptions of equity and justice.

These tentative moves to alleviate the position of women were soon abandoned, and after the 1930s the courts made no further efforts to interfere with customary law.[89] Instead they were content to treat women in the same way as common-law minors, an approach that was both misguided and prejudicial to its subjects. On the one hand, the common-law categories of minor and major cannot reflect the nuances and flexibility inherent in customary law, and, on the other, these categories were imposed on women not with a view to *protecting* them but with a view to *restraining* them.[90] The courts had no intention of progressively developing customary law nor did they try to bring it into line with the common law. Rather they sought to apply whatever common-law concepts seemed to be analogous with the African understanding of patriarchy.

Exclusion of customary law in favour of the common law, according to the conflict of laws rules in the manner of *Monaheng's* case above, was also shunned. Women were to be subjected to the full rigours of 'customary' law, whatever their lifestyle, and whatever actual competence they had demonstrated in leading

---

[89] A noticeable feature in other legal systems as well: Olsen (1983) 96 *Harvard LR* 1520–2.
[90] See Mbilinyi op cit n29 25 and n189 below.

an independent life. In the following case, for example, a widow sued unassisted for recovery of certain buildings in an urban area. Customary law was applied and the court refused her action.

[104] *MATSHENG v DHLAMINI & ANOTHER* 1937 NAC (N&T) 89 at 92–4

[The court held that, because the Black Administration Act of 1927 had entrenched the application of customary law] this Court is forced to the conclusion that native law governing the status of women is in force and must be recognised by this Court as indeed has been and is the practice, although moved by compassion in special cases the Court has in the past sought to apply "equity" to what is considered "hard cases".

It is a moot question whether this practice [alleviating hard cases] is sound for the utmost difficulty is experienced in deciding when this form of relief is to be accorded and what criteria should be present to take the incapacitated native female out of the status conferred on her by the law normally applicable to her; moreover, the dislocation, legal and social, which follows the indulgence in most cases, introduces complications far worse than the cure. There is a marked tendency especially among women to break away from the restraint of native law with complete subversion of native family life and institutions—a process of disintegration which it would not become this Court to expedite by recognition of the assumed position of such women. . . . [McLoughlin P then cited with approval the following passage from the judgment in *Dumalitshona v Mraji* 5 NAC 168 (1927) at 169.] "Until the proper authorities are satisfied that the time has arrived when various widely recognised customs which are practised daily by the native tribes of these Territories, e.g. polygamy, ukutwala, ukungena, etc., which admittedly fall short of civilised standards, should be abrogated, this Court is of the opinion that it should not interfere in matters of broad policy which is the prerogative of the executive, and that it would, therefore, not be justified in setting aside a custom which has long since become crystallized into law."

The refusal to allow relief from the customary-law regime, even where its application was patently inappropriate to the woman concerned, was explained in terms of the aphorism 'hard cases make bad law'. This was elaborated in the following case, where a woman sued for damages for her seduction and breach of promise. Both she and the appellant were educated and professing Christians. She was the unmarried daughter of a petty chief and a major. The appellant had promised to marry her by Christian rites. She claimed that he had seduced her, and without good cause had broken off their engagement. The Appeal Court refused her claim.

[105] *YAKO v BEYI* 1944 NAC (C&O) 72 at 76–9

Under Common Law a native adult female is conceived as having rights, personal to herself, which she can protect by unaided action in Court, the remedy being based on that designed by the Common Law for a people living under entirely different social sanctions and economic conditions—where these individual losses and obligations fall directly on the female, e.g. maintenance of an illegitimate child or loss of chances of a desirable marriage, etc.

In contrast the native system regards the female as a unit of the group, having no rights personal to herself, but being the ward of the group, whose interests are touched when a delict is committed against or with the woman. Being a ward of the group she is maintainable by the group—and in the present instance so also the fruit of the delict—the child is sometimes also maintained by the woman's group, on behalf of the natural father's group, to which payment of damages for the delict transfers the child, subject to compensation for such maintenance, etc.

When the first essay was made to proceed under Common Law, the Native Appeal Court, acutely conscious of the anomaly, evolved the formula that if the Native Law in such instances did not provide a remedy, recourse must be had to that law which did so provide a remedy, i.e. the Court, moved by the spirit of the times in advancing Common Law among the more enlightened natives gave a "remedy" when there was in actual fact no "right" which could or should have been remedied as between the woman suing in a personal private capacity and the wrongdoer. That right rested in the woman's guardian and not in her. . . .

It does not become this, or any other Court, to aid individuals to enrich themselves unjustly by departing from those standards and seeking abnormal gain by forcing the issue into a foreign mould. . . .

Reverting to the matter of a privileged class among rural (reserve) natives: the natives themselves attach no significance to those criteria which the plaintiff claims to entitle her to greater damages than the normal. Native Law, which regulates these matters, draws no distinction on the grounds of Christianity, square buildings, education and the like. What is considered is birth. Only a chief of consequence is entitled to higher damages—and these individuals are limited in number. . . . The number of the individuals who possess these qualifications is great to-day; but the legislation has not seen fit to exclude them as a class from the operation of Native Law—indeed the trend has been in the opposite direction as has repeatedly been shown in recent judgments of these Courts, which Courts owe their very being to that trend. And among the natives themselves the urge for retention of their laws and customs is strong. The introductory remarks in this judgment indicate clearly that it would be inequitable arbitrarily to single out individual cases for special concessions.

(a) Proprietary capacity

Access to property is one of the most sensitive indicators of power relations,[91] and the inferior position of women is especially evident in this regard. Although, as already noted, women play a vital role in food production and usually have unrestricted control over staple foodstuffs, they are denied control over the *means* of producing food, i e land and livestock.[92] Gender studies have revealed that post-marital residence rules are instrumental in restricting women's access to such property.[93] Wherever marriage is virilocal, the wife must leave her kingroup, which precludes her participation in the collective rights to the land of her natal family. Instead she becomes a stranger in her husband's group, liable to be returned to her own kin in times of marital discord;[94] in other words, her position is precarious.

The courts' ruling that women lack proprietary capacity is testimony to this restricted access to the means of production and to a lack of opportunity to acquire property. The concept of proprietary capacity, however, is a vague one, seeming to denote three things: the powers to acquire and dispose of real rights to property, and the liberty to use property without reference to any one else. In common law a minor's proprietary capacity is taken to mean only the latter two; in customary law, although a more generous interpretation would have been

---

[91] Hirschon op cit n13 1.
[92] See above, 304–5.
[93] Coontz & Henderson op cit n2 36.
[94] Chevillard & Leconte in Coontz & Henderson op cit n2 81.

possible, female proprietary capacity is taken to mean all three. As such, the concept overgeneralizes the position, thereby seriously disadvantaging women.

The following extract shows the considerable diversity of Swazi opinion regarding ownership of a woman's income.

[106] ARMSTRONG & NHLAPO *LAW AND THE OTHER SEX* 40–2

In brief, all property[1] in a household is held, generally speaking, in the name of the head of the household as in the case of the Roman "paterfamilias". . . . With married women, however, certain special rules apply.

First of all, two beasts (both of which are connected with the marriage ceremony) belong to the wife in full title. The first is the *liphakelo* beast, a cow settled on the bride by her husband to signify that she now has permission to eat sour milk at her new home—a delicacy previously forbidden her. The other is the *insulamnyembeti* beast. She gets this for each daughter who marries; it is earmarked from the rest of the lobolo cattle as her own personal consolation prize. Obviously, the more married daughters she has the wealthier she will be in this type of property.

In addition, "the earnings of the wife . . . and any property acquired by (her) through her own industry"[2] will fall into her estate. Statements such as this need further qualification. In the first place, a lot may depend on exactly what type of property is involved. Cooking utensils, personal clothing and even the modest profits from a roadside handicrafts or vegetable stall may belong to the wife, to control and use without interference. But controversy may well arise in the case of a thriving high-turnover business run by the wife, or a high salary brought in by a professional spouse. The problem here seems to be the ability of the wife, in present-day economic circumstances, to generate an income at least as high as that of her husband (if not higher): a circumstance that was unthinkable for the ordinary commoner at the time these traditional rules took root. In marked contrast to some East and West African societies, Swazi culture has not been habituated to the phenomenon of the entrepreneur wife who may rise to a position of great wealth and influence. This imbalance between economic reality and traditional expectations has already been known to cause some stress: the papers are forever reporting legal wrangles between widows and relatives of a deceased husband pursuing claims to property generated primarily by the wife. It is the sort of social stress that can only be eased by legislation.

Quite apart from the high-income wife, a further qualification to the rule that a customary wife owns her "minor" property must be mentioned. Our research revealed a significant minority viewpoint: namely that it all depends on the state of the marriage and the reasons why the topic of property has come up in the first place. If all is well with the marriage an indulgent husband may pursue a policy of total non-interference as far as his wife's activities are concerned. If, however, the issue of property arises because the marriage is breaking up, the woman may well be "sent to her parents in the clothes she stands in", as one respondent put it. This seems to be because the chain of control, power and authority still leads to the husband ultimately. As the same lady observed, "Even if my earnings come from handicrafts I make and sell, or from vegetables I grow . . . *who* gave me permission for that sort of activity, *who* bought me the original materials, *who* allocated the land to me . . .?"

Notes

1. R T Nhlapo *Women and the Law* 58.
2. C F Fannin *Preliminary Notes on Principles of Swazi Customary Law* 3.

The South African courts held that women can have outright ownership in only a very limited category of things: the ngquthu beast[95] and property of an intimate nature, such as traditional wearing apparel.[96] But they could have extended certain customary-law institutions to accommodate modern social practices in a way that would have benefited women considerably. According to some systems of customary law, for instance, if a woman were a diviner, herbalist or midwife, or if she brewed beer, made pots or other artifacts for sale, she would be entitled to keep any income she earned (or her own family could claim it on the ground that they had educated her).[97] The courts ignored such particularities, holding that *any* income a wife earned became house property,[98] with the consequence that her husband took control over it,[99] unless he chose to return it to her as a gift.[100]

The proprietary incapacity of women could have been construed to resemble that of minors under common law:[101] a person over the age of 7 has the capacity to acquire ownership of property if this will improve his or her position.[102] The guardian has a right only to administer the ward's estate and he or she is obliged to act bona fide and in the minor's best interests. Certain special rules have been adopted to protect the minor from dishonesty or inept management, such as the prohibition against alienation of immovables,[103] and the rule that damages received from suits for personal injuries must be paid into the Guardian's Fund or held in trust.[104] Most importantly, a parent has no general right to a minor's income.[105] All of these rules are protective in nature; none has been applied to African women.

Women have only a claim to maintenance.[106] In customary law the usual way of enforcing this was for the woman first to approach her husband's relatives, failing which, to return to her own family, and possibly to seek a divorce. In certain early decisions of the Transkeian courts, where the wife had been driven away from her husband's home, the house property was placed under her protection,[107] and on two occasions she was given ownership of her earnings

---

[95] *Mohlakula v Elizabeth* 1 NAC 56 (1902); *Mpongo v Mandlela & another* 3 NAC 34 (1913); *Sibiya v Sibisi* 1946 NAC (N&T) 60; *Mlaba v Mvelase* 1951 NAC 314 (NE); *Mbanjwa* 1964 BAC 122 (NE); *Khanyile da v Zulu* 1966 BAC 35 (NE); *Ndebele* 1971 BAC 70 (NE).

[96] *Xakaxa v Mkize* 1947 NAC (N&T) 85; *Dhlamini* 1967 BAC 7 (NE).

[97] Simons *African Women* 195.

[98] *Nomlota v Mbiti* 2 NAC 4 (1910); *Nomtewbulo v Ndumndum* 2 NAC 121 (1911); *Tantsi v Tabalaza* 4 NAC 107 (1922); *Ngexo v Tshopo* 1929 NAC (C&O) 9; *Mkwanazi* 1945 NAC (N&T) 112; *Mokoena v Mofokeng* 1945 NAC (C&O) 89; *Masondo v Butelezi* 1949 NAC 118 (NE); *Ntombela v Mpungose* 1950 NAC 150 (NE); *Mpantsha v Ngolonkulu & another* 1952 NAC 40 (S); *Mpungose v Shandu* 1956 NAC 180 (NE); *Sithole* 1967 BAC 18 (NE).

[99] Subject to the qualification that he should use it for the benefit of the family: *Tshobo & another v Tshobo* 4 NAC 142 (1920); *Tshemese* 4 NAC 143 (1921); *Ngcobo* 1946 NAC (N&T) 14.

[100] *Monelo v Nole* 1 NAC 102 (1906); *Mpafa v Sindiwe* 4 NAC 268 (1919).

[101] *Nomlota v Mbiti* 2 NAC 4 (1910); *Ndema* 1936 NAC (C&O) 15 at 19–20; *Mokgatle* 1946 NAC (N&T) 82; *Mpungose v Shandu* 1956 NAC 180 (NE).

[102] Spiro 94; Boberg 469–70.

[103] Section 80 of the Administration of Estates Act 66 of 1965.

[104] Boberg 489.

[105] *Chinnia v Dunna* 1940 NPD 384.

[106] See Poulter 171–2.

[107] *Meleni v Mandlangisa* 2 NAC 191 (1911).

when she had been deserted.[108] But a later judgment was careful to stress that this did not amount to giving the wife real rights in house property.[109]

It has been assumed that the wife's economic well-being is ensured by her personal right to support; and now that women routinely approach maintenance courts unassisted to sue for support, it might be argued that enough has been done to protect them. This is questionable. Rights to maintenance (if they are not to be enforced in court) depend on the durability of personal relationships formed by kinship and marriage. Where these relationships are weak or vulnerable, as they have become in southern Africa, the individual gains greater protection from having a real right to the property he or she has acquired.

Where a husband is away from home, he may leave his wife in charge of the household. And the courts have noted that as a result of migrant labour this has become an increasingly common arrangement. The woman then has authority as her husband's agent to dispose of property to meet the day-to-day requirements of the family.[110] If necessary, she may sue for the return of property.[111] But she is not permitted to dispose of valuable assets, like cattle, without first consulting one of her husband's senior male relatives, failing whom, a male in position of authority.[112]

Under s 26 of the Natal and KwaZulu Codes, the head of a family, while away from home, may delegate his powers to a fit and proper person. If he makes no formal appointment, his heir is deemed to be his representative: but if the heir is still a minor, his mother may take charge. These arrangements are supplemented by a further provision that a district officer may give written authorization to any appropriate person to protect the property of an absent family head or of a minor inmate.[113]

(b) Contractual capacity

A person who is not allowed to hold property is inevitably disabled from full participation in society. Hence the corollary of a proprietary incapacity is a contractual incapacity.[114]

In this case the courts have been more consistent in approximating the woman's status to that of a minor in the common law. According to Roman-Dutch law, a minor's contract creates a natural obligation, ie one enforceable at his or her option. The contract becomes fully binding if the minor has the assistance of a guardian.[115] This may be given expressly or it may be

---

[108] *Majomboyi & another v Nobeqwa* 2 NAC 63 (1911). Further see *Logose v Yekiwe* 4 NAC 105 (1919).
[109] *Sijila v Masumba* 1940 NAC (C&O) 42 at 46.
[110] *Cebekulu v Sitole* 1944 NAC (N&T) 48.
[111] *Mpahlwa v Mcwaba* 4 NAC 302 (1919). In *Bomela v Kobus* 1972 BAC 180 (S) the common law was applied.
[112] *Qolo v Ntshini* 1950 NAC 234 (S); and see *Ndlala d/a v Makinana* 1963 BAC 18 (S). See *Ndinisa d/a v Mtuzulu* 1963 BAC 74 (S) for the position of the widow.
[113] In *Ngubane v Hadebe* 1968 BAC 13 (NE) the commissioner's permission was not obtained; but this was not regarded as fatal because the woman had acted bona fide and reasonably.
[114] *Ndhlovu* 1954 NAC 59 (NE); cf *Komandisi v Mathuthu* 1943 NAC (N&T) 74, where the woman was in charge of the homestead, and *Mzwendayi v Busobengwe* 1921 NHC 62.
[115] Boberg 568.

implied, as where the guardian raises no objection to the contract.[116] Alternatively, assistance may take the form of ratification ex post facto.[117] In *Zwane v Dhlamini*,[118] it was held that a woman's contract could be ratified by her guardian. Moreover, and presumably this is in accord with the common-law rule that a minor may receive benefits under a contract but need not incur obligations, it was held that a woman could receive livestock in terms of sisa (nqoma) contracts.[119]

(c) Delictual capacity

The term 'delictual capacity' is often used loosely to refer both to the right to claim damages and to the duty to make compensation. But although a person's status might affect the ability to be a right/duty bearer, it would be wrong to confuse these concepts in the generic term 'delictual capacity'. Instead the following should be distinguished: the *capacity* to commit a delict, the *duty* to make compensation, and the *right* to claim compensation when a wrong has been suffered. Many legal systems keep these concepts analytically separate. In Roman Law, for instance, an infant was culpae incapax; once he became impubes, at the age of 7, he was capable of committing a delict, but he was not *liable* to make compensation. At all stages of his life, however, he would have a *right* to claim compensation, although his guardian would have to assert the claim on his behalf. This involved a different consideration, the child's locus standi.

Under the common law, a minor has delictual capacity. If over the age of 7, his or her capacity for fault is a question of fact that depends on the individual's maturity and the circumstances of the case.[120] The guardian becomes liable for the ward's delicts only where: there is vicarious liability flowing from a master/servant relationship; the child acted as an agent; or the guardian negligently failed to prevent the child from committing the act.[121]

The customary-law rules of delictual responsibility are quite different. They are bound up with the concept of 'kraalhead' liability, which closely resembles vicarious liability. The head of a household is liable for delicts committed by any of the inmates; this would include his wife and children.[122] (This rule is again a natural consequence of the inmates' proprietary incapacity.) Hence the family

---

[116] Boberg 572–3; Spiro 122.

[117] There are various statutory exceptions to these rules, eg, s 37(1) of the Insurance Act 27 of 1943 whereby a minor may insure his or her own life, and s 68(1) of the Building Societies Act 24 of 1965, which allows the deposit of funds in a building society. The applicability of these statutes to African women has not been judicially tested.

[118] 1938 NAC (N&T) 278.

[119] *Mambusha v Sigwadi* 3 NAC 203 (1912); *Luboko v Selani* 3 NAC 206 (1916).

[120] Spiro 173.

[121] Boberg 677.

[122] See below, 351ff.

head is personally liable for his wife's delictual actions.[123] The woman's capacity to commit delicts and her right to demand compensation have unfortunately not been judicially tested.

(d) Locus standi in judicio

Women in customary law have no locus standi in judicio.[124] It has been somewhat dramatically asserted that if women were allowed to bring actions in their own names, it would amount to such serious interference with tradition as to destroy the most widely recognized principle of customary law,[125] a principle that is said to go 'to the very root of Native custom'.[126]

Here the protective nature of the common-law institution of minority seems to have exerted some influence. On the assumption that women are not versed in the forensic arts, the common law requires a husband to sue on his wife's behalf, or to give his assistance.[127] The woman may sue on her own in matrimonial causes, actions for the custody or guardianship of her children, and actions arising out of her activities as a public trader.[128] If the husband is absent, incapable or unwilling to assist, the court may permit a wife to sue unassisted, or exceptionally a curator ad litem may be appointed for her.[129]

An African woman must be assisted by a person designated as her guardian according to customary law.[130] The courts do not seem to be overly concerned if the woman chooses some other male relative to help her,[131] but she (or any other party to the action) does not have an unfettered discretion to appoint whomever she wishes. The court may raise the issue of locus standi mero motu,[132] and it may decide to appoint a curator ad litem if her guardian does not appear.[133] In this regard a preference is shown for near relatives.[134]

The reason for denying women locus standi has never been clarified and the courts have allowed many exceptions. A woman may be given permission to sue unassisted[135] where her husband refused to help her[136] or deserted

---

[123] *Mabaso v Mtimkulu* 1915 NHC 124; *Mhlongo v Nzuza* 1935 NAC (N&T) 13; cf *Mlondleni v Magcaka* 1929 NAC (C&O) 10 and *Jali v Jali & others* 1969 BAC 1 (NE). A decision which held that the woman is personally liable, merely needing her guardian's assistance to appear in court—*Marshall v Chaka* 1950 NAC 63 (C) at 69—is clearly wrong: if she has has no property she cannot make compensation.

[124] *Dube & another v Ngwenya* 1935 NAC (N&T) 8; *Twala v Nzimande* 1938 NAC (N&T) 57; *Mathlaela v Lekoane* 1942 NAC (N&T) 15; *Cebekulu v Sitole* 1944 NAC (N&T) 48; *Saulos v Sebeko & another* 1947 NAC (N&T) 25; *Zweni* 1972 AC 56 (S); *Qubu v Jaca* 1973 AC 352 (C).

[125] *Kutuka v Bunyonyo* 4 NAC 302 (1920).

[126] *Mashinini* 1947 NAC (N&T) 25.   [127] Boberg 196.   [128] Boberg 221ff.

[129] Boberg 225.

[130] *Ngcamu v Majozi d/a Zondi* 1959 NAC 74 (NE); cf *Zondi v Southern Insurance Association Ltd* 1964 (3) SA 466 (N).

[131] *Nqayi v Figlane* 1943 NAC (N&T) 68.

[132] *Mashinini* 1947 NAC (N&T) 25; *Qubu v Jaca* 1973 BAC 352 (C); *Mthiyane v Ndaba* 1979 AC 268 (NE). Cf the inexplicable decision in *Dlamini v Mokoroto* 1970 BAC 73 (S).

[133] *Cele & another v Cele* 1957 NAC 144 (NE); *Ndlala da v Makinana* 1963 BAC 18 (S); *Phakathi d/a v Phakathi & another* 1966 BAC 48 (NE).

[134] *Twala v Nzimande* 1938 NAC (N&T) 57 at 59.

[135] *Tojani v Koza* 1942 NAC (N&T) 65.

[136] *Mangwane v Nontana & another* 3 NAC 98 (1914).

her;[137] or where she was left in charge of the homestead.[138] Aside from this, women have locus standi to sue for the dissolution of their marriages[139] and for the protection of house property.[140] In these cases, of course, the exception can be explained by the potential clash of interests between the woman and the person who would normally act as her guardian.

It is not clear from the cases whether the guardian's assistance is needed to cure some notional forensic infirmity peculiar to women. If this were the case, the guardian's intervention would be unnecessary if the woman could demonstrate her ability to conduct her own suit. Such a rationale could perhaps be inferred from a case where the guardian was not formally assisting a woman, but it was apparent that she was in fact being properly advised and the court raised no objection.[141] The other rationale may be that the guardian's assistance is necessary because he has an interest in his ward's case.[142] In the common law, a clear distinction is drawn between locus standi and the substantive right or obligation in issue. The minor, for example, is a party to the action, in that success or failure will enure to him, not to the guardian.[143] This means that the assistance of the guardian is necessary for procedural purposes only. It is not apparent whether this is the case regarding African women. Sometimes, where the woman sued for damages on the basis of common law, it was evident that the assistance of her guardian was merely a procedural requirement.[144] Similarly, where she sued for the recovery of her own property,[145] her guardian's presence was only a formality. But in many cases women have no locus because they have no substantive right of action; for example, a wife has no claim to the custody of her children born of a customary marriage[146] and unmarried women have no right to claim damages for seduction.[147] In these circumstances, the woman's incapacity cannot be cured because the right of action is not hers.

(3) Statutory reform

No country in Africa has legislated with the sole purpose of ameliorating the civil-law status of women.[148] While governments might have been sympathetic

---

[137] *Mamani & another v Mangele* 5 NAC 205 (1925). But normally the court will insist that she has a curator ad litem: *Tofu v Mntwini* 1945 NAC (C&O) 83.

[138] *Mpahlwa v Mcwaba* 4 NAC 302 (1919) and *Bomela v Kobus* 1972 BAC 180 (S), although here the claim was based on common law.

[139] *Ntambule v Nojojini* 3 NAC 168 (1914). But this principle was not upheld in *Nqambi* 1939 NAC (C&O) 57.

[140] *Sijila v Masumba* 1940 NAC (C&O) 42 at 46.

[141] *Marshall v Chaka* 1950 NAC 63 (C).

[142] A view that is implied in *Bangane v Tefu* 1935 NAC (N&T) 25.

[143] Boberg 682.

[144] See *Mbokazi* 1941 NAC (N&T) 117; *Shabangu v Lategele* 1955 NAC 91 (C); *Samente v Minister of Police & another* 1978 (4) SA 632 (E) at 636.

[145] *Mbutho v Cele d/a* 1977 AC 247 (NE); and compare *Masondo v Butelezi* 1949 NAC 118 (NE).

[146] *Tabede v Mlotywa* 1943 NAC (N&T) 71; although she must be cited as a party: *Nkosi v Ngubo* 1949 NAC 87 (NE).

[147] *Kumalo d/a Kumalo v Zungu* 1969 BAC 18 (NE); *Mkhombo v Mathungu* 1980 AC 79 (NE).

[148] Despite the growing momentum of the international women's rights movement, viz the UN Convention on the Elimination of All Forms of Discrimination against Women 1979, especially arts 5 and 15. Article 18(3) of the African Charter on Human Rights 1981 is more circumspect; it obliges states to

to the feminist cause, they could not afford to estrange the majority of their supporters, who in most cases were the conservative beneficiaries of the patriarchal tradition. Hence, even in countries espousing radical changes to the family structure, improvements to the status of women were incidental benefits, rather than a specific goal.

In Ivory Coast, for example, where in 1964 customary law was all but abolished in favour of a new code of civil law, the express purpose of the enactments was to replace the extended family with the nuclear family as the basic unit of society.[149] Despite the 'modernization' of the family, gender equality was not contemplated. Accordingly, while the status of women is no longer determined by customary law, women are still subordinate to men,[150] and the woman's proper role is still conceived to be that of wife and mother.[151] The same attitude is discernible in Malagasy legislation, where the husband was made head of the household[152] with overall power of administering the marital estate. Similarly in Tanzania (which was one of the few Anglophone countries specially to address the problem of marriage and the family), although wives are given full capacity,[153] the right to prevent subsequent polygynous unions,[154] and husbands may no longer inflict corporal punishment,[155] the intention was not to equalize the status of men and women.

There is perhaps an understandable scepticism about the efficacy of any far-reaching social reform.[156] Colonial legislation in Transkei,[157] for instance, which was specifically intended to improve the lot of women, remained on the statute-book for a century without appreciable effect.[158] A pessimistic commentator on Swaziland also observed that the country was not short of laws ameliorating the status of women, but that they were operating against a cultural background which was impervious to legal reform.[159]

In South Africa reform has been piecemeal and circumspect. The first modern enactment was an amendment to the Black Administration Act,[160] giving women the capacity to negotiate common-law contracts and locus standi to sue or be

---

eliminate gender discrimination 'as stipulated in international declarations and conventions'. See: Nhlapo (1989) *Int J Law & Family* 14; Howard in Welch & Meltzer *Human Rights and Development in Africa* ch 3 and Howard *Human Rights in Commonwealth Africa* ch 8.

[149] Law No 64–375, relating to marriage, and Law No 64–376, relating to divorce and judicial separation.

[150] Articles 58, 59 and 69 of Law No 63–375. See further Abitbol (1966) 10 *JAL* 158.

[151] Articles 58–61 and 56–7.

[152] Article 53 of Ord 62–089 of 1962.

[153] Section 56.

[154] Sections 20–2.

[155] Section 66.

[156] Ncube in Armstrong *Women and Law in Southern Africa* 193.

[157] The age of majority enactments above, 322.

[158] And, more recently, the principle of male authority has been even further entrenched by s 37 of the Marriage Act 21 of 1978, which provides that the wife falls under her husband's guardianship, whether her marriage was by civil or customary rites.

[159] Nhlapo in Armstrong op cit n156 51; see too: May op cit n7 chs 12 and 13.

[160] Section 5 of Act 21 of 1943.

sued for debts arising out of the common law. At the same time, however, the amendment confirmed the minority status of women married under customary law.

[107] SECTION 11(3) BLACK ADMINISTRATION ACT 38 OF 1927

The capacity of a Black person to enter into any transaction or to enforce or defend his rights in any court of law shall, subject to any statutory provision affecting any such capacity of a Black, be determined as if he were a European; Provided that—

(a) if the existence or extent of any right held or alleged to be held by a Black or of any obligation resting or alleged to be resting upon a Black depends upon or is governed by any Black law (whether codified or uncodified) the capacity of the Black concerned in relation to any matter affecting that right or obligation shall be determined according to the said Black law;

(b) a Black woman (excluding a Black woman who permanently resides in the province of Natal) who is a partner in a customary union and who is living with her husband, shall be deemed to be a minor and her husband shall be deemed to be her guardian.

Section 11(3) does not affect all the capacities of women. In terms of the first proviso, it applies only in respect of contractual capacity and locus standi,[161] and then only if it can be proved that the right or obligation in question arose out of common law. (Delictual and proprietary capacity continue to be governed by customary law.) Most important in this regard are the commercial contracts, all of which are governed by the common law.[162] So far as locus standi is concerned, certain delictual claims are also subject to common law, such as damages for assault[163] and sometimes damages for seduction.[164] Also, the courts have on occasion held that claims relating to property should be governed by common law, and so locus was determined by the same system.[165] Otherwise customary law applies.[166]

Before any question of capacity or locus standi can be considered, the court must decide whether customary law or the common law is to govern the claim. This involves the somewhat illogical procedure of hearing all the evidence and arguments regarding the main claim, before the preliminary issues can be settled.[167]

According to the second proviso to s 11(3), if a woman is married according to customary law and is 'living with her husband', she is deemed to be a minor

---

[161] Bennett 112–17.

[162] *Maphela v Seshea* 1943 NAC (C&O) 25; *Dlamini v Mokoroto* 1970 BAC 73 (S). Employment contracts, of course, are largely regulated by statute.

[163] *Mlondleni v Magcaka* 1929 NAC (C&O) 10; *Shabangu v Lategele* 1955 NAC 91 (C); *Xuza v Cingco* 1980 AC 37 (S).

[164] *Zulu v Mtolo NO* 1952 NAC 250 (NE); *Bujela v Mfeka* 1953 NAC 119 (NE); *Kumalo d/a Kumalo v Zungu* 1969 BAC 18 (NE); *Qubu v Jaca* 1973 BAC 352 (C).

[165] *Maqula* 1950 NAC 202 (S); *Nhlanhla v Mokweno* 1952 NAC 286 (NE); *Kunene* 1953 NAC 163 (NE); *Bomela v Kobus* 1972 BAC 180 (S); *Malaza v Mndaweni* 1975 BAC 45 (C) at 60.

[166] *Nzimande v Phungula* 1951 NAC 386 (NE); *Zweni* 1972 NAC 56 (S); *Khumalo v Zulu d/a* 1976 BAC 201 (NE); *Mkhombo v Mathungu* 1980 AC 79 (NE). Before Act 45 of 1988, in cases between Africans and Whites, the common law had to be applied, and so the African's capacity would be assessed in terms of the same system: *Zondi v Southern Insurance Association Ltd* 1964 (3) SA 446 (N).

[167] *Dsibande v Dlamini* 1947 NAC (N&T) 131; *Ex parte Minister of Native Affairs: In re Yako v Beyi* 1948 (1) SA 388 (A) at 402; *Nzimande v Phungula* 1951 NAC 386 (NE); *Guyana & another v Maroyana & another* 1962 NAC 69 (S).

and therefore lacking contractual capacity and locus standi, even in actions governed by the common law. The problem of defining customary marriage would make this subsection difficult to apply with precision, and the requirement that the woman be 'living with her husband' makes it needlessly restrictive. In *Tofu v Mntwini*,[168] the court was not prepared to construe the phrase literally (in which event it would presumably mean the actual physical presence of the husband) on the ground that it would lead to anomalies. By implication the husband must have deserted his wife deliberately and his assistance must be unobtainable. Even then the court said that the wife did not automatically acquire locus standi; she would need either a curator ad litem or she would have to get the leave of the court to sue unassisted.

A further problem of interpretation concerns a curious technicality of the conflict of laws. In terms of which system of law is the woman's guardian to be identified? Is it to be a guardian designated by customary law or one designated by the common law? The courts have held that the system of law generally pertaining to the person should be used.[169] This then involves a separate inquiry to determine the litigant's personal legal system, which could prove to be a complex matter (especially with regard to minors) in view of the refusal to give full recognition to customary marriages. The effect of denying them validity is to stigmatize offspring of such unions as illegitimate; the mother is accordingly deemed to be the guardian under the common law. In two cases, however,[170] the courts accepted the child's *father* as a curator ad litem. Had it been the child's mother, she would have acquired powers normally denied her by customary law. Conversely, even if the mother were designated guardian, because she herself is treated as a minor under s 11(3)(b), the child's father would still be required to appear in court—a remarkable irony.[171]

If the second proviso were interpreted simply as reducing the status of the wife to the level of a common-law minor, she would not be seriously disadvantaged. But in the context of customary law minority status has been used as a repressive device holding no benefit for the woman. There can be few arguments in favour of depriving the wife of a migrant labourer of the capacity needed to contract for household necessaries; and it seems almost punitive to deprive a wife of the powers required to work outside the family or to run a career.

By a 1985 amendment to the Black Administration Act the capacity of African women to perform 'any juristic act' with regard to the acquisition of a right of leasehold under the Blacks (Urban Areas) Consolidation Act[172] or the Black Communities Development Act[173] was subjected to the common law. Their capacity to dispose of such a right or to borrow money in respect of it was

---

[168] 1945 NAC (C&O) 83 at 84.
[169] *Ngcamu v Majozi d/a Zondi* 1959 NAC 74 (NE); cf *Zondi v Southern Insurance Association Ltd* 1964 (3) SA 446 (N); Kerr (1965) 82 *SALJ* 487.
[170] *Samente v Minister of Police & another* 1978 (4) SA 632 (E) and *Simayile v SA Mutual Fire and General Insurance Co Ltd* 1972 (2) SA 487 (E).
[171] Cf Kerr (1973) 90 *SALJ* 4.
[172] 25 of 1945.
[173] 4 of 1984.

similarly to be governed by the common law.[174] This provision was inserted to ensure that women would have no technical difficulties in procuring 99-year leaseholds from development boards in urban areas.

In Natal and KwaZulu the Codes have stipulated that wives fall under the marital power of their husbands provided that this power 'in civil marriage out of community of property may be excluded by an antenuptial contract'.[175] The concept of marital power may be thought to be an advance on the concept of minority, which used to be accorded wives under the earlier Codes.[176] But while it may appear appropriate to a married woman's status, it has little advantage to offer her. In the first place, marital power is an even less authentic representation of customary law than minority. Patriarchy gave the male plenary rights and powers over all members of his household, wives and children alike, and the concept of marital power is too limited to denote this.[177] In the second place, the powers of guardianship must be exercised in the interests of the minor. In contrast, the institution of marital power is conceived exclusively in the interests of the husband, allowing him decision-making authority over the family, control over his wife's person, and the right to administer the matrimonial estate.[178] (All, but the decision-making power may be waived by antenuptial contract.) In Roman-Dutch law the husband was permitted extensive powers to control his wife, including the right of chastisement and the right to restrict her freedom of movement. In the modern common law all that remains of this bundle of personal powers is the requirement that the husband assist his wife in court. It is not clear which of these rights and powers is denoted in the present Codes. They represent no improvement on earlier versions of the Natal Code, where a female was deemed to be 'a perpetual minor' with 'no independent powers save as to her own person'.[179]

Other reforms in Natal and KwaZulu are negligible. In KwaZulu s 11(3)(*b*) of the Black Administration Act was repealed[180] with the result that wives of customary marriages have the common-law contractual capacity and locus standi.[181] But in both territories it is provided that the inmates of a family home 'irrespective of sex or age are under the control of and owe obedience to' the family head in respect of all family matters.[182]

Potentially the most important piece of legislation affecting the status of African women was the Age of Majority Act. This statute, like its forerunners in the Transkei, has been hailed as a charter of emancipation.[183]

---

[174] Section 11A of the Black Administration Act 38 of 1927, inserted by s 1 of Act 90 of 1985.
[175] Section 27(3).
[176] Section 44(3) of Proc R195 of 1967.
[177] Armstrong & Nhlapo *Law and the Other Sex* 30–2.
[178] Hahlo 189.
[179] Section 27(2).
[180] By s 119 of the Code, Act 13 of 1984.
[181] The law in the rest of the Natal is unchanged.
[182] Section 22. See generally Dlamini *The New Legal Status of Zulu Women*.
[183] For example, in Zimbabwe: McNally (1988) 105 *SALJ* 437.

[108] AGE OF MAJORITY ACT 57 OF 1972

1. **All persons, whether males or females, attain the age of majority when they attain the age of twenty-one years.**

2. **Any person who has attained the age of eighteen years may, subject to the provisions of this Act, apply to the provincial division of the Supreme Court of South Africa having jurisdiction in the area within which such person is ordinarily resident ... for an order declaring him to be a major.**

Unfortunately it is uncertain whether the Act applies to persons subject to customary law. In some cases, the courts seem to have been assumed that it did,[184] and according to the general rule of statutory interpretation any enactment should supersede the common law and repeal prior legislation.[185] In this instance, however, there is no indication that the Legislature intended the Act to override customary law or to replace the earlier provision, s 11(3) of the Black Administration Act. In Natal and KwaZulu the problem had to be explicitly resolved by an amendment to the Codes,[186] which provided that the Age of Majority Act has overriding force. It is arguable that s 11(3) at least remains untouched, because although it is 'subject to any statutory provisions affecting such capacity of a Black person', this qualification is itself subject to the two provisos contained in subsections (a) and (b), and the latter clearly preserves the status of married women as minors.

In any event it is debatable whether the imposition of an age of majority can on its own have the desired effect, or even whether it should be used in this context. The transition from minor to major is predicated by the public/private dichotomy, a division reflecting the boundaries of what has long been thought to be the proper reach of the law: the family is supposed to be a reserved domain beyond the writ of the state.[187] What this actually meant was that the state delegated power and authority to the head of the family to deal with his dependants as he wished.[188] And in Africa this can be read as an implicit bargain struck between colonial governments and senior males, whereby the latter were given control over women 'as a form of security or pawn in exchange for male obedience and co-operation'.[189] Age of majority legislation reinforces rather than abolishes this social ordering.

It must be appreciated that the public/domestic distinction does not necessarily reflect social reality. For example, many wives are perforce wage or salary workers, and even if they are not, they may well have to participate in the broader economy outside the domestic sphere. They must operate bank accounts, purchase groceries, obtain credit, become members of pension schemes, claim under insurance policies, and so forth. Capacities cannot be

---

[184] *Mnyandu* 1974 BAC 459 (C); *Mpanza v Qonono* 1978 AC 136 (C) at 139 and *Khumalo d/a v Dladla* 1981 AC 95 (NE); and see clause 14(3) of the Bill proposed by the SA Law Commission *Marriages and Customary Unions of Black Persons*.
[185] Bekker (1975) 38 *THRHR* 394.
[186] Section 14.
[187] Cf Rose (1987) 14 *J Law & Soc* 61ff.
[188] O'Donovan *Sexual Divisions in Law* 57. See, too, Olsen op cit n89 1497.
[189] Mbilinyi op cit n29 1ff, especially 25.

granted for public transactions and withheld in family/marital relationships without creating friction and anomalies. And yet the granting of majority status does not alleviate the *domestic* position of women. African wives still suffer grave disabilities when suing for divorce, claiming maintenance, custody and guardianship of children, repelling the physical assaults of their husbands, or attempting to salvage property from a marriage.

Majority status alone is not enough to improve the lot of women.[190] While it obviously allows the woman *powers*, it is not proven that this leads to her acquisition of *rights* as well. For instance, even if a woman has the power to acquire property, it does not automatically follow that she also has a right to use it as she chooses without reference to her husband. Can the major woman sue for damages for her own seduction,[191] or prosecute her own divorce without reference to the bridewealth holder (who also has an interest to be protected)?

---

[190] See, eg, Jacobs & Howard in Afshar *Women, State and Ideology* 31.
[191] In Zimbabwe she can: Ncube in Armstrong op cit n156 201.

CHAPTER 8

Children

I PERSONALITY

In customary law a child was considered to be a person soon after birth; there was no question of attributing rights to a child en ventre sa mère.[1] On the other hand, personality did not terminate completely on physical death. The shades of the departed were the ever-present guardians of the living,[2] and their powers were pervasive.[3] Not all people qualified to become ancestral spirits.[4] A senior male was the most likely candidate (which can be gauged from the elaborate rituals surrounding his burial and succession); in comparison, the death of a youth or a female was a relatively insignificant affair.[5]

Personality was not a sharply demarcated status, measured physically, but rather a slow change of condition marked by various special rites de passage.[6]

---

[1] Because technical questions involving prenatal rights and duties never arose there is little writing on this topic. See: Allott in Gluckman *Ideas and Procedures in African Customary Law* ch 7; Myburgh (1965) 6 *Codicillus* 10.

[2] See Hammond-Tooke *Bantu-speaking Peoples* 324.

[3] Influencing, in particular, the way the land was to be dealt with and deceased estates were to be distributed. Several descriptions of customary law, eg, Elias *The Nature of African Customary Law* 162, take it for granted that land belongs to the ancestral shades of the community.

[4] Hammond-Tooke in *Bantu-speaking Peoples* 327.

[5] Conversely, the term 'ancestral spirit' might be attributed to a person who was still alive but very old. Hunter 231: 'Since the living person is a potential *ithongo* [ancestor] there is no hiatus between death and the possibility of the deceased influencing his descendants.'

[6] Hirst & Woolley *Social Relations and Human Attributes* 24–8.

[109] VAN TROMP *XHOSA LAW OF PERSONS* 1

A human being is in SiXhosa termed *umntu*. This term is applied to any human being surviving its birth, and has no juridical significance. If still-born or deceased before its umbilical cord (imfesane) has been cut off, a child is not considered to have been umntu.

An umntu is sometimes referred to as an *inja*, a dog, to show the relationship of legal dependence existing between Chief and subject, or between father and child. The word inja is used to denote both the responsibility of the father for the torts or misdemeanours of his child, and the lack of capacity of the child to acquire and maintain rights for itself: Inja yakho, i bambela wena inja i bambela umniniwe: the dog catches for its master. When used of the relations between chief and subject, it denotes the power of the Chief over his subject.

A human being, umntu, only gradually acquires the full legal status, according to his development in life.

II LEGAL CAPACITY

(1) Growing up

It would probably be true to say that every society withholds some, if not all, legal capacities from the young, until they have matured sufficiently to behave in a responsible manner. But childhood and adulthood are flexible concepts, decided according to cultural stereotypes of ageing and the constraints of social and economic circumstances. A long period of childhood is a luxury that cannot be afforded in subsistence societies, where the life span is short and survival is a struggle. In medieval Europe, for instance, the idea of childhood is said not to have existed at all;[7] and the poor today too cannot afford the prolonged period of time for training and educating the young that the more affluent can.[8]

[110] BURMAN *GROWING UP IN A DIVIDED SOCIETY* 8–11

A range of criteria may be used to distinguish the transition from childhood to adulthood. For some societies, for example, marriage has been regarded as the marker; in others some *rite de passage*; or, as in South African civil law, age may define who is and who is not a child. But in even so apparently unambiguous a definition as age are hidden many other assumptions. The stated justification for a definition of childhood by age is a socio-biological one—that people under a certain age are in general incapable or only partially capable of responsible judgement, and therefore cannot be held responsible or fully responsible for their actions and must be protected by society. Until the age of seven, for example, a child is presumed to be completely without criminal capacity, while until the age of twenty-one a person cannot be held to have contractual capacity if unassisted by his or her guardian. . . . The concept of adolescence . . . comes within this sphere of thought. The adolescent is a half-formed adult and so should be treated as partially responsible but also afforded some protection by society, not simply classed as an adult. Current scientific research supports this and the law therefore sounds eminently reasonable until one examines it more broadly. For example, eighteen is the minimum age for voters in South Africa and the age at which young white men become liable for military service. The implication is that at eighteen people are responsible enough to help decide the fate of their country and to kill, but not to order their own affairs unassisted. And are these voters and killers to be regarded as adults or children?

---

[7] Ariès *Centuries of Childhood* 128.
[8] Burman in Boonzaier & Sharp *South African Keywords* 167.

Another example of the ambiguity of the apparently unambiguous criterion of age is supplied by the state welfare system—a branch of the law. It provides that state maintenance for white and coloured children shall terminate when they reach eighteen years of age, while for African children it stops when they turn sixteen. One implication is that Africans are responsible and mature enough to finish school and enter the labour market two years before the rest of the nation's children. Welfare officials, when asked to justify this apparent anomaly, explain that Africans are not considered dependent at that age—so it would appear that financial dependence rather than irresponsibility is the legal criterion for deciding whether someone is immature enough to require financial support. This still begs the question, however, of what makes Africans of sixteen more independent than white or coloured children of that age. And what if the African aged sixteen is patently not self-supporting and unable to become so, being unskilled in an over-supplied market for unskilled labour? It makes no difference; the state maintenance grant stops. It would therefore seem that some other concept is involved when defining what causes an African to be treated as an independent adult at sixteen, while those who are white or coloured are not. While this finding may hardly surprise the reader, its policy implications are important for future governments pledged to equal treatment for children.

. . . [C]lashes between criteria used in defining childhood are not found only in the broader legal system. South Africa has a population with a richly varied assortment of values, traditions, religions, and ways of life. Not surprisingly, therefore, different criteria are in use among different groups. Sometimes these do not cause problems. . . . [A] Jew becomes classified as an adult after his or her barmitzvah or batmitzvah at the age of thirteen. However, it is clearly understood by all concerned that this reception into the adult community pertains only within a religious context, and that claims to be treated as an adult in any other would be given short shrift. In contrast, however, boys who have undergone initiation ceremonies in certain African communities, with examples ranging from the Transvaal to the Cape, are regarded as men within those societies and may no longer be disciplined by women, irrespective of the boys' physical age. Some are as young as six years of age; many are in their mid-teens. Yet, apart from exceptional cases . . . there is no question of most initiates becoming financially or legally independent of their families. They remain at home, under the control of the head of the family. . . .

[A] particular feature of South Africa which makes the study of its children so important is that it is a society in the throes of major and rapid social change. . . . In addition, there are the extensive effects of political unrest.

In such a situation the discontinuities of experience between children and their parents or grandparents rob the younger generation of the role models so essential for the transmission of values and experience which have been found useful for dealing with their world. The most extreme example presented in these studies is that of the resettlement camps, where . . . the transition from rural farming community to camp slum renders the accumulated expertise of the adult useless and thus liable to be rejected by the younger generation. However, changes in occupation and income can have much the same effect on a lesser scale. . . . Moreover, conditions resulting from urbanization and the effects of apartheid may disrupt family life to such an extent that old values and modes of behaviour can no longer be followed. . . . In other cases the normal role model may be removed from the child's life either by family break-up and the effects of apartheid or by the child's reactions to an unbearable home situation as [is shown in an] examination of street children who have run away from home. The recurrent theme is how children in many situations in South Africa are having to work out their own destiny, values, and life style to an extent far greater than is usual in more settled societies.

In literate societies, where accurate records can be kept, age can be precisely measured. As a result capacities can be attributed to people at fixed and predetermined ages. In preliterate societies, on the other hand, age is more directly related to physical processes, such as puberty, or social events, such as initiation.

In Africa age grades were ubiquitous. They cut across family and village loyalties, enabling chiefly rulers to maintain some degree of centralized control over the young and able-bodied. In its original sense, the age grade referred to the three sections into which society was divided on the basis of sociological age: the uninitiated, the initiated single men, and the elders. Different clusters of rights, duties and powers were associated with each of these statuses, in particular the duties incumbent on single, initiated men to render military service and to do public works.

Movement from one age grade to another was marked by social rituals or rites de passage, term coined by the Flemish anthropologist Arnold van Gennep[9] who maintained that in all simple societies ritual displays proclaimed transitions from one status to another or transformations in the affairs of a community. Initiation was a typical ceremonial occasion serving to distinguish

'the transition from childhood to socially recognized adulthood . . . the means of divesting a person of his status as a child in the domestic domain and investing him with the status of actual or potential citizen in the politico-jural domain'.[10]

[111] VAN TROMP *XHOSA LAW OF PERSONS* 1–7

According to Xhosa Law there are two stages in the life of a person which mark off his legal status. These stages are:
  (i) When he has reached the age of puberty, and undergoes the *initiation ceremony* (ukwaluka kwa makwenkwe),
  (ii) Marriage.

These two stages cover three periods: from birth to initiation; from initiation to marriage; from marriage onwards. . . .
1. The first period, from birth to initiation, may be divided into two stages:
  (*a*) from birth to the time when he is capable of herding the cattle, and
  (*b*) from the cattle-herding stage to initiation.
  (*a*) The Male: From birth to about six or seven years, that is when he begins to herd, a boy is not considered to have "eyes to see", that is, to do anything wrong: "A yi ka tungululi" he has not had his eyes opened. He cannot distinguish between right and wrong nor can he see his danger. If he should commit a wrong, eg allowing cattle to stray into the lands, or burning the veld, he is punished by the injured party or his parents and the matter is over. Where the mischief results in damage, the father or lawful guardian of the child is not responsible: "A yi ka tungululi." But the father or lawful guardian may, in order to preserve friendship and good relations, help to restore what has been damaged by his inja, child.
  (*b*) The boy has an enhanced social status from the cattle-herding stage to initiation. He is now considered to have more experience and better judgment, and is allowed to herd cattle and milk the cows. He has to do light jobs at the kraal (umzi), and help with the cultivation of the lands. His legal status, however, has not increased. From birth to the cattle-herding stage, and from this stage to initiation, the boy remains an *inkwenkwe*, a boy, and is in no way legally responsible for his actions though he may be punished by anyone who finds him committing a wrong. He has no hearing in any court, he cannot enter into a contract. If he receives

---

[9] *Rites of Passage* (1909).
[10] Gluckman *Essays in the Ritual of Social Relations* 16 and see his discussion of Van Gennep.

anything, by labour or otherwise, it falls to the household property of the hut, indlu (house), of which he is an inmate. He cannot be betrothed or married for, as a rule, only persons who have undergone the initiation ceremony are considered ripe for marriage. The initiation is the ritual transition from boyhood (ubukwenkwe) to manhood (ubudoda).

During the seclusion period the initiates, *abakhwetha*, are treated like iinyamezane, wild animals. They are not considered to be abantu, human beings, with a status or a say. Corporal punishment is common but they have no redress. They are guarded by one or more amakankatha (a kind of male nurse) representing the fathers of the initiates. The amakankatha nurse the wounds of the boys.

2. On initiation the boy acquires the status of a man. His eyes are opened and now that he has undergone the initiation ceremony he is accepted as an *indoda*, man. He can accept presents which belong to him though these may be controlled by his father. He is ripe for marriage, can be betrothed and can enter into a valid marriage.

The day he comes out of the isutu (itonto, ipempe) or seclusion hut, while at the umzi of the umnin'umzi (owner of the seclusion hut) the act or ceremony of *ukusoka* (presenting gifts), also takes place. This is the final ceremony in which his father, family and friends give him presents indicating his status, for these now become his own. Participation in the final ceremony is an essential for attaining the status of an indoda. For only then will he be an indoda in the true sense of the word. . . .

The short period from the time the abakwetha leave the isutu to the time they enter marriage, is an important one. They are called *amarwala*, sometimes abafana, meaning adolescents or young men. They can mix freely with the opposite sex, have sexual intercourse with amadikazi, loose women. In fact, in this irwala-period plans for a marriage are being started. Marriage is mainly a family affair and though the adolescent is allowed freedom in his choice, his father has a great say, especially with regard to the first wife he marries. Though he has the status of a man he is still under the control of his father as long as he is considered an inmate of his father's umzi.

Through initiation he attains greater rights and privileges. He takes part in his family court or inkundla where he can, discreetly, question the parties. When needful he may act for his father. He can now be selected by the Chief for work, perhaps as an umsengi, one who milks and provides milk for the calabashes of the Chief. He may go to the Great Place (Komkulu) and attend the Chief's Court.

In social life he has a higher status. He can attend beerdrinks and feasts with other young men of more or less his own age. He will not be pushed aside at these feasts and be branded a "kwedini" or child.

I met a middle-aged native undergoing this rite. He was married and had children. The reason why he underwent the ceremony, he told me, was because he was treated like a kwedini by other amadoda. At beerdrinks or feasts he was pushed aside and told to go and enjoy himself with the amakwedini, boys. And for all this treatment, treatment amounting to insult, Xhosa Law affords no remedy. Not only men look down upon an uninitiated male and treat him with contempt, but also women.

Once he is circumcised and has undergone the initiation ceremony, he can also sacrifice to the ancestral spirits, *izinyanya*. For only men can sacrifice and speak to the ancestral spirits. He is now a potential kraalhead and may one day sacrifice for his children.

The amaXhosa even hold that an uncircumcised male—being a kwedini—cannot inherit. He must be treated as a minor. He cannot therefore succeed his father. The Courts probably would not uphold this view, for they accept all persons of 21 years or more as majors, and will allow an uninitiated son to succeed his father, if he has reached the age of 21 years—or even before.

3. Marriage gives an initiated male the full status of a member of his umzi and tribe. He has a say in the family court as well as in the Chief's Court. His word now carries more weight. His first wife having been sanctioned and lobolaed by his father, he may hereafter marry freely as many wives as he can afford to lobola. With the consent of his

father he can build his own separate umzi, and thus become a kraalhead, umnin'umzi. The father is then no longer legally responsible, according to Xhosa Law, for the deeds of his son, but public opinion urges him to help his son in case of difficulty, and because he is his son's father he sometimes pays the fine for his son. While the son remained in the umzi of his father, the latter was responsible. Now that the son has his own umzi he can acquire anything and what he acquires he acquires for his umzi. He can enter into any contractual obligation and is responsible for his own acts and for those of his wife and children. . . .

From birth to marriage a female is under the guardianship of her father or his lawful heir and successor. Because she is a minor and a female, she cannot inherit. No female can in Xhosa Law become heir (indlamafa) or succeed her father or husband in his estate.

Puberty, marked off by the *intonjane* ceremony, brings a change in the female's social status. After the age of puberty the girl is taken more notice of, has a higher social status, can do more work, can take part in feasts where women are concerned, and can now be betrothed and married.

The intonjane ceremony is a kind of initiation similar in object to that of males. It is customary for girls to undergo this ceremony before marriage, but a female may marry even if she has not undergone it, and stigma will cling to her or to any of her children for neglecting it. When she reaches puberty she enters the domain of womanhood (ubufazi) and is now marriageable and ready to bear children.

Xhosa Law sanctions the intonjane ceremony and in certain cases insists that it shall be performed, for it is believed that upon its proper performance will depend successful maternity and the health of the children. Should the girl not have undergone this ceremony before marriage and certain mishaps, eg miscarriage (ukuphuma kwesisu) or the ill-health of the woman be ascribed to its non-performance, the father or lawful guardian of the woman is forced to take her back and put her through this ceremony at his own expense. In these circumstances the husband may also send his wife back to her people to put her through the ceremony and they may not refuse. Her family must support and maintain her and her baby, should she have one, while she is with them. . . .

Marriage changes the status of a woman, both socially and legally. She is now more respected and has greater authority and say among women in the affairs of the family. She has certain definite domestic rights and privileges. She is given and holds a piece of land to cultivate and to produce crops for her indlu. Until marriage she has no proprietary capacity and could not acquire anything for herself. After marriage, though she is under the guardianship of her husband, she has a proprietary capacity which, though limited, makes it possible for her, among others, to own the *ubulunga* beast (inkomo yobulunga) and those cattle given to her by her family at the time of her marriage, though she must consult her husband if she wishes to alienate them. She can also acquire household property.

When a woman has reached the menopause she is considered in many respects like a man. This change affects mainly her social status. She can now sit in the inkundla of her husband. This she could previously not have done. She may freely speak to older men. She has a say in the affairs of the umzi and her word is taken into consideration. She may now also go into and sweep that side of the indlu which is reserved for men. Because of all this a woman at this age is sometimes referred to as an indoda.

Widows seem to enjoy an even greater freedom. A widow has more say in the affairs of the umzi than she had during the life of her husband. The older she is, the greater her say. She may express her opinion, which is sometimes sought by the new umnin'umzi who has succeeded her husband, but her word cannot override his. Should a widow wish to return to her own people, she is at liberty to do so, but for dissolution of the marriage part of the lobola cattle must be returned to the deceased husband's umzi. When this is done she is free and again reverts to the guardianship of her father or his lawful heir and successor. She then is an *inkazana ya se khaya apha*, a woman of her father's umzi.

If she remains at the umzi of her deceased husband, the new umnin'umzi must care for her and maintain her.

The various stages described by Van Tromp should not be taken to suggest that maturing is a rigidly predetermined process.[11]

> 'Manhood is not attained at a single bound; one grows into it by imperceptible stages. There is no single criterion of adulthood and the maturity that is required cannot be given merely by a ritual act.'[12]

One of the first marks of enhanced capacity, a practice widespread amongst the Nguni in particular, was the piercing or slitting of an ear lobe. This was performed on a young child and was said to signify the 'opening of the ears', viz the child was taken to have sufficient intellectual ability to respond to reasoned instruction.[13] At about the age of 6 or 7, children were then introduced to a gender-based division of labour. Boys began to herd livestock and girls were instructed in domestic duties.

Dramatic rituals were occasioned by the onset of puberty and initiation (although the two did not necessarily coincide).[14] Groups of boys and girls of similar physical age were drafted into local age sets.[15] Each group was segregated from society to undergo special training and instruction. The function of the initiation schools varied.[16] With the Xhosa, initiation (described by Van Tromp above) was a parochial affair, conducted under the auspices of one of the local fathers; there was little emphasis on transcendent national values. Amongst the Sotho-Tswana, however, age sets were organized at the level of the chiefdom and considerable stress was laid on cultural knowledge and national identity. All the schools had this in common: they sought to inculcate in the recruits a more mature and responsible attitude towards social life.[17]

Formerly, a year or two after initiation or possibly at the same time that the age set was formed, boys would have been drafted into a military regiment.[18] The immediate purpose of these units was to provide a fighting force, but they were also used extensively for public works and for tending the king's crops and

---

[11] See further: Van der Vliet in Hammond-Tooke *Bantu-speaking Peoples* ch 7. For more specific accounts see: Ashton 30–40 and 46–60; Krige & Krige 102ff; Marwick 68ff and 140ff; Mönnig 98ff; Hunter 150ff; and Kuper *African Aristocracy* 134–6.

[12] Krige & Krige 115.

[13] Krige 81–7; Marwick 152–3; Junod 95.

[14] Initiation may include circumcision. On the function of this rite amongst Xhosa-speaking peoples, see: Ngxamngxa in De Jager *Man* 183ff esp 193.

[15] According to Eisenstadt (1954) 24 *Africa* 105, the existence of age sets is symptomatic of the development of a society from a kinship based socio-political organization to a more centralized political authority. Cf Schapera *Government and Politics in Tribal Societies* 216–17.

[16] Van der Vliet in Hammond-Tooke *Bantu-speaking Peoples* 234ff.

[17] Among the Northern Sotho and the Tswana, the first initiation ceremony would be followed by a subsequent or supplementary school: Mönnig 122–4; Schapera *Married Life* 231. See the Mayers' account of peer group socialization amongst the so-called 'Red' Xhosa in Mayer *Socialization* 159ff.

[18] Krige 106–17; Kuper op cit n11 119ff; Kuper 52ff; cf Krige & Krige 100 regarding the atrophy of regiments amongst the Venda.

cattle.[19] Women too were drafted into regiments. Marriage was then permitted only when the king decided to stand down the regiments, or special permission had been given.[20]

> 'In the old days people who had not yet been initiated could not marry or appear before a court as litigants, nor, if they were men, could they attend tribal meetings or even sit at the council place with their elders. These discriminations are no longer [ie in 1940] rigidly observed. . . . But membership of a regiment is still considered indispensable to full recognition as an adult.'[21]

Since the colonial conquest, the regiments have been disbanded and they have declined in importance.[22]

Full maturity was denoted by marriage and the establishment of an independent homestead.[23]

(2) Social transformations

The completely independent individual, capable of acting for himself and in his own interests, presupposed access to, and control of the material means of support. In the past, the authority structures of family and chiefdom placed only the heads of homesteads in this favoured position. They had plenary powers, and clearly all their legal dependants—women, unmarried sons, and even married sons who had not yet established their own homesteads—were denied capacity to interact with outsiders. The head of the household would be responsible for their wrongdoing; he would be required to argue their cases in court; and he was obliged to support them. Conversely, they had to submit to his discipline, and their acquisitions would be pooled as a family resource to be administered by him. This totality of powers and responsibilities was grounded on a strong ethic of family support, the coincidence of household and homestead, and a subsistence economy. The family needed little contact with outsiders; it was both a producing and a consuming unit whose dealings with neighbours and traders could be quite easily managed by a single representative. The rites of passage that marked the enhancement of status confirmed the interlinking values and belief systems; they taught respect for age, and engendered a sense of responsibility and loyalty to the domestic group.

In not one, but in many respects, this pattern has been disrupted. Urbanization and the lack of adequate housing in urban areas has fragmented the family and has forced people to live amongst strangers.[24] Wage labour has afforded juniors financial independence. The impoverishment of rural areas has reduced the self-sufficiency of the homestead and has made it dependent on the

---

[19] Kuper op cit n11 126–7 and 130; Schapera in Fortes & Evans-Pritchard *African Political Systems* 73–4. Guy in Marks & Atmore *Economy and Society in Pre-Industrial South Africa* 115–17 argues that this was a method of extracting surplus labour.

[20] Marwick 274; Schapera *Married Life* 231.

[21] Schapera *Married Life* 233.

[22] Roberts 24 on the Kgatla; and see Kuper 55.

[23] Roberts 17–18: even when a man had established his own house, his cattle remained with his father's herd and could not be dealt with without the father's consent. See further: Mönnig 329ff; Poulter 185ff; Duncan 3; and Hunter 25–6.

[24] And see Pauw 210 regarding tensions introduced by the housing allocation policy.

remittances of migrant workers. Christianity has militated against the performance of the elaborate rites de passage, which to many have become an
embarrassing reminder of a backward, rural culture.[25] And ritual itself has
tended to fall into desuetude in modern, urban settings.[26]

The rising number of illegitimate births and the cost of education and
upbringing has even provoked a change in the attitude towards children. They
are no longer unreservedly welcomed as new members of a family. There is
widespread complaint about the violence and irresponsibility of the young.
Lamenting the decay of parental discipline is doubtless a familiar theme
everywhere, but Africans commonly ascribe it to the insidious influence of
western culture and the failure to perform initiation rites under proper
supervision.[27] Whatever the cause, the widening generation gap and the
delinquent behaviour of the young have become serious social problems.

In the extract below, Mayer describes the urban gangs, the so-called tsotsis.[28]
He recounts a period of intergenerational conflict in East London in 1958, which
has parallels in contemporary political conflicts, where the initiative of defying
the government was taken up by school children.

[112] MAYER *TOWNSMEN OR TRIBESMEN* 83–5

The much slighter disturbances which occurred in 1958 grew out of attempted reprisals by
location citizens against the criminal gangs who burden their lives with fear and danger.
There was to be a clean-up which would teach a necessary lesson to the young robbers, the
pickpockets (*abakunthuzi*, lit "those who rub against one"), the dice boys, the wielders of
knife and dagger, the perpetrators of rape and murder. Most of the criminal and
semi-criminal gangs are made up of boys and youths, and most of these are *amakwenkwe*
(boys) in the technical Xhosa sense, ie have not yet been initiated. The counter-movement
was organized mainly by the mature men, fathers of families and solid characters.
Originally, therefore, this was a kind of inter-generation struggle.

Tsotsi activities are always expected to increase towards Christmas, when there are
extra opportunities to rob people of their wages or spending money. Towards the end of
November 1958 location people were talking about the murder of a widow's son, and the
murderer's alleged boast that this was neither his first nor his last victim. There was, as
usual, a feeling that the police are quite incapable of dealing with the tsotsi menace. Bills
began to be stuck up by tsotsis in location streets carrying the arrogant warning that
people must not be out of doors after 9 pm if they wished to be safe from attack. This
intensified anger as well as fear. "The tsotsis are trying to make their own curfew and pass
laws, and enforce these on their seniors."

On Thursday 27 November a young man returning from a beer drink at dusk was set
on in a street in the Amalinda Ward of Duncan Village—one of the most respectable parts
of the location—by a gang of youths. Men from near-by houses ran out to the rescue,
carrying their sticks. Most of the attackers escaped into the bush in Ngcabanga near by,
but one was caught. This slight incident turned out to be the genesis of the "clean-up"
movement. The avenging men—who included a member of the Headman's Committee of
Amalinda Ward—gave the youth a good hiding and took him to the police station. Here,
it is said, he was given another beating by the police and locked up for the night: but in

---

[25] Mayer in De Jager op cit n14 7ff.
[26] Gluckman op cit n10 38.
[27] Mayer in De Jager op cit n14 14.
[28] Cf Gluckman in Mayer op cit n17 187–8.

addition the men claimed that the police had thanked them for their manly action and given them permission to beat up any young hooligans they might find on the streets.

Meanwhile the gang reassembled, and their leader, according to report, called for terrible vengeance against the men who had taken their comrade to the police. Brandishing hatchets and knives they shouted that "blood would be spilt that night". The wife of one of the threatened men organized an escort party to see them home from the police station. It was discussion between the escorts and the original party which produced the idea of a public meeting to consider concerted action against young hooligans in general. The prime mover and organizer was the member of the Headman's Committee of Amalinda Ward, mentioned before. He is a country-born man in his 50's, who has made good money selling milk and snuff and has become a respected local figure, not least for his readiness to help people financially. He is a powerful speaker. His Red[1] sympathies are conspicuous; he wears his hair long and smokes a Xhosa pipe.

After two unsuccessful attempts a well-attended meeting was achieved on Sunday morning (30 November). The large crowd included both Red and less-educated School people, though "highly educated people" (it was widely remarked) showed no interest in this meeting and took no active part in subsequent events.

When the meeting had heard accounts of the Thursday evening's incident, the praise for the Amalinda men, someone proposed that men all over the location should now take it on themselves to beat any members of youthful gangs whom they might meet in the streets. This was enthusiastically received. There were loud acclamations and shouts of "that is the way to stop them!" A middle-aged townsman who insisted that the men could not take the law into their own hands, because they might beat the wrong boys, was received with groans and cries of "*Suka! suka!*" (Get away!). The consensus was "*Maka betwe*"—"they must be beaten". It is significant that at the meeting the talk was of beating boys, not of beating tsotsis, criminals or gangsters. It is also significant that the man who spoke up about the need to exempt innocent boys was a townsman. A real cleavage was about to open between the town-bred and the country-bred on this point. Meanwhile word ran round the location that "the men have declared war on the boys".

It is important to consider the relation between the generation categories on the one hand and the town-country categories on the other. Few country-born youths go to work in East London before being initiated, and few migrant men are able, under present regulations, to bring their young sons to live in towns with them. Thus the large majority of the *amakwenkwe* in town are necessarily either sons of townspeople, or, if they have country roots, sons of migrant (husbandless) mothers. In the category of mature men, on the other hand, the country-born element predominates. These facts created a possibility that any general conflict between men and boys might shape itself as a conflict between a migrant and a town faction. The possibility need not have been realized if the migrant men and the town-born men had really, as they at first imagined, felt common cause against the town boys. But in fact, although everyone (except the gangsters) resents gangsterism, the moral premises were quite different on the two sides. Two different concepts of discipline and morality, two different patterns of inter-generation relations, were implicitly involved.

To a rustic Xhosa—whether a Red or a traditionally minded Schoolman—boys as such are an essentially irresponsible and mischievous category. One reproaches a man when one says, "He has acted like a boy". All boys by nature require perpetual disciplining if they are not to fall into evil ways. It is not seen as a question of parental correction alone. A boy "is a dog" and should be corrected by any responsible-minded senior when occasion arises. The natural mode of correction is physical chastisement. Even an *umfana* (young man) may be beaten on occasion; how much more a mere boy. And whereas an *umfana* would be wronged if he were beaten on any grounds except proven guilt, the mere boy has no intrinsic dignity to lose. An occasional beating can be a good "lesson". In town surroundings a boy has all the more scope to learn wickedness, and it is for his own good that he should receive preventative "lessons" in good time. Moreover, among Reds especially, the boys of any neighbourhood are felt to have a kind of collective moral responsibility for one another, so that one need not be too fastidious about punishing only the active offenders. Through the organized life of the rural age-sets, run on a strictly local basis, "the boys of X" maintain their corporate identity vis-à-vis, say, "the men of X" or "the boys of Y", and a lapse by any individual member "gives a bad name to" the whole set. If the set want to keep a good name they must make it their own business to enforce proper standards on all their members by internal pressure.

In the eyes of the average country-born Xhosa, it is precisely the absence of this pervasive "communal" discipline in town that turns the town boy into something much worse than a dog, namely a tsotsi. In the eyes of Xhosa townsmen on the other hand, many of the rural ideas of discipline appear "old-fashioned" and "out of place". There may be admiration for the greater success of the rural and especially the Red father in controlling his children, but the supreme virtues of beating as a mode of discipline are not admitted. The stick is an essentially rural weapon. Town parents, also, are less ready to share with other adults the right of disciplining their own children. "In town every man goes his own way." The idea that "every man is a kind of policeman" is claimed by country Xhosa as specifically their own.

Mayer continues[29] to describe relationships between fathers and sons and new residential and social groupings.

Discharging kinship roles in absentia

It is basic to the Red ethic that the roles at home must never be repudiated. At first the migrant is probably earning money for his parents' sake, later for his own wife and dependants: all along (as was said) the morality of kinship is what sanctions the stay in town. The migrant's first problem—we might say—is how best to carry on discharging his kinship roles *in absentia*. Formidable as the task might seem, a Red man can go on being a fairly satisfactory member of his home circle in terms of weekly, monthly or even yearly visits. There are patterns of "proper" kinship behaviour for absentee sons, husbands and fathers.

A migrant son is being a good son as long as he sends money home regularly and visits whenever he can. If the father says he needs the money more than he needs the son's presence, that is an unarguable reason for staying longer in town. However this is always, in the background, the idea of having to go back "some day". On the death of the father all sons must come home for a sacrifice. The heir—if not the others—ought then to stay at home permanently. In Red peasants, accordingly, filial piety may strongly revive the urge to go home after it has been comparatively dormant for many years. Some old Red fathers visit their sons in town to reassure themselves that they are not going to "melt away" at the critical time.

Filial submission is made much of by Red Xhosa. The authoritarian aspects of the parent-child relationship are played up while (on the whole) the intimate aspects tend to be played down. The greater measure of success in keeping children obedient has been mentioned as one basis for the Red feeling of superiority over School people. The Red section emphasize not only the degree of filial submission but its duration. Even young adult sons and daughters may have to go on submitting to the parental thrashings which figure so largely in Red educational theory and practice; and even after marriage the Red Xhosa man is expected to regard himself as definitely "under" his parents. A not uncommon unit of residence here is the three-generation extended family in which the middle-generation individuals remain permanently junior. Among Red Xhosa such a homestead group appears as a unified pyramid with the grandfather at the apex, rather than (as in some other systems) an aggregation of nuclear-family cells. The "young" couple or couples have little separate domestic life. The Red Xhosa's emphasis on continued filial subordination after marriage was brought out when informants were

---

[29] Pages 96–7, 100–1 and 114.

asked to say which they thought were the closest kinship ties a man can have at various stages in life. Among Red respondents, almost without exception, it was stated that a man's closest ties are with his parents "always"—even after maturity, even after marriage. It is only among School people that the wife has begun to rival the parents as a man's "closest" relative.

These attitudes are mentioned here because they continue to manifest themselves when a Red man migrates to town. For instance, it is taken for granted that for a long time to come he will regard his earnings not as his own property but as his father's, or as the property of the homestead. Even young married men said that to spend all their own earnings would be wrong. The father must receive substantial and regular remittances. If he chooses to put part of the money away as a nest-egg for the son who earned it, that is his own affair: he is under no obligation to do so.

Domestic life

Owing to the acute shortage of accommodation [in town], even the tenant of a single room (*ibhoda*, "boarder") can have his pick of would-be sub-tenants, just as the owner of a house can have his pick of would-be room-tenants. The house occupants jointly share the water-tap and communal latrine with others in the same street, but the separate rooms of one house do not share facilities within it: there is no common kitchen for example. Each shack room being a combined kitchen, living-room, and bedroom, for the man or men who occupy it, "domestic relations" are those which involve staying in one room together, not staying in one house.

The Xhosa word for homestead (*umzi*) is used for a town house also, but in spite of the verbal equation of the owner of the house with the "head of the homestead", the role is fundamentally different. An English term is applied to the tenants who rent the rooms (*ibhoda*, "boarder"). Houseowner and tenants are not like "people of one homestead", a group with a common loyalty. They need only try "to be on good terms", and avoid major quarrels. Living in the same *room* is another matter. Besides being a domestic unit a group of room-mates must be regarded as a voluntary association. There is a financial element in the sense that sub-tenants contribute their shares of the rent, but the relation is not conceived of first and foremost as a commercial one. Red men say they choose to share rooms because they are "good friends", because they "like each other", because they "know they will be happy together". A man's room-mates, usually temporary, sometimes permanent, reflect his and their personal choice of companion, while his house-mates reflect only the decisions of his landlord, and his neighbours in the next-door shack must be accepted as an act of God.

In the domestic life of the average Red migrant two broad phases can be distinguished. In the first phase, while the man is young, sharing a room with another man or men (first as sub-tenant, then as host) is a matter of preference. It can re-create something of the "all-boys-together" atmosphere which *abafana* (young men) enjoy in the country. The second phase starts when the migrant grows older and begins to develop the outlook of an *indoda* (mature man). He now sets a higher value on peace and privacy, and although it costs more to keep on his room alone, he prefers to stay there by himself, or with a woman, or possibly with one steady male companion.

In town, where Xhosa from all districts meet together, age-grades and age-sets might—perhaps—have been used as a common denominator and basis for associational life, regardless of home origin. They are not so used. The inter-personal etiquette of seniority, of course, is a common code observed as far as practicable by all the Red men in East London, but the corporate organization based on age-groups is practically confined within *amakhaya* limits. It is simply an extension of the local organization which exists in the country.

Thus when Red migrants speak—as they so often do—of associating with their *iintanga* in town, they do not mean age-mates in general, but age-mates from the same home place. We have seen that this applies to sharing rooms: the friend with whom a migrant lodges is a "home person" first and foremost, and an *intanga* after that. The same principle is the one that forms the Red young men's "clubs" in town.

These clubs are, in effect, associations between groups of room-mates all of whom are *amakhaya*. Being the local parallel, or shadow, of the *abafana* clubs in the rural community, they are organized for the same functions; namely for sociability in the first place, and secondly for graver matters such as the settling of disputes between members. Each also, like the similar organization in the country, has its "leader".

Note

1. 'Red' denotes the conservative traditionalist; 'School' denotes the educated Christian, aspiring to western norms.

Even in the towns initiation rites have persisted to a remarkable extent.[30] In some rural areas they have been transformed by the demands of the economy: going to work on the mines or in the cities is regarded as supplementing or replacing the traditional ceremonies.[31] Yet everywhere formal education is now considered more important, since it is the only way of achieving position in the competitive capitalist society.[32] And, because fewer of the older generation had the same educational opportunities, this is deepening the division between old and young.[33]

The legal reaction to these changes has been negligible. Major shifts have occurred in domestic structures, notably from male to female-headed households and from the dependency of juniors to the dependency of seniors. These have been given no formal expression by the courts. Even more serious is neglect of questions posed by the children's rights movement.[34] Systems of western law nowadays interpret parental power as a protective device whereby children can be nurtured out of their condition of dependency and legal disability.[35] This means that parents are allowed only the powers necessary to supply a child's lack of physical/legal competence.[36] Customary law is still imbued with the idea that because children are wayward and irresponsible they need to be restrained and disciplined.

(3) The legal response

(a) *The age of majority: delictual and proprietary capacity*

In the early part of the last century in each of what are now the four provinces of South Africa, legislation was passed declaring the age of majority to be twenty-one years.[37] In the Cape, because customary law was not recognized, this enactment was applied to Africans, but elsewhere it was assumed to be

---

[30] Wilson & Mafeje *Langa* and Pauw 88–9.
[31] McAllister in Mayer *Black Villagers in an Industrial Society* 243; Hammond-Tooke 82.
[32] Gerber & Newman *Soweto's Children* 80 and see Hammond-Tooke 86ff.
[33] See Epstein *Urbanization and Kinship* 155–6.
[34] See below, 359–60.
[35] Dickens (1981) 97 *LQR* 462.
[36] Freeman *The Rights and Wrongs of Children* 1.
[37] Ordinance 62 of 1829 (Cape); Ord 4 of 1846 (Natal); art 123 Volksraad Resolution of December 1853 (Transvaal); Orange Free State Wetboek ch 89.

inapplicable.[38] Acts specifically directed at Africans were introduced only when the British annexed the Transkeian Territories.[39] Little thought seems to have been given to the consequences of imposing this rule.[40] Whatever their impact, the nineteenth-century enactments remained in force until 1972, when with the exception of the Transkeian proclamations, they were repealed and substituted by the Age of Majority Act.[41]

Despite the peremptory wording of all the age of majority legislation, the courts have been hesitant to apply it to those subject to customary law, with the result that their decisions are inconsistent and it is uncertain to what extent customary law has been preserved. Most of the cases concerned delictual liability.[42] Initially the courts refused to apply the rule of majority; they held that a father was liable for his son's delicts regardless of the son's age.[43] In one case, although an assessor had pointed out that application of the proclamations was mandatory, a majority decision still found the father liable.[44] It was held that the only way in which the head of a family could relieve himself of responsibility was formally to disinherit his son or to force him to set up his own homestead.[45]

So, instead of applying a common-law regime of liability for the delicts of minors (which was a logical implication of the age of majority legislation), the courts preferred the customary-law rule of 'kraalhead' liability. This meant that 'kraalheads' (the heads of families) were responsible for the actions of all the *inmates* of their homesteads.[46] They were excused liability only for the acts of visitors[47] and for delicts governed by the common law.[48] In consequence the courts became preoccupied with the definition of an 'inmate'. With the Southern Nguni, for instance, it was held that a son who had married and set up a homestead separate from that of his father, should be liable for his own delicts since he was no longer an 'inmate' of his father's 'kraal'.[49] A Natal decision held that the mere fact of the son leaving his father's homestead and building a

---

[38] And in Lesotho, according to Poulter 187–8 and Palmer *The Roman-Dutch and Sesotho Law of Delict* 74, it was declared inapplicable because the Cape Ordinance was enacted primarily to remedy a mischief of Roman-Dutch law.

[39] Although local customary law was generally preserved, Procs 110 and 112 of 1879 and Proc 140 of 1885 provided that all persons attained majority when they reached the age of 21.

[40] Although a Senate Select Committee of 1913 para 2 reported that 'The rights and privileges conferred by majority on women and girls are not generally known'.

[41] Section 9 of Act 57. See above, 336 regarding the argument whether this Act applies to Africans.

[42] There are no reported decisions regarding a son's powers of contractual capacity, apart from occasional comments that 'kraalheads' are not liable for the 'shop debts' of the inmates of their kraals: *Klaas v Mqweqwe* 1 NAC 19 (1897); *Sifuba v Mbaswana & another* 1 NAC 222 (1909).

[43] See especially *Klaas's* case supra; *Daniso v Makinana* 1 NAC 86 (1905); *Rubulana v Tungana* 1 NAC 90 (1905).

[44] *Daniso's* case supra. The proclamations were applied in only two cases: *Mfanekiso v Mpakana* 1 NAC 85 (1905) and *Bekwa v Nomandla & another* 3 NAC 144 (1914).

[45] *Mkeqo v Matikita* 1 NAC 242 (1909).

[46] *Saqoni & another v Ndiko* 3 NAC 138 (1916); *Mdingi & another v Wadonise* 4 NAC 178 (1919); *Thomas v Diniso & another* 1937 NAC (C&O) 214.

[47] *Fandesi v Ntsizi & another* 4 NAC 13 (1919).

[48] When capacity was governed by the same legal system: *Jele & another v Dlamini* 1982 AC 299 (NE).

[49] *Sabela & another v Ntutusile* 2 NAC 162 (1911). For the Pondo see *Fono v Tomose* 1930 NAC (C&O) 64 and *Mendwana v Biya* 1934 NAC (C&O) 59. For the Tembu see *Mgoma v Kulati & another* 1956 NAC 198 (S).

separate establishment would not suffice to break the bonds of kraalhead control.[50] With the Sotho on the other hand, marriage alone was enough to designate legal independence;[51] this rule was later deemed to be applicable to most other tribes.[52]

The term 'inmate' included people who were unrelated to the head of the family, implying that legal responsibility was based on residence[53] and not on blood ties.[54]

The question of proprietary capacity was handled differently. According to customary law, the head of a family 'owned' the earnings of all inmates.[55] A leading decision was *Mfanekiso v Mpakana*,[56] where it was held that once a son became a major under the proclamations he owned his own property. For a long time thereafter the courts ignored the nexus of proprietary and delictual capacity, although they realized that the ability of a kraalhead to pay compensation rested on his control of a joint family estate.[57]

[113] *MOTSEOA v QUNGANE* 1948 NAC 16 (S)

In this action respondent sued Moseane Motseoa and appellant, the latter in his capacity as kraalhead, for three head of cattle or their value, £15, as damages for seduction of his daughter Annie. Moseane consented to judgment and the case proceeded against second defendant alone.

The admitted facts in this case are as follows: Some twenty years ago appellant met a woman from Bechuanaland in Johannesburg. He brought her to Matatiele and lived with her as man and wife and paid local tax in respect of her until 1945 when she returned to her home. When appellant met her she had a small boy of about four years of age. This boy is Moseane (first defendant in this case). He grew up at appellant's kraal, assumed the latter's surname and looked upon him as his natural father; and appellant paid for the boy's education, had him circumcised and treated him as his son. Moseane who is now about 27 years of age, has been to work on the Rand and in Natal on a number of occasions and handed all his earnings to appellant. In 1946 Moseane returned from work in Natal and a few days after his arrival *twalaed* respondent's daughter and took her to appellant's kraal where he seduced her. He desired appellant to pay dowry for the girl but appellant refused, and, when Moseane declined to take her back to her people, appellant drove them both away. The girl thereafter returned to respondent's kraal.

In the Court below it was contended that according to Basuto custom a kraalhead is not liable for the torts of an inmate of his kraal who is not related to him. . . .

At the trial three expert witnesses were called. The evidence of two of them is to the effect that a kraalhead would be liable for the torts of an inmate only if the latter belongs,

---

[50] *Marala v Mbilana* 1917 NHC 32.

[51] *Gunyani v Modesane* 1 NAC 255 (1909).

[52] *Gonyela v Sinxoto* 2 NAC 69 (1910) and *Gqoboka v Magxaba & another* 3 NAC 135 and 274 (1913).

[53] See *Rweqana v Nganzana* 1929 NAC (C&O) 2 and *Mbambo v Swaai* 1931 NAC (C&O) 19.

[54] But see *Mtshekula v Singana* 1913 NHC 97. In *Mgedezi v Bontsa & another* 1958 NAC 73 (S) it was held that although the wrongdoer and his kraalhead were related as father and son by a civil marriage, the defence that such a common-law relationship should exclude kraalhead liability would not be entertained.

[55] *Ndopi v Sita* 1917 NHC 77; *Mtonto* 1921 NHC 45.

[56] 1 NAC 85 (1905).

[57] And see *Mcunu* 1916 NHC 116 and *Makoro & another v Seemane* 1948 NAC 60 (S). If a son is deemed not to have control over the property in his possession, there seems little point in holding him liable for his own delicts, as the assessors in *Mgoma v Kulati & another* 1956 NAC 198 (S) pointed out.

according to Basuto custom, to the head of the kraal. They state that the head would not
be liable for the torts of his own illegitimate son who had grown up at his kraal. The other
witness disagrees and states that the kraalhead is responsible for the torts of all the inmates
of his kraal whether they are related to the head or not.

We had no doubt that the third witness stated the law correctly, but as the Basuto Law
on the point has, as far as we are able to ascertain, never been decided, and as the expert
witnesses are divided, the matter was referred, at the request of Counsel for appellant, to
the Native assessors. . . . They are unanimous that the appellant is liable because he used
Moseane's earnings for his own purpose.

No doubt the opinion of the assessors was largely influenced by the fact that appellant
had received and appropriated the earnings of Moseane, but in my opinion the result is the
same if Moseane's earnings were not handed to appellant, because when a wrong has been
committed Native Law demands to know, not who received the wrongdoer's earnings, but
who is the head of the kraal where he resides. If his earnings were handed to his natural
father that is a matter between the father and the kraalhead and does not concern the
person who suffered the injury.

The obligation of the head to answer for those under his control is a fundamental
principle which has its roots deep in the legal system of the Bantu. Thus, it is well
established Native Law that the kraalhead is liable for the actionable wrongs of the
inmates of his kraal. Among most tribes a father is liable for the torts of his sons, whether
married or not, committed while living at his kraal. Among the Xosa speaking tribes of the
Cape the kraalhead is also liable for the wrongs of unrelated inmates of his kraal. . . .

The absence of any decisions restricting the liability of the kraalhead to the wrongs of
related inmates seems to indicate that the general principle of kraalhead responsibility has
never been questioned. Naturally if the inmate has his own property he himself must
satisfy the claim of the injured. But in Native Law an inmate of a kraal under tribal
conditions does not generally own property in an individual capacity. The people living at
a kraal form a collective unit with joint responsibilities and assets. All property and
earnings accruing to members of the kraal go into a common pool and are administered
by the kraalhead, for the general benefit of the permanent household. If an inmate by his
labour contributes to the general support of the kraal, the kraalhead cannot escape
liability on the ground that the inmate is unrelated. It would be illogical and inequitable
to hold otherwise.

For these reasons the appeal is dismissed with costs, but in order to make it clear that
the judgment is against the defendants jointly and severally the Native Commissioner's
judgment will be amended by inserting the words "jointly and severally with the first
defendant, the one paying the other to be absolved" after the words "defendant No. 2".

In keeping with *Motseoa's* case, but in complete disregard of both *Mfanekiso v
Mpakana*[58] and the age of majority legislation, the court in the following case
upheld the customary-law rule of proprietary incapacity. A son (presumably a
minor although this point was obscured by faulty pleadings) had sued his father
for delivery of four horses. At the son's request they had been purchased by his
father with money earned by the son while working away from home. The two
had quarrelled and separated. The question before the Appeal Court was
whether the earnings of a minor are the property of the head of the kraal at which
the minor resides.

---

[58] 1 NAC 85 (1905).

[114] *MFAZWE v MODIKAYI* 1939 NAC (C&O) 18 at 22–3

That principle [a minor's earnings accrue to his kraalhead] is basic in Native Law especially so in among the South Eastern Bantu, the Nguni tribes, which include the people of Zululand, Natal and the Cape.

To make doubly sure the following Pondo Assessors were consulted. . . . Their replies appended, clearly confirm the general principles. A minor's earnings accrue to his father. What is bought therewith becomes the property of the father. The father may earmark stock for such minor. He retains dominion in such stock and the minor has no claim should the father subsequently dispose of such stock.

These ideas are perfectly consonant with basic Native Law.

The Native Commissioner has endeavoured to subvert these principles on the plea of equity on reasoning which avoids the issue involved in the present case. There is no proof on record that it is "a practice fast becoming obsolete and which, carried to its logical conclusions, leads to an absurdity". Native law stands today more strongly entrenched in the legal system recognised by this Court than ever it did before, for the reasons I have set out in *Matsheng v Dhlamini* (1937 NAC (N&T) 89). Any change due to obsolescence or other reasons must come from the legislature and not from the bench.

This Court fails to see any inequity in a system of law which entitles a kraal head to the earnings of a minor who owes his very being to the care, protection and nurture he has received at the hands of that kraal head and its inmates [sic] during his tender years, plus a lobola exceeding the minor's possible contributions in the short period between attaining working age and his marriage. Native Law, however, goes deeper than this, regarding the family as a collective unit with joint responsibility and assets, so much so that the minor is entitled to a lobola from the kraal inmate in addition to other benefits received as a juvenile. Any attempt by a Native Commissioner to break down the Native system in a fatuous effort to introduce the European system of individualism is to be regretted as a retrograde step strongly opposed by the Natives themselves. . . . The Native system is a complete whole. Tampering with one aspect involves repercussions in various directions invariably destructive of their social system. To emancipate the minor would involve loss of that valuable asset in Native Law of Communal support, especially in the provision of a wife and in other directions, which in their present stage of advancement as a mass especially in Pondoland, would be most detrimental.

The remarks of Welsh, P. in *Dumalitshona v Mraji* 5 NAC at p. 169 may well be recalled here. . . .

> "In the opinion of this Court the statement of the Native Assessors is consistent with basic principles of Native Law and Custom which have long been recognised and followed by this Court; and though it may be contended that these principles do not reach the ethical standards which more civilised peoples have attained, this Court, which was established in order to preserve and give judicial recognition and effect to Native Law and Custom, feels that it would not be justified in reversing in the name of good morals, policy, justice or equity a long and weighty line of precedents unless it were satisfied that the Custom falls unequivocally within that category.
>
> To jettison Native Law and Custom in the circumstances disclosed would necessarily involve consequential issues such as the status of widows, their dowries (lobola), guardianship of their daughters and claims to the latter's dowries with the effects on the social life of the people entirely out of keeping with their habits, Customs and desires.
>
> Until the proper authorities are satisfied that the time has arrived when various widely recognised Customs which are practised daily by the Native tribes of these Territories, e.g., Polygamy, ukutwala, ukungena, etc., which admittedly fall short of civilised standards, should be abrogated, this Court is of opinion that it should not interfere in the matters of broad policy which is the prerogative of the executive, and that it would, therefore, not be justified in setting aside a Custom which has long since become crystallized into Law."

Eight years after *Mfazwe's* case,[59] the Appeal Court considered the relationship between delictual and proprietary capacity. It was faced with the difficult task of reconciling conflicting precedents. *Mfanekiso's* case, quite correctly in terms of the proclamations, had held that a son had full proprietary capacity once he turned 21. Another series of decisions ruled that a kraalhead was liable for the delicts of inmates regardless of their age. The court seriously contemplated overruling *Mfanikeso's* case in order to bring it into line with the decisions on delictual liability, but on the basis of proprietary rights already acquired by children, *Mfanikeso's* case was upheld.

Hence, once a person is over the age of 21, any property earned becomes his or hers, secured by a common-law capacity to acquire and alienate it at will. This liberty is subject to whatever personal duties the holder may have to support kinfolk and other dependants. Before the age of 21, however, the inmate of a homestead has no rights, real or personal, to property he or she may have acquired. Their acquisitions accrue to the head of the homestead, whose rights over it are tempered only by his duty to support dependants.[60]

The courts should have altered the rules of delictual liability to harmonize them with proprietary capacity, but they have not done so. This means that the head of a household may still be held liable for the delicts of any inmate, even though he no longer has a claim to that person's property. This anomalous situation is based on a shift in the courts' view of the underlying reasons for kraalhead liability. The economic responsibilities flowing from common residence are now not considered as significant as the head's duty to discipline persons living within his sphere of control.[61] The new rationale is plausible enough where the envisaged homesteads are geographically isolated, social contacts are few, and physical mobility is limited. But it makes little sense in a modern environment. In *Peter v Sango & another*,[62] however, the court said:

> 'The general rule is that a kraalhead is responsible for the delicts of any unemancipated person residing at his kraal whether related to him or not. . . . [M]any Bantu live in urban areas in property lawfully owned or occupied by themselves or in hired rooms or houses or with relatives of friends and to these persons the position applies that each head of a family is legally in control of its unemancipated members and property.'

Logically it would follow that where a delinquent inmate was living or working away from home, the head of the homestead could not be expected to exert any controls, and so the tortfeasor should be held liable for his or her own actions. In most cases such a finding would concur with the economic circumstances of the parties: a son living away from home would doubtless also be working, and would therefore be financially independent and so be able to pay for his delicts. Yet the courts were not prepared to go this far. In the following case the plaintiff (Nakani) sued a father and son jointly for damages

---

[59] In *Mlanjeni v Macala* 1947 NAC (C&O) 1. See above, [77].

[60] See above, 234.

[61] *Skenjana v Guza & others* 1944 NAC (C&O) 102; *Motseoa v Qungane* 1948 NAC 16 (S); *Makoro & another v Seemane* 1948 NAC 60 (S); *Mhlokonyelwa v Ngoma* 1950 NAC 197 (S); *Genge v Funani* 1961 NAC 33 (S); *Msenge v Ndzungu* 1962 NAC 75 (S); *Malie & another v Shiba* 1963 BAC 34 (S) and *Tumana v Mila & another* 1963 BAC 39 (S).

[62] 1972 BAC 185 (S).

caused by the seduction of his daughter. In an appeal against a commissioner's judgment in favour of the plaintiff, it was contended that the father should not have been joined as a defendant because his son was not living at home and the seduction had occurred at the son's place of work in a Potchefstroom township.

[115] *TOMBEEL & ANOTHER v NAKANI* 1947 NAC (N&T) 118

Steenkamp P [delivering a dissenting judgment]:

There is no doubt from various decisions and opinions expressed by Native assessors, that according to old Native law and custom a father is liable for his unmarried sons' torts irrespective of where the son is living or working at the time of the committing of the tort.

In the case of *Motloung v Motloung* 1939 NAC (C&O) 127, the point was raised but it did not become necessary to decide the extent of a father's liability for the torts of an absent son. This was a Free State case decided at Kroonstad but the principles are the same in the other provinces except in Natal. The Native assessors were asked the question:

"Is a father liable for the delicts or wrongdoings of his son when he lives at another kraal or is away at work?"

The reply was:

"A father is responsible for his son's wrongs if he is not married, if he is staying with his father or is away at work. If he is away at work, people must consult his father and say the son has done wrong. . . . A father ceases to be liable when his son marries."

McLoughlin (P) remarked in that case that while the statement given by the assessors undoubtedly reflects true Native law, it is a matter of consideration, whether in view of European contact and ideas of ownership, there has not resulted some changes which will require modification of the original custom.

As remarked above the point was not decided but the present appeal is a proper case calling for a decision and this Court will have to do so.

The Legislature has seen fit to introduce a modification in Natal where Native law and custom have been codified for many years. In the Proclamation No. 168 of 1932 the words "while in residence at the kraal" were inserted in Section 141(2)(b). The repealed Code contains no such provision. The Legislature therefore saw the wisdom, with change of conditions, to protect a father from liability for his son's delicts when the latter is working elsewhere and where the father cannot keep an eye over the son's behaviour.

I wish to make it clear that the Natal Code has no force or effect outside Natal and Zululand but I see no harm in using the provisions as a guide in appropriate cases, especially when a case from outside Natal has to be decided on the question whether the basic Native law is not opposed to the principles of natural justice.

Take the example of an extreme case. A father lives in a reserve at Middledrift, Cape, his unmarried son is working on a farm in the Lichtenburg district and there seduces a girl. Is it equity that the father who had no opportunity to keep an eye over his son, should be liable to pay the damages? It must not be overlooked that in ancient Native law, sons did not go away to work but the economic change of conditions makes this imperative and it would be most inequitable and contrary to natural justice to hold the father liable. It could be argued that a father gets the earnings of his son and is therefore liable for the torts but it is well known that sons do not always remit their earnings to the father and this Court would not be justified in drawing a line between a son who carries out his responsibilities and the one who does not do so. Such a line of demarcation will only lead to difficulties of application. . . .

Morgan [Member of Court—delivering the majority judgment]:

I agree with the learned President that the law to be applied in the present case is Fingo law. . . .

My own view in the matter now before this Court, following the Fingo law as given above and from personal experience in a Gaika/Fingo district, is that a father cannot relieve himself of his responsibilities for a tort committed by his son while the latter is temporarily away at work or on a visit. The rule would appear to be that all Fingoes are either kraal heads or are subject to a kraal head. The only way in which the father can relieve himself of his responsibility is, seemingly, by formally disinheriting his son or by making him set up an establishment for himself. This responsibility is usually acknowledged by the father unless his son has absconded and has lost touch with his father's kraal for a number of years. The father in the case of his son's abscondment will usually remark "uhilizile".

The practice is quite common for families living in a tribal area to come together and discuss the question of a fine for seduction in cases where the seduction itself took place in an urban area. Particularly is this the custom where the parents of both the man and the girl reside in the same district.

In the present case, the first defendant was working at Potchefstroom at the time he seduced the plaintiff's daughter. His father, the second defendant, was living on a farm in the district of Potchefstroom. It is, therefore, quite clear that the son was still a member of his father's kraal. To hold that the father in the circumstances of this case is not liable, jointly with his son, for the damages arising out of the seduction of the Plaintiff's daughter would, I feel, be too sweeping a change. It must be remembered in this connection, whatever other principles may be involved, that the father usually provides the lobolo for his eldest son's wife, and sometimes for his second son's wife, and that the fine for seduction merges with the lobolo cattle in the event of a marriage taking place after the fine has been paid.

It may be added that the kraal head's responsibility for the torts of an inmate may only be enforced in suits or proceedings involving questions of custom followed by Natives.

[Appeal was accordingly dismissed.]

As if to reinforce the new basis of kraalhead liability, the courts have rejected the argument that a father's responsibility should be limited to cases where his son continued to remit wages or to make any other financial contribution to the running of the homestead.[63] In a superficial way this might reflect traditional attitudes to childrearing, but it is incongruous in many modern contexts. The family head's customary-law remedy (to expel the delinquent from his homestead),[64] for instance, may not be legally possible where the offender is a tenant. More to the point is the problem of sustaining traditional authority structures in conditions of geographic mobility, especially labour migrancy. If the head of a family is away at work for long periods, he can hardly be expected to exert any control over members of his rural homestead. Conversely, where the nominal head of the family is dependent on the remittances of migrants, it is pointless to hold him responsible for their misdeeds because he does not have the money to pay compensation.

(b) Contractual capacity and locus standi

The Age of Majority Act affects not only delictual and proprietary capacity; it applies equally to locus standi and contractual capacity. But both of these powers are governed independently by s 11(3) of the Black Administration Act.[65] Under this provision contractual capacity and locus standi are regulated by the common

[63] *Penxa & another v Fani* 1947 NAC (C&O) 120.
[64] *Fono v Tomose* 1930 NAC (C&O) 48 and *Mendwana v Biya* 1934 NAC (C&O) 59.
[65] 38 of 1927. See above, [107].

law unless the right or obligation in question arises out of customary law, when the relevant capacities would have to be tested by the same system.[66]

Section 11(3) performed the (structurally) useful function of facilitating African participation in the capitalist economy. When an individual enters into any commercial contracts, his or her status is automatically regulated by common law, without the inconvenience (for the employer) of a plea that a customary-law incapacity pertains. In consequence, it is only in a few economically unimportant cases of delict that customary law has been preserved.

(c) Tacit emancipation

Assuming that the Age of Majority Act[67] is applicable to Africans, then like other people subject to a common-law regime, there is no reason why a minor may not anticipate the age of full majority by asking the court for an order declaring him or her to be a major.[68] Similarly, there is no reason why a minor might not be tacitly emancipated. This would involve proving economic independence, either by carrying on a business or by accepting paid employment, which is fairly easy to do where the person concerned is no longer living at home.[69] Although a tacitly emancipated minor is deemed capable of entering into any contract, and of being sued in court, he or she does not at the same time have full control of property, nor is such a person held liable for delictual actions.

In Zimbabwe the courts have grafted a modified concept of tacit emancipation onto customary law. They have held that a child who is physically and intellectually mature and who is financially independent may be held liable for his or her own delicts.[70] After denying that this institution existed in customary law,[71] the South African courts have not broached the issue again.

III LEGITIMACY

(1) The concept and its relevance

Ties of blood and socially approved relationships are the two basic determinants of family membership. Thus a child is deemed to be related to its biological parents only if they were partners of a valid marriage.[72] Most legal systems stigmatize the offspring of temporary sexual liaisons or other non-approved forms of cohabitation as illegitimate.[73]

Illegitimacy is said to have no place in customary law since 'birth in or out of wedlock is irrelevant to [the child's] status in the community or its legal rights and duties'.[74] The legal disadvantages of illegitimacy are indeed not as great in customary law as they used to be in western legal systems; and it is quite correct

---

[66] And if common law governs capacity, there is a better argument in favour of tacit emancipation.
[67] 57 of 1972.
[68] Section 2 of the Act.
[69] Boberg 384ff.
[70] *Mombeshora v Chirume* 1971 CAACC 30 and *Stewart a/b Patrick v Chigumbura* 1971 CAACC 35.
[71] *Gwenya v Madodeni* 1920 NHC 20.
[72] See Spiro 447ff.
[73] Krause (1976) 4 *IECL* ch 6 s2.
[74] Cotran & Rubin *Readings in African Law* v2 44.

to say that 'lawful wedlock' in its narrow, common-law sense is not a relevant consideration for determining legitimacy in customary law. But bridewealth certainly is. The relationship between a mother and child is socially close and obvious; the same is not necessarily true of the relationship between a father and child. Payment of bridewealth fixes and proclaims the link between men (or patrilines) and children. Hence the customary-law rule is that if bridewealth has been paid, the child will be attached to its father's family; otherwise it is part of the mother's family. The fortunate social consequence is, that unlike the filius nullius of early English law, the illegitimate child under customary law always has a home in some family.

There is an obvious functional connection between the concept of legitimacy and the social institutions considered appropriate for raising children. Yet in many early legal systems, and this is still true of customary law, the purpose of affiliating a child to a particular family or person was not to promote the child's interests. Rather, affiliation concerned the welfare of the family. Children were agents for the devolution of family fortunes, and they were expected to advance its interests by maintaining and adding to family property, influence, and prestige.[75] The rearing of the child—a responsibility of the family as a whole—was an incidental issue, and in any event the relatively free access to resources and the simple needs of a subsistence economy meant that upbringing did not pose a social problem.[76]

The law was a mirror of social practice. In England, for instance, parents had no legal duty to support their children until the sixteenth century, when mass unemployment and increased labour mobility began to threaten social stability.[77] In Europe the duty to care for children seemed so obvious that it was attributed to the natural law, and even at the turn of this century, a German lawyer could write:

> 'It is a plain precept of universal law that young and tender beings should be nurtured and brought up by their parents; and this precept have all nations enforced. So well secured is the obligation of maintenance that it seldom requires to be enforced by human laws.'[78]

Customary law, like the western legal systems of earlier times, was not conceived in the interests of children. They featured mainly as *objects* of the rights and powers vested in the head of the family. Affiliation was important because it forestalled potential conflicts arising out of competing family claims to children.

At the end of the twentieth century reliance on natural sentiment to secure the care of children would be thought unduly optimistic, and in developed countries both neglect and deliberate abuse of children have become major social issues.[79] A movement to foster children's rights (now amplified and codified in a United

---

[75] Eekelaar (1986) 6 *Oxford J Legal Studies* 163; Goode *The Family* 24: where there is no property to inherit and none to protect, there is less concern with legitimacy.

[76] Bennett 1980 *AJ* 117–18.

[77] Eekelaar op cit op cit n75 167; Eekelaar & Maclean in Meulders-Klein & Eekelaar *Family, State and Individual Economic Security* ch 6.

[78] Schouler *Treatise on the Law of Domestic Relations* v1 856 para 780; Krause op cit n73 para 103; and see Justinian's *Institutes* 1.2.pr.

[79] Freeman op cit n36 ch 1.

Nations Declaration)[80] has exerted considerable influence on western law.[81] An upshot of this movement is the call to eliminate any distinctions between legitimate and illegitimate children.

In most developed countries it is thought to be pointless and cruel to penalize children for their parents' sexual misdemeanours, and accordingly laws discriminating against illegitimate children have been abolished.[82] Equality of status is now widely regarded as a basic human right.[83] In South Africa the Law Commission[84] recommended removal of most of the disadvantages suffered by illegitimate children (principally in the area of succession) but it did not specially consider the implications for customary law.[85] (In any event, the abolition of the incapacity to inherit on intestacy[86] was not applicable to African estates.)[87]

The rules of affiliation—today the bulk of the remaining law on illegitimacy—function principally to allocate the duty of support. Where there is a high rate of illegitimacy and a low level of public welfare provision, as in South Africa, rules of affiliation can have a profound social impact. In the United States, for instance, where the number of illegitimate births amongst Whites is negligible when compared with those amongst Blacks, the traditional private-law rules affecting the illegitimate child have had the effect of discriminating most against black children.[88]

In South Africa there is a strikingly high incidence of illegitimate births amongst Africans, especially in the urban population.[89] This is often attributed to relaxation of the traditional code of sexual morality. Premarital pregnancy used to be considered a great disgrace[90] and young girls had to submit to regular inspections by older women or their age mates. Doubtless the decline of initiation schools and the diminishing control of elders have encouraged some moral laxity,[91] but this is only a partial explanation. More pertinent is the stability of marriage, because illegitimacy is a clear index of the general state of

---

[80] (1989) 28 *ILM* 1448. See Freeman op cit n36 41.
[81] Out of a diffuse concern to remedy various social ills, four particular issues can be isolated: rights to welfare, protection, and social justice, and a claim to greater freedom from parental control: Freeman op cit n36 40.
[82] See, especially, s 3(1) of the Status of Children Act 1969, New Zealand.
[83] Krause op cit n73 para 19. See: art 25(2) of the Universal Declaration of Human Rights 1948; art 10(3) of the International Covenant on Economic, Social and Cultural Rights 1966; and art 2 of the Convention on the Rights of the Child 1989.
[84] *Investigation into the Legal Position of Illegitimate Children* 38.
[85] Any work in this regard was complicated by the lack of comprehensive statistics (p 43), and the peculiar position of children in South Africa where, for the purposes of common law, the children of a customary marriage are deemed illegitimate (p 1).
[86] Section 1(2) of the Intestate Succession Act 81 of 1987.
[87] Section 1(4)(b) of the Act.
[88] Krause op cit n73 para 9.
[89] Africa Publications Trust *Children of Apartheid* 10; Simons *African Women* 221ff; Steyn & Rip (1968) 30 *J Marriage & Family* 511; Rip *Black Pre-marital Illegitimacy in Pretoria*.
[90] Schapera 171.
[91] See Krige & Krige 317; Krige (1936) 9 *Africa* 5–6.

marriage in a society.[92] In this regard the inflation of bridewealth may well have had a detrimental effect: as the amount demanded has increased, so has the possibility of early marriage become more remote, thereby encouraging casual or informal unions. The offspring of such unions are not necessarily illegitimate, because bridewealth may eventually be settled (even in later generations), but their status in the interim is ambiguous.[93] A complicating factor is the non-recognition of customary marriages; from the common-law point of view the children born of these unions are illegitimate.

The imposition of influx control legislation has had particularly deleterious social effects. Under the Blacks (Urban Areas) Consolidation Act[94] African children were permitted to live in urban areas only if their fathers could prove that: they personally had acquired rights under s 10(1)(a) or (b); the children were their unmarried, under 18 years old, sons or daughters (for this purpose, a customary marriage was given recognition); and that the family was lawfully and ordinarily resident there. Under s 11 of the Act fathers could be prosecuted for harbouring wives and children in contravention of these requirements.[95] Predictably, the difficulty of complying with these legal requirements and the threat of prosecution encouraged men to engage in temporary or casual (since there would be no intention of paying bridewealth) liaisons rather than bring their families to the cities.

In preconquest African societies illegitimate children apparently posed no problem. Regardless of whether the natural father was prepared to assume responsibility for his offspring, they would be incorporated into a homestead and looked after. With the high cost of rearing children relative to increasing poverty and unemployment,[96] and the scarcity of housing, the same accommodating attitude has disappeared. The burdens of childcare are no longer absorbed by an extended family; they must be borne by individuals, all too often single women.[97] The problem thus posed for modern customary law is not simply 'to which family should this child belong?' but 'who is liable to raise it?'

(2) Rules of affiliation

[116] HOLLEMAN *SHONA CUSTOMARY LAW* 242–59

Legitimacy in Shona Law has two aspects. The first concerns the question of parental rights and duties, amongst which are the right to have custody of the child, the duty to sustain and protect it, the right to receive marriage compensation for a daughter and the duty to provide a wife for a son, and the duty to accept responsibility for the child's

---

[92] Although Glendon *State, Law and Family* 102 says: 'The position of an illegitimate child in a stable *de facto* family is comparable to that of a child in a stable legal family, while the position of an illegitimate child in a one-parent household is often not unlike that of legitimate children of divorced or separated parents.'

[93] See above, 291.

[94] 25 of 1945.

[95] See the investigation of father–child relationships in the context of the migrant labour system: Reynolds *Men without Children*.

[96] See Reynolds op cit 3–4 and 6–8.

[97] See above, 166 and 316–17 regarding female-headed households.

actions. The second aspect concerns the child's membership of a patrilineage and his right
to succeed to the name and dignity of his father and other paternal ascendants.

Normally, when lawful marital relations exist between the child's parents, the child is
fully legitimate: it suffers no legal disabilities, and legitimacy is, so to speak, a single
indivisible concept. But when the child is born under irregular circumstances the two
aspects become separate issues which need not necessarily coincide. Parental rights and
duties will be determined by the question whether the child has been covered by the
payment of cattle to its mother's family or its legal guardian. Lineage membership is
determined by the question whether it has the same blood (*ropa*) as its legal father.

The discussion on legitimacy therefore falls into two parts. I shall first deal with the
acquisition of parental rights. After that the position of various classes of children will be
examined in order to ascertain whether they fail in either of the two aspects of legitimacy
mentioned above.

Acquisition of Parental Rights

Parental rights to a child born of a lawfully married or betrothed woman are vested in its
mother's husband or affianced groom by virtue of the affinition agreement between the
two families; but if the child is an adulterine child of such a betrothed or married woman,
the natural father may sometimes be allowed to obtain parental rights upon payment of
a compensation (*maputiro, butiro*) to the legal guardian of the child.

Parental rights to a child born of an unmarried or not-betrothed woman are vested in
its mother's family, but may be transferred to the natural father, either when the latter
subsequently marries the mother, or upon his payment of *maputiro*.

The position regarding parental rights of a father to the children he has raised with his
lawfully wedded or affianced wife needs little discussion. . . .

There is no specific act or token by which a father recognizes his child, but when he
comes to see his newly-born baby he has to give a token present (*cionesa*, from *kuona*, to
see) to the midwife. Such a present is, however, also given by any relative or friend who
wishes to see the baby, On the other hand, the refusal of a father to give *cioneso* is an
indication that he denies his paternity and is not interested in the child. . . .

I shall now deal with the acquisition of parental rights by a natural father to children
he has raised by women other than his lawfully married wife or affianced bride.

(i) Pre-marital children

The person who has unlawfully impregnated an unmarried woman may obtain parental
rights to his child either by marrying the woman or, if he refuses to marry her, by paying
adequate compensation to her family. The first alternative is in every respect regarded as
the most satisfactory. If the seducer is prepared to marry the woman there is seldom if ever
any question of an additional compensation for unlawful impregnation, except that the
woman's family may sustain their demand for a *mackorwa* or *mavunwa* (purification)
animal. If an agreement regarding a marriage is reached before the child is born, the
father's rights are covered by the normal marriage compensation payable to the woman's
family. Owing to the particular conception of the affinition agreement the child is
considered to have been born to lawfully "married" parents even if it is born before the
marriage has actually been contracted.

If the child is born before the affinition agreement has been reached, the parental rights
are vested in the mother's family and are, in principle at least, only transferable to the
natural father upon payment of *maputiro*. In practice, however, this time limit is not
always strictly adhered to. When for some reason or other the action against the seducer
has not been settled by the time the child is born, the defendant may, if he subsequently
agrees to marry the woman against a normal marriage compensation, be allowed to
assume his right to the child without an additional payment of *maputiro*. . . .

I have explained elsewhere that *maputiro*, the compensation covering parental rights to
an unlawfully begotten child, should be distinguished from the damages (*muripo*) payable
for unlawful impregnation—and also from the purification (*mackorwa*) animal which is

not, strictly speaking, a legal issue—although these may in practice often seem to form a single issue. The position can be briefly outlined as follows: The offender who unlawfully impregnates an unmarried woman whom he refuses to marry, is legally obliged to pay *muripo* for the delict—and in cases of first pregnancy he has no choice but to pay the purification animal as well, so that the woman can be re-accepted in her parents' home. The payment of *muripo* is not in itself sufficient to establish the defendant's right to the child, but it confirms his natural paternity and enables him to claim parental rights by tendering *maputiro* to the woman's family. Once the woman's family have accepted compensation for the delict they cannot deny the defendant's right to claim the child if he offers *maputiro*, unless he is deemed to have forfeited his claim; neither can they force the defendant to press his claim if he does not want the child.

Normally when an action on account of pre-marital impregnation is brought against a seducer who is unwilling to marry the woman, it is taken for granted that he intends to press his claim to the child when he agrees to pay damages. Often no specific term is given to the compensation payable to the woman's family. The defendant merely promises to pay two or three head of cattle, and, unless specifically stated to be otherwise, this amount covers both damages for the delict and parental rights to the child. . . .

If the defendant assumes custody of the child shortly after it is born, nothing more is payable. But if he leaves it in the care of its maternal grandparents for a considerable number of years he may be required to pay one (at the most two) head of cattle as compensation for its maintenance[1] before they allow him to take custody.

Under certain circumstances a natural father may forfeit his right to tender *maputiro*. The parents of a pre-maritally pregnant girl are obviously anxious to see her married before the child is born, and if the seducer is unwilling to marry her they may try to find another suitor who is prepared to give marriage compensation for her. The party who then marries the girl before her child is born, acquires parental rights to the child by virtue of the marriage agreement. It is a case of *ngombe ya vuya nouswa pa muromo*—"the cow comes with grass (wealth) in its mouth". It is on the one hand an emergency measure to protect the name and interests of the woman, her family and the child, but on the other hand a perfectly honourable marriage which in no way affects the dignity of the husband. Indeed, most informants subscribed to the view expressed in the above phrase and were of the opinion that marrying such a woman was something of a windfall. The woman's husband may, if he wishes, transfer his parental rights to the natural father against payment of *maputiro*, but this is said to be very uncommon. The natural father has lost his right to claim the child, and it would be regarded as a serious affront if he were to offer *maputiro* to the woman's husband after the child had been born in wedlock.

The natural father may also forfeit his claim to the child if he fails to give *maputiro* before the child is married. Amongst the Hera, probably more than elsewhere, it may happen that the defendant provides the purification animal and pays some compensation as *muripo* for unlawful impregnation, but delays paying *maputiro*, thus leaving the child after it is born with its maternal grandparents. The common excuse advanced for this delay is his inability to find the necessary cattle, but more often than not the real reason is that he wants to be certain of making a profitable transaction. It is generally admitted that a natural father "is more interested in the child when it is a girl, than in a boy. For a daughter he can get marriage cattle but for a son he has to provide a wife". And even when the child is born and proves to be a girl, he may hesitate to claim it until it has reached a marriageable age. Then he will claim his daughter by tendering *maputiro* in order to collect her marriage cattle. The maternal family apparently have no right to dispute his belated claim for parental control but are entitled to demand (apart from *maputiro*) adequate compensation (*uredzwa, marero*) for all the years they have looked after the child. . . .

Generally speaking, however, a man is expected to assume parental control of his natural offspring as soon as possible, and public opinion takes a poor view of a father who, for obviously mercenary considerations, postpones pressing his claims until the last moment. The child's maternal family will therefore urge an early settlement of *maputiro*. . . .

(ii) *Extra-marital children*

Parental rights to all children born during the subsistence of a valid affinition agreement are vested in the *vakuwasha*,[2] whether or not such children have been raised by the affianced groom or husband. The basic principle regarding children born as the result of the woman's adultery, is expressed in the popular maxim *gomba hari nomwana*—"a lover has no child", or more precisely, the lover of a formally betrothed or wedded woman has no right to the child he has raised by her.

Paternity of a child is rarely queried when a woman has committed adultery while living with her husband, but inevitably becomes an issue when she conceives either before normal conjugal relations have been established, or during her husband's absence.

The *mukuwasha* whose affianced bride has been unlawfully impregnated by another, can rightfully claim the child if he actually marries the woman—in which case he is also entitled to receive damages for unlawful impregnation from the offender. Generally speaking he should not object to marrying the woman if she has repented and promised to remain faithful to him, because such a marriage in no way impairs his dignity. If the woman is handed over to her husband before the child is born, the previously mentioned phrase *ngombe ya vuya nousa pa muromo* ("the cow comes with grass in its mouth") is applicable and expresses approval instead of ridicule.

If the *mukuwasha* refuses to marry his affianced bride on account of her adultery he can claim his *rovoro* back from the *tezwara*,[3] but he is then usually considered to have relinquished both his right to the child and his right of action against the guilty third party. These rights have now passed into the hands of the *tezwara* who can either claim damages from the offender (*gomba*) or allow him to marry his daughter. If the *gomba* marries the woman without undue delay he will normally be given the child without having to pay additional compensation. If he does not marry the woman but wants to have control of his natural offspring, he must pay the *tezwara* full compensation for unlawful sexual intercourse and a few head of cattle as *maputiro* (*kuputira mwana*, to cover the child), a total of about four or five head. . . .

Sometimes the *mukuwasha* decides to marry his bride but refuses to take the child. Under such circumstances he may allow the lover to take the child against a few head of cattle. The compensation payable by the lover then comprises: two or three head of cattle as *muripo* for adultery, and two or three head as *maputiro* for the child. The total number seldom exceeds five head of cattle and is commonly referred to as *maputiro*.

Informants expressed the opinion that the mother of the child, perhaps more than anyone else, will in practice determine to whom the child will go in case of dispute. Knowing that the child, although legitimate because it is covered by the *rovoro* paid by the *vakuwasha*, may nevertheless suffer certain disabilities in the family of its legal father because it is of different blood, she may urge her husband to leave the child to its natural father where she hopes it will meet with less prejudice. If the husband fears that he may lose his wife altogether if he does not heed her wishes, he may allow the natural father to take the child "so that he can keep his wife and raise his own children by her". . . .

Other exceptions to the rule that "a lover has no child" may be found when a married woman conceives during the absence of her husband and when there can be no doubt about the paternity of the child. In such cases the husband's family may occasionally agree to grant the child to its natural father against *maputiro*. The court has, however, no power to make such an order and will act only as an arbitrator and public witness to any arrangement reached by the parties. . . .

Notes

1. One of the Shona terms used for this is ngombe yokurera (from kurera, to bring up). Note the similarity to isondlo.
2. The Shona term for the husband's family.
3. The Shona term for the wife's family.

(a) Children born during marriage

As a general rule in customary law rights to a child accrue to the family to which the mother is attached.[98] If the mother is unmarried, the child becomes part of her family, unless the father marries her, in which case the child is then affiliated to him and his family.[99] Were the child to be born before the marriage took place, the husband might be required to pay isondlo to the mother's guardian (as recompense for rearing costs) when he claimed the child.[100]

Once a woman is married, any children she bears are automatically affiliated to the husband's family.[101] This rule is ascribed to the payment of bridewealth, which operates to transfer the woman's child-bearing powers to her husband.[102] In sociological terms, it is a particular manifestation of the widely accepted principle that all offspring born during the subsistence of a marriage are presumed legitimate. A Sotho maxim, like its common-law counterpart, puts it thus: 'a married woman has no bastard.'[103] This presumption has the effect of preferring a socially constituted family to a biological one.[104] In consequence it does not matter where the child was born,[105] or whether the husband took custody of it on birth;[106] in all cases his parental rights are assured.

There are, however, no hard and fast rules determining legitimacy.[107] Even where bridewealth was not been fully paid, provided that the parents had lived together for some time and some arrangement had been made to pay by instalments, the legitimacy of the children is seldom questioned.[108] Moreover, unless and until bridewealth is returned, any children a wife bears, even though she happens to be separated from her husband, are deemed to be his.[109] This rule is especially pertinent to a widow: she continues to bear children for her deceased husband's family[110] until the marriage is formally dissolved.[111]

---

[98] Schapera 172–3; Roberts 21–2; Van Tromp 139ff. In other words, bridewealth operates to transfer rights to all the children a woman bears: *Masheme v Nelani* 4 NAC 43 (1919).

[99] Van Tromp 146 adds that if the husband were to discover that the child were not his, he could sue the natural father for damages for seduction.

[100] *Ovolo v Tshemese* 3 NAC 121 (1912); *Ntshongole v Danti* 3 NAC 126 (1914); Schapera 172–3; Hunter 208–9.

[101] *Mdinda v Pahlane* 1917 NHC 56; *Koza v Zulu* 1935 NAC (N&T) 29; s 16(2) of the Natal and KwaZulu Codes; Hunter 208.

[102] Poulter 181–2; *Makwaba v Mhlango* 1947 NAC (N&T) 35.

[103] Poulter 181.

[104] Krause op cit n73 para 24.

[105] *Rangana v Mdingi* 6 NAC 6 (1928).

[106] *Lucingo v Mgiqika* 4 NAC 40 (1920).

[107] Because of the difficulty of defining a customary marriage. See, eg, *Zweni v Bonga* 1962 NAC 14 (S).

[108] Cf, eg, *Mnisi v Mnene* 1939 NAC (N&T) 152.

[109] *Mnanamba* 1937 NAC (C&O) 219; *Loliwe v Mnyuko* 1945 NAC (C&O) 14. And see s 16(4) of the Natal and KwaZulu Codes.

[110] *Motini v Selepi* 1941 NAC (N&T) 106 at 108; *Mcingana v Goniwe* 1944 NAC (C&O) 93; *Mfana v Ntlokwana* 1945 NAC (C&O) 69; *Mdumane v Mtshakule* 1948 NAC (C&O) 28; *Fubesi v Mandlaka & another* 1948 NAC 10 (S). Marriage between the widow and the natural father will not suffice to transfer rights to the new husband: *Koteni v Davis* 4 NAC 41 (1920).

[111] *Manunga v Yekiso* 1936 NAC (C&O) 87; *Guleni* 1944 NAC (C&O) 45; *Matingati v Lamba* 1947 NAC (C&O) 88. And see s 16(3) and (5) of the Natal and KwaZulu Codes.

The husband is not *obliged* to accept a child that he did not procreate. If he repudiates it, the child reverts to its mother's family[112] or the natural father may claim it.[113] But men are unlikely to reject their wives' children. To do so would be considered unusually drastic, normally a prelude to divorce on the ground of adultery.[114] Repudiation is more understandable where the child is discovered to be the product of an incestuous union; such children are believed to attract misfortune so there is a general reluctance to harbour them.[115]

(b) Rights of the natural father

Under customary law the natural father had no *automatic* right to the children he sired,[116] unless he were to marry the mother.[117] Instead, according to the rules stated above, the child would be affiliated to its mother's husband or her guardian.

In spite of this, most systems of customary law allowed the natural father to claim his child if he tendered a consideration to its guardian. Amongst the Pondo[118] and Swazi,[119] for example, payment of seduction damages (often confusingly referred to as a fine) entitled the offender to demand the child he had fathered. The Southern Nguni peoples required further consideration—isondlo (comparable with the Shona payment, maputiro). In part this signified compensation for bringing up the child,[120] and in part a transfer of rights.[121] A concomitant payment of seduction damages functioned to confirm paternity.[122] By way of contrast, under Southern Sotho law, payment of damages gave the natural father no rights,[123] and similarly, under Tswana law, the entire matter lay within the discretion of the mother's guardian.[124]

These rules and practices are difficult to reconcile with the common-law principle that the best interests of the child determine the person allowed custody. To this end, although the courts have the power to grant a legitimation order, they will not do so merely to satisfy some ulterior motive on the part of the applicant; and the predominant motive in the case of many men is acquisition

---

[112] *Tonono v Qobo* 3 NAC 120 (1912); *Kabi v Putumani* 1954 NAC 210 (S); *Ndyu v Nxoke* 1955 NAC 15 (S). And it should be noted that the husband is the only person entitled to reject the child: *Simono v Ngxenga* 3 NAC 123 (1915).

[113] Van Tromp 139–41.

[114] Roberts 21. The effect of repudiation is, of course, to disinherit the child: Mönnig 331.

[115] At best they can hope to find shelter with their mother's family: Van Tromp 146.

[116] *Kamani v Sigongo* 1940 NAC (C&O) 167; *Zwane v Dhlamini* 1951 NAC 353 (NE).

[117] *Montjoze v Jaze* 1914 AD 144 held that this was the only way in which he could acquire parental rights in Natal.

[118] Hunter 208 and *Mpeti v Nkumanda* 2 NAC 43 (1910).

[119] Marwick 90–1.

[120] Van Tromp 142–3; *Takayi v Mzambalala* 1 NAC 121 (1906); *Hlangabeza & another v Mgudlwa* 1943 NAC (C&O) 13. Further see Church (1979) 12 *CILSA* 329–30.

[121] See, eg, *Gujulwa v Bacela* 1982 AC 168 (S) at 173.

[122] In *Ngubentombi v Mnene* 4 NAC 49 (1919) and *Mayeki v Qutu* 1961 NAC 10 (S), however, it was held that payment of damages secures the father's right, which isondlo simply confirms. Accordingly, in *Mayeki's* case, once the damages were paid, the natural father acquired the right to his daughter's bridewealth.

[123] *Ludidi v Nongena* 1945 NAC (C&O) 59.

[124] Cf Schapera 173.

of a daughter's bridewealth.[125] Rather than order that a child be handed over to a person entitled by customary law,[126] the courts will give a declaration of property rights.

The welfare principle has taken on sharper definition in the courts' refusal to enforce transactions that smack of trafficking in children; these are condemned as being contra bonos mores and opposed to public policy and natural justice.[127] A strictly common-law construction means that *any* arrangement for the transfer of rights to a child against payment of a consideration would be unenforceable—a prohibition that comes dangerously close to refusing to recognize the legal effects of paying bridewealth. A situation frequently encountered was where a woman had been seduced by one man, had borne his child, and had then married another. The courts refused to give her husband the child merely because he had paid bridewealth. This they said amounted to trafficking in children.[128] Similarly, they held that a woman's second spouse, merely by paying bridewealth, obtained no rights to children she had borne during her first marriage.[129] And further, a court refused to enforce an agreement between a husband and his wife's guardian that the latter obtain rights in her children by giving the husband the full amount of bridewealth on dissolution of the marriage.[130]

Despite a preoccupation with the welfare of children, the courts' decisions have in fact tended to endorse the rules of customary law. Any children born to a woman have ultimately been affiliated to the family to which she was attached.[131] The courts are not prepared to sanction any agreement varying this arrangement unless custody/guardianship is claimed by the *biological* father.[132] The issue could have been differently interpreted: it was not so much a matter of commercial trafficking in children, as informal undertakings of adoption. The common law stipulates that adoption must be gratuitous and approved by a court order.[133] By implication any claim for payment of isondlo made against a person other than the natural father (or the guardian at customary law) is treated as unenforceable, unless, and this is a curious twist caused by a modern interpretation,[134] isondlo were deemed to be a form of maintenance.[135]

In attempting to secure the best interests of the children, do the courts play a sufficiently active role? Is nullity of these customary arrangements a sufficient

---

[125] *Mlotshwa v Ndwandwe* 1950 NAC 190 (NE).

[126] *Nyandeni v Mtshali* 1941 NAC (N&T) 1.

[127] *Ngxawum v Sibaca* 1949 NAC 144 (S).

[128] *Ndabankulu v Pennington* 4 NAC 171 (1919); *Matinise v Malote* 1936 NAC (C&O) 121 at 124; *Ndella v Butelezi* 1941 NAC (N&T) 38; *Pennington v Mcitwa* 1942 NAC (C&O) 45; *Nkambule v Shongwe* 1942 NAC (N&T) 2; *Mahlangu v Sibiya* 1954 NAC 42 (NE); *Mafulela v Mxezeni* 1970 BAC 15 (S).

[129] *Njapa v Makanya* 1937 NAC (N&T) 146; *Kubayi v Ngobeni* 1939 NAC (N&T) 52; and *Ndhlovu v Kanetse* 1940 NAC (N&T) 64.

[130] *Mathebe d/a Mathebe v Katima* 1944 NAC (N&T) 69; and see *Mhlala v Mohlala* 1938 NAC (N&T) 112.

[131] See, eg, *Msotwana v Sibeko* 1942 NAC (N&T) 17.

[132] *Luhleko v Langeni* 3 NAC 122 (1914); *Ciya v Malanda* 1949 NAC 154 (S).

[133] See below, 376–7.

[134] *Hlengwa v Maphumulo* 1972 BAC 58 (NE).

[135] See above, 279ff.

sanction? Whatever the answers to these questions, a more spiritedly interventionist policy seems, for the moment, out of the question.[136] Aside from the ethical and financial problems involved in monitoring domestic relationships, there is the difficulty of distinguishing permanent alienation of parental rights (adoption) from fostering,[137] a practice that is common throughout southern Africa.[138] Such arrangements are so numerous and so flexible that they cannot possibly be supervised by the state in the same way as other transfers of guardianship.

The courts have been careful not to impose the nuclear family structure as a general model on customary law.[139] This is evident from their studious neglect of the mother's right to her children. No mention is made of her in the affiliation cases, although presumably the rule in divorce actions holds good here: a young child should not be separated from its mother.[140]

Section 27(2) of the Natal and KwaZulu Codes, in a radical departure from customary law and the previous codes,[141] provides that an unmarried woman is the legal guardian of her minor illegitimate offspring, unless she herself is a minor, in which case the child falls under the guardianship of the mother's guardian.[142]

(c) Proof of paternity

In a society in which children are welcomed not only for the affective but also for the material benefits they may bring, men seek rather than deny paternity. Today, however, the responsibilities of parenthood are more burdensome, and especially where payment of maintenance is involved, there is a greater likelihood that paternity will be denied.

Customary law assumes that any child born to a married woman was fathered by her husband, and in the commissioners' courts (under the sway of common law) this was elevated to the status of a legal presumption.[143] It has the effect of casting an onus of proving the illegitimacy of a child born during a marriage onto the person alleging it.[144] Although the onus is said to be a heavy one,[145] in principle it should be no more difficult to discharge than the onus in any civil case, viz proof is on a balance of probabilities.[146]

---

[136] Gutto *Children and the Law in Kenya* 31 concludes his survey of custody and maintenance provisions on the breakdown of marriage by observing that although on paper the state is given sufficient room to intervene, it usually refuses or neglects to do so.

[137] See, eg, kin fostering in Ghana: Goody in Mayer op cit n17 51ff.

[138] See the distinction between adoption and fostering below, 377–8.

[139] In this regard the approach in maintenance cases can be distinguished. See below, 374–5.

[140] See above, 295.

[141] Section 30 of the previous version Proc R195 of 1967.

[142] Until the mother attains her majority. This provision echoes s 3(1)(*a*) of the Children's Status Act 82 of 1987. Presumably for the purposes of succession, however, s 16(1) of the Codes prevails, ie the child becomes a member of its mother's house.

[143] *Ntliziyombi* 1937 NAC (C&O) 233; *Kakaza* 1942 NAC (C&O) 36; *Mpela v Estate Mpela* 1944 NAC (N&T) 3; *Ndondo* 1944 NAC (C&O) 80; *Madubula v Mahlangu* 1974 BAC 449 (C).

[144] *Ntliziyombi's* case supra.

[145] *Mafuta v Ratshwa* 1939 NAC (C&O) 154; *Qwayimana v Manjezi* 1948 NAC 11 (S).

[146] *Mabutja v Maya* 1975 BAC 1 (C).

Foremost among the factors to be considered in contesting the husband's fatherhood would be his access to the mother[147] and whether he formally repudiated the child.[148] Conversely, admission of paternity can be inferred from payment of damages for adultery, the vimba (or ngquthu) beast,[149] and maintenance and lying-in expenses.[150] The mother's allegation regarding the identity of the father is naturally also relevant; but, although it does not require formal corroboration,[151] it should be weighed with care.[152] Under the common law, if a man admitted having intercourse, even at a time that was not relevant to the conception of the child,[153] he would be presumed to be the father.[154] This has now become a statutory presumption.[155]

(3) The rights of children

[117] HOLLEMAN *SHONA CUSTOMARY LAW* 252–9

The Rights of Children

We must now examine the rights of children with regard to the two aspects of legitimacy mentioned above, that is, first as members of a patrilineage, and then as dependants of their legal guardian and as claimants to his estate. Since females do not occupy a hereditary position in their patrilineage and normally cannot claim a share in the estate of their father (regardless of any other property rights which they may hold) the discussion will mainly be concerned with the rights of male children.

For the purposes of this section four classes of children are distinguished:

(*a*) children of lawfully married parents;
(*b*) children legitimized by their natural father by the customary *maputiro* compensation;
(*c*) adulterine children of a married woman under parental control of their mother's husband;
(*d*) children who are neither legitimized by their natural father nor recognized by their mother's husband.

(*a*) The first class of children comprises not only children conceived and born at a time when their parents were lawfully married, but also those born before the actual conclusion of their parents' marriage. Even when no formal affinition agreement has existed between the father's and mother's families at the time of birth, a satisfactory marriage agreement reached soon after the child is born, will normally transfer parental rights and control to the father's family, and the child is then considered to be fully legitimate as a matter of course. It has been explained before that in Shona law the correct and logical sequence of legal events is of relatively minor importance in comparison with the ultimate, satisfactory result of the transaction.

---

[147] *Mqadalana v Limani* 1941 NAC (C&O) 87. In case of doubt the presumption of legitimacy will prevail: *Mkwanyana* 1947 NAC (N&T) 106; *Madonela v Mpikeni* 1948 NAC 22 (S). If the child were born before the marriage took place, the husband is not deemed to be the father: *Gwatyu* 1952 NAC 283 (S); *Jim v Poswa & another* 1954 NAC 111 (S).
[148] *Nkwambi v Mgqobozi* 1941 NAC (C&O) 50; *Ngxawum v Sibaca* 1949 NAC 144 (S).
[149] *Mhlupeki v Bhoyi* 1912 (1) NHC 38.
[150] *Ngcobo v Dhlamini* 1970 BAC 86 (NE).
[151] *Mayer v Williams* 1981 (3) SA 348 (A) at 351–2.
[152] *Ngcobo v Makhubela* 1970 BAC 64 (C); *Silidana v Namane* 1982 AC 247 (C).
[153] *S v Swart* 1965 (3) SA 454 (A); *Motete v Lekhang* 1982 AC 339 (C).
[154] *Mntambo v Khoali* 1982 AC 138 (C); *Ngcobo v Nene* 1982 AC 342 (NE).
[155] Section 1 of the Children's Status Act 82 of 1987. And note, too, the presumption of paternity raised from a refusal to allow a blood test: s 2.

The children belonging to this class are fully legitimate. They are members of their father's patrilineage and the sons are therefore entitled to succeed to the name and genealogical position of their father and other paternal ancestors. The father and paternal family exercise full control over the children, who owe them obedience and filial support. Inversely, the father is legally responsible for their actions and he must feed, clothe and shelter his children to the best of his ability as long as they are dependent upon him. When they are ill the father must search for a remedy or consult a diviner or herbalist. Both sons and daughters belong to the unity of their father's family and estate, which means that the daughters are regarded as providers of cattle in which the sons have the right to share. To a Shona man, full legitimacy primarily means that he is a potential successor to his father's name and genealogical position, and that he can claim marriage cattle from the paternal estate.

(b) The second class of children result from the illicit pre-marital or extra-marital relations of their mother. If the mother, at the time the child is born, is neither married nor formally betrothed, parental rights to the child are vested in the maternal family. But the child is nevertheless assumed to be a member of the lineage of its natural father because it has the latter's blood and—if a boy—has a potential right of succession in such lineage. If the father pays the customary compensation (*maputiro*) to the maternal family (with or without additional compensation for maintenance) he can assume full parental control over the child.

If the child is born when the mother is legally betrothed or married to another than the natural father, parental rights are in principle vested in the family of the affianced groom or husband of the mother. In these cases the natural father has no rightful claim to the child but the legal guardian may sometimes agree to transfer parental rights to the natural father against the payment of *maputiro*.

Whenever the legal guardian has accepted *maputiro*, the child becomes the fully legitimate child of its natural father and, as far as the latter's patrilineage and estate are concerned, suffers no legal disabilities. When it is a boy he has the right to claim *rovoro* from his father's estate, and when he happens to be the first-born son (*danggwe, nevanje*) of his father, he has the right to succeed to his father's name after the latter's death. . . .

In practice, however, there may be difficulties because the other children of the father may regard such an extra-marital son as an intruder, a *mwana wefambi* (child of a loose woman), and therefore resent his succession to their father's name. In one or two cases it appeared that the half-brothers successfully sustained their objections, but the general opinion amongst informants was that by withholding such a legitimized son his right of succession, his paternal relatives were risking the mystical sanctions of their enraged father's spirit. The result is that more often than not such a son indeed succeeds to his father's name after the latter's death.

Another difficulty confronting an extra-marital son is due to the fact that he is not associated with any of the established "houses" of his father's wives, and that his step-mothers and half-brothers may sometimes succeed in denying the extra-marital son his rightful share in the common estate of the deceased father. . . .

(c) Regarding the third class of children—those resulting from the adultery of a formally betrothed or married woman. . . . Unlike the natural children of the husband, whose main practical obstacle lies in the fact that they are not associated with the house of any particular father's wife, the extra-marital child of a wife suffers no disability in this respect. Since the blood of a common mother establishes a closer unity amongst children than the blood of a common father, an extra-marital wife's son will meet no prejudice amongst the other children in his mother's house. He will have no difficulty in obtaining his rightful share in the estate of such a house. But since this child does not have the blood of the mother's husband it does not really belong to the latter's patrilineage. Even when the child is *pro forma* accorded the clan and sub-clan names of his legal father—which would normally establish his membership in his *rudzi* (lineage)—the fact that he has the "blood of another" (*ropa romumwe*) may disqualify him from succeeding to the name and dignity of his legal father or any other ancestor in the latter's lineage. In this respect

informants in the Wedza Reserve were generally outspoken in their opinion that such a son "cannot inherit the name of his father", and they were able to quote cases in support of their view. . . .

In the Narira Reserve, however, most informants were not prepared to accept as a fixed principle that such a "wife's child" cannot succeed to the genealogical position of his legal father on account of his different blood. Some were even inclined to take the view that since the legal father had given *rovoro* for the mother, the child was legitimate in every respect, and therefore not only entitled to share in his father's estate but was also eligible to succeed to his name and position in the lineage. They admitted, however, that "the other children would probably object to his getting the father's name and refuse to obey him" (*kunzwa*, literally, to "listen"). . . .

The question arose whether a son could succeed to the name and genealogical position of his natural father when the latter had not given *maputiro* for him. Informants argued that the question of *rudzi* (patrilineage) is determined by the blood of the father rather than by the payment of cattle. If there is no doubt about the paternity of the son he will be regarded as a member of the lineage of his natural father and as such be entitled to succeed to his father's name also if no *maputiro* has been given for him. Informants found an analogy in the case of a husband who has raised children by his wife but loses control over his children when he fails to fulfil his *rovoro* obligation. In such a case, when the marriage is dissolved, the son will nevertheless be eligible to succeed to his father's name. But it was also pointed out that failure to pay *maputiro* practically always implies that the natural father is not interested in the child, which is then brought up either by its maternal grandparents or mother's husband, away from its natural father. Only in exceptional circumstances will the latter's family consider such a child as the most eligible candidate for succession when his father dies.

(d) We must now consider the fourth-mentioned class of children, those neither legitimized nor recognized by their natural father or mother's husband. The majority of these children are born to unmarried or divorced women, and left in the care of their maternal grandparents because the father is either unknown (*rare*) or refuses to accept them. A few of them are born to married women but rejected by their legal father who denies paternity. They are usually boys, because girls represent a potential value in marriage cattle and are therefore as a rule either duly claimed by their natural father or retained by their mother's husband.

The common term usually employed with reference to such children is *mwana wegomba*, "lover's child". . . . Such a child falls under the control of, and is almost invariably brought up by, its maternal grandparents, who assume full responsibility, rights and duties in connexion with it. When it is a girl they can negotiate her marriage and accept her marriage cattle. When it is a boy they are expected to provide a wife for him, and are in return entitled to received his full filial support. When the natural father is unknown or cannot be traced the child may be given the clan and sub-clan names of the mother, but he is never regarded as a full member of his mother's patrilineage and cannot therefore succeed to the name of his *sekuru* (mother's father). As one Rozwi explained: "How can my daughter's child ever get my name? It would mean that I myself had raised the child with my daughter!"

(a) Succession

One of the functions of customary-law systems of succession is preservation of the purity of the family bloodline. Thus children who were genetically related to the deceased are normally preferred to anyone whose relationship was only of a social or legal nature.[156] As a result it is often said that a woman's illegitimate

---

[156] See Hunter 209 and 233.

offspring cannot succeed to her deceased husband.[157] But this statement stands subject to several qualifications.

Amongst the Southern Nguni, for example, an illegitimate son may succeed to the head of a household if there is no other male descendant[158] (and provided that he had not been repudiated by the deceased[159] or that his mother had not been driven away because of her adultery[160]). The illegitimate child of an unmarried woman also has rights of succession in her house, although again they are only 'ultimate' rights.[161] Similarly with the offspring of widows: when the head of a family dies his widow remains part of his household. The Southern Nguni do not allow levirate unions, but nor do they insist that the widow be chaste; any children she may bear as a consequence of her liaisons are treated in all respects as if they were legitimate,[162] again with the proviso that they cannot usurp the rights of the deceased's other heirs.[163] Finally, a man is free to institute[164] an illegitimate son as his heir[165] provided again that the rights of legitimate heirs are not ousted.[166]

No doubt influenced by principles of the common law, the courts expressed some doubt whether illegitimate children should be allowed to benefit from customary law. Two dissenting judgments urged strongly that customary law should not be followed on grounds of public policy and natural justice;[167] but later this contention was explicitly rejected,[168] and in view of the general trend to equalize the status of all children, it is unlikely to find favour today.

(b) Maintenance

Customary law was not concerned with the problem of deciding who had the duty to support children, whether legitimate or illegitimate.[169] They would be

---

[157] See Poulter 230 and 235–6; Marwick 92; *Mkwanazi* 1956 NAC 136 (NE); *Somabokwe v Sicoto* 2 NAC 118 (1911); *Mngcuka v Posiwe* 1930 NAC (C&O) 21; *Mbulawa v Manziwa* 1936 NAC (C&O) 76; *Mgijimi v Mgijimi & another* 1955 NAC 97 (S).

[158] Hunter 209; Van Tromp 142; *Baatje v Mtuyedwa* 1 NAC 110 (1906); *Ludidi v Msikelwa* 5 NAC 28 (1926); *Gebuza* 1938 NAC (C&O) 15; *Qakamba & another v Qakamba* 1964 BAC 20 (S). And see Coertze 284.

[159] *Ludidi's* case; *Madyibi v Nguva* 1944 NAC (C&O) 36.

[160] *Nkwambi v Mgqobozi* 1941 NAC (C&O) 50.

[161] In the sense that he may not usurp a legitimate heir: *Molefi v Khabo* 5 NAC 25 (1924); *In re Estate Late (Annie) Mzilikazi* 1933 NAC (N&T) 28 at 30; *Letlotla v Bolofo* 1947 NAC (C&O) 16.

[162] Such children must be born at the deceased husband's homestead: *Xelitole* 4 NAC 147 (1919); *Mazwana v Mongameli* 4 NAC 150 (1921); *Hahe v Nokayiloti* 1941 NAC (C&O) 115 at 119; *Tyali v Dalibango* 1942 NAC (C&O) 58 at 62; *Gade v Gqagqeni* 1944 (C&O) 85; *Tshaka v Betyi* 1951 NAC 301 (S).

[163] *Zibulale v Mtshisazwe* 3 NAC 120 (1913); *Gubevu v Gubevu & another* 3 NAC 127 (1914); *Djerman v Morris & another* 1949 NAC 132 (S). In other words, they have ultimate rights of succession: *Siqakaza v Mbulo* 2 NAC 66 (1910); *Madlongo v Nandi* 3 NAC 119 (1913); *Mazwana v Mongameli* 4 NAC 150 (1921); *Dumalitshona v Mraji* 5 NAC 168 (1927).

[164] This is a formal juristic act that must be publicly attested: *Matsolo* 1940 NAC (C&O) 177; *Mpolo v Nozihamba* 1964 BAC 73 (S).

[165] Ie a child who was not the offspring of a valid marriage. See, eg, *Mayekiso* 1963 NAC 13 (S).

[166] *Cakile v Tulula* 1 NAC 201 (1908); *Majiki v Sigodwana* 5 NAC 67 (1925); *Mkanzela v Rona* 1950 NAC 219 (S).

[167] *Ludidi v Msikelwa* 5 NAC 28 (1926); *Dumalitshona v Mraji* 5 NAC 168 (1927).

[168] *Madyibi v Nguva* 1944 NAC (C&O) 36.

[169] Bennett op cit n76 118–19.

absorbed into the family to which they were affiliated. In particular, the natural father had no responsibilities unless he had acquired guardianship.

The position is quite different in modern South African law. The Children's Act,[170] and its successor the Child Care Act,[171] were introduced to protect children, especially those in need of care, and to provide machinery for prosecuting neglectful parents.[172] In addition the Maintenance Act[173] established courts with jurisdiction to make maintenance orders against any person 'legally liable to maintain any other person'.[174] None of these statutes created substantive rights of maintenance; they were concerned only with enforcement of the duties.[175] The emphasis on procedure was a sensible one, for if social conditions are such that a child cannot expect as a matter of course to receive proper care and attention, some means must be found to compel those responsible for it to take action. These statutes give children the benefit of state protection.[176]

The statutory innovations in procedure were only partially complemented by developments in the substantive law. According to customary law, if a child is part of the mother's family, her guardian would be liable to provide for it (adulterine children would be the responsibility of their mother's husband). Even if these people did not perform their obligations, other members of the family could be relied upon; a child had the security of a powerful kinship ethic realized within an extended family. In 1943, however, the Deserted Wives and Children Acts and Ordinances[177] were made applicable to African children.[178]

The immediate effect was to extend the duty of support to the child's *natural* father.[179] Initially, in *R v Ngonyama*,[180] the court was hesitant to do so:

'As a matter of administration, it seems . . . to be highly desirable that cases which occur among natives living under tribal conditions in the traditional way should be regarded as covered by the Native Code . . . because it might seem to natives to be most unjust that the father, who has expiated his moral turpitude by payment of the correct number of beasts [ie seduction damages], should have to maintain a child who has fallen under the jurisdiction of a kraal head to the latter's great advantage.'

Despite this caution, a later series of Supreme Court decisions, based on prosecutions under s 16(2) of the Children's Act, freely held natural fathers

---

[170] 33 of 1960.
[171] 74 of 1983.
[172] Spiro 344ff. The latest Act clearly applies to African children (see, eg, ss 5(2) and (3) and 9(1)(a)) although the definition of 'Black' contained in s 1 pertains to the Population Registration Act 30 of 1950 and not to s 35 of the Black Administration Act. Section 5 establishes children's courts which are empowered to make orders for the care of children, who have no parents or guardians, or who happen to be in the custody of persons unfit or unable to look after them: see s 14 and generally Spiro 356 ff.
[173] 23 of 1963.
[174] Section 5(4)(a). This Act also specifically applied to Africans: see s 5(6) and generally Spiro 419ff.
[175] Boberg 292.
[176] With the result, of course, that maintenance is no longer an exclusively domestic concern. See Lowy in Roberts *Law and the Family in Africa* 15ff regarding litigants' choice of tribunals for enforcing paternity and maintenance claims in Ghana.
[177] Act 7 of 1895 (Cape); Act 10 of 1896 (Natal); Ord 44 of 1903 (Transvaal) and Ord 51 of 1903 (Orange Free State).
[178] Incorporated into the Black Administration Act as s 10*bis* by s 4 of Act 21 of 1943.
[179] Section 10*bis* was later repealed by the Maintenance Act 23 of 1963 'except in so far as it may impose any liability upon any person to maintain any other person'.
[180] 1944 NPD 395 at 398.

liable for the support of their illegitimate children.[181] In civil claims too, the new statutory obligations were implemented regardless of customary law.[182] Thus in terms of the acts and ordinances any child under the age of 15 was given a right to support from a father who had deserted it.[183]

If *non-statutory common law* is applied, the child's scope of support is extended beyond the age of 15, and it will include situations where the father had not technically deserted. In *Stamper v Nqolobe*[184] the court a quo had applied the common law to determine a natural father's liability to maintain his illegitimate child. The Appeal Court, however, found that both under s 11(1) of the Black Administration Act[185] and under the Maintenance Act,[186] the court had a discretion whether to apply customary or common law. It remarked obiter that until the natural father paid isondlo, he had no responsibility for maintenance; thereafter he became the legal guardian, and as such, he was liable to support the child.[187]

The role of the customary-law payment of isondlo has not yet been satisfactorily settled. On the one hand, it could be viewed as a species of maintenance,[188] on the other, as in *Stamper's* case, it could be treated as a token of the transfer of guardianship. The court in *Gujulwa v Bacela*[189] had to decide whether a natural father would be absolved of his obligation to pay maintenance because he had paid isondlo. It was held that he could not, by a 'subterfuge' of this nature, evade his common-law duties. The court said that isondlo was payable only where the natural father wanted to claim parental rights in the child; where he did not want the child—as in casu—liability for maintenance did not cease.[190]

There has been a discernible tendency in South Africa towards a 'redefinition of the group of relatives among whom legal support obligations exist', ie a shift in responsibility from the extended family to the natural parents.[191] The Child Care Act and most of the decisions of the courts cited above contemplate the nuclear family as the support unit.[192] But this process has not yet been carried through to its logical conclusion. In the first place, there are several decisions

---

[181] *R v Makwena* 1947 (1) SA 154 (N); *R v Rantsoane* 1952 (3) SA 281 (T); *R v Kumalo* 1952 (4) SA 638 (O); *R v Mofokeng* 1954 (1) SA 487 (O).

[182] *Mtaung v Mbonani* 1951 NAC 3 (C); *Nzimande v Phungula* 1951 NAC 386 (NE); *Sekgabi v Mahlangu* 1954 NAC 164 (NE); *Ngwane v Vakalisa* 1960 NAC 30 (S); *Yokwana v Bolsiki* 1963 NAC 41 (S); *Ngcobo v Nene* 1982 AC 342 (NE) at 348.

[183] For procedural purposes a distinction should be drawn between claims for maintenance under s 4 of the Maintenance Act and the common-law action for maintenance, because in the former case a full inquiry into the means of the father is necessary: *Qubu v Jaca* 1973 BAC 352 (C).

[184] 1978 AC 147 (S) at 156–9. This decision is in line with the approach of the court in *Sibanda v Sitole* 1951 NAC 347 (NE). See above, [34].

[185] Now s 1(1) of the Law of Evidence Amendment Act 45 of 1988.

[186] 23 of 1963.

[187] This decision was approved in *Gujulwa v Bacela* 1982 AC 168 (S) at 173.

[188] According to *Hlengwa v Maphumulo* 1972 BAC 58 (NE). See above, [92].

[189] Supra. He had received notification that a maintenance enquiry had been instituted under the Maintenance Act.

[190] See in this regard: *Xakaza v Zondi* 1961 NAC 1 (NE).

[191] Glendon *The New Family and the New Property* 47; and see *Tshiki v Ramncwana* 1963 NAC 87 (S).

[192] See Spiro 350.

revealing a reluctance to exclude the liability of the extended family completely[193] and there is as yet no decision requiring application of customary law if the common law fails to provide the child with a claim to maintenance.[194] (Obviously, a person should not be obliged to pay twice under two legal systems, but careful investigation will be necessary to avoid this, and the reverse situation, where a person escapes paying altogether.)[195] In the second place, for purposes of custody/guardianship, the nuclear family is not the legal model contemplated by the courts. Hence there is a contradiction: while the natural parents might be obliged to support their children, they will not necessarily be entitled to its custody or guardianship.

Worldwide there are difficulties with the enforcement of maintenance obligations,[196] difficulties that are exacerbated by poverty and the father's remarriage.[197] If a mother cannot rely upon regular remittances from her children's father or upon the support of her own family, then the only other source of income (apart from her own earnings) is state welfare.[198] Yet it is government policy in South Africa that parents should support children, which means that the state is prepared to accept responsibility only in exceptional circumstances.[199] Apartheid and the fragmentation of South Africa into homelands confirms this policy: many women and children must live in one of the national or independent states, in which case the South African government has no obligation towards them.[200] And further, beliefs and preconceptions about the extended family (principally that it functions as the African social security system) endorse this policy of self-reliance. The end result is that the system of state maintenance discriminates against Africans.[201]

IV ADOPTION

Adoption is a common-law concept[202] that is sometimes loosely applied in the context of customary law. It is doubtful, however, whether there is an exact correspondence. The customary-law institution resembles early Roman law adoptio,[203] the main purpose of which was the perpetuation of the bloodline. The modern common-law adoption, by contrast, is conceived mainly in the

---

[193] *R v Nxele* 1949 (1) SA 375 (N); *Marudu v Langa* 1949 NAC 106 (NE); *Sibanda v Sitole* 1951 NAC 347 (NE); *Dhlamini v Mabuza* 1960 NAC 62 (NE).
[194] *Gcumisa* 1981 AC 1 (NE).
[195] See conflict of laws approach above, 374.
[196] Glendon op cit n191 68–76.
[197] See Burman & Barry *Divorce and Deprivation in South Africa* 19.
[198] See: Burman & Barry op cit 11 and 19–21 regarding the difficulties mothers experience in claiming maintenance: and op cit 12 for the low awards given by the courts.
[199] See, eg, *House of Assembly* Debates 9 May 1983 col 6560 regarding the Child Care Act.
[200] They are likely to be nationals or citizens of these states: see s 3(c) of the Social Pensions Act 37 of 1973. They must be *legally* resident in South Africa in terms of the Aliens Act 1 of 1973.
[201] See Burman & Barry op cit n197 21ff for the requirements and the comparative table they provide 31. And see Horrell *The African Homelands of South Africa* 168–9.
[202] See *Helela v Maxinana* 1921 NHC 52, where it was held that adoption was unknown to customary law.
[203] Thomas *Textbook of Roman Law* ch 40.

interests of a parentless child.[204] Thus it is used to place a child in a home where it can be properly reared; the child's welfare is predominant and the interests of the genetic or the adoptive parents are a secondary consideration.[205]

Adoption in customary law is a private arrangement involving only the two families, whereas in common law it is a judicial act. In this way the court, as upper guardian of all minors, can supervise the arrangement. The adoption procedure, which includes a careful investigation by a social worker,[206] is now regulated by the Child Care Act.[207] Private adoption arrangements are not countenanced.[208]

[118] POULTER *FAMILY LAW AND LITIGATION IN BASOTHO SOCIETY* 237–9

Where a married man has no male issue he may adopt a minor son of one of his brothers or another close relative. All parental rights and duties will automatically be transferred to the adopter, and his child may later inherit as the adopter's heir when he dies. Adoption almost invariably occurs within the extended family and is practically unknown between strangers. The legal validity of the act depends upon the satisfaction of two conditions. First, there must be agreement between the child's natural father (or guardian) and the prospective adopter. There is no need for the agreement to be recorded in writing for purposes of evidence owing to the second requirement which is that full family publicity must be given to the event. In some cases it has been stated that the local chief must be notified, but while it would be desirable for the adopted child to be pointed out to the chief as the prospective heir for evidentiary reasons, it is not thought to be a sine qua non. However, it would seem essential that any person who would have inherited the deceased's estate but for the adoption should have been told.

It is not sufficient to show that the deceased brought up the child and treated him as his own, for instance by paying the expenses of his circumcision or compensation for his delicts or *bohali* on his marriage. These are equivocal acts and may represent no more than kindness and it is a very frequent occurrence for children to be reared by their uncles or grandparents or other relatives without the permanent transfer of parental rights or duties. This latter practice is often found convenient for personal or economic reasons and serves to cement family relationships; it is only temporary and the child may be recalled at any time by its parents. When the child eventually leaves, a single beast known as *khomo ea seotla* is payable to compensate the family which has looked after the child for the cost of its maintenance and upbringing. This is a fixed payment and no greater claim can be made on the basis that greater expenditure has actually been incurred unless this was expressly authorized.

Through the process of adoption even a child which was illegitimate at birth may come to inherit. He might, for instance, be adopted by his maternal grandfather, in which case he would inherit in his mother's family, or by his paternal grandfather or paternal uncle, in which case he would inherit in that family. In the latter case cattle may be paid to the family of the child's mother since the child is being transferred from one lineage to another in a manner similar to cases where the father of a pre-marital child pays extra *bohali* to "marry" the child with its mother. However, the payment of cattle would not seem to be necessary to make the adoption valid. Sometimes an adopted child will be allotted some stock by his natural father to take with him to his new home to give him a start in life.

---

[204] Krause op cit n73 para 149.

[205] Boberg 351.

[206] Boberg 351–2.

[207] 74 of 1983.

[208] *Van der Westhuizen v Van Wyk & another* 1952 (2) SA 119 (GW) at 121. See, too, *Sibiya v Commissioner for Child Welfare (Bantu), Johannesburg & others* 1967 (4) SA 347 (T) at 348.

In customary law adoption is normally resorted to in order to provide an heir for an otherwise heirless house. The child—obviously a boy—would be the offspring of a kinsman, preferably in the male line.[209] (Women may also be adopted, but because this does not affect rights of succession it does not occasion the same formalities,[210] and a simple agreement between the families suffices.) An analogous practice, in polygynous families, is the 'placing' of a son, ie the transfer of a son from one house to another to provide an heir.[211]

For evidentiary reasons it is essential that due publicity be given to the event.[212] The adoptive parent must call a family meeting at which the adoptive child is formally transferred, and of course the natural guardian must signify agreement.[213] In some cases the local chief should also be informed.[214]

On at least two scores customary law runs foul of the common law. Sometimes the natural parents are given a payment to compensate them for rearing the child. This brings the customary adoption procedure dangerously close to infringing the common-law prohibition on trafficking in children. Equally serious, from the common-law point of view, is the private nature of customary adoption; this contravenes the policy of state supervision.

Do the statutory provisions governing adoption override customary law? The court in *Zibi*[215] held that the institution of an heir (which does not necessarily involve a complete transfer of custody) is a custom peculiar to Africans, and on that account it was unnecessary to comply with the provisions of the Adoption of Children Act.[216] Section 18 of the current Child Care Act,[217] however, uses imperative wording: adoptions *must* be effected by order of a children's court, and s 27 makes it clear that the Act is intended to apply to Africans.[218] Aside from this, the Act contains several provisions that conflict with and presumably supersede customary law. Under s 18(4)(c), the adoption must serve the interests of the child; under s 18(4)(e), the child (if over the age of 10) must consent; and under s 24, no consideration may be paid.

Adoption is not practised by all peoples in southern Africa.[219] Fostering children, however, is ubiquitous. Children may be sent to live with relations, neighbours or close friends for various reasons: the child's parents might be too poor to raise it; there might be no women available to look after a child on breakup of a marriage; the foster parent might be lonely or might need help to run a household.[220] In all these cases it is understood that the child will eventually return to its own parents, so there is no intention to sever

---

[209] Duncan 8; Hammond-Tooke 154; cf Van Tromp 147.
[210] *Mokoatle v Plaki & another* 1951 NAC 283 (S).
[211] *Sibozo v Notshokovu* 1 NAC 198 (1908).
[212] On this basis fostering can be distinguished: *Kamani v Sigongo* 1940 NAC (C&O) 167.
[213] Van Tromp 147–8; Duncan 8; *Dlula v Zibongile* 1938 NAC (C&O) 64; *Mavuma* 1954 NAC 38 (S).
[214] Van Tromp ibid and *Dlula's* case.
[215] 1952 NAC 167 (S).
[216] 25 of 1923.
[217] 74 of 1983.
[218] See too: s 18(3), as read with s 40. See generally Spiro ch 3 and Boberg ch 17.
[219] Marwick 140; Coertze 303–4.
[220] Spiegel (1986) 45 *Afr Studies* 23–31.

relationships with the biological family, which typifies adoption.[221] Hence the child does not usurp rights of succession, or indeed acquire any rights at all in the foster parent's family.[222]

---

[221] Krause op cit n73 para 177.
[222] See Schapera 174 and Roberts 22–3.

CHAPTER 9

Succession

I DEATH AND BURIAL; SUCCESSION AND INHERITANCE

Death threatens family integrity. The disruption it poses is counteracted by burial and mourning rituals and by the rules of succession.

[119] KRIGE *SOCIAL SYSTEM OF THE ZULUS* 159–70

Death, the last act in the drama of life, not only robs the community of a valuable member, but by the conflicting emotions to which it gives rise, strikes at the very foundations of society by threatening its cohesion and solidarity. This demoralisation is counteracted, according to Malinowski, by the death and mourning ceremonies which provide a powerful means of reintegration of this shaken solidarity of the group. The mourning customs are the means by which the social sentiments of the survivors are slowly reorganised and adapted to the new conditions produced by the death, for the shock of the loss is a thing felt for a long time and many readjustments must be made. Being bound to the dead man, the relatives share in his ill fortune; they "have heavy knees and their bodies are weak", say the Zulus, and they must therefore be specially fortified with strengthening medicines. They are in a position of danger themselves and a source of pollution to the society, and therefore they may not take part in the normal life of the society till they have been purified after the mourning period, which is always longest for the nearest relatives. Hence death is a transition both for the deceased and for the relatives left behind. For the deceased it is a "passage" from the world of the living to that of the dead, the ancestors whom the Zulus worship; and for the living it marks a passage from one phase of life to another, for which some readjustment is necessary. We find therefore that for the deceased there are the separation rites of burial, and, among the Zulus, an aggregation into the group of the ancestors after a marginal period of about a year; while, on the other hand, the relatives are also cut off from society—they have their hair shaved and leave off all ornaments, and during the marginal period of mourning observe many taboos, till finally a cleansing beast is killed to take off the defilement of death and mourning. They are then purified with medicines and once more resume their normal life and occupations.

When a child dies, the funeral ceremonies are simple and do not affect a larger circle than the immediate family; but the death of a kraal head is accompanied by much more ritual and a much longer mourning period, for the higher the status of the deceased, the greater is the blow to society and the longer it takes to restore equilibrium. . . . The attack on social solidarity which takes the form of death is thought by the Zulus always to be due to some unnatural force, such as witchcraft, except in the case of senile decay when the person is deemed to be a spirit already and is not mourned. Indeed, the Zulus used, in the old days, to "help such a person home" by a custom known as *ukuGodusa*. If a man was too old and feeble to go to the king's kraal or join his regiment when called out, the king would send a troop of men to "send him home". They would pounce upon the old man and take him away, burying him alive or otherwise killing him. When women became too helpless to look after themselves, they were similarly "sent home" by their own people, often being merely abandoned in some deep donga far away from the kraal.

Burial[1]

After a death the first thought of those left behind is to get rid of the corpse, which is a source of pollution contaminating the whole kraal. . . .

The body is prepared for burial by having the face washed with preparations of leaves of a smelling shrub (*dippia asperifolia*), and the head is shaved, the hair being buried with the body. Before the corpse becomes stiff, the knees are drawn up under the chin, the arms are placed against the sides and the whole body bound firmly round with the blanket or hide mat of the deceased. Then the corpse is placed in a sitting posture with the back to one of the supports of the hut and covered up from view till burial. The women meanwhile will be wailing aloud, for immediately after the death has occurred, the funeral wail (*isililo*) is commenced, "a most mournful and dispiriting sort of dirge".

The time of burial was, in the old days, and in many instances even to-day, after sunset, especially when the body was buried outside the kraal, and this precaution was taken to prevent wizards from finding out the spot. If a wizard were to get hold of the body, more particularly if it is the body of a kraal head, he could with its assistance kill the whole family. . . .

The grave is dug by the closest relatives, usually brothers of the deceased, and in the case of a kraal head, the chief son and heir turns the first sod. . . .

In the funeral procession the men lead, the women following with hands crossed on the breast, in absolute silence. Then, while the chief son and heir stands at the head of the grave holding the principal assegai of his dead father, the body is placed in the grave by the brother of the deceased, who receives a consideration for his trouble. If he is not there, the chief wife places the body in the grave. Mats are spread out and the wooden head-rest, a snuff-box of snuff, and a small earthenware pot, which is sometimes filled with water, are placed in the grave. All the clothes of the deceased and the things he used are either buried with him or burnt, though articles of value are usually kept by the relatives. His sticks and assegais will be broken before being placed in the grave lest the deceased fight with the ancestors. . . .

For the deceased these burial rites are in the nature of separation rites, and after burial he enters upon a marginal period before being finally aggregated into the group of his ancestors by means of the *ukubuyisa* or "bringing home" of the spirit, which during this time is thought to be wandering round the veld or near the grave.

Taboos observed by the Living

When a death occurs, all the normal activities of the kraal are held up and a number of strict taboos are observed. On the day of a death, no one partakes of food or water nor is any cooking done, and if the cattle have not already been milked, they will not be milked that day. On this day no one speaks, except to say what is absolutely necessary, and anyone who were to make a noise or quarrel would turn mad or become a person who never stops talking. No work is done until the strictest part of the mourning is considered over, and on the death of a kraal head people do not work in the fields until after the funeral hunt, three weeks or a month after the death. All sexual intercourse is strictly taboo for the same period. For the first week or so, the closest relatives and the children hardly ever go outside the kraal. . . .

Mourning

The mourning period (*ukuZila*) begins at death; it is strictest until burial when nothing at all may be done in the kraal, but it relaxes slightly after this until the *iHlambo* about a month after the death, which lifts all the taboos on all the inmates of the kraal, except for the close relatives of the deceased. A husband or a wife mourns for a year. During the mourning period all unnecessary occupations cease; no one even works in the fields. There is no singing and no rejoicing, and marriages are held up. No finery is worn, grass ornaments taking the place of ordinary ones, the hair is allowed to grow, and men do not burnish their head-rings nor do the women smear ochre on their top-knots. No sexual intercourse may take place, and no food may be sent to any other kraal lest it be contaminated by the defilement of death, a taboo that lasts for six months. . . .

iHlambo and End of the General Mourning

If the deceased is a man or, in some localities, a chief wife, an *iHlambo* or ceremonial washing of spears takes place a month after the slaughter of the funeral goat. The spears are supposed to have grown rusty from disuse during the period of mourning. Much beer is prepared, and all the men of the neighbourhood set out to hunt, at the end of which they all wash in a stream with strengthening medicine, or at the kraal of the deceased with the water of that kraal. On their return home they sing the favourite anthems and praises of the deceased, and sometimes the girls will go forward to meet the men, chiming in occasionally with the refrain. . . .

Final Aggregation of Widows and Widowers

After the *iHlambo* things begin to run their normal course in the kraal except that the widows in the case of a man, or widower in the case of the death of a woman, continue their mourning for about a year. At the end of a year the widows are purified in the usual way by being smoked or steamed with roots and herbs (selected for this purpose by a doctor or some other person who knows what to do), by taking "white medicines" as an emetic in the morning, and washing in the stream after having been smeared with certain fats. . . . A widow may not re-marry before a year has passed, and if during this period there is any illicit intercourse on the part of any of the widows, this will bring defilement and disaster upon the whole kraal.[2] After the purification a year after the death, the widows are, however, ready for re-marriage. A widower will, at the end of a year, cleanse himself by slaughtering a goat, which shows that his mourning is over and that he may now re-marry if he wishes to. This is sometimes looked upon as a sort of private *iHlambo* for a deceased woman.

After a year, the widows will be courted by the brothers of the deceased who are eligible to *ngena* them in accordance with the custom of the levirate, and the widows are free to choose whom they wish, or decide not be be *ngena*'d at all and leave the husband's kraal for their own home. . . . When a widow is to be *ngena*'d a feast is held and a public declaration is made that the woman is being *ngena*'d by so-and-so, and she is now recognised as his wife for all practical purposes, though the resulting children will be considered children of the deceased. Beer is made, and a beast is slaughtered to inform the ancestors that the woman has chosen to abide with the people of the kraal and feels she may not depart, and they are asked to bless her and to reward her pleasing behaviour. The beast killed on this occasion is known as *inkomo yamahlangano* (the beast for bringing together for unity), and is taken from the estate of the deceased. Before any sexual intercourse may take place between the widow and her *ngena*'d husband, he must, however, undergo a process of fortification. . . .

The Ukubuyisa or Bringing Home of the Spirit of the Deceased

Equilibrium having been re-established in the group of the living, it remains for the deceased to be finally incorporated into the group of the ancestors. This is done by means of a ceremony known as *ukubuyisa idlozi*, the bringing home of the spirit of the deceased, which takes place a year or two after his death. There is no stipulated time when the *ukubuyisa* must be held and in some cases it is held three or four years after death. There is never an *ukubuyisa* for a woman, for it is only the male ancestors that are important, and while people may be remiss in holding the *ukubuyisa* of an ordinary man, they will always be very particular about "bringing home" the kraal head, for he it is who will look after the whole village in death as in life. For the *ukubuyisa* a large ox is killed and sometimes one or more goats, for it appears that in the case of an important man every one gives something, the important relatives providing beasts or goats, the lesser ones giving money or smaller gifts. . . . On this occasion the name of the deceased is included in the praises of the ancestors for the first time after his death, and he is specially asked, when the meat is placed at the *umsamo*, to come back to the village and look after his people. Often, as a further measure to ensure his return, the officiator, his eldest son, takes the branch of a tree and drags it from the grave into the house, by this process bringing him home. . . .

By the *ukubuyisa*, then, the deceased is incorporated into the group of the ancestors and his name called upon with theirs for the first time. It is a special feast for the deceased, who is by this means "brought home" to the village from the grave, and special means are taken to keep him there—hence the scattering of gall and the taboo against the sacrificial meat leaving the kraal. The *ukubuyisa* is therefore a very important ceremony, and one that secures the blessings and help of the deceased for the whole lineage. After the death of the head of a kraal, the whole village may be removed to a new site, but not till the period of mourning is over, for the grave must be carefully guarded against witches for that time.

Notes

1. See too: A E B Dhlodhlo (1984) 13 *Speculum Juris* 96ff.
2. And see Dhlodhlo op cit 99–100.

The burial ceremony is a rite de passage marking the deceased's separation from the community of the living. An intimate family affair, it seldom occasions any legal dispute. Recently in Kenya, however, the burial of a prominent lawyer— S M Otieno—became a cause célèbre that highlighted a basic difference between customary and common law: the person entitled to determine the mode and place of burial. The deceased's widow contended that the body should be buried near Nairobi (which she claimed to be the family home), while his eldest brother said that it should be buried near Lake Victoria, the land of his patrilineal Luo ancestors.[1] The Kenyan Appeal Court finally decided for the brother, by implication favouring 'the social solidarity of the clan [together with] traditionally based sex discrimination against the widow';[2] both lifestyle and form of marriage were disregarded.

In South Africa, according to the common law, if the deceased left no specific instructions concerning his or her burial,[3] the heir is entitled to decide the manner and place of the ceremony.[4] But the form of the deceased's marriage is another critical factor that must be taken into account. For example, where the deceased had been married by Christian rites, it was held that on policy grounds the widow should be preferred to the heir(s) designated by customary law.[5] The court seemed unaware that the heir (in terms of the admittedly complex rules of succession applicable in the case of civil/Christian marriages between Africans) was not the widow.[6] But it may be that her right to determine the burial derived from the consortium established by the marriage, not a formal entitlement as an heir.

The counterpart of the burial (in Xhosa and Zulu the ukubuyisa ceremony) takes place some weeks or months later. On this occasion the deceased's spirit is finally laid to rest and is united with the shades of the ancestors.[7] At the same time the heir is chosen, the estate is distributed, and the period of mourning ends. It is widely believed that until this ceremony has been performed, the spirit is in a state of limbo and is thus potentially dangerous to the living. After the ceremony the family can be reintegrated into the community.[8]

The system of succession facilitates continuation of the family as a corporate entity by providing rules for transmission of the deceased's rights and obligations to an heir.[9] The words 'succession' and 'inheritance' are often used as synonyms, but for analytical purposes they should be distinguished. The latter denotes transmission of rights to property only, and in those societies emphasizing material wealth (which will also have a highly evolved notion of property) inheritance predominates. Succession is more general; it implies the transmission of all the rights, duties, powers, and privileges associated with status. So in the case of customary law one should speak of a process of succession rather than inheritance.[10]

Certain statuses are functionally more important than others. The head of a family, for example, is a position of authority and control that must be occupied if the associated powers are to be realized. In order to find a suitable replacement, all possible male kinfolk may have to be considered; in this instance

---

[1] The case is fully described in Egan *S M Otieno, Kenya's Unique Burial Saga*; and see the analysis by Van Doren (1988) 36 *Am J Comp L* 329.

[2] Van Doren op cit 342–3.

[3] Which need not be contained in a will: *Sekeleni v Sekeleni & another* 1986 (2) SA 176 (Tk).

[4] *Mbanjwa v Mona* 1977 (4) SA 403 (Tk); Corbett 3.

[5] *Saiid v Schatz & another* 1972 (1) SA 491 (T) and *Tseola & another v Maqutu & another* 1976 (2) SA 418 (Tk).

[6] See below, 447ff.

[7] And only by this means can a person become a shade: Hammond-Tooke (1985) 44 *Afr Studies* 54.

[8] See Goody *Death, Property and the Ancestors* 34–5 and 36ff regarding definition of ritual.

[9] See Radcliffe-Brown *Structure and Function in Primitive Society* ch 2.

[10] See Radcliffe-Brown op cit 32ff.

the law of succession is at its most elaborate and complex. Other, socially less important statuses, are dealt with in more or less perfunctory ways. For example, there is no need to find a replacement for a young, unmarried inmate of a household, and there are no rules governing succession in such cases. A married woman, on the other hand, is a socially more important figure, so some institutionalized arrangement is normally made for the transmission of her responsibilities for the rearing of children.

All the customary-law systems of succession in southern Africa can be technically described as being patrilineal, universal and onerous. They are patrilineal in the sense that the heir is chosen on the basis of a relationship with the deceased that was determined by kinship through males. This does not imply that the heir must have been genetically linked to the deceased,[11] because other factors frequently intrude, notably adoption, residence in the family homestead, and behaviour towards the deceased.[12] Succession is universal in the sense that *all* the deceased's rights and duties are transmitted to the heir. This would be inevitable in a status-dominated society, particularly one in which property was not conceived of as a separate legal category.[13] Universal succession is usually denoted by the metaphor: 'the heir steps into the shoes of the deceased.' Having said this, it is in fact tautologous to add that succession is onerous, because it means that the heir inherits not only the property of the deceased but also his or her responsibilities.

II EXCURSUS: PROPERTY AND OWNERSHIP

(1) The absence of concepts

The title of this section 'property and ownership' begs the question whether customary law actually had a concept of ownership and a legal category of property. Sensitive use of language lies at the heart of this vexed question. The prudent scholar would be advised to discard technical, western terminology when attempting to describe customary law.[14] But Gluckman, a pioneer in the field of African jurisprudence, refused to do so. He claimed[15] that a word used by the Barotse—'bung'a'—could reliably be translated into English as 'ownership'. Challenging his approach, Bohannan argued for the use of vernacular terminology.[16] It is all too easy to dismiss this type of debate as merely academic and speculative (ie it all depends how broadly ownership is defined), but such a charge misses the point. Law is words, and through the application and understanding of words courts produce concrete results. If we are to understand the different accents and emphases of property holding in

---

[11] As Moore *Law as Process* ch 5 shows, descent functions as an ideology into which rights of succession may be built.

[12] ie bad behaviour could be grounds for disinheritance.

[13] See below, 393–4.

[14] See above, 37ff.

[15] *The Ideas in Barotse Jurisprudence* 140.

[16] In Nader *Law in Culture and Society* 401ff. He was in essence a proponent of the uniqueness of each culture. See above, [11].

different cultures, we must be aware of the language used and be prepared to modify our own language.[17]

Gluckman, of course, would claim that his translation did not distort customary law because the concepts he was describing were of universal occurrence; and indeed some hold that

> 'the phenomenon [of property] is a universal one, since there is no group who live so precariously that there is not some tool, some weapon, some bit of ornament or clothing that is not regarded as indisputably the possession of its maker, its user, its wearer'.[18]

According to this view ownership is so fundamental that it is *instinctual*, common to both animal and man. The contrary, and it would seem the more provocative view, calls for an explanation not of the want or desire for certain things, but of why other individuals, with similar wants or desires, should leave the holder in undisturbed possession.[19]

If it is acknowledged that ownership is a cultural artifact, then it is evident that Gluckman gives a false impression of Barotse categories of thought when he uniformally translates bung'a as ownership.[20] In fact, the context would frequently dictate a different meaning: for instance, the Barotse use bung'a to denote highly personal relationships, situations where 'ownership' is completely inappropriate. Similarly, the term 'ownership' does not convey the connotations of obligation and generosity that go hand in hand with the control of property and are always stressed in customary law.[21] Legal terms are historically and culturally specific, ie words do not have a priori meanings.[22] So the existence or absence of a special vocabulary about property rights reveals much about a society that we ignore at the risk of misconstruing customary law and misunderstanding its social context.[23]

Language is often treated as surface evidence of ownership. The economy on the other hand is believed to determine its existence or absence, and in this respect Marxism has been a productive source of ideas. Both Marx and Engels, in their numerous references to property, posited an original condition for mankind in which property was held communally.[24] Private (or individually held) property emerged with monogamy, the nuclear family, female subordination, and patrilineal succession. According to Engels,[25] these changes were occasioned by the introduction of herding and agriculture.[26] This was a turning point in legal history when property that had formerly had no more than a *use* value, acquired an *exchange* value.[27] Comestibles and personal belongings tend

---

[17] See Kiernan in Goody *Family and Inheritance* ch 10.
[18] Herskovits *Economic Anthropology* 327; and see Bentsi-Enchill (1973) 6 *IECL* ch 2 para 140, who says that there is no doubt that customary law knew 'dominium' of movables; the controversy centred only on immovables.
[19] Herskovitz op cit 328.
[20] MacCormack (1983) 21 *J Legal Pluralism* 10.
[21] See Hunter 121–30; Kuper *African Aristrocracy* 154–5; and Schapera 226–7.
[22] Allott (1961) 5 *JAL* 100.
[23] Regarding the approach of the courts see Bennett 1985 *AJ* 173ff.
[24] Bloch *Marxism and Anthropology* 41–3 and 46–7.
[25] *Origin of the Family, Private Property and the State* 45.
[26] See above, 304–5.
[27] Bloch op cit 90. See below, 393–4.

to have little worth aside from their intrinsic usefulness to the holder; but land and domesticated livestock were a means of production (ie they were capable of generating more property). Once this was recognized, the need arose to protect rights beyond the period of immediate use.[28]

To a large extent Engels' hypothesis is borne out in Holleman's account of the Shona estate below, although there is no *direct* relationship of cause and effect between productive resources and labour (ie the economy) and the legal construct of property.[29] Holleman shows that the Shona regarded wives and cattle almost as interchangeable assets. Their economy, like many others in southern Africa, was a mixed one: agriculture and herding, supplemented by hunting and gathering wild produce. Land was freely available (which is probably why it did not form part of a deceased estate), food resources were relatively abundant, technology simple, and opportunities to accumulate a surplus few.

[120] HOLLEMAN *SHONA CUSTOMARY LAW* 318–23

The traditional Shona conception of "wealth" differs from ours.

Material wants in pre-European times were very limited, and confined to the necessities of life: food, shelter, clothing, and the tools to help produce these. Little was needed to satisfy personal vanity or sense of beauty. It was a peasant population, and agriculture was the principal economic activity. Without exception, every able-bodied person was a farmer. Production was limited by the personal needs of the producers. Since every family unit was normally self-sufficient, there was no regular market for a surplus and hence little incentive to produce a surplus. In practically all other respects, too, the family was self-sufficient. Except for iron tools and weapons, produced by an exclusive guild of ironworkers, people provided their own utensils, as well as their clothing and housing. When necessary or expedient, the help of friends and neighbours was obtained on a reciprocal or communal basis. In some cases, however, individuals with a special skill in such lines as pottery, basket work or woodcraft, produced more than they personally needed and exchanged their products for some consideration in kind. But such exchanges never amounted to a regular trade. Production along these lines remained essentially a spare-time occupation and was never meant to provide the producer with a regular income. Even those relatively few individuals who were recognized as "professional" ironworkers, diviners or midwives, followed their professions as a side-line while devoting their main efforts to the production of food for their dependants. In short, the traditional economic pattern was on the whole aimed at self-maintenance and not at profit-making.

If we then find that, in spite of their very limited material needs, the people had a well-defined idea of "wealth" and strove to acquire wealth, it is clear that their conception of wealth must be interpreted in terms other than economic. It is no coincidence that the general term for livestock, *pfuma*, has the same root as the words for "wealth" (*upfumi*) and "to become rich" (*kupfuma*). Of all property, livestock and especially cattle were considered the most valuable. Whenever people found a demand for an occasional surplus of grain, or for the products of their manual skill, or for their "professional" services, they would seek to obtain small or big stock in return. In the old Shona society, however, livestock could hardly be regarded as economic property in Western sense, since its economic use was strictly limited. Milk and meat formed no regular part of the daily diet,

---

[28] Temporary control is never a property right; some degree of permanent access must be guaranteed before a society can be said to have a law of property: Herskovits op cit n18 324.

[29] Similarly Polanyi argued that the economy could not be said to be an autonomous system: Pearson *The Livelihood of Man* 51–2.

manure was not used as fertilizer, and until animal-drawn ploughs became popular about a generation ago, cattle had no function in the cultivation of crops. It is true that livestock always had a ready exchange value when a family had to replenish its exhausted stock of staple foods, but such exchanges (*kusunza*) were emergency transactions which formed no part of the normal pattern of family economy. The primary use of livestock was for the purposes of marriages and the propitiation of ancestral spirits. Even stock acquired by women was used for these purposes for the benefit of her own blood-relatives. In these purposes the traditional idea of wealth in Shona society is revealed. Wealth meant the capacity to maintain and reproduce one's own kin-group as an organic unit and to safeguard its spiritual and material well being by being able to propitiate the ancestral spirits. Prolific reproduction of the family was also the natural way to an enhanced social-status and political power. The acquisition of wealth for any other than these organic and primary needs was meaningless.

This particular conception of wealth established a very close correlation between livestock (especially cattle) and women. Cattle were thought of in terms of wives; wives meant children for one's kin-group; of these children the daughters represented a potential or actual value in cattle which provided wives for the sons and in this manner yet another generation of the family. In this sense cattle, wives and daughters, all having a procreative potentiality, were regarded as interchangeable values.

Nhaka, the Shona term for a deceased's estate, includes, besides livestock and other property, also a man's widows and daughters. This does not mean that women were ever regarded as "property" in the ordinary sense. But it does mean that the estate was primarily regarded as the capacity of the kin-group to reproduce itself, and that wives and children—that is, their reproductive value—were regarded as natural "assets" of the estate. Since the reproductive assets of the estate were by far the most important—in fact, at the *kurovaguva* ceremony of a deceased person the distribution of "non-reproductive" property was of relatively small importance—the Shona conception of estate was "organic" rather than "economic" in the Western sense.

Corresponding with these basic ideas, individual rights to property were largely limited to those goods which had a personal value rather than a reproductive value, such as clothing, weapons, tools, ornaments. In respect of such articles everybody, man, woman or child, could exercise a virtually unrestricted right of ownership.

As a rule a person was entitled to the fruits of his or her own labour and would be able to exercise ownership over property so acquired. But rights to property tended to assume a communal element, either when it resulted from the common efforts of members of the family, or when its usefulness was not confined to the individual, as in the case of foodstuffs and livestock. When property was of such a nature that it served the common interests of the family, these interests had to be considered. Individual claims on the ground of personal production or acquisition would still be recognized, but these claims could be overruled when the wider interests of the family prevailed.

In principle a father could claim the earnings of his unmarried children and exercise control over any property acquired by them. Children capable of doing productive work had to help their parents with the production of food and with other duties. But both boys and girls were encouraged to make their own toys and tools in their spare time, to cultivate their "own" tiny plots allotted to them by their father and to use the produce to barter their "own" fowls and small stock. The fruits of these special efforts were recognized as their own property, to be used for their own individual benefits, often with the idea of marriage in mind. The older boys and girls could thus contribute to their own *rovoro* or trousseau. On this modest scale parents stimulated the acquisition of personal property and duly respected their children's individual right to their possessions.

Sometimes a father gave his young son a goat or heifer in recognition of his services as a herd boy or farm hand or he would allot (*kugova*) such an animal to him to find out whether the child was "lucky" (*a na ropa rakanhaka*, he has good blood), in the hope that the animal would prove unusually prolific under the child's care. Such property, too, was individual in the sense that it was meant primarily as a nest egg for this particular child, the nucleus of his future *rovoro*, to which the child would be entitled in preference to all others.

A married woman could also acquire personal property by making a special effort *apart* from her duties and responsibilities regarding husband and children. When these activities did not interfere with her normal obligations as a housewife, her husband had no right whatever to *any* property which she acquired by making pots, acting as a midwife, or by growing surplus crops. . . .

Every person, however, would, even on the most modest scale, ultimately seek to invest in that kind of property which represented "wealth", i.e., livestock, whether small or big. But the essential value of livestock as property was not based on personal usefulness but on its inherent capacity to help maintain and reproduce the kin-group, and in this respect the interests of the individual owners merged with those of his or her blood-relatives. By acquiring livestock a person increased the potential reproductive capacity of the family estate. Consequently, even when such vital assets were individually acquired, the family of the owner (in the case of a married woman: her children and the children of her mother) naturally assumed a legitimate interest in them, thus curbing individual ownership. The owner could not, for instance, dispose of such property without at least consulting the head of his family. The measure of this control varied with the personal status of the owner and the importance attached to the property. An unmarried person would certainly not be allowed to dispose of a goat or calf acquired by his own efforts without the permission of his father. The father could in principle even overrule his child's right and make use of such property against the child's will, but he would in practice never do so except in an emergency when the interests of the family demanded it. Married men or women would also be expected to seek the approval of the head of their respective families before disposing of their own livestock, but since they were no longer directly dependent upon the support of their family they could, if they insisted, act against the advice of their elders. But even a married person could hardly maintain his individual right if the common interests of his family claimed his property. Under such circumstances, to deny one's family the benefit of one's personal property, would amount to a denial of the organic unity of one's family and reveal a complete misconception of "wealth" and estate.

In short, the *nature* of the property rather than the manner of its acquisition, determined the character of the rights pertaining to it. Individual rights could be freely exercised over property which had no value in connexion with the organic needs of the kin-group (such as personal clothing, tools, ornaments, weapons). But property such as livestock or essential foodstuffs, which served organic or ritual needs, had communal value and was therefore regarded as part of the family estate. Individual acquisition would give a person a claim to such property in preference to all others. But if the common interests of the family demanded it, these individual rights could be overruled because the very nature of the property precluded a strictly individual conception of ownership. . . .

In this connexion it should also be mentioned that land, whether cultivated or uncultivated, was never regarded as "wealth" or even "property" in the ordinary sense, and therefore did not form part of a person's estate. The kind of shifting cultivation practised by the Shona was not conducive to permanent land rights. Informants explained: "Land is not property (*cinhu*), it is something you use for a time and then abandon." And although a son or daughter might be given the plot cultivated by the deceased father or mother in preference to other relatives, such arrangements did not form part of the distribution of a deceased person's estate.

Systems of succession reveal what property is valued by the culture concerned. According to Holleman a Shona estate included only the items that facilitated *reproduction* of the family. Livestock, particularly cattle[30] with their diverse uses for food, draught, clothing, marriage,[31] and ritual, are of central importance in most African socio-economic systems.[32] Two other types of property can be distinguished: personal artifacts, like tools and clothing, and land. In the former individual rights are recognized,[33] but because such belongings have little significance in either the productive or reproductive processes, they are normally distributed as momento mori or are destroyed on the death of the holder.[34] In Holleman's account land did not form part of the estate but elsewhere in southern Africa there is evidence that rights of access (as opposed to the physical corpus) do become heritable.[35] Whether or not this happens depends largely on population density, land shortages and soil impoverishment.[36]

It is, of course, implicit in what has been said above that certain economic activities determine the social importance of particular types of property, and that the nature of property, together with the skill or labour involved in acquiring or creating it, yield legal rights.[37] Scarcity is a critical condition. In the case of land, shortage causes competition for diminishing resources, and thereby a need to regulate use and access. Whenever a living cannot simply be appropriated from the environment at will and emphasis has come to be placed on individual effort, ownership or a like institution will ensue. This proposition was recently demonstrated[38] in a study of two Malagasy peoples. The Merina conceived of property rights as relationships between persons and their land; their agriculture was based on a shortage of land and an abundance of labour, especially slave labour. The Zafimaniry, by contrast, conceived of property as a relationship between persons *in respect of* land. They, however, had free access to new lands and a relative shortage of labour.[39]

Valuable assets are invariably the mark of power and authority.[40] In this regard, in all parts of southern Africa, control of livestock and land confers social

---

[30] Because of bridewealth they are conflated with women in the reproductive process. It does not follow that women and cattle are dealt with in the same way. So far as deceased estates are concerned, rights to women are important because guardianship over them entitles the heir to their bridewealth when they marry: *Masuku* 1945 NAC (N&T) 41; *Ngcobo v Mkize* 1950 NAC 249 (NE).

[31] See above, 200.

[32] Kuper op cit n21 150–1; Soga 38–9; Krige 188. Note the linguistic relationship between wealth, authority and power: Kiernan in Goody op cit n17 366.

[33] Hunter 119 and 129–30; Schapera 228–9. See above, 238.

[34] As a symbol of the possessor's demise. See Kiernan in Goody op cit n17 368; Hunter 119.

[35] Schapera 202; Jeppe *Bophuthatswana: land tenure and development* 32.

[36] There are several accounts of customary-law systems, that previously did not countenance the inheritance of land, permitting heirs to take over the deceased's rights: Duncan 92; Ashton 149. Cf Hamnett *Chieftainship and Legitimacy* 77–82. Reader 71 ascribes this to a process of westernization. See further: Preston-Whyte & Sibisi (1975) 34 *Afr Studies* 283 and James (1988) 14 *Social Dynamics* 36.

[37] Bentsi-Enchill op cit n18 para 173.

[38] Bloch *Marxist Analyses and Social Anthropology* 203ff.

[39] This study confirmed the findings of Leach's *Pul Eliya*, an investigation of people engaged in rice agriculture in Sri Lanka. See too: Pashukanis *Law and Marxism* 122–4 and Seagle *The History of Law* 252–60.

[40] It was shown in the case of bridewealth, eg, that certain property is constituted marital property and is managed by the seniors to sustain their positions of power and control. See above, 199.

prestige.[41] In the following extract[42] Gluckman describes the intricate relationship between property and social relationships.

[121] GLUCKMAN in *IDEAS AND PROCEDURES IN AFRICAN CUSTOMARY LAW* 259–63

But no one owns a food or chattel absolutely, because his kinsfolk and even outsiders may
have claims upon it which he has difficulty in denying. The extreme form of a claim of this
kind is seen in the Lozi institution of *kufunda*, which is defined in the standard Lozi
dictionary as a "legal theft". *Kufunda* allowed any kinsman or kinswoman of a Lozi to take
anything belonging to the latter, without exposing himself or herself to the charge of
stealing which would be levied against outsiders. The Lozi attached such importance to
this privilege of kinship that when their king and council signed a treaty to come under
the protection of the British South Africa Company they specifically stated in it that
kufunda was to be allowed and not to be liable to prosecution. Many years later the king
ruled it to be theft, but I never heard of anyone prosecuting a kinsman for it, though
I knew of families that suffered severely under the depredations of ne'er-do-wells. They
accepted the depredations, even if with a lot of grumbling. Eventually one family sued in
the king's court to have a man of this sort declared no longer to be a kinsman of theirs:
while he was kin they felt they could not deny him this privilege; if he ceased to be a
kinsman he lost the privilege. The court agreed. *Kufunda* in this large African tribe
corresponds closely with what Firth calls "forced exchanges" in the small island of Tikopia
in Oceania. These are extreme forms of a rule which is very common, though the privilege
may be restricted to particular categories of kinsfolk.

In cattle-owning tribes it is almost impossible to work out who is the "real" owner of
cattle in a herd, for most cattle are also subject to claims by others for various reasons.
I illustrate this situation again from the Lozi. When a Lozi girl marries as an ostensible
virgin her bridegroom presents two beasts to her kin. He pays the first beast to make the
girl his wife, the second is for her untouched fertility. Should he divorce her and she has
not conceived, he is entitled to recover the second beast handed over with its progeny. This
is, therefore, called "the beast of herding", ie the bride's kin merely herd it for the husband
until he has impregnated their "daughter". They have the right to hold it and to sue for
it, against the world including the groom, but it is not theirs: it is still the husband's,
though he cannot claim it without divorcing his wife.

The husband's obligations are discharged provided he receives her from, and gives cattle
to, an apparently accredited guardian with whom she is living, whether this guardian be
of her paternal or her maternal kin. Whichever side of her family receives the two beasts
should give one to the other. Within each of these groups, if the recipient slaughters the
beast, he should divide the meat among his kin. Different kinsmen are entitled to specific
portions of the beast: the bride, for instance, gets the tongue, "for is she not the owner of
the beast since she brought it to the village?"

If a bride is not a virgin, only one beast is given. If it is killed by the person who receives
it, he should share the meat with the bride's kin on both sides according to fixed rules. If
the beast is kept to breed, say by the father of the bride, he must give the mother's family
the first and then all alternate calves. Thus he owns the beast but not all its offspring.

Courts will enforce all these claims by the bride's mother's family against the father's,
or vice versa: but claims within each family are not enforceable at law; they are moral
claims only, since kin should not sue one another. But any kinsman who feels he was
neglected could reject responsibility if the spouses or their children ran into difficulty. He
would say: "I know nothing of this marriage."

The rules for distribution of the marriage-cattle—which I have given in simple
form—show how a chattel, like land, may be subject to a cluster of rights held by different

---

[41] See the comment by Moore (1979) 7 *Int J Sociology L* 23.
[42] Another version of which can be found in *Politics, Law and Ritual in Tribal Society* 36–50.

persons in terms of their relationships within the network of kinship ties. In fact, their rights to claim on the marriage-cattle define their kinship relationships to the central parties. If they are not given their shares, this denies their kinship: hence they state they did not know of the marriage. The law of property is again intricately intertwined with the law of status. It means that to understand the holding of property, we must investigate the system of status relationships; and to describe the system of status relationships, we must deal constantly with relationships of property.

III IDEAS OF PROPERTY AND THE SOCIAL SENTIMENTS OF STATUS

Even among ourselves this is to some extent true. To describe family relations, we have to bring in the provision of goods and services by parents for children. If parents do not provide these they are liable to prosecution. But children no longer bear a corresponding *legal* obligation to provide goods and services for their parents, save when these are destitute, and siblings (brothers and sisters) have no such legal obligation to one another. In tribal society these obligations are strong and spread widely. A man's variegated relationships with others run through his chattels as well as his land; and the measure of how far he feels the correct sentiments in those relationships is the way he deals with his property and his produce. Anyone who feels he or she has been stinted will conclude that the other does not feel the right sentiments of love, demanded of their relationship. This is why in tribal life persons watch, apparently greedily, what their kinsmen do with their goods; and why bitter disputes can arise over amounts which appear negligible to us—such as being overlooked in the distribution of a small pot of beer. It is not the beer that counts: the invitation to drink is a symbol of recognition of kinship. The African has to eke out his distribution of his products with great skill, lest he offend some kinsman or woman. We ourselves feel hurt in similar situations: but however our kin and friends may offend us, it is not essential for our survival that they should feel the right sentiments and recognize their obligations to us. Our living depends on a wide series of impersonal relationships in the economic and political systems.

Another crucial fact arises from this situation. Ownership cannot be absolute, for the critical thing about property is the role that it plays in a nexus of specific relationships. Hence in Africa there is no clear definition of ownership: when an African court makes a decision on a dispute over property it states that X stands in a masterful position in relation to that specific object, privilege, or person, as against some other person who is counter-claiming—ie the decision is made as between persons related in specific ways.

Property law in tribal society defines not so much rights of persons over things, as obligations owed between persons in respect of things. Indeed, since there is relatively little in the way of goods, the critical property rights which a man or woman enjoys are demands on other persons in virtue of control over land and chattels—not as with ourselves, any set of persons, but persons related in specific long-standing ways with one another. Correspondingly, if new relationships are being established, this is done through transfers of property, which create and define these relationships, as I have illustrated with marriage-cattle. Men similarly make payments when they enter into allegiance to a superior. Indeed gifts are given at all changes of relationships, as we give them; but in tribal society these gifts are believed to recognize and validate the new relationship of giver and recipient. Goods take on a high symbolic value.

Once we look at the situation of property from this point of view, we understand why a man pays cattle or other goods for a bride. He is not purchasing a woman to be a concubine or a slave: a wife's rights are very different from those of such a person. He is validating the transfer of certain rights over the bride from her kin to himself, and establishing "friendship"—in-law relationship—with his wife's kin. The marriage-gifts also signify that he accepts the obligations of his status as husband, and that his own kin, who contributed to the payment, accept obligations to their new daughter- or sister-in-law and the rest of her family. We are misled if we think of a wife in this situation as a chattel of her father to dispose of as he pleases, to become a chattel to her husband.

Father or husband may speak of himself as "owner" of the woman: but this is shorthand for saying they have rights over her against each other, and accept duties towards her. The stress in this situation is on obligation to others. . . .

I believe that this analysis, with its emphasis on status and obligation, bears out Maine's century-old generalization, that "the movement of progressive societies has hitherto been a movement from *Status* to *Contract*".

The customary-law emphasis on person-to-person relationships and the seemingly incidental role afforded property should be compared with the emphasis that western legal systems place on a person's *right* to property. Gluckman notes that 'Barotse law defines not so much the rights of persons over things as the duties between persons in respect of things'.[43] In other words, property rights in customary law remain embedded in social relations: whether one is entitled to a certain thing is not thought of in terms of interdicts or vindicatory actions, but rather in terms of obligations generated by family relationships or torts.

The following case demonstrates a brief interaction between common and customary law. The suit involved the defendant's wife and a group of women who took an ox belonging to the plaintiff. Their reason for doing so was an entitlement arising from the plaintiff's seduction of the defendant's daughter. Although customary law would have permitted this, the court obviously disapproved, and condemned the act as an illegal spoliation. In a typically common-law fashion, preference was given to the security of property holding.

[122] *NOBANGULA v NONKOBE* 1948 NAC 64 (S) at 67–8

The custom of *isehewula* or *nqutu* is an accepted custom in Native Law but it is not practised by all tribes. . . .

The Assessors who were consulted in this matter and whose replies are appended unanimously state that this custom is foreign to the Tembu and Pondomise tribes and is practised by the Hlubi and Fingo tribes. . . .

It is specifically provided in section 11(1) of Act No. 38 of 1927 that the Native Commissioner is given a discretion to decide questions between Native and Native according to Native Law applying to the customs concerned except in so far as such Native Law shall have been repealed or modified. The Native Law applied however shall not be opposed to the principles of public policy or natural justice.

In *Mltoya v Mngayi* 1 NAC 182, it is stated that the nqutu custom being based on spoliation is no longer operative. In *Tlaba v Jordan* 3 NAC 207, and in *Mehlomane v Kwatsha* 1 NAC 33, it is clearly laid down that the custom in its true essentials does not permit of spoliation and amongst those tribes to whom the custom applies and provided the custom is followed under circumstances in which there is no suggestion of spoliation it would appear that the custom is on all fours with the right of action for damages at Common Law for seduction and might be considered to be in accordance with the principles of public policy and natural justice.

Now it seems that instead of this custom being repealed or modified there is evidence that its application is spreading to tribes which formerly did not apply it. This case is one in point. . . . It may therefore be accepted that the custom, not having been modified or repealed but rather extended in its application, is one in respect of which the Native Commissioner is entitled to take cognisance in the exercise of the discretion conferred on him by section 11(1) of Act No. 38 of 1927. From his judgment the Assistant Native

---

[43] Op cit n15 163. See too Krige & Krige 42.

Commissioner clearly applied Native Law and custom and there is nothing to say that in so doing he did not exercise his discretion judicially. That point was not raised in argument but we nevertheless feel it necessary to mention it.

Briefly the facts in this case are that defendant's daughter eloped with a man Mangwana and after a short absence was returned to her people and found to have been deflowered. From defendant's case it appears that some negotiations occurred and at the close thereof defendant's wife and some other women proceeded to plaintiff's kraal informed him that they demanded an isihewula beast and subsequently they took it off the commonage. This beast was slaughtered in accordance with custom and this action resulted therefrom. There is a conflict of evidence between that adduced by plaintiff and that adduced by defendant, the former denying the prior negotiations, liability as kraalhead for the seducer and that any opportunity was afforded him of replacing the seized beast with another. Defendant's case is that these essentials of the custom were followed but we are not required to decide which party is to be believed because our decision has been arrived at on other grounds (ie that according to the applicable customary law this entitlement did not exist).

This is not to deny that customary law may protect the immediate holder of property from undue disturbance of possession. But the popular conception of ownership as a nexus between a person and a thing is a peculiarly western idea.[44] The common-law notion of property is also distinguished by a tendency to expand the right of control to an 'absolute', viz a maximum power, classically expressed as the rights to use, enjoy and dispose of property.[45] The common law exhibits another tendency: to agglomerate these powers in a single person, preferably the one who happens to be in possession.[46] These are the popular connotations of the word 'ownership', which are implied by its companion epithet 'absolute'.

Ownership is a central organizing concept which is one of the bases for the division of the common law into different categories, such as persons, things, and obligations. The classification of rules is typical of mature legal systems. Customary law, by contrast, tends not to be differentiated.[47] It is generally supposed that the more complex a society becomes, the more complex its law becomes, and practicality dictates the need to sort rules into different groups. Classification is usually associated with specialist legal institutions, notably a judiciary and a legislature, having more or less exclusive responsibilities for applying and making rules.[48]

Recently interest was revived in Pashukanis, a Soviet legal theorist of the 1920s. He showed how commodity exchanges yielded the legal conception of property, and concomitantly contract and legal personality.[49] The emergence of these forms was occasioned by the capitalist mode of production. Before this, simple appropriation of property from the environment necessitated no more than a use-value conception. But when goods became involved in a system of

---

[44] One challenged only quite recently: Hohfeld *Fundamental Legal Conceptions* 76ff; Gluckman *Ideas and Procedures in African Customary Law* 94 and 149.

[45] Herskovits op cit n18 325.

[46] Donahue in Pennock & Chapman *Property* 32–4.

[47] A point made by Maine *Ancient Law* 152–3.

[48] At the same time as Hart's 'secondary' rules appear: see above, 4. See Moore op cit n41 17–19.

[49] Op cit n39.

exchanges, their value was no longer merely their usefulness to the holder; they acquired an abstract value relative to other commodities caught up in the exchange process. Exchange of commodities implied that their values were equivalent, and a relationship of equivalence was made possible by the existence of a particular commodity—cash. This was the universal means by which the value of every other commodity could be expressed.[50] The appearance of commodity exchange is, according to Pashukanis, accompanied by a more widespread and profound legal revolution. That commodities are

> 'exchangeable is a distinct quality, one solely dependent on the will of the possessor, and one which presupposes that they are owned and alienable. At the same time, therefore, that the product of labour becomes a commodity and a bearer of value, man acquires the capacity to be a legal subject and bearer of rights.'[51]

Hence a dichotomy between legal subject and legal object appears.[52]

Legal forms (and in this regard ownership is a good example) provide a simple conceptual apparatus, amenable to use in diverse social and economic contexts. Prior to the existence of ownership, customary law recognized a variety of highly specific rights in property, many of which existed concurrently in respect of the same thing. Commerce, however, requires property to be loosened from this complex network of conventional rights and obligations; property has to be freed of particularistic claims and entitlements so that it can be freely bought and sold in the market place.[53]

The transition from a subsistence to a market economy is the great watershed in legal development. It had not occurred in southern Africa before the colonial conquest,[54] which can be gauged, inter alia, from the absence of a category of property (and with it the legal form of ownership) in customary law. Property was still embedded in personal obligations. Any possibility of an endogenous growth of customary law was then thwarted by the introduction of common law.[55]

The market place has since exerted an irresistible force, ascribing an exchange (and thus cash) value to all types of property, notably land, labour, and marriage goods; and, in the face of competition from the market, the old symbolic values of property have disappeared.[56] Increasing poverty obviously tends to accentuate

---

[50] See Balbus (1976–7) 11 *Law & Soc R* 573–5.

[51] Op cit n39 112.

[52] Pashukanis' thesis has been criticized on various grounds. See Warrington (1981) 9 *Int J Sociology L* 1ff and the reply by Norrie (1982) 10 *Int J Sociology L* 419ff. One especially pertinent criticism is his assumption that commodity production existed prior to the legal construction of property: Warrington in Sugarman *Legality, Ideology and the State* 51–2. As Norrie op cit 423 says, the relationship is actually one of symbiosis.

[53] Thompson in Goody op cit n17 341.

[54] Reader 40–1; Marwick 178; Mönnig 184.

[55] The only detailed study of the impact on customary law of capitalism and the associated systems of western law is Snyder's *Capitalism and Legal Change*, a work on a people of the Casamance region of Senegal. He rejected any simplistic proposition that capitalism destroyed all indigenous economic and legal institutions. Cf Wolpe *The Articulation of Modes of Production* 1–3. Instead he argued that customary law had been *transformed*, a process whereby: the same legal form might serve different socio-economic functions; certain forms might disappear entirely; or new ones fashioned on capitalist models might appear.

[56] Gluckman op cit n42 270–1. And see above, 201 regarding bridewealth.

self-interested claims to property, thereby undermining the family ethic of generosity.[57] Moreover, because labour stresses the individual's productive effort, it tends to emphasize individual interest in the fruits of labour.[58] Family integrity, which could be expressed by building multiple interests in land and livestock, is not realizable in terms of cash. Money has little, if any, symbolic function. It is needed to gratify immediate needs, and is not regarded as a family fund in the way that livestock would be. So cash tends to be treated pragmatically as a means to an end.[59]

(2) The courts' response and 'new' property

The South African courts have been uncertain how to respond to the apparent lacuna of concepts in customary law. Rather than inquire into what was obviously a controversial topic, they avoided it altogether. This they could do by giving *remedies* whenever these seemed applicable,[60] even though it was doubtful whether customary law contained a spoliation remedy.[61] Another avoidance technique was simply to apply the common law, on the ground that customary law knew of no such thing as 'ownership'.[62] On the few occasions that the courts were compelled to pronounce on customary rights of land tenure, they borrowed heavily from the common law. Thus it was held that the tribe had an 'absolute' or 'allodial' title to land and that individuals had only 'usufructuary' rights.[63]

The common law of property itself is arguably in no position to articulate the fundamental social changes that have been occurring in respect of property. Some people now speak of the collapse of conventional or orthodox property law.[64] One of the reasons for this upheaval is the appearance of the so-called 'new' property.[65] The common-law concept of ownership was elaborated with reference mainly to tangible property, especially the products of individual labour. 'New' property consists of social welfare benefits, pensions, occupational licences, social insurance schemes, subsidies and the provision of housing and related services. According to conventional thinking none of this is considered to be property. Instead, it is treated as a gratuity from the state or corporate employer and a privilege for the recipient. By implication the 'new'

---

[57] Hunter 130–2 and 139–44 regarding consumer tastes and individual interests.

[58] See Mönnig 183.

[59] Reader 46.

[60] See, eg, *Ndamase v Sokwilibana* 1 NAC 230 (1909); *Nomosa v Njandini* 1944 NAC (C&O) 48 and especially *Yeko v Qana* 1973 (4) SA 735 (A), cited in *Mogodielo v Ntsoko* 1980 AC 165 (C).

[61] *Mazibuko v Kumalo* 1968 BAC 25 (NE).

[62] *Mhlonga v Dube & another* 1950 NAC 164 (NE); *Nhlanhla v Mokweno* 1952 NAC 286 (NE). See too the Zimbabwe cases: *Komo & another v Holmes NO* 1935 SR 86 at 94; *Dokotera v The Master & others* 1957 R & N 697 (SR) and *Gwebu* 1961 R & N 694 (SR).

[63] *Noveliti v Ntwayi* 2 NAC 170 (1911); *Dyasi* 1935 NAC (C&O) 1 at 9; *Gaboetloeloe v Tsikwe* 1945 NAC (C&O) 2; cf *Luke* 4 NAC 133 (1920).

[64] Grey and Donahue in Pennock & Chapman op cit n46 69ff and 56 respectively.

[65] Reich (1964) 73 *Yale LJ* 733ff.

property is revocable at the instance of the donor, and subject to any terms and conditions that the donor may choose to impose.[66]

Two decisions must be taken: whether to protect the recipient's right to such 'new' property generally, or (as at present) only in specific cases; and, if general protection is to be afforded, whether to do so via greater administrative regulation or by further development of the concept of private property (seemingly the more difficult course).[67] Bureaucratic regulation in fact appears to be the already established determinant of individual access to new property,[68] but this does not necessarily mean greater security for the individual:

'. . . [W]hile old property is insufficient, new property may be precarious. More loosely held in his family, more closely bound to the world of work, and furnished by the state with minimum subsistence, the individual appears less free than isolated; less secure than vulnerable—to the will of "distant majorities" and the upheavals of economic crisis.'[69]

III ESTATE DEBTS

Because succession in customary law is onerous/universal the heir inherits not only the deceased's assets but also his debts; this means that the estate could quite possibly be insolvent.[70] Customary law, however, gives no intimation whether an heir facing such a predicament could refuse to accept the estate. Instead it seems that he could be bound to pay the debts, if necessary out of his own pocket.

There is no easy method of determining insolvency in customary law because it has no winding-up procedure.[71] In any event the situation of the estate may improve, as income (such as daughters' bridewealth and the earnings of junior inmates) continues to accrue to it, or it may worsen as more debts come to light or are incurred. It is an open question whether the heir may use the common-law remedy of a declaration of insolvency to avoid meeting the estate obligations in full.[72]

The heir's burdens are exacerbated by the absence of any rule of extinctive prescription in customary law;[73] thus a debt incurred by the deceased survives him indefinitely. On this basis the courts have sustained a variety of highly personal claims: refund of bridewealth; return of a wife who had deserted her

---

[66] The significance of such 'assets' for a deceased estate becomes clear in the case of rights to urban accommodation in South Africa. In principle any permit or certificate will lapse on the death of a holder, although a dependant or heir has preference on the re-allotment of the site or dwelling: reg 17(2) of the Regulations Governing the Control and Supervision of an Urban Black Residential Area R1036 14 June 1968 *Reg Gaz* 976, as amended. Under the regulations governing rural land held by the state, s 52(2) of the Black Areas Land Regulations R188 11 July 1969 *Reg Gaz* 1154, the security of the widow's tenure is preserved until she dies or remarries.

[67] See Tay in Kamenka et al *Law and Society* 13–17.

[68] Glendon *The New Family and the New Property* ch 5.

[69] Glendon op cit 97.

[70] *Maguga v Scotch* 1931 NAC (N&T) 54; *Mekoa v Masemola* 1939 NAC (N&T) 61; *Letlotla v Bolofo* 1947 NAC (C&O) 16.

[71] Cf Kerr 134–7, who deals with *distribution* of the estate.

[72] See Poulter 255 and Ramolefe in Gluckman op cit n44 207.

[73] *Lequoa v Sipamla* 1944 NAC (C&O) 85; *Mafuleka v Dinga* 1945 NAC (N&T) 54; s 113(2) of the Natal and KwaZulu Codes; cf Labuschagne (1987) 50 *THRHR* 87ff.

husband;[74] return of livestock loaned in terms of a sisa or nqoma contract;[75] repayment of interhouse debts;[76] and damages for seduction or adultery.[77] In two cases it was held that a deceased's liability could not be transmitted to the heir because it was personal and died with him, but both involved delicts governed by Pondo law[78] which makes it difficult to extrapolate a general rule.

In view of some of the claims lodged against estates it is perhaps not surprising that one court held the principle of onerous succession is contrary to natural justice;[79] and there is a clearly discernible trend to limit its scope. Accordingly, in the case of common-law debts, the heir's liability is restricted to the assets of the estate.[80] Moreover, s 81(8) of the Natal and KwaZulu Codes provides that an heir is liable for estate debts only to the extent of the assets to which he succeeds;[81] but it has been held that because this provision overrides customary law, it must be strictly interpreted.[82]

Although there is no hard-and-fast rule in customary law specifying the time when outstanding debts should be paid, it is usual to make a demand at the ceremony at which the deceased's spirit is laid to rest.[83] A creditor should lodge his claim with the deceased's senior heir, and, if the debt involved a benefit received by one of the junior houses, the senior heir may arrange for reimbursement to be paid from the house concerned.[84]

IV SUCCESSION TO THE HEAD OF A FAMILY

(1) The order of succession

Rules of intestate succession are an adumbration of the kinship system concerned. From the pool of the deceased's relatives someone must be found to assume the responsibilities implicit in his status and to take over management of the family estate. This may involve several conflicting demands. On the one hand, there is a need for certainty in order to facilitate the transmission of rights and duties without the lengthy deliberation and discord that would be caused by rival claimants. On the other hand, a preordained heir might be tempted to usurp

---

[74] *Letlotla v Bolofo* 1947 NAC (C&O) 16; *Mahloane v Mohale* 1947 NAC (C&O) 95; *Hlatshwayo v Buthelezi* 1977 BAC 252 (NE).

[75] *Nompenxela v Manqomntu* 1952 NAC 142 (S).

[76] *Sijila v Masumba* 1940 NAC (C&O) 42; *Ngcobo* 1946 NAC (N&T) 14.

[77] *Mayekiso v Sifuba & another* 3 NAC 247 (1917); *Kawu v Meji* 5 NAC 85 (1924).

[78] *Ngiyafa v Nkwebane* 4 NAC 9 (1922); *Mgadlwa v Makupula* 1947 NAC (C&O) 22.

[79] *Santyisi v Msinda* 1935 NAC (C&O) 14; cf *Maguga v Scotch* 1931 NAC (N&T) 54.

[80] *Ngqandulwana v Gomba* 4 NAC 132 (1922); *Santyisi's case* supra; *Nompenxela v Manqomntu* 1952 NAC 142 (S). Conversely, however, if the heir succeeded in terms of the common-law rules of intestate succession, this will have no effect on his liability: *Mfubu v Cembi* 1947 NAC (C&O) 101.

[81] See: *Mhlengwa v Mhlawuli* 1920 NHC 30; *Ngcobo* 1946 NAC (N&T) 14; *Zulu v Mdheltshe* 1952 NAC 203 (NE); cf *Ngcobo v Mkize* 1950 NAC 249 (NE).

[82] *Ngcobo v Mkize* supra. The plaintiff creditor need not establish that the estate assets are sufficient to meet the claim. If the heir wishes to invoke s 81(8), he must show that there is not enough property in the estate: *Twala* 1956 NAC 137 (NE) at 139; *Zungu v Mlungwana* 1966 BAC 2 (NE).

[83] See Child *The History and Extent of Recognition of Tribal Law in Rhodesia* 101.

[84] Harries 46; Van Warmelo & Phophi 863, 873 and 903. But, as Bekker 300 admits, there is no way of knowing whether this is a general rule of customary law. He suggests that the creditor may sue the heir of the house concerned; if he does not know which house is involved, he may simply claim payment from the senior heir: *Ngogodo v Nqwili* 3 NAC 112 (1915).

his predecessor's position,[85] or might prove to be incompetent or unable to fulfil the roles expected of him.

Sufficient property must be left to maintain those members of the family who are not yet capable of looking after themselves. A rigid system of inheritance, which cannot take account of the individual circumstances of each member of the family at the time of death, could yield an inequitable distribution. One person might turn out to be more deserving of assistance than another; the concentration of power and property in the hands of one could provoke ill-feeling and work to the disadvantage of the family as a whole.

The customary-law systems of succession in southern Africa are far from being inflexible; they all contain various devices for avoiding the problems outlined above. In the first place, the common-law distinction between inheritance and inter vivos dispositions of property is arguably not apposite to customary law. In order to secure the coming generation, the head of a family may give a son property to establish an independent homestead or may provide his bridewealth. In other words, there is a *continuous* devolution of property from one generation to another, and it is artificial to consider one specific moment—inheritance—in isolation from the others.[86] In the second place, nearly all systems of customary law give the family some measure of freedom in selecting an heir,[87] at the very least the power to appoint a guardian for an immature heir. Finally, if a potential heir seems unsuitable, the head of a family may have him disinherited.

[123] ALLOTT (1970) 71 *ZEITSCHRIFT FÜR VERGLEICHENDE RECHTSWISSEN-SCHAFT* 112–14

Succession is the working out of the family system over time: one presupposes and depends on the other. African succession systems generally share the following features:

(a) Succession is *non-testamentary*. Wills are rare or unknown, though forms of dispositive succession, such as naming the principal heir, oral bequests, etc., are possible and practised in some of the systems. Because of limitations of space it is necessary to underplay the role of dispositive succession, as I have christened it, in some African customary laws. Thus in many of the southern Bantu societies *inter vivos* arrangements, allocations, earmarkings and distributions by the head of the family may have the effect of completing the framework for the re-distribution of the estate, at the will of the holder, during his lifetime.

(b) Succession is usually *elective* or *discretionary* rather than automatic. By this is meant that the mere fact of death does not usually automatically vest in the heirs the shares to which they are entitled by customary law. Typically there is designation of the successors after the decease by the administrator of the estate or the family group generally, or at least a formal installation of the heir or handing over of the property to the successors. Often the exact share of the estate to which any one person will be entitled will be specified by the family or administrator. The successory process is thus generally in the control of the family.[1]

(c) But discretion is by no means absolute; the range of choice is limited by various principles. Often there is a *preferential heir* or class of heirs, entitled to certain

---

[85] Before the latter's death: Kuper op cit n21 88–9.

[86] Goody op cit n8 311–12. Common law takes some account of inter vivos devolution through the obligation to collate.

[87] This is well illustrated in the case of the Swazi: Kuper op cit n21 88–9.

property unless there is good cause to the contrary. In polygamous households, especially those of the Southern African kraal type, the *inter vivos* allocations of land and cattle by the household head to his dependants, which, during his lifetime, do not pass the title but only concede the right to use, crystallize into vested interests at his death. This often means that each sub-unit or "house" now becomes an autonomous unit of a fraternal family kind.

(d) Most African succession systems are *plural*, by which is meant that a number of persons will be entitled to share, not necessarily on the same basis, in the estate. Where there is a multiplicity of successors, such sharing may take the form of sub-division between those entitled, or the maintenance of the estate as a common family fund, with ultimate title in the unit, but separated rights of use in the various sharers. A minority of African succession laws appear to follow the universal singular system, in which a sole inheritor "steps into the shoes" of the deceased, taking over all his rights and obligations; but it will generally be found that the successor's position is not on all fours with that of his predecessor, and others now have vested rights in the estate.

(e) Many laws recognize *onerous* succession (where there is succession to debts and duties as well as to assets).

(f) Succession often extends beyond the property sphere to the area of family responsibility, so that in the traditional system the principal successor might find himself saddled with the care of the widow(s) and children of the deceased.

(g) Succession often entirely *alters the legal basis* of the title to the estate, it ceasing to be individual property and becoming family property, by which is meant that succession creates a permanent overriding claim or title for the family in the inherited property. The "family" for this purpose is often the lineage as a whole, though with concurrent dependent rights vested in the immediate sub-lineage of deceased. In the alternative the "family" consists of the descendants of the original acquirer, so that different portions of property may be controlled by different sizes of lineage segment.

(h) In any case, succession is often a *continuing process* rather than an event. There is not a single distribution but a gradual handover of rights from the original holder to his successors. Such a handover may take place in the holder's lifetime, or after his death.

The significance of these and related features is that they lead to the creation and maintenance of a permanent family fund; once acquired, land is not lost by the family, except for disaster, emigration or alienation.

Note

1. Cf A K P Kludze (1972) 9 *Univ Ghana LJ* 116–22 and K Bentsi-Enchill (1972) 9 *Univ Ghana LJ* 130–3.

(a) Monogamous families

The rules of succession for monogamous families are the same in all systems of customary law in southern Africa. They are based on the principle of primogeniture.[88] The deceased's heir is his eldest son or, failing him, the eldest son's oldest male descendant, ie the oldest surviving grandson. Failing any male issue in the eldest son's line, succession passes to the second son and his male descendants, and so on through all the sons of the family head.

If the deceased had no male descendants, his father is heir. When the deceased's father is no longer alive, the family head's eldest brother is next in order of succession.[89] If the latter is dead, the eldest brother's eldest son or oldest

---

[88] *Sonti* 1929 NAC (C&O) 23. They may apply even when the deceased was married by civil/Christian rites.

[89] Cf Rubin (1965) 9 *JAL* 97: in Swazi law it would be the deceased's younger brother.

surviving male descendant is heir. Failing the eldest brother and his male descendants, the next brother in order of seniority and his descendants are in line of succession.

Failing any male issue in the first order of male ascendants, the deceased's grandfather succeeds, failing whom, the deceased's eldest paternal uncle or his eldest male descendant. Failing the paternal uncles, in order of seniority, or any of their descendants, the estate would pass to the next order of male ascendants.[90]

ORDER OF SUCCESSION

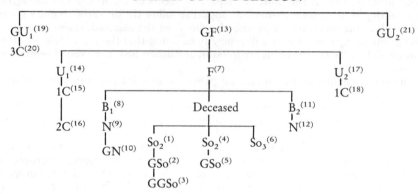

Primogeniture, a major characteristic of the kinship systems of the Southern Bantu, is one of the most hallowed principles of customary law. Yet this great verity has recently been challenged by a study of the inheritance patterns in a Lebowa village.[91] Several practices came to light which did not conform to the orthodoxy of customary law; these included treating land as a heritable commodity,[92] and allowing the *last-born* son to inherit it. The people in the village did not see this as a contradiction of their laws. Instead they treated it as a 'kind of bargain in which the provision of land is exchanged for the security of filial care for aged parents'.[93] For a son to acquire a stake in the limited land available in the homelands, he had to be prepared to acquiesce in the duty of parental support.[94] If he were not willing to do this, the land would be offered to one of the other sons. Ultimogeniture has been noted elsewhere in South Africa,[95] and there is a compelling logic to it. The last-born son is the last to leave home (his brothers have probably been migrants for some time), and in the circumstances, he is the one destined to stay with and care for his parents. He must be given both the means and an incentive to do so.

The Lebowa study introduces a measure of doubt regarding the rules of inheritance depicted above. It suggests that if primogeniture is not functionally

---

[90] A detailed account of the order of succession in South Africa can be found in Kerr 208–17; Olivier 438–40 and Bekker 274–5.

[91] James op cit n36 36ff.

[92] See above, 389.

[93] James op cit n36 32.

[94] James op cit n36 45.

[95] By Webster *Family and Household in KwaDapha, KwaZulu*: James op cit n36 45.

successful in securing family support and cohesion, it will be abandoned for a different rule.

In the unlikely event that the deceased had no male relatives, it seems that his chief could take over the estate, which he would be obliged to use for the care of the family.[96] Today the estate passes to the state.[97] Section 81(5) of the Natal and KwaZulu Codes provides that if there is no male heir any property in the estate devolves according to the rules of intestate succession applicable to a civil marriage. This, of course, would allow inheritance by the deceased's wife and/or daughter(s), an impossibility under customary law. In Lesotho too, customary law has been changed:[98] on failure of male descendants, the widow is entitled to inherit. If the widow is no longer alive, the deceased's father inherits or, failing him, the deceased's grandfather.[99]

(b) Polygynous families

In polygynous households each wife establishes a separate house when she marries, with the result that property accruing to her house must be kept strictly separate from other house property. The rules of succession outlined above are then modified to take into account the interests of the different houses.

Systems of polygyny have been classified as simple or complex.[100] According to the simple system,[101] the heir is the eldest son of the senior wife, or, if he is already dead, his oldest son. If he has no male descendants, the senior wife's second son is heir, or, failing him, his son. Failing any sons or their male descendants in the first house, the next in order of succession is the eldest son of the second married wife and his male descendants, and so forth.

With the Pedi, as with the Tswana and Sotho below, the ranking of wives/houses depends on the time of marriage. The woman whom the deceased married first is his senior wife; the second wife is subordinate to her, the third subordinate to the second, and so forth. The eldest son of the senior wife succeeds to the status of the deceased, together with the property in the great house and any unallotted family property. The oldest sons in each of the other houses inherit the livestock in the house concerned. If any junior house has no heir, it is inherited by the great house. Conversely, if the great house has no heir, it is inherited by the eldest son of the next senior house and so on.[102] Tswana law is the same: the eldest son of the first wife is the general heir, inheriting all the property in the senior house and any other unallotted family property.

---

[96] Cape Commission on Native Laws and Customs 1883 para 7079 p 395.

[97] *Myazi v Nofenti* 1 NAC 74 (1904); cf Kerr 125 who maintains that the estate nowadays passes directly to the state and not to a chief. Bekker 275, however, still supports the view that the estate goes to the chief.

[98] By the Laws of Lerotholi s 11(2).

[99] See Poulter 232.

[100] See above, 226–7.

[101] Followed, inter alios, by the Tsonga: Ramsay 9 and 26; *Maganu* 1938 NAC (N&T) 14; *Sijila v Masumba* 1940 NAC (C&O) 42.

[102] The principle of ultimogeniture is at play here too: the youngest son of each house inherits the purely domestic items in the house: Mönnig 336–7; Harries 39–40 and 42.

Otherwise the eldest son of each house is heir to that house.[103] In Lesotho[104] this regime has been enshrined in the Laws of Lerotholi:

> 'The heir . . . shall be the first male child of the first married wife, and if there is no male in the first house then the first born male child of the next wife married in succession shall be the heir.'[105]

The code introduced one significant departure from customary law: where a house has no male issue, the senior widow is heir.[106]

Under Venda law the wives are ranked as follows. The senior wife is the woman for whom the deceased's father paid bridewealth (in the normal course, she would be the deceased's first wife). The second (and junior) wife would be a maternal uncle's daughter, ie a cross-cousin. The third would be the wife for whom bridewealth was paid from the bridewealth received for the daughter of the first wife. Thereafter rank is decided according to the time of marriage.[107] The order of succession is much the same as above: the eldest son of the first wife is senior heir, and the eldest son of each house inherits the property in that house.

On the basis of a division of the homestead into two and sometimes three parts,[108] the following systems of polygyny are described as complex. A Southern Nguni homestead, for instance, may be divided into two sections: a great and a right-hand side.[109] If there are only two wives (and therefore two houses), the eldest son of each becomes heir to that house; but if one house has no male issue, the eldest son of the other inherits both. If the head of the family married a third wife, she would be affiliated (as a qadi or support) to the great house. The fourth wife would be attached to the right-hand house, the fifth wife to the great house, and so on. The order of precedence is normally established by the time of the marriage,[110] but it can be varied by a public declaration when the wedding takes place.[111]

If one of the houses has no heir, it is inherited by the most senior heir of the section of the homestead to which it was attached. In other words, the heir to a qadi of the great house would be the eldest son of the great house. Conversely, if the great house had no heir, it would be inherited by the heir of its qadis.[112]

---

[103] As a stamp of his authority, the general heir would be entitled to a beast from each of the other houses: Schapera 232–3; *Married Life* 293–5.

[104] Duncan 11.

[105] Section 11(1). Ambiguities in the wording of this section have been exploited to give the family council some latitude in choosing an heir. Hence, if the deceased died without a son, and one was born to a widow as a result of a levirate union, that child might become senior heir. Alternatively an adulterine child might be chosen as heir: Poulter 229ff.

[106] Section 11(2). According to custom, however, she would be expected to consult her deceased husband's relatives when administering the estate. See Poulter 288–9; Ramolefe in Gluckman op cit n44 201.

[107] Stayt 167–8; Van Warmelo & Phophi 817–23.

[108] See above, 224ff.

[109] Kerr 165–6; Cook *Social Organizations and Ceremonial Institutions of the Bomvana* 13–15 and 155–6.

[110] *Mndweza* 1937 NAC (C&O) 142 at 145.

[111] *Gcanga v Gcanga & another* 1949 NAC 137 (S).

[112] *Sonti* 1929 NAC (C&O) 23.

Where none of the houses in one section of the homestead has any heirs, the most senior heir of the other section inherits all of them.[113]

We are told that formerly, although very rarely, the Xhosa homestead could be divided into three sections: a great house, a right-hand house, and a left-hand house (ikohlo). For purposes of succession the left-hand house was considered to be affiliated and subordinate to the great house.[114] Hence if there were no heir in the great house, it could be inherited by the heir to the ikohlo.[115]

A Zulu homestead may be divided into three sections: a great house (indlunkulu), a right-hand house or support (iqadi), and a left-hand house (ikhohlwa).[116] As with the Southern Nguni, junior houses are affiliated to one of the senior houses, and the rank of the houses may be fixed by a public declaration at the time of the wedding.[117] The order of succession is as follows: if there are no sons in the iqadi or any of its affiliated junior houses, recourse is had to the indlunkulu and vice versa. Where the ikhohlwa and its junior houses have no heir, this section is inherited by the heir of the indlunkulu. If there is no heir in both the indlunkulu and iqadi, the heir of the ikhohlwa becomes heir to both sections.[118]

Apparently the homestead can be divided *after* the death of the family head. At a meeting of the family, an ikhohlwa house may be established in order to prevent all the property from being concentrated in one house.[119] Otherwise, s 70(2) of the Codes provides that if the homestead was not divided into sections during the family head's lifetime, the first married wife will be deemed to be the great wife, and the second married wife is deemed a senior wife bearing no specific name. Other houses continue to be ranked after these houses according to the time of the marriage. (See diagram on page 404.)

By way of contrast, the Swazi system of succession allows considerable flexibility in choosing an heir. After the death of the family head, a family meeting (lusendvo) is called at which the senior wife is chosen.[120] Her eldest son then becomes the main heir. In order of importance the considerations determining selection of the senior wife are: whether she was of royal blood; the mode of her marriage; whether she had the same clan name as the deceased's

---

[113] Kerr 217–18. Pondo law is a variation on the above. If there is no heir in the great house, its heir will be the eldest son of the right-hand house to the exclusion of any sons from the junior houses affiliated to the great house. The reverse is true where the right-hand house section has no heirs: *Mbulawa* 1956 NAC 104 (S); Hunter 120.

[114] Soga 54–6; Kerr 165.

[115] And see Bekker 276 regarding the ixhiba house.

[116] Krige 177–8. Section 68(1)(*b*) of the Natal and KwaZulu Codes suggests that commoners may not institute an ikhohlwa; but a better interpretation is that these sections are descriptive rather than mandatory.

[117] *Nkwanyana* 1958 NAC 4 (NE) at 6. Under s 69 of the Natal and KwaZulu Codes commoners may not alter the rank of the great wife (who is normally the first married wife) without special dispensation. There is considerable difficulty in interpreting the conflicting provisions of the Codes partly because of the vagueness of the terminology. See Kerr 169–83 and Stafford & Franklin 168ff.

[118] See Krige 180; *Mjana v Kuba* 1916 NHC 152; s 81(5)(*a*)–(*e*) of the Natal and KwaZulu Codes.

[119] See, eg, *Dhlamini & others v Dhlamini* 1939 NAC (N&T) 95 at 101.

[120] As Kuper op cit n21 91 says, power is inherited from men but it is transmitted through women. If it were to happen that the senior wife had produced no heir, the deceased's first born son could be placed in her house.

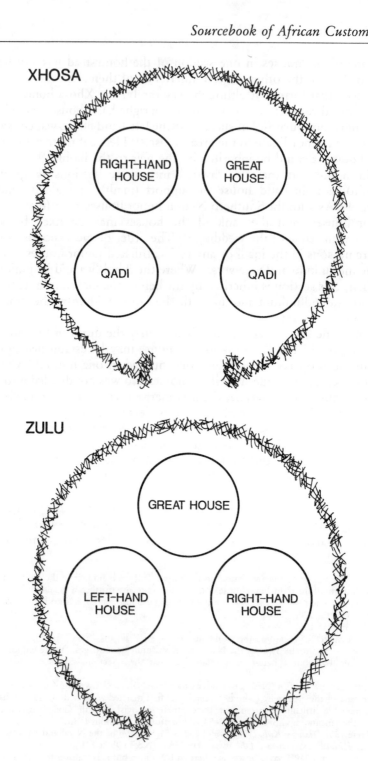

LAYOUT OF POLYGYNOUS HOMESTEADS

mother; and (for commoners) the time of marriage. More generally, the woman's character as well as that of her sons is taken into account. The other houses are each headed by their own heirs, who inherit the house property.[121] According to the Swazi this system has the advantage of suppressing the undue ambitions of offspring during the lifetime of the head of the family. They say that if the heir were known in advance, it could provoke family conflict, and might even tempt the heir to hasten his father's death.[122]

If there are no male descendants in a polygynous household, the order of succession follows the rules outlined in respect of a monogamous marriage, viz succession passes to the deceased's father or, failing him, to the deceased's brothers and their descendants in order of seniority.[123]

(2) Disinheritance

Most systems of customary law[124] permit disinheritance of the heir.[125] The practice bears little resemblance to a testamentary style of succession, however, because although a man may oust his heir, he is not free to choose a replacement. The person next in order of succession must succeed.[126]

The validity of an act of disinheritance depends upon compliance with the following rules. The family head must call a meeting of the family at which the matter is announced; reasons will be given and the issue can be debated. (There is no indication whether the heir has the right to answer any allegations made against him.) A report of the outcome of this meeting should then be sent to the local chief or headman.[127]

Under the common law, disinheritance is one aspect of the general power of testation, which in turn is derived from individual ownership of property. The testator is free to nominate whomever he or she wishes as heir; there is no need to give reasons for the choice and there is no accountability to dependants. In customary law the notion of the joint or family estate would preclude such wide-ranging powers, for the interests of the family must be taken into consideration. By implication the family head has only the very limited power to propose the disinheritance.

The courts have intervened to formalize disinheritance. As a result the nature of the procedure is now ambiguous: is it a private power, like the common-law testamentary freedom, or is it a judicial hearing instigated by the family head?

[124] *MNENGELWA* 1942 NAC (C&O) 2

Because of a son's persistent disregard for his father's authority and because of acute differences between them, the father called together certain members of his family and, in

---

[121] Rubin op cit n89; Kuper op cit n21 91–104; Marwick 48–9.

[122] Kuper op cit n21 88–9.

[123] The order of succession is described in Olivier 440–50 and Bekker 275–9.

[124] Except Swazi law: Rubin op cit n89 107 and Marwick 48. According to Poulter 239–41, this is an unsettled question in Lesotho.

[125] See Schapera 183–4; Van Warmelo & Phophi 743–63.

[126] *Sitole* 1938 NAC (N&T) 35 at 37 and see *Faro* 1950 NAC 224 (S). See generally: Kerr 151–8; Bekker 303–6; Olivier 474–83.

[127] Van Warmelo & Phophi 743–63; Hammond-Tooke 154; Mönnig 331; Whitfield 346–50.

the presence of the son, told them that his son had caused him a great deal of trouble, that he was disinheriting him and instituting another as his heir. [Counsel agreed that an opinion be obtained from African Assessors.]

After consultation the Native Assessors gave the following unanimous opinion which was expressed by Chief Jeremiah Moshesh:

"What we were asked about was Basuto custom. The heir is disinherited but that must be done in a proper way. The first thing a meeting is called and the one to be disinherited is scolded by his relatives for the wrong he has done. After doing that the matter is reported to the Chief. When he does it for the second time he is then brought before the Chief. His father then explains all the wrongs he has done. He is then given an opportunity of defending himself. If he is found guilty he is disinherited as he had been previously warned would happen if he again committed wrongs. There is no other way. If the Court finds the son guilty his father there and then appoints someone to take his place as heir. If we leave that procedure of the Court it would mean that the father of every child would do as he liked. This is to protect the heir.

That is the Basuto custom which we are here to give in this Court.". . . .

This Court considers that the opinion expressed by the Native Assessors goes far beyond the requirements of disinherison as laid down by previous decisions of the Native Appeal Court, and is not prepared to accept that opinion as being applicable at the present time even in the cases in which members of the Basuto tribe are concerned.

In none of the cases to which this Court has referred is it laid down that it is essential to the validity of an act of disinherison that an erring son should first be warned at a meeting of relatives and on repetition of his wrongdoing he should be brought before the Chief and there disinherited. The procedure of disinheriting an heir has been laid down in a number of cases, most of which stress the necessity for reporting to the Chief or Magistrate. In the earlier cases it was said that a father desiring to disinherit his son should call a meeting of the Chiefs and principal men of his clan and state publicly that he was discarding his son giving his reasons for doing so (see *Mbono v Sifuba* 1 NAC 137). . . . In *Tshobo* (4 NAC 140) and *Nvabeni v Sifumba* (5 NAC 65) it was held that a report had to be made to the Chief. . . . This necessity was again stressed in the case of *Nohele* (6 NAC 19) in which the Court said: "In Native Law and Custom a father has the right to disinherit his son for sufficient cause, and in so doing has two courses open to him, namely: (1) By calling together the members of his family, and in their presence and that of the son, publicly declaring that he was disinheriting him, and stating his reasons for so doing; thereafter reporting his action to the Chief or Headman of the clan. A son so disinherited was entitled to an opportunity of disproving his father's allegations. (2) By calling together the members of his family, and, after consultation with them, requesting the Chief to summon the son before him to show cause why he should not be disinherited. If the Chief was satisfied that the son had been guilty of conduct warranting his disinherison, it was competent for him to make the order asked for. If the son, after having been duly summoned, failed to appear before the Chief, it was competent for the order to be made in his absence. There was no appeal against either the declaration of the father or the order of the Chief, but the father had the right to revoke his declaration or apply to the Chief to rescind the order made by him.". . . . This Court is satisfied that it is part of the procedure for disinheriting a son that a report should be made to the Chief and failure to do so invalidates the alleged act of disinherison. It was argued that the report to the Chief was a mere technicality and not an essential, but this Court is not prepared to concede this. If the necessity for reporting to the Chief were done away with the heir would have no safeguard and might be disinherited at a hole-in-the-corner meeting. While a Chief might have no right to interfere with a declaration made by a father he would require to be satisfied that a proper meeting had been held and this would act as deterrent to caprice on the part of the father.

In the present case, even if the meeting referred to in the evidence can be regarded as a proper one, a point on which we consider there is some doubt, we are of opinion that failure to report to the proper authorities invalidated the proceedings. This being so the Native Commissioner was justified in entering a judgment of absolution from the instance.

Although it is apparent in this judgment that reasons must be given for disinheritance, it is not clear whether there is a closed list or whether any reason would suffice. Commonly cited examples are: incompetence of the heir (due to some mental or physical defect); serious antagonism between the heir and family head; persistent disobedience; and prodigality.[128]

It is not clear what purpose is served by the report of the family meeting, which the courts insist be sent to the local chief, headman, or commissioner.[129] In *Nohele*,[130] the court said that this was no mere technicality, and according to *Mnengelwa's* case, it publicizes the act of disinheritance. It is uncertain, however, whether the report provides an occasion for a review or appeal: does it give the heir an opportunity to contest the family council's decision? The requirement that reasons be given at the meeting would suggest that the heir does have some right of hearing. On the other hand, it has been held that disinheritance is not a judicial matter, but a private power vested in the head of the family.[131] If this is the case, his decision is not appealable.[132] It is still uncertain whether the decision-making power vests in the family or the head of family, and it is unclear whether the courts mean the decision of the family council alone, or that of the chief (or commissioner) too.

Presumably the family council must observe principles of natural justice. Thus, if the heir were not given a fair hearing or if the decision to disinherit were tainted by fraud, any customary rule precluding an appeal to a court could be disregarded.

An alternative procedure is a hearing before a chief or headman's court, where the heir can be summoned and complaints against him investigated. The disinheritance thereby becomes an order of the court.[133] In this case, if the heir does not appear, the court may make the order in his absence. There is no right of appeal from this decision. Any objection by a disinherited heir can be met by the argument that there was a court hearing, which is a guarantee of procedural fairness.

The Natal and KwaZulu Codes provide that disinheritance must be dealt with by way of formal application to a chief. From his decision an appeal lies to a district officer, whose decision in the matter is final.[134]

---

[128] See *Mhlonhlo* 3 NAC 114 (1913).
[129] *Mbekushe v Dumiso* 1941 NAC (C&O) 57 at 60.
[130] 6 NAC 19 (1928).
[131] *Silimo v Vuniweyo* 1953 NAC 135 (S) at 138.
[132] *Joel v Zibokwana* 4 NAC 130 (1919); *Mnengelwa* 1942 NAC (C&O) 2.
[133] *Nohele* 6 NAC 19 (1928).
[134] Section 81(9). Similarly, throughout the country disinheritance in respect of land held on quitrent tenure must be by way of a hearing before a commissioner: s 40(1) of the Black Areas Land Regulations Proc R188 of 1969. An appeal lies to the Chief Commissioner: s 40(3).

(3) Dispositions of property mortis causa

A fairer distribution of the estate, taking account of the individual needs of
family members, may be effected by a disposition of property mortis causa. The
occasion giving the disposition its force and effect is a family gathering, at which
an announcement is made by the head of the family in contemplation of his
death.[135] The force of the declaration is strengthened by a belief in the power of
the deceased's shade to vindicate his wishes;[136] notwithstanding, his instruction
will be ignored if it results in an indiscriminate allocation of property upsetting
the heir's inheritance.[137] In essence, a disposition should never depart too far
from the established order of succession. If it does, an appeal may be made to a
chief's court for redress.[138]

Despite a superficial correspondence between dispositions mortis causa and
the common-law privileged wills,[139] there are significant differences.
A customary-law disposition must be made publicly;[140] there must be a good
reason for it and it may not deviate too far from the established order of
succession. The written will, by comparison, is a product of literacy and
professional legal services. This might suggest that the informal customary
modes of disinheritance and disposition of property should be encouraged,
because they can serve the needs of poorer sections of society. But the
requirement of ratification by a family meeting is a problem. If the group of
kinfolk concerned has atrophied, there seems no point in requiring its
consultation; further, if property has become 'individualized', then there is no
reason why the owner should not dispose of it as he or she wishes.[141]

(4) Minority of the heir

If the heir happens to be too young to assume the deceased's responsibilities, the
estate must be administered for him during the period of his immaturity.

In a polygynous family a form of collateral succession asserts itself:[142] minor
heirs fall subject to the guardianship of the highest ranking major son of the
deceased (who is most likely to be the heir's oldest step brother). If the
household is divided into sections (i e the system of polygyny is a complex one),
the highest ranking heir of the same section becomes guardian. Conversely,
where there are no major sons in one section of the homestead, the highest
ranking heir in the other section acts as guardian. If the deceased's descendants

---

[135] See Duncan 15–17 and Ashton 185 regarding wills in Lesotho, and Poulter 309ff who examines these
dispositions in detail, showing how they may resemble the common-law will. See too: Mönnig 337–8;
Rubin op cit n89 106–8; and generally Kerr 143–51 and Olivier 450–3. The disposition may be intended
to take effect immediately or only after the death of the family head. It has been held that ownership in
the property concerned does not vest in the donee until the death of the donor: *Magadla* 3 NAC 28 (1915).

[136] Schapera 230 cites the Tswana maxim: *Lentswe la moswi ga le tlolwe* 'the word of a dead person is
not transgressed.' See too Cheater (1987) 57 *Africa* 181–2.

[137] *Ngungubele v Nomfedele* 1949 NAC 101 (S).

[138] *Zikalala* 1930 NAC (N&T) 139; *Nomatshaka & others v Mhlokonywa* 1933 NAC (C&O) 18 at 23.

[139] See Kerr 140 who cites *Mcunu* 1918 AD 323 at 329.

[140] A written document unannounced is of no effect: *Zikalala* 1930 NAC (N&T) 139 at 142.

[141] This in turn raises the question whether it would not be advisable to revive the common-law
privileged wills. Cf the Zimbabwe Wills Act 13 of 1987.

[142] Holleman 330–1.

are all too young, and also of course in the case of monogamous families, the estate is administered by one of the deceased's brothers.[143]

Customary law has been modified by two statutory provisions. First, in Natal and KwaZulu[144] the heir's mother becomes his guardian unless a district officer appoints some other 'suitable person'. Secondly, in Lesotho under the Laws of Lerotholi,[145] the principal heir is generally deemed to be guardian of any minor heirs, but if there is no major heir to perform this role, a guardian may be nominated by the deceased's relatives. Evidently it is quite common for widows to be appointed,[146] in which event they are automatically endowed with the capacities necessary to perform their duties.

The courts have never specified who the guardian should be, but despite this they do insist on conformity with the rules of customary law. In consequence, the deceased is not allowed to appoint a guardian of his own choice,[147] and presumably the family is similarly constrained.

The guardian does not act simply as an agent for or representative of the heir. He has a personal interest in the estate. Third parties enter into contracts with him, not with the heir;[148] and they must sue him directly[149] although the summons should disclose that the heir's interests are also at stake.[150] Yet, according to the decision in *Gcumisa*,[151] the guardian's responsibility extends only so far as *managing* the estate; he is not obliged to maintain the heir and other dependants out of his own pocket.[152]

In his dealings with the estate, the guardian should take care to consult the widow.[153] Especially before disposing of property, he should confer with her, the deceased's close male relatives, and the heir (if the latter is old enough to understand the significance of the transaction).[154] The effect of failure to consult, however, is unclear. Would a transfer of property or a contract be deemed void or voidable at the instance of an interested party? Here, as in other respects, the

---

[143] Poulter 281. Bekker 288 says that the deceased's *father* becomes administrator, but on the limited ethnographic evidence available, it seems that one of the deceased's siblings would be favoured.

[144] Under s 29(1) of the Codes and according to *Manqabeni v Kuyana* 1910 NHC 67.

[145] Section 12(3).

[146] Poulter 281–2.

[147] *Ximba & another v Mankuntwane* 1939 NAC (C&O) 142. Cf the appointment of guardians by will below. In *Ngozwane* 1944 NAC (C&O) 88, eg, it was held that the deceased's cousin could not act as guardian. In *Butelezi v Butelezi & another* 1964 BAC 124 (NE), however, the court did not object to a widow and heir being assisted by her own father. There are several possible reasons for this exceptional case: the locus standi of the parties had not been challenged; it was not apparent from the facts that any other male relative was available; and the presence of the widow's father might have been sufficient to cure what was seen as a purely procedural defect.

[148] *Ndinisa d/a v Mtuzulu* 1963 BAC 74 (S).

[149] *Kopo v Njenje* 4 NAC 271 (1920).

[150] See s 32 of the Natal and KwaZulu Codes which requires the permission of a district officer before a guardian may institute an action. In *Ngozwane* 1944 NAC (C&O) 88 he was rendered personally liable for the costs of an action.

[151] 1981 AC 1 (NE).

[152] This sounds suspiciously like a transposition of the common law.

[153] *Nobanjwa v Myuyu* 1948 NAC (C&O) 7.

[154] *Ndlala d/a v Makinana* 1963 BAC 18 (S).

full implications of the family interest in property have never been spelled out.[155]
In contrast, the remedies available against a guardian who had maladministered
the estate are clearly established. The suit may call for his removal from office,
a declaration of rights, or recovery of property he had purported to alienate.[156]

Any such action against the guardian would, in the first instance, probably
avail the widow, who has been called the 'natural protector' of her children's
interests.[157] For this purpose the courts allow her the necessary locus standi.[158]
If she is unable or unwilling to act, one of the deceased's senior male relatives
may sue on the heir's behalf.[159] The actions also avail the deceased's family,
namely, any elder, or coeval of the deceased who has an interest in the proper
administration of the estate.[160] As a last resort, the heir himself may sue,
provided that he is duly assisted by a curator ad litem appointed by the court.[161]
Under the Natal and KwaZulu Codes any person under guardianship may sue
his guardian without assistance, unless the court directs otherwise.[162]

The guardian may not be deposed by extracurial action, nor may the family or
widow install another person of their own choice. A new guardian must be
selected from the deceased's male relatives.[163]

V THE WIDOW

(1) Levirate unions and the status of widows

A man's death does not automatically terminate his marriage because, in
technical terms, marriage is a union of two families, not of two individuals. It
therefore endures until formal dissolution by settlement of the bridewealth. The
implication for the widow is that she must remain with her late husband's family
under the protection of the heir. (If he is not old enough, one of the deceased's
senior male relatives acts in his stead.) Few would demand that a young widow
be chaste; and particularly where the deceased died without a heir and she was
still young and capable of having children, another liaison would be positively
advantageous. To regularize the widow's status and to avoid her children
suffering any stigma of illegitimacy[164] she may enter a levirate union.[165] The
Sotho say that this gives the widow personal security and makes the bridewealth
fully productive.[166]

Levirate unions can be distinguished, on the one hand, from widow
inheritance, in that the levir does not father children for his own household but

---

[155] Cf West Africa: Coker *Family Property among the Yorubas* 86–7; Obi *Modern Family Law in
Southern Nigeria* esp 66–71.
[156] *Zakade & another v Zakade* 1951 NAC 288 (S).
[157] *Butelezi v Butelezi & another* 1964 BAC 124 (NE).
[158] *Nosentyi v Makonza* 1 NAC 37 (1900); *Manaso* 1949 NAC 144 (NE).
[159] *Mgodla v Galela & another* 3 NAC 200 (1917).
[160] *Sijila v Masumba* 1940 NAC (C&O) 42 at 47.
[161] *Zakade & another v Zakade* 1951 NAC 288 (S); *Ndlala d/a v Makinana* 1963 NAC 18 (S) and see
Sijila's case supra at 47.
[162] Section 31(2).
[163] *Mocumi v Mocumi & another* 1944 NAC (C&O) 107 at 110.
[164] Cf Roberts 33.
[165] Ukungena (Zulu); kenela (Sotho).
[166] Poulter 260.

for the deceased,[167] and, on the other hand, from marriages, because no more bridewealth need be paid.[168]

Where the deceased was married but died without a son (or more exceptionally where he was unmarried), one of his male relatives may arrange a 'seedraiser' union. The estate is used to provide bridewealth to acquire a woman, who is expected to consort with one of the deceased's brothers. Any son she bears is then considered to be the deceased's.[169]

These unions reflect the emphasis customary law places on social rather than genetic paternity: provided that bridewealth has been paid, all children accrue to the husband's family regardless of who fathered them.[170]

[125] PRESTON-WHYTE in HAMMOND-TOOKE *BANTU-SPEAKING PEOPLES OF SOUTHERN AFRICA* 189–92

In all the groups with the exception of Xhosa, Thembu and, possibly, the South Sotho,[1] should a married man die, an approved relative may assume responsibility for the widow and children. While in some cases the levir undertakes full domestic and marital duties in relation to the woman, in others he visits and provides some economic support for the widow, who remains in the homestead of her deceased husband. He may also help with the bridewealth needed by the sons of the dead man. The most important duty of the levir is to beget children for the deceased. No bridewealth is paid and the issue of the leviratic union refer to the deceased man as "father" (*pater*). Clearly this type of union is, like the sororate, viewed as a continuation of the original marriage. The levir is usually a younger brother or some other junior agnate of the dead man. He may be a son of the deceased, but not a son by the woman concerned. He is fulfilling an agnatic duty in ensuring the continuance of the house established by the marriage.

The levirate may have other important consequences. It serves to keep the woman, and hence her children, particularly if they are still young, under the effective control of her deceased husband's agnatic kin. Their position in the family and in the homestead remains virtually unchanged, and the security offered by legal marriage is ensured, even beyond the death of the husband and father. The Kriges report that among the Lobedu the main duty of a younger brother who takes his elder brother's widow is seen, not primarily in terms of "raising seed" to the dead man, but rather as of caring for the widow and her children and also, as in the case of the sororate, of *maintaining* intact the vital linkages created by marriage and the passing of marriage cattle.[2]

The levirate in its most developed form derives from the assumption that marriage is an exchange in which rights in the woman, both *in uxorem* and *in genetricem*, are transferred to the lineage of the man in return for the cattle which go to the group of the bride. Since it is the two groups which are important, rather than the individual bride and groom, it is logical that (as was the case until the reign of Mpande) a Zulu widow could not go and live with a man not related to her husband without being prosecuted. It must not be thought, however, that a leviratic union is inevitable for all widows. The Zulu chief, Mpande, ruled that a widow be permitted to go to the man of her choice but that the children should be retained by the agnatic group of her deceased husband.[3] Certainly, if a woman is beyond childbearing age when her husband dies, the levirate need not be enforced. She may merely remain on in her husband's homestead. It is usual, if fission of

---

[167] Gluckman in Radcliffe-Brown & Forde 183.

[168] Section 56(1)(*d*) of the Natal and KwaZulu Codes.

[169] Harries 43; Krige 182; Schapera 134. See the definition of 'ukuvusa' in s 1(1) of the Natal and KwaZulu Codes and *Mpengula v Mgqwayi* 1919 NHC 65.

[170] Mönnig 207. A further implication is the reinforcement of the unity of the sibling and lineal descent groups.

the family follows the death of a homestead head, for the widow to move with her eldest son to his new homestead, where she has a place of security and honour. Among the Cape Nguni she lives with her youngest son, who may take over his father's homestead.

Under certain circumstances, notably when there is property or position at stake, a form of marriage superficially similar to Nuer ghost marriage[4] may occur in some Bantu-speaking societies. E J Krige discusses the practice *ukuvusa* which occurs amongst the Zulu when a man of property dies without leaving a son. His natural heir, usually a full or half brother, instead of appropriating the property, may "from affection or fear of his spirit marry a woman to the dead man's name, and thus produce an heir".[5] A house of this nature ranks as a minor subordinate house in the homestead of the surviving brother. Gluckman mentions similar unions in which a brother marries a woman betrothed by a man before his death, or else "wakens" a dead kinsman by marrying and bearing children to his name.[6] Mönnig,[7] writing of the Pedi, reports that a marriage which is arranged on his behalf by the relatives of a man who has died without issue, is termed *tsosa leina la mohu*—raise the name of the deceased—and is contracted particularly among nobles and chiefs where succession is important and the death has occurred before the man could marry the woman designated as the bearer of his heir. This type of marriage occurs for specific purposes and is probably relatively rare. It is not mentioned in the literature on most other Bantu-speaking groups.

Yet another means of ensuring the continuity of a house in the absence of sons is through raising an heir to property or position by woman-to-woman marriage. In these cases the "wife" bears children for her "husband" either by an appointed lover or by a suitor of her own choice.

Woman-to-woman marriage may be undertaken among the South Sotho and Pedi by a childless widow in order to provide a son for her husband and an heir to his property.[8] Among the Lobedu a widow who has no sons may use the cattle coming into her house from the marriage of a daughter in order to marry a wife and provide an heir to her house.[9] Alternatively, if there are other daughters in the house, one of them may use the cattle and so provide the heir to her own line.[10] A similar situation is possible among the Zulu.[11] Van Warmelo points out that a Venda man may allot property to a house which has only daughters just as he does to one with sons. One of the daughters then marries a wife in order to raise an heir to the house.[12] The South Sotho use the term *lefielo* (broom) for a girl whose bridewealth has been paid by a wealthy man on behalf of his daughter.[13]

Among the Lobedu, Venda and Pedi woman marriages appear to be rather more frequent than in the other societies mentioned above. In the case of Lobedu and Venda a woman who has earned wealth from divining or trade may use this to marry a wife in her own right.[14] The children of such a union, though they may take the name of the wealthy woman's husband, belong essentially with their mother to the house of the principal woman and are under her control. In both Lobedu and Pedi groups another striking variant of woman marriage occurs. A woman is regarded as having a moral right to a daughter from the house which was established for her cattle-linked brother with the bridewealth obtained from her own marriage. Even if she has no son, and especially if her husband is dead, she "marries" the girl herself, using the bridewealth received from a daughter's marriage.[15]

Although undertaken primarily in order to raise an heir woman marriage may serve other purposes. The Lobedu Queen is sent wives by headmen and individuals of high birth who desire her favour. Some of these women remain at the royal court, but others are sent as wives to men elsewhere in the kingdom and some who are particularly favoured are placed as headmen of districts. In this way affinal ties centering on the queen are spread widely throughout the Kingdom and the network created by the institution of the queen's wives has important political connotations.[16] This kind of arrangement is, however, unusual and not found in other Bantu-speaking groups.

Notes

1. V G J Sheddick *The Southern Sotho* 39.

2. Krige & Krige 160–1.
3. Gluckman in Radcliffe-Brown & Forde 183.
4. E E Evans-Pritchard *Kinship and Marriage among the Nuer* 109–12.
5. Page 182. And see ss 57 of the Natal and KwaZulu Codes.
6. Op cit n3 184.
7. Page 206.
8. Sheddick op cit n1 38; Mönnig 206.
9. Krige in R F Gray & P H Gulliver *The Family Estate in Africa* 165.
10. Krige ibid.
11. Gluckman op cit n3 148.
12. *Venda Law* 391.
13. Jones in J Goody *Succession to High Office* 70.
14. Krige op cit n9 165; Stayt 143–5; Van Warmelo & Phophi 33.
15. Krige op cit n9 165; Mönnig 206.
16. Krige & Krige 173–7.

Most systems of southern African customary law allow levirate or kindred institutions. The Xhosa and Thembu law are exceptional. They regard intercourse between the widow and one of her deceased husband's relatives as incest.[171] Instead the widow is allowed to consort with approved strangers. Any children she bears, provided they were conceived and born at the deceased's homestead, even have ultimate rights of succession in his family.[172] Those conceived and born elsewhere are said to be 'off the mat', and are excluded.[173]

The choice of levirate partner is restricted by the dictates of the kinship system.[174] Normally the widow is expected to choose a younger brother of the deceased, and although certain peoples may permit her to take an older brother, this is generally prohibited because he stands in a father-like relationship to her.[175]

There is every indication that levirate unions are obsolescent. They are not popular with women[176] and certain churches have branded them as adulterous.[177] The tendency today is for widows to dissolve their first unions in order to contract new marriages.[178] The courts, however, adhere strictly to customary law. They assume that any union a widow contracts after her husband's death is

[171] Van Tromp 124.
[172] *Tshaka v Betyi* 1951 NAC 301 (S); *Dumezweni v Kobodi* 1971 BAC 30 (S).
[173] *Tyali v Dalibango* 1942 NAC (C&O) 58; *Gade v Gqagqeni* 1944 NAC (C&O) 85.
[174] See generally Stayt 169–7 and Hammond-Tooke 138–9.
[175] Ashton 84; Hunter 211; cf Krige & Krige 160; Kuper in Radcliffe-Brown & Forde 97; Mönnig 205; Junod 199–200; and Van Warmelo & Phophi 913ff. It is also believed that any children born of such a union would try to assert rights and privileges beyond those warranted by the deceased's status: Schapera in Radcliffe-Brown & Forde 153.
[176] Roberts 33.
[177] Schapera *Married Life* 285. See Ashton 83–5; Poulter 261 and Reader 154. In Lesotho the so-called 'ghost marriage' was prohibited under the Laws of Lerotholi s 34(3) Part II. And the High Court has held that it is contrary to morality: Poulter 163–6 and Ashton 195–6.
[178] Hunter 212. Even with her potential levirate partner: *Nkosi & another v Mkwanazi* 1945 NAC (N&T) 32. If she chooses to do so (which assumes that she has been transferred from her deceased husband's family back to her own family) her father would be entitled to her bridewealth: *Dobeni v Bako* 1 NAC 58 (1903). Section 61(3) of the Natal and KwaZulu Codes provides a different rule: the bridewealth for the second marriage goes to the house to which the widow belonged in her late husband's household.

a levirate union, with the result that someone asserting a new marriage is put to the proof.[179]

Surprisingly perhaps, the levirate union was never outlawed on the basis of repugnancy to public policy and natural justice.[180] Nevertheless, a widow will not be held to such a union unless she contracted it of her own free will.[181] In an influential decision, the court in *Nbono v Manoxoweni*[182] held that a widow must be free to decide her own future.

In the Cape Province the termination of customary marriage was deemed to emancipate women from their status of minority.[183] Similarly, in Natal and KwaZulu, under s 14 of the new Codes, women become majors on marriage.[184] Elsewhere, widows have been held to remain minors.[185] Now, of course, it could be argued that a widow, like any other person, is subject to the provisions of the Age of Majority Act,[186] and is thus a major, but there has been no decision on this.

A widow's status is unlikely to be contested. Problems arise incidentally, principally with regard to the bridewealth agreement: because the marriage contract involves two families, if the widow refuses to continue to perform her marital duties, the union should be dissolved by return of part of the bridewealth.[187] This rule has never been unreservedly implemented. In *Ngwekulu v Mano*[188] the court intimated that it was contrary to natural justice, and in *Sefolokele v Thekiso*,[189] it was held to be incompatible with the widow's majority status. Normally refund of bridewealth is required only where the widow remarries,[190] and if she is past child-bearing age, even remarriage will not oblige her guardian to return anything.[191]

The widow's guardian has everything to gain if his ward remains with her deceased husband's family: there will be no question of his having to refund bridewealth, and he will not be responsible for supporting her. It can readily be imagined, therefore, that he will not be favourably disposed towards her return or remarriage. In two early decisions[192] it was held that the widow's refusal to

---

[179] *Zulu* 1945 NAC (N&T) 27; *Magubane* 1948 NAC (N&T) 29.

[180] *Dube v Mnisi* 1960 NAC 66 (NE). And see: *Dumalitshona v Mraji* 5 NAC 168 (1927); *Madyibi v Nguva* 1944 NAC (C&O) 36 at 38 and s 37(6) of the Natal and KwaZulu Codes.

[181] *Lutuli* 1930 NAC (N&T) 132; and see s 56(1)(b) of the Natal and KwaZulu Codes. Cf the strange decision in *Moima* 1936 NAC (N&T) 15 at 19, where the court held that a Pedi rule to the effect that a widow is not permitted to remarry, and thus by implication is bound to accept a levirate union or remain single, was *not* contrary to natural justice and public policy.

[182] (1891) 6 EDC 62.

[183] *Xolo* 1931 NAC (C&O) 23; *Maqula* 1950 NAC 202 (S).

[184] Cf the former position: *Sibiya* 1949 NAC 61 (NE) and *Ntombela v Mpungose* 1950 NAC 150 (NE).

[185] *Macabangwana v Nompola* 1902 NHC 52; *Mhlongo & another v Sibeko* 1937 NAC (N&T) 34 at 36–7. Thus lacking locus standi: *Ngwenya d/a Ngwenya v Zwane* 1959 NAC 28 (NE).

[186] 57 of 1972; see above, [108].

[187] Deductions may be claimed: *Mgqongo v Zilimbola* 3 NAC 186 (1914).

[188] 1952 NAC 3 (C).

[189] 1951 NAC 25 (C).

[190] *Nomadudwana v Totsholo* 1938 NAC (C&O) 43; *White v Mxaseni & another* 1945 NAC (C&O) 41. This is a rule of Tembu and Pondo law: *Cosi v Nongomazi* 1941 NAC (C&O) 85 and *Ngqungiso v Gobo* 1946 NAC (C&O) 10.

[191] *Ngwekulu v Mano* 1952 NAC 3 (NE).

[192] *Nbono v Manoxoweni* (1891) 6 EDC 62 and *Mgqongo v Zilimbola* 3 NAC 186 (1914).

stay with her deceased husband's family did not render her guardian liable to refund any bridewealth. But in *Jobela v Gqitiyeza*,[193] this rule was qualified: only if the widow remarried and no bridewealth was paid for the second union would her guardian be absolved of his duty to refund bridewealth from the first marriage. Thus a maxim was coined: 'no man may hold two dowries for the same woman.'[194] Accordingly, in the normal case the widow's remarriage would render her guardian liable to repay part at least of the bridewealth.[195] This maxim, however, was a misconception of customary law, as the court below explained.

[126] *DESEMELE v SINYAKO* 1944 NAC (C&O) 17

The maxim—if it can be so termed—that "no man can hold two dowries for the same woman" appears first in one of the earliest reports—*Mqolora v Meslani* 1 NAC 97.

It is obviously a European misconception of Native Law for, in pure Native law, neither a wife nor a widow could remarry during the subsistence of the first union, and that union would continue until the first dowry was returned to the husband or his family, or, in rare cases, he publicly repudiated the woman and dissolved the union thereby forfeiting his dowry, thus freeing the wife to remarry.

A widow was and is still considered a "wife" of the husband's group, as indeed our Courts recognise by awarding her posthumous progeny to the husband's group. . . .

Native law required her continued residence at the kraal of her late husband for she was the wife of the group—"our wife" as the Natives express it. . . . She was dealt with as a deserter if she left the kraal and she could not remarry until her first lobolo had been restored to the group—*Ntame v Mbede* 3 NAC 94.

European ideas of so-called freedom of individuals being shocked by this "barbarity" the Eastern Districts Court in *Nbono v Manoxoweni* 6 EDC 62, ruled that a widow, being in the eyes of European law a major, was free to go where she pleased after the death of her husband without committing her family to refund of her lobolo. That case certainly did not decide that "the marriage was dissolved by the death of one of the parties to it", as set out in *Mgqongo v Zilimbolo* 3 NAC 186, which purported to follow *Nbono's* case, and which in return was relied on in *Jobela v Gqitiyeza* 1929 NAC (C&O) 15, as authority for overruling the decision in *Ntlongweni v Mhlakaza* 3 NAC 163.

What did happen, however, was that it became an accepted idea that the widow could contract a valid second marriage or union although her first lobolo had not been restored, and that has become fixed and recognised as law by our Courts. . . . Hence arose the position anomalous in pure Native law, that a father could hold two dowries for the same woman. Having coined a suitable maxim, as being the European's conception of Native law, the Courts proceeded to test claims for restoration of widows' first dowries by the new rule, overlooking the basic feature of the problem, namely, that Native law regards lobolo as the basis of a customary union, hence there can in Native law be no valid second union unless and until a second dowry had been paid. The maxim thus obviously can mean no more than that the first dowry is returnable when the widow contracts a valid second union, which terminates the rights of the former husband's group to her future progeny and thus vitiates the first lobolo contract. . . .

The fact that a valid second union has been contracted without the payment of a second dowry is no defence to the claim of the first husband's family that the contract with their group to transfer of the woman's reproductive powers to them had been frustrated by the

---

[193] 1929 NAC (C&O) 19.

[194] *Mqolora v Meslani* 1 NAC 97 (1905); *Nomadudwana v Totsholo* 1938 NAC (C&O) 43.

[195] *Ntlongweni v Mhlakaza* 3 NAC 163 (1915); and see *Ziqukwane v Tyaliti* 1933 NAC (C&O) 8; *Qabuka v Dlisondabambi* 1937 NAC (C&O) 187.

second union and they were, therefore, entitled to restoration of their (first) lobolo. Thus the criterion of restoration is certainly not that of the receipt of two dowries, but the breach of the first contract. A civil marriage without payment of dowry producing that result, the maxim is inapplicable and the Plaintiff is entitled to an order for restoration.

Since this decision it has been held that the widow's guardian is liable to return bridewealth if she remarries, even if both her marriages were by Christian rites,[196] and even if the woman's guardian was unaware of the second union.[197]

Although the court in *Nbono v Manoxoweni*[198] was anxious to ameliorate the widow's position—as it said, a state 'liable to gross abuse'—it is questionable whether much can be achieved by judicial intervention unless a consequential change is made to the rules governing refund of bridewealth. The mercenary considerations of the widow's family will always exert a strong influence on her to respect the status quo.

(2) Maintenance

It is a cardinal rule of customary law that women may not inherit from men.[199] If they were to do so, the family estate (which the customary law of succession is at pains to keep within the patriline) would pass out of the control of the deceased's family.[200]

None the less, a widow is not left destitute after her husband's death. The deceased's obligations to his dependants are transmitted to his heir, who becomes responsible for supporting the widow(s) and minor children.[201] And so, although the widow has no formal inheritance, she still has a claim for maintenance out of the estate.[202] Her claim is contingent upon continued residence at her late husband's homestead[203] or wherever else the heir chooses to place her,[204] which implies that she must continue to fulfil her wifely duties.[205]

---

[196] *Makedela v Sauli* 1948 NAC (C&O) 17.

[197] *Tobiea v Mohatla* 1949 NAC 91 (S).

[198] (1891) 6 EDC 62.

[199] *Madolo v Nomawu* 1 NAC 12 (1896); *Mbekushe v Dumiso* 1941 NAC (C&O) 57 at 61; *Mahashe* 1955 NAC 149 (S) at 153; and see *Mrhluli v Mbata* 1940 NAC (N&T) 19 at 20. In *Makabeni v Shuter* 1907 NHC 82 a testator left his estate to the women in his family; because this was such a drastic departure from custom, it was contended that he was of unsound mind!

[200] Even if the deceased were survived by no male relatives, his widow would not be entitled to his estate. In theory the woman would become a ward of the paramount chief: *Myazi v Nofenti* 1 NAC 74 (1904). This anachronistic rule seems to have survived; so today, on failure of all male relatives, the Supreme Chief, ie the State President, would be deemed heir and the widow would have to petition him for maintenance from the estate: *Kumalo v Estate Kumalo* 1942 NAC (N&T) 31.

[201] *Mnani* 1977 BAC 264 (S).

[202] In this respect customary law used to offer widows more than the common law, which allowed only the deceased's minor children a right to maintenance. Cf the recommendations of the South African Law Commission *Review of the Law of Succession* para 6 and the Maintenance of Surviving Spouses Act 27 of 1990. Illegitimate children can also claim under s 1(2) of the Intestate Succession Act 81 of 1987.

[203] *Sonamzi v Nosamana* 3 NAC 297 (1914); *Mavuma v Mbebe* 1948 NAC (C&O) 16; *Tulumane v Ntsodo* 1953 NAC 185 (S).

[204] *Ntsham* 1936 NAC (C&O) 128. See too: Schapera 166; Ashton 84; Harries 49 and Hunter 212.

[205] *Sibanda v Dlokweni* 1936 NAC (C&O) 61; *Mbekushe v Dumiso* 1941 NAC (C&O) 57 at 61–2; *Mocumi v Mocumi & another* 1944 NAC (C&O) 107 at 109–10; *Dodo v Sabasaba* 1945 NAC (C&O) 62; *Myuyu v Nobanjwa* 1947 NAC (C&O) 66; *Kgumare* 1948 NAC (N&T) 21. As Bekker 216 puts it: 'her position is no weaker nor stronger than that of a wife.'

This rule is qualified by certain exceptions in the widow's favour. The heir may not eject her at whim.[206] If he is not prepared to live with her, he should place a son at the homestead to keep an eye on the estate.[207] If he neglects or expels her, the widow may set up her own establishment.[208] Notwithstanding these provisos, the residential requirement is an unnecessarily literal interpretation of the continued marital obligations. It greatly restricts the widow's freedom of movement, and seriously erodes the improved status won for her in *Nbono v Manoxoweni*.[209]

The courts have been careful to point out that the widow has no proprietary rights in the estate,[210] and an early suggestion that she might have a usufruct was held to be wrong.[211] Following the logic of the common law, however, the courts were obliged to allow the widow to protect her *possession* of the estate by use of possessory interdicts.[212] In practice this is a valuable remedy, for she frequently needs protection immediately after her husband's death, when his relatives may demand transfer of some or all of the estate assets. Her title will not be questioned, giving her the advantage of not having to justify her claim in customary law.[213] So at least until the distribution of the estate at the ukubuyisa ceremony, the widow can be given undisturbed possession.

The heir, as universal successor to the deceased, may treat the estate as his personal property.[214] But this right is hedged around with many limitations. The first is a somewhat nebulous duty, already alluded to, of consulting the widow before disposing of estate assets.[215]

[127] *MYUYU v NOBANJWA* 1947 NAC (C&O) 66

The respective rights of the heir and the widow of a deceased Native in regard to the estate property may be stated as follows: Upon the death of a man the ownership of his movable property vests in his heir, who is entitled to the sole control of such property. The widows of the deceased are entitled to be supported out of the deceased's estate while they reside at the deceased's kraal or at a kraal approved of by the heir. As long as they are adequately supported they cannot interfere with the heir's right to exercise full ownership over the estate property. There are numerous decisions in which the Native Assessors have stated that where a widow is living at the kraal of her deceased husband she is entitled to be consulted in regard to dealings with the estate property. No doubt custom requires this, but we are at a loss to appreciate what legal effect failure to consult could have on the heir's right to deal with the property. No doubt a widow who has been left destitute has the right, as a last resort, to compel the heir by legal action to restore the estate property

---

[206] *Tonose* 1936 NAC (C&O) 103.

[207] *Gqalana* 1935 NAC (C&O) 51.

[208] *Mdyongolo & others v Mdyongolo* 1942 NAC (C&O) 121 and the heir loses control over any crops she produces.

[209] (1891) 6 EDC 62.

[210] *Xulu* 1938 NAC (N&T) 46 at 48; *Macubeni* 1952 NAC 270 (S).

[211] *Tetelwa v Mkatshane* 3 NAC 298 (1912); overruled in *Luke* 4 NAC 133 (1920). See too: *Rashula v Masixandu* 5 NAC 202 (1926) and *Sidubulekana v Somyalo* 1931 NAC (C&O) 12.

[212] See, eg, *Ncotama v N'Cume* (1893) 10 SC 207 and *Ngwenya d/a Ngwenya v Zwane* 1959 NAC 28 (NE).

[213] Stewart (1983–4) 1 & 2 *Zimb LR* 72ff.

[214] In *Dodo v Sabasaba* 1945 NAC (C&O) 62, eg, the heir could decide how lands were to be cultivated, what crops would be planted and whether portion of the land was to be leased.

[215] *Dlakiya* 2 NAC 87 (1910); *Letoao* 4 NAC 158 (1919). And see *Luke* 4 NAC 133 (1929).

or some of it to her husband's kraal for her support (*Zibuti* 6 NAC 21 (1928)), but so long as she is adequately maintained she has no right, in so far as she herself is concerned, to interfere with the heir's rights. If the heir is a minor, his guardian according to Native Law administers the estate property on behalf of the minor, and, since he acts for the heir, he is vested with the same rights, duties and obligations as the heir. He has the unfettered control of the estate property, he must support the deceased's family and upon demand by the heir (when a man) hand over the property to the latter and give a full and true account of his administration. Having done this he is entitled to something out of the estate for his services, generally a beast. But in administering the property the guardian must exercise care and apply the assets to the benefit of the minor and the deceased's family (*Malayikali v Ngoloti* 1945 NAC (C&O) 77). If he misspends or appropriates to himself the assets, or permits some other person to deal with the property to the detriment of the minor's interests, the Court will compel him to make restitution (*Vava* 1940 NAC (C&O) 15), and in addition, he can be removed from his position as guardian.

The heir's notionally unrestricted proprietary rights in the estate are further qualified by a series of personal actions that the widow may bring against him (or his guardian), all of which are aimed at securing her right to maintenance.[216] Thus she can insist that: the heir support her from the estate;[217] he place stock at her disposal;[218] he be removed from office;[219] he keep the estate intact at the deceased's homestead;[220] she be allowed to set up an independent homestead with stock from the estate under the control of another member of her deceased husband's family.[221]

In principle, because she has no proprietary rights, the widow has no authority over estate property.[222] But if she chose to exercise her personal rights against the heir, she could exert considerable control over its administration. In theory, she could even win complete independence from her husband's family by insisting on her own, separate homestead. But many questions remain unanswered. What is the effect of alienating an estate asset without prior consultation with the widow? Do other dependants of the deceased with an interest in the estate have the same rights as the widow, or must they exercise their rights through her? If the heir is removed from office, who may take his place?

The widow's position is a vulnerable one and it has been rendered even more precarious by the courts' insistence on preservation of the customary-law regime.[223] The requirements that the widow remain at her husband's homestead under the protection of the heir and that he keep the estate intact for her benefit, rely for their efficacy on the co-operation and good relationship of heir and widow. This in turn assumes the prevalence of a particular residential pattern (isolated, self-sufficient homesteads) and that the estate consists of land and

---

[216] She can bring these actions unassisted: *Khoapa* 1940 NAC (C&O) 16.
[217] *Myuyu v Nobanjwa* 1947 NAC (C&O) 66.
[218] *Macubeni* 1952 NAC 270 (S).
[219] *Selela & another v Selela* 1940 NAC (C&O) 68 obiter. Cf developments in Ghana in this regard: above, 237 n73.
[220] *Zepe* 1963 BAC 90 (S). And see *Duma v Swales NO* 1952 NAC 272 (NE) at 275.
[221] *Masokoto v Ntsonyana* 4 NAC 157 (1918); *Paula v Mangcukwana* 1930 NAC (C&O) 22.
[222] *Butelezi & another v Yende* 1937 NAC (N&T) 32.
[223] South Africa is not unique. Zambian courts have also done nothing to ameliorate the position of widows: Ndulo (1985) 18 *CILSA* 90ff.

livestock. Where *cash* is the main asset, one reason for these rules disappears. Cash must be invested and money can be managed from financial institutions anywhere in the country; there is no need for the widow to remain with the estate. Moreover, the overcrowded cities of southern Africa make nonsense of the residential rule; it may be physically impossible (not to mention unlawful) for the widow to remain living with the heir in the deceased's house.

On a more theoretical level, it seems that personal rights do little to assist the widow. Their efficacy is dependent on the survival of social relationships, and where these have been disrupted, the rights must be sued upon, which is a costly procedure. The widow would be better served by a proprietary claim on the estate, which would guarantee her an immediate source of income for the maintenance of herself and her dependent children.

VI SUCCESSION TO WOMEN

In a patriarchal society women cannot hold positions of authority. In consequence succession to a deceased woman, especially an unmarried woman, is of no great account; this is apparent from the abbreviation or complete omission of ceremonies to mark a woman's death and burial.[224] Her tasks in the family can be taken over by an older daughter or other unattached woman, and her unfinished duty to procreate may be performed by a sororal substitute. Women have fewer opportunities to acquire property, and so their estates tend to be less significant than those of men. Livestock or major assets are normally inherited by the woman's father, or guardian if she were single. Otherwise, any odds and ends that she accumulated would be distributed as mementoes amongst her children or members of her family.

(1) Sororate and cognate unions

The woman's child-bearing potential was thought to be her most important attribute. If she died or proved to be barren, the loss of this asset could be compensated by the institution of sororal polygyny.[225]

[128] PRESTON-WHYTE in HAMMOND-TOOKE *BANTU-SPEAKING PEOPLES OF SOUTHERN AFRICA* 189

In the case of the death of the wife without progeny, the family of the dead woman may send a substitute "to set up the house that has fallen".[1] Among the Zulu and Swazi, should no children have been born of a union, sending a substitute is a definite affinal obligation and no bridewealth need be passed.[2] The alternative is to return the bridewealth cattle so that the man may initiate a new marriage. Among the Zulu some cattle may be returned also if the wife bore up to two children, but if she bore three or more before her death, she is regarded as having fulfilled her duty and her family are absolved of the obligation to provide a substitute or to return the cattle.[3] The position is slightly different amongst the South Sotho and Lobedu where, even in the case of a death before the birth of any children, the widower has no absolute right to a substitute. As in the case of barrenness, it is usually his affines who initiate the sororate if they so wish. They can

---

[224] Krige 169, eg, says that no ukubuyisa ceremony is held for a woman.
[225] See further: Ashton 82–3; Van Warmelo & Phophi 823–5; Schapera *Married Life* 291–2.

expect full bridewealth, though may demand less or only half the amount of the first transaction if the man has proved a co-operative son-in-law and good father.[4] The Kriges suggest that this form of the sororate is motivated among the Lobedu mainly by the decision on the part of the dead woman's people to keep alive the links with the group of her husband and the fact that a woman has the right to a daughter of a union established with her bridewealth cattle.[5]

It must be remembered that the sororate occurs against a social background in which under normal conditions the wives of a polygynist are often sisters or classificatory sisters. Among the Zulu sororal polygyny is believed to be advantageous as less friction is thought to occur between sisters than between unrelated co-wives.[6] In this case the sisters are completely independent of each other and each establishes her own house, the relationship between these houses being subject to the normal rules of ranking. In this connection it may be noted that among the Tsonga there is a definite preference for a secondary marriage with the wife's younger sister or even the wife's brother's daughter[7] and this appears also amongst the Venda.[8]

Notes

1. Krige & Krige 159.
2. Gluckman in Radcliffe-Brown & Forde 185 and 188; Kuper 23.
3. Gluckman op cit 188.
4. Krige & Krige 159–60; V G J Sheddick *The Southern Sotho* 38.
5. Page 159.
6. Gluckman op cit n2 182.
7. Junod 260–2.
8. Stayt 179–80.

The term 'sororal polygyny' is often used loosely to include a new marriage but this is misleading. The purpose of a sororal union is to raise more children as legitimate heirs for the family head without creating a new house.[226] It denotes *continuation* of the marriage by a consortium of the widower with one of his deceased wife's sisters. A consideration might be paid but it is always less than a full bridewealth.[227]

The Southern Nguni do not countenance sororal polygyny. If a wife in one of the senior houses died childless, her family would not be expected to provide a sister as a substitute. Instead the husband would be obliged to contract a new marriage. The new wife would not found a house of her own, however; she would be incorporated into the vacant house to bear children for it.[228]

In those systems of customary law that require the deceased wife's family to provide a sororate partner, it follows that they would be in breach of their marital obligations if they could not, or would not do so. Strictly speaking, they would then have to return at least part of the bridewealth, especially if the deceased had been young and capable of bearing children.[229]

As with a customary marriage, the consent of the substitute wife is thought desirable but not absolutely essential, and predictably this occasioned the

---

[226] A substitute wife may be taken even if the deceased woman had borne children. In this event, her duty would be to raise the children: Ashton ibid; and see Poulter 157–60. Cf the Lesotho decision, cited by Duncan 32–3 and Poulter 159–60, where it was held that the offspring of such a union cannot oust the rights of a son of any other major wife who was married before the sororate union.

[227] Ashton 82–3. And see Campbell (1970) 3 *CILSA* 325–6.

[228] See Van Tromp 94–5 and Bekker 279–80.

[229] Unless the woman had actually died in childbirth: Krige 156; Harries 19 and 24; Stayt 152; Schapera *Married Life* 292.

intervention of the courts. They have held that any arrangement forcing an unwelcome union onto a woman is contrary to public policy and natural justice and will not be recognized.[230] They have also shown considerable reluctance to enforce any obligation to refund bridewealth, which they thought was mercenary and unfair.[231] In Transkei specific legislation was passed abolishing the duty to refund bridewealth on the death of a wife;[232] and the Natal and KwaZulu Codes similarly provide that if a woman dies within 12 months of her marriage, without having had children, the husband may recover a maximum of half of his bridewealth.[233] The same provision was invoked in a case arising outside Natal on the ground that, when assessing the refund, the wife's services and the husband's marital privileges should be taken into account.[234]

Sororate unions are now probably obsolete.[235] They belong to a different era when polygynous marriage was an ideal state. The emancipation of women and the influence of Christianity would not make them popular today. Yet, because the institution lingers on, if only as a potential, the more mercenary widower is afforded a justification for claiming refund of his bridewealth.

(2) The rules of inheritance

[129] HOLLEMAN *SHONA CUSTOMARY LAW* 350-8

Shona law governing the matri-estate is again mainly concerned with livestock, the kind of property which, owing to its particular nature, serves the essential spiritual and organic needs of the owners. With regard to livestock belonging to a woman, the proprietary rights and rights of succession, accordingly reveal a communal disposition similar to that which characterized the proprietary rights to the assets of the patri-estate. Other, personal belongings of a woman (excluding the stock of food in her granaries or in her garden) are considered to be of less importance and these articles may after her death be distributed amongst her daughters, sisters and other near-relatives as "consolation gifts" (*misodzi*, "tears"). In the following pages I shall therefore almost exclusively deal with the *dangga ramai* (lit. cattle kraal or herd of the mother): that is livestock acquired by a woman in her own right, as a legal entity completely separate from the estate of her husband and his patri-group.

The assets of the *dangga ramai*, matri-estate, may be divided into two different categories, dependent upon the manner in which they have been acquired. The first category comprises such livestock as have "naturally" accrued to a woman, ie on account of her capacity as mother of a married daughter....

The second category consists of any livestock and their natural increase which a woman may have acquired by her personal labour, for instance by selling or bartering grain, by acting as a mid-wife or herbalist, or by making and selling pottery.

The distinction between these two elements of the matri-estate is of great importance because different legal principles apply to them. The Shona refer to the first-mentioned category of animals as *dzingombe* (or *dzimbudzi*) *dsoumai*, ie cattle (or goats) "pertaining to motherhood". The second category is referred to by the general term *dzamavoko* (sing

---

[230] *Gidja v Yingwane* 1944 NAC (N&T) 4; cf s 37(a) of the Natal and KwaZulu Codes.
[231] In any event, this rule was evidently becoming obsolete in some systems of customary law. See Schapera 168 and Van Tromp 159.
[232] Proc 189 of 1922.
[233] Section 66(3). By implication if only one child is born, no bridewealth is recoverable.
[234] *Gidja v Yingwane* 1944 NAC (N&T) 4.
[235] See Poulter 157; Schapera 168; and Roberts 33.

yamavoko) ie "of the hands" (= as the result of manual labour). . . . For convenience' sake the terms *umai* ("motherhood") and *mavoko* ("hands") will be used as distinctive adjectives when I refer to, *(a)* the "naturally-acquired" elements of the matri-estate, or *(b)* those acquired by her personal labour.

Succession and control of the matri-estate

Participation in the matri-estate is, as a general principle, restricted to the *matrilineal blood-relatives* of the woman who has acquired the property. These relatives include in the first place the woman's full-brothers and full-sisters and her own children; but the benefit of her estate may, if necessary, be extended to other matrilineal relatives such as her children's children, the children of her full-brothers and full-sisters, or the full-brothers and full-sisters of her mother (or their children). *Excluded* from participation in the matri-estate are such relatives as the woman's half-brothers and half-sisters, or the children of the co-wives of her husband (unless, of course, their mother is a full-sister of her mother or herself) who fall outside her matrilineal blood-group. This principle applies to both the umai and mavoko stock, but is, as will be seen, more strictly enforced with regard to the former stock.

During her lifetime a woman has full control over her property. Whenever possible, she will keep her livestock and let them increase, but more often than not the essential needs of her children and other blood-relatives will force her to dispose of her stock before they have had time to increase, so that only in a minority of cases can a woman boast of a sizable herd of cattle or small stock by the end of her life.

[Umai gifts are presented to a woman in recognition of the procreative and mystical power which has produced a daughter. The woman's own brothers and sisters, as uterine siblings, are considered to be more closely connected to the woman than her children and thus in a better position to propitiate the spirit of the woman when she dies. Mavoko stock lacks the spiritual and 'organic' qualities of the umai stock, and rights to it are vested in the woman's own house to which her eldest son is the principal heir.]

The distinction between *mavoko* and *umai* stock is carefully maintained with regard to the offspring of the original animals as long as they remain in the possession of the woman or her heirs. As regards the legal implications of this distinction I found little or no confusion. In the course of the investigation literally hundreds of married women were asked how the assets of their matri-estate (if any) would devolve after their death. Almost without exception the answers were that the *mavoko* stock would be inherited by their sons while the *umai* stock would go to their full-brothers or full-sisters. A great number of women explained that their father or eldest full-brother would temporarily "look after" all their property "until my son has grown up and then he will be given my *mavoko* cattle". A few of them (all Christian) held that "all my property, even my *ngombe youmai*, must go to my son". Not a single woman, however, even considered the possibility that her husband might take control of her matri-estate after her death. The reason for this becomes clear when we consider the manner in which the matri-estate is controlled after a woman's death.

Immediately after his wife's death, the husband will point out all her property to her family and they will take control of such property. Informants state that instead of wishing to conceal any property belonging to his wife, a husband will rather be inclined to hand over more than is strictly necessary because "he fears his wife's spirit". He may thus transfer property in which he himself is lawfully interested, such as certain household utensils ("they belong to your sister because she used them"), or the grain in her granaries, the product of their joint labour ("it is all hers because she worked for it"). It is left to the discretion of the woman's relatives how much of this property they will leave with the husband. They are in principle entitled to half the amount of food jointly produced by the husband and wife, and to all the foodstuff produced by the woman on her own field. But in practice they will usually leave most of her share with the husband, especially when the latter will take care of the children. They may take a few pots or other utensils from her kitchen, leaving the rest as a "gift" to the husband or his daughters and sisters. But any cattle or small stock belonging to the matri-estate, including the *mavoko* stock, are as a rule driven to the village of the woman's father or brothers at the earliest possible moment, if only because the husband will refuse to accept responsibility for these animals.

The control of the matri-estate reveals a communal pattern similar to that described in connexion with the patri-estate. That is, the deceased's *fraternal* heir usually takes control of *all* the assets of her matri-estate for the benefit of her blood-group. He will, as far as possible, recognize the preferential claims of the individual relatives, but such individual claims may be overruled if the interests of the matri-group demand it.

There are nowadays instances in which the grown-up sons of a deceased woman claim the full control and benefit of their lawful share (ie the *mavoko* stock) of their mother's estate. They may sometimes argue: "We (ie our paternal family) paid full *rovoro* for our mother. Why should her family again receive cattle from her?" From a legal point of view this argument cuts no ice, but it is significant, in the first place because it reveals the modern individualistic attitude regarding the control of livestock, as opposed to the traditional, communal disposition; in the second place it stresses the fact that the members of the deceased's matri-group belong to different patrilineal units whose interests do not coincide. As members of their father's family and patrilineage (*rudzi*), the deceased woman's sons represent the interests of their own paternal unit, as against those of their maternal relatives who belong to a different patrilineage. As one Hera informant explained: "In such disputes it becomes a matter of one *rudzi* against another.". . .

Control of a deceased woman's estate is a precarious undertaking because it is firmly believed that her spirit will closely watch how her property is managed and will show her displeasure (by causing illness or other misfortune) whenever some of the stock is used for a purpose of which she disapproves. The spiritual supervision of, and mystical intervention in, matters concerning the deceased's livestock is a peculiar aspect of the matri-estate. This phenomenon is not altogether foreign to the patri-estate, but in connexion with the matri-estate it is revealed as a factor of dominant importance. Informants were unable to explain why a woman's spirit should be more concerned about her estate than a man's spirit about his patri-estate, but they left no doubt about their conviction that anyone in control of matri-stock would be well advised to "listen to the wishes of the (deceased woman's) spirit". Almost every informant could substantiate his view by relating one or more instances in which he himself or a near relative had experienced the mystical retributions of a woman's spirit on account of the (often inadvertent) mismanagement of her estate, and in particular her *umai* stock. For this reason, they stated, the heirs should not only try to keep at least one or two animals of the *umai* stock available for sacrificial purposes (and failing any *umai* stock, one or two *mavoko* animals), but they would be wise to ascertain the wishes of the spirit (by divination, *kukandira* or *kushopera*) before they disposed of a substantial portion of the estate, even when they believed that the proposed transaction would serve the best interests of the matrilineal kin-group.

The belief that the spirits are likely to enforce the legal principles governing the matri-estate, accounts for the fact that comparatively few claims concerning the matri-estate are brought before a formal court of law. In the majority of cases in which there is a question of misappropriation or a dispute about preferential claims, the issue is confined to the parties concerned and their families. Senior members of the matri-group act as arbitrators, interpreting points of law, weighing conflicting claims and interests, suggesting a solution. In doubtful cases the claimants will be more inclined to consult the spirit of the deceased owner than to submit the case to a tribal court which, it appears, is often reluctant to intervene. When the defendant refuses to comply with the recommendations of the family elders, or does not act in accordance with the spirit's alleged wishes, the matter is often left in abeyance, in the confident expectation that the spirit itself will apply such sanctions as it deems fit. Any misfortune which subsequently happens to a member of one of the interested parties (and not necessarily to the family of the party who is presumed to be guilty) is likely to be interpreted as evidence of the spirit's displeasure. With the help of a diviner the spirit's commands are revealed, and the fear of further retribution compels the offender to obey these commands. In this manner the law governing the control and distribution of the matri-estate is largely enforced by the fear of mystical sanctions.

Since the structure of Shona society is patrilineal, the unity of patrilineal groupings will endure and the identity of male ancestors is preserved because their names are transferred to their successive heirs. The possession of the ancestral name is closely associated with the legal interests pertaining to such a name. The heir is identified with the original bearer of the name and is lawfully entitled to assume the rights and responsibilities held by the latter. Unlike succession to patri-estates, the succession to the *matri-estate* is normally not accompanied by a succession to the name of the deceased owner. Moreover, matrilineal unity is bound to dissolve with the passage of time, if only because local groupings are based on paternal affiliations, and members of a matri-group therefore lose contact with each other. This has a profound influence upon the ultimate control and destination of the matri-estate.

Because female status is socially less significant than male status, it is probably better to speak of inheritance than of succession when a woman dies, since the main issue is the disposal of any property that she might have acquired. Be that as it may, a uniform system of rules governing the devolution of women's estates seems never to have evolved south of the Limpopo; and even an ethnographer as thorough as Schapera[236] confessed that there was considerable uncertainty. From the scanty data available the following rules have been pieced together.

Amongst the Tswana an unmarried woman's property goes to her mother or her sisters, any unmarried sisters having prior claim. If she had no sisters, her father inherits any cattle or, failing him, her linked brother. If she has children, they inherit all her property.[237] If the deceased woman was married, her personal belongings and domestic utensils go to her daughters; clothes, pots, baskets, etc go the family of her maternal uncle. The rest of her property is divided amongst her children according to age and sex. Huts, fields, and cattle remain under the control of her husband until his death, when they are divided amongst her children, the youngest being given priority. If the woman had no children, her property is inherited by her sister, if the latter had been taken as a sororate partner by her husband. Otherwise any property that the woman brought with her into the marriage reverts to her own family, and property that she was given by her husband remains with him.[238]

In Sotho law an unmarried woman's property is inherited by her parents. The personal belongings go to her mother and any cash or cattle go to her father, but they are obliged to share these out. If the woman was married, her personal effects are taken by her mother-in-law who may distribute them to the

---

[236] Pages 234–5.
[237] Cf Schapera 236.
[238] Schapera *Married Life* 296–7.

deceased's mother and brother's wife. Household utensils remain with her husband and can be used by her children.[239]

Principles of distribution and ultimogeniture are evident with the Pedi,[240] Venda,[241] and Pondo.[242] The bulk of the woman's estate is inherited by her youngest child (usually her son), but he may be obliged to share some of this with the other children or the woman's blood relatives.

In the case of the Swazi, an unmarried woman's property is inherited by her father or his heir. The property of married women and widows, on the other hand, goes to the heir of the house although it remains under the control of the husband during his lifetime. The principle of ultimogeniture governs the inheritance of livestock which accrued to the woman by virtue of her status as a wife and mother.[243]

In general the rules of inheritance are fragmentary and undeveloped. Although in earlier times succession to women was not a social issue, it is today. Women everywhere are expected to run households; sometimes they do this with the assistance of males, and sometimes they operate alone. De facto, whatever the courts' ruling on their proprietary capacity may be, they acquire and control property. What is to happen to this property on their death, and who will be responsible for rearing their children? It seems pointless to have two different systems of customary-law succession, distinguished only on the basis of the deceased's gender. Where the major purpose of succession is to provide material assistance for the rearing of surviving dependants, the estate should be transmitted to the person(s) actually responsible for discharging that duty. Previously, no doubt, this was unnecessary because children would be absorbed into the woman's extended family; but the erosion of kinship ties makes this less likely today.

VII WILLS

(1) Devisable property

Wills enable people to control the devolution of their property after death. A will is usually a written version of the deceased's wishes, as against the demands of potential heirs.[244] In southern Africa all people have testamentary capacity, even people subject to customary law. It is often hoped that by empowering people to dispose of property contrary to the order of intestate succession a more equitable distribution of property will be effected, especially in favour of widows and immediate dependants. But wills are no panacea of social ills. They presuppose a level of literacy and education which many people lack; execution and drafting normally require the assistance of a professional;

---

[239] Ashton 182, Poulter 226–7; cf *Faro* 1950 NAC 224 (S), where it was held that a widow's heir is the same as the heir of the deceased husband.

[240] Mönnig 338.

[241] Van Warmelo & Phophi 975ff.

[242] *Qomfa v Komfa* 4 NAC 105 (1918).

[243] Rubin op cit n89 105–6.

[244] Goody op cit n17 15.

and the common-law rule of freedom of testation offers no guarantee that a testator will make proper provision for dependants.

[130] BENNETT *THE APPLICATION OF CUSTOMARY LAW IN SOUTHERN AFRICA* 217–19

A will is a unilateral disposition of property mortis causa. As such it raises an important question of policy: to what extent should a person be allowed to disregard his or her personal law? It has always been assumed in southern Africa that people subject to customary law are free to make use of the common-law transactions, especially, of course, commercial contracts and the civil/Christian form of marriage. Apart from marriage it is further assumed that the rights and obligations arising out of the transaction are to be governed by the common law, irrespective of the parties' personal law. The argument is that by using a particular type of transaction the parties have implicitly agreed to the application of the law associated with the transaction. Excepting again the case of marriage, little thought seems to have been given to the repercussions that the transaction will have on third parties.[1] Yet, by making a will, the testator may upset the entire customary-law system of succession, especially the expectations of the intestate heirs.

Succession is concerned with rights to property, an area in which we have only the most rudimentary knowledge of customary law. The problem of inadequate information about traditional customary conceptions of property rights is compounded by the fact that the traditional law has doubtless been changed with the introduction of a capitalist economy. And together with capitalism came the common-law transactions which are predicated on the Western concept of ownership. One of the principal features of ownership is the idea that it is "absolute", ie an owner has the power to use and dispose of his property as he wishes. Consonant with this idea is the common-law freedom of testation which implies that a person is entitled to make whatever arrangements he chooses for the disposition of his property when he dies. If people subject to a customary-law regime are allowed to make wills, this assumes that they own the property they bequeath and that they may ignore the dictates of their personal law of intestate succession. The first assumption (which is more fully investigated below) may well be unfounded in view of the customary-law family interests in property; but because these customary interests are so poorly understood and formulated, they may not receive proper protection. Aside from this, the freedom of testation suggests that a person may disregard the expectations of his or her intestate heirs. It was for these reasons that the colonial powers in other parts of Africa were reluctant to give people subject to customary law the power to make wills.[2]

Customary law might not have known of the concept of a will but it was, none the less, possible for a person to vary, in some small measure, the rules of intestate succession. Prior to his death, a man could declare that he wanted certain property to be given to particular members of his family. . . . Moreover, customary law permitted the disinheritance of an heir. . . . None of this, however, compares with the common-law freedom of testation.[3]

In southern Africa no government seems ever to have seriously pondered the question whether people subject to customary law should be allowed to make wills. The Cape Colony was, perhaps, an exception: here succession was controlled by customary law in terms of the Native Succession Act.[4] Otherwise, Africans in the Transkei,[5] Natal[6] and the Transvaal[7] were permitted to make wills. Prior to 1953, each province in South Africa had its own legislation regulating the execution of wills and there was no mention of excluding Africans from the ambit of these enactments. Now the matter is controlled by the Wills Act,[8] which stipulates the method for executing the ordinary underhand will. . . . In Botswana the question was settled judicially in the leading case: *Fraenkel & another v Sechele*.[9] The testator here had married according to the common-law and had executed a will and codicil bequeathing his estate to his wife. His capacity to do so was contested on the ground that it was contrary to the Tswana customary law of succession and, further, that the testator did not fall within the proviso to s 3(*b*) of the Administration of Estates Proclamation,[10] ie he had not abandoned "tribal custom". The court rejected both arguments. It rightly pointed out that the Administration of Estates Proclamation deals only with the narrow issue of collecting the deceased's assets, paying his debts and then distributing his estate. This had nothing to do with the power to make wills, which was regulated (as in all the other southern African countries) by the Wills Proclamation,[11] where a general power was given to all people in the country to execute wills even if this meant upsetting the customary law of intestate succession. This judgment is, of course, of strong persuasive value in the other four countries. The leading Zimbabwean case—*Komo & another v Holmes NO*[12] although somewhat dated, is also relevant in this context. Here it was noted that the Administration of Estates Ordinance[13] implicitly contemplated the right to make a will. It was held that, in so far as any rule of customary law might prohibit the making of wills, such a rule would be inconsistent with the implications of the legislation and therefore inapplicable. Today, then, there is no doubt that people subject to customary law have full testamentary capacity, limited only by the common-law rules regulating such capacity.

Notes

1. Allott *New Essays* 240.
2. See below.
3. Although the common law is seen as supplementing customary law: *Maqetseba v Mgwaqaza* 1 NAC 163 (1907). See above, 405ff.
4. 18 of 1864. And see *Quvana v The Master & another* 1913 CPD 558.
5. By s 37 of Procs 110 and 112 of 1879, s 36 of Proc 140 of 1885, and by s 8 of Proc 142 of 1910. See *Nomveve v Mapini* (1892–93) 7 EDC 3; *Sigidi's Executors v Matumba* (1899) 16 SC 497; *Maqetseba's case* supra; *Mayekiso v Hermanus* 1908 EDC 53.
6. In *Zikalala* 1930 NAC (N&T) 139, however, the court held that it was permissible to dispose of kraal property only because the deceased was absolute owner of it.
7. By implication of s 70 of Proc 28 of 1902.
8. 7 of 1953, which repealed the various provincial enactments.
9. 1964 HCTLR 70 (reported in (1967) 11 *JAL* 51). See C M G Himsworth (1972) 16 *JAL* 12.
10. Chapter 83, which is the same as that in Lesotho.
11. 19 of 1957.
12. 1935 SR 86.
13. 6 of 1907, now ch 301.

In Ghana and Nigeria, colonial enactments providing for the execution and construction of wills were operative as statutes of general application. The institution they made available was freely used by Africans,[245] but courts and academics doubted whether the customary law of intestate succession could be so lightly disregarded.[246] In Kenya and Uganda, the legislature took a definite stand: the Indian Succession Act of 1865 (which had been imported into these countries in 1898 and 1906 respectively) was expressly declared not applicable to Africans, who in consequence had no testamentary capacity. It was only in 1972 that people subject to customary law in Kenya were given the power to make wills.[247] Similarly, in Zambia[248] and Malawi,[249] Africans were denied testamen-

---

[245] See Allott *Essays in African Law* 262–4.

[246] Morris (1970) 14 *JAL* 5. See the Nigerian case, *Yunusa v Adesubokan* (reported in (1970) 14 *JAL* 56–64 and (1972) 16 *JAL* 82–8), and the Gambian case *Saidy v Saidie* (reported in (1974) 18 *JAL* 183–98). The Ghanaian Wills Act 360 of 1971 does not apparently clarify the issue: Morris (1972) 16 *JAL* 65–70.

[247] Following from the 1968 Government Commission of Inquiry into Succession, for which see Ollennu (1969) 5 *East African LJ* 98–102.

[248] Regarding the position in Zambia see: Colson (1950) 2 *J Af Admin* 24ff and the Zambian Government Law Development Commission *Report on the Law of Succession* 1982.

[249] In Malawi testate succession for Africans was first introduced in 1967 by the Wills and Inheritance Act No 25.

tary capacity. In light of such a cautious policy elsewhere, the open-handed approach in southern Africa seems precipitate.

Testate succession is predicated by individual ownership of private property, and obviously where property is vested in a group the free disposal of it by an individual is bound to cause legal difficulties.[250] To allow people subject to customary law the power to make a will implies either that customary law has rights which approximate the common-law concept of ownership (a doubtful proposition), or that customary-law interests in property should be ignored. The executor of the will and the courts are put in a difficult position: how are they to take account of customary-law rights, especially when such rights are only half-understood?[251]

The Legislature has made some attempt to resolve this problem by specifying certain categories of property that can be disposed of by will.

[131] SECTION 23 BLACK ADMINISTRATION ACT 38 OF 1927

(1) **All movable property belonging to a Black and allotted to him or accruing under Black law or custom to any woman with whom he lived in a customary union, or to any house, shall upon his death devolve and be administered under Black law and custom.**

(2) **All land in a location held in individual tenure upon quitrent conditions by a Black shall devolve upon his death upon one male person, to be determined in accordance with tables of succession to be prescribed under sub-section (10).**

(3) **All other property of whatsoever kind belonging to a Black shall be capable of being devised by will.**

A literal reading of s 23(1) might suggest that all movable property must devolve according to customary law. The section is usually construed more narrowly, however, as a protection of house property, viz the house heir's expectation of inheriting when the head of a family dies has been ensured by a rule that such property cannot be disposed of by will.[252]

The second category of property, that mentioned in subsection (2), is land held upon quitrent conditions. Quitrent tenure has had a long history in South Africa. It was first applied to Africans in 1849 in what was then British Kaffraria, and it was then progressively extended to newly annexed territories, especially those in the Transkei.[253] Succession was regulated by statute.[254] Without departing from customary law, especially the principle of primogeniture, this

---

[250] Miller *The Machinery of Succession* 1–2.

[251] Only in the Natal case, *Zikalala* 1930 NAC (N&T) 139, does the court seem to have been fully aware of the problem.

[252] This provision is repeated in s 79(2) of the Natal and KwaZulu Codes. By the definition of 'intestate estate', in s 1(4)(b) of the Intestate Succession Act 81 of 1987, the customary-law regime of succession is left unaffected by the new act. This ruling does not affect the head of a family's right to disinherit an heir or to make dispositions of property mortis causa.

[253] See Brookes *The History of Native Policy in South Africa* 360–80.

[254] Derived from s 23 of Proc 227 of 1898, later reproduced in the Third Schedule to the Transkeian Proc 142 of 1910, and currently contained in Proc 188 of 1969. The latter is cited in full by Kerr 273–5. See too Bekker 325–30.

special regime ensured that land held under individual title would not be fragmented amongst a number of heirs on the death of the holder.[255]

This leaves two categories of disposable property: family and personal property.[256] As the name suggests, however, family property is not within the exclusive patrimony of the deceased. Can it be validly bequeathed? In most anglophone jurisdictions in Africa this would be impossible; only personal property can be willed.[257] But Roman-Dutch law allows a testator to dispose of things of which he is not the sole owner. Even property belonging to a third party may be bequeathed, provided that the testator was aware, when he made the will, that it did in fact belong to someone else.[258] This type of bequest naturally cannot create rights that the testator never had; it merely imposes an obligation on the executor to acquire the property or to pay its value over to the beneficiary.[259] Similarly, a testator may dispose of property that belongs to himself and others in common.[260] In this event it is presumed that the testator intended to bequeath only his share. If the property happens to be owned by the testator and the heir or legatee, the beneficiary acquires outright ownership in terms of the bequest.[261]

Although the legal difficulties regarding disposition of family property experienced elsewhere in Africa may be circumvented by the peculiarities of Roman-Dutch law, our systems of customary law have their own shortcomings. In the first place, given the poorly developed vocabulary to express customary-law property rights and the paucity of case law, how does a third party persuade an executor or a court to accept the validity of his or her claim? In the second place, the distinction that we draw between house and family property betokens a polygynous family structure in which each wife ran an independent house which the heir could expect to inherit. Today the monogamous family is the norm. The likelihood is that both spouses contributed to a joint estate that was used for the running of the family. Should this property be described as 'family' property, and thus devisable by will, or should it be designated 'house' property and preserved for the succession of the eldest son? Neither category seems helpful. What is more to the point is whether the family head should be permitted to dispose of property which his spouse helped him to acquire, and conversely, whether his wife should be allowed to bequeath

---

[255] These rules appear to be of application to land in rural areas only. The 99-year leases in urban areas (which closely resemble quitrent tenure) evidently can be disposed of by will: see s 6A(5)(c) of the Blacks (Urban Areas) Consolidation Act 25 of 1945. It is a moot question whether this section has survived the repealing acts, 4 of 1984 and 68 of 1986.

[256] See ss 108 and 79(1) and (2) of the Natal and KwaZulu Codes; *Ntukwini v Miso* 1918 NHC 216 and above, 237ff.

[257] Okoro *The Customary Laws of Succession in Eastern Nigeria* 226. Conversely, by will a testator may *create* family property by bequeathing his estate to the family as a group: *George & others v Fajore* (1939) 15 NLR 1.

[258] Corbett 224–6; *Receiver of Revenue v Hancke & others* 1915 AD 64 at 73; *Estate Brink* 1917 CPD 612; *Attridge NO v Lambert* 1977 (2) SA 90 (D).

[259] *Booysen v Colonial Orphan Chamber* 1880 Foord 48; *Hancke's* case supra at 73.

[260] *Estate Brink* and *Hancke's* cases supra at 73.

[261] *McMunn & others v Powell's Executors* (1896) 13 SC 27.

property that she obtained in her own right. These issues turn on the question of female proprietary capacity.

A related question is the fate of bridewealth received from the marriage of a daughter. This is often committed to provide bridewealth for a son. The common law could dismiss such a customary-law claim by invoking the principle of freedom of testation, or by adverting to the unenforceability of *pacta successoria*. Neither seems to be an adequate response.

A provision in a will directing that guardianship of the testator's child (or children) go to a specified person raises a problem analogous to disposition of property in which the testator does not have an exclusive right of ownership. Provided that bridewealth has been paid, the rights to children in customary law technically vest in the *family* of the father, not the father himself. What if the testator transferred these rights to a person outside the family? Or what if the testator were the mother, who in customary law would not be deemed to have any rights to the child at all? In Zimbabwe, this type of disposition is specially provided for in legislation,[262] but elsewhere in southern Africa it would presumably be invalid, unless guardianship were given to someone who had an independent entitlement under customary law.

(2) Interpretation of wills and conflict of laws

A will is a juristic act peculiar to the common law. As such it raises problems of conflict of laws: which legal system should be used to determine such questions as testamentary capacity, the validity of the document and its interpretation? In principle if a person elects to use a form peculiar to a particular legal system, then the dictates of that system must be obeyed. On this basis both formal validity of the will and capacity to execute it must be tested by the common law.[263]

It is not always obvious, however, which legal form a person intended to use. A written disposition of property *mortis causa* might fail to qualify as a common-law will,[264] but it might meet the requirements of a customary-law disposition.[265] Which legal system is to apply? In a Kenyan case on this question,[266] the court said that the testator intended to make use of an institution of the common law, and so the will had to be judged by that system. Strictly speaking this judgment is correct: if a person *intended* to dispose of an estate by common law, but did not observe the requirements, why should the disposition be upheld merely because of an accidental correspondence with the requirements of customary law? Yet it seems pedantic to insist on formalities—leaving aside

---

[262] Section 3 of the African Wills Act ch 240. Although the courts also would intervene to protect the best interests of the child: Stewart in Armstrong *Women and Law in Southern Africa* 94.

[263] Okoro op cit n257 228; Daniels *The Common Law in West Africa* 388. Section 11(3) of the Black Administration Act 38 of 1927 would be relevant here; see above, [107].

[264] But cf the privileged wills of Roman-Dutch law. In South Africa the soldier's will is now the only one allowed in terms of s 3(1) of the Wills Act 7 of 1953.

[265] A possibility contemplated in s 12 of the Zimbabwe Wills Act 13 of 1987.

[266] *Public Trustee v Wambui & others* (reported in (1978) 22 JAL 188).

issues of fraud—when to do so would defeat the testator's obvious purpose of bequeathing property in a particular way.[267]

With regard to the interpretation of wills, the general rule in common law is that the intention of the testator is of paramount importance.[268] Hence, where the terms of the will are clear and unambiguous, effect will be given to them, and no further evidence may be adduced to prove that the testator intended something other than what was written in the will. Words are given their ordinary meaning, unless they are legal or technical, in which event they will carry the special meaning usually attributed to them.

If a person subject to customary law executed a will, should it be construed according to his or her personal legal regime? In the leading Nigerian case in point, *George & others v Fajore*,[269] the testator had disposed of certain property in Lagos to twelve named persons 'their heirs and assigns for ever . . . as tenants in common without any power or right to alienate or anticipate the same or any part thereof'. The court interpreted this bequest in terms of customary law, because the will as a whole evinced an intention on the part of the testator that the property be held according to customary law.[270]

On the one hand, although it might seem reasonable to use the common law to construe a document that is peculiar to that system, there are good reasons for taking the testator's personal law into account. The common-law rule of interpretation itself allows a court to place itself, metaphorically, in the 'armchair' of the testator at the time that he executed the will. Hence it can consider all the relevant circumstances of which the testator would have been aware when he executed the will.[271] At the least this rule means that any ambiguity may be clarified by reference to such extrinsic factors as the testator's cultural affiliation. For instance, a bequest to 'my children', where there were issue from both a civil and a customary marriage, could be elucidated on this basis;[272] but in addition extrinsic evidence has been held to be admissible to explain circumstances where the will, on the face of it, was not ambiguous.[273]

Use of terms peculiar to a foreign legal system naturally suggests that that legal system should be used to interpret them.[274] In this regard, if the testator used vernacular terms, the application of customary law could clearly be implied.

VIII REFORM OF CUSTOMARY LAW

In Europe and North America, as the extended family shrank to the nuclear family, the concerns of the law of succession changed correspondingly, from

---

[267] See further: Poulter 315–24 and s 12 of the Zimbabwe Wills Act 13 of 1987, which makes special provision for the customary-law oral declarations.

[268] Corbett ch 21; Van der Merwe & Rowland *Die Suid-Afrikaanse Erfreg* 458ff.

[269] (1939) 15 NLR 1 at 3, cited by Daniels op cit n263 390–1 and Okoro op cit n257 27.

[270] Cf *Branco & others v Johnson* (1943) 17 NLR 70, cited by Daniels op cit n263 391 and Okoro op cit n257 227–8.

[271] Corbett 478–9.

[272] See *Momeen v Bassa & others NNO* 1976 (4) SA 388 (D) and the Nigerian cases, *Coker v Coker & others* (1938) 14 NLR 83 at 85–6 and *Sogbesan & others v Adebiyi & others* (1941) 16 NLR 26 at 27.

[273] *Ex parte Froy: In re Estate Brodie* 1954 (2) SA 366 (C) at 372; Corbett 480–2.

[274] Corbett 651.

preserving the blood line to providing economic maintenance for the deceased's spouse and immediate descendants.[275] The diminished range of support meant that the surviving spouse bore full responsibility for rearing minor children, and obviously he (and especially she) needed material assistance from the estate to discharge this duty.[276]

The customary-law widow in South Africa is in a vulnerable position.[277] Not only does she inherit nothing from her deceased husband's estate, but (because African women are denied proprietary capacity) any property she acquired during marriage is deemed to be her husband's and therefore part of his estate. In consequence the heir at customary law inherits it, and she loses her contribution.[278] In Natal and KwaZulu an attempt was made to alleviate widow's plight by applying the common law in cases of proved hardship.

[132] SECTION 81(6) NATAL AND KWAZULU CODES

(a) The district officer of the district in which the deceased husband resided may, where the assets in the estate have not been devised by will, at the request of the deceased's widow and upon notice to the heir according to Zulu law and custom or the members of the family of the deceased husband where no such heir appears to exist, administratively inquire into the estate with specific reference to the extent of the assets and liabilities, the extent of the widow's contribution towards the acquisition of such assets, the contribution or otherwise to such assets or welfare of the deceased's family by such heir or such families and other relevant factors, and if he is satisfied that it would be an injustice to the widow and would deprive her of the fruits of her labours if the assets were to be inherited by the heir and the widow be placed at the mercy of such heir, he may make an order that the estate shall devolve according to the law relating to intestate succession applicable to civil marriages.

[(b) A similar provision in favour of "any child of the deceased".]

(c) Any heir according to Zulu law and custom or the members of the deceased father's family aggrieved by a decision of the district officer may appeal against such decision to the Director-General, and if any of the aforementioned persons are aggrieved by the Director-General's decision an appeal may be made to the Minister whose decision shall be final.

(d) An appeal against the decision in terms of this section shall be made within a period of 21 days after such decision was made: Provided that if the person to whom an appeal in terms of paragraph (c) lies is satisfied that adequate grounds exist, he may, in his discretion, extend such period.

It should not be assumed that an appeal to the common law will necessarily resolve the accumulation of hardships currently borne by widows and dependants.[279] In the first place, the various statutory provisions in favour of

---

[275] There is a close analogy with African customary law: Glendon op cit n68 239.

[276] See Van Warmelo (1959) 21 *THRHR* 99.

[277] Simons 1960 *AJ* 329–33 and *African Women* chs 24 and 25.

[278] This was the early interpretation given to civil/Christian marriages as well: *Molefe* 1944 NAC (N&T) 8 at 10. The decision was later overruled by the Appellate Division in *Ex parte Minister of Native Affairs: In re Molefe v Molefe* 1946 AD 315.

[279] The Roman-Dutch law of succession was predicated on marriage in community of property; in most cases a widow was entitled to her half share of the joint estate when her husband died. The law had to be changed to allow a surviving spouse to inherit on a par with children, especially where the spouses had been married out of community: Succession Act 13 of 1934, now repealed and substituted by the Intestate Succession Act 81 of 1987.

surviving spouses apply only in cases of intestacy; because the common law allows a testator complete freedom of testation, a surviving spouse can still be disinherited with impunity.[280]

Over and above this, however, the common law of succession has become redundant in certain circumstances. First, modes of transmitting wealth from one generation to another have changed, bypassing wills and intestate succession. Whereas an affluent family's main assets (typically a farm or business enterprise) were formerly transmitted on the death of the owner, wealth now tends to be transferred inter vivos,[281] usually by providing for a child's education and by contractual investments in life insurance, pensions, and annuities.[282] Secondly, the law of succession cannot perpetuate rights that no longer exist. Nowadays much property that is critical to survival is the so-called 'new' property,[283] viz occupational licences, social welfare benefits, and other gratuities paid by the state. These benefits are withdrawn when the recipient dies, with the result that there is little left in the estate to benefit the survivors. The law of succession can do no more than effect a fair distribution of whatever assets remain; it cannot solve the problem of poverty.

Currently, western systems of law use two methods of ensuring a just distribution of property on the death of the holder. A surviving spouse may be guaranteed a fixed share in the estate (which may be varied according to the number of children born) by the rule of a 'legitimate portion'; a more flexible arrangement allows an administrative/judicial inquiry into the circumstances of dependants with a view to ordering an equitable sharing of the estate.[284] The legitimate portion, expressed as fractions of the estate or fixed sums, features in most of the civilian systems of law. It also used to be part of Roman-Dutch law,[285] but the South African Law Commission chose not to reintroduce it because it was too rigid.[286] In contrast, English law prefers a 'family maintenance' approach:[287] if the widow, children, and certain other dependants were inadequately provided for by will or on intestacy, they can apply to court for an order of periodic payment of maintenance out of the estate.[288] Two

---

[280] *Glazer v Glazer NO* 1963 (4) SA 694 (A). But now he or she can claim maintenance under the Maintenance of Surviving Spouses Act 27 of 1990.

[281] Like wills, however, these devices are the privilege of the relatively affluent, educated sections of society: Langbein (1988) 86 *Michigan LR* 724.

[282] Langbein op cit 722ff.

[283] See above, 395–6.

[284] Customary law, of course, gives the widow and children a claim for maintenance out of the estate which is similar. See above, 416ff.

[285] It was abolished by statute in the four provinces of South Africa around the turn of the century: Corbett 34.

[286] *Review of the Law of Succession* para 5.4.

[287] The Inheritance (Family Provision) Act of 1938, 1 & 2 Geo V c45.

[288] Important changes were introduced in 1975 by the Inheritance (Provision for Family and Dependants) Act ch 63 which put into effect recommendations made by the Law Commission. Provision for the surviving spouse was no longer to be limited to maintenance; instead he or she would be entitled to 'a fair share of the family property' in accordance with guidelines similar to those used in divorce proceedings. This approach has the advantage of allowing a distribution of the estate more neatly tailored to the actual circumstances of the deceased's family. This is the approach favoured by the South African Law Commission Report op cit n286 para 6.

features commend this approach in the context of customary law. First, children and spouses who would normally have no de jure claims on the deceased (ie partners in informal unions and illegitimate children) may be included in the distribution; and secondly, the estate is administered by an executor or the Master which puts its management on to sound basis.[289]

Post-colonial law reform in nearly all the anglophone African states has paid close attention to succession. Ghana paved the way with a White Paper on Marriage, Divorce and Inheritance[290] that put forth limited reforms in favour of the widow.[291] A proposal in 1964 to introduce new legislation regulating intestate succession was abortive, but eventually, under the Wills Act of 1971,[292] English-style family maintenance provisions were enacted in the case of testate succession. It was only in 1985, however, when a series of decrees aimed at improving the position of the nuclear family was promulgated[293] that the law of intestate succession was changed. Law reform in Kenya took a different route. Instead of family maintenance provisions, the Law Commission recommended that the surviving spouse (in particular widows) and both male and female children (whether legitimate or illegitimate) be entitled to a portion of the estate.[294] In 1972 these recommendations were finally translated into law.[295]

Zambia and Malawi both changed the rules of intestate succession and introduced the family maintenance approach. Malawi experimented with three successive reforms. The first two[296] were never brought into force, and in any event they were superseded by the Wills and Inheritance Act of 1967,[297] which introduced a flexible regime of intestate succession.[298] The main concern of the Act was to 'strike an acceptable balance between the demands of the customary heirs and those of the immediate family (ie spouses and children)'.[299] Either one half of the estate or two-fifths (depending on which part of the country the deceased came from) devolves on the widow and children; the rest goes according to customary law. And, if dependants of a deceased were not adequately provided for in his will, two-thirds of the estate can be used for their maintenance. In terms of the Bill produced by the Zambian Law Development

---

[289] Under customary law all such matters may be dealt with by the heir, an interested party.

[290] 3 of 1961.

[291] These were strictly limited to the self-acquired property of the deceased, and only in respect of persons married by civil/Christian rites who had died intestate: para 19 of the White Paper.

[292] See Morris op cit n246 65.

[293] Most important of these was the Intestate Succession Law No 111 which involved substantial alterations to customary law: Woodman (1985) 29 *JAL* 118ff.

[294] Not a mere right to maintenance which would not be inheritable. The Report was issued in 1968. See Ollennu op cit n247 101–2.

[295] Which came into force on 1 July 1981.

[296] The African Wills and Succession Ord 13 of 1960 offered Africans a simple procedure for making wills. The Wills and Inheritance (Kamuzu's Mbumba Protection) Ord 36 of 1964 repealed this enactment, and introduced testamentary succession for Africans in respect of personal property and land held under freehold or leasehold title. See Roberts (1966) 10 *JAL* 21ff.

[297] No 25.

[298] Accordingly, for purposes of intestate succession, two classes of estate must be distinguished: those to which customary law would not have been applicable prior to the Act and those to which it would have been applicable.

[299] Roberts (1968) 12 *JAL* 84.

Commission, on intestacy 25 per cent of the estate goes to the surviving spouse, 50 per cent to the children, and 25 per cent to any dependants. (The term 'dependant' is broadly defined to include any person living with the deceased prior to death.) The familiar English-law family maintenance rules apply to situations where a dependant has not been adequately provided for by will or on intestacy.[300]

Reform south of the Zambezi has been more timid. Only Zimbabwe and Bophuthatswana have squarely faced the shortcomings of customary law. In Zimbabwe family maintenance provisions based on the English model were introduced. Under the Deceased Persons Family Maintenance Act,[301] a 'dependant' is so defined that only members of the nuclear family and the deceased's parents are included; any such dependant may apply for an award of maintenance out of the net estate.[302] In Bophuthatswana, customary was excluded altogether:[303] the Roman-Dutch law of intestate succession applies to the deceased's children, and the surviving spouse is allowed a child's share of the estate.[304] Paler versions of these reforms exist in Botswana[305] and Swaziland.[306] The former introduced family maintenance provisions and the latter allowed the surviving spouse and children to inherit on intestacy; but neither Act is applicable to estates governed by customary law.[307]

---

[300] Report on the Law of Succession 1982, Part III of the Bill Contained in Appendix C; and see the commentary by Coldham (1983) 27 *JAL* 166–7.

[301] 39 of 1978.

[302] Section 3. The considerations that are used to guide the court are specified in s 7. See Stewart in Armstrong op cit n262 91–2.

[303] Succession Act 23 of 1982.

[304] Sections 1 and 2 of the Act. See Mohohlo 1987 *De Rebus* 31ff.

[305] Succession (Rights of the Surviving Spouse and Inheritance Family Provisions) Act 66 of 1970.

[306] Intestate Succession Act 3 of 1953 ch 104. Under s 4 it is provided that the Act does not apply to any African whose estate falls to be administered by customary law in terms of s 68 of the Administration of Estates Act 28 of 1902. This, in turn, applies to Africans, who during their lifetimes contracted a 'lawful marriage' or who are the offspring of parents 'lawfully married'. Because these terms can be interpreted to exclude customary marriages, it would imply that only unmarried persons or illegitimate children fall within the provisions of the Intestate Succession Act: Rubin op cit n89 95.

[307] In South Africa the Maintenance of Surviving Spouses Act 27 of 1990 does not apply because 'survivor' is defined to mean the spouse of a *marriage* dissolved by death; and marriages do not normally include customary unions.

CHAPTER 10

Civil/Christian Marriage

I CHURCH, CULTURE, AND THE CONFLICT OF LAWS

Christianity was part and parcel of the European cultural export to Africa. Marriage was taken to be an overt sign of religious commitment and Christian marriage was used as a vehicle for transporting colonial ideas of civilization to the subject peoples; hence the assumption that if a person married according to a certain form, he or she had opted in favour of a particular culture.

Christian marriages contracted by people normally subject to customary law generated diverse legal problems, all of which had this question in common: to what extent should the *form* of the marriage be allowed to determine the spouses' status. Marriage affected not only the spouses' relations inter se, but also their relations with their children, their families, and the world at large. In formal terms this was a conflict between the European legal system associated with the marriage and the spouses' erstwhile customary-law regime. The answer to these awkward choice of law problems naturally depended upon the extent to which customary law was recognized. In South Africa, for instance, it was never allowed free rein; civil/Christian marriage and common law were given absolute primacy.[1] In Lesotho, by way of comparison, customary law had a much wider scope of application, and here the form of the marriage has far less effect on the spouses' personal legal regime.[2]

Within terms of these two broad approaches, courts have tended to favour one of two policies. The first was to say that if the spouses chose the civil/Christian form of marriage, it would be 'sufficient to show that it was their intention that the marriage contract and all the consequences flowing therefrom should be regulated exclusively by English law'.[3] In other words, the act of participating in a culturally marked ritual (the marriage ceremony) would determine choice of law in respect of all related rights and duties. Construed in this way, marriage functioned as a type of exemption from customary law. And Christian marriage could offer certain secular benefits, such as enhancing the status of women.[4] In South Africa the incentive lay in having a fully recognized legal union that would allow spouses to qualify, inter alia, for urban accommodation.[5]

Yet the relationship between a marriage ceremony and such relatively remote issues as the settlement of property on divorce or the devolution of a deceased estate,[6] is too tenuous to justify this simplistic choice of law rule.[7] Unvarying application of common law might have the advantage of giving a single, straightforward answer to all potential conflict problems, but it often does not accord with the parties' actual expectations, and in some cases it yields quite arbitrary results. For example, why should the spouses' children and heirs be subjected to the common law merely because their parents had entered a Christian form of marriage?[8]

Africans may contract a Christian marriage as a matter of conscience. They need have no intention of opting out of customary law, nor might it be possible for them to transcend their existing social networks.[9] The tenacity of customary law is apparent from the almost invariable companion to a Church marriage—a bridewealth agreement—and the continued observance of traditional ceremonies.[10] Aside from this, no spouse can reasonably be expected to understand the full legal implications of his or her marriage.

---

[1] And automatically terminated prior customary unions: *Nkambula v Linda* 1951 (1) SA 377 (A); Peart (1983) 16 *CILSA* 40–1.

[2] In fact there is much confusion as to which should prevail, especially in situations of dual marriage: Bennett 197ff; Maqutu (1983) 16 *CILSA* 374.

[3] *Cole* (1898) 1 NLR 15; *Asiata v Goncallo* (1900) 1 NLR 41.

[4] Most importantly perhaps their spouses' right to engage in adulterous unions and/or to take polygynous wives was checked. See Burman in Hirschon *Women and Property/Women as Property* 123; Phillips 29; Poulter *Legal Dualism in Lesotho* 34.

[5] Only couples who had a civil marriage or a registered customary marriage with documentary proof thereof would be allocated housing: Burman 1984 *AJ* 98.

[6] In Nigeria, eg, the fact that a deceased person had contracted a marriage under the Marriage Ordinance meant that the husband's intestate estate would be distributed according to the common law: *Cole* (1898) 1 NLR 15.

[7] *Coleman v Shang* 1959 GLR 390 at 401, confirmed on appeal to the Privy Council [1961] AC 481.

[8] The rule in Natal under s 15 of Act 46 of 1887.

[9] See the case study of Christian marriage in Lagos in the 1930s: Mann in Hay & Wright *African Women and the Law* 151ff and Poulter op cit n4 35–6.

[10] See Pauw 128 and 130; Raum & De Jager *Transition and Change in a Rural Community* 55ff; Koyana *Customary Law in a Changing Society* 27ff; Coertze 237.

It was to meet these objections that the first approach was modified to take account of the actual expectations of the parties. In a leading Nigerian case, the court said:

> 'It would be quite incorrect to say that all the persons who embrace the Christian faith or who are married in accordance with its tenets, have in other respects attained that stage of culture and development as to make it just or reasonable to suppose that their whole lives should be regulated in accordance with English laws and procedures.'[11]

According to this view, the selection of a particular form of marriage does not necessarily entail application of the legal system associated with it. This is especially true of Christian unions, because although most churches will induce their members to have their union properly solemnized, this has no *necessary* connection with a personal status under the common law. As the churches have been freed from their ties to colonial government, Christian marriage has started to lose its cultural connotations, a process that has been hastened by the growth of independent African churches.[12]

The result of this thinking, however, has been to deprive the courts of any hard-and-fast choice of law rule. In some measure their difficulties have been resolved by the provision of specific statutory choice of law rules, but where the legislature has given no guidance the courts have been hard pressed to find a unifying principle to direct the solution of the multifarious conflict problems they encounter.

II ENGAGEMENT, CAPACITY AND FORMALITIES

(1) Engagement

There is a marked difference in the attitude of customary and common law to engagement agreements. In customary law the prospective spouses' undertaking to get married has no legal consequence,[13] whereas under the common law failure to fulfil a promise to marry could ground an action for damages.

If a couple have decided to get married in a church or registry office, the courts have had no hesitation in applying the common law and allowing actions for breach of promise.[14] But if the parties' intentions were not clearly evinced, as for example where they wanted to celebrate their marriage by both customary and Christian forms, the choice of law is not so obvious. In these circumstances, the courts could seek additional connecting factors (such as lifestyle) to ascertain with which legal system the agreement has its closest connection; and where a dual marriage was contemplated, the court could ascertain which was to be the predominant form of marriage.[15]

---

[11] *Smith* (1924) 5 NLR 102 at 104.

[12] Although marriages in these churches had no legal effect. See eg: Welsh *The Roots of Segregation* 255.

[13] See above, 183–4.

[14] *Lupusi v Makalima* 2 NAC 163 (1911); *Nzalo v Maseko* 1931 NAC (N&T) 41; *Roqoza* 1965 BAC 1 (S).

[15] *Mabitle v Mochema* 1971–3 LLR 271; and see Poulter op cit n4 50. See generally Bennett 143–7, 190–1 and 208.

(2) Capacity

The capacity of Africans to marry by civil or Christian rites is governed by common law.[16]

(3) Formalities

In South Africa it has been taken for granted that only Africans have the choice of marrying by either civil/Christian or customary rites. It is assumed that Whites must marry according to civil or Christian rites, the form being dictated by their personal law.[17] But this assumption seems entirely without foundation. Both forms of marriage are available to all people in the country.

Once the parties have decided to marry in church or a registry office, they have to comply with the various requirements of the common law.[18]

If the priest officiating at the ceremony is a member of an independent African church, the couple will not be deemed to be validly married, because under the Marriage Act these functionaries are not recognized marriage officers.[19] The union, however, might be accorded the status of a customary marriage if the necessary requirements for that form have been met. People who are aware of this problem sometimes choose a civil marriage;[20] but it is not a popular option because the civil ceremony is regarded as 'cheap', and couples who choose it are suspected of doing so in order to avoid paying bridewealth.[21]

Because of the far-reaching effects of the transition from a customary to a common-law regime, certain additional formalities are required of prospective spouses who happen to be African.[22]

[133] SECTION 22 BLACK ADMINISTRATION ACT 38 OF 1927

(3) No marriage officer shall solemnize the marriage of a Black man unless he has first taken from him a declaration to the effect that he is not a partner in a customary union with any woman other than the one he intends marrying.

(4) Any person contravening sub-section (3) shall be guilty of an offence, and shall, upon conviction, be liable to a fine not exceeding fifty rand, or, in default of payment, to imprisonment for a period not exceeding three months.

(5) A Black man who wilfully makes a false declaration to a marriage officer with regard to the existence or not of a customary union between him and any woman, shall be guilty of an offence and liable on conviction to the penalties which may by law be imposed for perjury.

It is difficult to see what purpose is served by making this declaration a mandatory requirement. Presumably it acts as a check on the man who thinks

---

[16] In this regard s 11(3) of the Black Administration Act 38 of 1927 is relevant. See above, [107].

[17] The question whether Whites could conclude valid customary marriages arose only briefly at the turn of the century: *In re Bethell* (1888) 38 ChD 220 and *Canham's Estate v The Master* (1909) 26 SC 116.

[18] See ss 21–22 and 29–30 of the Marriage Act 25 of 1961. Traditional requirements, however, are not completely ignored: Reader 214–21.

[19] Section 11 of Act 25 of 1961.

[20] Phillips 39–40.

[21] Raum & De Jager op cit n10 62; Shropshire *Primitive Marriage and European Law* 68 and 72; Pauw 128. For a contrasting view, see Phillips 40.

[22] See, eg, the 'enabling certificate' in Zimbabwe under s 12(1) of the African Marriages Act ch 238 (borrowed from Natal): Bennett 207. See generally: Bennett & Peart 1983 *AJ* 145ff.

that polygyny is permissible in civil/Christian marriages. But the effect of failing to make the declaration, or of making a false declaration is obscure; and there is good authority for arguing that the validity of the marriage is unimpaired.[23]

III CONSEQUENCES

A marriage by civil/Christian rites in South Africa has the general effect of imposing a new personal status on the spouses, one governed by the common law. The general matrimonial obligations are not that different from customary law: the spouses are under a duty to live together, to afford each other marital privileges, and to be faithful to one another.[24] The common-law consortium, however, implies that the wife does not establish a house, as she would if married under customary law,[25] and that she has a right to be with her husband, who is not free to place her at a homestead of his choosing.[26]

The same legal regime has been extended to other members of the immediate family, which is now conceived to be a nuclear unit. Hence the parent-child relationship is governed by common law,[27] the legitimacy of the children is tested by the same system,[28] and *both* parents have a duty to maintain their children, and vice versa.[29] Technically, more remote members of the extended family (who under customary law could expect maintenance from the head of a household) would be excluded from the scope of this duty. Nevertheless, it seems that as a result of ingrained attitudes and the payment of bridewealth, men tend to be called upon to support any relatives who would have had claims under customary law; and case studies indicate that people are usually prepared to accommodate their distressed relatives.[30]

Relationships with third parties are legally more problematic. A delict arising from impairment of the marital consortium is always governed by the common law. This involves a considerable departure from the customary-law regime since the husband's duty to remain monogamous is one of the hallmarks of civil/Christian marriage. Hence any secondary union contracted by the husband will be deemed adulterous.[31] And at common law both the husband and the wife have rights of action against any person who commits adultery; in customary law

---

[23] *Malaza v Mndaweni* 1975 BAC 45 (C) at 55–6.

[24] Hahlo 130. The customary-law attitude to the marital infidelities of the husband, however, is a point of difference.

[25] *Mrasi & another v Majavu* 1932 NAC (C&O) 4 at 7; *Titi* 1936 NAC (C&O) 101 at 103; *Tonjeni* 1947 NAC (C&O) 8; *Francis* 1967 AJ 152.

[26] *Sishuba* 1940 NAC (C&O) 123 at 129–30. And see *Tzanibe* 1950 NAC 34 (C) and *Ngake v Mahahle en 'n ander* 1984 (2) SA 216 (O) at 221.

[27] *Ntoyi* 4 NAC 172 (1920); *Dlakiya v Nyangiwe* 4 NAC 173 (1921); *Mdema v Garane* 5 NAC 199 (1923); *Ngcobo* 1944 NAC (C&O) 16; *Morai v Morai & another* 1948 NAC (C&O) 14; *Mosehla* 1952 NAC 105 (NE); *Msomi* 1968 BAC 29 (NE) at 32; *Ramokhoase* 1971 BAC 163 (C) at 167; *Madlala* 1975 BAC 96 (NE) at 99.

[28] *Sgatya v Madleba* 1958 NAC 53 (S) and *Ledwaba* 1951 NAC 398 (NE).

[29] Boberg 267.

[30] They found it especially difficult to refuse help to members of the husband's family who might have helped to pay bridewealth: Burman op cit n5 99.

[31] And of no legal effect. Even so, it seems that many men disregard the strictures of the common law: Allott *Essays in African Law* 203; Maqutu op cit n2 275; and in Transkei, polygynous civil/Christian marriages are now permitted: s 3 of the Transkei Marriage Act 21 of 1978. See below, 459.

only the husband would have such a right. The method of calculating damages and the quantum are also quite different. The common law similarly applies to cases of abduction or enticement[32] on the understanding that these actions arise out of an interference with conjugal rights established by the marriage.[33]

Before the common law (ie Roman-Dutch law) was altered by statute in 1984, although the wife attained her majority on marriage[34] she was subject to her husband's marital power,[35] and the spouses were automatically deemed to be married in community of property and of profit and loss. If they wished, the spouses could vary these consequences by entering into an antenuptial contract. When the Black Administration Act was passed in 1927, Africans were given a special dispensation to save them from being caught unawares by a matrimonial property system that would probably be unfamiliar to them.[36]

[134] SECTION 22(6) BLACK ADMINISTRATION ACT 38 OF 1927

A marriage between Blacks, contracted after the commencement of this Act, shall not produce the legal consequences of marriage in community of property between the spouses: Provided that in the case of a marriage contracted otherwise than during the subsistence of a customary union between the husband and any woman other than the wife it shall be competent for the intending spouses at any time within one month previous to the celebration of such marriage to declare jointly before any magistrate, Commissioner or marriage officer . . . that it is their intention and desire that community of property and of profit and loss shall result from their marriage, and thereupon such community shall result from their marriage except as regards any land . . . held under quitrent tenure such land shall be excluded from such community.

In the ordinary course the marriage would be out of community of property and of profit and loss, but the husband's marital power was left unaffected.[37] This regime was derived from earlier Transkei legislation[38] that modelled the consequences of the marriage as closely as possible on customary law.[39] The spouses were free, however, to choose community of property and of profit and loss simply by making a prenuptial declaration to that effect. This had to be done one month prior to the wedding before a magistrate, commissioner or marriage officer.[40] It was an inexpensive method of varying the matrimonial proprietary

---

[32] Poulter op cit n4 64–5.
[33] *Mdodana & another v Nokulele* 2 NAC 138 (1911); *Mtshengu v Mawengu* 1954 NAC 172 (S); Poulter ibid finds this reasoning simplistic.
[34] Age of Majority Act 57 of 1972; Bekker 250 and s 14 of the Natal and KwaZulu Codes.
[35] Section 37 of the Transkei Marriage Act 21 of 1978 provides that the wife is invariably subject to her husband's guardianship irrespective of the form of marriage.
[36] Bekker 250; Bennett 155; but the regime is not a customary-law one: *Ex parte Minister of Native Affairs: In re Molefe v Molefe* 1946 AD 315.
[37] *Ex parte Minister of Native Affairs* supra.
[38] Section 5(1) Proc 142 of 1910.
[39] In Lesotho the court simply applied customary law to decide the property consequences of marriage: *Khatala* 1964 HCTLR 97. Poulter op cit n4 72–4 applauds choice of law based on life style rather than marriage. Similarly, in Swaziland, under s 24 of the Marriage Act 47 of 1964, in Botswana, under s 7(1) of the Married Women's Property Act 69 of 1970, and in Zimbabwe, under s 13 of the African Marriages Act ch 238, the property consequences of civil/Christian marriage continue to be governed by customary law.
[40] This right was denied the man who chose to 'discard' one or all of the wives that he had already married by customary law.

regime, although if the spouses wanted to enter into an antenuptial contract there was nothing to prevent them from doing so.[41]

Section 22(6) did not purport to incorporate customary law into the marriage[42] nor did it change the common law governing the marital relationship any more than was specified. Thus in terms of common law, the husband continued to have marital power over his wife[43] and this power would not be excluded in the prenuptial declaration, although it could be by antenuptial contract.[44] Because the marital power was retained, the wife's status remained very much the same as it would have been under customary law. For example, she had no locus standi in judicio;[45] her contractual capacity was limited;[46] and so too was her delictual capacity.[47]

The *common law* regarding matrimonial property and marital power was changed by the 1984 Matrimonial Property Act,[48] but this legislation had no effect on civil/Christian marriages contracted by Africans.[49] It was provided that chapters 2 and 3 (which governed abolition of the marital power and the powers of spouses married in community) did not apply to Africans. Similarly, chapter 1, which introduced an accrual regime for those married out of community, applied only to marriages where the community regime had been excluded by an antenuptial contract. In practice very few Africans executed antenuptial contracts because their marriages were automatically out of community. This meant that de facto at least the accrual regime was virtually inapplicable. Only the provisions of chapter 4 of the Act were applied to Africans: under s 21(1) a husband and wife (whether married before or after commencement of the Act) could apply to the court for permission to change their matrimonial property system, ie postnuptial variation was permissible.

This legal regime, despite being carefully designed to harmonize with the spouses' cultural expectations, seems in fact to have worked to the disadvantage of African women.

'This leaves the African woman with neither the financial protection of a joint estate with her husband, nor the freedom to control her own property, even though she is recognised as having the legal capacity to own it. Yet by marrying by civil law, the African woman also loses the protection of the customary law. Civil law introduces into the centre of African family life the concept of outright ownership, rather than the African Customary law concept of the head of the family as manager of a joint family estate, with rights and obligations to other family members, providing them with guaranteed economic support in need. Thus, while in theory the civil law gave women more control over their own fate, it may be argued that in practice their position was, if anything, worse during the marriage (and sometimes after it was ended) than if they had been married by customary law. Given

[41] Bennett 156.
[42] *Ex parte Minister of Native Affairs: In re Molefe v Molefe* 1946 AD 315 at 319.
[43] *Figlan* 5 NAC 70 (1924); *Mambi v Mtshisa* 5 NAC 98 (1927).
[44] And see s 27(3) of the Natal and KwaZulu Codes.
[45] *Rabotapi v Nkonyane* 1946 NAC (N&T) 72; *Twala v Nsuntsha* 1954 NAC 35 (C); *Mtonjana v Jaxa* 1972 BAC 91 (S). Her lack of capacity could, of course, be remedied by the appointment of a curator ad litem or a grant of venia agendi: *Mototsi v Mamabolo* 1934 NAC (N&T) 71.
[46] *Rabotapi's* case supra; *Mpushu & others v Mjolo* 1976 (3) SA 606 (E).
[47] Cf *Malunga v Zilwana* 1947 NAC (N&T) 64.
[48] No 88.
[49] Section 25(1). See Sinclair *Introduction to the Matrimonial Property Act 1984* 62–3 for criticism.

the reluctance of many African men to pool their earnings with their wives, and the low earning capacity of most African women, this introduction of absolute ownership into the marriage can leave the woman in a very disadvantageous position. It is therefore interesting to note that community of property marriages are increasingly frequent, appearing in about 50 per cent of marriage certificates. Antenuptial contracts among Cape Town Africans are so rare as to be virtually non-existent: in a sample of 400 divorce cases, not one had an antenuptial contract, and both lawyers and the officials of the (African) Southern Divorce Court confirm this fact.'[50]

When the South African Law Commission examined African marriages, it recommended that the consequences of civil/Christian marriage should be the same for all people in the country.[51] It also proposed that spouses married prior to the 1984 Matrimonial Property Act should be entitled to change their property regime and exclude marital power if they wished.[52] Both these proposals were translated into law by the Marriage and Matrimonial Property Law Amendment Act.[53] Section 22(6) of the Black Administration Act was repealed, with the implication that the accrual regime now applied to Africans,[54] and chapters 2 and 3 of the Matrimonial Property Act were also made applicable to African civil marriages.[55]

As a result all marriages are automatically *in* community of property and of profit and loss and the husband's marital power is *excluded*. This regime may be varied by antenuptial contract only; but where the marriage is out of community of property, the accrual system may be made applicable.[56] The 1988 Matrimonial Property Law Amendment Act is, like its predecessors, not retrospective. Yet provision is made[57] to allow spouses whose matrimonial property system was governed by s 22 of the Black Administration Act, to harmonize the consequences of their marriage with the new law by execution and registration of a notarial contract. They were given two years after the commencement of the 1988 Act[58] within which to do this.

IV DISSOLUTION BY DIVORCE

(1) Courts and procedure

In other African countries the dissolution of a civil/Christian marriage is processed in the ordinary courts, but in South Africa special tribunals were constituted for this purpose.[59] They were authorized

---

[50] Burman in Hirschon op cit n4 124. Coertze 241 also found that among the Bafokeng few couples made the prenuptial declaration.

[51] *Marriages and Customary Unions of Black Persons* para 11.8.4.

[52] Paragraph 11.8.7.

[53] 3 of 1988.

[54] Section 1(e).

[55] Section 3.

[56] Section 3 of Act 3 of 1988; the decision must be exercised within two years of 2 December 1988.

[57] Section 4 of Act 3 of 1988, inserting s 25(3) into Act 88 of 1984.

[58] 2 December 1988.

[59] Act 9 1929.

'to hear and determine suits of nullity, divorce and separation between Blacks domiciled within their respective areas of jurisdiction in respect of marriages and to decide any question arising therefrom . . . '.[60]

The Supreme Court retained concurrent jurisdiction, but at the same time it could act as a court of appeal.[61]

The areas of jurisdiction coincided with those of the former Black Appeal Courts. Hence when Transkei, Ciskei, Venda and Bophuthatswana were given independence, the Divorce Courts lost much of the territory over which they were previously competent. They retain jurisdiction only in respect of citizens/domiciliaries of the independent states where: the husband was domiciled within their area of jurisdiction; or the plaintiff/applicant wife was ordinarily resident in the area for at least one year prior to the action (and was a South African citizen or had been domiciled in the Republic immediately prior to the marriage).[62]

These special courts were originally established to provide a cheap and accessible forum for the hearing of matrimonial actions. Empirical research, however, revealed that they were unpopular with potential litigants, who distrusted their association with the apartheid administration. In practice divorce orders were often sought here for ulterior purposes, principally to secure custody of children and urban housing rights.[63] In any event the Hoexter Commission[64] found that the proliferation of courts and the fragmentation of adjudication in domestic matters was not conducive to the preservation of the family as a social unit. Accordingly, it recommended the abolition of the Black Divorce Courts and the transfer of their powers to the proposed Family Courts.[65] But until the Family Courts are established the Divorce Courts continue to function.

(2) Grounds for divorce

It is generally accepted that a civil/Christian marriage may be dissolved only on the basis of common law. In an early Zimbabwean case, the court reasoned that:

'The parties were married by Christian rites, and it seems to me that the marriage must be subject to the ordinary law of the land. That being so, the parties having openly entered into the marriage, must stand or fall according to our law dealing with marriage.'[66]

Such thinking also seems to underlie the courts' decisions in South Africa; at any rate, the application of common law has never been seriously questioned. It follows that the wife may sue in her own name and that she has the locus standi necessary to do so[67] even if she is under her husband's marital power.[68]

This somewhat simplistic approach to choice of law ignores the cultural orientation of the parties.

---

[60] Section 10(1). See above, 85ff.
[61] Section 10(5).
[62] Section 2(1) of the Divorce Act 70 of 1979.
[63] Burman 1983 *AJ* 171ff.
[64] Inquiry into the Structure and Functioning of the Courts *Fifth Report* 31 para 3.5.2.
[65] Paragraph 4.6.4.
[66] *Sikwela* 1912 SR 168 at 170.
[67] This would also follow from s 11(3) of the Black Administration Act 38 of 1927.
[68] Hahlo 237.

'Might there not be advantages in making the law of divorce fit the general social values, beliefs, needs and circumstances of the life of the parties since these have provided the framework of their married lives?'[69]

Under current South African divorce laws, these considerations can be taken into account, if only to establish the fact of an irretrievable breakdown of the spouses' marriage.[70] This would allow the courts to pay serious attention to certain African norms and beliefs (notably, in the latter regard, witchcraft) that may have influenced the marital relationship.[71]

(3) Consequences of divorce

In South Africa the common law governs the proprietary consequences of dissolution. In Zimbabwe, by contrast, customary law applies. Inflexible choice of law rules like these are too general to do justice to the subtleties of individual cases, and the courts have on occasion been driven into tortuous reasoning to justify application of a law that blatantly conflicts with the choice of law rule, but is more equitable on the facts.[72] This has prompted certain countries to adopt a more flexible approach. In Botswana, for instance, the common law is generally applicable[73] with a proviso that,

'if it shall appear to that court on application made to it that regard being had to the mode of life of the spouses or to any disposition of the property made by either of the spouses during the subsistence of the marriage it would not be just and equitable that such property should be dealt with according to customary law'

the court may apply customary law.[74]

In South Africa, under the common law, if the marriage was out of community each spouse is entitled to his or her separate estate. If the marriage was in community, the decree of divorce operates as an order dividing the joint estate into halves. It is then open to an aggrieved spouse to apply for a decree of forfeiture of benefits.

Section 7(3) of the Divorce Act[75] authorizes the court, when granting a divorce, to order a division of assets in respect of a marriage out of community entered into in terms of an antenuptial contract. However, because the out of community regime under s 22(6) of the Black Administration Act was automatic and not the result of an antenuptial contract, s 7(3) was, prima facie at least, inapplicable. The court in *Mathabathe*,[76] however, held that African marriages must be included within this section. Subsequently, under the Matrimonial Property Law Amendment Act,[77] the Divorce Act was amended to cater

---

[69] Poulter op cit n4 92.
[70] Section 3 of the Divorce Act 70 of 1979. Many African marriages are adversely affected by economic pressures and male sexual infidelity, factors which lead to breakdown: Burman in Hirschon op cit n4 129; Phillips 42.
[71] Burman (1985) 14 *Quaderni Fiorentini* 185–6.
[72] See *Jirira v Jirira & another* (reported in (1975) 15 *RLJ* 17).
[73] Under s 2(1) of the Dissolution of African Marriages (Disposal of Property) Act Chapter 29:06.
[74] Similarly, in Lesotho, the courts adopted a flexible approach: *Khatala* 1964 HCTLR 97 at 100; and see Poulter op cit n4 75.
[75] 70 of 1979.
[76] 1987 (3) SA 45 (W).
[77] Section 2 of Act 3 of 1988.

specifically for African civil/Christian marriages and particular mention was made of the husband's obligations in respect of a so-called 'discarded' spouse.[78]

Custody and guardianship of children is also governed by the common law,[79] although no good reason has ever been advanced for this choice of law rule. Under the Divorce Act,[80] a court may not grant a decree of divorce until it is satisfied that proper provision has been made for the children; and it is further provided that the child's best interests are of paramount importance. The latter rule is, of course, an overt expression of public policy and on this ground customary law may be rendered inapplicable.[81]

Maintenance is claimable under the common law,[82] although in practice the Divorce Court does not grant maintenance orders unless embodied in consent papers.[83]

V DISSOLUTION BY DEATH

(1) General effect on status

In the eyes of the common law, if either spouse were to die, the marriage would be terminated, together with most of the rights and obligations which had regulated their relationship.[84] Once the marriage ends it can be argued that the personal law of the surviving spouse and children should revive to regulate their status. If this were the case, under customary law the widow would be obliged to remain with her deceased husband's family and possibly to enter into a levirate union. Were she to do so, she could claim support from her deceased husband's estate and her levirate partner would be responsible for maintaining her and her minor children until the heir came of age. Conversely, if the widow wanted to return to her own family, she would fall under the guardianship of her father (and might make him liable to restore part of the bridewealth); but the children she had borne during the marriage would remain as part of her husband's family (provided that bridewealth had been duly paid).

Neither logic nor expediency has prevailed to dictate the choice of law on death. The courts have held that the marriage is at an end, but for certain purposes the common law continues to apply. Thus rights of custody and guardianship to minor children are determined by the common law.[85] And if the widow decides to enter into a levirate union, and if she bears more children for

---

[78] Under s 22(7) of the Black Administration Act.
[79] *Ledwaba* 1951 NAC 398 (NE); *Nombida v Flaman* 1956 NAC 108 (S); *Mzamo* 1956 NAC 121 (NE).
[80] Section 6(1) of Act 70 of 1979.
[81] See *Mathenyane v Mathenyane & another* 1954 NAC 66 (C) and *Msomi* 1968 BAC 29 (NE). For Lesotho, see *Seotsanyana* 1981 (1) LLR 64 and Poulter op cit n4 94–5; for Botswana, see *Ex parte Veen* 1978 BLR 43 at 50; and for Zimbabwe, see Bennett 211–13.
[82] *Lekaba* 1974 BAC 454 (C); *Metsi* 1979 AC 177 (NE). For Zimbabwe see *Machongwe v Farusa* 1972 CAACC 21.
[83] Women wanting to claim child maintenance were referred to the local maintenance court: Burman op cit n63 176–7.
[84] *Magcoba* 6 NAC 17 (1928); *Tobiea v Mohatla* 1949 NAC 91 (S).
[85] *Dlakiya v Nyangiwe* 4 NAC 173 (1921); *Mdema v Garane* 5 NAC 199 (1923); *Nombida v Flaman* 1956 NAC 108 (S); *Ramokhoase* 1971 BAC 163 (C) at 167.

her deceased husband's family, they are deemed to be illegitimate.[86] On the same basis, it could be argued that if the woman died and her husband chose to replace her with a 'seedraiser', this union would have no formal validity in the eyes of the common law.[87]

Under the common law, if a spouse were a minor before getting married, marriage would operate as an emancipation, and he or she would not revert to minority status if the union were later dissolved. Apart from this, under the Age of Majority Act,[88] persons automatically attain the age of majority when they turn 21. Early cases from the Transkei confirm that these rules apply in the case of African marriages too,[89] but there is no clear authority for the rest of the country.

(2) Succession

Section 23(1) of the Black Administration Act provides that house property[90] must devolve according to customary law.[91] Civil/Christian marriages, which do not create 'houses', were not contemplated in this provision.[92] Prima facie therefore the section seems to be inapplicable to the estates of such marriages.

Section 23(2) of the Act stipulates that land held under quitrent tenure shall devolve according to tables of succession,[93] which by preserving the principle of primogeniture attempt to reproduce customary law. Unfortunately the language used in these tables is again unsuitable for civil/Christian marriages. For example, para 1 provides that 'the deceased's eldest son of the principal house or, if he be dead, such eldest son's senior male descendent, according to Black custom' shall inherit. As a civil/Christian marriage does not create a house, the eldest son of such a union would, on a literal reading, be disqualified because he was not a house member under customary law. In *Ex parte Minister of Native Affairs: In re Magqabi v Magqabi & others*,[94] however, the court held that the sons of civil/Christian marriages were not disqualified; in the event of competition between the sons of more than one marriage, of whatever form, it would simply be the deceased's *oldest* son who would inherit.[95]

Section 23(3) provides that all property, apart from house property and land held under quitrent tenure, may be devised by will. And if the deceased has left a will,[96] the common law then applies to the devolution of the whole estate.[97]

---

[86] *Mrubata & another v Dondolo* 1949 NAC 174 (S) at 176.
[87] On the other hand, there would be nothing to prevent either spouse from contracting a subsequent customary marriage.
[88] 57 of 1972.
[89] In *Nolanti v Sintenteni* 1 NAC 43 (1901), *Nosaiti v Xangati* 1 NAC 50 (1902), and *Xolo* 1931 NAC (C&O) 23, the decisions were based on s 38 of Proc 140 of 1885.
[90] See above, 232ff.
[91] And see s 79(2) of the Natal and KwaZulu Codes.
[92] *Tonjeni* 1947 NAC (C&O) 8; *Ngcwayi* 1950 NAC 231 (S) at 232.
[93] Proclamation R188 of 1969.
[94] 1955 (2) SA 428 (A).
[95] See the discussion by Kerr 225–30.
[96] No matter whether he or she died partially or wholly testate: s 23(9).
[97] Bekker 319ff.

More detailed choice of law rules governing succession to property not covered by s 23 are provided in regulations.[98]

[135] REGULATION 2 GN R200 OF 1987

If a Black dies leaving no valid will, so much of his property, including immovable property, as does not fall within the purview of subsection (1) or subsection (2) of section 23 of the Act shall be distributed in the manner following:

(a) If the deceased was, during his lifetime, ordinarily resident in any territory outside the Republic other than Mozambique, all movable assets in his estate after payment of such claims as may be found to be due shall be forwarded to the officer administering the district or area in which the deceased was ordinarily resident for disposal by him.

(b) If the deceased was at the time of his death the holder of a letter of exemption issued under the provisions of section 31 of the Act, exempting him from the operation of the Code of Zulu Law, the property shall devolve as if he had been a European.

(c) If the deceased, at the time of his death, was—

    (i) a partner in a marriage in community of property or under antenuptial contract; or

    (ii) a widower, widow or divorcee, as the case may be, of a marriage in community of property or under antenuptial contract and was not survived by a partner to a customary union entered into subsequent to the dissolution of such marriage, the property shall devolve as if the deceased had been a European.

(d) When any deceased Black is survived by any partner—

    (i) with whom he had contracted a marriage which, in terms of subsection (6) of section 22 of the Act, had not produced the legal consequences of a marriage in community of property; or

    (ii) with whom he had entered into a customary union; or

    (iii) who was at the time of his death living with him as his putative spouse; or by any issue of himself and any such partner, and the circumstances are such as in the opinion of the Minister to render the application of Black law and custom to the devolution of the whole, or some part, of his property inequitable or inappropriate, the Minister may direct that the said property or the said part thereof, as the case may be, shall devolve as if the said Black and the said partner had been lawfully married out of community of property, whether or not such was in fact the case, and as if the said Black had been a European.

(e) If the deceased does not fall into any of the classes described in paragraphs (a), (b), (c) and (d), the property shall be distributed according to Black law and custom.

Regulation 2(c) contains the provisions most pertinent to persons married by civil/Christian rites. The common law applies if the deceased: at the time of death was married in community of property or with an antenuptial contract; or at some time before death had been the partner of such a marriage and was not survived by the partner of a customary marriage.[99] Conversely, customary law is to apply if the deceased: were survived by the partner of a customary union which had been entered into after the dissolution of a civil/Christian marriage; or were a widow(er) or a divorcé(e) of a marriage in community of property and had left a surviving spouse of a civil marriage (which was out of community of property). Because very few Africans make antenuptial contracts or availed themselves of the prenuptial declaration under s 22(6) of the Black Administra-

---

[98] The provisions of the Intestate Succession Act 81 of 1987 are excluded in terms of s 1(4)(b).

[99] *Molefe* 1944 NAC (N&T) 8; *Lentsoe* 1946 NAC (N&T) 80.

tion Act, the common law scarcely ever regulates succession in cases of civil/Christian marriage.

More usual (at least before the Matrimonial Property Law Amendment Act of 1988) are marriages in which community of property was automatically excluded, and here in terms of subsection 2(e) as read with 2(d)(i) of the Regulations, the customary law of succession applies.[100] The rationale for this rule seems to have been a desire to prevent the spouses from being caught unawares by the consequences of their marriage, in other words, their personal law would continue to apply. But where the parties to the marriage were sufficiently familiar with the common law to make a prenuptial declaration or an antenuptial contract, there would be no harm in applying the common law—the parties could be presumed to be cognizant of its consequences.

That leaves only one situation in which the common law can be applied in respect of marriages out of community. If the application of customary law would be inappropriate or inequitable, potential beneficiaries may petition the Minister of Development Aid for a directive that the common law be applied. This saving provision is hardly satisfactory. Choice of law is left to the discretion of an administrative official, and while this no doubt saves the cost of litigation it may preclude argument from all interested parties.[101]

Natal and KwaZulu have enacted special provisions that override the Black Administration Act and regulations. The Codes stipulate that estates of Blacks married by civil rites are to devolve according to the Succession Act of 1934.[102] Bophuthatswana too has introduced the common law of intestate succession.[103] Elsewhere in southern Africa succession is governed by customary law on the understanding that if the spouses had wanted to opt out of that system they should have executed a will.[104]

For all intents and purposes the widow of a civil/Christian marriage in southern Africa is in the same vulnerable position as the widow of a customary marriage.[105] The South African Law Commission recommended general application of the common law of intestate succession except to the devolution of house property and land held under quitrent tenure.[106] Widows stand to

---

[100] *Danana v Sotatsha* 1947 NAC (C&O) 48; *Duma v Swales NO* 1952 NAC 272 (NE) at 274; *Shabango v Ngabi* 1953 NAC 111 (NE); *Msomi* 1963 BAC 94 (C); *Mnani* 1977 BAC 264 (S).

[101] Cf Bennett 170.

[102] No 13. Section 79(3) of the Codes. Unfortunately this precludes the current Intestate Succession Act 81 of 1987.

[103] Succession Act 23 of 1982.

[104] For Botswana see s 7(1) of the Married Women's Property Act 69 of 1970, s 2(1) of the Dissolution of African Marriages (Disposal of Property) Act Chapter 29:06, and s 7 of the Customary Law (Application and Ascertainment) Act 51 of 1969. For Zimbabwe see s 13 of the African Marriages Act Chapter 238. Lesotho has a more flexible approach: s 3 of the Intestate Succession Proc 2 of 1953 provides that the enactment is applicable only where a deceased estate is administered under the Administration of Estates Proc 19 of 1935. Section 3(b) of this Proclamation provides in turn that it applies only to the estates of those Africans who have 'abandoned tribal custom and adopted a European mode of life and who, if married, have married under European law'. See: *Mokorosi v Mokorosi & others* 1967–70 LLR 1 at 6; *Hoohlo* 1967–70 LLR 318 at 323; and the commentaries by Bennett 196–7 and Poulter op cit n4 24–9.

[105] See above, 416.

[106] *Marriages and Customary Unions of Black Persons* para 11.7.2. This proposal is anomalous in one respect: civil/Christian marriages do not create houses.

benefit most, however, from the Maintenance of Surviving Spouses Act;[107] s 2(1) provides:

> 'If a marriage is dissolved by death after the commencement of this Act the survivor shall have a claim against the estate of the deceased spouse for provision of his reasonable maintenance needs until his death or remarriage in so far as he is not able to provide therefor from his own means and earnings.'

VI BRIDEWEALTH AGREEMENTS

Nearly all Africans who contract civil/Christian marriages conclude companion bridewealth agreements. They would not consider themselves properly married unless they did this.[108] There is nothing to prevent people from coupling bridewealth and civil marriage,[109] but the courts have declared that bridewealth is not essential to the validity of the union.[110] And as a consequence, the wife's guardian may not insist on the payment of bridewealth as a condition for giving consent to his daughter's marriage.[111]

Because bridewealth and the church or civil ceremony are both aimed at procuring a marriage, the parties will probably not see any incompatibility between them,[112] but technically there are profound differences. To begin with, different parties are involved. The marriage is exclusively the concern of the bride and the groom, whereas bridewealth involves the groom (or his guardian) and the bride's father (or his heir).[113] In the event of a conflict of obligations under the marriage and the bridewealth agreement, which is to prevail? Or put in different terms, what law is to govern the bridewealth?[114]

[136] *GOMANI v BAQWA* 3 NAC 71 (1917)

President of the Court: Plaintiff sues for return of dowry paid by him to Defendant whose daughter he married according to Christian rites. This marriage has been dissolved by the Court of the Chief Magistrate on the ground that the wife had committed adultery.

Exception to the summons was taken in the Magistrate's Court on the ground that it disclosed no cause of action inasmuch as the dowry was paid under Native law and custom and that adultery on the part of a wife does not entail the return of dowry under Native law and custom. The Magistrate upheld the exception holding that the dissolution of the Christian marriage has nothing to do with the question of the return of dowry and that the Plaintiff should rely on purely Native custom and sue for restoration of his wife failing which return of dowry paid, which practically leaves him without a remedy....

The point to be decided on this argument is whether a contract to pay dowry can be held to arise out of a Christian marriage. Such a contract is no part of a Christian marriage,

---

[107] 27 of 1990.
[108] Burman in Hirschon op cit n4 125; Dlamini 405.
[109] See the proviso to the recognition of customary law in s 1(1) of the Law of Evidence Amendment Act 45 of 1988. Regarding the history of recognition of bridewealth agreements see: Harries in Phillips 360–5.
[110] *Tobiea v Mohatla* 1949 NAC 91 (S); *Ntsimango* 1949 NAC 143 (S); *Ntabeni v Mlobeli & another* 1949 NAC 158 (S).
[111] See *Letabe v Ralithlalo* 1949 NAC 26 (C) and *Letaba v Ralithlalo* 1950 NAC 12 (C).
[112] Poulter op cit n4 35–6, however, argues that there are two marriages. And see Pauw 128.
[113] Bennett 147.
[114] See generally: Bennett 147–54; Bennett & Peart op cit n22 145–69; and Peart (1984) 47 *THRHR* 158ff.

and is entered into under an entirely separate law from the law governing such marriage, it must be dealt with quite apart from a Christian marriage, and cannot for the purposes of the section quoted be regarded as arising out of the Christian marriage. It is a contract made under Native law and custom, and as such should be dealt with under Native law. . . .

In this case it is alleged that the woman committed adultery with one Luswazi, deserted the Plaintiff, and thereafter cohabited with Luswazi. If her conduct has been such as would entitle the Plaintiff to the return of his dowry under Native custom no difficulty would present itself.

A man whose marriage is dissolved through no fault of his is entitled to return of his dowry.

In this case the marriage has been dissolved on the ground that the wife has misconducted herself. Even if it were held that her conduct would not under Native law and custom entitle the husband to the return of the dowry paid it would be repugnant to justice and equity to say that a woman and her father, who was a party to the contract, should be allowed to benefit by the woman's misconduct.

The marriage has been dissolved on the ground of the woman's misconduct, and the husband is entitled to claim from the Defendant the dowry he paid under a contract, a condition of which was that the woman should be faithful to her husband.

The appeal is allowed with costs, and the case is returned to the Magistrate to be tried on its merits.

Dissenting Judgment by Walter Carmichael

. . . I now come to the question whether the summons discloses any ground of action.

It alleges that during the subsistence of the Plaintiff's marriage with the Defendant's daughter "by Christian rites", she committed adultery with one Thomas Luswazi, deserted the Plaintiff, and thereafter cohabited with the said Luswazi in the district of Mount Currie, that the Plaintiff divorced her in the Chief Magistrate's Court, and now "by reason of the dissolution of the said marriage is entitled to the return of the dowry". To this the Defendant, now the Respondent, pleads that "the dowry was paid under Native law and custom, and that adultery on the part of a wife does not entail the return of dowry under Native law and custom". Here, agreeing at the outset with the dictum in the majority judgment of this Court that "the dowry transaction was a contract under Native law and custom and as such should be dealt with under Native law and custom", I am forced to apply this test as well to the summons as to the Proclamation. One cannot, it seems to me, hold at once that the question is resolvable under Native law and that it is to be construed in terms of a separate European marriage contract. At this stage, indeed, the majority judgment prepares itself to jettison Native law in the name of "justice and equity", if not "public policy and good morals"—the more usual formula for such occasions. Such a course raises very debatable questions, whatever one's personal opinion may be, one cannot overlook the fact that to a large portion of the ecclesiastical world divorce from a Christian marriage is itself an immoral proceeding, the heinousness of which would be aggravated by an attempt to profit therefrom by recovering dowry. Moreover there is much to be said for the view that a woman is less vagrant of instinct than a man and that a husband has only himself to blame if he loses the affections of his wife. But it is well nigh impossible for a Court of Justice to resolve such delicate and complicated issues; the only safe course appears to me to adhere strictly to the law and judge of the claim by the nature and intention of the Native dowry contract without endeavouring to import into it ethical ideas foreign thereto.

Predictably, in view of the favoured status of civil/Christian marriage, Carmichael's dissenting judgment has not prevailed:[115] in the event of any

---

[115] See further: *Peme v Gwele* 1941 NAC (C&O) 3.

conflict between the bridewealth agreement and the marriage, common-law obligations are preferred.

[137] *MBONJIWA v SCELLAM* 1957 NAC 41 (S)

Whilst, as conceded by Counsel for appellant, there can be no doubt that *lobola* paid or agreed upon in respect of a customary union is purely a Native law transaction, the same cannot, as contended by him, be said of *lobola* agreed upon or paid in connection with a civil marriage, as is the case here; for, although the Native Appeal Court decisions have not been consistent in this respect, the preponderant weight of authority is to the effect that a *lobola* agreement or payment made in connection with a civil marriage must be regarded as ancillary to, and modified by, the legal principles underlying such a marriage .... But such *lobola* agreement or payment remains essentially a Native law transaction and the Native Appeal Courts have regarded it as such and given effect to its incidents as are dictated by Native law in so far as they are not in conflict with the principles underlying the civil marriage.

Other countries in southern Africa have also subordinated bridewealth agreements to the exigencies of civil/Christian marriages.[116] But this is not the only possible solution, and arguably it does not coincide with the parties' expectations. The parties probably regard themselves as married under both systems of law. If their views are to be respected, neither the bridewealth agreement nor the marriage should be treated as superior. In this case the most principled way of solving conflicts between the two is to refer to the lifestyles of the parties, ie obligations under the bridewealth agreement must be assessed in terms of the law signified by their cultural predilections.[117] Even this approach is not without difficulty. Whose lifestyles are to be taken into account: the spouses' or the wife's guardian's in addition? Possibly for this reason, and no doubt also because the inquiry is complex and potentially inconclusive, this line of argument has not been followed.

The courts have based their decisions on the premise that bridewealth agreements are ancillary to civil/Christian marriages and are modified by the principles underlying the union. In particular situations, however, they have oscillated between treating the bridewealth agreement as a basically common-law contract[118] (with implied terms governed by customary law) or treating it as an African agreement governed by customary law (unless in conflict with the principles of the marriage).[119]

The wife's guardian cannot assume that his ward's marriage includes a bridewealth agreement. Bridewealth must be expressly agreed upon, and if the courts have no evidence of a contract they will not enforce a claim for payment.[120] This follows logically from the non-essential nature of bridewealth.[121] It has been suggested, however, that where the parties belong to

---

[116] For Swaziland, see *Khoza v Malambe & another* 1976 SLR 380 at 384; for Zimbabwe, see *Muchenje v Kunaka* 1912 SR 207; and for Lesotho see *Maqutu v Hlapane* 1971–3 LLR 36.

[117] See above, 127ff.

[118] Kerr 1960 *AJ* 337.

[119] Peart op cit n114 167.

[120] *Mbonjiwa v Scellam* 1957 NAC 41 (S).

[121] *Ntabeni v Mlobeli & another* 1949 NAC 158 (S).

a tribe, who by convention fix the quantum of bridewealth (and where there is *some* evidence that the husband had agreed to pay) the amount customarily paid would be the amount implied in the contract.[122]

Theleka is one right that the wife's guardian will quite obviously lose; and with it the corresponding duty of phuthuma disappears.[123] Theleka has been construed as the equivalent of malicious desertion.[124] Prior to the 1979 Divorce Act, desertion would have grounded an action for divorce, but it has been argued that this rationale is misguided for two reasons.[125] The first is the one advanced in *Mbani*;[126] the court said that although the wife might have left her husband, this did not necessarily mean that she had intended to *desert* him in the sense of having the animus deserendi required for malicious desertion. The second reason is that a court may now grant divorce on the ground of an irretrievable breakdown of the marriage,[127] and theleka does not suggest that the prospect of restoring the marriage is hopeless. On the contrary, it is a method of prompting the husband to restore the consortium by reminding him of his obligations.

It is probably more appropriate to disallow theleka in the context of civil/Christian marriage on the ground that it gives the wife's guardian a right to interfere in the spouses' relationship: the continuance of the marriage depends upon the bridewealth agreement and not vice versa.[128] This does not mean that the wife's guardian loses his only method of enforcing payment, since he now has an action to sue for bridewealth in court.[129]

In terms of the common law, the death of either spouse automatically terminates the marriage, but under customary law, strictly speaking, the union continues until liquidated by a bridewealth settlement. According to some systems of customary law, if the principal reason for the marriage were frustrated because the wife died while still young and capable of bearing children, her family would be expected to provide a substitute wife ('seedraiser'). If they failed to do so, the wife's guardian would be obliged to return some at least of the bridewealth.[130] Conversely, if the husband were to die when his wife was still capable of bearing children, she would be expected to enter into a levirate union, and if she refused to do so and returned to her own family, her guardian would have to return part of the bridewealth.[131]

There is good reason for arguing that the surviving spouse should be free of any bridewealth obligations. So far as the widow is concerned, she was never a party to the agreement, and there is no reason why her freedom of action should

---

[122] See *Cheche v Nondabula* 1962 NAC 23 (S) 27–8 and Kerr 1963 *AJ* 49.
[123] *Ngake v Mahahle en 'n ander* 1984 (2) SA 216 (O); and see Verloren van Themaat (1986) 49 *THRHR* 100ff. See above, 261.
[124] *Ntsimango* 1949 NAC 143 (S) at 144.
[125] Peart op cit n114 169–70.
[126] 1939 NAC (C&O) 91 at 93.
[127] Section 4(1) of the Divorce Act 70 of 1979.
[128] See *Cheche v Nondabula* 1962 NAC 23 (S) at 28.
[129] *Sihuhu v Ntshaba* 1 NAC 62 (1903); *Njengaye v Mbola* 3 NAC 76 (1917); *Skweyiya v Sixakwe* 1941 NAC (C&O) 126; *Tonya v Matomane* 1949 NAC 138 (S).
[130] See above, 419ff.
[131] See above, 410ff.

be circumscribed by it.[132] More generally, however, it is clear that when the parties enter into a marriage accompanied by bridewealth the coexistence of two marriages is not implied. The courts have held that there is only one union—the civil/Christian marriage[133]—and that the bridewealth agreement is ancillary to it. This suggests that the bridewealth should be treated as an ordinary contract dependent for its existence on the marriage. It follows that when the marriage ends the accessory contract must also end.

A more expedient approach (and one probably more in accord with the parties' expectations) is to allow the continuation of the bridewealth agreement.[134] On these terms posthumous children borne by the widow have been awarded to the husband's family, and his heir has been given the right to bridewealth paid for any daughters.[135] Similarly, it has been held that while a widow is free to do as she wishes, if she chooses to leave her husband's family, she will render her guardian liable to restore portion of the bridewealth.[136]

The issue most litigated about is return of bridewealth, especially where one of the spouses committed adultery. In customary law the husband's adultery gives his wife (and her family) no cause for complaint, and in the normal course it would not justify termination of the marriage. Even adultery committed by the wife, provided that it was not persistent or aggravated in some other way, is not necessarily a good cause for ending the marriage.[137] In terms of the common law, on the other hand, an act of adultery by either spouse may lead to an irretrievable breakdown of the marriage.

The courts have tended to use the common law as a general yardstick for assessing return of bridewealth. In the early case of *Gomani v Baqwa*,[138] it was held that although the bridewealth was governed by customary law, on grounds of justice and equity, common law must determine its restoration. In a later decision—*Fuzile v Ntloko*[139]—the decision was more straightforward: the wife's adultery must be judged in terms of the common law. In consequence a husband's adultery results in his forfeiture of bridewealth, while his spouse's entitles him to its return.[140]

Viewed in context, this conclusion is an odd one. For several reasons the marriage and the bridewealth contract are treated quite separately on divorce: the divorce action is brought in the Black Divorce Courts and the bridewealth action is brought in a magistrate's (formerly commissioner's) or chief's court. The

---

[132] See *Nbono v Manoxoweni* (1891) 6 EDC 62 and above, 414.

[133] *Tobiea v Mohatla* 1949 NAC 91 (S); *Sgatya v Madleba* 1958 NAC 53 (S) at 56.

[134] *Mrubata & another v Dondolo* 1949 NAC 174 (S) at 176. In *Tobiea's* case supra, dissolution by death and by divorce was distinguished; it was held that where the marriage had ended in divorce the bridewealth agreement was cancelled by the divorce decree.

[135] *Mrubata's* case supra.

[136] *Ntlongweni v Mhlakaza* 3 NAC 163 (1915); *Makedela v Sauli* 1948 NAC (C&O) 17; *Tobiea's* case supra. Cf the case where the *wife* dies. Here the court has wavered on the question of returning bridewealth: *Somzana v Bantshi* 4 NAC 84 (1921).

[137] Bekker 364ff.

[138] 3 NAC 71 (1917).

[139] 1944 NAC (C&O) 2 and see *Sicence v Lupindo* 3 NAC 164 (1914).

[140] *Sicence's* case supra; *Mpoko v Vava* 3 NAC 198 (1912); *Cobokwana v Mzilikazi* 1931 NAC (C&O) 44; *Nkuta v Mathibu* 1955 NAC 47 (C) at 49. And see *Gwala v Cele* 1978 AC 27 (NE).

various deductions allowed the wife's guardian must be determined by customary law.[141] Customary law is excluded in one respect only—determining which spouse was at fault in causing the breakdown of the marriage. The reason for excluding customary law in this regard seems obtuse in light of the 1979 Divorce Act, which was supposed to have abolished fault (in the form of adultery and malicious desertion) as the basis of divorce. If the Act prohibits consideration of the reasons for the breakdown of marriage, then why should prestatutory reasons provide the sole criteria for return of bridewealth?[142]

The Law Commission proposed that a decree of divorce should operate to end any bridewealth agreement appended to the marriage, and that the court granting the divorce should have the power to make an order regarding restoration of bridewealth.[143]

One final area in which customary law is not applied to the bridewealth agreement involves parental rights to children. Under customary law a father's rights are determined by the due payment of bridewealth.[144] In case of a civil/Christian marriage the courts have held that custody and guardianship are to be decided by common law, and as a result the payment or non-payment of bridewealth is irrelevant.[145] The courts have raised no objection, however, to the bridewealth holder claiming bridewealth for a daughter on her marriage.[146]

VII DUAL MARRIAGES

Customary marriages are, of course, potentially polygynous, and it quite often happens that a husband marries more than one woman under different rites. (Less frequently, a wife purports to take more than one husband.) Various questions concerning the validity and effect of the second union then arise. The answers to these questions have generally depended on the extent to which customary marriage is recognized. In South Africa, for example, where the customary union enjoys very limited recognition, a marriage by civil/Christian rites used to terminate a subsisting customary marriage automatically. In Lesotho, on the other hand, the courts treat customary and civil marriages as equally valid and so the one cannot override the other.[147]

Four different situations should be considered: first, where the husband of a subsisting customary union takes another wife by civil/Christian rites (including the situation where a polygynist decides to marry one of his customary wives by civil/Christian rites); secondly, where the spouses of a customary marriage celebrate their union again, this time by civil/Christian rites; thirdly, where the *wife* of a customary marriage contracts a civil/Christian union with another man;

---

[141] *Qotyane v Mkhari* 1938 NAC (N&T) 192; *Phalane v Lekoane* 1939 NAC (N&T) 132 at 134; *Raphela v Ditchaba* 1940 NAC (N&T) 29; *Fuzile v Ntloko* 1944 NAC (C&O) 2.

[142] It is only in s 4(2)(b) of the Divorce Act that fault finds minor expression: if the defendant committed adultery and if the plaintiff found such behaviour irreconcilable with a continued marital relationship, this may be used to show irretrievable breakdown.

[143] *Marriages and Customary Unions of Black Persons* para 11.8.9.

[144] See above, 289.

[145] *Morai v Morai & another* 1948 NAC (C&O) 14 and *Madlala* 1975 BAC 96 (NE) at 99.

[146] *Dlakiya v Nyangiwe* 4 NAC 173 (1921).

[147] Maqutu op cit n2 378.

and fourthly, where the partner to a subsisting civil marriage marries a third person by customary rites.

(1) Civil/Christian marriage by the husband of a subsisting customary union

Until recently the rule in South Africa was that the civil/Christian marriage superseded and extinguished the prior customary union(s). This naturally led to great hardship for the 'discarded' wife and children. The husband was afforded an easy method of ridding himself of his family without the obligation of making any financial or proprietary provision for them, and without submitting to any court procedures; he had only to contract another marriage.

Some legislative protection was given to the discarded wife (or wives) and children under s 22(7) of the Black Administration Act which preserved 'the material rights of any partner' of a subsisting customary union. According to the Appellate Division in *Nkambula v Linda*,[148] however, this section did not protect the discarded wife's *conjugal* rights. The civil marriage was strictly monogamous and continued cohabitation with the discarded spouse constituted adultery.[149] The Court went further; it held that the husband's civil marriage was an act of repudiation freeing his customary-law wife's guardian from the duty to return any bridewealth.[150]

Section 22(7) was aimed at protecting property which might have been allotted to a house before the civil marriage. It ensured that such property did not become a windfall for the second wife. But the husband was obviously not obliged to continue adding to this property, and once it had been exhausted, the discarded wife had nothing from her previous marriage with which to support herself. Her position was precarious in the extreme. At best s 22(7) entitled her to property which happened to be in her possession when her marriage ended; and if her former spouse sent her away, she could take this property with her.

The discarded family received its greatest measure of protection from s 22(7) when the husband died. Then customary law 'revived', as it were, to govern devolution of the deceased estate. This meant that the widow and children of the civil marriage were deemed to be the equivalent of a customary-law wife and children for the purposes of succession. By implication the former had no preferred position; they ranked with any prior discarded wife (or wives) and their children. Potentially, this provision could do greater harm than it sought to avoid. After the law had declared that the customary wife was no longer married, she might (possibly many years later) regain her status. In effect the customary marriage was resuscitated. The unfortunate corollary was that the civil-law spouse, who had enjoyed the benefits of a common-law regime (again possibly for many years), would find that her position was suddenly downgraded to that of a customary-law wife. And her husband could not cushion the blow by

---

[148] 1951 (1) SA 377 (A).

[149] The Black Appeal Court took this further, holding that in urban areas at least the discarded wife is not entitled to remain in her husband's house. He may bring an order of ejectment against her: *Malaza v Mndaweni* 1975 BAC 45 (C).

[150] See too: *Bucwa v George* 1964 BAC 110 (S).

bequeathing her property in his will because this was said to contravene s 22(7).[151]

The Law Commission rightly condemned this anomalous situation. It recommended that no spouse of an existing customary marriage be allowed to contract a common-law union.[152] (The converse—that the spouse of a common-law marriage was not competent to contract a customary-law union—was already the rule.) This recommendation became law in 1988.

[138] SECTION 1 ACT 3 OF 1988 (amending s 22 of the Black Administration Act)

(1) A man and a woman between whom a customary union subsists are competent to contract a marriage with each other if the man is not also a partner in a subsisting customary union with another woman.

(2) Subject to subsection (1), no person who is a partner in a customary union shall be competent to contract a marriage during the subsistence of that union.

. . .

(7) No marriage contracted after the commencement of this Act but before the commencement of the Marriage and Matrimonial Property Law Amendment Act, 1988, during the subsistence of any customary union between the husband and any woman other than the wife shall in any way affect the material rights of any partner of such union or any issue thereof, and the widow of any such marriage and the issue thereof shall have no greater rights in respect of the estate of the deceased spouse than she or they would have had if the said marriage had been a customary union.

Although partners to a customary union may marry one another by civil rites, a spouse may not contract a valid civil/Christian marriage with a third person (including a polygynous wife). This amendment is not retroactive, so the discarded spouses of customary marriages dissolved prior to 2 December 1988 continue to receive the dubious protection of s 22(7) of the Black Administration Act.

(2) Civil/Christian marriage by the spouses of a customary union

Where the spouses to a customary marriage decide to celebrate their union anew under civil rites, the first union is extinguished, and the parties' status is thenceforth determined by the common law.

Minimum violence is done to the spouses' relationship inter se;[153] but their relations with third parties are another matter, although the extent to which these relationships are affected is still uncertain.[154] One case, for example, held that the bridewealth agreement was automatically subordinated to the exigencies of the civil marriage, with the suggestion that it had been novated.[155] In another case it was clear that the bridewealth agreement had suffered no change at all.[156] And in

---

[151] Bennett 181.

[152] Op cit n143 para 11.2.7.

[153] Although one consequence is that any children born before the civil marriage are automatically legitimated: *Mtyelo a/b Sibango v Qotole* 4 NAC 39 (1920); *Ngqovu v Mciza* 4 NAC 42 (1920); *Ledwaba* 1951 NAC 398 (NE) at 402.

[154] And here it should be remembered that customary marriage is technically a union of two families.

[155] *Sgatya v Madleba* 1958 NAC 53 (S) at 56.

[156] *Matchika v Mnguni* 1946 NAC (N&T) 78 where it was held that there was still an action for recovery of bridewealth after dissolution of the civil union.

the most recent decision, the court upheld an action for damages for adultery, a right left over from the extinguished customary marriage.[157]

The inclination to protect acquired rights, especially in the last situation, is superficially appealing, but given the general preference for the civil marriage it is difficult to assert any rights or duties generated by the customary union.[158] And it must be remembered that a continued assertion of rights and duties acquired under the customary marriage may work to the disadvantage of the new civil-law family.

(3) Civil/Christian marriage by the wife of a customary union

Where the wife of a customary union enters a civil/Christian marriage with a man other than her customary-law spouse, her second union automatically terminates the customary marriage.[159] By implication any children she might have had in an adulterous liaison with a man who subsequently becomes her husband under the common law are legitimated.[160]

In general, however, the effect of the marriage is not as harmful as when the husband takes another wife by civil rites. Because customary law encodes the principle of patriarchy, the status of men is relatively better than that of women; and men are in an economically stronger position than women. Men accordingly do not need the same material protection that women do. So it is of little concern that men have no rights under s 22(7) of the Black Administration Act.

Under the Matrimonial Property Law Amendment Act of 1988 women are now also prohibited from contracting a civil/Christian marriage with a person other than a customary-law husband.[161]

(4) A customary marriage by a partner to a subsisting civil/Christian marriage with a person other than the civil-law spouse

If the spouse of a civil/Christian marriage purports to enter into a customary union with a person other than the spouse at common law, the second union is null and void.[162] It has been described as an immoral contract because it contravenes the common-law precept of monogamy. As a result, in situations where both parties are in pari delicto, the courts have invoked the principle that

---

[157] *Kumalo v Jonas* 1982 AC 111 (S).
[158] For instance, it is most unlikely that the courts would ever allow the wife's guardian to *theleka* her.
[159] *Gqamse v Stemele* 1 NAC 113 (1906); *Mtyelo a/b Sibango v Qotole* 4 NAC 39 (1920); *Zondi v Gwane* 4 NAC 195 (1919); *Njombani v Tshali* 1952 NAC 62 (S).
[160] *Ngqovu v Mciza* 4 NAC 42 (1920); *Guma* 4 NAC 220 (1919).
[161] Section 1 of Act 3.
[162] *Mnduze v Mdlimbi* 1 NAC 27 (1898); *Matee v Njongwana* 1 NAC 272 (1909); *Tutu* 2 NAC 167 (1911) at 169; *Moshesh v Matee* 4 NAC 78 (1920); *Ntonga v Dulusela* 4 NAC 80 (1921); *Mda v Mda & others* 4 NAC 127 (1921); *Mpande v Mdingi* 1929 NAC (C&O) 27; *Mlumbi & another v Salayi* 1930 NAC (C&O) 27; *Gwalata* 1932 NAC (N&T) 51; *Ntseki* 1933 NAC (C&O) 61; *Xalisa* 1942 NAC (C&O) 103; *Zulu v Mcube* 1952 NAC 225 (NE); *Sogoni v Jacisa* 1970 BAC 76 (S); *Qitini v Qabu* 1981 AC 42 (S).

the position of the possessor should be the stronger.[163] Thus the 'husband' may not reclaim any bridewealth he had given to his intended spouse's guardian, and the 'wife's' guardian cannot enforce his claim to the promised bridewealth. It has also been suggested that the courts should refuse to entertain a claim by the prospective 'wife's' guardian for damages for seduction, because in this case the principle of volenti non fit iniuria would be applicable.[164] But if one of the parties to the second union were not culpable (as for example where the 'husband' was unaware of his intended 'wife's' existing civil marriage) a claim may be successful.[165]

The second union is not bigamous. A customary marriage is not recognized as a marriage by the common law, and so the requirements for the crime of bigamy are not met.[166]

(5) Transkei

This is the only territory in southern Africa where an attempt has been made to devise a code of marriage law that is uniformly applicable to all persons in the country regardless of their personal legal regime. The 1978 Marriage Act[167] was inspired by the Tanzanian Law of Marriage Act,[168] but it did not go as far as the latter in harmonizing personal laws. By drawing on the rules of both customary and common law, the Tanzanian government sought to create a hybrid code applicable to all marriages. The Transkeian Act is not as bold as this. The integrity of the two forms of marriage has been preserved with certain exceptions, viz property consequences, the status of the wife, and divorce procedures.

The most dramatic innovation is the freedom given to husbands of civil/Christian marriages to contract additional customary marriages.[169] The introduction of polygynous civil marriages was a radical departure from the orthodoxy of western Christianity. To placate the established Churches, however, s 9 of the Marriage Act allows a minister of religion to refuse to solemnize a marriage that would not conform to the dictates of his religion.

The husband may enter a subsequent customary marriage only if a civil marriage is out of community of property; and conversely a husband may contract only a civil marriage that is out of community of property during the subsistence of a customary union. By implication polygynous marriages are not permitted in the following circumstances:

(i) a man who is party to a civil marriage may not contract another *civil* marriage (presumably with a woman other than his spouse);

---

[163] *Matee, Moshesh* and *Ntonga's* cases supra; *Sogayise v Mpahleni* 1931 NAC (C&O) 13; *Qitini's* case supra at 44. This rule has been modified by the decision in *Jajbhay v Cassim* 1939 AD 537: *Cele v Soni* 1942 NAC (N&T) 78; *Gule v Kuzwayo* 1950 NAC 56 (C); *Mlaba v Ciliza* 1951 NAC 391 (NE); *Zulu v Mcube* 1952 NAC 225 (NE).

[164] Bekker 272 and Olivier 249.

[165] *Sogoni v Jacisa* 1970 BAC 76 (S).

[166] *Zonyane v Rex* 1912 EDL 361.

[167] No 21. For general commentary see: Bekker 255–62 and Van Loggerenberg 1981 *Obiter* 1.

[168] 5 of 1971. For general commentary see: Read (1972) 16 *JAL* 19.

[169] Section 3.

(ii) a man who has a civil marriage in community of property may not contract a customary marriage with another woman;

(iii) a man who is party to a customary marriage may not contract a civil marriage with another woman which will produce the consequences of a marriage in community of property.

The Act says nothing about the status of these forbidden unions. They are obviously void, but it is not clear whether the man has also committed bigamy. This crime always seems to be out of place in a legal system that allows polygyny, which is especially true of the Transkeian Marriage Act, where the offence is not simply marrying another woman during the subsistence of a prior marriage, but marrying *in community of property*, a precondition that makes bigamy irrelevant in the context of the offence that the Transkeian legislature intends to punish.[170]

Any rights acquired during the subsistence of a customary marriage are protected by s 3(2). In other words, one marriage does not automatically terminate another, which then gives rise to a problem of conflicts between the rights and duties generated by the two marriages. The Act resolves this in a characteristically trenchant fashion by ruling that the civil union is to be treated in the same manner as a customary marriage. Hence, if a man becomes party to more than one marriage (irrespective of whether one of the marriages is a civil one), the status of his wives and children is to be regulated by customary law.[171]

The Act provides that all marriages are on an equal footing[172]—a reaction to the South African prejudice against customary marriage. Here the Act is partly retrospective in effect. It attempts to save customary marriages, which under the pre-independence law would not have been recognized. Section 2(1) provides that any customary 'union' (to use the South African terminology) that subsisted prior to the commencement of the Act is deemed to be a valid marriage. And s 2(2) allows spouses of customary unions that had been superseded by civil/Christian marriages under the law inherited from South Africa to apply to have their unions registered as valid marriages.[173]

If persons subject to different systems of personal law decide to marry, which system of law should be applied to the consequences of their marriage? (Since the repeal of the Prohibition of Mixed Marriages Act[174] this has become more likely in South Africa, and Transkei can provide a model for future development.) The general choice of law rule contained in the Act[175] provides that if a person subject to customary law contracts a marriage with a person who is not so subject, customary law applies. There are other, more specific choice of law rules governing particular cases viz: the prohibited degrees of affinity are determined

---

[170] There is no question of a woman being allowed to contract more than one marriage at a time. The customary-law prohibition on polyandry has been preserved: s 49(ii).

[171] Section 38.

[172] Section 1 of the Act, which contains all the definitions, makes this clear.

[173] The status of the wife and children will then be governed by customary law: s 38.

[174] 55 of 1949 by Act 72 of 1985.

[175] Section 51.

in accordance with the personal law of the female;[176] bridewealth agreements are subject to the customary law applicable to the father or guardian of the female;[177] the place and manner of consummation of a customary marriage are governed by the customary law applicable to the prospective groom.[178]

Some of the consequences of marriage are common to both customary and civil marriages. Women are invariably deemed to be under the guardianship of their husbands.[179] All marriages, whether customary or civil, are out of community of property.[180] Parties to a civil marriage, however, may establish a community regime in one of two ways: either they can conclude an antenuptial contract, or they can make a prenuptial declaration before a magistrate or marriage officer.[181] It is specially provided that the antenuptial contract or prenuptial declaration shall not affect the husband's marital power over his wife and shall not impose a community regime on land held in individual tenure under quitrent conditions. As a result of these provisions the wife has proprietary capacity, but she is denied contractual and delictual capacity and locus standi.[182] Chapter 5 of the Act deals, inter alia, with the dissolution of marriages by divorce. The grounds for divorce, applicable to both customary and civil marriages, are the same as those in South Africa prior to the passing of the 1979 Divorce Act.[183] A man may not contract another civil marriage without obtaining a certificate from the Master of the Supreme Court to the effect that proper provision has been made for the maintenance of the wife and the children of the prior marriage.[184] Custody and guardianship of children on divorce are regulated by the common law.[185] The court may, as it deems just, order that the guilty spouse pay the innocent spouse maintenance until the death or remarriage of the innocent spouse, whichever occurs first.[186]

The Marriage Act does not contain any provisions regulating intestate succession. Instead, s 23 of the South African Black Administration Act has been retained.

(6) The self-governing territories and independent states

The scope of application of South African statutes directed towards Africans raises pressing and complex questions of the conflict of laws. People move freely

---

[176] Section 28.
[177] Section 30.
[178] Section 31.
[179] Section 37. This term is more familiar to customary law. In the common law the term 'marital power' could have been used. The two terms are not synonymous, and Van Loggerenberg op cit n167 11 suggests that in the context of a civil marriage 'guardianship' should be construed to mean 'under marital power'.
[180] Section 39(1). Under s 38 it is provided that in the case of polygynous marriages the rights of wives and children are to be governed by customary law.
[181] Section 39(2).
[182] To protect the wife the Act imposes a series of restrictions on the husband's powers derived from the South African Matrimonial Affairs Act 37 of 1953.
[183] Act 70.
[184] Section 44.
[185] Section 45.
[186] Section 46.

across 'borders' to keep family and social contacts alive; the various entities making up the southern African region are economically interdependent which demands a constant traffic of people and goods. Yet formally this area is divided into fourteen legal territories.

It is presumed that no enactment has extraterritorial effect unless expressly stated; thus statutes such as the Marriage and Matrimonial Property Law Amendment Act[187] do not apply in the *independent* states (or, of course, in Lesotho, Botswana and Swaziland). For matters of personal status, however, the common law considers the domiciliaries of a state to be bound by the laws of that state, no matter where they happen to be.[188] On this understanding, spouses domiciled in Transkei at the time of marriage, for example, are bound by the laws of Transkei governing matrimonial property, even when they sojourn or work in South Africa;[189] and conversely South African domiciliaries are bound by the provisions of its matrimonial property laws even when they are in Transkei.

The position of the self-governing territories is different. Because they are not independent sovereign entities, the laws of South Africa, in principle, remain applicable within their territories. Yet their legislative assemblies have authority within the areas for which they were established to legislate over certain matters of personal law regarding their *citizens*.[190] A contrario, the South African legislature lacks competence in the same area, viz over citizens of the national states. On this reasoning the Marriage and Matrimonial Property Law Amendment Act[191] does not apply to citizens of the self-governing territories,[192] although such citizens might simultaneously be domiciliaries of South Africa. The applicability of personal law has been conceived in terms of two different, and potentially conflicting, connecting factors, domicile and citizenship. This legislative inadvertence knows of no straightforward solution.

---

[187] 3 of 1988.

[188] Forsyth 102–3.

[189] If they have not executed an antenuptial contract: Forsyth 252–6.

[190] Section 3 of the National States Constitution Act 21 of 1971, as read with s 26 of the First Schedule which provides that legislative competence exists for births, deaths, marriage and customary unions.

[191] 3 of 1988.

[192] Section 30(3) of the National States Constitution Act; and see Bekker 249. The term 'citizen' is defined in s 3 of the National States Citizenship Act 26 of 1970 to mean any person born in a particular national state, born of parents from that state, speaking the language of that state, or having an association with the population of that state by virtue of a particular cultural or racial background.

Index